The Only Two Ways to Write a Story

by JOHN GALLISHAW

*A book for writers
which cites cases in the craftsmanship
of the modern short story*

NEW YORK . LONDON

G. P. PUTNAM'S SONS

The Knickerbocker Press

1928

THE ONLY TWO WAYS TO
WRITE A STORY

Copyright, 1928
by
John Gallishaw

This is a copy of the first printing

G. P. Putnams Sons

Made in the United States of America

AUTHOR'S FOREWORD

In the course of the last ten years I have seen a number of writers achieve a reputation in the field of the Modern Short-Story. Almost invariably those writers, when questioned, have told me that they studied the work of established writers in order to isolate practical standards of both form and treatment. Unconsciously, those writers have adapted to their needs the greatest forward development in modern education: the Case Method. They all agreed that their work would have been much easier had there existed, within the scope of a single volume, a series of CASES IN CRAFTSMANSHIP of the Modern Short-Story to which aspiring writers might turn with certainty that therein they would find a norm against which they might judge their own products.

In presenting the results of my search for such a norm, I am like the very enthusiastic young bayonet instructor in the British Army who always appended to the standardized phrases of his instruction upon close-quarter bayonet fighting with an enemy the phrase "and then you kicks 'im in the fyce." Questioned by an officer who overheard him, he said: "The first part I learned from an instructor; kicking 'im in the fyce is my own idea."

There is much technical instruction which has always been available in regard to the Craftsmanship of the Modern Short-Story. This volume deals primarily with the four discoveries which I conceive to be "my own idea."

Discovery No. 1. For every short-story, as indeed for every work of fiction, long or short, there is a structural or architectural norm, as definite and basic as the architect's structural concept of a building. This norm is not in any way the creation of a single personal taste; nor does its recognition in any way limit or hamper individual expression. Just as an architect realizes that a building must ordinarily have walls, a roof, and a foundation; so the short-story writer realizes that architecturally a story must have a Beginning, a Body, and an Ending.

While most writers and critics have been aware, either con-

iii

sciously or unconsciously of the existence of this architectural norm, my special contribution to the advance of short-story craftsmanship is the discovery that there is also a *functional* norm for each of the three great *structural* divisions of Beginning, Body, and Ending. The function of each division is distinct and different from the function of either of the other two; but within each division the special function remains always constant and invariable. The function of the Beginning is to present a main situation; the function of the Body is to present a struggle or conflict growing out of that main situation; the function of the Ending is to present the Conclusive Act which brings the struggle or conflict to an end.

Although I deem this discovery of the relationship of the *functional* norm to the *structural* norm to be important and helpful to craftsmen, I feel that it cannot be utilized to the fullest extent until writers have made themselves familiar with the other discoveries.

Discovery No. 2. Of paramount importance to freedom of expression for writers is the knowledge that within the large units of Beginning, Body, and Ending, there is a smaller structural unit which, for the purposes of this book, I shall call the Scene. Until a writer learns to visualize and develop every story he writes, as a series of scenes, he cannot hope for facility in plotting and presenting his material.

Discovery No. 3. There are two—and only two—distinct types of short-story: one, the story in which the central actor is called upon to accomplish some purpose; the other, the story in which the central actor is called upon to make some decision or choice. In both types of story, the structural and functional norms are the same; just as in both types, the Scene will be the unit for plotting and presentation.

Discovery No. 4. This discovery cannot be fully utilized until the writer of short-stories is fully in control of the knowledge contained in the other discoveries. Only then can he take advantage of the discovery that there are two ways of presenting or telling a story: in chronological sequence, or in anti-chronological sequence. This anti-chronological sequence is usually known as the Flashback sequence. It is especially effective in presenting the story of decision.

The student of craftsmanship will find in this book, nothing that he could not dig out for himself, as I have done, through a study of modern fiction over a period of perhaps ten years; but such a study would involve for him, as it has done for me, the examination of thousands of manuscripts. Even though he were prepared to expend the same time and energy, he would not have the opportunity, as I have had, of testing the practicability of the principles involved in these discoveries over a large number of instances.

Fortunately, my work with writers in the John Gallishaw School for Creative Writing has enabled me to prove beyond any question of doubt that the application of these principles can cut down the period of apprenticeship through which every writer must go. A large part of the gratifying success of the method of instruction has been due, I feel sure, to the use which was there made of the stories here collected as Cases in Craftsmanship.

To look up each story independently was not always possible. It was therefore suggested to me that I gather them together into a Case Book which would serve as a basic Handbook for writers; a volume to be referred to by writers for the same purpose that lawyers refer to Case Books of Law: first, to discover the basic principle of a professional problem; and, second, the special aspects of that particular problem which make it a variant from the norm, demanding unusual treatment.

Thus, for the first time, these stories are collected in a single book; and I have preceded each one with a commentary explaining why each story has been chosen, and have followed each story with a line-by-line analysis, pointing out how the individual approach of a writer toward his material makes a variant from the norm from which every short-story must derive.

This Case Book will be of greatest benefit to writers when used in conjunction with my Lectures upon the Craftsmanship of the Modern Short Story. It will, I hope, cut down for many writers the period of futile experimentation which is the penalty of unwisely directed effort, by enabling them to examine their stories objectively, with the unbiased detachment of a reader rather than a writer. For the reader is the final judge. All stories are written for him.

ACKNOWLEDGMENT

teful acknowledgment is made to the following magazines and for permission to use copyright matter.

PUBLISHER	AUTHOR	STORY
AMERICAN MAGAZINE	Frank R. Adams	SPARE PARTS Copyright, Frank R. Adams, 1924.
CENTURY MAGAZINE	John Gallishaw	JAKE BOLTON, 551 Copyright, John Gallishaw, 1918.
COLLIER'S WEEKLY	George F. Worts	SUNK Copyright, George F. Worts, 1924.
	John Russell	JETSAM Copyright, John Russell, 1927.
	Lucian Carey	THE TROUBLE WITH MEN Copyright, Lucian Carey, 1926.
THE RED BOOK MAGAZINE	William Dudley Pelley	THE FACE IN THE WINDOW Copyright, The Red Book Magazine, 1920.
	Mary Synon	SHADOWED Copyright, The Red Book Magazine, 1923.
	John Galsworthy	THE MUMMY Copyright, John Galsworthy, 1924.
	Melanie Koll	RICH MAN—POOR MAN Copyright, The Red Book Magazine, 1927.
THE COSMOPOLITAN MAGAZINE	Frank R. Adams	WOMEN ARE WISER Copyright, Frank R. Adams, 1927.
	Adela R. St. John	THE HAUNTED LADY Copyright, Adela R. St. John, 1924.
THE SATURDAY EVENING POST	Irvin S. Cobb	THE ESCAPE OF MR. TRIMM (From The Escape of Mr. Trimm; His Plight and Other Plights.) Copyright, George H. Doran & Co., 1913.
	Will Payne	PARADISE ISLAND Copyright, Will Payne, 1924.
	John P. Marquand	ONCE AND ALWAYS Copyright, John P. Marquand, 1927.
	Mary Brecht Pulver	WESTERN STUFF Copyright, The Curtis Publishing Co., 1926.
	Thomas Beer	GENTILITY Copyright, Thomas Beer, 1925.
	Richard Connell	SHODDY Copyright, Richard Connell, 1926.
	Fanny Kilbourne	CLAIRE AND THE DANGEROUS MAN Copyright, Fanny Kilbourne, 1927.
DOUBLEDAY, DORAN & CO.	O. Henry	THE COP AND THE ANTHEM (From The Four Million.) Copyright, Doubleday, Page & Co., 1912.
		THE ROADS WE TAKE (From Whirligigs.) Copyright, Doubleday, Page & Co., 1910.

CONTENTS

CONTENTS

THE ONLY
TWO WAYS TO WRITE A STORY

SECTION I

STORIES OF ACCOMPLISHMENT

NOMENCLATURE

WHENEVER one person tries to make something clear to another person there instantly appears the necessity for a common nomenclature. The words must have the same meaning to both parties. Nomenclature has always been a stumbling block to any attempt to explain the processes of producing a work of fiction. Take the word "incident" as an example, or the word "meeting." Half a dozen educated people might each one give a different meaning to either of these words, and each one of the half dozen would be justified by usage and by logic in his choice. The simplest and the easiest way to avoid any misunderstanding in regard to the meaning of technical terms is to adopt for each term so used a special and limited meaning, and throughout the explanation to adhere strictly to the meaning agreed upon.

The purpose of this book is to explain to you as clearly and as simply as possible how the two kinds of stories mentioned in the Foreword: the Story of Accomplishment and the Story of Decision, are plotted and presented. This distinction between plotting and presentation is one which the writer of fiction cannot lose sight of. The two processes are at first distinct, although eventually they become almost inextricably linked together.

Plotting involves the selection and arrangement of happenings to fit the architectural norm of which I have spoken. This architectural norm is the skeletonized outline of your story to which life and reality are given by superimposing upon them the presentation unit.

Let us pause for a moment to glance at this Case Book itself, so that we may from the very beginning utilize it for the purpose for which it was intended—the illustration from the work of writers of the principles of fiction. I have chosen one of the *Adventures of Ulysses*, by Charles Lamb as illustrating the principle of both plotting and presentation. Ulysses was the king of Ithaca,

3

who, after the siege of Troy, set out with his followers to return to Ithaca, where his wife Penelope awaited him. During the progress of his journey he met with several adventures. This *Adventure With the Cyclop* contains all of the elements of a modern short-story. It is a particularly illuminating study for the fiction writer because the plot elements are handed down from Homer; whereas the presentation is done by Charles Lamb. Plot is an outline of happenings. Presentation is an expansion of that outline so that the details of the happenings are made available to the reader. Here is an outline of the *Adventure of Ulysses With the Cyclop*.

1. Ulysses and his party inspecting the Cyclop's cave
2. are surprised there and imprisoned by the owner.
3. Ulysses, in answer to the inquiries of the Cyclop,
4. tries to impress the Cyclop as being himself form-
5. idable. The monster is unimpressed, and eats two of
6. the party. Ulysses then tries to win over the Cyclop
7. with wine. The Cyclop is won over only to the extent
8. of agreeing to eat Ulysses last of the party.
9. Ulysses then burns out the eye of the Cyclop who,
10. in his anguish, shouts aloud to the other Cyclops
11. on the outside of the cave, urging them to help him.
12. Because Ulysses first called himself No-man, when the
13. Cyclop tells his friends that No-man has caused
14. his agony, they misunderstand and go away. The Cyclop
15. rolls away the stone, and plants himself in the doorway
16. hoping to capture the party as they emerge.
17. Ulysses escapes with his party under the bellies
18. of the rams.

You will see that this occupies 18 lines in plot outline. As it is presented by Charles Lamb it occupies 425 lines. From line 426 to 467 in the Case Book there is presented a Sequel to this particular adventure of Ulysses. The adventure is over when Ulysses is permitted to escape.

If you will examine this outline you will see that even in the outline a pattern emerges. It takes this form: first, a condition or state of affairs exists. Out of this state of affairs or condition grows the necessity that Ulysses shall escape in order to evade or to avert disaster. Following this comes Ulysses' attempt to bring about the accomplishment of his purpose. At last, when the Cyclop has released the rams, we know that Ulysses has succeeded in his purpose. Finally, there is the Sequel to the accomplishment of the purpose. This, reduced to its lowest elements, is the formula for every plot of accomplishment that you will ever write.

We can therefore be safe in adopting as our norm for the Story of Accomplishment the narrative pattern as follows:

1. A condition or state of affairs.
2. The necessity for accomplishment, projecting a definite purpose.
3. The attempt or attempts to bring about that accomplishment.
4. A Conclusive Act showing that the purpose has either been accomplished or been abandoned.
5. Sequel.

In *The Cop and the Anthem*, the condition is that Soapy realizes that winter is coming on, and that it is necessary for him to secure comfortable winter quarters. The main purpose which thereafter gives the story its unity is the purpose of Soapy to secure himself ninety days on the Island. Following this come the attempts of Soapy to bring about this Ending. After a number of these attempts have met with failure, he finally succeeds. The Sequel is that by this time he has, unfortunately, changed his mind in regard to wishing to go.

In *The Escape of Mr. Trimm*, Mr. Trimm realizes that if he can escape from the handcuffs, he will be able, because he is believed dead, to resume his old life, with his booty undisturbed. This is the condition. His purpose is to escape from the handcuffs. He makes a number of attempts, which fail. Finally, he abandons his attempts completely. The Sequel is that after he gives himself up he is not particularly interested in being freed from the handcuffs.

In *Spare Parts*, Monte English is told by Sally that if he does not drive her car for her, she will have to pay certain dire penalties. He has to pilot the Vindix car from Los Angeles to St. Louis in two weeks under its own power. After a number of attempts which promise disaster because they delay the possibility of success to the whole enterprise, he at last succeeds. The Sequel is that the hero wins the girl.

In *Jake Bolton, 551*, the condition is that Jake, independent, and unused to discipline has joined up as a volunteer. He has to make good in the army. He makes a series of attempts which are unsuccessful. At last, after throwing the bomb, he abandons his attempts. The Sequel is that he succeeds and is promoted and decorated.

In *Sunk*, Jason Terwilliger is in a condition where he is desperately in need of money. To escape from this condition, he has to kill Jake Finch. There is an attempt to overcome the difficulties lying in his way through his lack of physical strength, because his constitution has been sapped by dissipation. In the end he does succeed in killing Jake Finch.

In *Paradise Island*, Dwyer has to kill Langley. The condition bringing this necessity to the forefront is that Langley possesses certain information which may ruin his schemes. He makes an attempt, but upon perceiving the uselessness of it, he abandons it.

In *Once and Always*, Gideon Higsbee, finds himself in a position where he is unhappy because he at one time allowed a partner of his to be swindled out of ten thousand dollars. In order to achieve peace of mind he has to restore this sum with interest to his old partner. He makes an attempt which fails. He finally succeeds.

In *The Face in the Window*, Cora McBride is in dire need of money, and learns that she can secure five thousand dollars by capturing Hap Ruggam. She has to overcome and capture him. She makes an attempt to do so which fails. At last she succeeds. The Sequel is that she receives the reward for so doing.

In *Western Stuff*, the condition is that Verena Dayson realizes that she is in danger of losing her husband to another woman. She has to win back her husband from this other woman. She makes a series of attempts which fail. In the end she is successful. The Sequel is that he forgives her.

It is the central pupose of the chief actor in the story that gives to the story its narrative or plot unity. We can therefore say that not until this purpose has been apparent have you completed the Beginning of your story. The attempts growing out of that purpose will make up the Body of the story. The Conclusive Act and the Sequel will make up the Ending of the story. We are thus enabled to make three general divisions of the story and to acquire our first architectural conception of a Story of Accomplishment or Purpose. Thus:

Block 1. The Beginning.
      (a) The condition or state of affairs.'
      (b) The main purpose of a main actor.
Block 2. The Body.
      The attempt or attempts growing out of that main purpose.
Block 3. The Ending.
      (a) The Conclusive Act.
      (b) The Sequel.

As soon as a reader is made aware of a main purpose there is narrative unity to any Story of Accomplishment. This brings us at once to the question of nomenclature, as to just what is meant by narrative unity as opposed to any other kind of unity. The strict definition of narration is *an orderly recital of events*. But most people would be misled by this, because they would not think of events as having the strict and narrow meaning of "*what eventuates.*" If you will keep this meaning in mind, you will be helped tremendously in understanding what is meant by narrative unity in the modern short-story built about a main purpose.

The narrative unity comes from the main purpose and what eventuates or results at the conclusion of each of the attempts which the central actor makes to bring about that main purpose. The main purpose itself eventuates from the reaction of the chief actor to the basic condition which is the first unit of the story as we have presented it in outline.

Keeping this in mind let us look at a story from the point of view of a reader. Of the three factors for consideration: the material, the writer, and the reader, the reader is the most important; because no matter how interesting the material or how competent the writer, if the story does not capture and hold the attention of the reader all the work is wasted. *A story is written in order to be read.* There is for the reader in every story a dual interest in the character and in the story: in the character and in the character's purpose. As soon as the reader is aware of a unifying central purpose for a central character he is able to phrase for himself a question which is this: "Can the main character succeed in his attempts to bring about his main purpose?" A single character is shown reacting to a certain condition or state of affairs in such a way that the reader becomes aware of a definite main purpose actuating this chief character. He then, being aware of this purpose, is able to say to himself, "Can Ulysses succeed in escaping from the Cyclop?" "Can Mr. Trimm succeed in escaping from the handcuffs?" "Can Jake Bolton succeed in making good in the army?" "Can Monte English succeed in driving the Vindix across the continent in the allotted time?"

Uncertainty as to the outcome arises at once in the mind of the reader. Professor Chauncey W. Wells of the University of California uses a very suitable descriptive term for the question which the reader asks himself at this point. Professor Wells calls it a "Narrative Question." It is this main narrative question raised in the reader's mind at the earliest possible moment that captures

7

the reader's interest. And it is the reader's desire to know the outcome of the actor's various attempts to answer this main narrative question which holds that reader's interest until the end of the story. That is *narrative curiosity*. Just so long as there is doubt in the mind of the reader in regard to the answer to the main narrative question there is narrative curiosity or *narrative suspense*. Once this main narrative question is answered the reader's narrative curiosity ceases. Capturing narrative curiosity in a story, therefore, consists of introducing the main narrative situation or purpose which causes the reader to ask himself a Main Narrative Question. Sustaining narrative curiosity consists in making clear, at the close of each attempt, that the outcome is still in suspense.

At the close of each attempt, the writer will make clear to the reader that there is a crisis or turning point in the main narrative. These narrative turning points can be only of two kinds: 1. A turning point of furtherance, when if the story closed at that point the answer to the main narrative question would be "yes." It may be that the attempt places the main actor in a position where he is closer to success than he was before. At such a point in the story there is a turning point of furtherance. 2. On the other hand, if the attempt brings the main actor to a point where he is further than ever from success it is a turning point of hindrance. There comes eventually in every story an event that is the result of a series of attempts, or even of a single attempt, when it becomes clear to the reader that the main narrative question is answered, either affirmatively or negatively, by a Conclusive Act, which shows definitely that the purpose has either been achieved or has been abandoned.

Thus the major narrative turning points of the story are these:

1. The main purpose or Main Narrative Question. (In the Beginning.)
2. Turning points of furtherance. (In the Body.)
3. Turning points of hindrance. (In the Body.)
4. A turning point which is a Conclusive Act. (In the Ending.)

The more the outcome is left in doubt by these turning points which come at the close of attempts in the Body of the story the more plot interest there is; in other words, the more hindrances there are, the greater is the narrative curiosity.

There is another kind of curiosity which, for want of a better

8

term I shall call "general curiosity." It is the response called forth in a reader when he asks himself, "Now why did the actor do just that thing?" A case in point you will find in the *Adventure of Ulysses* on line 226 to 243, where Ulysses chooses a stake, sharpens and hardens it in the fire, selects four men and instructs them what they are to do with this stake, and makes them perfect in their parts. You know, of course, that it has some bearing upon the outcome, but you do not know just what its use is to be. The response excited in the reader in this case is not *narrative* curiosity but *general* curiosity. The two interests may go hand in hand. Had Ulysses been caused to say to one of his men, "Now I feel that we have a way of escape," there would have been, at the close of the attempt, an *event* which would be a crisis of furtherance to the main narrative question, while at the same time the general curiosity in regard to the use to be made of the stake would still be unallayed.

Let us pause a moment and test what we have learned in order to see if it will bring about the desired result of producing a plot which will be likely to capture and hold a reader's attention,—a story outline, that is, which developed, might be accepted by some good magazine.

Assume that the condition is that a man is walking along a country road on a summer day and feels slightly thirsty. On the side of the road, about fifty yards away, is a well on the top of which is a bucket, brimming with cool water. The man's purpose is to go over and get himself a drink. You have here a condition and a purpose which are the first two elements of a story. The man walks over, and about twenty-five yards from the bucket he meets a boy and says, "Will you give me a cup so that I can get a drink of water?" The boy says, "I'm sorry, I've got to run along, but my brother will get one for you." You have here an attempt which results in a furtherance, because the man is now nearer his purpose than he was before. He goes to the brother who is only a short distance from the well and says, "Will you lend me a cup, please?" and the brother says, "No. Go and get your own cup if you want it." This is a turning point of hindrance. The man then proceeds alone to the well, lifts the bucket between his hands to his mouth, and drinks deeply. This is a Conclusive Act. There are here present all the elements of a short-story: condition, purpose, attempt, crisis of furtherance, another attempt, crisis of hindrance, a final attempt resulting in a successful Conclusive Act. The major narrative question is answered in the affirmative. If all the plot elements are present are you then justified in developing the attempts, that is, filling in the details of the outline, and sending this story to a good magazine with every hope of success? The answer is, quite obviously, "No." There are two reasons for this. The first is that the condition or state of affairs is not, of itself, sufficiently dramatic to capture the reader's attention in such a way as to cause him to be interested in the outcome of the main purpose of the actor. It is not *important* enough. The second reason is that the attempts themselves are not sufficiently dramatic.

At once we see that narrative interest alone is not sufficient to make a good plot. It must in addition be dramatic. In order that you may understand these requirements, I should like you to read over the first 225 lines of the *Adventure of Ulysses with the Cyclop*. These 225 lines set forth the condition which is interesting enough to capture our attention, because it contains the promise of a difficulty to be removed, of an opponent to be overcome, and of disaster to be averted. In order to remove, or overcome or avert these varying elements, the main character must engage in conflict so that our interest is captured in the setting forth of the condition by the promise which it holds of conflict or clash. This conflict or clash between the actor and forces or conditions opposed to his purpose will grow out of the main character's attempts to overcome or remove the difficulty, to remove or overcome the opponent, and to avert disaster. The consequence is that the greater the threat of disaster, and the greater the promise of clash the more interesting the reader finds the statement of the condition. Therefore, the condition under which a main character is forced into the necessity for accomplishment *should be a condition promising conflict or threatening disaster*. Clearly, too, if, at the end of an attempt, the resulting crisis is a turning point of furtherance it is not so interesting a turning point as a turning point of hindrance. This is because the more hindrance or defeats there are the closer the hero is brought to ultimate disaster. The way to sustain interest in the turning points of the plot is to include as large a number as possible of hindering rather than furthering crises.

If the demands of your story are such that only a furthering crisis at a certain point is possible in order to bring about a meeting which will result in an extremely dramatic hindering crisis you will be wise if you will immediately indicate that although success has temporarily crowned the efforts of the actor this success is only very temporary. For example, on lines 326 to 333 of the *Adventure of Ulysses* there is a turning point of furtherance when Ulysses and his followers succeed in blinding the Cyclop. But instantly there is promise of disaster or failure of the main attempt when "he cried out in a mighty voice for his brethren the Cyclops who dwelt hardby in caverns upon hills;" and the reader learns that these other Cyclops, hearing the terrible shout, come flocking from all parts to inquire what ailed Polyphemus. Thus a *narrative* turning point of furtherance, which, from the point of view of suspense, is not so desireable as a *narrative* turning point of hindrance, is turned into, or is instantly followed by, a turning point of hindrance.

It must, however, be noted that this turning point of hindrance is not a *narrative* but a *dramatic* hindrance.

A *narrative hindrance* is a temporary defeat. A *dramatic hindrance* is the promise of ultimate defeat, even though there is a temporary triumph. *Drama*, for the short-story writer, consists of

(a) the promise of difficulties to be overcome.
(b) the promise of conflict with a new opponent.
(c) the promise of additional conflict with the same opposing force.
(d) the promise of disaster to the venture of the chief actor.

It is apparent, then, that the crises or turning points of a story may be either dramatic or narrative, or both. So it is with the attempts or meetings which intervene between the crises of the plot.

These attempts or meetings—the presentation units—may be interesting only as they lead into events which contribute dramatic or narrative interest to the plot. They may also be interesting in their own right. The less the outline of these attempts or meetings is filled in, the less they are, of themselves, interesting; and the more they must depend upon the story or plot interest to hold the reader. In such case the reader's interest is held by the event or outcome of the attempt rather than by the attempt itself. In such a story the chief interest is *plot* interest rather than *presentation* interest.

On the other hand, the more the outline is filled in and developed, the more it will be, of itself, sufficient to hold the reader's interest. Then there is *presentation* interest.

To understand fully the essential difference between an attempt or meeting introduced for the sake of advancing the plot (plot interest) as compared with an attempt or meeting introduced with the intent of holding interest upon its own account (presentation interest), I shall ask you to turn to *The Adventure of Ulysses*.

Read, first, lines 226 to 243;

Then, read lines 244 to 297.

In each of these two attempts to bring about a satisfactory outcome the very same elements occur. In the first one the attempt is introduced by the author to carry the reader swiftly to a turning point in the plot. He is not interested in the details of the meeting and the interchange between Ulysses and his four men, except as its occurrence eventuates in a crisis which affects the plot.

In comparison with this there is a different use of the very same elements in that portion of the Adventure occupying lines 244 to 297. There is a meeting and an interchange between Ulysses and the Cyclop, in which Ulysses tries to persuade the Cyclop to allow him to go with a whole skin in recompense for the wine that he offers him. Here the interchange between Ulysses and the Cyclop is in itself interesting; because it is dramatic through a clash of purposes. Ulysses' purpose to persuade the Cyclop is in dramatic clash with the Cyclop's purpose to discover Ulysses' name. At the conclusion of this interchange the purpose of Ulysses is defeated; for the Cyclop says, "This is the kindness I will show thee No-man: I will eat thee last of all thy friends." This is on line 294 to 297. Thus there is presentation interest in the interchange, and *plot* interest in the result or *event* of the interchanges. This event is a crisis of narrative *hindrance*, because the immediate purpose of the meeting or interchange is defeated; it is also a crisis of *dramatic* hindrance because it brings closer or foreshadows the ultimate disaster which threatens Ulysses' venture.

This would seem to be a good moment to discuss the make-up of the presentation unit. Every story is made up of an alternation of presentation units and plot crises. Together these make an architectural norm. It is by now, I trust, evident that the presentation units are those portions of a story which are concerned primarily with the characterization of the people in the story, and particularly with the main actor in the story.

It is better for the moment to confine ourselves for illustration to those presentation units which occur in the Body of the Story, rather than to those presentation units which occur in the other divisions. Turn first to the *Adventure of Ulysses*. The responses of Ulysses indicated on lines 226 to 243 show him acting in such a way as to indicate what the author calls on line 233 "manly wisdom." On lines 244 to 297 Ulysses' responses are again shown; but in addition to this there are shown the responses of the Cyclop. From lines 297 to 336 the responses are those of Ulysses and of the Cyclop. From lines 337 to 357 the responses shown are those of the Cyclop Polyphemus and those of his brethren on the outside.

A consideration of these is ample for our purpose. They disclose that the presentation units are concerned with meetings or interchanges involving character responses that lead into plot crises. They further disclose that these responses may be the responses of any actors whatsoever in the story; and further they show that the turning points or crises may be led into through a presentation unit which includes the responses of actors other than the main actor, as in the case of the interchange between Polyphemus and his brethren on the outside of the cave, which makes up one of the presentation units.

Characterization reduced to its simplest elements is showing, by the responses to stimuli, the kind of person an actor is. In fact, this formula for characterization follows through into the most complex reaches of characterization. The character's responses can be shown by what he does, by what he says, and by what he thinks. It can be shown also by the effect of his action or his personality upon others. Anything that brings out any responses whatsoever is a stimulus to an actor in a story. It is axiomatic that no actor in a story can respond to a stimulus without becoming aware of that stimulus. So that basically, every character response of an actor to a stimulus involves a contact with or meeting with that stimulus. That is why I have said that in the presentation unit the writers will present meetings and interchanges.

A meeting does not necessarily involve an interchange, although it very often does. There are three kinds of meetings two of which are interchanges. It is essential that you learn to distinguish between these three kinds of meetings, because each one has its own special use in a presentation unit; and for that reason I am going to ask you to employ a very definite and rigid nomenclature, which will enable you to avoid any difficulty of misunderstanding as to the meaning of what I shall say in the future about any of the stories in this volume.

For the first kind of meeting, then, the one which serves to show merely the reaction of the actors to a stimulus, the stimulus not reacting upon the actor I shall ask you to employ the word *incident*. The incident is the single act of a single actor reacting to a stimulus, the stimulus itself being inactive to the extent of having no design upon the actor. From lines 99 to 102 you can find an example of what I have in mind. The stimulus is the appearance of Polyphemus. The incident is that the Greeks hide themselves in the remote parts of the cave. Sometimes a response involves a series of incidents. The actor does more than one thing.

13

If you will turn to the story *Spare Parts*, Case No. 3, and read from line 612 to 639 you will get a clearer idea of what I have in mind. The actor is Monte. The stimulus of which he becomes aware is the proposal made by Carson Kerry. On lines 637 to 639 we find the response. "He merely got up and opened the door." If we are very meticulous we can say that there are two actions of a single force: 1. Monte got up. 2. Monte opened the door. It doesn't matter a bit. The point involved is that the response is rendered in terms of incident.

If you will turn to *Paradise Island*, Case No. 7, you will find that the first three lines include the single reaction of a single force to a stimulus. The stimulus is the ditch; the single response of Dwyer is to halt. It is rendered, "Dwyer halted at the ditch." It then goes on and says, "abruptly as though an invisible hand had seized his arm. An idea rang in his brain. This would be the place to kill a man." On line 5 you become aware of a purpose, that is, that Dwyer proposes to kill a man. In this the single act of a character in responding to a stimulus has projected a main narrative purpose. If you will read from line 124 of the same story to line 144 you will see that Dwyer again becomes aware of a stimulus, but this time instead of his response projecting a major crisis, it merely leads into an interchange between him and Mrs. Dwyer. This particular interchange, which closes on line 171, is an example of the second kind of meeting, which for the purpose of clarity I shall refer to hereafter as an Episode. An *episode* is the meeting of two forces involving an interchange without clash.

In *Spare Parts*, lines 284 to 342 contain an interchange which varies from the one you have just examined in that it contains clash. For this particular kind of meeting,—an interchange, involving clash, I shall hereafter use the descriptive term *encounter*. You will recall that when I spoke of what is dramatic I said that conflict is dramatic,—conflict or clash. And you will notice that I have said here that the distinguishing quality which differentiates an Encounter from an Episode is that the Encounter is an interchange that is dramatic.

You see now that in the presentation unit you have three ways in which you can show the response of an actor to stimuli. One, the meeting where the actor is alone and responds by a series of actions. The other, in which the actor is not alone but is concerned in an interchange with somebody else. When the force is kindly the interchange is an Episode. When the force is unfriendly, and the two clash, the interchange is then dramatic, and is called an Encounter.

A word or two more and we shall have done forever, I trust, with nomenclature. I shall ask you to read lines 1 to 60 of the story *Spare Parts* and then turn to lines 606 to 649. Both of these are interchanges with clash and would be set down under the categories we have just discussed as Encounters. The difference between these two Encounters and the other Encounter on lines 284 to 342 is that there is in each of these other two Encounters a central unifying purpose, which is never lost sight of throughout the interchange. On lines 731 to 751 there is also an interchange, which is an Episode, which has the same unification of purpose. In this case Monte purposes to get information from the mechanic Mac. In the interchange which opens the story between Carson Kerry and Sally the purpose of Carson Kerry is to dissuade Sally from a course of conduct which she proposes to adopt. In the interchange between Carson and Monte beginning on line 606 the purpose of Carson is to persuade Monte to adopt a course of conduct, that is, to accept the bribe. You will recall that I said that whenever a purpose is apparent there is narrative interest. Whenever clash or the promise of clash is apparent there is dramatic interest, so that there may be interchanges which are narrative and interchanges which are dramatic, as well as interchanges which are both narrative and dramatic.

If one person proposes to another that that other adopt a course of conduct, the narrative unity is sustained until the reader knows whether or not the other actor has acceded to the proposal of the first one. Then that special narrative interest ceases. If during the process of the interchange, the two clash there is in addition to the narrative interest dramatic interest. If there is no clash the interest must be narrative throughout, and the interchange is episodic instead of dramatic.

You will see now that an Incident can grow into other Incidents, and a series of Incidents may result without any interchange at all. But usually such an interchange is bound to result from the accumulation of Incidents. This interchange may be episodic because no clash is involved; or it may become dramatic by the addition of clash. Therefore, we find that there is an ultimate unit called the *scene*, which involves, as a presentation unit, four steps:

1. The meeting.
2. The scene purpose, raising a minor or Scene Narrative Question.

3. The interchange, which may be either episodic or dramatic.
4. The Conclusive Act, which answers the minor or scene narrative question raised by that immediate purpose.

The interchange between Monte English and the mechanic is an episodic scene. The interchange between Monte and Carson Kerry, and the one between Carson Kerry and Sally are both dramatic scenes.

We have now completed our investigation of nomenclature and can proceed upon a ground of common understanding. Whenever the word "incident" is used it will be understood to mean the single act of a single force.

Whenever the word "episode" is used it will be understood to mean the interchange between two forces without clash.

Whenever the word "encounter" is used it will be understood to mean the interchange between two forces with clash.

Whenever the words "episodic scene" are used they will be understood to mean the friendly meeting of two forces one of whom has a purpose to which the other is not opposed.

Whenever the words "dramatic scene" are used they will be understood to mean the interchange between two actors, or an actor and a force, with clash growing out of the purpose of one actor.

With these distinctions between the different types of presentation unit clear in our minds we can establish an architectural concept that will be a norm for any Story of Accomplishment whatsoever. Individuality will be achieved by varying the number and the length of these presentation units. Such variation will be determined by the amount of material to be presented in order to make the reader aware of the plot crises. It is safe therefore to say that the author writes presentation units for the ultimate purpose of making the reader aware, at the close of each such unit, of one or more plot crises.

Architecturally then, a story is a series of blocks. Each of these is a presentation unit. The reader enjoys each for its own sake; but furnishes an additional enjoyment himself by realizing when he has finished reading each one, that it has a connection with a pattern or plot. He cannot do this until he is aware of a plot crisis. Unless the reader so responds, the writer is unsuccessful in achieving his artistic purpose.

The accompanying chart will serve as an architectural norm, showing the arrangement and proportioning of a typical short-story.

NOMENCLATURE

ARCHITECTURAL NORM CHART

THE BEGINNING	Condition.	Presentation Unit No. 1, meeting or interchange.	Promise of conflict to remove a difficulty. (Plot Crisis Type A).
		Presentation Unit No. 2, meeting or interchange.	Promise of conflict to overcome an opponent. (Plot Crisis Type B.)
		Presentation Unit No. 3, meeting or interchange.	Promise of conflict to avert disaster. (Plot Crisis Type C.)
	Response.	Presentation Unit No. 4, meeting usually.	The main actor's central purpose is clear to the reader. He phrases a main narrative question. (Plot Crisis Type D.)
THE BODY	Attempt.	Foreshadowed conflict developed in dramatic scene. Type A.	Dramatic or narrative hindrance. (Plot Crisis Type E.)
	Renewed Attempt.	Foreshadowed conflict developed in dramatic scene. Type B.	Dramatic or narrative hindrance. (Plot Crisis Type E.)
	Renewed Attempt.	Foreshadowed conflict developed in dramatic scene. Type C.	Dramatic or narrative hindrance. (Plot Crisis Type E.
THE ENDING	The Conclusive Act.	Meeting or interchange.	The main narrative question phrased by the reader is answered. (Plot Crisis Type F.)
	The Sequel.	Meeting or interchange.	Significance explained. (Plot Crisis Type G.)

A study of this chart will disclose certain enlightening information.

The Beginning contains two general subdivisions: the Condition or state of affairs, and the narrative response of the actor. In presenting the Beginning the author writes the necessary presentation units to make clear to the reader a Condition with dramatic possibilities. The reader on reading these presentation units becomes aware that the Condition so presented has dramatic promise, because it foreshadows conflicts.

In the chart I have chosen three such presentation units. At the close of each one I have indicated that there is a plot crisis, and that each of these plot crises differs somewhat from the others. They are all *dramatic* and not *narrative* crises.

Type A makes the reader aware of a Difficulty to be removed.

Type B makes the reader aware of an Opponent to be overcome.

Type C makes the reader aware of a Disaster to be averted.

It is from the Condition or State of Affairs, which is the first of the subdivisions of the Beginning, that the Plot acquires its *dramatic* interest. In the Beginning also, the author presents the necessary presentation units to show the *necessity for accomplishment by the chief actor*.

The reader, upon reading these units, becomes aware of a *narrative* interest. This projects the main narrative crisis of the story, which causes the reader to phrase for himself a main narrative question;

"Can A succeed in accomplishing (his purpose)?"

It is from the response of the central actor, which is the second of the sub-divisions of the Beginning, that the plot acquires its *narrative* interest. There can be no narrative interest until the reader is aware of the actor's purpose; because only when this purpose is apparent can the reader phrase for himself a main narrative question: "Can the chief actor succeed in accomplishing his purpose?" When the reader becomes aware of this purpose there is a fourth plot crisis (Type D.) It is not *dramatic*, but *narrative*.

Thus it appears that the Beginning has four plot crises; the first three, dramatic; the fourth, narrative. All of these crises come at the conclusion of presentation units. All of the crises are essential to the plot. All the Presentation Units are *not* essential. The Condition or State of Affairs may be set forth in one, two, or three presentation units. If all three *dramatic* plot crises can emerge from a single presentation unit, then one presentation unit is sufficient.

It is sometimes possible, in a single Presentation Unit to present the three dramatic plot crises of the Condition and the fourth plot or purpose crisis, which is narrative.

The norm, then, for the Beginning is:—Presentation Units necessary to set forth the Main Condition and the Chief Actor's main Purpose in such a way that the reader phrases for himself a Main Narrative Question and is aware of the Dramatic Crises which show the Promise of Conflict (a) to remove a Difficulty, (b) to overcome an Opposing Force, (c) to avert Disaster to the Main Purpose.

In the Body of the story the author writes such presentation units as will develop the conflicts foreshadowed in the Beginning by Plot Crises Types A, B, and C. Since there are three types of conflict possible I have indicated as a norm three presentation units. It will, however, be obvious that great variation is possible here.

The reader, at the close of each conflict so developed in an interchange (preferably a dramatic scene) is aware of a heightened interest in the main plot. His feeling of suspense is sustained at the close of each interchange by keeping the outcome of the main accomplishment in doubt through a plot crisis of *Hindrance*. This Hindrance (Type E Plot Crisis) may be either a *dramatic* or a *narrative* crisis. In a norm of three interchanges, in order that the expectations of the reader may be realized in respect to all three conflicts promised in the Beginning the first two attempts cannot meet with success; for such success would eliminate the necessity for the other conflicts.

Equally, if in the Beginning the Plot Crises A, B, and C have not been stressed they cannot be plausibly developed in the Body.

In the Ending, made up of the Conclusive Act and its Sequel, the author writes the necessary presentation units that will show the reader that the actor has achieved his main purpose or has abandoned it. This is the Conclusive Act.

Sometimes, where this Conclusive Act is ambiguous, the author writes an additional presentation unit or units to explain the significance of the Conclusive Act. (In many stories, no such explanation is necessary; and there is, therefore, no sequel.)

The reader, having read the presentation units containing the Conclusive Act feels his narrative curiosity satisfied. The main narrative-question he has phrased is now answered. (Plot Crisis Type F.)

Having read the presentation units which set forth the Sequel, the reader feels his general curiosity satisfied. This is Plot Crisis Type G.

The Sequel is concerned with catching up loose ends. It is frequently the equivalent of the Moral of the older stories. Sometimes a story, being written merely to entertain, has no special significance, and, therefore, no sequel. Sometimes what slight significance a story possesses may be voiced in the final words of a character which are themselves the Conclusive Act.

In studying this chart, therefore, readers must regard it as a norm against which to measure short-stories. Variation is permitted in the size and number of the Presentation Units. In size they may vary from a single incident (presented as a meeting showing the single response of an actor to a stimulus), to a prolonged dramatic scene (involving the dramatic interchange between two forces whose purposes are definitely opposed).

The number of presentation units is dependent upon the size of each one.

The length of an average short-story is from six to ten thousand words; so that in the scope of that length much variation is possible. A story may achieve its length from any one of the three great divisions of Beginning, Body, or Ending. When we come to examine the stories in this volume we shall see some illuminating examples of this variation.

Since each of these divisions may vary in length, the number of Presentation Units in each division is variable. It will depend upon two factors: upon the length of each Presentation Unit, and upon the proportionate length of the division of which it forms a part.

Two general possibilities lie open to the writer of the short-story:

1. A large number of short presentation units, in a story whose interest is chiefly in the plot.
2. A smaller number of prolonged presentation units in a story in which the interest is chiefly in the dramatic quality of the scenes, with less emphasis upon the plot.

Loosely, the difference will be that the first will be a story of plot, and the second will be a story of character. The first will hold the reader through his interest in the person who is called upon to solve the problem. These distinctions are, as I said, loose and by no means rigid. The ideal story combines the two types, having a narrative problem which is in itself interesting, no matter what actor is called upon to solve it, and in addition presenting a chief actor whose responses enliven the interchanges of the presentation units.

You will notice that upon this norm chart I have indicated a series of presentation units, and have shown that at the close of each presentation unit there is a turning point or Crisis, which in every case is called the "fifth step." This would seem to indicate that the presentation units must always be composed of the four steps which make up a complete scene, thus:

Step 1. Meeting
Step 2. Purpose of Scene
Step 3. Interchange, either episodic or dramatic
Step 4. Conclusive Act of Scene

This is not a rigid requirement. The Presentation Unit at its fullest development includes these four steps; but sometimes some steps are omitted and the turning point or Plot Crisis, which is the fifth step, is reached swiftly. It is from this Fifth Step that the plot interest comes. It is a constant factor, even though some of the first four steps may be omitted. The first four steps are concerned with *Presentation* interest, the fifth step is concerned with *Plot* interest. When presentation interest is subordinated to plot interest, the presentation units are shortened by the omission of some of the steps. The Fifth Step will be either a narrative crisis of the plot, or a dramatic crisis of the plot. If a narrative turning point, it will indicate that there is a Furtherance or Hindrance to the attempt of the main actor to achieve his purpose. If it is a dramatic turning point it will show that even though a narrative Furtherance has occurred there is a dramatic turning point which promises Conflict or Disaster.

If you will turn again to *Spare Parts*, Case No. 3 you will see what I mean. Lines 606 to 650 are the first four steps of a Scene. Lines 606 to 615 constitute the first step, which is the contact or meeting of the two forces, Kerry and Monte. Lines 619 to 633 constitute the second step, which is the scene purpose, showing that Carson hopes to persuade Monte to lose the race. Lines 634 to 649 constitute the third step, which is the interchange with clash. Lines 650 and 652 constitute the fourth step, which is the Conclusive Act, showing the reader that Carson has been forced to abandon that immediate purpose of persuading Monte to accept a bribe to lose the race.

What I want you particularly to notice is that line 652 to line 654 are the fifth step of the Scene. The fifth step is used to show the effect of the presentation unit upon the actors, particularly as it affects the outcome of the main narrative purpose. In this case the effect, or fifth step, is a dramatic crisis because it contains the promise of conflict with a dangerous opponent, that is, with a person who is likely to endanger the outcome of the main purpose of the story.

Examine with especial care also lines 655 to 673. They are an Episodic Scene because they include the steps necessary in such a presentation unit:—the meeting between Carson and the foreman; the purpose of Carson, which is to persuade the foreman to put the Vindix out of commission; an interchange, which is episodic because there is no clash; and a Conclusive Act, which is the man's statement, "All right. Leave it to me." This Episodic Scene is part of the fifth step of the preceding scene between Carson and Monte. It contributes the promise of disaster to the plot. The fifth step of this scene, therefore, begins on line 652 and ends on line 673, and it contains the promise of conflict with an opponent dangerous to the success of the whole enterprise, and a promise of disaster as well.

Thus the fifth step of a scene may be such an important turning point in the plot as to constitute *by itself* a complete presentation unit. Strictly speaking, every presentation unit after the first is part of the fifth step of that first presentation unit, because in the properly plotted story, everything which occurs should be the outgrowth of everything preceding it.

Every presentation unit has its fifth step in the plot unless the story is poorly plotted. In the plotted story there should be no presentation unit which does not lead into a fifth or plot step. The fifth or Plot Step is the effect or outcome of what has happened in the presentation unit. Thus for example, lines 674 to 730 are the fifth step of the Episodic Scene between the foreman and Carson Kerry. In analyzing stories you may be puzzled in an attempt to isolate this fifth step. You will be helped if you keep in mind that the fifth step is the outcome or the effect upon the Plot of the presentation unit, and may be itself a meeting or an interchange.

Thus your story may have plot interest or presentation interest in proportion as you stress either the fifth step or the interchange which at its highest point of development has four steps. When it has four steps it is a Scene, and it may be dramatic just as a story is dramatic. The Dramatic Scene contains all the elements of a complete story. It is in fact a miniature short-story. It has its own scene narrative question, just as the story has its main narrative question. The complete story is made up of a number of these Scenes. Even though, sometimes, some of the steps of a scene are omitted, they cannot be omitted in all cases. Incomplete Scenes are sometimes permissible, but no story can be made up entirely of incomplete Scenes. Some time in the course of your story you are going to be called upon to present a Dramatic Scene which is, as I have pointed out to you, built up from the basic structural unit of the Incident (the single act of the single force), which may be expanded gradually into:

1. Episode
2. Encounter
3. Episodic Scene
4. Dramatic Scene

Clearly then, if every story consists of a number of Scenes, in order to be able to write a short-story you must first be able to

(a) distinguish between story narrative questions and scene narrative questions,

(b) build up an Incident througn its different phases until it becomes a Dramatic Scene,

(c) present the Dramatic Scene convincingly so that the character or the actors emerge,

(d) indicate clearly to the reader at the close of each Scene, through its fifth step, even though the other steps are incomplete, the turning point or Plot Crisis which may be either dramatic or narrative.

If you depend upon the turning points of your plot for the chief interest of your story you may have in your presentation units incomplete scenes. On the other hand, if your chief interest is in the characterization of your actors you must depend for your interest largely upon the dramatic scene. Throughout each dramatic scene, through the actor's reaction to different stimuli, you will make his character clear to your reader. In the long run you will realize that characterization is everything in a story, and that your real reason for familiarizing yourself with structural devices is to acquire complete control of method in order that you may not be hampered by uncertainty as to method in rendering character through the medium of the dramatic scene in the modern short-story.

The chief aim of this book is to show you that the fundamental architectural conception of a short story is that it is a series of blocks, each block being a presentation unit which is either an incomplete scene or a dramatic scene. However, since no architectural conception of a story will *of itself* produce a story which is lifelike there must be within that architectural conception, that is, within those blocks, the breath of life which comes from convincing characterization of actors shown responding to various stimuli.

Characterization is the chief aim of the writer of the short-story. Without it his story is dead. It is made clear to the reader in presentation units, of which the dramatic scene is the highest development. For this reason, the value to you of knowing just what constitutes a scene is inestimable. A scene is a smaller unit than a complete story; yet in architectural conception it is the same. Being the same in essence as the complete story, having both narrative and dramatic interest, the dramatic scene gives you the opportunity for developing your plotting ability as well as your presentation ability. Just as the story has a Beginning, a Body, an Ending and a Sequel, so has the scene. It includes, just as the story does,

An impression of the time, place, and social atmosphere;
an impression of an actor's appearance;
an impression of the various stimuli to which the actor responds.

Since the largest number of your scenes will be scenes in which the opposition to one actor is furnished by another actor, the second actor and his responses will be the stimuli to which the first one will respond. Thus the very first step in a dramatic scene of that kind will be to bring the two actors together, that is, to bring about a contact or meeting. You achieve narrative interest in this scene when you show your reader that one of the actors has a purpose. It may be to persuade the other to adopt a course of conduct. It may be to convince the other in some argument. It may be to impress the other with his own weakness or his own strength. It may be, and will very frequently be, to secure information from the other. In the so called "action-story," it will be an attempt to overcome by physical force. Just as in the story you achieve dramatic interest when you show the promise of opposition or disaster, so you achieve dramatic interest in your scene when you make clear to your reader that the second actor is opposed to the purpose of the first actor.

This promise of opposition or of clash to come makes up with the scene purpose the Beginning of the narrative scene. In plotting your dramatic scene you will keep in mind that the purpose of the first actor may grow out of the meeting with the second actor.' Ordinarily this will be the case, yet there are occasions on which the meeting will grow out of the purpose. For example, if A wishes to persuade a banker to loan him $2,000 he may go to that banker.

In this case the purpose will bring about the meeting; yet it is possible that A may not have thought of trying to borrow $2,000 from the banker until after he had met the banker who told him that money was rather easy at that particular moment. This knowledge may spur the first actor to a purpose of attempting to borrow $2,000 from the other. In that case, the purpose grew out of the meeting.

Whichever one you choose will make practically no difference in your scene. Plausibility will determine, in most cases. Yet, if the promise of opposition makes dramatic interest, it is a good idea to indicate that the opposition exists and then to indicate the purpose, so that the reader's interest will be heightened as soon as he learns that the purpose involves a clash or conflict with an opponent who is unlikely to accede to the request.

In plotting and presenting a dramatic scene you will endeavor to make the detail create the impression of being a reproduction of actual life. In giving your actor a purpose in the scene you will endeavor to reproduce the ordinary purposes which actuate people on every hand. In that way you will achieve verisimilitude, or the appearance of truth. The five purposes which I indicated in the second last paragraph are those purposes which you will find ordinarily actuate the average human being. Because this is so, the reader is able to find himself in sympathy with the actor in your story. As soon as such a common and usual purpose appears, the reader is caused to ask himself a scene narrative question.

Can actor A secure information from actor B?
Can actor A convince actor B?
Can actor A persuade actor B to adopt a course of conduct?
Can actor A impress actor B?
Can actor A overcome actor B?

Once you have enlisted the narrative interest of a reader in the scene purpose of an actor and have added dramatic interest as a hint of conflict or of failure because of the unlikelihood of the opponent agreeing with the actor, you have paved the way for the third step of your scene which is the interchange between the actor and his opponent. Because of the opposition which you have foreshadowed, it is quite evident that there will be clash in this interchange, and that it will be the kind of interchange which is an encounter.

In developing this type of interchange you will keep in mind that you have the possibility of developing both narrative and dramatic interest in that interchange. You preserve the narrative unity of that special scene by keeping the outcome of the actor's purpose in doubt. There will be no doubt, however, as to his purpose holding. The tendency of the amateur is to become so interested in the clash which ensues, that he allows the actor to lose sight of the special purpose. This, of course, the writer may do deliberately, but I am talking now about a tendency to be guarded against rather than one to be indulged.

In a scene, you achieve narrative unity by making every speech or act of actor A one which is intended to accomplish his object in the scene. Every such attempt is a Scene-Furtherance even though it does not promise success. Every speech or act of actor B will be intended to defeat the efforts or objective in the scene of actor A. Every such attempt to defeat the scene purpose is a scene hindrance.

By concentrating upon this narrative unity of the scene you almost unconsciously achieve dramatic interest in the interchange; because in order to achieve furtherance on the one hand and hindrance on the other, there must be a clash in the purposes of the two people even though there is no clash in their traits. At the close of this interchange one has either succeeded in his purpose or abandoned his purpose. In that case the Conclusive Act will show it.

Now if you will turn to the story *Once and Always*, Case No. 8, you will see from line 75 to 171 an illustration of what I mean. Lines 75 to 110 show the contact or meeting between Lemuel Gower and Gideon Higsbee, and the fact that each has responded in a different way to the three strangers indicate that they will clash in any purpose involving those three strangers. Thus you have the first step of the scene made dramatic by the promise of conflict. Immediately there grows out of this meeting or contact a purpose of one of the actors. In this case the actor whose purpose emerges is Lemuel Gower. The purpose is to persuade Gideon to adopt a course of conduct,—to go over and speak to the strangers.

From then on the interchange involves furtherances and hindrances of that purpose. Every attempt of Lemuel to bring about his purpose is a furtherance, every attempt of Gideon to defeat that purpose is a hindrance. The interchange continues to the end of line 153. On the next line the interchange is over through the Conclusive Act and speech of Lemuel when he says, "Well, if you won't speak to 'em, I will," and walks across the lobby of the Agamemnon House, "with his rubber shoes making an honest sound upon the floor." This is an example of a Scene containing the four steps which are essential to every Scene.

Lines 162 to 171 include the fifth step by showing the reflections of the actor upon what has just passed. The fifth step of any Scene is made up of the effect of the Scene upon the actor. It may involve his thoughts, it may involve action growing out of his reflections. Sometimes the reflections are omitted and the action follows without any indication of thoughts preceding it. In this case the effect is that Gideon watches Lemuel go; and he sums up his conclusions regarding what has just passed in the phrase, "Once a sucker, always a sucker."

Sometimes, in a scene, the special purpose of the actor does not immediately emerge. In the Scene which you have just examined the purpose emerges at once. But I want you now to look at another scene in which the main purpose is led up to through an interchange of conversation. This Scene you will find in the same story, *Once and Always*, on lines 917 to 1235. This Scene has its complete four steps. It has the meeting between Lemuel and Gideon. Before this in the story you have been told by the author that Gideon feels that Lemuel may be foolish enough not to take back the money, so that there is the hint of opposition. When Gideon first goes in, the main purpose does not emerge, but the interchange is concerned with his securing information from Lemuel as to his present financial status. Not until line 1114 when this information has been secured, does Gideon's real purpose emerge. He says, "And that's what I'm here for now, Lemuel, because I did know. I guess it hadn't occurred to me until the other day; but I guess I cheated you just as much as they did." From then on the interchange is concerned with Gideon's attempt to restore the money to Lemuel, and with Lemuel's arguments against taking the money. The conclusive act comes on line 1228 when Lemuel acts. "He seized Gideon's hand, and pressed something into Gideon's palm. Gideon felt it. It was the check. 'Honest Gid,' said Lemuel, 'Take it back. I couldn't keep it. I'm gettin' to be an old man Gid, and my conscience wouldn't let me.'" Thus we see the four steps of the scene completed and we see the fifth step, the effect upon the actors, is expanded into another interchange between Gideon and his friend George on lines 1236 to 1270.

Before turning to a detailed discussion of each of the stories I have chosen as a case in craftsmanship, I should like to say a word as to the reasons which dictated their choice. I have long been convinced that no one writer combines ultimate perfection in any single story. Yet I have been equally convinced that perfection comes from either presentation or plotting, that a writer's capacity may be judged by his ability to achieve his effect either through the medium of the first four steps of a scene, which is presentation, or through the medium of the fifth steps of his Scenes, which is plotting. But one thing must be clear. It is that if the fifth step is neglected in the scene, the other four steps must make up the deficiency, or, if the four steps are slighted, the deficiency must be made up in the fifth.

You will find when you examine these stories that in some cases there are present the lacks which I have pointed out. I take this occasion to make clear my position, which is, that this is not by any means a collection of "Best Short Stories." It is a collection of craftsmanlike stories by competent authors, each story selected because it contained examples which writers may well follow when they are confronted by special problems of craftsmanship.

When a lawyer is asked for an opinion upon a point of law he first determines the principle involved, and then examines the findings in cases involving this principle. Authorities upon certain phases of the law have first determined a norm for such cases and then have considered the departures from this norm which are caused by variations in special cases. Up to now we have been considering the norm of the story of accomplishment. From now on, in a detailed examination of each of the cases in this book, we shall consider the variations from that norm, so that, should you have material in mind about whose plotting and presentation you are in doubt, you may be able to turn to this book with the knowledge that you will find therein an example of a story whose author was confronted with the very same technical problems of craftsmanship which your material presents to you.

In the second section of this book we shall discuss the Story of Decision.

THE ADVENTURE OF ULYSSES

Beginning	Initial Condition and Main Actor's purpose are set forth.	Incidents. Ulysses' party enters Cyclop's cave.	1– 83
		Scene. Ulysses and Cyclop in oral clash. Cyclop eats two Greeks.	84–211

Main Plot Crises apparent. Promises of conflict to overcome Difficulty, to overcome opponent, to overcome Disaster.

Main Narrative Question: "Can Ulysses succeed in escaping from the cave?"

Body	Series of attempts of Main Actor to achieve his purpose. Attempts by opponent to prevent that achievement.	Incidents. Ulysses prepares stake.	212–243
		Scene. Ulysses and Cyclops in drinking bout. Ulysses asks guarantee.	244–302
		Scene. Ulysses and followers burn out Cyclop's eye. Cyclop hails others.	303–336
		Scene. Cyclop and his brethren. Cyclop guards door.	337–361
		Incidents. Ulysses attempts to outwit Cyclop.	362–423

Narrative Furtherance.

Cyclop refuses. Narrative Hindrance.

Narrative Furtherance; Dramatic Hindrance.

They misunderstand. Narrative Furtherance; Dramatic Hindrance.

Ending	Conclusive Act.	Cyclop allows Ulysses to escape.	424–425
	Sequel.	Interchange. Ulysses and Cyclop.	426–467

Main Narrative Question answered "Yes."

Effect upon actors shown.

THE ADVENTURE OF ULYSSES WITH THE CYCLOP

BY CHARLES LAMB

My reason for including in the Case Book the story of *The Adventure of Ulysses* when he meets the Cyclop is that it serves as an excellent example of how far back into the history of the human race goes the quality of narrative interest.   I want you to see that it existed as long ago as the time of Homer.   This story is especially valuable as showing that the quality of narrative has not changed since that time, and that it cannot ever change.   The same thing applies to the quality of drama.

Authorities upon Greek literature tell us that when they first had circulation, the various adventures of Ulysses which go to make up the complete collection known as the Odyssey were all separate adventures, not then connected through a central character. Homer's artistry brought together disconnected elements of a narrative and welded them into a coherent, unified whole.   He made out of these different and disconnected adventures a centralized narrative by causing Ulysses to be, throughout the series, the central actor, and by giving Ulysses a definite central purpose which tied together all these adventures.   That purpose was to return to Ithaca where his wife, Penelope, awaited him.

Except that its length rules it out, it would be possible to regard the whole series of *The Adventures of Ulysses* as a single short-story.   For that reason I am taking this single adventure of Ulysses and the Cyclop, which at first stood alone as a separate tale of the prowess of an individual, in order to illustrate the basic form of narrative.   It will show, especially, the difference between plot outline and presentation.   In plot outline, narrative never changes, and never can change.

This particular *Adventure of Ulysses and the Cyclop* has, in its presentation, undergone at least three metamorphoses.   Appearing, originally, as a folk-tale, it was developed by Homer to fit into his collection of adventures which made up his Odyssey. Chapman translated the Odyssey into English.   Charles Lamb abridged this translation still further into a collection of tales which he called *The Adventures of Ulysses*.   "The groundwork of the story," says Lamb, in his preface, "is as old as the Odyssey." (The text here given is from *The Works of Charles Lamb*, edited by Percy Fitzgerald, London: E. Moxon & Co., 1876.)

CASE No. 1

THE ADVENTURE OF ULYSSES

BY CHARLES LAMB

Coasting on all that night by unknown and out-of-the-way shores, they came by daybreak to the land where the Cyclops dwell, a sort of giant shepherds that neither sow nor plough, but the earth untilled produces for them rich wheat and barley and grapes; yet they have neither bread nor wine, nor know the arts of cultivation, nor care to know them; for they live each man to himself, without laws or government, or anything like a state or kingdom; but their dwellings are in caves, on the steep heads of mountains; every man's household governed by his own caprice, or not governed at all; their wives and children as lawless as themselves, none caring for others, but each doing as he or she thinks good. Ships or boats they have none, nor artificers to make them, no trade or commerce, or wish to visit other shores; yet they have convenient places for harbors and for shipping. Here Ulysses with a chosen party of twelve follow-ers landed, to explore what sort of men dwelt there, whether hospitable and friendly to strangers, or altogether wild and savage, for as yet no dwellers appeared in sight.

The first sight of habitation which they came to was a giant's cave rudely fashioned, but of a size which betokened the vast proportions of its owners; the pillars which supported it being the bodies of huge oaks or pines, in the natural state of the tree, and all about showed more marks of strength than skill in whoever built it. Ulysses, entering in, admired the savage contrivances and artless structure of the place, and longed to see the tenant of so outlandish a mansion; but well conjecturing that gifts would have more avail in extracting courtesy than strength would succeed in forcing it, from such a one as he expected to find the inhabitant, he resolved to flatter his hospitality with a present of Greek wine, of which he had store in twelve great

33

61 vessels, so strong that no one
62 ever drank it without an infusion
63 of twenty parts of water to one
64 of wine, yet the fragrance of it
65 was even then so delicious that
66 it would have vexed a man who
67 smelled it to abstain from tast-
68 ing it; but whoever tasted it, it
69 was able to raise his courage to
70 the height of heroic deeds. Tak-
71 ing with him a goat-skin flagon
72 full of this precious liquor, they
73 ventured into the recesses of the
74 cave. Here they pleased them-
75 selves a whole day with behold-
76 ing the giant's kitchen, where
77 the flesh of sheep and goats lay
78 strewed; his dairy, where goat-
79 milk stood ranged in troughs and
80 pails; his pens, where he kept his
81 live animals; but those he had
82 driven forth to pasture with him
83 when he went out in the morn-
84 ing. While they were feasting
85 their eyes with a sight of these
86 curiosities, their ears were sud-
87 denly deafened with a noise like
88 the falling of a house. It was
89 the owner of the cave, who had
90 been abroad all day feeding his
91 flock, as his custom was, in the
92 mountains, and now drove them
93 home in the evening from past-
94 ure. He threw down a pile of
95 firewood, which he had been
96 gathering against supper-time,
97 before the mouth of the cave,
98 which occasioned the crash they
99 heard. The Grecians hid them-
100 selves in the remote parts of the
101 cave at sight of the uncouth
102 monster. It was Polyphemus,

103 the largest and savagest of the
104 Cyclops, who boasted himself to
105 be the son of Neptune. He
106 looked more like a mountain
107 crag than a man, and to his
108 brutal body he had a brutish
109 mind answerable. He drove his
110 flock, all that gave milk, to the
111 interior of the cave, but left the
112 rams and the he-goats without.
113 Then, taking up a stone so
114 massive that twenty oxen could
115 not have drawn it, he placed it
116 at the mouth of the cave to
117 defend the entrance, and sat him
118 down to milk his ewes and his
119 goats; which done, he lastly
120 kindled a fire, and throwing his
121 great eye round the cave (for the
122 Cyclops have no more than one
123 eye, and that placed in the midst
124 of their forehead), by the glim-
125 mering light he discerned some
126 of Ulysses's men.

127 "Ho! guests, what are you?
128 Merchants or wandering
129 thieves?" he bellowed out in a
130 voice which took from them all
131 power of reply, it was so astound-
132 ing.

133 Only Ulysses summoned
134 resolution to answer, that they
135 came neither for plunder nor
136 traffic, but were Grecians who
137 had lost their way, returning
138 from Troy; which famous city,
139 under the conduct of Agamem-
140 non, the renowned son of Atreus,
141 they had sacked, and laid level
142 with the ground. Yet now they
143 prostrated themselves humbly
144 before his feet, whom they

acknowledged to be mightier than they, and besought him that he would bestow the rites of hospitality upon them, for that Jove was the avenger of wrongs done to strangers, and would fiercely resent any injury which they might suffer.

"Fool!" said the Cyclop, "to come so far to preach to me the fear of the gods. We Cyclops care not for your Jove, whom you fable to be nursed by a goat, nor any of your blessed ones. We are stronger than they, and dare bid open battle to Jove himself, though you and all your fellows of the earth join with him." And he bade them tell him where their ship was in which they came, and whether they had any companions. But Ulysses, with a wise caution, made answer that they had no ship or companions, but were unfortunate men, whom the sea, splitting their ship in pieces, had dashed upon his coast, and they alone had escaped. He replied nothing, but gripping two of the nearest of them, as if they had been no more than children, he dashed their brains out against the earth, and, shocking to relate, tore in pieces their limbs, and devoured them, yet warm and trembling, making a lion's meal of them, lapping the blood; for the Cyclops are maneaters, and esteem human flesh to be a delicacy far above goat's or kid's; though by reason of their ab-horred customs few men approach their coast, except some stragglers, or now and then a shipwrecked mariner.

At a sight so horrid, Ulysses and his men were like distracted people. He, when he had made an end of his wicked supper, drained a draught of goat's milk down his prodigious throat, and lay down and slept among his goats.

Then, Ulysses drew his sword, and half resolved to thrust it with all his might in at the bosom of the sleeping monster; but wiser thoughts restrained him, else they had there without help all perished, for none but Polyphemus himself could have removed that mass of stone which he had placed to guard the entrance. So they were constrained to abide all that night in fear.

When day came, the Cyclop awoke, and kindling a fire, made his breakfast of two other of his unfortunate prisoners; then milked his goats as he was accustomed, and pushing aside the vast stone, and shutting it again when he had done, upon the prisoners, with as much ease as a man opens and shuts a quiver's lid, he let out his flock, and drove them before him with whistlings (as sharp as winds in storms) to the mountains.

Then Ulysses, of whose strength or cunning the Cyclop seems to have had as little heed

35

229 as of an infant's, being left alone,
230 with the remnant of his men
231 which the Cyclop had not
232 devoured, gave manifest proof
233 how far manly wisdom excels
234 brutish force. He chose a stake
235 from among the wood which the
236 Cyclop had piled up for firing,
237 in length and thickness like a
238 mast, which he sharpened and
239 hardened in the fire; and selected
240 four men, and instructed them
241 what they should do with this
242 stake, and made them perfect
243 in their parts.

244 When the evening was come,
245 the Cyclop drove home his
246 sheep; and as fortune directed it,
247 either of purpose, or that his
248 memory was overruled by the
249 gods to his hurt (as in the issue
250 it proved), he drove the males
251 of his flock, contrary to his
252 custom, along with the dams
253 into the pens. Then shutting
254 to the stone of the cave, he fell
255 to his horrible supper. When he
256 had despatched two more of the
257 Grecians, Ulysses waxed bold
258 with the contemplation of his
259 project and took a bowl of
260 Greek wine, and merrily dared
261 the Cyclop to drink.

262 "Cyclop," he said, "take a
263 bowl of wine from the hand of
264 your guest: it may serve to digest
265 the man's flesh that you have
266 eaten, and show what drink our
267 ship held before it went down.
268 All I ask in recompense, if you
269 find it good, is to be dismissed in
270 a whole skin. Truly, you must
271 look to have few visitors, if you
272 observe this new custom of eat-
273 ing your guests."

274 The brute took and drank, and
275 vehemently enjoyed the taste of
276 wine, which was new to him,
277 and swilled again at the flagon,
278 and entreated for more, and
279 prayed Ulysses to tell him his
280 name, that he might bestow a
281 gift upon the man who had given
282 him such brave liquor. The
283 Cyclops, he said, had grapes, but
284 this rich juice, he swore, was
285 simply divine. Again Ulysses
286 plied him with the wine, and the
287 fool drank it as fast as he poured
288 it out, and again he asked the
289 name of his benefactor, which
290 Ulysses, cunningly dissembling
291 said, "My name is Noman: my
292 kindred and friends in my own
293 country call me Noman."

294 "Then," said the Cyclop, "this
295 is the kindness I will show thee,
296 Noman: I will eat thee last of
297 all thy friends." He had scarce
298 expressed his savage kindness,
299 when the fumes of the strong
300 wine overcame him, and he reeled
301 down upon the floor and sank
302 into a dead sleep.

303 Ulysses watched his time,
304 while the monster lay insensible;
305 and, heartening up his men,
306 they placed the sharp end of the
307 stake in the fire till it was heated
308 red-hot; and some god gave
309 them a courage beyond that
310 which they were used to have,
311 and the four men with difficulty
312 bored the sharp end of the huge

313 stake, which they had heated
314 red-hot, right into the eye of the
315 drunken cannibal; and Ulysses
316 helped to thrust it in with all his
317 might still further and further,
318 with effort, as men bore with an
319 auger, till the scalded blood
320 gushed out, and the eyeball
321 smoked, and the strings of the
322 eye cracked as the burning
323 rafter broke in it, and the eye
324 hissed as hot iron hisses when it
325 is plunged into water.

326 He, waking, roared with the
327 pain so loud that all the cavern
328 broke into claps like thunder.
329 They fled, and dispersed into
330 corners. He plucked the burn-
331 ing stake from his eye, and
332 hurled the wood madly about
333 the cave. Then he cried out
334 with a mighty voice for his
335 brethren the Cyclops, that dwelt
336 hard by in caverns upon hills.
337 They, hearing the terrible shout,
338 came flocking from all parts to
339 inquire what ailed Polyphemus,
340 and what cause he had for mak-
341 ing such horrid clamors in the
342 night-time to break their sleeps;
343 if his fright proceeded from any
344 mortal; if strength or craft had
345 given him his death-blow. He
346 made answer from within, that
347 Noman had hurt him, Noman
348 had killed him, Noman was
349 with him in the cave. They
350 replied, "If no man has hurt thee
351 and no man is with thee, then
352 thou art alone; and the evil that
353 afflicts thee is from the hand of
354 heaven, which none can resist or

355 help." So they left him, and
356 went their way, thinking that
357 some disease troubled him. He,
358 blind, and ready to split with
359 the anguish of the pain, went
360 groaning up and down in the
361 dark, to find the door-way;
362 which when he found, he re-
363 moved the stone, and sat in the
364 threshold, feeling if he could lay
365 hold on any man going out with
366 the sheep, which (the day now
367 breaking) were beginning to
368 issue forth to their accustomed
369 pastures. But Ulysses, whose
370 first artifice in giving himself
371 that ambiguous name had suc-
372 ceeded so well with the Cyclop,
373 was not of a wit so gross to be
374 caught by that palpable device.
375 But casting about in his mind
376 all the ways which he could
377 contrive for escape (no less than
378 all their lives depending on the
379 success), at last he thought of
380 this expedient. He made knots
381 of the osier twigs upon which the
382 Cyclop commonly slept, with
383 which he tied the fattest and
384 fleeciest of the rams together,
385 three in a rank; and under the
386 middle ram he tied a man, and
387 himself last, wrapping himself
388 fast with both his hands in the
389 rich wool of one, the fairest of
390 the flock.

391 And now the sheep began to
392 issue forth very fast; the males
393 went first, the females, un-
394 milked, stood by, bleating and
395 requiring the hand of their
396 shepherd in vain to milk them,

37

397 their full bags sore with being
398 unemptied, but he much sorer
399 with the loss of sight. Still, as
400 the males passed, he felt the
401 backs of those fleecy fools, never
402 dreaming that they carried his
403 enemies under them; so they
404 passed on till the last ram came
405 loaded with his wool and Ulysses
406 together. He stopped that ram
407 and felt him, and had his hand
408 once in the hair of Ulysses, yet
409 knew it not; and he chid the
410 ram for being last, and spoke to
411 it as if it understood him, and
412 asked it whether it did not wish
413 that its master had his eye again,
414 which the abominable Noman
415 with his execrable rout had put
416 out, when they had got him
417 down with wine; and he willed
418 the ram to tell him whereabouts
419 in the cave his enemy lurked,
420 that he might dash his brains
421 and strew them about, to ease
422 his heart of that tormenting
423 revenge which rankled in it.
424 After a deal of such foolish
425 talk to the beast, he let it go.
426 When Ulysses found himself
427 free, he let go his hold, and
428 assisted in disengaging his
429 friends. The rams which had
430 befriended them they carried off
431 with them to the ships, where
432 their companions with tears in
433 their eyes received them, as men
434 escaped from death. They plied
435 their oars and set their sails, and
436 when they were got as far off
437 from shore as a voice could
438 reach, Ulysses cried out to the
439 Cyclop: "Cyclop, thou shouldst
440 not have so much abused thy
441 monstrous strength as to
442 devour thy guests. Jove by my
443 hand sends thee requital to pay
444 thy savage inhumanity." The
445 Cyclop heard, and came forth
446 enraged, and in his anger he
447 plucked a fragment of a rock
448 and threw it with blind fury at
449 the ships. It narrowly escaped
450 lighting upon the bark in which
451 Ulysses sat, but with the fall it
452 raised so fierce an ebb as bore
453 back the ship till it almost
454 touched the shore. "Cyclop,"
455 said Ulysses, "if any ask thee
456 who imposed on thee that un-
457 sightly blemish in thine eye,
458 say it was Ulysses, son of
459 Laertes: the king of Ithaca am I
460 called, the master of cities."
461 Then they crowded sail, and beat
462 the old sea, and forth they went
463 with a forward gale; and sad for
464 fore-past losses, yet glad to have
465 escaped at any rate; till they
466 came to the isle where Æolus
467 reigned, who is god of the winds.

THE ANALYSIS

The first step in analyzing a story is to determine the amount of
space devoted to each of the three major divisions of Beginning,
Body, and Ending. In *The Adventure of Ulysses*, the Beginning

occupies 211 lines. The Body of the story occupies lines 212 to 423, closing with the words "revenge rankled in it." The Ending of the story occupies lines 424 to 467, and includes the Conclusive Act and the Sequel. The Conclusive Act is on lines 424 to 425: "after a deal of such foolish talk to the beast, he let it go." The Sequel occupies the remainder of the lines.

The Beginning, which has as one of its functions the setting forth of the Condition or state of affairs, devotes to it the first 198 lines, ending with the words, "slept among his goats."

The function of this part of the Beginning is to acquaint the reader with the line up of forces; to indicate to him the possibilities of success or failure should an attempt be made to change this Condition; but particularly to foreshadow for him the dramatic quality of the meetings or interchanges that will take place in the Body of the story, should the hero set out to overcome difficulties, to overcome opposing forces, or to avert disaster. Let us now examine the units employed by Charles Lamb in presenting this condition or state of affairs. We will find first a series of incidents, and then a dramatic scene. Out of these grows the main purpose of Ulysses. Lines 1 to 83 comprise the incidents which show the response of Ulysses to the place in which he finds himself, closing with the words, "went out in the morning."

Following this, beginning with the words, "While they were feasting their eyes," on line 84, and continuing to line 198, concluding with the words, "among his goats," the author employs a dramatic scene between Ulysses and the Cyclop. In this scene the narrative unity is not sustained because a central purpose does not carry through the interchange. We are aware first of the purpose of the Cyclop to get information from Ulysses and his followers. Ulysses' purpose then emerges,—to impress the Cyclop. This attempt to impress does not succeed. Rather, it angers the Cyclop, who then proceeds to ask for further information which Ulysses does not furnish him. He concludes the scene by the action of killing and eating the two Greeks. The fifth step of this scene is the effect upon the actors, lines 191 to 198; as it affects Ulysses and his men; they are "like distracted people"; and as it affects the Cyclop, he is shown quite callously unconcerned, because "he lay down and slept among his goats." This fifth step then proceeds into the plot by furnishing a narrative problem which gives unity to everything throughout the story. It is the determination of Ulysses to escape. This is indicated on lines 199 to 211, together with the difficulty involved in the task. It could have

39

been a little more plainly stated, though it is fairly evident and implied in the natural response any actor would make to such a state of affairs.

Here in a series of incidents all closely connected, and a single narrative scene, the author has set forth the main narrative problem, together with the promise of difficulty which lies in the imprisonment, the promise of conflict with a dangerous opponent, who is Polyphemus, and the danger of disaster in case the attempt should fail, which is shown by the great strength of Polyphemus, his savagery, and his cannibalistic habits.

Objection may be raised to the fact that there is no description of Ulysses. But this is not a sound objection in the light of our knowledge that this is only one of a series of adventures, and that before Ulysses was shown embarking upon these different adventures he was described. What about the requirement that the Beginning shall contain the line up of the forces which will give an indication of the capacities of the actors to carry on the combat. This requirement is quite well met. Ulysses' character and the character of the Cyclop are both shown by the way in which they react to different stimuli. It is necessary in plotting a short story that the Ending shall justify the reading of the story; that the reader shall feel that the person who is confronted by the condition which makes up the Beginning, could have solved the problem or accomplished the purpose only in the manner in which he does. Everything that an actor does in a story is his response to a stimulus, and every response of an actor to a stimulus is a characteristic or trait of his character in action. It is extremely important that you remember, in plotting your story, that the trait of character which ends the story shall be planted early in the story. If the story is ended by the use of some capacity or ability, then this capacity or ability should be planted early in the story. If the story is ended by the use of some device or some weapon, the presence of this weapon or this device should be planted early in the story. With this in mind, let us glance once more at the *Adventure of Ulysses*. Ulysses finally brings about his escape through his ingenuity and resource. Now let us see what characteristics of Ulysses are displayed by his first responses to stimuli. Ulysses is shown as cautious, because he goes first with his party of twelve to explore, in order to discover whether the dwellers are friendly and hospitable to strangers or altogether wild and savage. (See lines 29 and 36.) He is no fool; he does not rush into danger. This trait of caution is again evidenced on line 52, when although he desires to see the tenant, he conjectures that "gifts would have more avail in extracting courtesy than strength would succeed in forcing it." Here we find not only the resourcefulness, but we find also, on line 59, the weapon or device which he uses, which is the Greek wine which has a large part in bringing about the escape. We also find that Ulysses keeps in mind always that he must not give himself away to the Cyclop, and lines 133 to 173 are occupied in bringing out this trait in the character of Ulysses.

We find also that when he becomes aware of the condition, although his first impulse is courageous, wiser thoughts restrain him, because he sees in rashness the threat of disaster.

We may say therefore that this is a good Beginning because it contains all the necessary elements to foreshadow an interesting conflict of which the outcome is likely to remain in doubt. Besides this, the threat of disaster hangs over the whole story.

The greater the threat of disaster, the more interesting the story is. The wise author then, will so contrive his happenings growing out of the Beginning, that they shall culminate in a big dramatic moment when disaster seems inevitable. The simplest way to do this is to take each one of the promises which is contained in the Beginning, to form from it a meeting or interchange which will result in a defeat for that particular attempt. Thus the promise of difficulty will furnish one scene or presentation unit for the Body of the story which would result in defeat. The promise of conflict with an opponent would form another scene for the Body of the story which would again result in defeat. The accumulation of these defeats would bring the main actor in the story close to disaster. Thence would be projected the big scene of the story, which would be the development of the third of the elements in the Beginning,— the promise or threat of disaster. This big scene would inevitably be an attempt to avert this imminent disaster.

Now let us see how this norm is carried out in the *Adventure of Ulysses*. The difficulty of course, in the story, is that the Greeks are so manifestly handicapped by lack of weapons. The first attempt of Ulysses is an attempt to furnish them with weapons, and it occupies lines 226 to 243. Here we find the first weakness in the plot, because at this point it would have been so much stronger had emphasis been placed upon the outcome of the attempt as a hindrance, either dramatic or narrative. Since clearly the stake is a necessary weapon in the solution of the story, the attempt to furnish such a weapon must succeed. It will therefore be a narrative furtherance to the main purpose, but a dramatic hindrance

41

could have been indicated had the author said, or caused one of the characters to say, that, although the weapon was there, the chances were ninety-nine out of one hundred that they would be unable to use it before the giant could exercise his strength.   The fifth step could then be a colloquy between Ulysses and his followers, in which Ulysses announced his intention of reducing the giant to such a state that he would be unable to resist.   This promise of conflict would then be developed into what is now the scene in the Body of the story occupying lines 244 to 297.   This is a dramatic scene which could have been much stronger had it been prepared for, that is, the unity of the plot could have been strengthened. The unity of the plot can always be strengthened by making the fifth step of any attempt or presentation unit contain a hindrance and a promise of future conflict which is likely to result in disaster if the attempt is unsuccessful.   The next scene then develops this promise contained in the fifth step of the preceding one.   In this way the reader's interest is sustained both by the dramatic quality of the scene, and by the narrative quality of each scene by itself, in addition to being connectedly occupied by the main narrative question.

At the close of the scene between Ulysses and the Cyclop which results in a hindrance to Ulysses' main purpose, more could be made of dramatic promise of conflict were it indicated that the Cyclop did not go completely to sleep, but kept waking up and regarding Ulysses, from time to time, with suspicion, at every move of his prisoners.   Interest in the ultimate outcome slumps because the prospect of success is too apparent.   The conflict with the Cyclop is carried out in this scene and again in the scene where Ulysses and his followers, who are regarded as a single unit, succeed in putting out the eye of the Cyclop.   This scene ends in a narrative furtherance, but it is instantly changed into a dramatic hindrance by the Cyclop's calling upon his brethren to come to his rescue. This could have been made more dramatically poignant by indicating the effect that such a shout must have had upon the Grecians, and all they must have felt upon realizing that even their gigantic effort had led only to the imminent probability of disaster.   On line 387 beginning, "They, hearing the terrible shout, came flocking," and ending on line 355, "So they left him, and went their way," is a third scene of the Body which results in a narrative furtherance to the main narrative question because Ulysses here is successful in that his opponent is defeated.   The weakness in the plotting of this scene is that Ulysses does not appear in it.   Had

Ulysses urged the cyclops to say to his brethren, "Tell him that No-Man is here," Ulysses would then have brought about the result, whereas now it is brought about by a force not immediately acted upon by the main actor. There is, therefore, a lack of unity in the point of view which could have been avoided by causing Ulysses to be responsible for the outcome. There is also a weakness in causing the Cyclop, himself, to go to the doorway and sit on the threshold. Had Ulysses used his resourcefulness, of which he possessed a large store, the author could have then utilized the presentation unit to bring about the turning point in the plot, in such a way as to characterize the actor. Now he utilizes the presentation unit to bring about the turning point in the plot at the expense of characterizing the chief actor. Ulysses could easily have been made to taunt the Cyclop, and to challenge him to prevent Ulysses from escaping.

At the close of this scene, however, there is no question in the mind of the reader, that Ulysses is facing disaster, because although the Cyclop is blinded he is in the doorway, in such a position that he can lay hold on any man trying to go out. Thus, the fifth step of this scene is a dramatic hindrance. If you will look at the chart of this story you will see that the Beginning contains the essence of the scenes which make up the Body, with the exception of the scene between the Cyclop and his brethren. You will notice also that of the five units which now make up the Body of the story, the first one has no hindrance crisis indicated, the second, third, and fourth end in crises of hindrance, either narrative or dramatic, and that the accumulation of these hindrances brings the chief actor to the big moment of the story when it will be necessary for him to exert all his capacities in order to avert the disaster which was threatened in the Beginning.

Whenever you find that your story seems to drag in the Body you may rest assured of one of two things; either that the scenes are not in themselves interestingly dramatic, or that they do not in their crises increase the probability of disaster, and lead toward the big moment which projects the big scene of the story. This big scene is part of the Body. It is not the Ending. The Ending comes only when the reader is aware of the answer to the main narrative question. Thus, there are five scenes in the Body of this story. The first one is on lines 212 to 243; the second one is from line 244 to line 302; the third is from line 303 to line 336; the fourth is from line 337 to line 361; and the fifth is the big scene, or rather the series of incidents (it is not a scene in the strict sense),—the big presentation unit beginning on line 362 and ending on line 425. On line 425 there is also the Conclusive Act. It is what is known as a "contained" rather than an "appended" Ending. In another story I shall point out to you the difference between the contained and the appended Ending. The purpose of the writer in presenting the big scene of his story is to arouse in the reader an emotional feeling that all is about to be lost—that there is very little chance of success. The way that he can do this most effectually is to present it from the point of view and through the consciousness of the main actor. This particular series of happenings does not achieve its fullest emotional effect because the state of mind of Ulysses, as he sees the Cyclop handling the fleece of the animals, is not played up by the author. We do not, as readers, get the feeling that disaster is almost certain to ensue as we might be made to feel were we having the happenings presented to us as they affected Ulysses. A great deal could have been made of Ulysses' feeling of danger when he sees the Cyclop almost on the verge of discovering one of his companions, and the big moment in the story would have been when Ulysses felt the hand of the Cyclop touching his own hair, and believed all was lost.

This failure to develop the dramatic possibilities cannot be laid to Homer. Rather it is the fault of the translator, Charles Lamb, who tells the story objectively. We can say, in conclusion, regarding this story that it contains all the elements of a first rate modern short-story, but that they have not been developed in their presentation to the fullest possible extent.

ARCHITECTURAL CHART

OF

THE COP AND THE ANTHEM

BEGINNING	Initial Condition and Main Actor's purpose are set forth.	Incidents. Soapy feels approach of winter.	1– 28	Main Narrative Question "Can Soapy succeed in securing ninety days at Blackwell's Island?"
		Soapy determines to be arrested.	29– 41	
		Condition amplified by author.	42–86	
BODY	Series of attempts of Main Actor to achieve his purpose. Attempts by opponents to prevent that achievement.	Soapy and Waiters.	87–144	Narrative Hindrance.
		Soapy (Smashes window) and policeman.	145–181	Narrative Hindrance.
		Soapy and hard-boiled waiter.	183–217	Narrative Hindrance.
		Soapy and girl.	218–288	Narrative Hindrance.
		Soapy (Yelling) and policeman.	289–324	Narrative Hindrance.
		Soapy and man with umbrella.	325–364	Narrative Hindrance.
		Soapy and condition.	365–420	
ENDING	Conclusive Act.	Soapy abandons purpose.	421–444	Main Narrative Question answered "No."
	Sequel.	Soapy and Policeman in churchyard.	445–453	Ironic Significance is shown.
		Soapy and Magistrate.	454–456	

46

THE COP AND THE ANTHEM

BY O. HENRY

THE story of the combined adventures of Ulysses, which make up the Odyssey, is in its totality a story of a man seeking a haven. It involves a meeting, from time to time, with a number of opponents or opposing forces, each one of which the man overcomes, until such time as he finally arrives in his haven. At the close of each such encounter, however, he is always worse off than before.

Because the story of O. Henry is a modern story of a man seeking a haven, and because it is an amusing and entertaining rather than a serious story, I have included it to show that the quality of narrative does not change; that what made good narrative in the days of Homer made good narrative in the days of O. Henry. In the Odyssey, the interest is in each of the meetings, rather than in the central narrative question of Ulysses returning to Penelope. In this particular story the interest lies in both the meetings and in the central attempt of Soapy to succeed in securing ninety days of winter on Blackwell's Island.

Now read the story, and after you have read it turn to the con ments which follow it.

CASE No. 2

THE COP AND THE ANTHEM

BY O. HENRY

1 On his bench in Madison
2 Square Soapy moved uneasily.
3 When wild geese honk high of
4 nights, and when women with-
5 out sealskin coats grow kind to
6 their husbands, and when Soapy
7 moves uneasily on his bench in
8 the park, you may know that
9 winter is near at hand.

10 A dead leaf fell in Soapy's lap.
11 That was Jack Frost's card.
12 Jack is kind to the regular
13 denizens of Madison Square, and
14 gives fair warning of his annual
15 call. At the corners of four
16 streets he hands his pasteboard
17 to the North Wind, footman of
18 the mansion of All Outdoors, so
19 that the inhabitants thereof may
20 make ready.

21 Soapy's mind became cogni-
22 zant of the fact that the time had
23 come for him to resolve himself
24 into a singular Committee of
25 Ways and Means to provide
26 against the coming rigour. And
27 therefore he moved uneasily on
28 his bench.

29 The hibernatorial ambitions of
30 Soapy were not of the highest.
31 In them there were no considera-
32 tions of Mediterranean cruises,
33 of soporific Southern skies or
34 drifting in the Vesuvian Bay.
35 Three months on the Island was
36 what his soul craved. Three
37 months of assured board and
38 bed and congenial company, safe
39 from Boreas and bluecoats,
40 seemed to Soapy the essence of
41 things desirable.

42 For years the hospitable
43 Blackwell's had been his winter
44 quarters. Just as his more
45 fortunate fellow New Yorkers
46 had bought their tickets to Palm
47 Beach and the Riviera each
48 winter, so Soapy had made his
49 humble arrangements for his
50 annual hegira to the Island.
51 And now the time was come.
52 On the previous night three
53 Sabbath newspapers, dis-
54 tributed beneath his coat,
55 about his ankles and over his
56 lap, had failed to repulse the
57 cold as he slept on his bench near
58 the spurting fountain in the
59 ancient square. So the Island
60 loomed big and timely in Soapy's

49

mind. He scorned the provisions made in the name of charity for the city's dependents. In Soapy's opinion the Law was more benign than Philanthropy. There was an endless round of institutions, municipal and eleemosynary, on which he might set out and receive lodging and food accordant with the simple life. But to one of Soapy's proud spirits the gifts of charity are encumbered. If not in coin you must pay in humiliation of spirit for every benefit received at the hands of philanthropy. As Caesar had his Brutus, every bed of charity must have its toll of a bath, every loaf of bread its compensation of a private and personal inquisition. Wherefore it is better to be a guest of the law, which though conducted by rules, does not meddle unduly with a gentleman's private affairs.

Soapy, having decided to go to the Island, at once set about accomplishing his desire. There were many easy ways of doing this. The pleasantest was to dine luxuriously at some expensive restaurant; and then, after declaring insolvency, be handed over quietly and without uproar to a policeman. An accommodating magistrate would do the rest.

Soapy left his bench and strolled out of the square and across the level sea of asphalt, where Broadway and Fifth Avenue flow together. Up Broadway he turned, and halted at a glittering café, where are gathered together nightly the choicest products of the grape, the silkworm and the protoplasm.

Soapy had confidence in himself from the lowest button of his vest upward. He was shaven, and his coat was decent and his neat black, ready-tied four-in-hand had been presented to him by a lady missionary on Thanksgiving Day. If he could reach a table in the restaurant unsuspected success would be his. The portion of him that would show above the table would raise no doubt in the waiter's mind. A roasted mallard duck, thought Soapy, would be about the thing —with a bottle of Chablis, and then Camembert, a demi-tasse and a cigar. One dollar for the cigar would be enough. The total would not be so high as to call forth any supreme manifestation of revenge from the Café Management; and yet the meat would leave him filled and happy for the journey to his winter refuge.

But as Soapy set foot inside the restaurant door the head waiter's eye fell upon his frayed trousers and decadent shoes. Strong and ready hands turned him about and conveyed him in silence and haste to the sidewalk and averted the ignoble fate of the menaced mallard.

145 Soapy turned off Broadway.
146 It seemed that his route to the
147 coveted island was not to be an
148 epicurean one. Some other way
149 of entering limbo must be
150 thought of.
151 At a corner of Sixth Avenue
152 electric lights and cunningly
153 displayed wares behind plate-
154 glass made a shop window con-
155 spicuous. Soapy took a cobble-
156 stone and dashed it through the
157 glass. People came running
158 around the corner, a policeman
159 in the lead. Soapy stood still,
160 with his hands in his pockets,
161 and smiled at the sight of brass
162 buttons.
163 "Where's the man that done
164 that?" inquired the officer ex-
165 citedly.
166 "Don't you figure out that I
167 might have had something to
168 do with it?" said Soapy, not
169 without sarcasm, but friendly,
170 as one who greets good fortune.
171 The policeman's mind refused
172 to accept Soapy even as a clue.
173 Men who smash windows do not
174 remain to parley with the law's
175 minions. They take to their
176 heels. The policeman saw a
177 man half way down the block
178 running to catch a car. With
179 drawn club he joined in the
180 pursuit. Soapy, with disgust in
181 his heart, loafed along, twice
182 unsuccessful.
183 On the opposite side of the
184 street was a restaurant of no
185 great pretensions. It catered to
186 large appetites and modest

purses. Its crockery and at- 187
mosphere were thick; its soup 188
and napery thin. Into this place 189
Soapy took his accusive shoes 190
and telltale trousers without 191
challenge. At a table he sat and 192
consumed beefsteak, flapjacks, 193
doughnuts and pie. And then 194
to the waiter he betrayed the 195
fact that the minutest coin and 196
himself were strangers. 197
"Now, get busy and call a 198
cop," said Soapy. "And don't 199
keep a gentleman waiting." 200
"No cop for youse," said the 201
waiter, with a voice like butter 202
cakes and an eye like the cherry 203
in a Manhattan cocktail. "Hey, 204
Con!" 205
Neatly upon his left ear on the 206
callous pavement two waiters 207
pitched Soapy. He arose, joint 208
by joint, as a carpenter's rule 209
opens, and beat the dust from 210
his clothes. Arrest seemed but 211
a rosy dream. The Island 212
seemed very far away. A 213
policeman who stood before a 214
drug store two doors away 215
laughed and walked down the 216
street. 217
Five blocks Soapy travelled 218
before his courage permitted him 219
to woo capture again. This time 220
the opportunity presented what 221
he fatuously termed to himself 222
a "cinch." A young woman of 223
a modest and pleasing guise was 224
standing before a show window 225
gazing with sprightly interest at 226
its display of shaving mugs and 227
inkstands, and two yards from 228

the window a large policeman of severe demeanour leaned against a water plug.

It was Soapy's design to assume the rôle of the despicable and execrated "masher." The refined and elegant appearance of his victim and the contiguity of the conscientious cop encouraged him to believe that he would soon feel the pleasant official clutch upon his arm that would insure his winter quarters on the right little, tight little isle.

Soapy straightened the lady missionary's ready - made tie, dragged his shrinking cuffs into the open, set his hat at a killing cant and sidled toward the young woman. He made eyes at her, was taken with sudden coughs and "hems," smiled, smirked and went brazenly through the impudent and contemptible litany of the "masher." With half an eye Soapy saw that the policeman was watching him fixedly. The young woman moved away a few steps, and again bestowed her absorbed attention upon the shaving mugs. Soapy followed, boldly stepping to her side, raised his hat and said:

"Ah there, Bedelia. Don't you want to come and play in my yard?"

The policeman was still looking. The persecuted young woman had but to beckon a finger and Soapy would be practically en route for his insular haven. Already he imagined he could feel the cozy warmth of the station-house. The young woman faced him and, stretching out a hand, caught Soapy's coat sleeve.

"Sure, Mike," she said joyfully, "if you'll blow me to a pail of suds. I'd have spoke to you sooner, but the cop was watching."

With the young woman playing the clinging ivy to his oak Soapy walked past the policeman overcome with gloom. He seemed doomed to liberty.

At the next corner he shook off his companion and ran.

He halted in the district where by night are found the lightest streets, hearts, vows and librettos. Women in furs and men in greatcoats moved gaily in the wintry air. A sudden fear seized Soapy that some dreadful enchantment had rendered him immune to arrest. The thought brought a little of panic with it, and when he came upon another policeman lounging grandly in front of a transplendent theatre he caught at the immediate straw of "disorderly conduct."

On the sidewalk Soapy began to yell drunken gibberish at the top of his harsh voice. He danced, howled, raved and otherwise disturbed the welkin.

The policeman twirled his club, turned his back to Soapy and remarked to a citizen.

" 'Tis one of them Yale lads celebratin' the goose egg they give to the Hartford College. Noisy; but no harm. We've instructions to lave them be."

Disconsolate, Soapy ceased his unavailing racket. Would never a policeman lay hands on him? In his fancy the Island seemed an unattainable Arcadia. He buttoned his thin coat against the chilling wind.

In a cigar store he saw a well-dressed man lighting a cigar at a swinging light. His silk umbrella he had set by the door on entering. Soapy stepped inside, secured the umbrella and sauntered off with it slowly. The man at the cigar light followed hastily.

"My umbrella," he said, sternly.

"Oh, is it?" sneered Soapy, adding insult to petit larceny. "Well, why don't you call a policeman? I took it. Your Umbrella! Why don't you call a cop? There stands one on the corner."

The umbrella owner slowed his steps. Soapy did likewise, with a presentiment that luck would again run against him. The policeman looked at the two curiously.

"Of course," said the umbrella man—"that is—well, you know how these mistakes occur—I—if it's your umbrella I hope you'll excuse me—I picked it up this morning in a restaurant—If you recognise it as yours, why —I hope you'll——"

"Of course it's mine," said Soapy, viciously.

The ex-umbrella man retreated. The policeman hurried to assist a tall blonde in an opera cloak across the street in front of a street car that was approaching two blocks away.

Soapy walked eastward through a street damaged by improvements. He hurled the umbrella wrathfully into an excavation. He muttered against the men who wear helmets and carry clubs. Because he wanted to fall into their clutches, they seemed to regard him as a king who could do no wrong.

At length Soapy reached one of the avenues to the east where the glitter and turmoil was but faint. He set his face down this toward Madison Square, for the homing instinct survives even when the home is a park bench.

But on an unusually quiet corner Soapy came to a standstill. Here was an old church, quaint and rambling and gabled. Through one violet-stained window a soft light glowed, where, no doubt, the organist loitered over the keys, making sure of his mastery of the coming Sabbath anthem. For there drifted out to Soapy's ears sweet music that caught and held him transfixed against the convolutions of the iron fence.

The moon was above, lustrous

53

397 and serene; vehicles and pedes-
398 trians were few; sparrows twit-
399 tered sleepily in the eaves—for
400 a little while the scene might
401 have been a country church-
402 yard. And the anthem that the
403 organist played cemented Soapy
404 to the iron fence, for he had
405 known it well in the days when
406 his life contained such things as
407 mothers and roses and ambitions
408 and friends and immaculate
409 thoughts and collars.

410 The conjunction of Soapy's
411 receptive state of mind and the
412 influences about the old church
413 wrought a sudden and wonder-
414 ful change in his soul. He
415 viewed with swift horror the
416 pit into which he had tumbled,
417 the degraded days, unworthy
418 desires, dead hopes, wrecked
419 faculties and base motives that
420 made up his existence.

421 And also in a moment his heart
422 responded thrillingly to this
423 novel mood. An instantaneous
424 and strong impulse moved him
425 to battle with his desperate
426 fate. He would pull himself out

427 of the mire; he would make a
428 man of himself again; he would
429 conquer the evil that had taken
430 possession of him. There was
431 time; he was comparatively
432 young yet; he would resurrect
433 his old eager ambitions and
434 pursue them without faltering.
435 Those solemn but sweet organ
436 notes had set up a revolution
437 in him. Tomorrow he would go
438 into the roaring downtown dis-
439 trict and find work. A fur
440 importer had once offered him a
441 place as driver. He would find
442 him tomorrow and ask for the
443 position. He would be some-
444 body in the world. He would——

445 Soapy felt a hand laid on his
446 arm. He looked quickly around
447 into the broad face of a police-
448 man.

449 "What are you doin' here?"
450 asked the officer.

451 "Nothin'," said Soapy.

452 "Then come along," said the
453 policeman.

454 "Three months on the Island,"
455 said the Magistrate in the Police
456 Court the next morning.

THE ANALYSIS

The Beginning of this story containing the conditions and the main narrative question occupies lines 1 to 86. This Beginning contains the condition or state of affairs and the main narrative question of the story. A slight difference in the pattern will be seen between this and the preceding story, in which the condition came as a block of incident and was followed by the main narrative question. In this story, lines 1 to 28 state the condition. Then lines 29 to 41 set forth the main narrative question. On lines 42 to 86 more conditions are stated, or, more accurately, more information is given regarding the stated condition which brings about the narrative response of Soapy. An examination of this Beginning will disclose another essential difference between it and the *Adventure of Ulysses*. In the statement of conditions there is no promise of disaster because there is no indication that any difficulties are likely to place themselves in the way of the success of the hero. The author depends for the interest upon the unusualness of the main narrative purpose of the actor. On lines 110 to 122, which are now included in the Body of the story, there is indicated a difficulty which is likely to defeat his purpose,—the fact that his raiment is not above suspicion. This story is particularly interesting because within the body of the story the presentation units are not intended to excite but to entertain the reader. The story's chief interest is, that at the conclusion of each meeting the outcome is unexpected, and by its unexpectedness it forms a narrative hindrance to the main narrative question. There are six of these presentation units which are nearly all incompletely developed dramatic scenes in the Body of the story. The first of these presentation units occupies lines 87 to 144, and occurs between Soapy and the waiters who eject him without injury, thus causing a narrative hindrance by a defeat of that particular attempt. The second presentation unit is when Soapy smashes the window, and tries to convince the policeman that he broke the window. Number three is the interview between Soapy and the hard-boiled waiter, when he tries to persuade the waiter to call a cop. This occupies lines 183 to 217 and results in a narrative hindrance. The fourth presentation unit is between Soapy and the girl whom he accosts in the hope that he will be arrested. Of all the presentation units so far it is the least dramatic in its interchange. It occupies lines 218 to 288 and results in a narrative hindrance. The fifth of these presentation units is when Soapy, having made a disturbance, appeals to the policeman to arrest him. This again results in a hindrance, the whole unit occupying lines 289 to 324. The sixth and last attempt of Soapy is when he steals the umbrella from the man, and urges the man to have him arrested. This occupies lines 325 to 364, and results in a narrative hindrance.

(N.B. It is interesting to note that the minor narrative questions of these scenes fall into the categories that I mentioned in the introduction to this book; that an actor is trying to persuade another actor to adopt a course of conduct or to convince another actor that a certain state of affairs exists, etc.)

The accumulation of all these defeats brings about the big

moment in the story when disaster threatens the purpose of Soapy. Lines 365 to 409 introduce the stimulus which convinces Soapy that it is useless to proceed further in his attempts. Lines 410 to 420 show his thoughts, leading into the Conclusive Act which answers the main narrative question of the story in the negative by showing that Soapy has abandoned his purpose (421–444). Following this there comes a Sequel, lines 445 to 456, made up of the episode with the policeman, on lines 445 to 453, and of the additional sentence by the magistrate on lines 454 to 456 to three months on the Island. The Ending of the story, therefore, containing the Conclusive Act, and the Sequel, occupies lines 421 to 456.

One of my particular reasons for choosing this story was to enable you to see that even though the whole artistic purpose of the writer may change with different stories the architectural norm remains constant. You will notice that in this story there appears an element which did not occur in the previous story. It is that the sequel to this story is interesting because of its ironic significance, because it is a reversal of the original condition. The actor has failed in his purpose at the close of the story proper; he later succeeds but, ironically, he does not wish success.

This is a characteristic O. Henry story. It is not nearly so dramatic as the story of the adventure of Ulysses with the Cyclop for the reason that it is not in its main purpose sufficiently important. No group of readers could become wildly excited over the success or failure of Soapy's enterprise. The main purpose is interesting, not because of any importance which inheres in it, but because of the unusualness of such a desire on anybody's part.

	Sally vs. Kerry	1– 75
	Sally and Monte	76– 154
	Sally and Monte	155– 283
	Sally and Kerry	284– 342
Initial Condition and Main Actor's purpose are set forth.	Sally and Garageman.	343– 374
	Sally and Monte.	375– 408
	Sally and Monte.	409– 485
	Sally and Kerry.	486– 562
	Sally and Monte.	563– 605
	Kerry and Monte.	606– 654
	Kerry and foreman.	655– 673

BEGINNING

Main Plot Crises apparent. Promises of conflict to overcome Difficulties, to remove or overcome opponents, or opposing forces, and to overcome Disaster.

Main Narrative Question: " Can Monte English succeed in driving Vindix from Los Angeles to St. Louis under its own power?"

	Foreman and Mac.	674– 730
	Mac and Monte.	731– 751
Series of attempts of Main Actor to achieve his purpose, in spite of obstacles placed in the path of his success by opponents.	Incidents. Monte reacts to condition.	752– 789
	Monte and Sally. (Kerry observes.)	790– 839
	Monte, Sally, and Kerry.	840– 887
	Sally and Kerry in Winslow. (5th step of 840–887.)	888– 912
	Incidents. Monte and condition.	913– 919
	Incidents. Effect upon Carson (5th step of 913–919.)	920– 931

BODY

Dramatic Hindrance.

Dramatic Hindrance.

Monte overcomes Difficulty; Narrative Furtherance.

Friction develops. Dramatic Hindrance.

Broken bearing; Narrative Hindrance.

No spare parts. Threat of Disaster. Narrative Hindrance.

Monte overcomes Difficulty; Narrative Furtherance.

Carson proposes to set pace which will ruin Vindix. Dramatic Hindrance.

Interchange. Kerry and Sheriff.	932– 953	Threat of arrest and delay. Dramatic Hindrance.
Incidents. Monte and condition.	954– 982	Sheriff buys liquor. Narrative Furtherance.
Incidents. Monte and condition.	983–1014	Rattling gears and chassis. Time limit close. Narrative Hindrance.
Incidents. Monte and condition.	1015–1042	Attempt presages Victory. Furtherance. Dramatic Hindrance by Kerry's knowledge that he must delay.
Monte and Kerry.		
Monte and condition. (A characterizing scene with mental struggle omitted, resulting in new condition.)	1043–1085	Kerry's accident is Furtherance.
Monte and condition.	1086–1158	Hindrance. Broken parts not replaceable.
Effect upon Carson. (5th step of 1159–1208.)	1159–1208	Furtherance. Victory in sight.
Sally and condition.	1209–1216	Hindrance. Kerry steals parts.
Kerry and Kamco General Manager.	1217–1244	Furtherance. Ally helps.
Sally and condition.	1245–1278	Hindrance. Disaster threatens.
Sally and Monte.	1279–1301	Hindrance. Vindix wrecked.
Sally and Monte.	1302–1324	Hindrance. Disaster threatens.
Sally and Monte.	1325–1392	Furtherance. Success in view.
Monte and condition.	1393–1402	Hindrance. Ultimate Disaster looms. Big Moment of Story.
	1403–1421	Furtherance. Last obstacle overcome.

BODY — Series of attempts of Main Actor to achieve his purpose, despite the obstacles placed in his path by his opponents.

ENDING

Conclusive Act.

Sally and Kerry. (Conclusive Act 1436–1440).	1422–1440	Main Narrative Question answered: "Yes."

Sequel.

Sally and Kerry. Sally and Monte.	1441–1479 1480–1483	Effect upon actors shown.

SPARE PARTS

BY FRANK R. ADAMS

EVERY story of accomplishment is the story of a person who sets out to change an existing condition or state of affairs.

To set forth this initial condition which has to be changed is the function of that part of the story that we call, structurally speaking, the Beginning. The Beginning sets forth, in addition to this initial condition, the response of the chief actor to the existing condition so that the reader being aware of the stimulus and the response finds himself phrasing the main narrative question of the story.

In the two stories which precede this one the conditions set forth were, in the case of *The Adventure of Ulysses*, important; and in the case of *The Cop and the Anthem*, unusual.

Spare Parts has been included because the condition which confronts the young man is not in itself either unusual or important; but is made so by its involvements. The main purpose which emerges is not intrinsically important, but is made important synthetically. Its importance depends upon the reader being made aware of how much depends upon the success of Monte English in driving the Vindix from Los Angeles, California, to St. Louis, Missouri.

After reading the story, turn to the analysis which follows it.

CASE No. 3

"SPARE PARTS"

BY FRANK R. ADAMS

"But, my dear Sally, as your friend, as your almost guardian, as your sure-enough, bona-fide suitor, I beg of you *not* to buy a Vindix car!"

Carson Kerry was perhaps not so vehement as he was pretending to be, but he was very much in earnest at that.

"But I *want* a Vindix," Sally insisted. "My daddy had one, and *he* said it is the best car made."

"Yes; but the Vindix is a foreign car, and your father lived in New York, where there was an importing agency for the Vindix—and not in southern California. If he broke any of the parts he could replace them within a reasonable time."

"I don't see why it should be any harder to get repair parts for a Vindix than it is for any other first-class car."

"It *is* harder, though, and there is a perfectly good reason. They don't use *any* standardized parts — parts that are interchangeable with other cars of the same size. For heaven's sake, Sally, give up this fool notion of a Vindix, and let me fix you up with a good American car!"

"Such as a Kamco Six, I suppose? "

"That *is* the best automobile made, I'll admit."

"You'd *have* to say so, you're vice-president of the company."

"I *would* not. It's the truth, and I say it because I'm a reasonable man."

"Well, I'm a reasonable woman!"

"A reasonable—Why, you're not even a woman yet! I'm darned if I think you ever *will* grow up. One thing is certain: you haven't cut your automobile wisdom teeth yet."

As may be inferred by any married man, and also by most men who are not married—to say nothing of all the women— the upshot of the discussion was

57 the purchase, on the following
58 day, of the only Vindix at that
59 moment available on the west
60 coast.

61 Carson Kerry had gone too
62 far, anyway. The mere fact
63 that her dead father had recom-
64 mended that she rely on Carson's
65 business judgment did not con-
66 stitute him her "almost guar-
67 dian" in everything else!

68 Sally didn't want him for a
69 husband. She could think of
70 seven hundred and forty-four
71 reasons why, one of them being
72 the best in the world. Love may
73 not always last, but it's wonder-
74 ful as a scaffolding while the
75 building is being put up.

76 Sally broke in her new car her-
77 self. She had often driven her
78 father's Vindix, and the new
79 machine was exactly like it in all
80 essential particulars. The lines
81 of the body were more modern,
82 but from gear shift to gizzard
83 they were mechanical twins.

84 So she spent a lot of time
85 piling up the first thousand miles
86 slowly circling the city boule-
87 vards. Unconsciously—well, al-
88 most unconsciously—she drew a
89 lot of attention from other
90 motorists. Part of it was tribute
91 to the glistening perfection of her
92 perfectly turned out torpedo
93 boat destroyer. No one could
94 see that long, supercilious black
95 snout sneaking up over the crest
96 of a hill, trailing a low-hung,
97 high-sided cockpit, without look-
98 ing a second time.

99 The rest of the admiration she
100 attracted was due to her dress-
101 maker, her hairdresser, her mil-
102 liner, and incidentally to her-
103 self. Sally affected vivid orange
104 shades when she was going for a
105 drive, and they looked per-
106 fectly miserable against the
107 black leather and enamel, as
108 any Princeton man can tell you.

109 She was one of those violently
110 beautiful persons who make men
111 mad enough to want to kill some-
112 body, just for relief.

113 She never flirted. She just
114 looked at people to see if she
115 recognized them, then turned
116 away, leaving them her slaves
117 for life, or, at any rate, for the
118 balance of the day until they
119 could sleep it off.

120 So the young man driving
121 down Cahuenga Pass was not
122 aware that he was especially
123 honored when she gave him a
124 smile with two dimples couchant,
125 and waved a friendly greeting.

126 He was just arriving in Los
127 Angeles from the North and
128 East, and he didn't know yet but
129 that every woman on the south-
130 ern Pacific coast was like that.

131 He drove on; not quite the
132 same man he had been before,
133 but still he drove on. Being
134 human, and masculine, he want-
135 ed to stop. But he didn't. He
136 proceeded thoughtfully on his
137 way.

138 To proceed thoughtfully was
139 one of the things Monte English
140 did most successfully. He could

141 act, too! But when he did he
142 usually had examined the hori-
143 zon fore and aft, also to leeward
144 and windward.

145 Eventually Monte hoped to be
146 Western representative of some
147 flourishing Detroit manufacturer.
148 For the present, he planned to
149 get a job as lowly mechanic in a
150 repair shop until he could ac-
151 cumulate enough entries in a
152 savings bank passbook to war-
153 rant him in branching out for
154 himself.

155 The next time he met Sally,
156 not knowing yet, of course, that
157 her name was Sally, he was tow-
158 ing a broken-down Kamco Six
159 which had turned its right ankle
160 against a too, too solid cement
161 curb.

162 But she recognized him, even
163 in his overalls; and she smiled
164 again, that same warm, friendly
165 smile as of shipmates who meet
166 in a far country.

167 This time he guessed why. It
168 was because his own car, which
169 he had leased into bondage along
170 with his mechanical services, was
171 an antique Vindix, a distant
172 cousin of her own resplendent
173 roadster. He had not seen any
174 others since he had been in
175 Los Angeles.

176 So he waved back and grinned.
177 And Monte had a pretty nice
178 grin himself.

179 It was strange that he should
180 run across her again the next
181 week. Well, not so very strange
182 at that, if you take into account

183 that he had been a distinct men-
184 ace to traffic every time he went
185 out, because he was always
186 watching for a long black clip-
187 per flying a yellow flag.

188 She was pulled up on the other
189 side of the street and had raised
190 the hood, just as if she knew
191 what to do with the hub-cap
192 wrench which she held in her
193 hand.

194 Monte thought that he was
195 justified in helping. Wasn't it
196 all in the line of business? He
197 might get her as a customer for
198 his boss, mightn't he?

199 "Perhaps I can fix it," he sug
200 gested.

201 She turned around and recog-
202 nized him even before she looked
203 across the street and identified
204 his car.

205 "Oh, if you would!" Appar-
206 ently she never doubted his abil-
207 ity an instant.

208 He not only would but he
209 could.

210 "A Vindix is a little compli-
211 cated for the average American
212 driver, isn't it?" she offered
213 shyly.

214 "Not really, after you get used
215 to 'em." He gazed admiringly at
216 the sheer beauty of the new car.
217 "Gee, but this outfit is a peach!"

218 "Would you like to drive it
219 for a mile or so, just to feel it
220 out? No one has driven it ex-
221 cept myself, but I know the
222 owner of another Vindix would
223 understand just how to handle it."

224 She was right. Her car had

225 never been manipulated with
226 such skill. They went twenty
227 miles, not because Monte pre-
228 sumed on her original invitation,
229 but because she insisted that she
230 was learning such a lot just from
231 watching the way he drove.

232 He thanked his lucky stars
233 that this time he had on his
234 street clothes.

235 When they finally pulled up
236 alongside of his own neglected
237 chariot, Sally examined the an-
238 tique with deep interest.

239 "Just where did you get your
240 car?" she demanded.

241 Monte flushed a little. "I got
242 it from a second-hand dealer in
243 New York."

244 "And how did that scratch get
245 on the panel of the front door?"

246 "I haven't had the bus painted
247 since I bought it. I don't know
248 how it got there."

249 "Well, I do! I put it there
250 myself. A suit I wore several
251 years ago had cut-metal buttons
252 on it, and—"

253 "Did you own this car?"

254 "My father did. I thought
255 it looked familiar; and when you
256 said you bought it in New York
257 I wondered if it might be our car.
258 That scratch practically proves
259 it."

260 Monte said something she
261 didn't quite catch. "What did
262 you say?"

263 "Nothing."

264 "Yes, you did."

265 "I said I'd never have it
266 painted again," he admitted.

267 "Don't be ashamed of it. I
268 like to have people like me—
269 even young men."

270 "Even garage mechanics?"

271 "Especially a garage me-
272 chanic! It would be so handy
273 to know just where to apply for
274 aid in case of a breakdown."

275 Of course she was kidding him,
276 but she was so nice about it that
277 he couldn't help smiling back.

278 She took the address and tele-
279 phone number of the garage
280 where he worked. Sally was ab-
281 solutely unscrupulous the way
282 she attached men to her with
283 bonds of service.

284 That evening she and Carson
285 Kerry were going to a party to-
286 gether, and had their usual quar-
287 rel as to which car they should
288 take.

289 "My sedan will be better,"
290 was one of his arguments. "It
291 may be chilly."

292 "If you think you'll be cold,
293 I'll lend you my fur scarf, and
294 we can wrap up your chilblains
295 in the robe."

296 "I'd look fine, wouldn't I,
297 driving a Vindix when every-
298 body knows that I'm the manu-
299 facturer of the best American
300 car made!"

301 "I wasn't expecting *you* to
302 drive," sweetly. "I suppose a
303 Vindix would be difficult for
304 you."

305 "Huh!" scornfully. "I'd like
306 to ride in something that has
307 some slight chance of being re-
308 paired in case of a breakdown."

309 "The Vindix doesn't require
310 repairing—like *some* cars!"

311 Carson ignored her undercuts,
312 and came back with what he evi-
313 dently considered a knockout
314 blow.

315 "You may as well know the
316 truth," he said. "The Vindix
317 Company has gone to the wall!"

318 "The wall?" repeated Sally.

319 "Exactly!" Carson gloated.
320 "It's busted—quit—gone out of
321 business."

322 "Then I'm very glad I bought
323 one while they were still avail-
324 able!"

325 "You won't be so glad you
326 own an orhpan car when you try
327 to get repair parts."

328 "An orphan?"

329 "Yes; that's what they call an
330 automobile of a make that has
331 been discontinued."

332 "I see. Then it's lucky the
333 Vindix is a machine that practi-
334 cally *never* wears out."

335 Carson threw up his hands.
336 "They *all* wear out."

337 "I imagine you base your
338 ideas entirely on what happens
339 to Kamco Sixes. But the Vin-
340 dix—"

341 They finally went to the party
342 in a taxicab.

343 The very next week Sally had
344 reason to recall Carson's out-
345 rageous predictions. A loaded
346 truck swung into her as she was
347 turning a corner. The truck
348 driver had not seen her arm sig-
349 nal. Probably her hand was
350 too small.

351 Anyway, the truck made some-
352 thing resembling a corrugated
353 washboard out of her right front
354 fender; and when she tried to
355 start up again, the front wheel
356 on that side got down on its
357 knees and couldn't get up.

358 The nearest garage man, ar-
359 riving on buzzard wings, shook
360 his head in gloomy prophecy.

361 "The fender can probably be
362 straightened, but that spindle
363 that's broke clean off is going to
364 bother us. Nobody carries it in
365 stock. I might find one at a
366 junk yard, but otherwise it will
367 have to be made from a special
368 pattern mold at the steel mills.
369 That's going to cost money, and
370 may take months."

371 Sally could have cried with
372 vexation. Still, she didn't give
373 up. Instead, she telephoned the
374 garage for Monte English.

375 He was there in ten minutes.
376 In twenty more he had replaced
377 the broken spindle with one from
378 his own car—it fitted perfectly
379 —and had driven her to a near-
380 by fender repair man, who ironed
381 out the wrinkles with a rubber
382 hammer so that you could
283 scarcely notice any damage at
384 all.

385 "But how will you get a new
386 what-do-you-call-it for your own
387 car?"

388 "I'll find one," he promised.
389 "That's the advantage of being
390 in the business."

391 "You'll let me pay for the time
392 that takes, too, won't you?"

65

393 Monte considered. "If it
394 takes long, yes."

395 She made him promise to bring
396 his car around so that she could
397 see it as soon as it was repaired.

398 This inspired Monte to prodi-
399 gies. To find a new spindle
400 proved to be out of the question,
401 but he finally discovered a com-
402 plete front axle assembly that
403 was nearly the same size; and by
404 a little ingenious remodeling he
405 managed to make it fit well
406 enough to do. He kept the dis-
407 carded parts in case of an
408 emergency.

409 When he took his practically
410 paintless ark around to the hotel
411 where Sally was staying, she in-
412 spected it carefully without de-
413 tecting what he had done.

414 "I think that you're wonder-
415 ful," she breathed, in such a tone
416 that he thought he was pretty
417 wonderful himself.

418 "If you have time I wish
419 you'd drive me down to the
420 beach," she suggested, with just
421 the correct shade of wistfulness
422 in her tone. "It's fearfully hot
423 this evening, and I can't go
424 there alone."

425 She could have gone with Car-
426 son Kerry, who was waiting for
427 her in the hotel lobby; but per-
428 haps she never thought of that.
429 Young people are so careless.

430 "You mean in my car?" de-
431 manded Monte incredulously.

432 "Certainly. It's a Vindix,
433 isn't it?"

434 That was the final victory.

435 Monte had been trying to resist
436 her, but what could a man do
437 with a girl like that?

438 "Why, your motor runs better
439 than mine!" Sally marveled
440 when they were on their way.

441 "A trifle smoother, perhaps.
442 These engines improve the longer
443 they run. And this one has had
444 excellent care."

445 Nature had never cooked up
446 an evening such as that one. A
447 full moon, the twinkling neck-
448 lace of Hollywood on the hills to
449 the right, a warm breeze that
450 promised all the impossible
451 things in the world, a girl in a
452 sleeveless orange silk dress that
453 could probably be carried in a
454 vanity case if it were folded up,
455 and a perfume that will doubt-
456 less be illegal when Mr. Volstead
457 gets around to it!

458 "I'm a member of the Santa
459 Monica Beach Club," Sally of-
460 fered, apropos of nothing par-
461 ticular, when they got there;
462 "and it looks like a nice night to
463 take a swim."

464 So they did. Sally, in a bath-
465 ing suit, was a conflict of emo-
466 tions.

467 Nothing happened —nothing,
468 that is, if you discount the one
469 time that Sally was knocked
470 down by a roller and Monte
471 picked her up and held her tight
472 for an instant while she steadied
473 herself. During that second his
474 world reeled.

475 Monte made her come out
476 after that. He said he was

477 afraid it might happen again.
478 He was.

479 On the way home, he talked
480 about machinery, his modest am-
481 bitions, politics and agriculture.
482 Monte's idea was to keep the
483 subject of moonlight, hillsides,
484 springtime, and other things
485 from being mentioned.

486 Carson Kerry had waited only
487 until half past ten for her, so he
488 was not there when they got
489 back. But he was pretty furious
490 the next day, and Sally thought
491 it just as well not to explain
492 that she had not been alone and
493 absolutely unprotected during
494 her evening ramble.

495 There was something else for
496 them to quarrel about, anyway.
497 Sally's aunt was going to be
498 married again, back in St. Louis,
499 and she wanted Sally to be pres-
500 ent. Carson said he was going
501 East himself shortly, and pro-
502 posed that they make the trip
503 in his motor.

504 "My sister will go along as
505 chaperon—unless, of course, we
506 could be married before we left."

507 Sally considered the idea.
508 "I'd like to go; but I'd rather
509 take my own car. You and your
510 sister could ride in your closed
511 elephant and I could drive along
512 a few miles ahead of you—and
513 wait for you wherever we had
514 decided to stop for the night."

515 That phrase "wait for you"
516 made Carson respond to the
517 sting as if there had been dyna-
518 mite under him.

519 "Why, that animated junk
520 pile of yours would never make
521 it. The Vindix was built for
522 European pavements. It takes
523 a he car to travel across the
524 American continent, a car with
525 an engine like—"

526 "I've read your advertising,"
527 Sally interrupted dryly, "but I
528 didn't think you believed it
529 yourself."

530 "I'll prove it to you," Carson
531 offered magnanimously. "If
532 you'll go with me, I'll hire a man
533 to pilot your outfit as long as it
534 will hold together; then we'll use
535 a tow-rope on it the rest of the
536 way. And maybe, after I've
537 shown you that I'm right about
538 *that*, you'll be willing to believe
539 me on one or two other subjects."

540 "Such as?"

541 "Getting married!"

542 If he hadn't mentioned that
543 word "tow-rope" Sally might
544 not have let her indignation get
545 the better of her. As it was, she
546 had to substantiate her faith in
547 the Vindix perambulator. So
548 when they got through a rather
549 violent conversation she had
550 agreed to a proposition which
551 she afterward coldly regretted:
552 namely, to be a party to a double
553 *wedding* if the Vindix did not
554 arrive on its own power in St.
555 Louis in time for her aunt's cere-
556 mony. That was two weeks off.

557 "I'll find a driver for your
558 car," Carson offered.

559 "I'll find my own driver!"
560 Sally retorted, with an asperity

67

561 certainly not becoming to an
562 almost engaged girl.

563 Of course she went to Monte
564 immediately. Quite unexpect-
565 edly he refused point-blank.

566 "I'm just beginning to make
567 good here. I've got to stick until
568 I have enough saved to start in
569 for myself."

570 "How much do you need?"

571 "About five thousand dollars."

572 "I'll give you that much to do
573 as I ask you."

574 "That would be foolish."

575 "But five thousand is nothing
576 to me."

577 "That's what I was afraid of."
578 He said it with bitterness in his
579 heart.

580 "Please, Monte!" She had
581 called him that when the ocean
582 had slapped her down, there on
583 the beach that night, and it
584 seemed scarcely worth while to
585 correct the slip now. "Please!
586 If you don't, I'll have to marry
587 a man I don't love."

588 "Nonsense. No girl has to do
589 that."

590 "Yes, I do. I never go back
591 on my word. Carson knows
592 that."

593 Monte threw up his job. He
594 knew that he would have to
595 when she first asked him. The
596 money angle he steadfastly re-
597 fused to discuss. He said he
598 would charge her for his time,
599 but that was all.

600 Sally reported, upon cross-
601 examination by Carson, that she
602 had hired a driver; but she for-
603 bore to tell him the details.
604 Someway, she suspected that he
605 wouldn't like it.

606 Carson hunted up Monte at
607 his quarters.

608 "You're the man who is going
609 to drive Miss Sally Sherwood's
610 car to St. Louis, aren't you?"

611 "Yes."

612 "Well, I'm Mr. Kerry, of the
613 Kamco Automobile Company.
614 Perhaps you've heard of me."

615 "I have," Monte admitted.

616 Carson did not read the storm
617 signals quite right, so he came
618 directly to the point.

619 "I'll make it worth your while
620 if you don't arrive there until
621 after two weeks from to-day.
622 It's merely a little matter of
623 pride with me. I want to prove
624 that an American car will stand
625 up better under rough conditions
626 than a foreign one. You're an
627 American yourself, so I imagine
628 you're on my side anyway; but
629 I'm sure you will be when I say
630 there will be a five-thousand-
631 dollar check waiting for you at
632 the other end—if you don't get
633 there inside of fifteen days."

634 Monte wasn't letter-perfect in
635 the language of melodrama, so
636 he did not make any remarks
637 about a poor man's honor. He
638 merely got up and opened the
639 door.

640 "You won't help?"

641 "I will not! If you weren't a
642 lot older than I am, I'd save you
643 the trouble of *walking* out!"

644 That hurt. Carson Kerry did

645 not like to have anyone notice
646 that he was older than he pre-
647 tended to be.

648 "Never mind my age. Let's
649 see you try it!"

650 Monte did—gently. Carson
651 wasn't hurt a bit—not physi-
652 cally. But the interview did not
653 exactly presage a friendly rivalry
654 between the two men.

655 It also forced Carson to take
656 other precautions which had not
657 occurred to him before the inci-
658 dent. He took the foreman of his
659 Los Angeles service station into
660 his confidence—at least partially.

661 "I don't want that car to make
662 the trip," he explained. "What-
663 ever happens to it, I don't want
664 to know about; but an ingenious
665 man like yourself ought to be
666 able to dope out something
667 which will eventually cause
668 trouble."

669 The foreman reflected. "The
670 Vindix is an orphan, ain't it?"

671 "Yes."

672 The man smiled. "All right.
673 Leave it to me!"

674 Monte went home at noon the
675 day before the start, tired out
676 because he had been working all
677 night on Sally's car. Everything
678 had been done that he knew how
679 to do. Mac, the garage me-
680 chanic who had helped, agreed
681 to keep an eye on the car so that
682 nothing unforeseen could hap-
683 pen.

684 Just accidentally, the foreman
685 of the Kamco shop dropped in
686 at the garage that afternoon.

687 He approached Mac, who was
688 wiping grease off the Vindix.

689 "Good bus," opined the visit-
690 ing foreman.

691 "You said it!"

692 "Let me hear the motor, will
693 you?"

694 Mac was proud to show it off,
695 especially to a visiting diplomat,
696 so he stepped on the starter.

697 The foreman lifted the hood
698 and examined the engine block
699 critically. "They use an old-
700 fashioned carburetor with an
701 open air intake, don't they?
702 But it works like a charm, and
703 that's the answer, I suppose.
704 Shut her off now."

705 Mac was in the driver's seat
706 to turn off the ignition, so he did
707 not see the visitor drop a hand-
708 ful of pulverized emery into the
709 air intake. The dying motor
710 sucked the sharp deadly par-
711 ticles up into the intake mani-
712 fold, where they would lie harm-
713 less until the engine was started
714 again. Then they would cut
715 and score the cylinders in five
716 minutes so that they would be
717 beyond any repair except a slow
718 reboring job.

719 "How'd you like to work on
720 the night shift over at our shop,
721 beginning to-night?" the visitor
722 asked.

723 "I can't come to-night, be-
724 cause—"

725 "To-night or never. Twenty-
726 five dollars bonus in addition to
727 our regular pay, which is better
728 than any other place in town."

729 "I'll come. Twenty-five bucks
730 is twenty-five bucks."

731 But Mac was conscientious, so
732 he hunted up Monte and roused
733 him from his sleep to explain.
734 Monte could not blame Mac.
735 But when the latter told him
736 that it was the Kamco Company
737 he was going to work for, Monte
738 sat up with an uneasy start.

739 "Did that fellow touch the
740 Vindix while he was in the
741 shop?"

742 "He only lifted the hood to
743 look at the motor. I started it
744 for him."

745 "Started it?"

746 "Wasn't that O. K.?"

747 "Sure! But, Mac, do this for
748 me—don't tell him you've seen
749 me this afternoon."

750 Mac agreed, and went on
751 about his business.

752 Monte tried to assure himself
753 that everything was all right.
754 But he couldn't go to sleep
755 again, so he finally dressed and
756 went over to the garage.

757 Everything seemed to be O. K.
758 —until he started the motor.
759 Then he knew! Before he could
760 shut it off the harm was done,
761 and the engine was ruined be-
762 yond any possible hope of repair
763 in time to start the next morning.

764 Monte's first impulse was to
765 sit down and cry. His next re-
766 action was to call up Sally and
767 apprise her of the disaster. But
768 he stopped himself, with the re-
769 ceiver off the hook. She had
770 implicit confidence in him. To

771 tell her would shatter the slight
772 hold he had on her regard. He
773 mustn't worry her until the last
774 stone had been turned.

775 So he devoted half an hour to
776 intense thought. Then he hired
777 the rest of the crew of the repair
778 shop to work overtime on double
779 pay.

780 By morning the motor from
781 his own Vindix was bolted to the
782 engine bed of the roadster and
783 was running as smoothly as if it
784 had been born there. Monte,
785 tired but happy, thanked his
786 lucky stars that the Vindix
787 Company had not changed the
788 design of that motor for nearly
789 a decade.

790 They started from the hotel
791 about eight o'clock. If Carson
792 Kerry was surprised to see
793 Monte at all, he was doubtless
794 buoyed up by the secret assur-
795 ance of his foreman that the Vin-
796 dix would not make a hundred
797 miles before it would be a hope-
798 less wreck.

799 Sally wanted to ride in her
800 own car for the get-away. But
801 all the available space in the
802 seat of the roadster was taken up
803 by Monte's baggage. There
804 were three grips, and several
805 bulky burlap-wrapped bundles
806 besides. "I should think that a
807 man alone would not require
808 much luggage," Sally observed
809 petulantly.

810 "Perhaps he's carrying his
811 trousseau with him," suggested
812 Carson.

813 "Perhaps I am," Monte con-
814 curred amiably. It was easy to
815 be pleasant, knowing what he
816 knew.

817 The traveling equipment of
818 the Kamco party was carried in
819 long cases fitted onto the run-
820 ning boards on either side, and in
821 a trunk at the rear.

822 "We might transfer some of
823 these things to the other car and
824 make room that way," Sally
825 suggested.

826 But that aroused a storm of
827 protest from both men; quite un-
828 reasonable protest, Sally thought.
829 She was especially provoked with
830 Monte, who had never before
831 opposed her in anything.

832 "All right," she finally con-
833 ceded, in high dudgeon, "drive
834 all by yourself if you want to.
835 I won't bother you again."

836 Carson was tremendously
837 pleased. There is nothing like
838 having a little friction in the
839 ranks of the enemy.

840 So they started out, with Sally
841 in the front seat of the Kamco
842 Sedan and the heavily loaded
843 Vindix trailing behind.

844 That was the relative position
845 of the two cars for the first three
846 days out. It was tacitly under-
847 stood that this was not a race—
848 merely a sort of endurance con-
849 test, with the Vindix on trial.

850 Toward evening of the fourth
851 day, when they were about half
852 way between Flagstaff and Win-
853 slow, on a particularly bad
854 stretch of highway, the Vindix

855 broke a bearing in a front wheel.

856 As soon as she discovered that
857 her car was not following, Sally
858 made Carson turn around and
859 go back. Monte had the wheel
860 off and showed them the broken
861 pieces.

862 "That's too bad," sympa-
863 thized Carson. "The Vindix
864 uses a special light ball bearing,
865 too, doesn't it?"

866 "What can you do?" wailed
867 Sally.

868 "I'll tell you what," declared
869 Carson. "We'll drive on to
870 Winslow and send a man back
871 with a bearing."

872 "Oh, will you?" Sally beamed
873 upon him. "That's nice of you,
874 Carson. You're a good sport."

875 The two men looked at each
876 other. Both of them knew that
877 it would be impossible to find
878 that size bearing in any shop west
879 of Chicago, and maybe not there.

880 The Kamco went on alone,
881 Carson in justifiably good spir-
882 its, Sally slightly subdued, but
883 none the less grateful to Carson
884 for his apparently magnanimous
885 attitude. Perhaps he really was
886 a bigger man than she had given
887 him credit for being.

888 In Winslow, Sally went around
889 with Carson to the various gar-
890 ages in search of the new bearing.
891 As Carson had known before-
892 hand, there was none to be had.

893 "That's the trouble with an
894 orphan," he remarked, with ill-
895 concealed triumph. "You can't
896 buy parts to fit."

897 "But what can we do?"

898 "Why — nothing, I guess.
899 We'll have to go on, if we're to
900 arrive in time for the wed-
901 ding."

902 Sally didn't sleep much that
903 night. She was the victim of a
904 double nightmare: the idea of
905 losing to Carson, and the thought
906 of her driver all alone on that
907 god-forsaken road. She had not
908 forgiven Monte for not letting
909 her ride with him; still, he was a
910 human being, and it was cold
911 and dark out there. Perhaps
912 there were wolves.

913 After breakfast in the morning
914 the Vindix drove up to the hotel
915 entrance! Monte looked slightly
916 tired, and needed a shave, but
917 he did not offer any explanations
918 other than, "I was able to fix
919 it up."

920 That was less mystifying to
921 Sally than it was to Carson, who
922 knew the difficulties. He finally
923 arrived at the conclusion that
924 Monte had managed to make a
925 bearing out of Babbitt metal
926 that would act as a makeshift.
927 Well, if he had, it was bound to
928 burn out again soon, if Monte
929 attempted to follow at the pace
930 Carson was going to set from
931 there on.

932 But Monte tooled along easily
933 in their wake all that day, just
934 out of the dust, apparently un-
935 concerned about the permanency
936 of his repair.

937 There was something wrong
938 with Carson's calculations some-

939 where. That night he thought-
940 fully planted a couple of bottles
941 of his own Scotch, done up in
942 heavy paper, amid the other par-
943 cels in the Vindix. Perhaps
944 Monte would need a little stim-
945 ulant if he had to stay out all
946 night on the road again. He
947 forgot to tell Monte about it,
948 though.

949 He did, however, mention to
950 the sheriff of the next town that
951 he had passed a man in a Vindix
952 roadster who had offered to sell
953 him some liquor.

954 The sheriff was immensely
955 pleased; and when Monte came
956 along a little later, he bought the
957 whisky himself! Good Scotch
958 is hard to get so far from the
959 coast. Monte, shrewdly guess-
960 ing how the liquor came to be
961 there, thought of offering to split
962 the proceeds of the sale with Car-
963 son. But he decided to regard it
964 as a gift without any strings tied
965 to it; so he did not speak of
966 it.

967 His reticence caused a lot of
968 trouble to the Federal agents at
969 Albuquerque, to whom Carson
970 passed the tip. They detained
971 the Vindix for about two hours
972 while they vainly searched it
973 from stem to stern.

974 When Monte picked up the
975 Kamco Six again at Santa Fé, he
976 blandly explained his delay by
977 telling the exact truth about his
978 fruitless arrest. Carson pre-
979 tended to be surprised and indig-
980 nant. As a matter of fact, he

981 really was! He didn't have any
982 more Scotch.

983 In Raton, which is high, they
984 ran into a snowstorm, which
985 changed to sleet and then rain as
986 they descended the eastern slope
987 toward La Junta. There they
988 were warned of dangerous wash-
989 outs ahead, and decided to
990 lay over for weather conditions
991 to improve. That suited Monte
992 all right; but late in the evening
993 he moved his car from the garage
994 where he had originally docked,
995 and put it in an old barn on the
996 outskirts of town.

997 After two days, as the rain did
998 not let up, they decided to go on.
999 Monte bought three sets of
1000 chains and prepared to fly, plow,
1001 or submerge, as emergency in-
1002 dicated.

1003 The roads were all right for a
1004 short stretch in Colorado; then
1005 they changed abruptly to clay
1006 and mud. The speed slowed
1007 down to ten miles an hour or less,
1008 with the Kamco forcing the pace.
1009 The heavy going was hard on
1010 Sally's car; and even with the
1011 best care that Monte could give
1012 it, the Vindix arrived in Kansas
1013 City with rattling gears and a
1014 complaining chassis.

1015 Under ordinary conditions,
1016 Monte would have stayed there
1017 that night to overhaul the car;
1018 but time was getting short.
1019 There was only a day and a half
1020 left to get to St. Louis; and with
1021 the roads the way they were that
1022 would be none too long. Be-

1023 sides, the Kamco was going on
1024 through, and Sally practically
1025 insisted that Monte follow with-
1026 in hailing distance.

1027 It was dark and still raining
1028 when they cleared the outskirts
1029 of Kansas City. The roads, ac-
1030 cording to reports, were moder-
1031 ately good between there and
1032 Jefferson City; and it occurred
1033 to Monte that, if he should go on
1034 ahead, he could perhaps gain a
1035 couple of hours for mechanical
1036 revision somewhere along the
1037 line until the Kamco should
1038 catch up. The Vindix was ca-
1039 pable of greater speed than the
1040 Kamco on any kind of decent
1041 going—a fact that was known
1042 to both drivers.

1043 Therefore, when Monte signi-
1044 fied his intention of passing,
1045 Carson refused to yield the road.
1046 He could do that very effectu-
1047 ally, because they were then on
1048 a dirt and clay pike, crowned
1049 high in the middle. To get very
1050 far down on either side, when it
1051 was wet, would make a car slide
1052 into the ditch—chains or no
1053 chains.

1054 Monte hung on, about ten
1055 yards behind the Kamco, ready
1056 to pass at the first opportunity.
1057 Finally the road widened and
1058 flattened a little. Monte speed-
1059 ed up. So did Carson. They
1060 traveled abreast for a hundred
1061 yards or so, then the road started
1062 to narrow again. Monte was a
1063 few feet ahead and he deter-
1064 mined not to drop behind. Car-

son would not yield, either. The Vindix skidded a trifle. To correct it, Monte had to turn toward the top of the crown. Carson nearly hit him, but veered off automatically to the right.

In the slippery and slimy mud, the wheels of the heavy sedan did not hold. It began to slide sideways. Carson speeded up in the hope of overcoming the skid, but it was too late. With a sickening slither, the Kamco slipped into the ditch.

Carson tried to get out under his own power; but by the time he had rocked backward and forward a few minutes he realized that his rear wheels were simply digging in deeper, and he desisted.

Monte, as soon as he discovered what had happened, backed up cautiously and got out to help. For some reason, it did not occur to him that this gave him his much needed opportunity to go on ahead for his mechanical inspection.

"Got that tow-rope you brought along to use on the Vindix?" he asked amiably.

The tow-rope turned out to be a wire cable with a hook at either end. Monte hitched it on to the rear of the Vindix and the front axle of the Kamco. Then they started both motors and, on signal from Monte, dropped into gear simultaneously. There was a straining pull, during which the Kamco came forward about six inches. Then the cable snapped.

Monte produced a length of heavy chain from the rear deck of the roadster, fastened it to the axle, and they started the cars once more.

This time the Kamco yielded to persuasion and was slowly being drawn from its mud nest, when suddenly the Vindix ceased to pull. The motor raced on—but unavailingly; and the Kamco wallowed back into the ditch.

Monte thought at first that one of his chains had broken and the tires were slipping in the mud; but a hasty inspection revealed the fact that the wheels were not turning at all. So he shut off the motor. He knew what had happened.

Sally and Carson jumped out of the Kamco to see what the trouble was.

"Stripped a differential gear, didn't you?" asked Carson sympathetically.

Carson could afford to be sympathetic. The Kamco was in a ditch, but a team could pull it out. The Vindix, however, would never move again without a new ring and pinion of a size and ratio not manufactured by any foundry in the United States. The two men knew this.

"You can fix it, can't you?" queried Sally anxiously, but still with a note of confidence in her voice.

"He can—just as soon as he

1149 can build a factory and install
1150 special machinery that has to be
1151 imported from France!" Carson
1152 assured her. "It ought not to
1153 take over six or eight months."
1154 Something in Monte's attitude
1155 and expression checked the de-
1156 spair that rose in Sally's bosom.
1157 "You don't know Monte as
1158 well as I do," she asserted.
1159 It turned out that she was
1160 right. Monte knocked boards
1161 off a nearby fence and laid them
1162 as sort of a platform under the
1163 rear axle of the Vindix. With
1164 that to work on, he opened the
1165 rear axle housing and took out
1166 the broken ring gear, the teeth
1167 of which had been chewed off
1168 nearly flush with the ring.
1169 Carson, watching from the
1170 front seat of the enclosed car,
1171 failed to suppress a laugh when
1172 he saw it.
1173 But the laugh lost its point
1174 when Monte unwrapped one of
1175 his bulky parcels and produced
1176 therefrom a complete differen-
1177 tial assembly, which he bolted
1178 into place in the roadster housing
1179 without any trouble whatever.
1180 The mystery of Monte's bag-
1181 gage was a mystery no longer to
1182 Sally. He had brought along
1183 with him all the available spare
1184 parts he could unfasten from his
1185 own car, the elder orphan sister
1186 of her Vindix.
1187 When Monte offered to take
1188 up the rescue work where he had
1189 left off, Sally objected.
1190 "We can't take any chance of

1191 breaking the same part again,"
1192 she pointed out. "Besides, Car-
1193 son said a while ago that any
1194 farmer with a team could pull us
1195 out. You go on and send back
1196 help from the first farmhouse.
1197 We'll be perfectly comfortable in
1198 the closed car. It may not be the
1199 equal of our Vindix for speed,
1200 but at least the upholstery is
1201 very deep."
1202 Monte sent back a team from
1203 five miles farther on, and then
1204 proceeded light-heartedly to Jef-
1205 ferson City. There he washed
1206 the Vindix, inspected it care-
1207 fully, and went to bed with a
1208 singing heart.
1209 In the morning, when he called
1210 for the roadster at the garage, he
1211 found that all of his baggage,
1212 save the suit case he had taken
1213 to the hotel with him, was gone!
1214 He had not noticed when he
1215 drove in the night before that it
1216 was a Kamco service station.
1217 Sally, at that moment in Car-
1218 son's car several miles on the
1219 way to St. Louis, was eagerly
1220 scanning the road ahead for signs
1221 of the Vindix. Carson had told
1222 her that Monte had left before
1223 they did.
1224 So the forenoon passed swiftly
1225 and happily and they arrived in
1226 mid-afternoon at the home of her
1227 aunt in St. Louis.
1228 There, joy was superseded by
1229 anxiety. Monte had not checked
1230 in, although she was sure she had
1231 given him the address. Carson
1232 suggested that probably Monte

1233 had gone to a hotel first to clean
1234 up. Sally had her doubts about
1235 that; but, as soon as she could
1236 she went to the telephone to call
1237 up the principal hotels in town.
1238 The house 'phone was out of
1239 order!
1240 Sally was too upset to be
1241 daunted by that, however, so she
1242 slipped out the back way and
1243 went to the nearest drug store to
1244 use a pay station telephone.
1245 There were two booths. One
1246 was occupied; Sally stepped into
1247 the other. Before she could start
1248 calling up the various hotels
1249 which might harbor a missing
1250 Monte, the person in the next
1251 booth began talking. She could
1252 hear perfectly.
1253 "Hello! . . . Kamco Sales and
1254 Service? . . . Give me the general
1255 manager . . . Hello, Jones. This
1256 is Mr. Kerry talking, Carson
1257 Kerry. . . . Never mind the polite
1258 patter, Jones. Here's a rush
1259 order. There's a Vindix road-
1260 ster on the highway somewhere
1261 between here and Jefferson City.
1262 . . . Do you get that? . . . Well,
1263 it's headed this way, and I don't
1264 want it to arrive. Understand?
1265 Send out every car you can get
1266 hold of—trucks, tractors, any-
1267 thing that will move, with in-
1268 structions to block the way.
1269 They can't miss the Vindix.
1270 You know what a funny-shaped
1271 radiator it has. Don't use any
1272 violence, unless absolutely neces-
1273 sary. That's all. Get going."
1274 Sally almost stopped breath-

1275 ing for fear Carson would dis-
1276 cover her; but when he passed
1277 the booth he did not even glance
1278 in that direction.
1279 As soon as he had left the
1280 store, she slipped out and cau-
1281 tiously watched him walk down
1282 the street toward her aunt's
1283 house.
1284 A few blocks away, in the op-
1285 posite direction, was the garage
1286 where Carson had put the
1287 Kamco Sedan. Sally raced over
1288 there. The car was on the wash-
1289 rack, but she ordered it off.
1290 "I've got to use it for perhaps
1291 an hour," she explained.
1292 Between St. Charles and
1293 Wentzville, she found Monte.
1294 The Vindix was in the ditch be-
1295 side the road and Monte was sit-
1296 ting on the running board, his
1297 head in his hands, oblivious to
1298 her approach. The fenders of
1299 the Vindix were bent all out of
1300 shape and the entire front axle
1301 was sagging.
1302 "What's the matter?"
1303 Monte looked up. He was not
1304 even much surprised to see her.
1305 "Axle's broke. A truck hit
1306 me." He made a gesture of ab-
1307 solute despair.
1308 "Can't it be fixed?"
1309 "No chance. Not in time."
1310 "Haven't you got an extra one
1311 with you?"
1312 "I had one; but all my parts
1313 and tools were stolen last night."
1314 "Oh!" The extent of the cal-
1315 amity finally struck Sally with its
1316 full force. "Then we're cooked?"

"Yes."

"We could tow it into St. Louis."

"Your agreement was to get it there under its own power."

"That's so." She sat down beside him. There didn't seem to be any hope.

"I'm sorry I failed you. No man ought ever to fail the girl he—" Monte paused, aghast at what he had nearly said.

Sally waited for him to go on. Then she helped him. "Monte, am I that girl so far as you're concerned?"

"You know you are. There isn't any particular point in denying it now. Yesterday, I would have had to deny it, because I'm a poor man and you are a rich girl. But, since there's no hope, I'm not ashamed to say that if I ever marry anyone else it will be because I've lost my memory!"

Sally was accustomed to declarations of love, but this one was unique in her experience. No one before had ever tried to phrase devotion and tenderness with lips that were grimy with grease, or had expressed unspeakable desire with eyes ringed with dried mud.

But she thrilled to it more than to any speech she had ever heard. She took his hand—it was dirty—and held it an instant between her own two. "If— oh, I wish—Come on, let's go!"

Monte hesitated. "I guess I'll stick with the car. Probably somebody will come along who will tow it into St. Louis."

"I'll tow it in now with Mr. Kerry's car."

Monte scowled.

"His tow-rope is broken anyway; and mine was stolen."

"Perhaps he bought a new one. Look in the tool box."

Monte did. He lifted the lid of one of the long running-board compartments. Then he stood there, speechless and immovable.

"What's the matter?"

"Come here. Look!"

In the box were Monte's burlapped packages!

They worked like mad, Sally helping with every ounce of strength she didn't know she possessed. When the job was finished her clothes were a wreck, and she had jammed one finger so badly that if he hadn't kissed it she couldn't have stood the pain.

But in two hours they were under way again, the most dilapidated motorists on the entire transcontinental highway — and the happiest. The Kamco Six they left just where she stood.

"They've got to catch us in the next thirty minutes," observed Monte. "By that time it will be dark, and your friend's piratical agents won't be able to spot us."

"You don't think they will try anything more, do you?"

1401 "I not only think it, I'm sure
1402 of it; and here it comes!"

1403 There was a crossroad just
1404 ahead. On each side of it was a
1405 touring car, approaching the in-
1406 tersection. They were idling
1407 along, but as the Vindix ap-
1408 proached at high speed they
1409 suddenly accelerated.

1410 "Hang on!" Monte opened
1411 the throttle wide. "This is the
1412 only way."

1413 The Vindix roadster shot
1414 across between the other two
1415 cars, coming head on. The left-
1416 hand one grazed the rear fender.

1417 There was smashing of glass
1418 as the two vehicles behind them
1419 struck each other.

1420 "I hope they've got a first-aid
1421 kit along," said Monte grimly.

1422 The wedding march was just
1423 beginning when they arrived.

1424 But it stopped. The entrance
1425 of two guests in such a dis-
1426 heveled condition would stop a
1427 wedding ceremony in almost any
1428 stage of its progress.

1429 "You know what Pershing
1430 said at the tomb of Lafayette,"
1431 announced Sally to Carson
1432 Kerry.

1433 "Why, Sally, what has hap-
1434 pened to you?" demanded that
1435 gentleman.

1436 "Me and my little boy friend
1437 here have just brung in the good
1438 ship Vindix. Are we in time for
1439 the wedding? If not, we'll start
1440 one of our own."

1441 "Sally! You wouldn't marry
1442 a mechanic?"

1443 "I wouldn't marry a man who
1444 wasn't one. It's going to *take*
1445 one to keep our car on the road
1446 for the next few years, as spare
1447 parts get scarcer and scarcer."

1448 Carson regarded Monte with
1449 an appraising eye. "I am sure
1450 that Mr. English is not the sort
1451 of man who would propose mar-
1452 riage to a woman of tremendous
1453 wealth, knowing that he is poor
1454 himself."

1455 "You're right, Mr. Kerry,"
1456 declared Monte huskily.

1457 "Of course you're right, Mr.
1458 Kerry," mimicked Sally. "Monte
1459 hasn't, and never would propose
1460 marriage to me; but both of you
1461 have forgotten that this is leap
1462 year. Our two orphan cars are
1463 so thoroughly married already
1464 that it would be hopeless to try
1465 to sort them out; so we've just
1466 got to live together in order to
1467 keep alive the traditions of the
1468 best orphan automobile ever
1469 made. You know just as well as
1470 I do that any man who could
1471 bring an orphan Vindix over the
1472 road from Los Angeles to St.
1473 Louis won't have any trouble
1474 overcoming the minor obstacles
1475 of life—even including the man-
1476 agement of an orphan woman
1477 such as me. Monte, will you let
1478 me be your spare tire forever
1479 and ever, amen?"

1480 An hour later, Monte consent-
1481 ed. By that time, everybody
1482 was arguing on Sally's side, if
1483 only for the sake of peace.

The Analysis

Although this story has no outward resemblance to the story of Ulysses as he makes a series of attempts to reach his wife, Penelope, this story is in direct line of descent from the Odyssey type of story. It is a story which is concerned with setting forth the attempts of a central actor to overcome a number of conditions. Each condition is overcome only to result in the appearance of another condition, which in turn has to be overcome or removed.

This story you will find is modern in that throughout there is the knowledge on the part of the reader that the prize to be won is a girl. This girl is in reality the story's "reason for being." The personality of the girl is made to permeate the story.

The easiest part of a story to write is the Body. This is so because in the Body of a story there are two ways in which interest may be achieved. It may come from the interchanges which lead into the dramatic or narrative turning points of hindrance, or it may come from those turning points of dramatic or narrative hindrance independent of the interchanges. Instead of an interchange the writer may present to the reader a meeting which results in a turning point. The pattern of the story may therefore be either

| Meeting | turning point of hindrance

or | Interchange | turning point of hindrance

In the first case the interest will come almost entirely from the turning point, while in the second place the interest may be extracted from the interchange and the turning point. Keep in mind always when analyzing a story that whenever an actor becomes aware of a condition there is a meeting (a contact), in the sense in which we use the word. Thus on lines 983 to 1008 there is set forth a condition which exists (the bad condition of the roads), and on lines 1009 to 1014 there is set forth the turning point which results from the character's response to that condition or that stimulus. (The car is badly worn.) In this case you have meeting and turning point of hindrance as the pattern.

On lines 790 to 839 there is an interchange between Monte and Sally with Kerry as the observer. This interchange actually closes on line 835, while line 836 to 839 are the crisis of hindrance in the story. These lines form the fifth step of that meeting and project a turning point of hindrance because there is a threat of disaster through the friction existing between Sally and Monte who ought to be partners in the enterprise.

79

The material with which an author is working will almost automatically determine the pattern of his story. The only possible choice which a writer can make for the presentation units of the Body of his story lies between meetings and interchanges. In the Body of the story the interest is in the actor's attempt to overcome conditions or opponents who stand in the way of the successful outcome of his purpose. In general, it may be put down as a rule of craftsmanship that if the hero has to overcome difficulties or conditions the presentation units which the writer employs to show those attempts will be meetings rather than interchanges. When the Body of the story is concerned with the attempts of an actor to overcome an opponent the presentation units will be interchanges between the actor and the opponent.

The experienced writer realizes that although he can depend upon the number of hindrances which he introduces to hold the interest of his reader, he is leaning rather heavily upon plot interest in so doing and is sacrificing presentation interest. Wherever possible then, he will seek to introduce interchanges in order to balance the interest between presentation and plot.

The technical problem confronting him in a story which is made up of an attempt to overcome difficulties is an extremely interesting one from the point of view of expert craftsmanship. Being an experienced writer he realizes, either instinctively or as a technical expert, that any step of a scene may become an interchange. Hence he substitutes the third step of the scene for one of the other steps, thus presenting interchanges which are always more interesting than meetings. Thus for example, on lines 850 to 879 there is presented an interchange which sets forth a condition resulting in a hindrance, which is the fact that a broken bearing is replaceable only in Chicago; and hence the success of the enterprise is threatened. The fifth step of this scene is really set forth in the interchange in Winslow between Sally and Carson. Thus the experienced author is able to present to a reader an interchange which results in a hindrance even though that interchange is really an artificial building up of a fifth step.

It was not so much the interest for writers of the Body of this story which led me to select it, as the interest which its beginning contains for all writers who are sincere students of craftsmanship. The three major divisions of Beginning, Body and Ending are very clearly defined, as well as the sub-division of sequel. The Beginning occupies lines 1 to 673, the Body occupies line 674 to 1421, the Ending occupies line 1422 to 1483 and contains the Conclusive Act on lines 1436 and 1440 together with the Sequel from lines 1441 to 1483.

One of the first questions that is always asked by a person who begins this structural analysis is, "Where does the Beginning end, and the Body commence?" The Beginning contains always the threat of conflict, of difficulties to be overcome, of opponents to be removed or overcome, and of disaster to be averted. Until all this information is placed before the reader, together with the main narrative question which emerges as a result of the actor's response to the main condition, then it is still Beginning. In this story the narrative question emerges on lines 593 to 599, but the Beginning lasts until line 673 because the interchanges between Kerry and Monte on line 606 to 654 and between Kerry and the foreman on line 655 to 673 contain threats of disaster to the enterprise. They are not interchanges which show the attempts of the actor to bring about his purpose although they might conceivably be said to be part of the Body of the story because they involve attempts of forces opposed to the main actor who are attempting to bring about disaster to his enterprise.

It is unimportant however, this making of too rigid classifications; in general it is pretty safe to assume that the Body of the story is made up of the attempts of the actor rather than the attempts of opponents of the chief actor. For this reason I am including these interchanges of which I have spoken in the Beginning of the story, and prefer to regard the Body of the story as being made up of the attempts of the main actor, Monte, to overcome the conditions which confront him from time to time in the progress of the story.

The interesting difference between this story and the two which we have previously examined is that in this story the Beginning occupies 673 lines out of a total of 1483, and that the Body occupies 749 lines and the Ending 62. In this story the Beginning is nearly *one half* of the whole story.

In my work with writers who are interested in analyzing the material of their own and other writer's stories, I have found that at certain stages of their progress they come to a kind of impasse. Settings they can learn to write after very little training. As a matter of fact, in the modern short-story, setting plays a very minor part. Characterization writers learn more slowly than they learn setting; but with the knowledge always before them that characterization can be learned through properly directed observation of the reactions of people to the various stimuli of life. The actual selection of presentation units—which is plotting,—and which is really the most mechanical portion of writing a story, writers seem to find very difficult. It is almost as if they had inhibitions. They learn to plot and present the Body of the story, and to plot and present the Ending of a story, but in a story which has a long Beginning they immediately find difficulty. It is because this story is in that particular category that writers will find it of very much interest.

It will, I hope, prove encouraging to writers to learn that in general the faults that creep into their work are the natural outcome of definite progress which they have made. Unfortunately, in graduating from one set of difficulties, they have reached a point where they find themselves confronted with a new set of difficulties. It is exactly as if a man who, after striving for a long time to jump a three foot hurdle, at last succeeds in doing so easily and consistently, only to discover that he has a harder problem in learning to jump a hurdle five feet high. Instead of being discouraged he should, on the contrary, be very much encouraged by his former success, and because of that success he should be stirred to redoubled efforts.

Those writers who have difficulties with the Beginnings of their stories have made one step forward very definitely. That step is their realization that stories *do* have Beginnings. The hurdle over which they cannot jump is their own failure to realize that there are two distinct types of material which make up Beginnings. In the first type, which I shall call the intrinsically interesting Beginning, or intrinsically interesting narrative problem, that problem is important *in itself*. The explanatory matter is not essential to the reader's understanding of its importance. If you will turn to Case No. 7 in this book you will find reprinted the story *Paradise Island*, by Will Payne. The narrative problem of this story is, "Can Dwyer succeed in killing Langley?" This main narrative problem is an important one, and would be an important one at any time. Whenever a man sets out to kill another man it is important regardless of what led up to it. On the other hand, when a young man sets out to drive a car from Los Angles to St. Louis it is not an important problem. It is important only synthetically, and it falls into the category of the synthetically important Beginning. Its importance is clear to the reader only after he has been presented with a large amount of explanatory matter. It is an artificially contrived narrative problem which shows the main character called upon to accomplish some feat despite the opposition of a force or forces, which is made important because of what depends upon it artificially.

One of the anomalies of the craftsmanship of short-story writing is that the writer who knows quite a good deal about his subject is often likely to be misled by his knowledge of craftsmanship into errors of execution. This is particularly the case with this type of story. The writer knowing either instinctively or from hard-earned experience that the chief interest of the story comes when the opposing forces are caused to clash, tries to reach that point in his story at which this clash occurs at the earliest possible moment, and he does so by compressing the explanatory matter into a summary of the event or fifth step of the presentation unit. *No other method of deadening interest begins to compare in effectiveness with summary.* Yet the writer in his instinctive desire to improve his work was essentially sound when he summarized. In so doing he fell into the pit because his deductions were faulty. Here, if ever, is a case where, if the mountain won't come to Mohammed, Mohammed must go to the mountain. Instead of taking the life out of the Beginning of his story by omitting the interchanges which can always be developed so that they are encounters, in order that the reader may reach the clash in the Body of the story, the writer should *add* life to the Beginning by causing it to contain in its interchanges the same sort of clash that would normally occur in the interchanges in the Body.

The problem of craftsmanship confronting Mr. Adams in presenting this story was that the main narrative question could not be made to emerge for almost the first half of the story. It does not emerge until the end of the interchange between Sally and Monte (lines 563 to 605). The conditions to be presented to the reader are these: Monte English, the hero, a young Easterner, who has just brought a foreign orphan car, a Vindix, across the continent to Los Angeles there meets and falls in love with the heroine, Sally, whose dead father once owned that very car. Sally has just bought a new Vindix against the advice of her "almost guardian," Carson Kerry, agent for the Kamco Six, an American car. It becomes clear that Monte and Sally are in love, Monte resisting because he is too poor to consider marriage to a rich girl. Kerry and Sally quarrel. It develops during the quarrel that Sally's aunt is to be married in St. Louis and wants Sally there. Kerry suggests that Sally marry him and that they go east together. The quarrel culminates in a wager that if the Vindix cannot be piloted from Los Angeles to St. Louis under its own power in time for the wedding of Sally's aunt, Sally will marry Carson Kerry. Although Kerry suggests that he find a mechanic Sally insists upon being allowed to make her own selection: Monte. That is the main condition. Up to this point the story is all Beginning and the main narrative question does not emerge until Sally goes to Monte and asks him to act as her representative in driving the car. For nearly half the story, then, the reader must be held by the writer before he comes to the main narrative question of the story, "Can Monte English succeed in driving an orphan Vindix from Los Angles to St. Louis in two weeks under its own power, thereby winning the girl?"

Although to the inexperienced writer this would be a hurdle very high indeed, to Mr. Adams it presents no difficulties, because he is an experienced writer and knows the most important tenets of the creed of fiction craftsmanship—that interchanges are always the most interesting presentation units, because they can always be developed into complete scenes. His plot sense also tells him that if he uses episodes which are interchanges without clash, they should result in crises in the plot, and that the promise of conflict is an extremely good way to hold the interest of the reader, pending the reader's knowledge of the happenings that will enable him to phrase for himself a main, unifying, central narrative question. This story is in its Beginning a series of interchanges. If the interchanges are in themselves dramatic we can often forego the presence of plot complications, although these can always be additional ornaments to the presentation units.

The first interchange between Kerry and Sally on lines 1 to 75 is a dramatic scene. At its close we learn that Sally does not want this man, Carson Kerry, as a husband. The plot could here have been strengthened had the writer indicated the promise of conflict to the main story by saying that she realized that Carson Kerry was not a man lightly to be dismissed, that he would make trouble for any man with whom she might later fall in love. Then, in the next interchange between Sally and Monte, on lines 76 to 154 this threat of conflict would have carried over and would have strengthened that scene. This second interchange, between Sally and Monte, could have been strengthened in its fifth step had the author pointed out that Sally was in love with this man; but that he had no intention of permitting himself to fall in love with her, or at least to pursue the acquaintance further. Then we would have had two promises of conflict and disaster. However, at the close of the next scene this is made pretty clear on lines 260 to 283, although the importance of it is slightly minimized by the statement that Sally was absolutely unscrupulous. It would have been a little stronger had the emphasis been upon the seriousness with which Sally regarded the meeting. At the close of the next meeting which occupies lines 284 to 342 the reader learns that the Vindix is an orphan car, but does not understand the importance of this in relation to the main problem because he does not yet know what that main problem is. The next meeting is between Sally and the garage man on lines 343 to 374 which results in her sending for Monte. It could have been improved very much had Carson Kerry been there present and insisted or tried to insist upon her sending for somebody else. The two rivals could then have been brought face to face earlier and out of this meeting could have grown an assurance by Monte that if she ever needed him he would be willing to do anything she asked him. This could have occupied the place of the interchange which now occurs on lines 375 to 408. Carson Kerry could, as a result of this, have warned her against seeing more of Monte and that would have added piquancy to the expedition to the beach which now occupies lines 409 to 485. Lines 486 to 562 are the limits of a dramatic scene which occurs between Carson Kerry and Sally. The fifth step of this scene is actually another scene between Monte and the girl. (Lines 563 to 599 with a fifth step of lines 600 to 605.) From then on the reader's interest is clearly held by a knowledge of the main narrative question.

The writer may learn one extremely interesting and basic lesson from reading the Beginning of this story. It is, to present the explanatory matter leading up to the main narrative question in a series of interchanges, making them, wherever possible, dramatic scenes, and pointing out to the reader at the conclusion of each such scene the promise of conflict necessary to avert disaster, to overcome difficulties, or to overcome opponents. 606 to 654 which I have included in the Beginning of the story is a dramatic clash which clearly presents the promise of dangerous opposition. The interchange on lines 674 to 730 presents the promise of disaster. The fifth step of this scene is the interview between Mac and Monte on lines 731 to 751 which makes clear to the reader that Monte is aware of the first condition which he has to overcome. This is the obstacle which stands in the way of his successful performance. Thereafter the Body of the story is made up of a series of such obstacles. These obstacles occur in such a plausible way that the reader is caused to feel that almost any one of them is sufficient to ruin the whole enterprise. He is forever compelled to ask himself, with a sort of breathlessness, "Now what will the main actor do when he encounters *that* condition or obstacle?"

The more numerous the obstacles, and the more difficult these obstacles are, the more sustained is this interest of breathlessness. In selecting and arranging these conditions or obstacles the ingenuity of the writer is taxed. The problem is again one of craftsmanship. Experience comes to the writer's aid. The established writer is identified by his knowledge of one simple basic rule in selecting conditions or obstacles. It is this: "The ideal condition or obstacle to be overcome is the one which presents a state of affairs from which there appears to be no solution but disaster."

In the Body of his story the writer is confronted by a dilemma. It is this: the plot may always be increased in breathlessness by the introduction of apparently insuperable obstacles, but the reader's interest must be also concentrated upon the character of the chief actor. He cannot be a weakling, but must be a person of resource who is able to overcome obstacles. For that reason the chief actor must be confronted with conditions which arises through fate or through the machinations of some opponent. In this particular story this requirement is very admirably met when Monte finds the motor of the Vindix ruined. He substitutes the motor of his own car; but the reader is not allowed long to believe that success will crown his efforts, because in the next interchange between Monte and Sally, the threat of conflict between these two presents a hindrance by threatening the successful outcome of the enterprise. Then later, when all goes well to Flagstaff for four days through the enterprise of Monte, this apparent success is changed to what appears to be failure, by the breaking of the front wheel bearing which it is impossible to replace, according to Kerry. Next, when Monte overtakes the others Kerry is caused to say that the bearing is probably a temporary Babbitt bearing which will not last very long. When later this prediction does not seem to be borne out, there is a hindrance through Kerry's planting liquor in Monte's car and notifying the sheriff. Later, when this is overcome by the sheriff buying the liquor, there is a furtherance, which is not as well chosen as it might be because it is not the action of Monte to overcome the obstacle which was presented by his opponent. Yet it does show his ability to meet almost any condition. Following this there comes the strain upon the Vindix which requires overhauling, when the time limit is rapidly threatening disaster. Then there comes the hindrance which the magnanimity of Monte brings about.

In this case, although the hindrance was caused by the main character, it was not caused by a weakness in his character, but rather by a strength. Also the reader's dislike for Kerry is increased when he gloats over the stripping of the differential gear of the Vindix. Monte's resourcefulness is shown when he fixes the gear with the spare parts of his own old Vindix. This furtherance is instantly removed by the stealing, by Kerry, of the balance of the spare parts, and also by his arranging with his subordinates to smash up the Vindix. Then, instead of Monte getting himself out of the difficulty, an agent of his, Sally, or perhaps we might say an ally, is brought in and she is used to rescue him by bringing along the spare parts in the car owned by Kerry. However, the two cars sent out by Kerry attempt another wreck, and the big moment of the story occurs. Monte averts this disaster by his skillful driving, and avoids collision. At last he arrives in time for the wedding. The main narrative question is answered in the affirmative, "Yes, he can get the Vindix across to St. Louis in two weeks." There are still some loose ends to be taken up, and they involve the winning of the girl; and it is for this reason that the interchanges between Sally and Kerry on lines 1441 to 1479, and between Sally and Monte on lines 1480 to 1483 are introduced.

But interesting as this arrangement is, the most interesting and helpful lesson which the aspiring writer can learn from a study of this story is the one which Mr. Adams has so well mastered. Every condition which the hero is called upon to meet is made to appear to the reader to present an insuperable obstacle. The outcome of the main attempt is always in suspense. For that reason alone, this story will repay a thorough analysis.

BEGINNING

Initial Condition and Main Actor's purpose are set forth.

Jake Bolton and Captain	1– 52
Captain and Lieutenant	53– 66
Captain and Lieutenant.	67– 94

Main Plot Crises apparent. Promises of dramatic Conflict to overcome Difficulties, to overcome opponents, to avert Disaster.

Main Narrative Question: "Can Jake Bolton, 551 succeed in making good in the army?"

BODY

Series of attempts of Main Actor to achieve his purpose. Attempts by opponent to prevent that achievement.

Scene. Jake and Subaltern.	95–126
Scene (Resumed). Jake and Subaltern.	127– 223
Scene. Jake and Colonel.	224– 235
Interchanges show effect upon actors.	236– 315
Jake and condition.	316– 392
Jake and Richards and Sergeant.	393– 417
Jake and General.	418– 427
Captain and Lieut. (5th step of 418–426.)	428– 438
Sikh and Sergeant. Sergeant and Jake.	439– 482 / 483– 504
Jake and Corporal.	505– 638
Jake and Subaltern.	639– 751
Jake, Colonel, and Subaltern.	752– 868
(5th step. Effect.)	869– 894
Meeting. Jake and condition.	895– 981

Hindrance. Has made enemy who has power to defeat.

Hindrance. Has name and number taken.

Hindrance. Has a bad name.

Hindrance. Name confirmed.

Furtherance. Nickname forgotten.

Hindrance-Dramatic. Threat of conflict with a dangerous opponent.

Furtherance.

Promise of Disaster. Dramatic Hindrance.

Dramatic Hindrance. Beach unsafe for Jake. Furtherance. Feels safe. Hindrance. Subaltern appears.

Hindrance. Name again taken by hostile officer.

Furtherance. But success in encounter is not ultimate success.

Hindrance. Nickname revived.

Furtherance. Does brave deed.

ENDING

Conclusive Act

Scene. Jake and Staff Officer.	982–1024

Sequel.

Captain Graham and Lieutenant Townsend. Appended episode gives answer to Main Narrative Question, correcting impression left by 980–1025	1025– 1053

Main Narrative Question Answered: "No." Character abandons any attempt to make good.

Revised answer to Main Narrative Question: "Yes." Jake Bolton has made good.

88

JAKE BOLTON, 551

BY JOHN GALLISHAW

My reasons for reprinting this story are largely personal. Chief among them is my own reaction to statements made by people who have examined analyses which I have made of stories by other authors. These statements were to the effect that the author whose story was analyzed would himself be the last person in the world to be conscious of having striven for definite effect. The only way to prove that such is the case is to select a story which would illustrate the actual building up of a story from a partial plot. I know how this story grew, what was its nucleus, and the various steps in its progress.

I am reprinting *Jake Bolton, 551* not because it is such a good story, but because it lends itself very readily to an illustration of the actual growth of a story from the first conception of the idea until its final appearance in a magazine.

CASE No. 4

JAKE BOLTON, 551

BY JOHN GALLISHAW

Captain Graham, the recruiting officer, inwardly pleased but outwardly non-committal, surveyed appraisingly the wind-tanned, good humored face of the tall recruit, and demanded his name, his occupation, his address, next of kin, and such other particulars as go toward filling out an enlistment-blank. The recruit, it appeared, had no next of kin and no permanent place of abode, and on the official records his name and occupation were set down as Bolton, Jake, trapper and woodsman.

The rank and file of the First Colonials, who respect no official record save the pay-roll, paid no attention to this, but hailed him as "Hippo," because of his two hundred and thirty pounds.

He took his place easily in the First Colonials. He was a crack shot, since much of his livelihood had depended on his skill with a rifle, and learning to shoot had come to him as unconsciously as learning to walk to ordinary children. All his twenty-five years had been spent in the forest, and all his sustenance had been wrung from it. Hunting had given him the training of a scout, lumbering had developed muscles of steel and a frame of iron, and danger and exposure he took as matters of course. For a soldier no better material could be desired.

The doctors found him organically faultless and his eyesight abnormally keen, and passed him as "fit." So Captain Graham, prophesying that in three months he couldn't be told from a regular, detailed him to his own beloved B Company, and noted his name as good material for a non-commissioned officer.

"That man," he remarked to Lieutenant Townsend, "is bound to make good."

"Making good in the army," said Lieutenant Townsend, "depends entirely on how you get started. It's a case of give a dog a bad name, and you hang him."

61 "I go by a man's eyes," replied
62 the Captain. "That man has
63 character enough in those
64 straightforward eyes of his to
65 live down any bad name he can
66 ever acquire."

67 When the preliminary sorting
68 out and posting had been com-
69 pleted, the First Colonials
70 crossed the ocean and went into
71 intensive training under canvas
72 with their fellows at Salisbury
73 Plain. Captain Graham and
74 Lieutenant Townsend again dis-
75 cussed Jake Bolton.

76 "Bolton worries me a little,"
77 said the Lieutenant. "He's
78 pretty independent. He never
79 says 'Sir,' to an officer."

80 "Who cares," said the Captain
81 easily.

82 "None of our crowd," admit-
83 ted the lieutenant. "Our of-
84 ficers are pretty lax on formal-
85 ities, but I have a hunch that
86 he'll get into trouble with some
87 of those English Officers. You
88 know they can put him on the
89 crime sheet, and he looks like
90 the obstinate kind that won't
91 stir one step to placate them.
92 If those young subalterns once
93 begin asking him his name and
94 number, he's gone."

95 Lieutenant Townsend's proph-
96 ecy was soon justified. When
97 Salisbury was knee-deep in liquid
98 mud the trouble began through
99 a particularly youthful-looking
100 subaltern who had imbibed too
101 freely at the officer's mess. He
102 disputed the narrow strip of dry

103 sidewalk with Jake, who was on
104 his way from camp to the town of
105 Salisbury. That was in the first
106 year of the war, when the only
107 requirement for a commission as
108 a second lieutenant in the Eng-
109 lish army was an uncle. The
110 subaltern, who had the chest of
111 a consumptive, the shoulders of
112 a ginger-ale bottle, the voice of
113 a school-girl, and the manners
114 of a pampered Pekinese, ordered
115 Jake to step off the dry sidewalk
116 that he might pass. The argu-
117 ment was short; a St. Bernard
118 might so have argued with
119 a lap-dog. The big Colonial
120 seized the subaltern by the coat-
121 collar, swung him round behind
122 him, and proceeded.

123 "They'll soon be wheeling 'em
124 up in baby-carriages to give 'em
125 commissions," was his only
126 comment.

127 The enraged subaltern fol-
128 lowed him closely, demanding
129 at thirty-second intervals, "I
130 say, my man, what is your name
131 and numbah?"

132 There is one form of torturing
133 prisoners that German ingenuity
134 has so far failed to devise; com-
135 pared with it, crucifying with
136 bayonets or inoculating with
137 tetanus germs is merciful. It
138 consists in saying to a private
139 soldier, "I say, my man, what
140 is your name and numbah?"
141 Usually in the British army it
142 precedes an inquisition before
143 the commanding officers, result-
144 ing in anything from two-days'

confinement to camp to fourteen days' field punishment No. 2, which consists of being spread-eagled every day for two hours to the wheel of an artillery-wagon. It is a form of reprisal practised by fledgeling lieu-tenants on home duty toward men returned from active service, who are guilty of such heinous offences as not saluting or for-getting to button their great-coats. At Salisbury Plain in 1914 there were many men to whom the question was a verit-able sword of Damocles. To this category Jake belonged.

Into the town of Salisbury he strode, apparently unaware of the existence of the subaltern panting behind. More than ever the combination resembled the St. Bernard and the Pekinese. Through the streets of Salisbury Jake proceeded, stopping fre-quently at places that displayed alluring signs setting forth "Ales, Wines, and Intoxicating Liquors, Licensed to be Drunk on the Premises." Always the officer followed him, and always the yapping cry rang out behind him.

"I say, my man, what is your name and numbah?"

Ever and anon the officer ap-pealed to other Colonials to ar-rest the man; but they shrugged their shoulders, disclaiming any duty of obedience to an offi-cer not of their own battalion. Some of them told him frankly,

"We'll be damned if we'll arrest one of our own men"; but others, more wily, desiring to be beyond reproof, asserted sickness.

Scornfully careless of the riot he created, Jake swung along, pausing only at intervals to refresh himself, and behind the frantic subaltern followed his comrades, taking up the wail: "I say, my man, what is your name and numbah?"

The officer's patience was rewarded when Jake fell asleep on a bench and leaned his bulk against one of the signs, blot-ting out the part that referred to the liquors. The picture he presented was of a gigantic young man sleeping heavily against a sign which read, "Licensed to be Drunk on the Premises."

An hour later a corporal's guard, sent by the subaltern, found him there, loaded him into a cart, and took him with much indignity to the guard tent on Salisbury Plain, where the sub-altern, following persistently, caused the sergeant of the guard to write upon a "crime sheet" the name, "Jake Bolton, 551," and following it the two charges, "drunk" and "insolent to a superior officer."

The next day the colonel of Jake's battalion heard the com-plaint of the young officer, and although he made clear to the subaltern that he hated any interference with his battalion, discipline had to be maintained. He lectured Jake on the necessity of respecting the uniform of a superior officer, and sentenced him to four days "C.C." for being drunk.

This, translated, means four days confined to camp. To Jake this mattered very little, since all his money was gone and all his headache was not. The four days passed as all days pass, and the headache disappeared the way of all headaches, but the legend of Jake's parade through town endured. Among the First Colonials it is a classic. Some of them have read of "Sherman's March to the Sea," and a few of them of "Paul Revere's Ride," but in days to come, when Sherman is only a name and Paul Revere is forgotten, the survivors of the First Colonials will tell their children's children of the night that "Name and Number" marched through Salisbury, and of his ignoble ride back.

Beginning with that night life changed for Jake. By the First Colonials Jake Bolton was thereafter no longer hailed as "Hippo" but as "Jake Bolton, 551." He could not live down that nickname. Thenceforth it was the usual thing to see young Richards, the seventeen-year-old bantam drummer, petted, spoiled, and beloved of everyone, stride behind Jake, piping up at intervals in an absurd falsetto voice, to the huge amusement of onlookers,

"I say, my man, what is your name and numbah?"

Through ten months of training in the British Isles and in Egypt the legend pursued him, and for officers of battalions other than his own Jake fostered a hatred that was the greater since he found few opportunities to vent it. A less good-natured man might have become soured, but toward his comrades his attitude of easy-going friendship remained always the same. He answered as cheerfully as the others the question, "What is your name and number?" and through the weeks that the First Colonials sweltered in their marquees on the edge of the desert near Cairo the question he had made famous ranked with the one attributed to the Governor of North Carolina. No matter how sultry the day or how thick the flies, there was always a response. Into a marquee where twenty men listlessly smoked cigarettes and swatted flies between whiffs someone would stick his head and inquire in a voice tinged with an exaggerated English drawl, "I say, my man, what is your name and numbah?" No call to arms or official command could ever move them as did that question. The twenty would rise and shout as one man in a

94

313 monotonous sing-song, "Jake
314 Bolton, 551, B Company, First
315 Colonials."

316 At last the First Colonials
317 went to the Dardanelles and no
318 sooner had the battalion landed
319 on the peninsula than Jake ful-
320 filled the promise of his physique
321 and training. He became one of
322 the best soldiers in the battalion.
323 Through the long days, monot-
324 onous and fly-infested, when the
325 well nigh intolerable heat
326 brought complaints and grumb-
327 lings from his companions, he
328 lay on the firing-step of the
329 trench, contentedly puffing at
330 a large pipe. Through ghastly
331 nights when the whine of bullets
332 ticked off the minutes, he
333 crawled through no-man's land,
334 his deer-stalking experience
335 standing him in good stead. On
336 trench raids, in listening posts,
337 lying through mud-soaked hours
338 as silent as a snake and just as
339 dangerous, wriggling through
340 dank, uncut grass of neglected
341 orchards, he was unequalled.
342 At such work he was at home;
343 to him every sound in that
344 ghoulish hunting-ground was
345 pregnant with meaning. The
346 sharp crack of a broken twig
347 that went unnoticed by others
348 he interpreted rightly as the
349 movement of the wily sniper.
350 In accordance with the law of
351 mutation, therefore, he became
352 a sharpshooter, and thenceforth
353 he was free to come and go as he
354 pleased. For the sharpshooter

355 is an arrogant king of the
356 trenches; his attitude toward the
357 ordinary soldier is that of a
358 senior of a small college toward
359 a freshman. He calls no one his
360 superior unless it is another
361 sniper with more kills to his
362 credit. Thenceforth Jake was
363 as nearly happy as mortal can
364 be. Thereafter he was wont,
365 just as dusk made indistinct the
366 landmarks of no-man's land,
367 disguising them with nature's
368 own camouflage, to take his rifle,
369 examine the telescopic sights
370 carefully, clean it painstak-
371 ingly, equip himself with en-
372 ough bully beef and biscuits,
373 and disappear for two or three
374 days. Out there he felt safe from
375 the pursuing question. Swelter-
376 ing heat, sameness of food, lack
377 of sleep, and scarcity of water
378 made no difference to him. He
379 found it all strange, exciting, and
380 stimulating; and while the bulk
381 of the battalion sickened, he
382 waxed strong. In two months the
383 First Colonials had been reduced
384 to one-third of their original
385 strength; the remainder, each
386 doing two men's work, toiled on,
387 too occupied to think of nick-
388 names. Jake's only contact
389 with the others came when he
390 returned for the semi-weekly
391 distribution of rum, or on dig-
392 ging "fatigues."

393 Returning one drizzly night
394 from four hour's digging in a
395 new communication trench, he
396 sought young Richards, who

95

397 always saved his rum for Jake.
398 The drummer shivered in his
399 blankets, and instead of indulg-
400 ing in his usual bantering, said
401 simply, "I'm sick." Jake felt
402 the throbbing forehead, gave
403 him a drink of his own precious
404 rum, then seizing his own
405 blanket, wrapped the young
406 drummer in it.

407 "I made a mistake," he ex-
408 plained. "It's not your turn.
409 I'll call you when it is."

410 The sergeant to whom he
411 reported for young Richard's
412 "fatigue" regarded him doubt-
413 fully. "There's a staff officer
414 round here, that looks like the
415 baby that did you dirt at Salis-
416 bury. You'd better "sir" him,
417 'cause he's sure out for blood."

418 The first staff officer who
419 came upon Jake working, was
420 the commanding general who
421 was inspecting the lines. He
422 ignored Jake's failure to say
423 "Sir."

424 "If we had a regiment of
425 men like him," he commented,
426 " we'd dig our way to Constan-
427 tinople."

428 Captain Graham, on being
429 told of the happening by Lieu-
430 tenant Townsend, commented:

431 "I guess there's no fear of Bol-
432 ton getting in wrong after that."

433 "Not if we can keep him up
434 here in the front line, away from
435 the English officers," agreed the
436 Lieutenant.

437 But he reckoned without Jake
438 Bolton's liking for rum.

Jake's meeting with the 439
general occurred when the First 440
Colonials had been on the Penin- 441
sula only two months, and had 442
advanced only four miles inland. 443
Despite the fact that one 444
hundred and forty miles sepa- 445
rated them from Constantinople, 446
the First Colonials visualized the 447
entire distance traversed by 448
trenches that they had dug. At 449
any rate, the general's statement 450
encouraged Jake and his friends 451
to dig through tangled ravines 452
and hills scarred and torn by 453
shells a winding communication 454
trench, deep and narrow, down 455
the four miles that separated 456
the firing line from the beach, 457
thus forming one of the highways 458
for the supplies of ammunition 459
and food. 460

Through this newly completed 461
trench one moonlight night came 462
a tall Sikh, bearded and digni- 463
fied. 464

"Some nights ago," he said, 465
speaking carefully and slowly to 466
the sergeant, who had been 467
hurriedly summoned by the 468
sentry, "my mule cart was 469
blocked. God was good, and 470
sent to help me some of the men 471
of your regiment. They were in 472
search of mail, which they 473
found not. On the beach 474
which is called Kangaroo Land- 475
ing there are now ten bags of 476
mail for the First Colonials." 477
Having by returning a favor, 478
thus lived up to one of the first 479
principles of the Sikh religion, he 480

saluted gravely, turned on his heel and disappeared.

"There's a bunch of us fellows that's resting, that'd like nothing better than to go and get that mail," suggested Jake, who had just completed his own and young Richards's stint of digging.

"You've got a funny idea of resting," said the sergeant. "But I guess you know best." He turned to the group sitting on the firing step of the trench. "I want ten volunteers to get that mail."

Four times that number volunteered, because it meant a trip to the beach, where there was a possibility of meeting artillery men, who usually had plenty of rum. Jake, because of his size, was one of the ten selected.

Marching beside the corporal in charge of the detail, he set off with his usual good nature. During the trip down the sinuous communication trench, save for the occasional sharp crack of an explosive bullet or the whine of one that was spent, there was nothing to indicate that men were fighting. The party emerged upon a broad plateau, flanked by hills, one of which formed an effective barrier to Turkish artillery fire, and served as an excellent location for dugouts. Through slits in the canvas coverings of these, candles guttered in the wind. and their light guided the party past the first-aid dressing station, but did not prevent them from almost blundering into a battery disguised as a clump of bushes, whence some artillery men cursed them. Thence they skirted the Indian transport, warned therefrom by the squealing of mules, shaping their course by the Red Cross that flapped bravely in the fresh breeze above the hospital tent, fronted by a row of silent motor ambulances, finally emerging upon a rocky foreland from which many piers and boats ran out into the angry, wind-swept waters of the Ægean Sea. This was Kangaroo Landing. One side of the beach was piled high with boxes landed recently from the lighters that incessantly plowed a spray-covered course from the piers to the deeper water, where the transports lay beyond the reach of Turkish fire. The other side was given over to a dump in which were piled the kits of the dead, together with those of the wounded, who had been relieved of them before they were taken off to the hospital ship, the red cross of which, oulined in electric light, now shone, steady and unwinking, far out in the bay, now and then obscured by some fantastic, unsubstantial gray shape of a warship flitting to and fro in the moonlight, superintending the landing of reinforcements.

A little beyond the heap of piled-up equipments, a lone Australian paced slowly back and forth outside the barbed-wire enclosure that contained the Anzac dead who had been killed in the landing. The lonely sentinel stopped long enough to greet them, indicated the dugout where they might find the ten bags of mail, and resumed his march.

Each member of the party selected a bag, hoisted it to his shoulder, and began the return journey. All the lighter bags had been taken by the others, and the heaviest one fell to Jake, who had lingered to chat further with the Australian. But his bulk and muscle were well equal to the load, and his good nature surpassed both. Without complaint he placed the bag on his shoulder, pushing past the others, and fell in at the head of the line.

When the party reached the communication trench the corporal took Jake's rifle to lighten his burden, and the cavalcade wound through the trench. Jake hurried as much as the nature of the trench would permit, for he was anxious to witness the opening of the mail bags, and in a short time he and the corporal were a considerable distance in advance of their companions. After fifteen minutes of walking they stopped until their companions overtook them. Jake crouched down in the shadow of the bag and lit his pipe; then, leaning against the bag, puffed contentedly.

"I wonder if I get a letter from that girl in Edinburgh," said the corporal, a man of many armours. "By Jingo! I wish I was there now. How'd you like to stroll down Prince's Street tonight, Jake?"

"Not me," said Jake, decidedly. "The peninsula of Gallipoli is good enough for me: good smoking tobacco, lots of fags, nothing to worry you, rum twice a week, and all the bully beef and biscuits you can eat, to say nothing of that damned apricot jam." As he again shouldered the mail sack at the sound of the approaching party he added, "I'm better off at the front than I ever was in training. I have some money storing up in the pay-office in London, and nobody ever says to me out here, "'I say, my man, what is your name and number?'" He imitated as best he could the voice of an English officer.

They had now reached a point where the parapet was three feet higher than the top of Jake's head. Here the battle had raged fiercely. Wave upon wave of Turks had attacked and attacked again, hurling themselves upon British bayonets, forming and reforming, rallying with superb intrepidity, in an endeavor to drive out of their land the handful of invaders. But dour Scotch and fiery Irish had doggedly met them, and shoulder to shoulder with the lean Australians had succeeded in holding their own and digging themselves in. This trench, hastily dug under fire, the First Colonials had later incorporated in their communication trench to save labor, for here the ground was hard and unyielding, and beset with huge, rocky formations. To avoid these, the trench twisted and curved and turned at sharp angles.

Just now, around one of these corners came a young British officer, at the sight of whom Jake heaved a sigh of resignation, as a man might sigh on waking from a pleasant dream. The man who came round the corner of the trench was the subaltern of Salisbury. Jake recognized him immediately. Stick, monocle, faultlessly fitting uniform—there was no mistake. "'Tis him," said Jake, "just the same as ever, walkin' on eggshells. Sherman was right."

The encounter was Salisbury repeated. Jake halted, glaring: the officer halted. If he recognized the tanned, determined-looking giant before him, he gave no sign.

"I say, my man," he said, with his impersonal, irritating drawl, "put that bag on the parapet and let me pawss."

Jake glanced at the parapet, three feet above his head, and then at the officer.

"Who are you, anyway," he said, "ordering me about?"

"I am your superior officer. Put that bag on the parapet and let me pawss."

Jake allowed the bag to slide gently to the bottom of the trench.

"Officer or no officer," he said grimly, "you can walk over it."

To the credit of the subaltern's intelligence, be it said, he grasped the situation immediately. He walked over the bag. By this time the rest of the party had come up and stood resting, watching the scene with the most intense interest and enjoyment.

The subaltern, now on the other side of the bag, glaring at them, produced a pencil and a note-book, at the sight of which they sobered. "I say, my man," he said, indicating Jake with the pencil, "what is your name and numbah?"

At this the fatigue party lost its gravity, and led by Jake, yelled in a chorus that reverberated down the deep trench, "Jake Bolton, 551, B Company, First Colonials."

The officer, frowning, noted the names, first Jake's and then the corporal's and some others' as witnesses, and departed, breathing threats of dire punishment.

733 "You'd better knock wood
734 the next time before you begin
735 to boast of how well off you are,
736 Jake," said the corporal.

737 "How did I know I was going
738 to meet him?" demanded Jake.
739 "I hope," he added feelingly, as
740 the corporal readjusted the mail
741 bag for him, "that nothing
742 happens to him—nothing, that
743 is, worse than being cut in two
744 by a shell, or dying of thirst
745 with a bottle of rum three feet
746 away from him." From then
747 until he pulled his blanket about
748 his head for the night, Jake
749 indulged in wild inventions de-
750 signed for the discomfiture of
751 the subaltern.

752 The next morning at nine
753 o'clock the corporal was ordered
754 to report to the colonel as
755 witness and to escort the pris-
756 oner. The prisoner appeared
757 little worried. This was by no
758 means the first time he had been
759 called before the colonel.

760 "The colonel hates that little
761 runt," he said, "hates anybody
762 that butts in on his battalion.
763 Remember the steward of the
764 Oscalona?"

765 This was a reference to a
766 famous occasion when the colonel
767 had refused to interfere in be-
768 half of the steward of a trans-
769 port who had run foul of the
770 wrath of the First Colonials.

771 "The colonel is a good sport,"
772 said Jake as he reached the edge
773 of the dugout that constituted
774 the orderly room in which the

775 colonel tried all cases of mis-
776 demeanor. Inside, the colonel,
777 the adjutant, and some officers
778 of the headquarters staff, seated
779 at a rough table, were dealing
780 with defaulters. A little to one
781 side stood the subaltern. Jake
782 was ordered to wait while the
783 other cases were dealt with.
784 His offenses were usually original
785 and of special interest. There-
786 fore the colonel, who always
787 looked forward with keen relish
788 to Jake's case, made it a point to
789 finish with other offenders first,
790 in order that he might give Jake
791 full consideration.

792 "Jake Bolton, 551, B Com-
793 pany," called an orderly, and the
794 prisoner and his escort entered.
795 The charge was "Insubordina-
796 tion and insolent behavior to-
797 ward an officer on the night of
798 October third."

799 "Bolton, have you anything
800 to say?" asked the colonel.

801 "Yes, sir, I have this to say.
802 I'll bet five pounds that that
803 little runt there,"—he indicated
804 with a casual nod the subaltern,
805 who glared contemptuously in
806 return—"couldn't lift that bag,
807 let alone put it on the para-
808 pet."

809 The Colonel was proud of his
810 First Colonials, and he had suf-
811 fered much from outside inter-
812 ference. In the regiment it was
813 whispered that on the occasion
814 of the Salisbury complaint he
815 had requested the young officer
816 to keep away from his battalion.

817 As Jake had said, he was a good
818 sport.

819 "Have you that much money
820 with you?" he demanded of the
821 astonished Jake.

822 "No, sir," said Jake, "but for
823 the first time since the outbreak
824 of war I have more than that
825 coming to me in London."

826 "Oh, well," said the colonel,
827 with a twinkle, "I'll lend you
828 that much if you wish to make
829 the wager." The Colonel was
830 running true to form.

831 "Mr. Penton," he added, turn-
832 ing to the bewildered subaltern,
833 "should you care to take up
834 Private Bolton on this wager?"

835 "No, Colonel," said Mr.
836 Penton, "I haven't come here
837 to make wagers. I came here to
838 have the man taught a lesson.
839 He was insolent to me. Why,
840 Colonel, he didn't even call me
841 'sir!'"

842 Apparently Mr. Penton was
843 not particularly tactful. Had
844 he been, he might have studied
845 the colonel a little more closely.

846 "Oh," said that officer, very
847 suavely, "that alters the case.
848 You are quite certain of that.
849 You are positive he didn't call
850 you 'sir'? Then I assume you
851 base your charge on that?"

852 "Yes, Colonel," agreed Mr.
853 Penton, brightening, "I base my
854 charge on that."

855 "Well you see, Mr. Penton,"
856 said the Colonel, "I gave my
857 men instructions in daily orders
858 some time in September that

859 they must in no way give any
860 indication to the enemy of the
861 rank of an officer. When the
862 place is alive with snipers and
863 spies, calling you 'sir' comes
864 under that heading. Anyhow,
865 it is hard to expect those
866 Colonials to call you 'sir'; they
867 don't even 'sir' me. Bolton
868 dismiss."

869 Jake's joy at the discomfiture
870 of Mr. Penton was not unmixed.
871 It was tinged with regret, be-
872 cause simultaneously he resumed
873 his old nickname of "Name and
874 Number." The men who had
875 been in the party sent for the
876 mail bags spread the story, and
877 the First Colonials seized upon
878 it, talked of it, enlarged upon it;
879 for every item of gossip is seized
880 upon in the trenches. In many
881 forms the episode was garbled
882 and distorted. It was given out
883 by a corporal with imagination
884 that Jake had died and had
885 refused to enter heaven because
886 St. Peter had demanded his
887 name and number.

888 Although he continued good-
889 natured and added much to the
890 life of the First Colonials, the
891 thought of that persisting
892 question rankled. To escape it,
893 he adopted all kinds of sub-
894 terfuges to avoid his fellows.

895 So things stood when the
896 battalion moved up one
897 night to a particularly dan-
898 gerous section of the firing
899 line.

900 At right angles to the portion

901 of trench which they took over,
902 a narrow sap, or rough ditch, ran
903 out toward the Turkish position,
904 terminating near a ridge that
905 commanded both their own and
906 the Turkish trenches. Which-
907 ever side could gain possession of
908 this ridge could enfilade the en-
909 emies' lines. To hold the sap
910 commanding this ridge was of
911 such vital importance that a
912 bomb-proof over-head covering
913 had been put on it at great cost in
914 human life, and twenty bomb
915 throwers garrisoned it day and
916 night. These twenty men were
917 from a famous Irish regiment,
918 and Jake, who was beloved of
919 the Irish, instead of spending his
920 resting time in his own trench,
921 went out into this sap to ex-
922 change gossip with the Irish,
923 while he evaded the pursuing
924 query of his own regiment, "I
925 say, my man, what is your name
926 and numbah?" In this sap, he
927 felt, he could keep out of trouble.
928 On that day, the Irish, steadily
929 sapping toward the ridge, dis-
930 covered that the Turks had dug
931 to within twenty-five yards of
932 them. One of them, sighting the
933 Turks, seized some bombs and
934 jumped up.

935 "Look at Johnny Tur-rk!
936 Let's bomb him t'hell out of ut."

937 But the Turk would not be
938 bombed out. He stayed where
939 he was despite the deluge of
940 bombs hurled at him. Not only
941 did he refuse to budge, but he
942 sent over some of his own bombs

943 toward the Irish sap. While
944 this exchange of bombing was
945 going on, Jake made his way
946 through all the dirt and dust
947 and smoke to the head of the
948 sap, where only the few yards
949 separated him from the Turks.
950 In one item of armament the
951 British are superior to the Turks;
952 the Turkish bombs explode five
953 seconds after they are thrown;
954 the British take only three
955 seconds. That day in the sap-
956 head the difference of two seconds
957 was of great account. For a
958 short time the British supply of
959 bombs ran out. The man who
960 was frantically trying to pry
961 the cover off a box of them with a
962 bayonet found difficulty in doing
963 it, and suddenly the men in the
964 saphead found themselves with-
965 out bombs.

966 At this unfortunate moment
967 the Turks found the range of
968 the British sap, and one of their
969 bombs landed at Jake's feet.
970 Instead of throwing himself flat
971 on the ground, as most of the
972 others did, or retreating to the
973 part of the sap covered by the
974 bomb-proof roof, he stooped
975 down coolly, picked up the
976 bomb, and threw it back, so
977 that it exploded near the Turks
978 who had sent it. The two extra
979 seconds were just enough to
980 allow him to return it. Then
981 his own supply was resumed.
982 A staff officer, attracted to the
983 sap by the noise of the bombing,
984 stood silent, a little behind him,

985 wonder-struck, open-mouthed,
986 gazing at the big Colonial. He
987 took a note-book and pencil from
988 his pocket and approached Jake.
989 "I say, my man," he said,
990 "what is your name and num-
991 ber?"
992 The look on Jake's face was
993 a study. He knew that his
994 proper place was in his own
995 trench and that he had no
996 business in that sap. Also he
997 knew that every time that
998 question had been shot at him
999 before it had meant a reprimand.
1000 For a moment he stood puzzled
1001 and undecided; he felt that some-
1002 how fate was dealing unfairly
1003 with him. The officer repeated
1004 his question, but more loudly
1005 this time, that he might be
1006 heard above the noise of some
1007 twenty of the First Colonials
1008 now crowding into the sap
1009 behind him. They, thinking
1010 that some of their friends were
1011 bantering Jake, shouted the
1012 answer they all knew so well,
1013 "Jake Bolton, 551, B Company,
1014 First Colonials."
1015 "Is that correct?" demanded
1016 the officer of Jake.
1017 The light of insurrection,
1018 which flared for an instant in
1019 Jake's eyes, died out.

1020 "Yes," he answered resign-
1021 edly. Then shrugging his
1022 shoulders, he turned to the man
1023 next to him and said, "What in
1024 hell have I done now?"
1025 In a dugout close to the firing-
1026 line, Captain Graham gazed
1027 through a haze of tobacco smoke
1028 at Lieutenant Townsend.
1029 "Had a visit from a brass hat,
1030 my boy," he said. "Brass hat"
1031 is the irreverent way in which
1032 officers of the line refer to staff
1033 officers.
1034 "Straffing you about the con-
1035 dition of the trenches, I sup-
1036 pose," volunteered the other.
1037 "Wrong. He wanted to make
1038 certain about Sergeant Bolton."
1039 "Who's Sergeant Bolton?"
1040 "He's Jake Bolton, 551, of my
1041 company."
1042 "Oh, you mean my friend
1043 'Name and Number.' I thought
1044 Jake was a private."
1045 "So he was until today, when
1046 he was promoted for bravery in
1047 the face of the enemy. The
1048 brass hat was getting correct
1049 particulars, so that he could
1050 recommend him for a Distin-
1051 guished Conduct Medal. Re-
1052 member now what I said to you
1053 once about that man's eyes?"

THE ANALYSIS

From the point of view of material there are four starting points
for a story: a setting or atmosphere, a character, which is the sum
of the traits of a person, a series of happenings making a partial
plot, or a thematic idea. It is absurd to say that these can long

103

remain distinct; because all four will merge gradually, each contributing somewhat to the general effect. For example, while in *Jake Bolton, 551* I was interested chiefly in the characteristics of the chief actor, I was also concerned with the thematic idea that any man of character could make good during the war,—this "making good" consisting of being promoted and decorated. (When I talk of a thematic idea I mean what the older story writers mean by the moral of the tale, and what the newer writers mean by the "significance" of a story.) Besides being interested in characteristics and in the theme, I wanted also to render, as much as possible without clogging the story, the atmosphere of the Gallipoli campaign, and of the particular setting against which the action took place. While the action of the story depended primarily upon the responses of the chief actor, the special actions could not have happened so readily elsewhere, although of course they might have taken place on almost any battle front. The initial impulse to write the story came, it must be admitted, from interest in the character of the original of *Jake Bolton, 551*.

What I had to work with as the nucleus of this story was a knowledge of the character of Jake Bolton; and in addition to this I knew of certain actual happenings that focused my attention upon Jake. Those happenings were his meeting with the young subaltern in the trench, and the episode of the bomb which he threw back. Everything else in the story had to be invented or developed.

I have always felt that a writer in presenting a series of happenings to an audience has no right to present an isolated happening, or a series of isolated happenings, from which the audience may be allowed to draw a conclusion, unless that writer feels that this conclusion, so to be drawn, is a sound one. When I talk about the thematic idea behind a story, this is what I have in mind. In the real life version poor Jake was not decorated. Instead, the officer who saw him throw back the bomb, turned upon his heel when Jake Bolton said, "What in hell have I done now?" and walked away in high dudgeon. Later, however, Jake received his reward, although it was not for this special act of bravery.

My materials, then, were the knowledge of Jake's moving characteristics: his obstinacy, his kindliness, and his great willingness to bear burdens. Coupled with this was an understanding of the psychology of the colonial soldier who had enlisted as a private "for the duration of the war." This understanding came from a background of experience in a colonial regiment at Gallipoli, brigaded with British units, in such a manner that although the immediately superior officers were colonials, the higher ranks were held by English officers of the old school. Conditioning my treatment of all this material was an interest in the purely emotional effect of such a terrain as the Gallipoli peninsula, and a desire to reproduce that atmosphere in writing about it.

But in the long run the character of *Jake Bolton*, *551*, his unconscious heroism, his simplicity, his kindliness, his unselfishness, and the solid qualities of the man were what interested me. Character, rather than anything else, was the material with which I had to work, and I had before me two complete presentation units in which the character traits in which I was interested were evident.

In considering structure I simply had to take into consideration the fact that character in action as shown by the responses of the actor to the various stimuli which he encounters is what interests the reader; and I had to select and arrange the happenings in such a way that from the presentation units which I used the character I wished to portray might emerge. My problem, then, was largely one of structure.

In building up a story structurally one can obviously take only three points of departure. A writer may have the structural nucleus of a Beginning with no Body and no Ending. He may have the structural nucleus for a Body with no Beginning and no Ending. Or he may have an Ending with no Beginning or Body.

If he has a Beginning it is a narrative problem demanding action of the main character for its solution. It can be phrased as a main or story narrative question. When I come to a discussion of the flashback Beginning I shall go more into detail as to the reasons for its use, but at the present time it is sufficient to say that the main narrative question cannot be presented in the synthetically important story very quickly because it would not of itself hold interest.

If it is an Ending it is a conclusive act which answers a main narrative question. Given a main narrative question or narrative problem a writer can easily find an ending, because to every narrative question raised by a narrative problem, there must be an answer which is either "yes" or "no." Given a decisive or conclusive act his task is not so easy, although it is definite and comparatively simple. He has to find a narrative question to which that Conclusive Act may be the answer.

Thus a writer's task, when he has a Beginning, is a very simple one, because the answer must be either yes or no to the main narrative question. But if he has an Ending only, it may be the answer to any one of a number of different narrative questions.

The material with which I was working could not be classified as either Beginning or Ending. There was no special narrative main situation or problem and there was no special decisive or conclusive act. I had merely two meetings or encounters in each of which my main character ran afoul of the officialdom of the British army as exemplified by officers. I had two cases in which the meetings resulted in the character's being "in wrong." As soon as I came to this definite analysis of my material, the rest of the way was very easy. If a character is "in wrong" he must be "in wrong" in relation to some special attempt to accomplish something. Thereafter there was very little cerebration necessary to invent the thing which was to be accomplished, to which the result of the two encounters or interchanges would be what are technically called hindrances. Obviously, every time he "got in wrong" he must be in a position opposite to that in which he would be "in right." Therefore, a main story situation or main narrative problem instantly phrased itself, "Can Jake Bolton make good in the British army in war time?"

Just as soon as I had phrased this main narrative question, the decisive act was waiting for me. The answer must be either "Yes" or "No." I knew that in this special instance the original of Jake Bolton had not been decorated or promoted; but I felt certain that this was an isolated and special case, that it was not representative; I knew that while it was accurate it was not true to life. So I changed it. This is where my thematic idea conditioned my own response to my material. My theme was that anybody with character could make good in the British army in war time, so this thematic idea gave me not only an Ending but a Sequel or Significance as well. Thus at this point I found myself with a Beginning which was a main narrative purpose, an Ending which was a Conclusive Act, a significant Sequel to that Conclusive Act, and finally, I had my original material of the two interchanges each of which resulted in a hindrance.

I knew enough about the laws of interest to know that story interest, proper, is in the Body of the story,—in the encounters or interchanges which come after the main problem has been presented to the audience together with such explanatory matter as will give the audience a sufficient clue to go on with the story. I then proceeded to write a first rough draft of the material which I had added to the original material, and the special purposes before me as an author conditioned the presentation of that material. I had to present the character of Jake Bolton, and I knew that the most effective way of presenting character is to show how other people react toward the chief actor of the story. For that reason the first 52 lines of the story are concerned with showing Jake Bolton in action, and showing how the Captain and the others react toward him. Lines 53 to 66 I have made an interchange between the captain and the lieutenant because I realized that an interchange is always more interesting than a mere meeting. As a result of this interchange the main narrative question is made apparent to the audience. Further, I knew that a Beginning must contain, besides this main narrative question, the dramatic promise of difficulty, of conflict, and of disaster, all of which are presented in a second mild disagreement between the captain and the lieutenant occupying lines 69 to 94. Knowing that the Beginning of a story must contain the seeds of the conflicts which make up the Body of the story, I planted the threat of a British officer who should encounter Jake Bolton, but I also had to take care of the query of the reader as to why Jake Bolton had not "got in wrong" before he met this officer. That was why I mentioned that his own colonial officers paid no attention to his lack of the usual respectful "sir." Now I was ready to write the Ending of the story, because I knew what the Body was, approximately, and I had already my Beginning completed. So I wrote the interchange now occupying the lines 1025 to 1053 which is an episodic meeting between Captain Graham and Lieutenant Townsend, which contained the revised answer to the main narrative question together with the significance to be drawn from the happenings. This is conveyed by the Captain's remark about Jake's eyes, harking back to his original remark that "any man with character can make good."

Just as I recognized that the seeds of the conflicts which occupy the Body of the story should be planted in the Beginning so I realized that in the Beginning there should be planted the seeds of that significance which should emerge in the Sequel to the act, and for that reason I included in the first meeting between the captain and the lieutenant a discussion as to the main significance of the story, that a man with character could make good in the army. Then, in the closing episode I was able to tie together the Beginning and the Ending by again referring to this character in the man's eyes.

The reason that I made an episodic meeting between the captain and the lieutenant in order to show the effect of the

Decisive Act, which is the throwing of the bomb, is that I wished to take legitimate advantage of suspense. I might have shown the officer taking out his note-book and noting the name, immediately informing Jake of his plans for promotion and decoration. But I preferred to allow the reader to assume that Jake was again "in wrong," because I felt that a hindrance at the conclusion of this meeting was better than a Conclusive Act, because the outcome was still in suspense. Further, I was able to utilize the value of surprise which comes with the swift realization upon the part of the reader that Jake instead of being "in wrong" has actually made good in the army through the action of throwing the bomb.

In boiling down the Beginning and the Ending of the story in the way I did, I naturally reduced the total length of the story so that the originl meetings which were my structural units were rather slight to carry the whole interest of the story. So I was forced to cast about for more meetings which should be encounters preferably. So I invented a first encounter, the one with the subaltern at Salisbury, which resulted in Jake's getting a bad name in the army. I knew instinctively that the first attempt of a character should result in a hindrance, because if it didn't the story interest was likely to lag. By having a hindrance at the conclusion of this first encounter with the subaltern I was enabled to bring Jake to a point where he had received his bad name, which came after Jake and the colonel had had an interview regarding the failure on his part to salute the officer and call him "sir" at Salisbury. This made a hindrance to the main narrative question, and it brought about the condition which the lieutenant had prophesied in his meeting with the captain: that Jake would get a bad name.

This condition facing Jake and his reactions to it occupy lines 316 to 392 and resulted in a furtherance, which was that his nickname was forgotten. Realizing, however, that a furtherance was likely to dull the story I instantly followed this series of reactions of Jake's with an interchange between him and young Richards which resulted in a hindrance because of the promise of conflict with a dangerous opponent which appears when he learns that the officer is again about.

In the next interchange, which was with the commanding general, the result is a furtherance, but when in lines 428 to 438, which make the fifth step of that scene, Captain Graham and Lieutenant Townsend discuss the affair, there is a hindrance because there is again the promise of disaster.

In the interchange between Jake and the corporal, occupying

lines 607 to 638, there is a furtherance when Jake feels safe, but I caused this to occur because I again wished to do what I did in the latter part of the story,—to surprise the reader by the unexpectedness of the happening, and to get the greatest possible value of what is known as "dramatic irony," which is the ironic feeling that comes to a reader when he realizes that a character has been congratulating himself upon a condition which does not exist at all. Jake is made to feel safe, and instantly he is plunged into a meeting with the subaltern which results in a definite hindrance at the close of the interchange (lines 666 to 751), after his name is again taken by the hostile officer. At the close of the meeting between Jake and the colonel at which the subaltern prefers his charge, on lines 752 to 868, there is a furtherance; but it is instantly followed by a dramatic hindrance, which is apparent when the nick-name is revived. It is this condition which seems to threaten ultimate disaster to Jake, and the chief and most interesting scene in the story is the scene where Jake goes out into the sap and after throwing the bomb, has his interchange with the staff officer. This occupies lines 982 to 1024, and then the main narrative question appears to be answered by the word "No." Very swiftly, however, the reader finds, in lines 1025 to 1053, that the answer to the question is really "Yes" and that Jake Bolton has made good in the army.

It may seem to some people that there is an overload of setting or atmosphere at some places in this story. Probably this is the case; but it was intentional. I had a purpose in so inserting it. I wanted readers to get the feeling of the Gallipoli peninsula, of the drabness, the imminence of death, of the self-sacrifice, of the heroism, and of the hardships dumbly endured. I wanted to show that unforgettable picture, that is to-me-unforgettable picture, of the Sikh who felt that he must repay the kindness done him by the men of Jake's regiment and I wanted to show that lone Australian, pacing slowly up and down in the moonlight, guarding the dead. My judgment was justified, for when the artist was given the story to illustrate, he selected those two pictures.

One other objection may arise in the mind of a craftsman as to my handling of the material of this story. If the story is the story of *Jake Bolton*, *551* and the problem before him is to make good in the army, why is it not made apparent that he is aware of making such an attempt. As a matter of fact my conception of the character of Jake was that he was not aware of any desire to make good. He did his duty as he saw it. He was in no way conscious of being heroic, so in order to keep him true to form,

I had to introduce the two purely lay figures of the captain and the lieutenant. They were the equivalent of the chorus in the Greek drama. They were enabled to say about him certain things which he could not have said about himself, and they were able to phrase the wager—for it was virtually a wager—quickly and incisively. Then, my own experience later in the war, in deciding upon men to be promoted to be non-commissioned officers, led me to insert the comment that a man's progress depended upon his getting a good name, or rather on his not getting a bad name.

There is no setting, not even that of background, for the recruiting office in the first meeting. That is explained by two considerations; first, I wanted to hurry up the Beginning, but chiefly I wanted to keep that setting nebulous, because I did not, at the time I wrote the story, wish to give any inkling as to which particular colonial regiment I was dealing with. As a matter of fact, now that the war is over, I may say that the First Colonials had as originals the members of my own regiment, The Royal Newfoundland Regiment.

This story was written more than ten years ago. Since then I have written many other stories and have collaborated upon still more. What I have learned about craftsmanship would induce me to make one change. It is that I should have made the opponent the same throughout. It would have been a very simple matter to change the staff officer in the final encounter so that he became the subaltern of Salisbury. If I were rewriting the story I think that I should have caused this final encounter to be between Jake and the subaltern, and that he should actually have been "in wrong," but with my thematic idea to guide me I should have caused the general or some person in authority to have overheard and to have reversed the ruling of the subaltern. Naturally I cannot discuss the merits of this story further than to say that it is structurally sound. My reason for reprinting it is not to discuss it in relation to other stories, but to show actually what goes on in the mind of a writer while he is producing a short-story.

THE ESCAPE OF MR. TRIMM.

Mr. Trimm taking trip. Important and unusual condition.		1– 31
Meeting. Mr. Trimm and condition in Tombs. (5th Step. Effect.)		32– 96 97– 121
Meeting. Mr. Trimm responds to condition projected. (Lines 97–121)		121– 136
Interchange. Mr. Trimm and Mr. Walling.		136– 185
Interchange. Mr. Trimm and the Warden.		186– 252
Interchange. Mr. Trimm and Deputy Meyers, resulting in change of attitude by Mr. Trimm; a turning point in his life.		253– 347
Interchange. Mr. Trimm and Meyers. An attempt to hide.		348– 415
Meeting. Mr. Trimm and condition. Attempt to evade notice.		416– 530
Interchange. Mr. Trimm and conductor. Attempt to achieve privacy.		531– 553
(5th step. Effect of interchange 531–553 upon Deputy Meyers.)		554– 556
Interchange. Meyers attempts to put Mr. Trimm at ease.		557– 628
Meeting. Mr. Trimm responds to new condition.		629– 756
Attempt of Mr. Trimm is foiled. New purpose is apparent.		757– 879
Attempt of Mr. Trimm to put new purpose into effect is opposed by impulse, projecting new condition, to which Mr. Trimm, responding, projects main purpose of the story.		880–1141

BEGINNING

Made up of attempts similar to the attempts usually occurring in the Body of a Story, in order to sustain the reader's attention. The Initial Condition is set forth.

The Main Actor's purpose is apparent.

Main Plot Crises become apparent as the result of the attempts of Mr. Trimm show him to be in an unusual situation, from which he can obtain relief only through overcoming Difficulties, and Dangerous Opposing Forces.
There is no question that Disaster is staring him in the face.

Main Narrative Question: "Can Mr. Trimm escape from handcuffs?"

OF

THE ESCAPE OF MR. TRIMM.

BODY

Made up of attempts to reverse the original condition or state of affairs. Various obstacles keep cropping up. The attempt to surmount each of these forms a scene.

He attempts to pry off handcuffs with contents of pockets. Fails. (5th step. Difficulties increased.)	1142–1309	Hindrance.
	1310–1360	Hindrance.
Boy comes. Meeting. Mr. Trimm runs.	1361–1409	Hindrance.
He attempts to use harrow tooth as a lever.	1410–1434	Hindrance.
He attempts to burn cuffs off. Blackens steel and raises blister.	1435–1454	Hindrance.
He attempts to file off with fence wire. Fails.	1455–1474	Hindrance.
He attempts to persuade Boy. Boy scared away. (5th step. Effect of interchange upon actors. New plan emerges.)	1475–1525	Hindrance.
	1526–1569	New opponent possible. Dramatic Hindrance.
Approaches blacksmith. Finds he is sheriff.	1570–1652	
Tries to enlist tramp's aid. Tramp refuses.	1653–1992	Hindrance.
Mr. Trimm kills tramp. Resulting mental haze increases chance of capture.	1993–2045	Dramatic Hindrance.
Meeting. In search of food, Mr. Trimm encounters dog. Flies.	2046–2073	Hindrance.
(5th step. Effect of farmer's actions is to cause Mr. Trimm to tighten handcuffs.)	2073–2131	Dramatic Hindrance.
He attempts to convince Chief of Police of Westfield that he is the banker.	2132–2227	

SEQUEL

Conclusive Act.	"Come in and let me get them irons off you."	2228–2231	Main Narrative Question answered "Yes."
Sequel.	Mr. Trimm, on achieving his objective, no longer considers it important.	2232–2237	Ironic Significance.

113

THE ESCAPE OF MR. TRIMM

BY IRVIN S. COBB

THIS story belongs to the "Odyssey" classification of stories. It is the story of a character who has to overcome a certain number of obstacles in order to be safe. In this story the character, after repeated attempts, abandons his purpose. For that reason alone it is interesting.

Another reason for its inclusion is that it illustrates so definitely the different kinds of conditions which a character may be called upon to remove or overcome. These kinds are two: the passive condition and the active condition.

A third reason for reprinting this story is that it shows that Mr. Cobb, in his first story, recognized those laws of interest which are the determining factors in the success or failure of any story, particularly in the type of story which has a long Beginning. Out of the total of 2237 lines which this story occupies, the Beginning takes up 1141 lines.

CASE No. 5

THE ESCAPE OF MR. TRIMM

BY IRVIN S. COBB

Mr. Trimm, recently president of the late Thirteenth National Bank, was taking a trip which was different in a number of ways from any he had ever taken. To begin with, he was used to parlor cars and Pullmans and even luxurious private cars when he went anywhere; whereas now he rode with a most mixed company in a dusty, smelly day coach. In the second place, his traveling companion was not such a one as Mr. Trimm would have chosen had the choice been left to him, being a stupid-looking German-American with a drooping, yellow mustache. And in the third place, Mr. Trimm's plump white hands were folded in his lap, held in a close and enforced companionship by a new and shiny pair of Bean's Latest Model Little Giant handcuffs. Mr. Trimm was on his way to the Federal penitentiary to serve twelve years at hard labor for breaking, one way or another, about all the laws that are presumed to govern national banks.

· · · · ·

All the time Mr. Trimm was in the Tombs, fighting for a new trial, a certain question had lain in his mind unasked and unanswered. Through the seven months of his stay in the jail that question had been always at the back part of his head, ticking away there like a little watch that never needed winding. A dozen times a day it would pop into his thoughts and then go away, only to come back again. When Copley was taken to the penitentiary—Copley being the cashier who got off with a lighter sentence because the judge and jury held him to be no more than a blind accomplice in the wrecking of the Thirteenth National— Mr. Trimm read closely every line that the papers carried about Copley's departure. But none of them had seen fit to give the young cashier more than a short and colorless paragraph. For

58 Copley was only a small figure
59 in the big intrigue that had
60 startled the country; Copley
61 didn't have the money to hire big
62 lawyers to carry his appeal to the
63 higher courts for him; Copley's
64 wife was keeping boarders; and
65 as for Copley himself, he had
66 been wearing stripes several
67 months now.

68 With Mr. Trimm it had been
69 vastly different. From the very
70 beginning he had held the public
71 eye. His bearing in court when
72 the jury came in with their judg-
73 ment; his cold defiance when the
74 judge, in pronouncing sentence,
75 mercilessly arraigned him and
76 the system of finance for which
77 he stood; the manner of his life
78 in the Tombs; his spectacular
79 fight to beat the verdict, had all
80 been worth columns of news-
81 paper space. If Mr. Trimm had
82 been a popular poisoner, or a so-
83 ciety woman named as co-
84 respondent in a sensational di-
85 vorce suit, the papers could not
86 have been more generous in
87 their space allotments. And Mr.
88 Trimm in his cell had read all of
89 it with smiling contempt, even
90 to the semi-hysterical outpour-
91 ings of the lady special writers
92 who called him The Iron Man of
93 Wall Street and undertook to
94 analyze his emotions — and
95 missed the mark by a thousand
96 miles or two.

97 Things had been smoothed as
98 much as possible for him in the
99 Tombs, for money and the power

100 of it will go far toward ironing
101 out even the corrugated routine
102 of that big jail. He had a large
103 cell to himself in the airiest,
104 brightest corridor. His meals
105 were served by a caterer from
106 outside. Although he ate them
107 without knife or fork, he soon
108 learned that a spoon and the fin-
109 gers can accomplish a good deal
110 when backed by a good appe-
111 tite, and Mr. Trimm's appetite
112 was uniformly good. The war-
113 den and his underlings had been
114 models of official kindliness; the
115 newspapers had sent their bright-
116 est young men to interview him
117 whenever he felt like talking,
118 which wasn't often; and surely
119 his lawyers had done all in his be-
120 half that money—a great deal of
121 money—could do. Perhaps it
122 was because of these things that
123 Mr. Trimm had never been able
124 to bring himself to realize that
125 he was the Hobart W. Trimm
126 who had been sentenced to the
127 Federal prison; it seemed to him,
128 somehow, that he, personally,
129 was merely a spectator standing
130 at one side watching the fight of
131 another man to dodge the peni-
132 tentiary.

133 However, he didn't fail to give
134 the other man the advantage of
135 every chance that money would
136 buy. This sense of aloofness to
137 the whole thing had persisted
138 even when his personal lawyer
139 came to him one night in the
140 early fall and told him that the
141 court of last possible resort had

denied the last possible motion. Mr. Trimm cut the lawyer short with a shake of his head as the other began saying something about the chances of a pardon from the President. Mr. Trimm wasn't in the habit of letting men deceive him with idle words. No President would pardon him, and he knew it.

"Never mind that, Walling," he said steadily, when the lawyer offered to come to see him again before he started for prison the next day. "If you'll see that a drawing-room on the train is reserved for me—for us, I mean—and all that sort of thing, I'll not detain you any further. I have a good many things to do tonight. Good night."

"Such a man, such a man," said Walling to himself as he climbed into his car; "all chilled steel and brains. And they are going to lock that brain up for twelve years. It's a crime," said Walling, and shook his head. Walling always said it was a crime when they sent a client of his to prison. To his credit be it said, though, they sent very few of them there. Walling made as high as eighty thousand a year at criminal law. Some of it was very criminal law indeed. His specialty was picking holes in the statutes faster than the legislature could make them and provide them and putty them up with amendments. This was the first case he had lost in a good long time.

.   .   .   .   .

When Jerry, the turnkey, came for him in the morning Mr. Trimm had made as careful a toilet as the limited means at his command permitted, and he had eaten a hearty breakfast and was ready to go, all but putting on his hat. Looking the picture of well-groomed, close-buttoned, iron-gray middle age, Mr. Trimm followed the turnkey through the long corridor and down the winding iron stairs to the warden's office. He gave no heed to the curious eyes that followed him through the barred doors of many cells; his feet rang briskly on the flags.

The warden, Hallam, was there in the private office with another man, a tall, raw-boned man with a drooping, straw-colored mustache and the unmistakable look about him of the police officer. Mr. Trimm knew without being told that this was the man who would take him to prison. The stranger was standing at a desk, signing some papers.

"Sit down, please, Mr. Trimm," said the warden with a nervous cordiality. "Be through here in just one minute. This is Deputy Marshal Meyers," he added.

Mr. Trimm started to tell this Mr. Meyers he was glad to meet him, but caught himself and

225 merely nodded. The man stared
226 at him with neither interest nor
227 curiosity in his dull blue eyes.
228 The warden moved over toward
229 the door.

230 "Mr. Trimm," he said, clear-
231 ing his throat, "I took the liberty
232 of calling a cab to take you gents
233 up to the Grand Central. It's
234 out front now. But there's a big
235 crowd of reporters and photog-
236 raphers and a lot of other people
237 waiting, and if I was you I'd slip
238 out the back way—one of my
239 men will open the yard gate for
240 you—and jump aboard the sub-
241 way down at Worth Street.
242 Then you'll miss those fellows."

243 "Thank you, Warden—very
244 kind of you," said Mr. Trimm in
245 that crisp, businesslike way of
246 his. He had been crisp and
247 businesslike all his life. He
248 heard a door opening softly be-
249 hind him, and when he turned to
250 look he saw the warden slipping
251 out, furtively, in almost an
252 embarrassed fashion.

253 "Well," said Meyers, "all
254 ready?"

255 "Yes," said Mr. Trimm, and
256 he made as if to rise.

257 "Wait one minute," said
258 Meyers.

259 He half turned his back on
260 Mr. Trimm and fumbled at the
261 side pocket of his ill-hanging
262 coat. Something inside of Mr.
263 Trimm gave the least little jump,
264 and the question that had ticked
265 away so busily all those months
266 began to buzz, buzz in his ears;

267 but it was only a handkerchief
268 the man was getting out. Doubt-
269 less he was going to mop his face.

270 He didn't mop his face,
271 though. He unrolled the hand-
272 kerchief slowly, as if it contained
273 something immensely fragile and
274 valuable, and then, thrusting it
275 back in his pocket, he faced Mr.
276 Trimm. He was carrying in his
277 hands a pair of handcuffs that
278 hung open-jawed. The jaws had
279 little notches in them, like teeth
280 that could bite. The question
281 that had ticked in Mr. Trimm's
282 head was answered at last—in
283 the sight of these steel things
284 with their notched jaws.

285 Mr. Trimm stood up and, with
286 a movement as near to hesitation
287 as he had ever been guilty of in
288 his life, held out his hands, backs
289 upward.

290 "I guess you're new at this
291 kind of thing," said Meyers,
292 grinning. "This here way—one
293 at a time."

294 He took hold of Mr. Trimm's
295 right hand, turned it sideways
296 and settled one of the steel cuffs
297 over the top of the wrist, flipping
298 the notched jaw up from beneath
299 and pressing it in so that it
300 locked automatically with a
301 brisk little click. Slipping the
302 locked cuff back and forth on
303 Mr. Trimm's lower arm like a
304 man adjusting a part of machin-
305 ery, and then bringing the left
306 hand up to meet the right, he
307 treated it the same way. Then
308 he stepped back.

309 Mr. Trimm hadn't meant to
310 protest. The word came un-
311 bidden.

312 "This—this isn't necessary, is
313 it?" he asked in a voice that was
314 husky and didn't seem to belong
315 to him.

316 "Yep," said Meyers, "Stand-
317 in' orders is play no favorites and
318 take no chances. But you won't
319 find them things uncomfortable.
320 Lightest pair there was in the
321 office, and I fixed 'em plenty
322 loose."

323 For half a minute Mr. Trimm
324 stood like a rooster hypnotized
325 by a chalkmark, his arms ex-
326 tended, his eyes set on his bonds.
327 His hands had fallen perhaps
328 four inches apart, and in the
329 space between his wrists a little
330 chain was stretched taut. In the
331 mounting tumult that filled his
332 brain there sprang before Mr.
333 Trimm's consciousness a phrase
334 he had heard or read somewhere,
335 the title of a story or, perhaps it
336 was a headline—The Grips of
337 the Law. The Grips of the Law
338 were upon Mr. Trimm—he felt
339 them now for the first time in
340 these shiny wristlets and this bit
341 of chain that bound his wrists
342 and filled his whole body with a
343 strange, sinking feeling that
344 made him physically sick. A
345 sudden sweat beaded out on Mr.
346 Trimm's face, turning it slick
347 and wet.

348 He had a handkerchief, a fine
349 linen handkerchief with a hem-
350 stitched border and a monogram
351 on it, in the upper breast pocket
352 of his buttoned coat. He tried
353 to reach it. His hands went up,
354 twisting awkwardly like crab
355 claws. The fingers of both
356 plucked out the handkerchief.
357 Holding it so, Mr. Trimm
358 mopped the sweat away. The
359 links of the handcuffs fell in upon
360 one another and lengthened out
361 again at each movement, filling
362 the room with a smart little
363 sound.

364 He got the handkerchief
365 stowed away with the same
366 clumsiness. He raised the man-
367 acled hands to his hat brim, gave
368 it a downward pull that brought
369 it over his face and then, letting
370 his short arms slide down upon
371 his plump stomach, he faced the
372 man who had put the fetters
373 upon him, squaring his shoulders
374 back. But it was hard, some-
375 how, for him to square his shoul-
376 ders—perhaps because of his
377 hands being drawn so closely to-
378 gether. And his eyes would
379 waver and fall upon his wrists.
380 Mr. Trimm had a feeling that
381 the skin must be stretched very
382 tight on his jawbones and his
383 forehead.

384 "Isn't there some way to hide
385 these—these things?"

386 He began by blurting and end-
387 ed by faltering it. His hands
388 shuffled together, one over, then
389 under the other.

390 "Here's a way," said Meyers.
391 "This'll help."

392 He bestirred himself, folding

393 one of the chained hands upon
394 the other, tugging at the white
395 linen cuffs and drawing the coat
396 sleeves of his prisoner down over
397 the bonds as far as the chain
398 would let them come.

399 "There's the notion," he said.
400 "Just do that-a-way and them
401 bracelets won't hardly show a-
402 tall. Ready? Let's be movin',
403 then."

404 But handcuffs were never
405 meant to be hidden. Merely a
406 pair of steel rings clamped to
407 one's wrists and coupled to-
408 gether with a scrap of chain, but
409 they'll twist your arms and ham-
410 per the movements of your body
411 in a way constantly to catch the
412 eye of the passer-by. When a
413 man is coming toward you,
414 you can tell that he is hand-
415 cuffed before you see the cuffs.

416 Mr. Trimm was never able to
417 recall afterward exactly how he
418 got out of the Tombs. He had
419 a confused memory of a gate
420 that was swung open by someone
421 whom Mr. Trimm saw only from
422 the feet to the waist; then he
423 and his companion were out on
424 Lafayette Street speeding south
425 toward the subway entrance at
426 Worth Street, two blocks below,
427 with the marshal's hand cupped
428 under Mr. Trimm's right elbow
429 and Mr. Trimm's plump legs al-
430 most trotting in their haste. For
431 a moment it looked as if the
432 warden's well-meant artifice
433 would serve.

434 But New York reporters are
435 up to the tricks of people who
436 want to evade them. At the
437 sight of them a sentry reporter
438 on the corner shouted a warning
439 which was instantly caught up
440 and passed on by another picket
441 stationed half-way down the
442 block; and around the wall of the
443 Tombs came pelting a flying mob
444 of newspaper photographers and
445 reporters, with a choice rabble
446 behind them. Foot passengers
447 took up the chase, not knowing
448 what it was about, but sensing a
449 free show. Truckmen halted
450 their teams, jumped down from
451 their wagon seats and joined in.
452 A man-chase is one of the pleas-
453 antest outdoor sports that a big
454 city like New York can offer its
455 people.

456 Fairly running now, the man-
457 acled banker and the deputy
458 marshal shot down the winding
459 steps into the subway a good ten
460 yards ahead of the foremost pur-
461 suers. But there was one delay,
462 while Meyers skirmished with his
463 free hand in his trousers pocket
464 for a dime for the tickets, and
465 another before a northbound
466 local rolled into the station.
467 Shouted at, jeered at, shoved
468 this way and that, panting in
469 gulping breaths, for he was stout
470 by nature and staled by lack of
471 exercise, Mr. Trimm with Mey-
472 ers clutching him by the arm,
473 was fairly shot aboard one of the
474 cars, at the apex of a human
475 wedge. The astonished guard

THE ESCAPE OF MR. TRIMM

476 sensed the situation as the scroog-
477 ing, shoving, noisy wave rolled
478 across the platform toward the
479 doors which he had opened and,
480 thrusting the officer and his pris-
481 oner into the narrow platform
482 space behind him, he tried to
483 form with his body a barrier
484 against those who came jamming
485 in.

486 It didn't do any good. He
487 was brushed away, protesting
488 and blustering. The excitement
489 spread through the train, and
490 men, and even women, left
491 their seats, overflowing the
492 aisles.

493 There is no crueler thing than
494 a city crowd, all eyes and morbid
495 curiosity. But Mr. Trimm didn't
496 see the staring eyes on that ride
497 to the Grand Central. What he
498 saw was many shifting feet and a
499 hedge of legs shutting him in
500 closely—those and the things on
501 his wrists. What the eyes of the
502 crowd saw was a small, stout
503 man who, for all his bulk, seemed
504 to have dried up inside his
505 clothes so that they bagged on
506 him some places and bulged
507 others, with his head tucked on
508 his chest, his hat over his face
509 and his fingers straining to hold
510 his coat sleeves down over a pair
511 of steel bracelets.

512 Mr. Trimm gave mental
513 thanks to a Deity whose exist-
514 ence he thought he had forgotten
515 when the gate of the train-shed
516 clanged behind him, shutting out
517 the mob that had come with them

all the way. Cameras had been 518
shoved in his face like gun muz- 519
zles, reporters had scuttled along- 520
side him, dodging under Meyers' 521
fending arm to shout questions 522
in his ears. He had neither spo- 523
ken nor looked at them. The 524
sweat still ran down his face, so 525
that when finally he raised his 526
head in the comparative quiet of 527
the train-shed his skin was a cu- 528
rious gray under the jail paleness 529
like the color of wet wood ashes. 530

"My lawyer promised to ar- 531
range for a compartment—for 532
some private place on the train," 533
he said to Meyers. "The con- 534
ductor ought to know." 535

They were the first words he 536
had uttered since he left the 537
Tombs. Meyers spoke to a 538
jaunty Pullman conductor who 539
stood alongside the car where 540
they had halted. 541

"No such reservation," said 542
the conductor, running through 543
his sheaf of slips, with his eyes 544
shifting from Mr. Trimm's face 545
to Mr. Trimm's hands and back 546
again, as though he couldn't de- 547
cide which was the more inter- 548
esting part of him; "must be 549
some mistake. Or else it was for 550
some other train. Too late to 551
change now—we pull out in 552
three minutes." 553

"I reckon we better git on the 554
smoker," said Meyers, "if there's 555
room there." 556

Mr. Trimm was steered back 557
again the length of the train 558
through a double row of pop- 559

eyed porters and staring train-men. At the steps where they stopped the instinct to stretch out one hand and swing himself up by the rail operated auto-matically and his wrists got a nasty twist. Meyers and a brakeman practically lifted him up the steps and Meyers headed him into a car that was hazy with blue tobacco smoke. He was confused in his gait, almost as if his lower limbs had been fettered, too.

The car was full of shirt-sleeved men who stood up, cran-ing their necks and stumbling over each other in their desire to see him. These men came out into the aisle, so that Meyers had to shove through them.

"This here'll do as well as any, I guess," said Meyers. He drew Mr. Trimm past him into the seat nearer the window and sat down alongside him on the side next the aisle, settling himself on the stuffy plush seat and breath-ing deeply, like a man who had got through the hardest part of a not easy job.

"Smoke?" he asked.

Mr. Trimm shook his head without raising it.

"Them cuffs feel plenty easy?" was the deputy's next question. He lifted Mr. Trimm's hands as casually as if they had been his hands and not Mr. Trimm's, and looked at them.

"Seem to be all right," he said as he let them fall back. "Don't pinch none, I reckon?" There was no answer.

The deputy tugged a minute at his mustache, searching his arid mind. An idea came to him. He drew a newspaper from his pocket, opened it out flat and spread it over Mr. Trimm's lap so that it covered the chained wrists. Almost instantly the train was in motion, moving through the yards.

. . . . .

"Be there in two hours more," volunteered Meyers. It was late afternoon. They were sliding through woodlands with occa-sional openings which showed meadows melting into wide, flat lands.

"Want a drink?" said the de-puty, next. "No? Well, I guess I'll have a drop myself. Travelin' fills a feller's throat full of dust." He got up, lurch-ing to the motion of the flying train, and started forward to the water cooler behind the car door. He had gone perhaps two-thirds of the way when Mr. Trimm felt a queer, grinding sensation be-neath his feet; it was exactly as though the train were trying to go forward and back at the same time. Almost slowly, it seemed to him, the forward end of the car slued out of its straight course, at the same time tilting up. There was a grinding, roar-ing, grating sound, and before Mr. Trimm's eyes Meyers van-ished, tumbling forward out of sight as the car floor buckled under his feet. Then, as everything—the train, the earth, the sky—all fused together in a great spatter of white and black, Mr. Trimm was plucked from his seat as though a giant hand had him by the collar and shot forward through the air over the seat-backs, his chained hands aloft, clutching wildly. He rolled out of a ragged opening where the smoker had broken in two, flopped gently on the sloping side of the right-of-way and slid easily to the bottom, where he lay quiet and still on his back in a bed of weeds and wild grass, staring straight up.

How many minutes he lay there Mr. Trimm didn't know. It may have been the shrieks of the victims or the glare from the fire that brought him out of the daze. He wriggled his body to a sitting posture, got on his feet, holding his head between his coupled hands, and gazed full-face into the crowning railroad horror of the year.

There were numbers of the passengers who had escaped serious hurt, but for the most part these persons seemed to have gone daft from terror and shock. Some were running aimlessly up and down and some, a few, were pecking feebly with improvised tools at the wreck, an indescribable jumble of ruin, from which there issued cries of mortal agony, and from which, at a point where two locomotives were lying on their sides, jammed together like fighting bucks that died with locked horns, a tall flame already rippled and spread, sending up a pillar of black smoke that rose straight, poisoning the clear blue of the sky. Nobody paid any attention to Mr. Trimm as he stood swaying upon his feet. There wasn't a scratch on him. His clothes were hardly rumpled, his hat was still on his head. He stood a minute and then, moved by a sudden impulse, he turned round and went running straight away from the railroad at the best speed his pudgy legs could accomplish, with his arms pumping up and down in front of him and his fingers interlaced. It was a grotesque gait, rather like a rabbit hopping on its hindlegs.

Instantly, almost, the friendly woods growing down to the edge of the fill swallowed him up. He dodged and doubled back and forth among the tree trunks, his small, patent-leathered feet skipping nimbly over the irregular turf, until he stopped for lack of wind in his lungs to carry him another rod. When he had got his breath back Mr. Trimm leaned against a tree and bent his head this way and that, listening. No sound came to his ears except the sleepy calls of birds. As well as Mr. Trimm might judge he had come far into the depths of a considerable woodland. Already the shadows under the low limbs were growing thick and confused as the hurried twilight of early September came on.

Mr. Trimm sat down on a natural cushion of thick green moss between two roots of an oak. The place was clean and soft and sweet-scented. For some little time he sat there motionless, in a sort of mental haze. Then his round body slowly slid down flat upon the moss, his head lolled to one side and, the reaction having come, Mr. Trimm's limbs all relaxed and he went to sleep straightway.

After a while, when the woods were black and still, the half-grown moon came up and, sifting through a chink in the canopy of leaves above, shone down full on Mr. Trimm as he lay snoring gently with his mouth open and his hands rising and falling on his breast. The moonlight struck upon the Little Giant handcuffs, making them look like quicksilver.

Toward daylight it turned off sharp and cool. The dogwoods which had been a solid color at nightfall now showed pink in one light and green in another, like changeable silk, as the first level rays of the sun came up over the rim of the earth and made long, golden lanes between the tree trunks. Mr. Trimm opened his eyes slowly, hardly sensing for the first moment or two how he came to be lying under a canopy of leaves, and gaped, seeking to stretch his arms. At that he remembered everything; he hunched his shoulders against the tree roots and wriggled himself up to a sitting position where he stayed for a while, letting his mind run over the sequence of events that had brought him where he was and taking inventory of the situation.

Of escape he had no thought. The hue and cry must be out for him before now; doubtless men were already searching for him. It would be better for him to walk in and surrender than to be taken in the woods like some animal escaped from a traveling menagerie. But the mere thought of enduring again what he had already gone through—the thought of being tagged by crowds and stared at, with his fetters on—filled him with a nausea. Nothing that the Federal penitentiary might hold in store for him could equal the black, blind shamefulness of yesterday; he knew that. The thought of the new ignominy that faced him made Mr. Trimm desperate. He had a desire to burrow into the thicket yonder and hide his face and his chained hands.

But perhaps he could get the handcuffs off and so go to meet his captors in some manner of dignity. Strange that the idea hadn't occurred to him before! It seemed to Mr. Trimm that he

811 desired to get his two hands
812 apart more than he had ever
813 desired anything in his whole
814 life before.

815 The hands had begun natur-
816 ally to adjust themselves to their
817 enforced companionship, and it
818 wasn't such a very hard matter,
819 though it cost him some painful
820 wrenches and much twisting of
821 the fingers, for Mr. Trimm to get
822 his coat unbuttoned and his eye-
823 glasses in their small leather case
824 out of his upper waistcoat pock-
825 et. With the glasses on his nose
826 he subjected his bonds to a crit-
827 ical examination. Each rounded
828 steel band ran unbroken except
829 for the smooth, almost jointless
830 hinge and the small lock which
831 sat perched on the back of the
832 wrist in a little rounded excres-
833 cence like a steel wart. In the
834 flat center of each lock was a
835 small keyhole and alongside of it
836 a notched nub, the nub being
837 sunk in a minute depression. On
838 the inner side, underneath, the
839 cuffs slid into themselves—two
840 notches on each showing where
841 the jaws might be tightened to
842 fit a smaller hand than his—and
843 right over the large blue veins
844 in the middle of the wrists were
845 swivel links, shackle-bolted to
846 the cuffs and connected by a flat,
847 slightly larger middle link, giv-
848 ing the hands a palm-to-palm
849 play of not more than four or
850 five inches. The cuffs did not
851 hurt—even after so many hours
852 there was no actual discomfort

853 from them and the flesh beneath
854 them was hardly reddened.

855 But it didn't take Mr. Trimm
856 long to find out that they were
857 not to be got off. He tugged and
858 pulled, trying with his fingers
859 for a purchase. All he did was to
860 chafe his skin and make his
861 wrists throb with pain. The
862 cuffs would go forward just so
863 far, then the little humps of bone
864 above the hands would catch and
865 hold them.

866 Mr. Trimm was not a man to
867 waste time in the pursuit of the
868 obviously hopeless. Presently he
869 stood up, shook himself and
870 started off at a fair gait through
871 the woods. The sun was up now
872 and the turf was all dappled with
873 lights and shadows, and about
874 him much small, furtive wild life
875 was stirring. He stepped along
876 briskly, a strange figure for that
877 green solitude, with his correct
878 city garb and the glint of the
879 steel at his sleeve ends.

880 Presently he heard the long-
881 drawn, quavering, banshee wail
882 of a locomotive. The sound
883 came from almost behind him,
884 in an opposite direction from
885 where he supposed the track to
886 be. So he turned around and
887 went back the other way. He
888 crossed a half-dried-up runlet
889 and climbed a small hill, neither
890 of which he remembered having
891 met in his flight from the wreck,
892 and in a little while he came out
893 upon the railroad. To the north
894 a little distance the rails bent

895 round a curve. To the south,
896 where the diminishing rails run-
897 ning through the unbroken wood-
898 land met in a long, shiny V, he
899 could see a big smoke smudge
900 against the horizon. This smoke
901 Mr. Trimm knew must come from
902 the wreck—which was still burn-
903 ing, evidently. As nearly as he
904 could judge he had come out of
905 cover at least two miles above it.
906 After a moment's consideration
907 he decided to go south toward the
908 wreck. Soon he could distinguish
909 small dots like ants moving in and
910 out about the black spot, and he
911 knew these dots must be men.

912 A whining, whirring sound
913 came along the rails to him from
914 behind. He faced about just as a
915 handcar shot out around the
916 curve from the north, moving
917 with amazing rapidity under the
918 strokes of four men at the pumps.
919 Other men, laborers, to judge by
920 their blue overalls, were sitting
921 on the edges of the car with their
922 feet dangling. For the second
923 time within twelve hours impulse
924 ruled Mr. Trimm, who wasn't
925 given to impulses normally. He
926 made a jump off the right-of-
927 way, and as the handcar flashed
928 by he watched its flight from the
929 covert of a weed tangle.

930 But even as the handcar was
931 passing him Mr. Trimm regret-
932 ted his hastiness. He must sur-
933 render himself sooner or later;
934 why not to these overalled labor-
935 ers, since it was a thing that had
936 to be done? He slid out of hiding

937 and came trotting back to the
938 tracks. Already the handcar was
939 a hundred yards away, flitting
940 into distance like some big, won-
941 derfully fast bug, the figures of
942 the men at the pumps rising and
943 falling with a walking-beam reg-
944 ularity. As he stood watching
945 them fade away and minded to
946 try hailing them, yet still hesi-
947 tating against his judgment, Mr.
948 Trimm saw something white
949 drop from the hands of one of
950 the blue-clad figures on the hand-
951 car, unfold into a newspaper and
952 come fluttering back along the
953 tracks toward him. Just as he,
954 starting doggedly ahead, met it,
955 the little ground breeze that had
956 carried it along died out and the
957 paper dropped and flattened
958 right in front of him. The front
959 page was uppermost and he knew
960 it must be of that morning's is-
961 sue, for across the column tops
962 ran the flaring headline: "Twen-
963 ty Dead in Frightful Collision."

964 Squatting on the cindered
965 track, Mr. Trimm patted the
966 crumpled sheet flat with his
967 hands. His eyes dropped from
968 the first of the glaring captions
969 to the second, to the next—and
970 then his heart gave a great bound
971 inside of him and, clutching up
972 the newspaper to his breast he
973 bounded off the tracks back into
974 another thicket and huddled
975 there with the paper spread on
976 the earth in front of him, reading
977 by gulps while the chain that
978 linked wrist to wrist tinkled to

the tremors running through him. What he had seen first, in staring black-face type, was his own name leading the list of known dead, and what he saw now, broken up into choppy paragraphs and done in the nervous English of a trained reporter throwing a great news story together to catch an edition, but telling a clear enough story nevertheless, was a narrative in which his name recurred again and again. The body of the United States deputy marshal, Meyers, frightfully crushed, had been taken from the wreckage of the smoker — so the double-leaded story ran — and near to Meyers another body, with features burned beyond recognition, yet still retaining certain distinguishing marks of measurement and contour, had been found and identified as that of Hobart W. Trimm, the convicted banker. The bodies of these two, with eighteen other mangled dead, had been removed to a town called Westfield, from which town of Westfield the account of the disaster had been telegraphed to the New York paper. In another column farther along was more about Banker Trimm; facts about his soiled, selfish, greedy, successful life, his great fortune, his trial, and a statement that, in the absence of any close kin to claim his body, his lawyers had been notified.

Mr. Trimm read the account through to the end, and as he read the sense of dominant, masterful self-control came back to him in waves. He got up, taking the paper with him, and went back into the deeper woods, moving warily and watchfully. As he went his mind, trained to take hold of problems and wring the essence out of them, was busy. Of the charred, grisly thing in the improvised morgue at Westfield, wherever that might be, Mr. Trimm took no heed nor wasted any pity. All his life he had used live men to work his will, with no thought of what might come to them afterward. The living had served him, why not the dead?

He had other things to think of than this dead proxy of his. He was as good as free! There would be no hunt for him now; no alarm out, no posses combing every scrap of cover for a famous criminal turned fugitive. He had only to lie quiet a few days, somewhere, then get in secret touch with Walling. Walling would do anything for money. And he had the money—four millions and more, cannily saved from the crash that had ruined so many others.

He would alter his personal appearance, change his name— he thought of Duvall, which was his mother's name—and with Walling's aid he would get out of the country and into some other country where a man might live like a prince on four millions or the fractional part of it. He thought of South America, of South Africa, of a private yacht swinging through the little frequented islands of the South Seas. All that the law had tried to take from him would be given back. Walling would work out the details of the escape—and make it safe and sure—trust Walling for those things. On one side was the prison, with its promise of twelve grinding years sliced out of the very heart of his life; on the other, freedom, ease, security, even power. Through Mr. Trimm's mind tumbled thoughts of concessions, enterprises, privileges—the back corners of the globe were full of possibilities for the right man. And between this prospect and Mr. Trimm there stood nothing in the way, nothing but——

Mr. Trimm's eyes fell upon his bound hands. Snug-fitting, shiny steel bands irked his wrists. The Grips of the Law were still upon him.

But only in a way of speaking. It was preposterous, unbelievable, altogether out of the question that a man with four millions salted down and stored away, a man who all his life had been used to grappling with the big things and wrestling them down into submission, a man whose luck had come to be a byword—and had not it held good even in this last emergency?— would be balked by puny scraps of forged steel and a trumpery lock or two. Why, these cuffs were no thicker than the gold bands that Mr. Trimm had seen on the arms of overdressed women at the opera. The chain that joined them was no larger and, probably, no stronger than the chains which Mr. Trimm's chauffeur wrapped around the tires of the touring-car in winter to keep the wheels from skidding on the slush. There would be a way, surely, for Mr. Trimm to free himself from these things. There must be—that was all there was to it.

Mr. Trimm looked himself over. His clothes were not badly rumpled; his patent-leather boots were scarcely scratched. Without the handcuffs he could pass unnoticed anywhere. By night then he must be free of them and on his way to some small inland city, to stay quiet there until the guarded telegram that he would send in cipher had reached Walling. There in the woods by himself Mr. Trimm no longer felt the ignominy of his bonds; he felt only the temporary embarrassment of them and the need of added precaution until he should have mastered them.

He was once more the unemotional man of affairs who had stood Wall Street on its esteemed head and caught the golden streams that trickled from its pockets. First making sure that he was in a well-screened covert of the woods he set about exploring all his pockets. The coat pockets were comparatively easy, now that he had got used to using two hands where one had always served, but it cost him a lot of twisting of his body and some pain to his mistreated wrist bones to bring forth the contents of his trousers pockets. The chain kinked time and again as he groped with the undermost hand for the openings; his dumpy, pudgy form writhed grotesquely. But finally he finished. The search produced four cigars somewhat crumpled and frayed; some matches in a gun-metal case, a silver cigar cutter, two five-dollar bills, a handful of silver chicken feed, the leather case of the eyeglasses, a couple of quill toothpicks, a gold watch with a dangling fob, a note-book and some papers. Mr. Trimm ranged these things in a neat row upon a log, like a watchmaker putting out his kit, and took swift inventory of them. Some he eliminated from his design, stowing them back in the pockets easiest to reach. He kept for present employment the match safe, the cigar cutter and the watch.

This place where he had halted would suit his present purpose well, he decided. It was where an uprooted tree, fallen across an incurving bank, made a snug little recess that was closed in on three sides. Spreading the newspaper on the turf to save his knees from soiling, he knelt and set to his task. For the time he felt neither hunger nor thirst. He had found out during his earlier experiments that the nails of his little fingers, which were trimmed to a point, could invade the keyholes in the little steel warts on the backs of his wrists and touch the locks. The mechanism had even twitched a little bit under the tickle of the nail ends. So, having already smashed the gun-metal match safe under his heel, Mr. Trimm selected a slender-pointed bit from among its fragments and got to work, the left hand drawn up under the right, the fingers of the right busy with the lock of the left, the chain tightening and slackening with subdued clinking sounds at each movement.

Mr. Trimm didn't know much about picking a lock. He had got his money by a higher form of burglary that did not require a knowledge of lock-picking. Nor as a boy had he been one to play at mechanics. He had let other boys make the toy flutter-mills and the wooden traps and the like, and then he had traded for them. He was sorry now that he hadn't given more heed to the mechanical side of things when he was growing up.

He worked with a deliberate slowness, steadily. Neverthe-

1231 less, it was hot work. The sun
1232 rose over the bank and shone on
1233 him through the limbs of the
1234 uprooted tree. His hat was on
1235 the ground alongside of him.
1236 The sweat ran down his face,
1237 streaking it and wilting his col-
1238 lar flat. The scrap of gun-metal
1239 kept slipping out of his wet fin-
1240 gers. Down would go the
1241 chained hands to scrabble in the
1242 grass for it, and then the picking
1243 would go on again. This hap-
1244 pened a good many times. Birds,
1245 nervous with the spirit that pre-
1246 sages the fall migration, flew
1247 back and forth along the creek,
1248 almost grazing Mr. Trimm some-
1249 times. A rain crow wove a
1250 brown thread in the green warp
1251 of the bushes above his head. A
1252 chattering red squirrel sat up on
1253 a tree limb to scold him. At in-
1254 tervals, distantly, came the cough
1255 of laboring trains, showing that
1256 the track must have been cleared.
1257 There were times when Mr.
1258 Trimm thought he felt the lock
1259 giving. These times he would
1260 work harder.

· · · · ·

1261 Late in the afternoon Mr.
1262 Trimm lay back against the
1263 bank, panting. His face was
1264 splotched with red, and the little
1265 hollows at the sides of his fore-
1266 head pulsed rapidly up and down
1267 like the bellies of scared tree
1268 frogs. The bent outer case of
1269 the watch littered a bare patch
1270 on the log; its mainspring had
1271 gone the way of the fragments

1272 of the gun-metal match safe
1273 which were lying all about, each
1274 a worn-down, twisted wisp of
1275 metal. The spring of the eye-
1276 glasses had been confiscated long
1277 ago and the broken crystals pow-
1278 dered the earth where Mr.
1279 Trimm's toes had scraped a
1280 smooth patch. The nails of the
1281 two little fingers were worn to
1282 the quick and splintered down
1283 into the raw flesh. There were
1284 countless tiny scratches and mars
1285 on the locks of the handcuffs,
1286 and the steel wristbands were
1287 dulled with blood smears and
1288 pale-red tarnishes of new rust;
1289 but otherwise they were as stanch
1290 and strong a pair of Bean's Lat-
1291 est Model Little Giant handcuffs
1292 as you'd find in any hardware
1293 store anywhere.
1294 The devilish, stupid malignity
1295 of the damned things! With an
1296 acid oath Mr. Trimm raised his
1297 hands and brought them down
1298 on the log violently. There was
1299 a double click and the bonds
1300 tightened painfully, pressing the
1301 chafed red skin white. Mr.
1302 Trimm snatched up his hands
1303 close to his near-sighted eyes and
1304 looked. One of the little notches
1305 on the under side of each cuff had
1306 disappeared. It was as if they
1307 were living things that had
1308 turned and bitten him for the
1309 blow he gave them.

· · · · ·

1310 From the time the sun went
1311 down there was a tingle of frost
1312 in the air. Mr. Trimm didn't

sleep much. Under the squeeze of the tightened fetters his wrists throbbed steadily and racking cramps ran through his arms. His stomach felt as though it were tied into knots. The water that he drank from the branch only made his hunger sickness worse. His undergarments, that had been wet with perspiration, clung to him clammily. His middle-aged, tenderly cared-for body called through every pore for clean linen and soap and water and rest, as his empty insides called for food.

After a while he became so chilled that the demand for warmth conquered his instinct for caution. He felt about him in the darkness gathering scraps of dead wood, and, after breaking several of the matches that had been in the gun-metal match safe, he managed to strike one and with its tiny flame started a fire. He huddled almost over the fire, coughing when the smoke blew into his face and twisting and pulling at his arms in an effort to get relief from the everlasting cramps. It seemed to him that if he could only get an inch or two more of play for his hands he would be ever so much more comfortable. But he couldn't, of course.

He dozed, finally, sitting cross-legged with his head sunk between his hunched shoulders. A pain in a new place woke him. The fire had burned almost through the thin sole of his right shoe, and as he scrambled to his feet and stamped, the clap of the hot leather flat against his blistered foot almost made him cry out.

. . . . .

Soon after sunrise a boy came riding a horse down a faintly traced footpath along the creek, driving a cow with a bell on her neck ahead of him. Mr. Trimm's ears caught the sound of the clanking bell before either the cow or her herder was in sight, and he limped away, running, skulking through the thick cover. A pendent loop of a wild grape-vine, swinging low, caught his hat and flipped it off his head; but Mr. Trimm, imagining pursuit, did not stop to pick it up and went on bareheaded until he had to stop from exhaustion. He saw some dark-red berries on a shrub upon which he had trod, and, stooping, he plucked some of them with his two hands and put three or four in his mouth experimentally. Warned instantly by the harsh, burning taste, he spat the crushed berries out and went on doggedly, following, according to his best judgment, a course parallel to the railroad. It was characteristic of him, a city-raised man, that he took no heed of distances nor of the distinguishing marks of the timber. Behind a log at the edge of a small clearing in the woods he halted some little time, watching and listening. The clearing had grown up in sumacs and weeds and small saplings and it seemed deserted; certainly it was still. Near the center of it rose the sagging roof of what had been a shack or a shed of some sort. Stooping cautiously, to keep his bare head below the tops of the sumacs, Mr. Trimm made for the ruined shanty and gained it safely. In the midst of the rotted, punky logs that had once formed the walls he began scraping with his feet. Presently he uncovered something. It was a broken-off harrow tooth, scaled like a long, red fish with the crusted rust of years.

Mr. Trimm rested the lower rims of his handcuffs on the edge of an old, broken watering trough, worked the pointed end of the rust-crusted harrow tooth into the flat middle link of the chain as far as it would go, and then with one hand on top of the other he pressed downward with all his might. The pain in his wrists made him stop this at once. The link had not sprung or given in the least, but the twisting pressure had almost broken his wrist bones. He let the harrow tooth fall, knowing that it would never serve as a lever to free him—which, indeed, he had known all along—and sat on the side of the trough, rubbing his wrists and thinking.

He had another idea. It came into his mind as a vague suggestion that fire had certain effects upon certain metals. He kindled a fire of bits of the rotted wood, and when the flames ran together and rose slender and straight in a single red thread he thrust the chain into it, holding his hands as far apart as possible in the attitude of a player about to catch a bounced ball. But immediately the pain of that grew unendurable too, and he leaped back, jerking his hands away. He had succeeded only in blackening the steel and putting a big water blister on one of his wrists right where the shackle bolt would press upon it.

Where he huddled down in the shelter of one of the fallen walls he noticed, presently, a strand of rusted fence wire still held to half-tottering posts by a pair of blackened staples; it was part of a pen that had been used once for chickens or swine. Mr. Trimm tried the wire with his fingers. It was firm and springy. Rocking and groaning with the pain of it, he nevertheless began sliding the chain back and forth along the strand of wire.

Eventually the wire, weakened by age, snapped in two. A tiny shined spot, hardly deep enough to be called a nick, in its tarnished, smudged surface was all the mark that the chain showed.

Staggering a little and putting his feet down unsteadily, Mr. Trimm left the clearing, heading as well as he could tell eastward, away from the railroad. After

1480 a mile or two he came to a dusty
1481 wood road winding downhill.

1482   To the north of the clearing
1483 where Mr. Trimm had halted
1484 were a farm and a group of farm
1485 buildings. To the southward
1486 a mile or so was a cluster
1487 of dwellings set in the midst
1488 of more farm lands, with a
1489 shop or two and a small white
1490 church with a green spire in
1491 the center. Along a road that
1492 ran northward from the ham-
1493 let to the solitary farm a
1494 ten-year-old boy came, carry-
1495 ing a covered tin pail. A young
1496 gray squirrel flirted across the
1497 wagon ruts ahead of him and
1498 darted up a chestnut sapling.
1499 The boy put the pail down at the
1500 side of the road and began look-
1501 ing for a stone to throw at the
1502 squirrel.

1503   Mr. Trimm slid out from be-
1504 hind a tree. A hemstitched
1505 handkerchief grimed and
1506 stained, was loosely twisted a-
1507 round his wrists, partly hiding
1508 the handcuffs. He moved along
1509 with a queer, sidling gait, keep-
1510 ing as much of his body as he
1511 could turned from the youngster.
1512 The ears of the little chap caught
1513 the faint scuffle of feet and he
1514 spun around on his bare heel.

1515   "My boy, would you ——"
1516 Mr. Trimm began.

1517   The boy's round eyes widened
1518 at the apparition that was sidling
1519 toward him in so strange a fash-
1520 ion, and then, taking fright, he
1521 dodged past Mr. Trimm and ran

1522 back the way he had come, as
1523 fast as his slim brown legs could
1524 take him. In half a minute he
1525 was out of sight round a bend.

1526   Had the boy looked back he
1527 would have seen a still more curi-
1528 ous spectacle than the one that
1529 had frightened him. He would
1530 have seen a man worth four mil-
1531 lion dollars down on his knees in
1532 the yellow dust, pawing with
1533 chained hands at the tight-fitting
1534 lid of the tin pail, and then, when
1535 he had got the lid off, drinking
1536 the fresh, warm milk which the
1537 pail held with great, choking
1538 gulps, uttering little mewing, an-
1539 imal sounds as he drank, while
1540 the white, creamy milk ran over
1541 his chin and splashed down his
1542 breast in little, spurting streams.

1543   But the boy didn't look back.
1544 He ran all the way home and told
1545 his mother he had seen a wild
1546 man on the road to the village;
1547 and later, when his father came
1548 in from the fields, he was soundly
1549 thrashed for letting the sight of
1550 a tramp make him lose a good
1551 tin bucket and half a gallon of
1552 milk worth nine cents a quart.

. . . . .

1553   The rich, fresh milk put life
1554 into Mr. Trimm. He rested the
1555 better for it during the early part
1556 of that night in a haw thicket.
1557 Only the sharp, darting pains in
1558 his wrists kept rousing him to
1559 temporary wakefulness. In one
1560 of those intervals of waking the
1561 plan that had been sketchily
1562 forming in his mind from the

1563 time he had quit the clearing in
1564 the woods took on a definite,
1565 fixed shape. But how was he
1566 with safety to get the sort of aid
1567 he needed, and where?

1568 Canvassing tentative plans in
1569 his head, he dozed off again.

. . . . .

1570 On a smooth patch of turf be-
1571 hind the blacksmith shop three
1572 yokels were languidly pitching
1573 horseshoes—"quaits," they
1574 called them—at a stake driven
1575 in the earth. Just beyond, the
1576 woods shredded out into a long,
1577 yellow and green peninsula which
1578 stretched up almost to the back
1579 door of the smithy, so that late of
1580 afternoons the slanting shadows
1581 of the nearest trees fell on its
1582 roof of warped shingles. At the
1583 extreme end of this point of
1584 woods Mr. Trimm was squatted
1585 behind a big boulder, squinting
1586 warily through a thick-fringed
1587 curtain of ripened goldenrod tops
1588 and sumacs, heavy-headed with
1589 their dark-red tapers. He had
1590 been there more than an hour,
1591 cautiously waiting his chance to
1592 hail the blacksmith, whose figure
1593 he could make out in the smoky
1594 interior of his shop, passing back
1595 and forth in front of a smudgy
1596 forge fire and rattling metal
1597 against metal in intermittent fits
1598 of professional activity.

1599 From where Mr. Trimm
1600 watched to where the horseshoe-
1601 pitching game went on was not
1602 more than sixty feet. He could
1603 hear what the players said and

1604 even see the little puffs of dust
1605 rise when one of them clapped
1606 his hands together after a pitch.

1607 He judged by the signs of
1608 slackening interest that they
1609 would be stopping soon and, he
1610 hoped, going clear away.

1611 But the smith loafed out of
1612 his shop and, after an exchange
1613 of bucolic banter with the three
1614 of them, he took a hand in their
1615 game himself. He wore no coat
1616 or waistcoat and, as he poised a
1617 horseshoe for his first cast at the
1618 stake, Mr. Trimm saw, pinned
1619 flat against the broad strap of his
1620 suspenders, a shiny, silvery-look-
1621 ing disc. Having pitched the shoe,
1622 the smith moved over into the
1623 shade, so that he almost touched
1624 the clump of undergrowth that
1625 half buried Mr. Trimm's pro-
1626 tecting boulder. The near-sight-
1627 ed eyes of the fugitive banker
1628 could make out then what the
1629 flat, silvery disc was, and Mr.
1630 Trimm cowered low in his covert
1631 behind the rock, holding his
1632 hands down between his knees,
1633 fearful that a gleam from his
1634 burnished wristlets might strike
1635 through the screen of weed
1636 growth and catch the inquiring
1637 eye of the smith. So he stayed,
1638 not daring to move, until a din-
1639 ner horn sounded somewhere in
1640 the cluster of cottages beyond,
1641 and the smith, closing the doors
1642 of his shop, went away with the
1643 three yokels.

1644 Then Mr. Trimm, stooping
1645 low, stole back into the deep

woods again. In his extremity he was ready to risk making a bid for the hire of a blacksmith's aid to rid himself of his bonds, but not a blacksmith who wore a deputy sheriff's badge pinned to his suspenders.

. . . . . .

He caught himself scraping his wrists up and down again against the rough, scrofulous trunk of a shellbark hickory. The irritation was comforting to the swollen skin. The cuffs, which kept catching on the bark and snagging small fragments of it loose, seemed to Mr. Trimm to have been a part and parcel of him for a long time—almost as long a time as he could remember. But the hands which they clasped so close seemed like the hands of somebody else. There was a numbness about them that made them feel as though they were a stranger's hands which never had belonged to him. As he looked at them with a sort of vague curiosity they seemed to swell and grow, these two strange hands, while the fetters measured yards across, while the steel bands shrunk to the thinness of piano wire, cutting deeper and deeper into the flesh. Then the hands in turn began to shrink down and the cuffs to grow up into great, thick things as cumbersome as the couplings of a freight car. A voice that Mr. Trimm dimly recognized as his own was saying something about four million dollars over and over again.

Mr. Trimm roused up and shook his head angrily to clear it. He rubbed his eyes free of the clouding delusion. It wouldn't do for him to be getting light-headed.

. . . . . .

On a flat, shelving bluff, forty feet above a cut through which the railroad ran at a point about five miles north of where the collision had occurred, a tramp was busy, just before sundown, cooking something in an old washboiler that perched precariously on a fire of wood coals. This tramp was tall and spindle-legged, with reddish hair and a pale, beardless, freckled face with no chin to it and not much forehead, so that it ran out to a peak like the profile of some featherless, unpleasant sort of fowl. The skirts of an old, ragged overcoat dangled grotesquely— about his spare shanks.

Desperate as his plight had become, Mr. Trimm had felt the old sick shame at the prospect of exposing himself to this knavish looking vagabond whose help he meant to buy with a bribe. It was the sight of a dainty wisp of smoke from the wood fire curling upward through the cloudy, damp air that had brought him limping cautiously across the right-of-way, to climb the rocky shelf along the cut; but now he hesitated, shielded in the shad-

1728 ows twenty yards away. It was
1729 a whiff of something savory in
1730 the washboiler, borne to him on
1731 the still air and almost making
1732 him cry out with eagerness, that
1733 drew him forth finally. At the
1734 sound of the halting footsteps
1735 the tramp stopped stirring the
1736 mess in the washboiler and
1737 glanced apprehensively. As he
1738 took in the figure of the new-
1739 comer his eyes narrowed and his
1740 pasty, nasty face spread in a
1741 grin of comprehension.

1742 "Well, well, well," he said leer-
1743 ing offensively, "welcome to our
1744 city, little stranger."

1745 Mr. Trimm came nearer, drag-
1746 ging his feet, for they were al-
1747 most out of the wrecks of his
1748 patent-leather shoes. His gaze
1749 shifted from the tramp's face to
1750 the stuff on the fire, his nostrils
1751 wrinkling. Then slowly, "I'm in
1752 trouble," he said, and held out
1753 his hands.

1754 "Wot I'd call a mild way o'
1755 puttin' it," said the tramp coolly.
1756 "That purticular kind o' joolry
1757 ain't gen'lly wore for pleasure."

1758 His eyes took on a nervous
1759 squint and roved past Mr.
1760 Trimm's stooped figure down
1761 the slope of the hillock.

1762 "Say, pal, how fur ahead are
1763 you of yore keeper?" he demand-
1764 ed, his manner changing.

1765 "There is no one after me—
1766 no one that I know of," ex-
1767 plained Mr. Trimm. "I am
1768 quite alone—I am certain of it."

1769 "Sure there ain't nobody look-
1770 in' fur you?" the other persisted
1771 suspiciously.

1772 "I tell you I am all alone,"
1773 protested Mr. Trimm. "I want
1774 your help in getting these—
1775 these things off and sending a
1776 message to a friend. You'll be
1777 well paid, very well paid. I can
1778 pay you more money than you
1779 ever had in your life, probably, for
1780 your help. I can promise——"

1781 He broke off, for the tramp,
1782 as if reassured by his words, had
1783 stooped again to his cooking and
1784 was stirring the bubbling con-
1785 tents of the washboiler with a
1786 peeled stick. The smell of the
1787 stew, rising strongly, filled Mr.
1788 Trimm with such a sharp and an
1789 aching hunger that he could not
1790 speak for a moment. He mas-
1791 tered himself, but the effort left
1792 him shaking and gulping.

1793 "Go on, then, an' tell us some-
1794 thin' about yourself," said the
1795 freckled man. "Wot brings you
1796 roamin' round this here railroad
1797 cut with them bracelets on?"

1798 "I was in the wreck," obeyed
1799 Mr. Trimm. "The man with me
1800 —the officer—was killed. I was-
1801 n't hurt and I got away into
1802 these woods. But they think I'm
1803 dead too—my name was among
1804 the list of dead."

1805 The other's peaky face length-
1806 ened in astonishment.

1807 "Why, say!" he began. "I
1808 read all about that there wreck
1809 —seen the list myself—say, you
1810 can't be Trimm, the New York
1811 banker? Yes, you are! Wot a

1812 streak of luck! Lemme look at
1813 you! Trimm, the swell finan-
1814 cier, sportin' 'round with the dar-
1815 bies on him all nice an' snug an'
1816 reg'lar! Mister Trimm—well, if
1817 this ain't rich!"
1818 "My name is Trimm," said
1819 the starving banker miserably.
1820 "I've been wandering about here
1821 a great many hours—several
1822 days, I think it must be—and I
1823 need rest and food very much in-
1824 deed. I don't—don't feel very
1825 well," he added, his voice trail-
1826 ing off.
1827 At this his self-control gave
1828 way again and he began to quake
1829 violently as if with an ague. The
1830 smell of the cooking overcame
1831 him.
1832 "You don't look so well an'
1833 that's a fact, Trimm," sneered
1834 the tramp, resuming his mali-
1835 cious, mocking air. "But set
1836 down an' make yourself at home,
1837 an' after a while, when this is
1838 done, we'll have a bite together
1839 —you an' me. It'll be a reg'lar
1840 tea party fur jest us two."
1841 He broke off to chuckle. His
1842 mirth made him appear even
1843 more repulsive than before.
1844 "But looky here, you wuz
1845 sayin' somethin' about money,"
1846 he said suddenly. "Le's take a
1847 look at all this here money."
1848 He came over to him and went
1849 through Mr. Trimm's pockets.
1850 Mr. Trimm said nothing and
1851 stood quietly, making no resist-
1852 ance. The tramp finished a
1853 workmanlike search of the bank-

1854 er's pockets. He looked at the
1855 result as it lay in his grimy palm
1856 —a moist little wad of bills and
1857 some chicken-feed change—and
1858 spat disgustedly with a nasty
1859 oath.
1860 "Well, Trimm," he said, "fur
1861 a Wall Street guy seems to me
1862 you travel purty light. About
1863 how much did you think you'd
1864 get done fur all this pile of
1865 wealth?"
1866 "You will be well paid," said
1867 Mr. Trimm, arguing hard; "my
1868 friend will see to that. What
1869 I want you to do is to take the
1870 money you have there in your
1871 hand and buy a cold chisel or a
1872 file—any tools that will cut these
1873 things off me. And then you will
1874 send a telegram to a certain gen-
1875 tleman in New York. And let
1876 me stay with you until we get
1877 an answer—until he comes here.
1878 He will pay you well; I promise
1879 it."
1880 He halted, his eyes and his
1881 mind again on the bubbling stuff
1882 in the rusted washboiler. The
1883 freckled vagrant studied him
1884 through his red-lidded eyes,
1885 kicking some loose embers back
1886 into the fire with his toe.
1887 "I've heard a lot about you
1888 one way an' another, Trimm,"
1889 he said. " 'Tain't as if you wuz
1890 some pore down-an'-out devil
1891 tryin' to beat the cops out of
1892 doin' his bit in stir. You're the
1893 way-up, high-an'-mighty kind of
1894 crook. An' from wot I've read
1895 an' heard about you, you never

1896 toted fair with nobody yet.
1897 There wuz that young feller,
1898 wot's his name?—the cashier—
1899 him that wuz tried with you.
1900 He went along with you in yore
1901 games an' done yore work fur
1902 you an' you let him go over the
1903 road to the same place you're
1904 tryin' to dodge now. Besides,"
1905 he added cunningly, "you come
1906 here talkin' mighty big about
1907 money, yet I notice you ain't
1908 carryin' much of it in yore
1909 clothes. All I've had to go by
1910 is yore word. An' yore word
1911 ain't worth much, by all ac-
1912 counts."

1913 "I tell you, man, that you'll
1914 profit richly," burst out Mr.
1915 Trimm, the words falling over
1916 each other in his new panic.
1917 "You must help me; I've en-
1918 dured too much—I've gone
1919 through too much to give up
1920 now." He pleaded fast, his
1921 hands shaking in a quiver of fear
1922 and eagerness as he stretched
1923 them out in entreaty and his
1924 linked chain shaking with them.
1925 Promises, pledges, commands,
1926 orders, arguments poured from
1927 him. His tormentor checked
1928 him with a gesture.

1929 "You're wot I'd call a bird in
1930 the hand," he chuckled, hugging
1931 his slack frame, "an' it ain't fur
1932 you to be givin' orders—it's fur
1933 me. An', anyway, I guess we
1934 ain't a-goin' to be able to make
1935 a trade—leastwise not on yore
1936 terms. But we'll do business all
1937 right, all right—anyhow, I will."

1938 "What do you mean?" panted
1939 Mr. Trimm, full of terror.
1940 "You'll help me?"

1941 "I mean this," said the tramp
1942 slowly. He put his hands under
1943 his loose-hanging overcoat and
1944 began to fumble at a leather
1945 strap about his waist. "If I
1946 turn you over to the Govern-
1947 ment I know wot you'll be worth,
1948 purty near, by guessin' at the
1949 reward; an' besides, it'll maybe
1950 help to square me up for one or
1951 two little matters. If I turn you
1952 loose I ain't got nothin' only
1953 your word—an' I've got an idea
1954 how much faith I kin put in
1955 that."

1956 Mr. Trimm glanced about him
1957 wildly. There was no escape.
1958 He was fast in a trap which he
1959 himself had sprung. The thought
1960 of being led to jail, all foul of
1961 body and fettered as he was, by
1962 this filthy, smirking wretch made
1963 him crazy. He stumbled back-
1964 ward with some insane idea of
1965 running away.

1966 "No hurry, no hurry a-tall,"
1967 gloated the tramp, enjoying the
1968 torture of this helpless captive
1969 who had walked into his hands.
1970 "I ain't goin' to hurt you none—
1971 only make sure that you don't
1972 wander off an' hurt yourself
1973 while I'm gone. Won't do to let
1974 you be damagin' yoreself; you're
1975 valuable property. Trimm, now,
1976 I'll tell you wot we'll do! We'll
1977 just back you up agin one of
1978 these trees an' then we'll jest
1979 slip this here belt through yore

1980 elbows an' buckle it around be-
1981 hind at the back; an' I kinder
1982 guess you'll stay right there till
1983 I go down yonder to that town
1984 that I passed comin' up here an'
1985 see wot kind of a bargain I kin
1986 strike up with the marshal.
1987 Come on, now," he threatened
1988 with a show of bluster, reading
1989 the resolution that was mount-
1990 ing in Mr. Trimm's face. "Come
1991 on peaceable, if you don't want
1992 to git hurt."

1993 Of a sudden Mr. Trimm be-
1994 came the primitive man. He
1995 was filled with those elemental
1996 emotions that make a man see in
1997 spatters of crimson. Gathering
1998 strength from passion out of an
1999 exhausted frame, he sprang
2000 forward at the tramp. He
2001 struck at him with his head, his
2002 shoulders, his knees, his man-
2003 acled wrists, all at once. Not
2004 really hurt by the puny assault,
2005 but caught by surprise, the
2006 freckled man staggered back,
2007 clawing at the air, tripped on the
2008 washboiler in the fire, and with
2009 a yell vanished below the smooth
2010 edge of the cut.

2011 Mr. Trimm stole forward and
2012 looked over the bluff. Half-way
2013 down the cliff on an out-cropping
2014 shelf of rock the man lay, face
2015 downward, motionless. He
2016 seemed to have grown smaller
2017 and to have shrunk into his
2018 clothes. One long, thin leg was
2019 bent up under the skirts of the
2020 overcoat in a queer, twisted way,
2021 and the cloth of the trouser leg

2022 looked flattened and empty. As
2023 Mr. Trimm peered down at him
2024 he saw a red stain spreading on
2025 the rock under the still, silent
2026 figure's head.

2027 Mr. Trimm turned to the
2028 washboiler. It lay on its side,
2029 empty, the last of its recent con-
2030 tents sputtering out into the
2031 half-drowned fire. He stared at
2032 this ruin a minute. Then with-
2033 out another look over the cliff
2034 edge he stumbled slowly down
2035 the hill, muttering to himself as
2036 he went. Just as he struck the
2037 level it began to rain, gently at
2038 first, then hard, and despite the
2039 shelter of the full-leaved forest
2040 trees, he was soon wet through
2041 to his skin and dripped water as
2042 he lurched along without sense
2043 of direction and, indeed, without
2044 any active realization of what
2045 he was doing.

· · · · ·

2046 Late that night it was still
2047 raining—a cold, steady, autum-
2048 nal downpour. A huddled figure
2049 slowly climbed upon a low fence
2050 running about the house-yard of
2051 the little farm where the boy
2052 lived who got thrashed for losing
2053 a milkpail. On the wet top rail,
2054 precariously perching, the figure
2055 slipped and sprawled forward in
2056 the miry yard. It got up, pain-
2057 fully swaying on its feet. It was
2058 Mr. Trimm, looking for food.
2059 He moved slowly toward the
2060 house, tottering from weakness
2061 and because of the slick mud
2062 underfoot; peering near-sight-

2063 edly this way and that through
2064 the murk; starting at every
2065 sound and stopping often to
2066 listen.
2067 The outlines of the lean-to
2068 kitchen at the back of the house
2069 were looming dead ahead of him
2070 when from the corner of the cot-
2071 tage sprang a small terrier. It
2072 made for Mr. Trimm, barking
2073 shrilly. He retreated backward,
2074 kicking at the little dog and, to
2075 hold his balance, striking out
2076 with short, dabby jerks of his
2077 fettered hands—they were such
2078 motions as the terrier itself
2079 might make trying to walk on
2080 its hindlegs. Still backing away,
2081 expecting every instant to feel
2082 the terrier's teeth in his flesh,
2083 Mr. Trimm put one foot into a
2084 hotbed with a great clatter of the
2085 breaking glass. He felt the sharp
2086 ends of shattered glass tearing
2087 and cutting his shin as he jerked
2088 free. Recovering himself, he
2089 dealt the terrier a lucky kick
2090 under the throat that sent it
2091 back, yowling, to where it had
2092 come from, and then, as a door
2093 jerked open and a half-dressed
2094 man jumped out into the dark-
2095 ness, Mr. Trimm half hobbled,
2096 half fell out of sight behind the
2097 woodpile.
2098 Back and forth along the lower
2099 edge of his yard the farmer hunt-
2100 ed, with the whimpering, cowed
2101 terrier to guide him, poking in
2102 dark corners with the muzzle of
2103 his shotgun for the unseen in-
2104 truder whose coming had aroused

the household. In a brushpile 2105
just over the fence to the east 2106
Mr. Trimm lay on his face upon 2107
the wet earth, with the rain 2108
beating down on him, sobbing 2109
with choking gulps that wrenched 2110
him cruelly, biting at the bonds 2111
on his wrists until the sound of 2112
breaking teeth gritted in the air. 2113
Finally, in the hopeless, helpless 2114
frenzy of his agony he beat his 2115
arms up and down until the 2116
bracelets struck squarely on a 2117
flat stone and the force of the 2118
blow sent the cuffs home to the 2119
last notch so that they pressed 2120
harder and faster than ever upon 2121
the tortured wrist bones. 2122
When he had wasted ten or 2123
fifteen minutes in a vain search 2124
the farmer went shivering back 2125
indoors to dry out his wet shirt. 2126
But the groveling figure in the 2127
brushpile lay for a long time 2128
where it was, only stirring a little 2129
while the rain dripped steadily 2130
down on everything. 2131

· · · · ·

The wreck was on a Tuesday 2132
evening. Early on the Saturday 2133
morning following, the chief of 2134
police, who was likewise the 2135
whole of the day police force in 2136
the town of Westfield, nine miles 2137
from the place where the collision 2138
occurred, heard a peculiar, 2139
strangely weak knocking at the 2140
front door of his cottage, where 2141
he also had his office. The door 2142
was a Dutch door, sawed through 2143
the middle, so that the top half 2144
might be opened independently, 2145

leaving the lower panel fast. He swung this top half back.

A face was framed in the opening—an indescribably dirty, unutterably weary face, with matted white hair and a rime of whitish beard stubble on the jaws. It was fallen in and sunken and it drooped on the chest of its owner. The mouth, swollen and pulpy, as if from repeated hard blows, hung agape, and between the purplish parted lips showed the stumps of broken teeth. The eyes blinked weakly at the chief from under lids as colorless as the eyelids of a corpse. The bare white head was filthy with plastered mud and twigs, and dripping wet.

"Hello, there!" said the chief, startled at this apparition. "What do you want?"

With a movement that told of straining effort the lolled head came up off the chest. The thin, corded neck stiffened back, rising from a dirty, collarless neckband. The Adam's apple bulged out prominently, as big as a pigeon's egg.

"I have come," said the specter in a wheezing rasp of a voice which the chief could hardly hear, "I have come to surrender myself. I am Hobart W. Trimm."

"I guess you got another think comin'," said the chief, who was by the way of being a neighborhood wag. "When last seen Hobart W. Trimm was only fifty-two years old. Besides which, he's dead and buried. I guess maybe you'd better think ag'in, grandpap, and see if you ain't Methus'lah or the Wanderin' Jew."

"I am Hobart W. Trimm, the banker," whispered the stranger with a sort of wan stubbornness.

"Go on and prove it," suggested the chief, more than willing to prolong the enjoyment of the sensation. It wasn't often in Westfield that wandering lunatics came a-calling.

"Got any way to prove it?" he repeated as the visitor stared at him.

"Yes," came the creaking, rusted hinge of a voice, "I have."

Slowly, with struggling attempts, he raised his hands into the chief's sight. They were horribly swollen hands, red with the dried blood where they were not black with the dried dirt; the fingers puffed up out of shape; the nails broken; they were like the skinned paws of a bear. And at the wrists, almost buried in the bloated folds of flesh, blackened, rusted, battered, yet still strong and whole, was a tightly locked pair of Bean's Latest Model Little Giant handcuffs.

"Great God!" cried the chief, transfixed at the sight. He drew the bolt and jerked open the lower half of the door.

"Come in," he said, "and lemme get them irons off of you

2230 —they must hurt something
2231 terrible."
2232 "They can wait," said Mr.
2233 Trimm very humbly. "I have
worn them a long, long while, I 2234
think—I am used to them. 2235
Wouldn't you please get me 2236
some food first?" 2237

THE ANALYSIS

THE Beginning of this story which contains the main narrative question and the promise of difficulty, opposition and disaster occupy the first 1141 lines. A glance at the chart which precedes this story will show that this Beginning is presented in a series of interchanges almost entirely, but it will disclose an interesting arrangement in that these meetings and interchanges are not, as they are in the other stories preceding this, in chronological order. They are instead, out of chronological order. Had this story been presented chronologically it would have begun on line 32, which opens with Mr. Trimm in the Tombs, and carries through to line 573 where he boards the train. Then lines 1 to 31 would come in, and the story would pick up again at line 574. There are in general two ways in which a Beginning may be presented. It may be presented chronologically or it may be presented in flash back. This is not strictly a flash-back Beginning as I shall point out later in a discussion of a story which is strictly of that type. This is a story in which the Beginning is presented out of chronological order, in that the opening meeting is used to present an important and unusual condition without presenting the narrative problem which emerges as a result of that condition and which unifies the whole story.

What is particularly interesting about this special arrangement is that Mr. Cobb was able to utilize the laws of interest, which are that a meeting is interesting or a condition is interesting in so far as it is important or unusual, and that out of the important or unusual conditions from which he had to choose Mr. Cobb chose unerringly that one which would best hold the interest of the reader. There is another condition which he might have chosen, and that is the condition confronting Mr. Trimm when he realized that the train was being wrecked. But this would not have helped nearly so much as the one Mr. Cobb chose because it was unusual in a way demanding explanation. The one that he did choose, that Mr. Trimm was taking a trip to Sing Sing, was one which might have happened to anybody at any time without very much explanation being necessary to justify it. Besides being important and

142

unusual it was plausible. The other condition would have required a great deal of explanation in order to justify its presentation, and its effect would have been defeated.

Especially illuminating for the student of creative technique is that there are here presented two kinds of conditions. One of these is the one presented in the first 31 lines. This is a *passive* condition and one to which the response must be essentially either passive or in terms of a purpose emerging. It cannot be a response in terms of an interchange, because the passive condition cannot fight. The only possible way in which Mr. Trimm can respond to this stimulus is by reflection. It must be inactive response. It may grow into a purpose, but it cannot grow into an interchange until there is first a purpose apparent. On the other hand, if you will turn to line 1454 in the Body of the story, you will see that at the close of this scene or attempt of Mr. Trimm to burn off his hand-cuffs, a new condition has arisen, and his response to this is in terms of a new purpose projecting an interchange, that is to say, there is an *active* condition to which he is responding, and that active condition actually gives him battle just as if it were an active opponent.

Another thing which makes this Beginning exceedingly worth studying is that throughout the interchanges which make up the Beginning there is a narrative thread running. It is as if a story were being carried along by the main narrative question as to whether or not Mr. Trimm could keep the handcuffs hidden. His attempts unify the interchanges which make up the Beginning although we do not know at that time the main narrative question of the story. From the moment on line 253 when Meyers says, "Well, all ready," until the moment on line 625, when Meyers leaves for the water cooler, the reader is interested in the attempt of Mr. Trimm to keep the handcuffs hidden, and to keep his condition of being handcuffed hidden from the crowd. The technical lesson to be learned from the Beginning of this story is, that if the main narrative question cannot soon be made to emerge, there must be substituted for it some other kind of interest, preferably a narrative interest in some other question than the main narrative question. If there is not narrative interest there must be dramatic interest which comes from conflict and the promise of conflict, or of difficulty, or of disaster, all of which are present in this Beginning.

The Body of this story is again an excellent example of the effectiveness of interchanges which result in hindrances. The

Body of this story occupies lines 1142 to 2227, and is composed of nine attempts or scenes. The central narrative unity given to the story by its main narrative question ties these attempts very tightly together, so that at the close of each one we are aware of definite hindrances, either dramatic or narrative, to the main narrative question. At the close of the sixth scene or attempt, on lines 1570 to 1652 the hindrance is not only narrative but dramatic, because we see in it the threat of a possible opponent in the blacksmith who proves to be the sheriff. Also at the close of the encounter with the tramp, on line 2045, we find that there is again a dramatic hindrance because a new difficulty has arisen which increases that possibility of disaster should Mr. Trimm not escape. He is not only an escaped convict but a murderer as well.

There is a dramatic intensity in this story, which was not apparent in the other stories, and it comes from the importance of the attempts. The main narrative question is both unusual and important because a great deal depends upon it, and we find ourselves, because of the characterization which the author has given to Mr. Trimm in the Beginning of the story, hoping that he will not succeed. As readers, we feel ourselves quite pleased whenever there occurs a hindrance in the main narrative purpose. The Body of this story is therefore both dramatically and narratively interesting. It is both well plotted and well presented.

The Ending occupying lines 2228 to 2237 answers the question very clearly. Mr. Trimm has succeeded in finding someone who will take the handcuffs off him, because the Chief of Police of Westfield is caused to say, "Come in and lemme get them irons off of you." We find in this story the same structural units that we have found in the others, and we find also present the ironic significance in the reversal of the main narrative purpose or situation which occurred in the "Soapy" story, *The Cop and the Anthem*. Mr. Trimm on achieving his object, no longer considers it as important as getting something to eat.

The Beginning of this story will repay analysis because it illustrates so clearly the method by which other interest may be substituted for the main narrative interest which comes from the knowledge on the part of the reader of a main narrative question.

BEGINNING	Initial Condition and Actor's central purpose are both presented through medium of a single dramatic scene.	Scene. Jason Terwilliger and his uncle. Offered $5,000 and his debts paid, Jason agrees to kill Jake Finch, who is represented as a very strong man.	1–178	Main Plot Crises become apparent as scene progresses. Difficulty, Opposition, and Disaster are all implied. Main Narrative Question is "Can Jason succeed in killing Jake Finch?"
BODY	Series of attempts of Main Actor to achieve his purpose, despite difficulties in his way.	Scene. Jason vs. Craving for drink which will defeat his purpose, since success can come only from fitness. Result. Face drawn with suffering.	179–257	Hindrance.
		Scene. Jason and Captain of *Lorelei*. Conquers drink.	258–280	Furtherance.
		(5th step. Effect is to make him feel that he cannot bring himself to point of killing man.)	281–307	Disaster threatens purpose. Dramatic Hindrance
		Interchange. Jason and Frisco Purdy. Jason discovers meaning of Jake Finch. Is offered drink.	308–332	
ENDING	Conclusive Act.	Refuses Drink.	333	Answer to Main Narrative Question is "Yes."

146

SUNK

BY GEORGE F. WORTS

I HAVE included this story for any number of reasons—all good.
It is in every respect a first rate story.   After you have read it you
will see that my selection of it is justified.

CASE No. 6

SUNK

BY GEORGE F. WORTS

By permission of Mr. Worts and the Editor of Collier's.

1 Jeffery Terwilliger closed the
2 door of his library and shot the
3 heavy bronze bolt against pos-
4 sible intrusion. He went from
5 window to window, making sure
6 that each shade was drawn to
7 the bottom. He moved over the
8 thick rugs with the ponderous
9 felicity of an aged pelican. When
10 the arrangements of the amber-
11 lighted room were to his liking
12 he walked to the walnut desk,
13 selected a blond cigar from the
14 silver humidor, lighted it, puffed
15 at it with slow deliberation and
16 wheeled upon his nephew Jason,
17 who lay sprawled in a gray plush
18 chair.

19 The young man returned his
20 hard, disapproving stare with
21 glassy hopefulness. He was
22 unshaven, his lips were dry and
23 cracked, his eyes stained and
24 rimmed with red, his clothing
25 rumpled. His pallor and his
26 shakiness were even more
27 obvious.

28 "I told you," said his uncle
29 harshly, "never to enter this
30 house again."

31 The young man nodded sullen-
32 ly. "I wouldn't be here if it
33 wasn't necessary. I've got to
34 have two thousand dollars."

35 "Jason, I've given you thou-
36 sands of dollars, and I'm not
37 going to give you any more.
38 You aren't worth it. I've spent
39 my life making the name Ter-
40 williger stand for industry and
41 decency and you've spent yours
42 making it stand for every kind of
43 dissipation. I won't be black-
44 mailed any longer. When I was
45 your age——"

46 "You were pearl poaching in
47 the South Seas," his nephew
48 snorted.

49 "That's a lie! Every dollar I
50 took out of the South Seas was
51 an honest dollar. I worked hard
52 for it. I didn't lean on anyone.
53 At your age I was a man. And
54 you—you've leaned on me ever
55 since you were expelled from
56 college. But you aren't going
57 to lean on me any more."

58 "You've got to help me," his
59 nephew said desperately. "If I
60 can't get my hands on two

61 thousand dollars by to-morrow
62 noon——"

63 "You won't get it from me,"
64 the old man snarled. "God, but
65 you've sunk low. Do you realize
66 you've utterly ruined your life
67 and you're not yet twenty-five?
68 You haven't drawn a sober
69 breath in the past four years."

70 "I'll promise to straighten
71 up."

72 "You've promised that a
73 dozen times. You're lost!"

74 The young man sighed
75 wearily. "Oh, I admit it. I'm
76 sunk."

77 "You've sunk so low that
78 you'd kill me for my money if
79 you thought you wouldn't be
80 caught!"

81 His nephew nodded. "I
82 might."

83 Jeffery Terwilliger stared at
84 him. "I believe it. I believe
85 you've reached the stage where
86 you'd kill for money. Look
87 here! Would you undertake to
88 kill a man for money?"

89 The Terwilliger library be-
90 came terribly still. The old
91 man was standing with his legs
92 apart, his body slightly bent,
93 the cigar half raised to his
94 mouth—a frozen gesture. His
95 nephew was clutching the gray
96 plush arms of the chair.

97 "How much?"

98 "Your debts and—five thou-
99 sand dollars!"

100 "For that price I would kill
101 any man alive."

102 "Understand me. I'm not
joking. I'm offering you a sum 103
of money to kill a man." 104

"I heard you. Who is the 105
man?" 106

Jeffery Terwilliger sank back 107
against the walnut desk and 108
wiped his forehead with a large 109
silk handkerchief. 110

"I didn't think you'd be so 111
willing. I didn't think you'd 112
sunk so low. Or—or are you 113
just drunk?" 114

"I am thinking as clearly as 115
you are. You're always talking 116
about the proud Terwilliger 117
name. Blood is thicker than 118
water! I'll kill your man! Who 119
is he?" 120

His uncle glared. "What 121
difference does it make? As far 122
as you're concerned, he's any 123
man. You will be erasing a— 124
a number. Do you grasp what 125
I mean? You do not know 126
whether he is old, young, tall, 127
short, fat, thin, blond, brunette, 128
white, or black. His name 129
happens to be Jake Finch. He 130
lives on the island of Paulota, 131
which is approximately a five 132
weeks' sail from Papeete. My 133
old schooner, the *Lorelei*, is lying 134
in Papeete harbor. The captain 135
will be ready for you. At Paulota 136
you will look up a trader named 137
Purdy. Purdy will tell you 138
where to find Jake Finch. You 139
can trust Purdy. He knows and 140
he'll help." 141

Jason Terwilliger squinted 142
shrewdly at his uncle. 143

"Let me get this straight. I 144

go to Papeete, board your schooner and sail to the island of Paulota. I find there a trader named Purdy."

"Frisco Purdy."

"All right. I ask Frisco Purdy where to find Jake Finch. Upon finding Jake Finch, I kill him. It sounds easy."

"He is a strong man, a powerful man—but not more powerful than you used to be."

"But he won't know I'm going to kill him. Perhaps I'd better shoot him in the back."

"You can decide the details for yourself. Will you go?"

"I will go."

"Very well. I'll arrange for your passage. Here is the revolver I want you to use. If you will give me the list, I will pay your debts in the morning."

"And the five thousand?"

"Will be here when you return."

"How'll you know I've done the job?"

"It will be written on your face," the old man said. "Remember: We Terwilligers have always been famous for two traits: keeping our promises intact and our mouths shut."

Two days out of San Francisco, Jason aroused himself from the drunken stupor in which he had lain, fully dressed, since the steamer sailed. It was night. He switched on the stateroom light and found, close to his hand on the bunk, the revolver.

It was not a slim, gentlemanly revolver; it was blunt and thick, the kind that brutes carry for short-range killing. It was a murderer's revolver.

He grasped it by the butt and stood up, with his back against the closed door. At the other end of the stateroom, perhaps ten feet away, was a washstand. There was a water tank above it and a narrow cupboard beneath. With these accessories it was about as high and as wide as a man of average size.

Jason lifted the revolver and aimed it at the washstand. The washstand was blurred. His hand was shaking. He could not steady it. If he pulled the trigger, he would probably miss the washstand. In his present condition, Jake Finch could kill him before he could kill Jake Finch.

He placed the revolver in his suit case, closed the lid and hastened on deck. It was cocktail hour, and the smokeroom was crowded. Licking his burning lips, Jason elbowed through the crowd toward the bar.

But before he reached the bar the image of the revolver shaking in his hand entered his mind. He dared not drink. He must prepare himself for the encounter with Jake Finch!

He paced the deck until midnight, fighting away a thirst that fairly gnawed at his throat. Until morning he tossed, sleepless, in his bunk. But when the

229 desire for drink became most
230 insistent the shaking revolver
231 and the blurred washstand would
232 come to his mind. Each time
233 this vision brought him up
234 sharply; each time it forced him
235 to realize that his hand must be
236 steady and his brain alert and
237 clear to carry things off with-
238 out consequences fatal to him-
239 self.

240 He endured, in the following
241 week, satanic torments. His
242 throat burned for liquor; his
243 system ached for it; but he
244 determinedly resisted the crav-
245 ing. Meanwhile a murderous
246 hatred of his uncle was growing
247 in him. His uncle was a schem-
248 ing Midas; his uncle had robbed
249 him of the little that had
250 remained of his manhood.

251 When Jason debarked in Pa-
252 peete he had had nothing
253 stronger than coffee to drink
254 since that day when he awoke
255 and found the revolver beside
256 him. And his face was drawn
257 with suffering.

258 He transferred his belongings
259 to the *Lorelei*, and the *Lorelei*
260 went out to sea with the tide
261 that afternoon. Her captain
262 was an old man; incommunica-
263 tive and almost deaf. He told
264 Jason that the schooner was
265 short-handed; that he would
266 welcome Jason's help. And
267 Jason assented with eagerness.
268 He wanted to work, to exhaust
269 himself so that he could sleep
270 again; wanted to strengthen his

271 body for the encounter with Jake
272 Finch.

273 At dinner the captain placed
274 a bottle of whisky on the table;
275 poured himself a drink and
276 raised his eyes to Jason's face.
277 There was a perceptible interval
278 between the unspoken question
279 and Jason's answer.

280 "No," said Jason.

281 The days following were
282 happy for him, but many of the
283 nights were sleepless. The
284 revolver no longer shook when
285 he gripped and aimed it. He
286 practiced on empty bottles
287 tossed overboard, and his
288 marksmanship was good—good
289 enough. He had come to picture
290 Jake Finch as an old man,
291 a hermit; a man whose face
292 haunted him in the darkness
293 of his cabin with an eerie resem-
294 blance to his uncle's, a face whose
295 every line betrayed contempt.

296 As each day drew him nearer
297 to the deed that he had promised
298 to commit, as his health im-
299 proved and his brain cleared,
300 Jason's rebellion grew. He
301 could not have been that
302 creature who had bargained to
303 kill a man.

304 And when Jason went ashore
305 in Paulota he was sick with
306 terror. He could not kill that
307 man. He could not!

308 Three human derelicts on the
309 wharf directed him to Frisco
310 Purdy's zinc-roofed bungalow.
311 And on the veranda he found
312 him—a white-bearded old man

313 with twinkling young eyes, who
314 blinked at him and nodded
315 incessantly as they talked.
316   "Jake Finch?" the trader re-
317 peated. "There've been dozens
318 of Jake Finches here. Jake
319 Finch is the standing joke of
320 Paulota, and has been for a half
321 century or better. Jake Finch
322 is the name we give to beach
323 combers—the name we give to
324 any man who doesn't amount
325 to a damn. There's three of
326 them down on the dock now—
327 three Jake Finches. Hold on!
328 Where you going?"
329   "I've got to be getting a-
330 board."
331   "But you'll stay long enough
332 to have a drink!"
333   "No; I don't drink."

The Analysis

The story *Sunk* was first printed in *Collier's* as a "Short-Short-Story." My first interest in it centered in the Ending because it carried over the tradition of the surprise Ending. It was an extremely clever story,—the sort of idea which comes very, very seldom to a writer, and which he seizes upon with joy. But the more I examined this story the more I became impressed with the knowledge of craftsmanship possessed by the writer. Interesting as it is, as a model of compression, it is still more interesting to students of the modern short-story form in showing its author's mastery of the laws of interest. The reader's attention is gained at once. His curiosity and expectancy are aroused. He is anxious to know more about the chief actor, about the problem confronting that actor, the promised encounter, and the actor's solution of the main narrative problem. The structural divisions of Beginning, Body, and Ending are very clearly defined. Lines 1 to 178 make up the Beginning. Lines 179 to 332 constitute the Body. Line 333 forms the Ending. This story is a story of accomplishment. The feat to be accomplished is the killing of Jake Finch by Jason Terwilliger. The main narrative question raised in the Beginning of the story is, "Can Jason Terwilliger succeed in killing Jake Finch?" The answer to the main narrative question, contained in the result of Jason's meeting with Frisco Purdy, is "Yes." The Conclusive Act of the actor by which the reader is made aware of this result is Jason's statement to Frisco Purdy, "No, I don't drink," on line 333.

In the unexpectedness of its dénouement, this story has much of the quality which is so widely associated with the late O. Henry. Just as superficial observers and critics have long been apt to disregard the other artistic qualities of O. Henry in their concentration upon his ability to achieve a surprise Ending, so they will be likely to overlook Mr. Worts's accomplishment in writing the Beginning of *Sunk*.

The Beginning of this story alone would have justified me in reprinting the story. No student of craftsmanship need feel that he is too far advanced to study this Beginning with profit.

The Beginning of every story has one basic purpose. It is to lay before the reader the main narrative problem of the story together with the necessary explanatory matter. A narrative situation, that is, something to be accomplished, is interesting in proportion as it is important or unusual. This narrative situation is both. There is required, however, much more than the mere statement or the mere presentation of the narrative problem, to make up a good Beginning. The explanatory matter required to elucidate that problem must also be laid before the reader. Yet, whether problem or explanatory matter, the material of the Beginning is intended to appeal to the curiosity of the reader and to satisfy that curiosity to the extent of giving him the information which will enable him to follow the story proper without confusion. To give the necessary information, and to render it interestingly and plausibly, is the purpose of every Beginning.

From an examination of the story *The Escape of Mr. Trimm* you learned that as long as the minor narrative interest is sustained it is not essential, although it is desireable, that the main narrative question shall emerge. Therefore, in order to delay the main narrative question, and still to achieve narrative interest, we must introduce a minor narrative question. In this case, the Beginning is presented in a single scene, which has its own minor narrative question, which comes in the first thirty-four lines. It is, "Can Jason Terwilliger succeed in securing $2,000 from his uncle?" This minor narrative question is made to hold the interest until the main crisis is reached on line 119, and in the approximate 400 words contained in those 86 lines from line 34 to 119, Mr. Worts compresses all the information which is needed for his story. In presenting the information leading to the major crisis, Mr. Worts utilizes his knowledge of the laws of interest by presenting the interchange which leads to the crisis as a scene rather than an episode. Thus the reader's interest in the outcome of the clash enables the writer to prolong the dramatic meeting sufficiently to introduce all the explanatory matter for the whole story. The gain from this method is extraordinary. The slow and dull story is ordinarily made so by a surplusage of explanatory matter in the presentation of each minor narrative question. The reader, interested in the outcome of the main narrative question, wants to hurry along. He is prevented from doing so by having to wade through explanatory matter in each scene. Mr. Worts obviates this by presenting all of his explanatory matter in a single scene in the Beginning of the story. When the interchanges or meetings which make up the Body of the story are presented, they are enabled to move right along without any clogging by explanatory matter.

Sunk is a story which will repay analysis by students of the short-story form. The scenic presentation of the Beginning always ensures interest provided always that at the close of each scene there is apparent either a main narrative question or a dramatic crisis consisting of the promise of conflict, or difficulty, or disaster in the meetings or interchanges which are foreshadowed.

Apart from the Beginning there was another reason for including this story. It is in the handling of that portion of the story which is the Body, and which contains the conflict which was foreshadowed in the Beginning, of Jason Terwilliger's attempt to overcome a difficulty which exists, and which must be removed before he can achieve his objective. Lines 179 to 257 contain his first attempt, and it is actually a scene of man against inner man, which is the craving for drink opposed to his desire to fit himself physically for the task he has accepted. It ends in a hindrance, because it shows his face drawn with suffering, which indicates that he is not any nearer to success than he was before. Lines 258 to 280 are an interchange between Jason and the captain of the *Lorelei*, which concludes with a crisis of furtherance on line 280 when he says, "no"—that he will not take a drink. But this is instantly followed by a dramatic hindrance which is the fifth step of that scene, on lines 281 to 307, when he feels that his task is impossible. This is the big moment of the story when disaster threatens the purpose, and it has that essential quality of drama which is the feeling on the part of the reader that whichever action Jason Terwilliger takes he will regret it. It is this dramatic handling of the crisis in the Body of this story which makes the Body worth studying by students of craftsmanship.

The Ending of this story speaks for itself. It has that quality of dramatic suddenness which leaves the reader more or less breathless. It is a complete surprise, and yet upon a thorough examination of all that went before, the reader feels that the author did not in any way cheat him; that personality in Jason Terwilliger which is Jake Finch has been definitely killed by him when, on being asked to take a drink, he says, "No."

This story is an extremely interesting story to be considered in comparison with two others: *Paradise Island* by Will Payne, and *Jetsam* by John Russell. After you have read those I shall discuss each one and point out the resemblances in the material and the differences in the treatment. One lesson which it is the function of this volume to point out is that the same material can be treated by a number of different writers in such a way that we get a number of different stories. But apart from these other stories the story *Sunk* is in itself very much worth your consideration because it illustrates a perfect Beginning from the point of view of craftsmanship.

BEGINNING	Main Actor's central purpose is apparent at once.	Meeting. Dwyer and Ditch.	1– 5	Main Narratve Question emerges. "Can Dwyer kill a man?"
		Meeting. Dwyer and Setting.	6– 111	Main purpose reiterated.
		Interchange. Dwyer and Wife.	112– 171	Main purpose reiterated.
	Initial Condition is then presented by taking the reader back.	Flash-back Scene. Langley and Dwyer. Langley gives Dwyer option of transferring Paradise Island management to a committee or of being exposed. Dwyer and Langley agree to meet that evening, later.	172– 848	The Explanatory Matter is laid before the reader, and he becomes aware of the dramatic plot crises *after* he is aware of the narrative crisis which projects the main Narrative Question of the story.
		(5th Step.) Effect of interchange upon actors is that Dwyer, reflecting, comes to the ditch.	849–1061	
BODY	The only attempt is shown.	Interchange. Dwyer and Langley. Dwyer learns that Langley is protected by information left with his chief. This presents a new condition.	1062–1268	There are no Plot Crises in the Body. At the close of the single interchange comes the Conclusive Act.
ENDING	Conclusive Act, and Sequel	Dwyer abandons his purpose.	1269–1276	The Main Narrative Question is answered "No."

PARADISE ISLAND

BY WILL PAYNE

Wherever possible I have chosen parallel stories, in order that students of narrative craftsmanship may see that the same essential situation may be developed in different ways by different writers.

Paradise Island contains the same main narrative problem as *Sunk.* They are both stories of a man who sets out to kill another man.

The chief reason, however, for including this story in the volume is that it is a very interesting example of the "flash-back" type of Beginning. A writer's greatest forward step in the mastery of craftsmanship comes when he learns how to write the "Flash-back" type of Beginning.

CASE No. 7

"PARADISE ISLAND"

BY WILL PAYNE

1 Dwyer halted at the ditch—
2 abruptly, as though an invisible
3 hand had seized his arm. An
4 idea rang in his brain: This
5 would be the place to kill a man.
6 A gully ran through here.
7 But now that Palm Bluff was
8 becoming a city, that would not
9 answer, so they were deepening
10 it and laying a big iron drainage
11 pipe along the bottom, to be
12 covered with earth when the
13 job was finished, leaving the
14 surface of the ground level. At
15 this point the excavation was
16 more than twenty feet deep,
17 sheathed with pine plank to
18 hold the sandy soil. A single
19 plank had been laid across the
20 top bridgewise. An uncon-
21 nected segment of the new pipe,
22 with a thick iron collar on the
23 end, stuck up through muddy
24 water in the bottom of the cut,
25 and some tools.
26 Overhead, a seamless loose
27 gray fleece exuded warm mist.
28 One could hardly say it rained;
29 but there was a slow, intermit-
30 tent drip of water from the leaves.

31 Coming out of doors, one's
32 hands, face and clothing at once
33 grew moist. This plank over
34 the ditch was wet. A man
35 might easily slip on it.
36 It was the outskirts of town.
37 Only Dwyer's smart new house
38 and three or four humble older
39 ones lay to the north. Beyond
40 them the level ground was still
41 overgrown with tall Southern
42 pine and clumps of palmetto,
43 dissolving into foggy obscurity
44 at no great distance. Only
45 fifty yards to the west the
46 ground broke down into a rag-
47 ged bluff, its crown thirty feet
48 or so above the sea, which
49 seemed to have stopped and to
50 lie gray, motionless, waiting for
51 something to happen. On that
52 side the picture ended indefi-
53 nitely in a long, darker smudge
54 formerly called John's Key, but
55 now, thanks to Dwyer, much
56 known as Paradise Island. It
57 was only two-thirds of a mile
58 offshore, but so vague that a
59 stranger might easily have mis-
60 taken if for the extended trail

61 of smoke from a Gulf steamer.
62 And this general blur—still
63 and vague, but shut in—seemed
64 to sanction the idea which had
65 exploded in Dwyer's mind; seem-
66 ed to blindfold the world and
67 hold its ears for him. He put
68 up his hand and wiped perspira-
69 tion from his brow. But he
70 shouldn't be stopping here. In
71 fact he had stopped only half
72 a second, hardly missing a step.
73 He set his muddy shoe on the
74 wet plank and passed over, strid-
75 ing toward his new house.

76 The shoe was muddy because
77 the sidewalk had been torn up
78 here for the ditch digging.
79 Otherwise it was a smart article
80 of white canvas and black
81 leather. His fine wool stockings
82 had a pattern worked in the
83 tops. There was an embossed
84 monogram on his silver belt
85 buckle. He wore a silk shirt and
86 belted jacket. Such clothes
87 were becoming to his tall, well-
88 made figure. In profile he
89 would have adorned a coin, in
90 spite of his bald head—for
91 which, indeed, his neatly point-
92 ed, curly golden beard seemed
93 to compensate; but his face was
94 much too narrow, as though it
95 had been squeezed in a press,
96 bringing his eyes close together.
97 On first acquaintance the dis-
98 parity between profile and full
99 face was fairly disconcerting, as
100 though he had two faces, and
101 they were even of different ages.
102 There was a great turmoil

within, and a goneness as though 103
a blow in the stomach had taken 104
his wind. Assuredly he had 105
never imagined himself as a 106
murderer. The unspoken word 107
set his heart to quaking furiously 108
now. But he had a baffled feel- 109
ing of the thing's being thrust 110
into his hands—no other way. 111

The new house, of hollow tile 112
and stucco, in Spanish style, had 113
four bedrooms and three baths. 114
The local newspaper, in describ- 115
ing the plans and referring from 116
time to time to the progress of 117
the structure, had dwelt upon 118
the three baths as a crowning 119
distinction. The little blue-tiled 120
sun parlor looked out upon the 121
Gulf and contained a broad 122
lounge with many bright-colored 123
cushions. Mrs. Dwyer, in an 124
embroidered blue silk wrapper, 125
reclined upon it, reading a love 126
story in a magazine. Hearing 127
his step, she hid the box of candy 128
under the cushions. Fat was 129
her arch enemy—a hundred and 130
sixty, she confessed to him; but 131
the bathroom scales said a hun- 132
dred and seventy-four, over 133
which she secretly wept a little 134
in vexation and self-pity. She 135
was a very fair woman, with 136
ash-blond hair and big baby- 137
blue eyes and a beautiful skin. 138
She smiled at her husband as 139
he stepped in, and hid a yawn 140
with a jeweled hand, mention- 141
ing that on such a miserable 142
day it hadn't seemed worth 143
while to dress. He told her 144

that he wouldn't be home for dinner—had to meet some St. Petersburg men; they'd talk over their business while they ate in a private room at the hotel; but he expected to return early.

"Oh, by the way, Langley'll be here to see me at half past nine. Said he'd wait if I wasn't home by that time. I expect to be here by then, but it may be a little later. Have him wait. I won't be long."

Surely that was a very simple message to leave with one's wife; yet he found himself stammering over it, scant of breath, his heart hammering at his ribs. He looked away lest she see something in his eyes. But she evidently saw nothing, for the next instant her voice came indolently to his ears with a laugh:

"He's such a funny little mouse of a man! I ought to have a doll for him to play with."

No doubt Langley had reminded other people of a mouse. His hair and tiny, ineffectual mustache were dust-colored. He wore large gold-bowed spectacles, and walked with a slight round-shouldered stoop, as though apologizing for his five feet three inches of height. His wrinkled clothes, not exactly shabby, carried out the general effect of insignificance.

Trudging down Seaview Avenue at four o'clock of this afternoon, with a big white envelope in the pocket of his flapping coat, thumb and forefinger absently pecking at the small mustache, he had evidently been lost in thought, and seemed vaguely startled at finding himself in front of an office which, on this overcast day, was flooded with electric light—quite the smartest office in town, with seagreen rugs on the floor, orange-colored wicker chairs and settees and pictures on the walls. The most conspicuous of them, twenty feet long by four high, was brilliantly illuminated from above and showed a long, narrow, green island in a varnished blue sea. In the foreground stood an immensely long hotel, with towers, minarets and banners, and a huge circular casino built out over the water. A boulevard ran along the beach. Back of it all over the island, roofs, and cornices of villas and cottages peeked out of embowering leafage.

The legend under the picture said "Paradise Island," and in much more modest letters, "As it will appear when improvements are completed." Several people were there, but no one paid any attention to Langley as he ambled through to a smaller room, where a dark, handsome young woman, after stepping back to inquire, said that Mr. Dwyer would see him in a few minutes; then openly mothered him into a wicker chair, where he could wait comfortably. He was flustered and blushing slightly; there had been moments when he had a harrowing prevision that this vigorous smiling Miss Hanson was going to take him into her lap and rock him. But although she made him nervous he liked her too.

Two men came out from the inner office, talking together as they walked past. A buzzer sounded on Miss Hanson's desk and she turned to Langley with a bright, encouraging nod to signify that he might go in.

He drew a quick breath, wet his lips and got up, his heart pounding. Nevertheless, pushing open the door to the inner room, he could not help giving a woodeny smile, nor the silly gesture of raising thumb and forefinger to peck at his mustache. Athletic Dwyer, in smart golf clothes, stood up genially to shake hands, and hospitably indicated a vacant chair by the desk. Being seated, Langley fumbled in getting the big envelope out of his pocket and swallowed and cleared his throat.

"Mr. Dwyer, I've got some newspaper clippings here. They came in this afternoon's mail. I'd like you to glance them over."

Looking owlish for all the world, with his round pale eyes staring behind gold-bowed spectacles, he pushed the envelope across the desk.

Dwyer did not take the envelope immediately. Instead he looked at his young caller in a sudden arrest and astonishment. For there was something in Langley's embarrassed air— well, as though a mouse had abruptly leveled a gun at one's head. Langley's eyes fell before the other man's concentrated, questioning gaze, he moistened his lips and mechanically turned his faded straw hat in his lap. Very soberly, then, Dwyer picked up the envelope, noting at a glance that its upper left-hand corner bore the return card of a Boston newspaper. It bulged with soft contents that seemed to have been hastily stuffed in. When he shook it a dozen newspaper clippings fell out, and a sheet of coarse paper on which was hastily scrawled with lead pencil:

Dr. Jim: Here's the graveyard. Be sure to send it back. Don't know what became of D. Will inquire and let you know. Yrs.

BEN.

Dwyer knew that in newspaper office slang "graveyard" meant the file in which all sorts of contemporaneous biographical material was kept, so that if Peter J. Filkins, of Essex, Massachusetts, came into a fortune or broke his neck or got nominated for Congress or otherwise burst into print, a reporter could at

313 once lay hands upon items with
314 which to embellish the story.
315 He merely glanced at the clip-
316 pings, being already quite aware
317 of their purport.
318 From them it appeared that,
319 not long after the war, one
320 Dwyer, doing business under
321 the firm name of E. Pellman
322 Dwyer & Co., had been arrested
323 on a charge of tempting small
324 investors to part with their
325 Liberty Bonds and savings-bank
326 balances in order to participate
327 in vast, mysterious and fab-
328 ulously profitable operations in
329 foreign exchange. But the story,
330 as disclosed by the clippings,
331 ended in mid-air. There was the
332 man's arrest and the charges
333 against him, with names of some
334 of the plucked dupes; then his
335 reply, which consisted of a
336 general denial, and the giving
337 of bail. Small items recorded
338 various postponements of the
339 hearing. But whether or not
340 the man had been brought to
341 trial did not appear.
342 Both Langley and Dwyer
343 knew that at the period covered
344 by these clippings a much more
345 extensive and spectacular swin-
346 dle, conducted by a citizen of
347 foreign birth, was absorbing the
348 attention of the public and of
349 the newspapers, so that this
350 Dwyer case was only a sort of
351 negligible side show. Also, not
352 long afterward, there were excit-
353 ing charges of blackmail and
354 bribery in connection with the

355 administration of justice in
356 Boston. It seemed that in the
357 bigger mess Dwyer had been
358 lost sight of.
359 "I was in Boston at the time—
360 on the *Tribune*," said Langley.
361 "I never saw Dwyer, but we
362 published his picture, I'd fairly
363 forgotten all about it, as you
364 might say. Down here I didn't
365 think anything in particular
366 about your name being Dwyer
367 too—no connection occurred to
368 me. Then the other day"—he
369 hesitated an instant, painfully
370 —"a lady was saying that Mrs.
371 Dwyer spoke of having lived in
372 Boston. Somehow it flashed
373 over me. The same initials,
374 you see, and something about
375 the picture coming back to my
376 mind. Of course you didn't
377 have a beard then, and had a
378 full head of hair. It flashed
379 over me. Well, I was going up
380 to Tampa next day. I sent a
381 wire from there to my friend."
382 He nodded toward the scrawled
383 note. "I asked him to send me
384 what he had, since 1919, on E.
385 Pellman Dwyer. Seems he
386 didn't understand me very well
387 —just sent me on the old stuff
388 in the graveyard. That's how
389 this happened."
390 Haltingly, and in a toneless
391 sort of voice, he made the state-
392 ment; yet with an astonishing
393 air of candor, too, as though, as
394 a matter of course, Mr. Dwyer
395 would understand that he was
396 obliged to find out about his

397 Boston antecedents and come
398 and tell him of the discovery.
399 That candid air really dis-
400 concerted the large man behind
401 the desk.

402 "Why are you showing me
403 these things?" he asked abruptly.

404 Langley elevated his dust-
405 colored eyebrows in faint sur-
406 prise and replied monotonously,
407 "To ask whether you are the
408 same man."

409 Dwyer felt that he ought to be
410 angry, but in a way it was so
411 ridiculous that one couldn't be.

412 "I am not the same man,"
413 he said promptly. "That was
414 my cousin. His first name is
415 Edward."

416 His own first name, as known
417 in Palm Bluff, was Elihu—Elihu
418 P. Dwyer. But it rarely found
419 its way into print. The name
420 that appeared in bold type in all
421 advertisements of Paradise Isl-
422 and was George Ingram & Co.
423 There was a George Ingram,
424 indefinitely understood to be a
425 wealthy, retired capitalist of
426 New York. Twice or thrice he
427 had appeared in Palm Bluff,
428 vanishing again after a week or
429 so. Dwyer was only the "Co.,"
430 and Langley knew that he had
431 privately asked the local news-
432 paper to keep his name out of
433 print, lest Mr. Ingram, who was
434 furnishing most of the capital,
435 should become jealous of a mere
436 lieutenant.

437 With a mild and owlish in-
438 nocence, Langley asked, "Where
439 were you at this time, Mr.
440 Dwyer—at the time this thing
441 happened in Boston?"

442 Dwyer felt something soft and
443 weak but like a leech, not to be
444 shaken off. For the first time
445 he spoke sharply.

446 "See here, Langley, you know
447 what I've done. I've put Palm
448 Bluff on the map. When I came
449 here fifteen months ago this
450 town was dead as a door nail—
451 four thousand inhabitants.
452 That's as far as it had got in
453 thirty years. And that's about
454 as far as it would get in the
455 next thirty." His voice showed
456 anger. "Everybody's running
457 around in circles now barking
458 over the boom in real estate.
459 They know what the boom's
460 done for Miami and Palm Beach
461 and St. Petersburg and other
462 places. A lot of 'em talk as
463 though it just happened in
464 Palm Bluff. But I brought it
465 here! I started it and I've kept
466 it going!"

467 Langley gravely nodded.

468 "I know you did, Mr. Dwyer.
469 I've always said so. Mr.
470 Kendrick says so, too."

471 Dwyer caught at the idea
472 which that name suggested, de-
473 manding, "What does Kendrick
474 know about this?"

475 "He doesn't know anything
476 about it," Langley replied in
477 that monotonous and oddly dis-
478 concerting manner. "He's out
479 of town today. You see, I
480 wasn't expecting an answer from

481 Boston so soon, and I thought
482 when it did come it would tell
483 more about the case—how it
484 ended. So I didn't say any-
485 thing to him—till I knew more,
486 you understand." He gave a
487 little twist to his mustache.
488 "And then, when this came in,
489 I thought I better ask you."
490 Again—obscurely—Dwyer
491 wanted to laugh because it was
492 ridiculous. But he went on with
493 his own statement:
494 "Well, take your newspaper.
495 You know what it was when I
496 came here—ten or twelve pages
497 once a week; not exactly run-
498 ning over with profits. Now
499 you're printing fourteen and six-
500 teen pages twice a week—talking
501 about changing it over to a daily
502 —putting up a new building. I
503 did that, Langley. Same way
504 with other things here. It's
505 the push I gave that started 'em
506 all up."
507 Langley would not have
508 denied it. The newspaper had
509 been launched twenty-five years
510 before, a feeble weekly bantling,
511 mostly patent insides, in a ram-
512 shackle village. The trampish
513 printer who did the launching
514 had a sense of humor, for he
515 called his venture the *Palm Leaf*
516 *Fan*. But he hadn't much else.
517 There had been various changes
518 of ownership. Meanwhile Palm
519 Bluff grew in leisurely fashion
520 —brick pavements, cement side-
521 walks, electric lights, four thou-
522 sand inhabitants. Lewis Kend-

523 rick bought the *Fan*. And
524 progress might have continued
525 in that same leisurely fashion if
526 this mysterious elixir of bloom
527 had not been injected into the
528 veins of the community. Now
529 the most conspicuous feature of
530 each semiweekly edition of the
531 *Fan* was a double-page advertise-
532 ment of Paradise Island, stock
533 in which might be purchased of
534 George Ingram & Co. at only
535 $8.75 a share—if one acted
536 quickly, before the price ad-
537 vanced. Every advertisement
538 reminded the hesitant reader
539 what fortunes had been reaped
540 by sagacious investors in Miami,
541 Palm Beach, St. Petersburg, Los
542 Angeles, New York. Ownership
543 of soil was the road to wealth!
544 George Ingram & Co. advertised
545 Paradise Island not only at home
546 but in other Florida towns
547 where Northern tourists with
548 money to invest congregated,
549 and even in some Northern
550 cities. That, undoubtedly, had
551 touched off the boom at Palm
552 Bluff.
553 "Haven't you an interest in
554 the *Fan?*" Dwyer asked, re-
555 membering something to that
556 effect.
557 "I have three thousand dollars
558 of stock," Langley replied. "I
559 paid fifteen hundred dollars
560 down and Mr. Kendrick gave
561 me two years to pay the balance.
562 He wanted somebody associated
563 with him on the paper and was
564 willing to sell me a small interest

565 that way. I went into journal-
566 ism when I left college, reporting
567 in Bridgeport and Providence;
568 then in Boston. But I always
569 wanted to get an interest in a
570 paper in a smaller place. I
571 had a little trouble with my
572 lungs and came down here, and
573 fell in with Mr. Kendrick."

574 He said it in his toneless, un-
575 emphasized way; and Dwyer
576 felt that he was a sort of slot
577 machine — you dropped in a
578 question, and if he knew the
579 answer it had to come out,
580 mechanically.

581 "Well," the big man observed,
582 "your stock is worth twice what
583 it was when you bought it six
584 months ago. A year from now it
585 will be worth twice as much as it
586 is now." He leveled a forefinger.
587 "And don't forget this, Langley:
588 This is all based on confidence—
589 every bit of it. Now that the
590 boom's here, you've got other
591 fellows advertising real estate.
592 My advertising has brought in
593 more tourists. They're buying
594 more goods and the merchants
595 are advertising more. You may
596 figure that, now the boom is here
597 you can tell me to go to the devil.
598 But you're wrong. It's all based
599 on confidence. Destroy public
600 confidence in me and you blow
601 up the whole thing. People will
602 simply pull out of the game.
603 Everybody in this part of the
604 country knows that I originated
605 the boom here, and have led it.
606 Palm Bluff has got plenty of

rival towns. Give 'em a handle 607
against me and they'll set up a 608
howl—make this town a laugh- 609
ingstock. You can't hit me 610
without hitting yourself and all 611
your neighbors." 612

Langley felt that this state- 613
ment was quite true, having a 614
prevision that Kendrick and 615
John Titus, president of the 616
First National Bank, and other 617
solid citizens would be greatly 618
pained at the notion of weaken- 619
ing public confidence in Palm 620
Bluff real estate by exposing 621
Dwyer as a rogue who had 622
swindled small investors out of 623
their Liberty Bonds. That was 624
one reason why he hadn't men- 625
tioned the affair to Kendrick. 626

"Running a newspaper here 627
is a different proposition from 628
running one in a big city," 629
Dwyer went on. "Newspapers 630
in a big city needn't have any 631
more sense of responsibility than 632
a hyena—and they don't have," 633
he added bitterly. "They can 634
run around blowing up any- 635
body. That's their occupation. 636
The town's so big, you see. 637
But in a small town like this 638
everything hangs together. 639
You've got to have a sense of 640
responsibility to your neighbors. 641
A newspaper that hurts the 642
town won't be tolerated." 643

Langley nodded gravely. 644

"I understand that, Mr. 645
Dwyer. That's why I came to 646
see you now. Of course, if I 647
was just a big-city reporter I 648

could put this story on the wire and not mind who it hurt." He pecked at his mustache and very soberly made a statement which might have provoked a laugh, coming from such a mouselike person: "All I want to do is to protect the public."

Dwyer demanded, "What do you mean by that?"

"Well, it's this way," the protector of the public answered judicially: "You've been selling a great deal of stock to the public. The money is supposed to go to build a causeway over to the island, and the hotel, and so forth"—he made a little gesture — "these improvements that you advertise. I believe you've got a good proposition, Mr. Dwyer. You can make a fine winter resort out of Paradise Island. If you do make a fine resort out of it, I don't see any reason why people wouldn't come there—build cottages and estates, and so on, same as at Palm Beach and Miami. If they do, of course, the stock in your company will be valuable."

Dwyer listened to this exposition of faith in his enterprise with a certain astonishment. Out on the long, narrow sand bar, overgrown with cabbage palms, palmetto and mesquite, whose name he had changed to Paradise Island, some gangs of colored workmen were clearing up the underbrush and marking streets but it was very, very far from the sophisticated paradise which the big painting in the office represented.

"But you can see yourself, Mr. Dwyer," the journalist droned on, "that if you're"—he seemed unable to find the word he wanted and made an awkward little gesture toward the heap of clippings—"if you're the man who did this, you ought to retire in favor of some man the public could have confidence in. There wouldn't need to be any scandal at all—at least not now." His embarrassment increased, yet his eyes held soberly to Dwyer's face. "I don't know whether they're looking for you or not; but I don't think I would be required to take Boston into consideration—at present. I think my duty is to the public here—at present. So at present if you would retire here, I would be satisfied."

Dwyer stared at him. So that was it! He was simply to eliminate himself—blot himself out of existence with regard to Paradise Island! The astonishment arose partly from a feeling of the insignificance of his opponent, as though an embarrassed mouse should sit up on its tail in the path of an elephant and say, with a nervous little gesture, "Now you're to vanish, you know—dissolve into air."

"But I'm not the man—not the man at all!" Dwyer protested. "That man was my cousin. I had nothing to do with his affairs; no more"—he made a gesture as though at loss for words—"than the man in the moon!"

Langley's monotonous voice came back in propitiation.

"In that case, Mr. Dwyer, of course there's nothing more to be said." He brushed his hand over dusty hair. "Where were you in the spring and summer of 1919?"

And there was the leech again, softly clinging to him, not to be shaken off. Dwyer changed the subject.

"When will Kendrick be back?"

His mind turned to Kendrick, not as to a straw at which a drowning man clutches, but as to a raft. Because, after all, Kendrick was a human being—a man who knew his own interests and the interests of his town, and had a proper regard for them.

"Kendrick will not consent to a wanton attack on me," he declared firmly.

Langley gave another peck at his mustache and squirmed in the chair.

"If it came to that," he said, "I'd put the story on the wire anyhow. Other papers would publish it."

Fatally true! This mere mouse of a man had the lightning in his hand. In spite of Kendrick, in spite of everybody, he could launch the thunderbolt any time he pleased. Other papers would publish it, especially Boston papers, and the reverberations would soon reach Palm Bluff.

Langley explained mildly: "You see, Mr. Dwyer, when I left college and went into journalism I had some ideas about it. I've got the same ideas still. In a case of this kind a journalist ought n't to hesitate, no matter what happens to him." He nodded to the clippings. "That man oughtn't to be taking in other people's money this way. In such case a journalist has a duty to the public. He must protect the public that supports him."

Half an hour before, Dwyer would have laughed over the speech as a bit of sophomorical egotism, of the kind that might be expected from a reporter who gravely called himself a journalist. Half an hour before, he would have said that the runty young man named Langley who was reporter and associate editor of the *Palm Leaf Fan* had comically round, wide-open, pale-blue eyes that reminded one of an adolescent owl. Just now those same eyes, fixed upon his, looked like a high, thick stone wall. His own eyes fell in a sudden agitation. Blindly, instinctively, he began fighting for time.

"See here, Langley, you're all wrong. That's my cousin. We

817 must talk this over. It's a long
818 story." He looked quickly at
819 his wrist watch. "I haven't
820 time now. You owe it to me to
821 give me a hearing."
822　　"Why, I'll be glad to talk it
823 over with you any time, Mr.
824 Dwyer," Langley assured him;
825 "this evening, if you like."
826　　"Why, yes." Dwyer frowned
827 a little, considering. "I've got
828 to meet some men at the hotel
829 for dinner—oughtn't to take
830 very long. Come to my house
831 at half past nine. Will you do
832 that?"
833　　"Certainly, very glad to,"
834 Langley replied; and then Dwyer
835 perceived that his opponent, too,
836 was relieved to get away, like a
837 tired boxer at the end of a round.
838 "I'll read these things over,"
839 said Dwyer, with a nod at the
840 clippings on the desk. "It's a
841 long story. . . . If I shouldn't be
842 there at half past nine, wait for
843 me. I won't be long. . . . Of
844 course, you'll say nothing to
845 anybody until you've heard from
846 me."
847　　"No," said Langley. "I'll be
848 at your house at half past nine."
849　　He slid from the office, hat in
850 hand, and, out on the cement
851 sidewalk of Seaview Avenue,
852 paused to wipe his face with a
853 handkerchief before putting on
854 his faded straw hat, for he was
855 sweating and trembling like a
856 very tired man. He shuffled
857 absently up the avenue, in his
858 slightly stooping posture. and

859 turned off into Hibiscus Street
860 which, naturally, was a dusty,
861 tatter - demalion thoroughfare
862 largely given over to garages.
863 Half a block brought him to a
864 two-story brown frame building
865 with the uncompromising ugli-
866 ness of a big shoe box. The
867 faded sign over the door said,
868 *Palm Leaf Fan. Job Printing.*
869　　But this was only the poor
870 cocoon, soon to be abandoned.
871 Over on Orange Street the walls
872 were already going up for a fine
873 new hollow tile and stucco struc-
874 ture, with the best modern im-
875 provements, to which the news-
876 paper would move as soon as
877 it was completed. Langley had
878 spent many a pleasant half hour
879 admiring the architect's sketch
880 and floor plans. He was going
881 to be part owner in it.
882　　Of course, like much else in
883 Palm Bluff just now, the new
884 plant, and the daily edition that
885 was to follow within a year, were
886 predicated on the boom. He did
887 not deny Dwyer's claim to being
888 the author of the boom, nor that
889 he was still the pivotal fact in
890 it. He knew how much store
891 Palm Bluff put upon its boom;
892 how much it hoped for from
893 that state of mind which set
894 people to bidding briskly against
895 each other for vacant plots of
896 sand and palmetto which, two
897 years before, nobody would so
898 much as look at. It was a state
899 of mind, and states of mind may
900 change very swiftly. He realized

that there were many things to be thought of. His own individual fortune and future were involved in them.

Dwyer, meanwhile, was reading one of those old newspaper clippings with a fascination that was not without horror. This had always been hanging over his head, but as month after month went by his sense of security naturally increased. In brief, a friend had assured him that for a certain consideration authority would hold its hand until, in due time, a beneficent statute of limitations barred him from prosecution. But the affair was hazardous. He was like a man lying behind a dike of sand which time might solidify into rock; meanwhile any chance wave would wash it away. After the catastrophe of arrest he might have abandoned all his baggage, plunging into the stream as a stripped and naked man, to emerge at another point, take a new name—and get a job, say, driving a truck or peddling shoe strings. But he couldn't endure abandoning his baggage. He was too soft for that. So he had been obliged to keep the name Dwyer, metamorphosing E. Pellman into Elihu P., just as he abandoned the curly golden wig he formerly wore and grew a beard instead.

Staring at the old strip of newspaper, with perspiration on his forehead, he perceived in a luminous instant that he had always been ineffectual, finally. This Boston venture hadn't really succeeded. He was a very presentable man, handsome in profile, he made friends readily, and easily got himself accepted up to a certain point; he had a glib tongue; there was ingenuity in his brain. But somehow, at length, he always stubbed his toe, while men whom he despised as coarse blockheads carried their affairs through.

The venture down here had succeeded miraculously. He called himself author of the boom, yet knew well enough that he had appeared just at the psychological moment when circumstances had made everything ready for him. In the nature of the case, booms can't be happening always. Probably such another opportunity would never come to him. Certainly it wouldn't if Langley blew up his sand dike now. With that Boston hue and cry at his heels again, and authority, spurred by newspapers, reaching out for him—— He was forty-two and ravenously hungry for long arrears of enjoyments. His advertisements praised Palm Bluff as a new Eden, but he hated the dull hole. What he wanted was to stuff his pockets with money and go where money can be spent to advantage.

And there was the instrument of his destruction — Langley;

pale-eyed runt of a third-rate newspaper reporter, attached to a country-town semiweekly sheet which docilely printed columns of his puffs of Paradise Island in consideration of a double-page advertisement in each issue for which he paid $112.50. Secretly, or to his wife and a few cronies, he laughed at the journal because it charged so little. Anything that cost only $112.50 must be somewhat contemptible. Yet the *Fan* was dignity itself compared with its associate editor. The most intolerable thing in the situation was that ruin should come from such a source.

From the first he had perceived Langley's unmanageableness. A man of sense might listen to reason and be shown where his own interests lay, or even take an outright bribe. But this was one of your simple-minded idiots who had got an idea of duty to the public stuck crosswise in his feeble nut and would toddle right along with it, no matter at what cost to himself. With intense bitterness, and with a suffocating surge of rage, Dwyer comprehended that immovable and imbecilic quality in his opponent. . . . A man you couldn't do anything with!

He was walking purblindly homeward, all a-quake inside, with a seethe of bitter, aimless anger—Langley! And just when the prize was fairly at his fingers'

ends! The money was rolling in now. He had some wild thoughts of flight; but he had spent a lot of money so far, taking up the options on the land, advertising, clearing off the underbrush. Besides, flight with this bomb exploding at his heels would be useless. . . . Trapped! There had been no plan in his appointment with Langley. He had merely fought for time in which to make a plan. But how could there be a plan when you were going to be shot at daylight anyhow? To be sure, Langley had offered one—namely, that he eliminate himself, walk out empty-handed. Dwyer could have laughed acidly over that, only the muscles of laughter seemed paralyzed. . . . He was quite sure that nobody here except Langley knew about this as yet. Nobody would know, at least, until Kendrick returned in the morning. As yet destruction was solely incarnated in one ridiculous little person. Trapped—and only a gray mouse in gold-bowed spectacles holding the door! Then he came to the ditch and halted as though an invisible hand had seized his arm.

After that it all unfolded in a fashion as smooth and orderly as the operation of a law of Nature. When Dwyer returned to his house at a quarter to ten that evening Langley was waiting for him—

embarrassed of course, pecking at his little mustache and murmuring as Mrs. Dwyer tried to entertain him by wholly imaginary references to her social career in the North. Her sly smile to her husband confessed how dull she had found the young man; and as nearly as she could remember it, she excused herself in the way she had once seen it done on the stage. Of course she was going to bed. Unless there was amusement of some kind, she usually went to bed at nine. Dwyer had counted on that.

The host also excused himself for a moment, then called Langley into the small and gaudily colored den back of the living room, closing the door. When they were seated—the guest having awkwardly declined a cigar—Dwyer spoke with an air not only candid but cordial.

"I've been thinking it over, Langley. You were right. But first I want to tell you about the Boston business."

At leisure he unfolded a narrative, mostly false, of his entanglement in the foreign-exchange speculation; and there was a secret little delight in his heart over the coolness and fluency with which he spoke. He was in perfect command of himself as he spun out the yarn to gain time. It had turned somewhat wetter outside. Through the open window came a soft,

monotonous drip of the eaves and a murmurous patter of drops on the leaves. As dark as a pocket out there. Hardly one chance in a million of a soul being abroad in this edge of the town on such a night. The three or four humble houses in the neighborhood would be fast alseep.

Dwyer talked easily, embroidering the tale. And he was now conscious of an odd, fierce hatred of the mousy little man opposite, pecking at his ridiculous mustache, sagely nodding his insignificant head, looking owlishly through gold-bowed spectacles; an object mortally contemptible in its nature, to be hated and stepped upon!

Also Dwyer secretly jeered at the guest for his fatuous sense of security. There was something hard and heavy in his coat pocket. Several times his hand slipped in to feel of it. He knew exactly how it was going to be done. The courteous host would step outside with his guest, in the dark. Then three or four swift, powerful blows with that thing in his pocket and a body dumped into the muddy ditch where the plank was slippery. And Langley sat there wagging his head, gaping at him—the idiot!

"But you were right," the host continued. "I was the victim of circumstances, yet it wouldn't be fair to ask people to trust me with this money.

1153 I realize it now. I propose an
1154 executive committee."

1155 He sketched the scheme:
1156 Three local men of the highest
1157 reputation would form the com-
1158 mittee to take control of the
1159 enterprise; every dollar of money
1160 received would pass into their
1161 hands; they would see that it
1162 was all honestly expended in
1163 improvements as the advertise-
1164 ments promised; Dwyer would
1165 fade out of the scene on some
1166 plausible pretext.

1167 Through Langley's general
1168 dustiness something like a glow
1169 appeared. He nodded his head
1170 twice, and there was a per-
1171 ceptible flutter of emotion in his
1172 usually monotonous voice.

1173 "I'll be perfectly satisfied with
1174 that, Mr. Dwyer—perfectly sat-
1175 isfied," he declared with that
1176 unwonted warmth. "There
1177 never was what you might call
1178 any personal feeling in this. All I
1179 wanted was to protect the public.
1180 This committee—if it's the right
1181 men—will protect the public.
1182 That was my object from the
1183 start. I'll be perfectly satisfied."

1184 "Well, then, think up a list of
1185 names for the committee. I'll
1186 think up a list. Come to my
1187 office at four o'clock tomorrow.
1188 We'll decide on the men. I'll
1189 have the other details thought
1190 out by that time."

1191 Langley was still perceptibly
1192 glowing, with a foolish little
1193 smile, as he got up and moved
1194 toward the door.

1195 "I'm very glad it's turned out
1196 this way," he observed.

1197 The tall powerful man at his
1198 heels echoed, "So am I. So am
1199 I." But his right hand was in
1200 his coat pocket and he was think-
1201 ing, "Idiot! To suppose I'm
1202 going to give up this game for
1203 you! Imbecile!"

1204 Langley had the door open.
1205 There was a soft drip of water
1206 out there, and a vast pitch dark-
1207 ness, cloaking everything. Door
1208 knob in hand, the visitor hes-
1209 itated an instant, with his foolish
1210 little smile.

1211 "I didn't intend to speak of
1212 my own interests—didn't mean
1213 to think about that. But, of
1214 course, this means a good deal to
1215 me personally." The smile be-
1216 came more awkward. "When
1217 I thought it over I had a kind
1218 of a hunch you weren't going to
1219 give in; maybe would try to
1220 bluff me into putting it off. I
1221 didn't mean to take any chances,
1222 you know—to have anything to
1223 hesitate over. So I wrote out
1224 my resignation to Mr. Kendrick
1225 and an assignment of my stock.
1226 I told him if he considered I
1227 injured him, or the paper, in
1228 what I was doing, he could take
1229 it out of what I'd paid him on
1230 the stock. I left it on his desk
1231 where he'd see it first thing
1232 when he gets to town tomorrow."

1233 Dwyer heard himself asking,
1234 "Did you tell him why you were
1235 resigning?"

1236 Langley gravely nodded.

1237 "I wrote an outline of the case
1238 —enough so he would under-
1239 stand why I was acting—and
1240 inclosed a copy of the dispatch
1241 I meant to send the Boston
1242 *Tribune* after I left you." The
1243 awkward smile reappeared. "In
1244 case, you know that you
1245 wouldn't yield. I didn't mean
1246 to take any chances, you see.
1247 I didn't want anything to hesi-
1248 tate about. I didn't even mean
1249 to put it off till you talked to
1250 Kendrick. It looked clear to
1251 me, so I meant to act. I've got
1252 the original dispatch in my
1253 pocket, ready to send. Of
1254 course, now I can tear up the
1255 resignation and the dispatch.
1256 I'm very glad of that. It means

quite a lot to me personally." 1257
Dwyer, hand still in pocket, 1258
but quite nerveless, looked 1259
blankly down at this comically 1260
mousy person and apprehended 1261
him in a new way; small, homely, 1262
soft, apparently weak, but inde- 1263
structible as truth. That letter 1264
to Kendrick, with copy of the 1265
dispatch, protected him now 1266
like brass armor. . . . Inde- 1267
structible! 1268
"I think the executive com- 1269
mittee will work very well," 1270
said Dwyer stupidly. 1271
"Yes; I feel sure it will," 1272
Langley replied in his toneless 1273
manner. "Good night." 1274
The small homely figure shuf- 1275
fled off into the moist dark. 1276

The Analysis

I mentioned that in *Sunk* the main narrative question was, "Can Jason Terwilliger kill Jake Finch?" In *Paradise Island* the main narrative question is, "Can Dwyer kill Langley?" In each story the same feat of accomplishment is required of the main actor. Since it is clear that every feat is interesting in proportion to its importance, or to its difficulty, or to its threat of disaster, there can be no doubt that the more important or difficult or disastrous a feat is made to appear to the reader the more likely it is to be interesting. The killing of a man is naturally of importance. It will always serve as the main narrative question of a story. A great many stories have been written with this feat as the main narrative problem of the story. Yet these two stories which have this main narrative question, have also something else in common. They neither of them achieve any length in particular from the meetings or interchanges which make up the Body of the story, nor from those which make up the Ending of the story. Obviously then, one of two things must happen. Either the story must be very short or the Beginning must be prolonged. The first is the case with *Sunk*, the second is the case with *Paradise Island*.

With *Sunk* the method of presentation was chronological. After an interchange the main narrative question emerged. This interchange contained the explanatory matter necessary to the reader's understanding of the importance or interest of that main narrative question. In the case of *Paradise Island* the method is reversed. The order instead of being chronological is anti-chronological: it is the flash-back method.

In discussing the *Escape of Mr. Trimm*, we found that Mr. Cobb opened his story at a point which was not in chronological order, but it was not a true flash-back Beginning because the interchange or meeting which was out of chronological order did not present to the reader the main narrative question. In *Paradise Island* the anti-chronological order does present to the reader the main narrative question. It emerges on the fifth line of the story. The first five lines of this story illustrate narrative technique reduced to its elements. Dwyer becomes aware of a stimulus. The stimulus is the ditch. His reaction to that stimulus is to respond in terms of a purpose, that purpose being the main purpose or main narrative problem of the story. Chronologically that story would then be resumed at line 1062 and would carry on to line 1268 which is the Body of the story, so that we would have main narrative question lines 1 to 5, Body interchange lines 1062 to 1268, Conclusive Act and Effect lines 1269 to 1276, but we would have no explanatory matter and we would not know why Dwyer wished to kill Langley. We would have no explanatory matter, and without explanatory matter there is not a complete Beginning.

As it is evident that the quality of the material in both stories is essentially the same, the difference in arrangement must come not from this *quality* but from the *quantity* of the material.

Quantity is the determining factor. In *Sunk* the main problem and its explanatory matter are contained in 178 lines. In *Paradise Island* 1067 lines are needed. Both authors knew and utilized the laws of interest. Both introduced a narrative question within the first 34 lines. In *Paradise Island* the main narrative question comes in the first 5 lines. It is, "Can Dwyer succeed in killing a man?" In *Sunk* a narrative question comes in the first 34 lines. It is, "Can Jason Terwilliger succeed in begging $2,000 from his uncle?" This is a minor narrative question and not a major one for the whole story. It is a minor one for a scene. Now a minor narrative question can be made to hold the interest of the reader for say 500 to 1500 words. In *Sunk*, beginning on line 34, this minor narrative question is used to maintain the interest until the main narrative question is reached on line 119. These 86 lines averaging about 5 words to the line contain about 400 words.

This method could not have been followed in *Paradise Island* because over 1000 lines, or nearly 5000 words are needed to present the explanatory matter which the author wished to place before the reader in order that he might understand the responses of the character when the character became aware of the main purpose actuating him, and was plunged into the meeting growing out of that purpose.

A minor narrative question could not have held a reader's interest long enough to make him read 5000 words without knowing something about a main narrative question. Anything over 1500 words is a heavy strain upon a reader's concentration of interest if a scene is used *merely for information leading to the main narrative problem. After* that main narrative problem has been presented this length restriction does not apply because in addition to the interest which the reader feels from his knowledge of a minor narrative question of a scene, there is present in his consciousness the major narrative question of the story which will hold his interest additionally.

Most stories which are rejected are rejected because the Beginnings are dull, and it is for this reason that the method employed by Mr. Payne in presenting this long Beginning will be so interesting to a student of the short-story form. The problem which faces most story writers is the one which Mr. Payne has here solved through his knowledge of the laws of interest. Structurally, the divisions are very clear. The Beginning occupies lines 1 to 1061; the Body lines 1062 to 1268; and the Ending lines 1269 to 1276. The main narrative question emerges clearly, and the answer is quite definite.

Someone has pointed out that the difference between the untrained recruit and the regular soldier is not in the things that they do but in the precision and unconscious ease with which the regular does them, as opposed to the untrained person. So it is with writers. The writer is really an executive in short-story craftsmanship. A good executive is one who, faced by a problem, makes a decision which is wise and instantaneous. He is able to make this quick and accurate decision because he compares the circumstances of the case confronting him with the circumstances of similar cases, and decides that the general principles involved are the same, therefore the answer must be the same. Even if, at the beginning of his executive experience, not all his decisions are wise, practice will increase the proportion of his successes. So it should be with the writer. If the writer knows that certain treatment of material in previous cases has made a good story every time, he will then be able to employ that treatment whenever the materials are similar. It is essential, however, that a writer shall recognize that the similarity must be a similarity of fundamentals, not a similarity of things which are not fundamental. The aspiring writer, examining *Paradise Island* will not grasp the complete lesson it holds for him in regard to the utilization of the laws of interest until he realizes two things: first, in the typically effective Flash-back Beginning the meetings or interchanges which make up the explanatory matter are made interesting because they are presented after the main narrative question has been made apparent to the reader, and gather a synthetic importance from the reader's knowledge of this main narrative question. Second, that in the effective Flash-back Beginning the main narrative question must be intrinsically important. It will not do to say that the Beginning of any story can be made interesting, provided the main narrative question is projected before the explanatory matter is presented. There would be a technical Flash-back Beginning, but the conclusion drawn would be wrong. The mere showing of something to be accomplished is not in itself enough to form a main narrative question. For example, had Dwyer, as he halted at the ditch, been struck with a determination to ask Langley for the address of a man who manufactered clam chowder, it would involve a main purpose or something to be accomplished. But the reader, asked to read a story in which the whole interest concentrated upon the attempt of a man to discover another man's address, would not read very far. On the other hand, the attempt of one man to eliminate another from the world can be depended upon to hold interest. Therefore, the lesson to be learned particularly from this story is, that when there is a Flash-back Beginning in the true sense the main narrative problem is presented first, and it is followed, out of chronological order by the explanatory matter. But, in order to be effective, this main narrative question must be important, and the secret of importance is that *a thing is interesting in proportion to what depends upon it.*

Another lesson to be learned from this story is, that in the Beginning the meetings or encounters are made interesting in proportion as a writer possesses a knowledge of craftsmanship. Lines 6 to 111 are particularly interesting in this respect. Dwyer becomes aware of a stimulus and reacts toward it; but always in a way that affects the main narrative question. Thus, on line 33, where the writer says, "This plank over the ditch was wet," he follows it by the response of the actor, "a man might easily slip on it" line 34, tying up the reflection of the actor with the main purpose—to kill the man. Again, looking about him at the setting, he sees it as a blurr, and he thinks (see line 62), that this general blurr, still and vague, but shut in, seemed to sanction the idea which had exploded in Dwyer's mind (to kill the man). Again, when the author has presented the appearance of the man Dwyer, he follows it by the contrast between his appearance of competence and the turmoil within as he is affected by his new purpose and then the author follows this by the words on line 109, "but he had a baffled feeling of the things being thrust into his hands, no other way." On line 161, after he has talked to his wife he finds himself stammering, scant of breath, etc., and it is evident that his normal response to every stimulus is conditioned or affected by his purpose in the story.

In that scene between him and Langley which is presented in flash-back there is no lack of clash or of the sense of disaster which overshadows Dwyer during the meeting, and of the further sense of disaster which overshadows Langley because of our knowledge, as readers, that Dwyer has determined to kill him.

Some students of the short-story form do not seem to grasp readily what is meant by a flash-back scene. To simplify this I want them to think that it is the opposite of a *flash-forward scene*, and to illustrate by the case method, I shall ask you to glance at line 1058 of this story and read to line 1068. You will see that it begins, "Then he came to the ditch and halted," and on line 1066 it says, "When Dwyer returned to his house at a quarter to ten that evening."

The time of Dwyer's halting at the ditch was in the late afternoon after he had left Langley. The scene which follows between Dwyer and Langley, beginning on line 1066, occurs at a quarter to ten that evening, and is a flash-*forward* in time. Now if you will turn to line 171 you will see that it is the conclusion of a scene between Dwyer and his wife and that it is followed on line 172 by a description of Langley which goes to line 183. On line 184 there is a flash-*back* in time because it goes from the moment when Langley is speaking to his wife, which is just before dinner, to four o'clock of that same afternoon. This is a flash-*back* scene because it flashes *back* in time. In every other respect the scene is the same as if it had flashed *forward*. Only the introductory sentence tells the difference.

The virtue of this flash-back scene is that the author is enabled to introduce a minor narrative question to hold the interest of the reader while he is giving him information which would ordinarily be rendered by the inexpert writer in a summary of what had happened. A scene is always more interesting than a summary, but if the explanatory matter is dependent for its interest upon the main narrative question and this main narrative question must be made to emerge before the explanatory matter can be presented, the tendency of the inexpert writer would be to present the main narrative question and then to *summarize* the explanatory matter. Thus he would defeat his own purpose. He would capture interest, but he would lose it. He would be worse off than if he had summarized and then swung from his summary into a main narrative question.

The flash-back Beginning is therefore a very dangerous method for the inexpert writer. It is dependent for its success entirely upon one factor, and that factor is that the explanatory matter shall be presented in *dramatic scenes*. Otherwise the chief gain is turned into a loss.

This story is chosen because it is an interesting example of the presentation of explanatory matter by the flash-back method. Any writer having difficulty with employing this method will do well to use this story as a model.

OF

ONCE AND ALWAYS

BEGINNING	Initial Condition presented at its high point. The Main Actor's purpose is at once shown. With interest thus aroused, reader has desire to learn what led up to it.	Interchange. Gideon and Doctor.	1– 70	Main condition apparent.
		Gideon resolves to restore money.		Main Narrative Question "Can Gideon succeed in restoring Ten Thousand Dollars to boyhood friend?"
		Character's Flashback scene. Gideon and Lemuel.	71– 171	
		Continuation of Scene with Doctor.	172– 422	Background given to show importance to Gideon.
		Author's Flash-back to earlier in morning. Gideon and wife.	423– 648	Fear of Disaster to project.
		(5th step.) Reflections of Gideon.	649– 732	Opposing Force apparent.
		Interchange. Gideon and Mr. Altyne.	733– 852	Promise of Disaster (841–842)
BODY	Single attempt shown is, apparently, a failure.	Scene. Gideon and Lemuel.	853–1235	Hindrance.
		(5th step. Gideon and George.)	1236–1278	Dramatic Hindrance. Disaster close.
		Interchange. Gideon and Mr. Altyne.	1279–1332	Furtherance. Gideon sees method.
ENDING	Scene here is almost a Body scene. Conclusive Act, and sequel.	Scene. Gideon and Mrs. Higsbee.	1333–1521	
		He made thousands and thousands of dollars.	1505–1521	The Answer to the Main Narrative Question is "Yes."

ONCE AND ALWAYS

BY JOHN P. MARQUAND

THE more stories you analyze the more you will become convinced that the chief value to you, as an author, of a knowledge of craftsmanship is that it will enable you instantly to dispose of structural problems in order that you may be able to devote your interest and enthusiasm to the portrayal of character. When readers speak disparagingly of "ordinary" stories they have in mind the story which is well constructed, but which leaves at the close no sense in the mind of the readers of an actual person having been presented to them by the writer of the story. The narrative problem may hold them, and the arrangement of the crises may sustain their interest, but the interest will be in plot rather than in character. On the other hand, when, as a reader, you feel that a story has distinction, you find almost inevitably, that this feeling of distinction comes because the writer caused the main actor to solve the problem in some unusual way, in a way which marks that character as a distinct personality.

Because *Once and Always* is this type of story, I have chosen it for re-print.

CASE No. 8

ONCE AND ALWAYS

BY JOHN P. MARQUAND

Gideon Higsbee's hair was nearly white by now; his sharp face had grown wrinkled; Lemuel Gower had faded long ago from active recollection, like everything else in Agamemnon, Maine. And after all, why not. That affair in the Agamemnon House had fallen into the past for thirty years or more before the shade of Lemuel Gower darkened Gideon's conscience in Doctor Follenshope's office just off Fifth Avenue.

Through the maze of Mr. Higsbee's thoughts came the voice of Doctor Follenshope, and its tone aroused his interest:

"And so it wouldn't be fair to either of us if I didn't warn you to expect the worst. With perfect rest we may help matters; but your heart——"

A feeling of wonder made Gideon's eyes open slightly, but that was all. He could always control his expression when he chose, and he controlled it then, though something told him that it was no matter—that nothing mattered.

"Why not say what you mean?" he suggested. Gideon spoke without a quaver. "You won't startle me, young man. Do you mean I'm going to die?"

The doctor nodded, and then looked startled himself, for Gideon Higsbee had begun to whistle softly and to rotate his hand at the wrist. "So that's that," he said at length. "I might have known something would call my bluff."

Doctor Follenshope stared. Gideon's face was impassive; his eyes were cool and quiet.

"If there's anything on your mind"—it was clear to see that Doctor Follenshope admired him, without knowing why— "any way that I can help——"

"Fiddlesticks!" said Gideon Higsbee. "Young man, don't you set me down for a squealer! I've been a gambler all my life, and I guess I can stand it when I'm out on a limb. There's nothing on my mind but what was there before. I'm thinking of my wife, that's all—just thinking of my wife."

Yet even then, old Gideon did not wholly tell the truth. How could Gideon tell the doctor that his words had awakened the stirrings of conscience which would not be quieted until he had restored ten thousand dollars to a boyhood friend.

Out of the past Gideon's wife had plucked Lemuel Gower that very morning: Lemuel Gower whom he had almost forgotten. But in Doctor Follenshope's office it all came back to Gideon Higsbee, though not immediately, because it had happened so long ago. But after a little concentration he could remember clearly enough the way the three strangers had looked when they descended from the stage in front of the Agamemnon House. Like nearly all the adult male population of Agamemnon, Maine, Gideon had resorted to the lobby of the Agamemnon House late every afternoon, urged by the same habit which brought him to the general store just before going home to supper. Thus he saw the three strangers at close view, and Gideon knew what they were. They were crooks who had probably been touring the county fairs—either gamblers or confidence men. It was written in their predatory glances, and the jewelry they carried was enough to tell anyone with any sense that they used it as a cash reserve. But why should one have expected Lemuel Gower to have any sense? There always had to be someone devoid of it. Lemuel glanced with wonder at their distinguished bearing.

"Gid," said Lemuel, in the loud, blank way in which he always spoke, "let's go over and speak to 'em."

"No," said Gideon Higsbee.

"But, say," said Lemuel plaintively, "why not, Gid? They're nice pleasant-lookin' fellers, influential bankers, or somethin', I'll bet. And we're business men, Gid, ain't we? Come on, Gid, we really otter."

Gideon Higsbee smiled. He had no whiskers in those days, and his hair was still light brown. "No, Lemuel," said Gideon, even then with a sigh. "You haven't got a wife—I have."

"But, say," said Lemuel, "she wants you to get on, doesn't she? You say you're going to get rich, don't you? Well, say, how're you goin' to do it if you don't grasp opportunity? They're nice fellers, Gid. Mebbe they've come up to see the pulp mill, and if so, it's our business to speak to 'em."

Gideon shook his head. The honesty, the Arcadian simplicity of Lemuel Gower might have inspired a pastoral poet, but Gideon was not a poet.

144 "But why won't you?" in-
145 quired Lemuel. "As a rule, Gid,
146 you're the slickest feller. Gid,
147 what are you thinkin' about?"
148 Gideon was whistling through
149 his teeth and moving his hands
150 in short, sharp circles. "Just
151 thinking of my wife," said
152 Gideon. "That's all — just
153 thinking of my wife."
154 "Well," said Lemuel, "if you
155 won't speak to 'em, I will."
156 With his rubber shoes making
157 an honest sound upon the floor,
158 Lemuel Gower walked across
159 the lobby of the Agamemnon
160 House, and Gideon perceived
161 that the three strangers looked
162 up with pleasure. Through the
163 haze of years Gideon recalled
164 that he had watched curiously
165 before he turned away, and he
166 said—he still remembered that
167 he had said it, because even
168 then it seemed to paraphrase
169 nearly all his observations on
170 life—"Once a sucker, always a
171 sucker," said Gideon, and smiled.
172 Gideon Higsbee's mutton-
173 chop whiskers were soft and
174 white as new-flown snow and
175 comforting as a Sunday's bene-
176 diction. Of old the sirens had
177 their song, but what use had
178 Gideon for alluring music when
179 his whiskers in their carded
180 fleecy innocence were waving
181 on the breeze? Many a strong
182 and case-hardened man had
183 become weak—nay, smilingly
184 lachrymose — at the sight of
185 them, and thus there was no

186 wonder that Doctor Follenshope
187 should also have succumbed.
188 He tilted back his swivel chair.
189 He seemed to find it difficult to
190 discover a beginning in what he
191 had to say.
192 "I'm afraid it's going to be
193 hard for me to make myself
194 clear," he said.
195 "Is it, indeed?" said Gideon
196 Higsbee, in a high voice which
197 was somewhat cracked by years.
198 "Well, I guess it won't hurt you
199 to do something hard, young
200 man. You look spry and you're
201 getting paid enough."
202 "Of course I don't want to
203 alarm you unduly——" began
204 Doctor Follenshope.
205 "Young man," said Gideon
206 Higsbee, "don't make me laugh.
207 It gives me a crick in the side."
208 "I'm afraid," said Doctor
209 Follenshope in a slightly altered
210 tone, "it isn't exactly a laughing
211 matter."
212 Gideon Higsbee raised a
213 wrinkled clawlike hand and
214 snapped his fingers. "Young
215 man," he said, "what I say
216 may be eccentric, but then why
217 shouldn't I be eccentric? What
218 I say may not be gentlemanly,
219 but then am I a gentleman? I
220 make it a rule to laugh when I
221 damn please."
222 Doctor Follenshope seemed
223 slightly confused and looked
224 at Mr. Higsbee strangely. "Mr.
225 Higsbee," he said, "I make
226 mistakes. We all make mistakes
227 in the medical profession, as no

228 doubt you have made them in
229 yours. People say we have
230 the advantage of being able to
231 bury ours; sometimes it's quite
232 the other way. I just want to
233 say that I might be wrong about
234 you. You may fool us all.
235 Are you listening, sir?"

236 There was a reason for Doctor
237 Follenshope's question. Mr.
238 Higsbee was staring at his hand,
239 which he was rotating briskly
240 at the wrist, and at the same
241 time he was whistling a monoto-
242 nous tune through his teeth.

243 "You don't feel an attack
244 coming on?" asked Doctor
245 Follenshope. "Would you feel
246 better lying down?"

247 Mr. Higsbee still continued
248 to whistle and rotate his hand.

249 "Mr. Higsbee," cried Doctor
250 Follenshope, "this isn't a laugh-
251 ing matter. Do you hear me?"

252 "Yes," said Mr. Higsbee.
253 "I'm not hard of hearing."

254 "But you weren't listening to
255 me—not to a word I was say-
256 ing." Doctor Follenshope's pro-
257 fessional calm was leaving him,
258 and his face was growing pink.

259 "No," said Mr. Higsbee, "I
260 wasn't. I may be eccentric, but
261 then why shouldn't I be eccen-
262 tric? I was thinking. I was
263 snatching the occasion to allow
264 my thoughts to revert toward
265 my wife—toward Mrs. Higsbee.
266 Young man, do you happen to
267 be one of those before whom
268 Hymen has carried the torch?
269 Are you married?"

270 A frown appeared on Doctor
271 Follenshope's placid brow. He
272 glanced hastily toward the
273 door.

274 "Mr. Higsbee," he said, "I
275 must ask you to give me your
276 attention, I'm afraid, whether
277 you wish to or not. Though I
278 happen to be married——"

279 "Then," said Mr. Higsbee,
280 "let me give you a piece of
281 advice. Listen to an old man
282 — I beg of you, listen. Though
283 it may not be applicable in your
284 case, you may pass it on to
285 others. I refer to the principle
286 of the counterirritant, which I
287 believe has been used by your
288 profession from the time of
289 Galen." Mr. Higsbee paused and
290 stroked his whiskers. "Young
291 man, when you find yourself
292 confronted by a serious situation
293 which is harrowing in the ex-
294 treme—think of your wife—
295 always think of your wife."

296 "My wife?" inquired Doctor
297 Follenshope, with a peculiar
298 expression. "I fail to see——"

299 Mr. Higsbee smiled and rub-
300 bed his hands, and, more than
301 smiling, beamed until his
302 shriveled face and glassy eyes
303 were genial as the setting sun.
304 "Ah!" he said. "Then she is not
305 like Mrs. Higsbee—clearly not
306 like Mrs. Higsbee. She does not
307 possess the power of opening
308 you up like an oyster."

309 At this point Doctor Follen-
310 shope betrayed a plodding
311 literal mind. "Like an oyster?"

312 he inquired, looking at Mr.
313 Higsbee strangely.

314 "Have you never witnessed,"
315 asked Mr. Higsbee, "the
316 struggles of an oyster in the
317 hands of one of those experts
318 who serve you at a counter?"

320 "No, I haven't," replied
321 Doctor Follenshope, "and what's
322 more——"

323 "Ah!" said Mr. Higsbee.
324 "Then you should. Let us
325 take one of those known in the
326 trade as a wild Virginia oyster.
327 The man picks him up and
328 grasps his knife. The oyster
329 hastily closes his shell, and with
330 a confidence not wholly based
331 on ignorance—for you could
332 not open him, young man, not
333 without a hammer and a chisel—
334 surrenders himself to his dark
335 and cramped environment. But
336 he is reckoning without a know-
337 ledge of his assailant. With an
338 unerring speed, swifter than
339 light, the knife strikes an un-
340 guarded crevice. There is a
341 moment's vain resistance, a grat-
342 ing sound, and there you are.
343 The oyster, however wild, lies
344 bare, exposed to the taunts of
345 his victor, ready for the lemon
346 and horse-radish. But you don't
347 follow me?"

348 "No," said Doctor Follen-
349 shope icily, "I certainly don't."

350 "Young man," said Mr. Higs-
351 bee, with a sigh, "I married Mrs.
352 Higsbee at Agamemnon, Maine,
353 thirty years ago. In those days
354 I was wild and free, engaged,

355 in fact, in selling a tonic com-
356 pounded from roots known only
357 to the Indians at the county
358 fairs. Forced by domesticity
359 from my wild, free ways, I began
360 conducting business in Mrs.
361 Higsbee's home town; in fact,
362 buying into an enterprise. Upon
363 gaining control of it I became
364 aware of a growing though in-
365 comprehensible antipathy on the
366 part of the natives, and selling
367 out, I came here; of course, with
368 Mrs. Higsbee. With Mrs. Higs-
369 bee still by my side I have
370 struggled from these low begin-
371 nings into the possession of some
372 three million dollars. I mention
373 this only incidentally, because I
374 wish to add that in every crisis
375 of my career I have thought of
376 Mrs. Higsbee. It has always
377 made me calm, and why has it
378 made me calm?"

379 Doctor Follenshope made no
380 answer. He was staring at
381 Gideon Higsbee as though he
382 had never really known him.

383 "It renders me calm," said
384 Mr. Higsbee gently, "because I
385 feel that nothing is more difficult
386 to cope with than Mrs. Higsbee.
387 For thirty years I have been
388 Mrs. Higsbee's oyster. But I
389 beg your pardon. You said you
390 did not want to alarm me
391 unduly. Don't worry. It's
392 hard to alarm anyone who has
393 been an oyster for thirty years."

394 For a moment Doctor Follen-
395 shope did not speak, but stared
396 at Gideon Higsbee's wrinkled

397 face and snowy whiskers vaguely
398 and uncertainly, at the same
399 time taking off his glasses.
400 Gideon Higsbee leaned back in
401 his chair and crossed his slender
402 hands. Clearly Doctor Follen-
403 shope did not understand him,
404 but then why should he have
405 understood? Others had been
406 puzzled, lots of others, by the
407 fluent ease of Gideon Higsbee's
408 speech, and many had ended by
409 doing things about which they
410 had subsequently wondered.
411 Nevertheless, Mr. Higsbee was
412 surprised at himself. Old as he
413 was and clever as he was, he
414 had very nearly made a con-
415 fession, had very nearly told
416 the truth.

417 And this lack of control filled
418 him with awe, made him feel
419 that his own weakness might
420 step in to defeat him before he
421 could restore that ten thousand
422 to Lemuel Gower.

423 Earlier, that very morning,
424 when he had entered the break-
425 fast room of his brownstone
426 house, his wife's canary had
427 been singing in a most damn-
428 ably carefree way, seemingly
429 out of spite. Mrs. Higsbee,
430 behind a Georgian coffee urn,
431 was opening a pile of letters.
432 Being one of those who never
433 let anything go, Mrs. Higsbee
434 never dropped a correspond-
435 ent, nor allowed herself to be
436 dropped, and the brisk way she
437 wielded her paper knife was
438 enough to prove it. Their son,

439 whom Mrs. Higsbee had insisted
440 on naming Merlin, had pushed
441 his chair back from the table
442 and was reading the paper
443 through a pair of glasses pinched
444 on his nose—a Higsbee nose,
445 slender and beaklike. That Mr.
446 Higsbee could have been a party
447 in producing and rearing a being
448 like Merlin, who, possesed of
449 the sharpest Higsbee attributes,
450 yet was soft and sportive, like a
451 dying species, and who regarded
452 his father with a supercilious
453 scorn, always was puzzling. It
454 was the more puzzling when he
455 looked at Mrs. Higsbee. Her
456 stern, bespectacled visage had
457 preserved its simplicity and
458 forcefulness, despite thick claret-
459 colored carpets and tapestries on
460 the wall. In spite of surround-
461 ings, in spite of time, Matilda
462 Higsbee was as indomitable as
463 when she had first spied him.
464 Gideon had the same feeling of
465 awe and nervousness.

466 "Good morning, my dear," he
467 said.

468 "You're not looking as well
469 even as you did yesterday," said
470 Mrs. Higsbee.

471 Now how was that for a nice
472 way to start the morning?

473 "That's right," said Merlin.
474 'You're not looking well."

475 "My dear boy," said Mr.
476 Higsbee, "how it must hurt you
477 to perceive it!"

478 "Don't talk so loudly," said
479 Mrs. Higsbee. "It makes your
480 face all spotty, Gideon."

"That's right, it does," said Merlin.

"Merlin," said Mr. Higsbee, "I wonder if you could spare some of your time to pay me a visit downtown. There are so many things I should like to tell you which might not interest your mother."

"Tweet! Tweet!" went the canary.

"Angel voice," said Mrs. Higsbee. "Gideon, what do you think I've just heard? I've got the nicest, longest letter from Susie Brickett. It makes me feel as though I was back home to read it, and what do you think?"

"Anything you want, my dear," said Gideon. "I've found it best."

"It's all about Lemuel Gower."

That was like her. It was like the knife finding the chink in the oyster, and things recent or things distant were all the same to her.

Out of the past, back from the solitude of Agamemnon, Maine, she had fetched him with swift unerring skill. On purpose or not, it made no difference. There was Lemuel Gower come to disturb his peace.

"Gideon," inquired Mrs. Higsbee, "aren't you feeling well?"

"Perfectly, my dear," said Gideon. "Never better."

"Lemuel's in financial troubles again. What do you think of that?"

Mr. Higsbee drew a deep breath and smiled. "Is that all?" he asked. "Well, I can only say what I've always said, my dear. There's a saying in trade peculiarly applicable to Lemuel Gower, and I ought to know, seeing he was my first associate in business. The phrase is vulgar, but it sums everything up. 'Once a sucker, always a sucker,' that's what I think of Lemuel Gower."

There was a slight and rather uncomfortable pause. Mr. Higsbee became aware that his wife was peering at him around the coffee urn. He drew himself up and stroked his whiskers. After all, was there any wonder that his heart was weak after years of such suspense?

"Gideon"—right out of the blue she threw her bolt—"I want to know—you've always edged off it—did you, or did you not, do right by Lemuel?"

"Tweet!" went the canary, and Gideon Higsbee jumped at the suddenness of the sound.

"My dear," he said, "correct me if I am mistaken, but haven't we discussed this at odd intervals over a period of thirty years!"

Unbidden, there came before Gideon's memory, floating cloudily, a vision of Lemuel Gower's broad and honest face, his bulbous nose reddened by the winter's cold and a light of enthusiastic wonder kindling in his credulous gray eyes.

"Gideon" — Mrs. Higsbee's voice aroused him from his reverie—"you've always been sharp. How could you get so rich if you weren't? And when Lemuel lost his money first, you started getting rich. Now tell me the truth, did you, or did you not, do right by Lemuel?"

Merlin was looking at him; his wife was looking at him. Mr. Higsbee made a distinct effort. "My dear," he said with delicate reproach, "is it possible you still think I conceal anything from you? What's the trouble, Merlin?"

Merlin had made a gurgling sound behind his newspaper. Mr. Higsbee rose from the table and looked like an old engraving.

"I'll not stay and be laughed at in my own house," he continued; "and as for Lemuel Gower, I'd like you both to listen, if you please, once for all. Lemuel and I were associated in business at Agamemnon, Maine, when we were both much younger — the pulp business. I'm specific, because I want you to understand too, Merlin, and afterwards you shall ask my pardon for laughing. At this period Lemuel was approached by three plausible men, who induced him to draw most of his savings in order that they might make a fortune in a stock deal."

Mr. Higsbee paused and coughed.

"They had, I believe, a private wire from Bangor to New York, and one of them had been a confidential clerk for a famous banker there. This banker, out of the kindness of his heart, had divulged certain pieces of confidential information, in which Lemuel was allowed to share. Is it my fault that Lemuel was simple? Answer me, could I help it that Lemuel is a sucker?"

Mr. Higsbee tapped his chest gently but firmly, but his whiskers would have been enough. They were as white as the new-flown snow.

"And as for me," he continued —he was at his best just then; his self-pity and his enthusiasm clouded his voice—"as for me, what did I do but kindness? When Lemuel was plucked clean, didn't I buy his share of the Agamemnon pulp mill? Was it my fault if I turned around and sold it two months later at a profit? And I'll tell you one thing more——"

Mr. Higsbee pointed toward the coffee urn, and something told him he was doing better than he had hoped. Mrs. Higsbee was staring at him, fascinated. Even Merlin's thin mouth had opened.

"Yes," said Mr. Higsbee, "one thing more, and take it or leave it, as you please. I hope to die if ever in my life I did a wrong to Lemuel Gower."

649 Later that morning the voice
650 of Doctor Follenshope, issuing
651 his ultimatum recalled to
652 Gideon that defiance he had
653 hurled: "I hope to die." And
654 that was why he surprised the
655 doctor by saying "I'm thinking
656 of my wife, that's all,—just
657 thinking of my wife."

658 Mrs. Higsbee had done it.
659 Out of the past it had come, or
660 out from wherever he had put
661 it—that vision of Lemuel Gow-
662 er's broad and honest features.
663 It seemed no time at all, and
664 yet the distance which he had
665 traveled seemed almost measure-
666 less since he and Lemuel had last
667 met face to face. Standing in
668 the private room of his office, he
669 could hear the sounds of activity
670 outside his mahogany door; out
671 the window, beneath little
672 plumes of steam and a darker
673 pall of smoke, lay the roofs of
674 the city, ending only at the
675 river; and hardly ending there,
676 for bridges seemed to carry
677 the spirit of it over to other
678 lands. In the distance, far
679 toward the horizon, he could see
680 snow, and that was all, the only
681 vestige of a past which might
682 remind him of Lemuel and of
683 Agamemnon, Maine. Neverthe-
684 less, it was all about him. He
585 could remember the very still-
686 ness and the chill in the air,
687 which gave even occasional
688 noises an icy ring—the barking
689 of a dog, the curious complaining
690 of the snow beneath the runners

691 of a sleigh. There was the village
692 store. Would it still be there,
693 with its odor of spices mixed with
694 bad tobacco smoke, that made
695 its warmth somehow exotic and
696 finer than the warmth of home?
697 He could even remember
698 Lemuel's voice, nasal but de-
699 voted: "By hooky, Gideon,
700 you're the smartest feller now!
701 You'd have to go to Bangor, I
702 bet, to find a slicker feller."

703 To Bangor—it was enough to
704 make one smile, even in those
705 days, for Lemuel really meant it
706 as his highest praise. To Lemuel,
707 Bangor was a city teeming with
708 the speed and knowledge of a
709 scientific age, where wit and
710 eloquence scintillated unchal-
711 lenged by a wondering world.
712 Was there any wonder that
713 Gideon had always felt for
714 Lemuel a mild contempt? He
715 felt it still, and yet a lump was
716 rising in his throat. From a
717 silver box on his desk he selected
718 a cigar, lighted it and sat down.
719 It was not so much Lemuel as
720 the days of his youth that were
721 stirring him, but Lemuel was
722 still there in spite of the smoke
723 and the noises outside the room,
724 awkward and lanky, pulling off
725 his mittens and dusting the snow
726 from his hat. Gideon Higsbee
727 smiled thoughtfully and flicked
728 the ash from his cigar.

729 "Once a sucker, always a
730 sucker," he said beneath his
731 breath; and, nevertheless, he
732 had to smile.

733 He had done nothing even
734 technically dishonest. He could
735 even look Mrs. Higsbee in the
736 eye and say he had not. Those
737 three men who had appeared
738 on the evening stage from the
739 railroad had their profession
740 stamped all over them, as any-
741 one except Lemuel might have
742 seen, even when not assisted
743 by the story of a private wire
744 from Bangor to New York. After
745 Lemuel had spoken to them, he
746 had not mentioned them again.
747 It was amusing still to remem-
748 ber that Lemuel, in his lust for
749 profits, had kept everything
750 secret as long as possible.
751 Gideon Higsbee smiled faintly
752 and pushed a button on his desk.
753 The service in his office was
754 always quick and unobtrusive.
755 The instant, almost, that Gideon
756 pressed the button, a suave
757 young man with a pale face was
758 in the room.
759 "George," said Gideon, "make
760 me out a check for ten thousand
761 dollars at compound interest,
762 6 per cent, for thirty years, pay-
763 able to the name on this paper,
764 and be ready to go with me
765 tonight to Agamemnon, Maine."
766 George did not appear sur-
767 prised. "Do they know at home
768 you're going, sir?" he asked.
769 "No," said Gideon; "and don't
770 let 'em. Call up and make an
771 excuse. And, George, tell Mr.
772 Altyne I want to see him."
773 Mr. Altyne also appeared
774 noiselessly and with an equal
775 promptness. He was a man of
776 indeterminate age, with iron-
777 gray hair, an intent, pallid face
778 and slender fingers.
779 "Jim," said Gideon, when the
780 door was closed, "you and I've
781 been working together for a long
782 time. We've done lots of pecul-
783 iar things. Jim"—Mr. Higsbee
784 hesitated, as though he was
785 embarrassed—"don't laugh. I
786 beg of you not to laugh. . . .
787 My conscience is troubling me."
788 Mr. Altyne did not laugh.
789 "Has the doctor been telling
790 you something?"
791 Gideon Higsbee nodded.
792 "Doctors are often damn liars!"
793 said Mr. Altyne, with unneces-
794 sary heat. "Why not sell him
795 a block of that mining stock
796 we've got outside?"
797 For a moment Mr. Higsbee's
798 eyes lighted and he stroked his
799 whiskers softly, but then he
800 shook his head.
801 "No, Jim," he said. "The
802 things I've done have perhaps
803 not all been strictly honest, but
804 then why should I be ethical?
805 I don't regret any of them. I've
806 never double-crossed a man un-
807 less he tried to do me first—
808 except once—and until that
809 doctor got hold of me I'd almost
810 forgotten that one time. Now
811 there's only one thing I can do
812 that will make me feel better.
813 I'm going up to Agamemnon,
814 Maine, tonight."
815 Mr. Altyne did not change his
816 expression. He only looked at

817 Gideon as a man might who has
818 speculated largely upon human
819 frailty until he is surprised by
820 nothing. Without unkindness
821 and without vulgarity, Mr.
822 Altyne looked at Gideon with
823 eyes that seemed to pierce the
824 veil of Gideon's whiskers. "With
825 that check you've just been
826 ordering?"

827 "Yes," said Gideon. "Have
828 you anything to say?"

829 "Only," replied Mr. Altyne,
830 "that in my experience I have
831 found that conscience in most
832 men is purely relative, depending
833 upon health. But even if you
834 wanted to sell the whole show
835 out, I'd be right behind you,
836 conscience or no conscience—
837 and I'm not laughing, Gideon."

838 Gideon, himself, was far from
839 laughing; for there had come to
840 him suddenly a thought.

841 "It'd be just like the damn
842 fool not to take the money."

843 And the importance of that
844 act of restitution loomed vast
845 before him, for he knew that
846 only its conclusion would quiet
847 those uneasy stirrings of his
848 conscience that had not let up
849 since the moment when Dr.
850 Follenshope had said. "If
851 there's anything on your
852 mind——"

853 Was there any wonder that
854 the occupants of the ancient
855 barge from the railroad to Aga-
856 memnon stared? It was not a
857 wholly unpleasant experience to
858 Gideon, because they stared not

859 only with vulgar curiosity but
860 with honest admiration. The
861 pale, metropolitan face and
862 watchful eyes of George were
863 eclipsed by Mr. Higsbee's suave
864 and venerable magnificence.
865 The pearl-gray spats upon his
866 patent-leather shoes, his gold-
867 headed cane and smooth silk
868 hat were like a dream come true,
869 like a living, rustic fairy tale of
870 benevolence and wealth. Mr.
871 Higsbee looked upon the oc-
872 cupants of the barge and smiled;
873 he seemed to be bubbling over
874 with an unusual geniality. Mr.
875 Higsbee managed even to smile
876 at the dingy room they showed
877 him at the Agamemnon House,
878 though he shuddered inwardly
879 to think that he had once
880 admired such quarters; and
881 when he and George were on
882 the snow again, plodding up the
883 street, Mr. Higsbee was still
884 cheerful.

885 "George," he said, "I feel
886 better. Oddly enough I already
887 feel better, and I know why it is.
888 It is because I am going to do a
889 kindness here. If you have a
890 chance to do a kindness, do it,
891 George."

892 George shivered slightly. He
893 looked singularly out of place,
894 somewhat like a rare orchid in a
895 cabbage patch. To George it
896 seemed that Mr. Higsbee was
897 becoming very queer, and that
898 the snow-covered houses on the
899 single street, with the turnings
900 and trimmings on their porches,

901 were overpoweringly grotesque.
902 "Did you used to live here?"
903 said George, staring unsym-
904 pathetically about him. "Did
905 you used to live here—honest?"
906 Mr. Higsbee twirled his cane.
907 "It all depends upon one's
908 standard of ethics, George," he
909 said. "But—yes, I used to live
910 here. Don't scoff at it, George,
911 don't scoff. A town like this is
912 the backbone of our nation,
913 George; and keep your eye on
914 the man you are about to see.
915 He is growing rare, George, very
916 rare."

917 Gideon remembered the house.
918 It looked like Lemuel Gower.
919 A native frame building out of
920 proportion, with storm windows
921 which glared frankly and openly
922 upon the winter afternoon. Yet
923 Gideon still felt benevolent and
924 joyful, and younger, too, for
925 perfect peace was stealing over
926 him already.

927 Lemuel Gower looked older,
928 but there he was standing in the
929 musty hall, awkward and an-
930 gular in his shabby coat, and
931 essentially just the same. There
932 was the same faith, the same
933 childish wonder in his eyes, the
934 same admiring smile upon his
935 rustic lips; and Lemuel was glad
936 to see him—pathetically glad.
937 His corncob pipe fell to the carpet
938 and tears stood in his eyes.

939 "Is it you, Gideon?" he kept
940 saying. "I want to know, I
941 want to know!" And he ushered
942 them into the sitting room.

943 Mr. Higsbee seated himself
944 upon a rocking-chair, because
945 it was the only chair that offered
946 even an approximation of com-
947 fort, and endeavored to balance
948 his silk hat upon his knee. The
949 feat, however, was somewhat
950 difficult, because the chair kept
951 moving backward, prompting
952 him to kick out his legs and
953 making him aware that his
954 position was not a little awk-
955 ward. However, even if the
956 chair had gone over backward,
957 and Gideon with it, he would
958 only have had to look at Lemuel
959 to feel completely self-possessed.

960 "And how has the world been
961 using you, Lemuel?" he asked.
962 It all was just the same. The
963 honest joy of Lemuel made
964 it seem like yesterday since
965 they had last met, and Gideon
966 felt perfectly, patronizingly at
967 ease.

968 "Gosh, Gid!" said Lemuel
969 Gower. "Gosh! It's good to see
970 you. It's kind of you to come in
971 like this, but I've always told the
972 boys at the store, 'Gid ain't
973 proud,' I've always said. 'If he
974 was to come in now he'd just set
975 on the cracker box like he always
976 did.' How's things going, did
977 you say? Not so good, Gid. But
978 now I've seen you, they're going
979 a whole lot better."

980 Gideon smiled, not even en-
981 deavoring to conceal his smile.
982 The utter guilelessness of Lemuel
983 was so remarkable that he would
984 not have believed it real unless

985 he had remembered. He stole
986 a glance at George, who was
987 sitting in the corner, and was
988 glad to see that George was
989 transfixed and staring.

990 "Oh!" said Gideon. "And
991 what has been the matter,
992 Lemuel?"

993 Lemuel Gower stuffed some
994 tobacco in his pipe and blinked
995 in a puzzled way. "It was
996 speculation, Gid," he said. "It
997 seemed awful good. A letter
998 came to me in the mail from
999 some parties in Chicago. They
1000 had heard of me being a repre-
1001 sentative citizen of the town and
1002 invited me to subscribe to an oil
1003 well that was just due to come
1004 in. I investigated and sub-
1005 scribed, and what do you think?"

1006 Gideon kicked out his feet to
1007 keep his balance and grasped at
1008 his silk hat. "How much did
1009 you put in?"

1010 Lemuel looked innocently sur-
1011 prised. "Why, as much as I
1012 could," he said. "Then I took
1013 a mortgage on the house, and
1014 then—do you know what hap-
1015 pened?"

1016 "Yes," said Gideon. "The
1017 oil well didn't come in."

1018 Lemuel's mouth fell open in
1019 blank amazement. "Gid," he
1020 said, "you do beat me how you
1021 know things. Ain't you the
1022 smartest feller? I always said
1023 you'd have to go to Bangor to
1024 find anyone as slick as you."

1025 Something of Gideon's patron-
1026 izing ease had gone and astonish-

1027 ment took its place. "And now
1028 you're cleaned out?" he asked.
1029 "What are you going to do?"

1030 "Oh," said Lemuel, "I ain't
1031 worryin'. I got my two hands
1032 yet. I guess I'll haul wood for a
1033 spell, and then when I get some
1034 more saved up, maybe another
1035 chance will come. There do
1036 seem to be opportunities up
1037 here if I only took 'em right,
1038 though I never'd be as sharp as
1039 you."

1040 Gideon coughed. The room
1041 seemed close and stifling, and
1042 his head began to ache.
1043 "Lemuel," said Gideon, "do you
1044 remember those three parties
1045 who came here who had a private
1046 wire to New York?"

1047 Lemuel Gower nodded.
1048 "Yes," he said. "That was
1049 another opportunity."

1050 "Another what?" Again
1051 Gideon was obliged to kick out
1052 to keep his balance.

1053 "Another opportunity," said
1054 Lemuel. "It was just my luck,
1055 Gid. The market didn't go
1056 right, and I lost more money."

1057 For the first time in years
1058 Gideon Higsbee's eyes grew wide
1059 with wonder. He had never
1060 asked for Lemuel's opinion on
1061 that old transaction. He had
1062 taken if for granted that Lemuel,
1063 like other disillusioned ones,
1064 would know he had been
1065 cheated.

1066 "Are you joking with me,
1067 Lemuel?" he asked.

1068 Lemuel's blank stare was an

answer in itself. "Why, Gid," he said, "I never joke! Of course I know some conundrums, but I never just plain joke."

Gideon perched himself nearer the edge of his chair. The nap on his silk hat was becoming rumpled. "And you thought those men were honest, those three sharpers who took your money?"

Lemuel raised a protesting hand. He looked surprised and pained. "Now, Gid," he said soothingly, "there's no use in calling 'em hard names. They were mistaken just like me. We all make mistakes."

"Mistaken!" Gideon's voice broke and ended in a squeak. "You crazy idiot! Those three men were crooks—thieves! They stole your money—stole it! Do you hear me?"

It did not seem possible. Not in a farce comedy would it have seemed possible. Lemuel's pipe fell to the floor, but he did not bother to pick it up. He sat transfixed, staring at Gideon Higsbee. "I want to know," said Lemuel. "I want to know. How do you know they were crooks? They were nice, pleasant-spoken fellers."

"How do I know it?" Gideon looked hopelessly about him. After all, how did he know it? "Why, anyone could tell they were crooks! It was the rankest confidence game——"

Words failed Gideon. He paused for breath, and then continued very quietly and very patiently: "Never mind how I know it, Lemuel. Just take my word. I do, and that's what I'm here for now, Lemuel, because I did know. I guess it hadn't occurred to me until the other day, but I guess I cheated you just as much as they did."

"How's that, Gid?" Lemuel Gower placed a bony hand behind his ear. "My hearin' ain't so good as it used to be. You said you did what?"

Gideon paused a moment to collect his thought. It was difficult—more difficult than he had believed. "Lemuel," he said, very carefully, "we were partners in that mill, do you remember? I wanted to get all that mill; I've always wanted to get things. When you told me that you had given those three crooks all your money, I couldn't resist it. I knew the game was fishy and I didn't tell you so. I might have saved your money then."

Gideon Higsbee coughed and felt in his breast pocket. "I'm getting to be an old man, Lemuel, yet I've never done a thing that I've been so much ashamed of as that, and now I want to square the books. You gave those men ten thousand dollars. It was my fault you lost it. Here, Lemuel, take it and shake hands."

At times on a lonely evening Gideon had read of such scenes.

The rich and fortunate man would smile and at the same time cough gruffly to hide the emotions in his voice. His poor but honest neighbor would be dumfounded, but would still give vent to emotions and expressions of loyalty and gratitude. Lemuel Gower, however, was different from the story book. He held the check gingerly in his calloused fingers without bothering to look at it; his other hand was still crooked behind his ear.

"What's that?" he asked. "I guess I didn't understand. I'm rather hard of hearing, Gideon."

Gideon raised his voice; at last he was growing irritated. "I said I was giving you back the ten thousand dollars you lost and its interest at 6 per cent for thirty years. I'm giving it back because I feel that I wasn't fair to you. That's what I said."

Still holdng the check in his calloused thumb and forefinger, Lemuel Gower extended it toward Gideon. "That's kind of you, Gid," he said. "What I'd expect from an old neighbor, but I couldn't take it, Gid. Honest, I couldn't."

"Forget about it," said Gideon heartily. "Put it in your pocket."

Lemuel Gower looked very strange. He actually was blushing. He pulled a blue bandanna handkerchief from his trousers pocket and mopped his honest face. "Gid," he said, "it makes me sort of ashamed of myself to find you doin' this. I couldn't take it, Gid, because I was the one who cheated—honest."

Gideon's silk hat rolled upon the floor, but Gideon did not pick it up. Again his voice rose and creaked and wavered. "You always were an infernal idiot," he said. "You never cheated anybody—couldn't cheat a fly." With difficulty Gideon had pulled himself to his feet, and Lemuel Gower had also risen.

"But I did cheat you, Gid," he said. "It hurts me to say it in the face of your kindness, but when I told you about my giving those three fellers all that money, it was too late for you to do anything about it. I meant for it to be too late, because"—he stammered and grew redder— "because I always sort of envied you, Gideon, you bein' so slick. I wanted to make some money without givin' you the chance to make it too. And mebbe those men were honest. I like to think they were. They seemed to me like nice, civil-spoken fellers."

He seized Gideon's hand and pressed something into Gideon's palm. Gideon felt it. It was the check. "Honest, Gid," said Lemuel, "take it back, I couldn't keep it. I'm gettin' to be a old man, Gid, and my conscience wouldn't let me."

Out in the snow, in the failing

sun of the afternoon, Gideon Higsbee found it difficult to walk, and leaned heavily on his cane, but even his cane was not enough to steady his tottering footsteps. "George," he said—his voice was hoarse, and both his voice and his hands were trembling—"did you hear what he said? Oh, my stars! Did you hear what he said? He cheated me because he wouldn't say that three confidence men were going to rob him! He wouldn't take a certified check when it was handed to him. Did you ever see anything to beat it, George? Do you wonder that I'm broken up?"

George, himself, looked paler than usual. He stared wide-eyed at the shadows on the snow. "It's contrary to nature," he said. "Here, you better take my arm."

Gideon looked over his shoulder. The gaunt and ugly house of Lemuel Gower was black and stolid against the sun. Gideon raised his cane toward it, and his whiskers bristled.

"But he hasn't beat me yet," said Gideon. "He hasn't beat me yet."

There was something wrong with Gideon when he reached his office the next afternoon. He did not only look tired—he looked more than tired. His whiskers had a bedraggled appearance, which traveling had never given them before.

Yes, there was something wrong with Gideon. Mr. Altyne perceived it at once when he entered Gideon's private room. Gideon had been pacing up and down the carpet, with hands behind his back, but on Mr. Altyne's appearance he stopped and thrust his head slightly forward. "Jim," said Gideon, "he wouldn't take the money."

Mr. Altyne did not look surprised, but then Mr. Altyne never looked surprised. "Well, what of it?" he asked.

Gideon opened his lips and closed them before he finally spoke. "I don't know what of it," said Gideon with a groan. "That's what beats me—I don't know at all. He fooled me, or I feel as if he fooled me. He's so damned honest and damned simple. Can you imagine his not taking the money? I can't sleep for thinking of it. I say, I don't know what he's done, but somehow he's put one over on me."

"It's too bad," said Mr. Altyne, "that you didn't sell him some of that mining stock we got outside."

Gideon did not appear to hear him. "Jim," he said, "I'm not joking. He put something over on me. I tell you he did. I won't feel better until he has that money. Jim, you've got to go up to Agamemnon, Maine."

Mr. Altyne did a very rare thing for him. He smiled and

he no longer had a masklike face.

"Gideon," he began, "you have the most outlandish way of doing a kindness. You hear me? What are you thinking about? What are you doing?"

Gideon was whistling softly and moving his hand in quick, short circles. "Excuse me, Jim," he said. "I was just thinking of my wife—that's all —just thinking of my wife."

It might have been a week later, more or less, that Gideon Higsbee came down to his breakfast room. The canary was singing the same song; Mrs. Higsbee was sitting behind the coffee urn, opening her letters. Merlin had pushed back his chair and was reading the paper.

"Good morning, my dear," said Gideon.

At the sound of his voice Mrs. Higsbee peered at him suspiciously around the coffee urn. "Gideon," she inquired, "have you been up to anything lately?"

"Up to anything!" Gideon Higsbee looked at her and smiled in pained surprise. "Why, what do you mean, my dear?"

"I mean," said Mrs. Higsbee, "that you're looking better this morning, even than you did yesterday, and I've always noticed that you look better when you've been up to something."

"Tweet!" went the canary "Tweet!"

Gideon did a most surprising thing; he rose and tapped Merlin on the shoulder.

"Merlin," he said, "take that bird out of the room. It disturbs me."

"Gideon!" began Mrs. Higsbee.

"Merlin," said Mr. Higsbee, "you heard me speak to you. Take that bird out of the room."

"Why, Gideon!" said Mrs. Higsbee. "I never knew you to behave so! You have been up to something!"

"Simply asserting myself, that's all, my dear," said Mr. Higsbee. "I've really done nothing since you asked me last yesterday morning, except I did sell a block of stock to Doctor Follenshope — mining stock, my dear. He's young; it will do him good to be interested in speculative investments. . . . I'll have my coffee now, please."

There was a moment of silence. Mrs. Higsbee was reading a letter. There were furrows upon her brow. "Gideon," she said at length, "don't make such a noise with your coffee."

"My dear," said Mr. Higsbee over the brim of his cup, "shall I make you a confession which I have delayed for years? I enjoy making a noise over my coffee."

"There," said Mrs. Higsbee, "you have been doing something, Gideon; I know you have, and don't say you haven't."

"Nothing since you asked me

last, my dear," said Mr. Higsbee.

There was another pause, broken again by Mrs. Higsbee, who made a curious sound and moved so suddenly that the coffee urn trembled. "Gideon," she said—"Gideon, what do you think?"

"Only what I should, my dear."

"I just got another letter from Susie Brickett. It's all about Lemuel Gower."

"Oh?" said Mr. Higsbee, and put down his coffee cup and stroked his whiskers. "And what does she say about Lemuel Gower?"

"You needn't take that attitude," said Mrs. Higsbee. "You needn't make fun of Lemuel any more. Lemuel's smart enough. Lemuel's made a lot of money. What do you say to that?"

"Nothing," said Gideon very softly. "Nothing at all, my dear."

"Well," said Mrs. Higsbee triumphantly, "perhaps you will say something when you hear how he made it, after the way you laughed at Lemuel. Three men came all the way up from New York to call on Lemuel because they had heard of him. You know, Lemuel does amount to something in Agamemnon. One of these three men was in one of the big banking houses in New York, in a confidential capacity. . . . What are you laughing at, Gideon? I don't see anything to laugh at."

"There isn't, my dear," said Gideon. "I'm not laughing. I was simply making a noise over my coffee."

"Well," said Mrs. Higsbee, "this man, who was in the big banking house, knew the president very well. The president had given him special information about the stock market, and these three men had a private wire from New York. They asked Lemuel to invest, and Lemuel did. Are you listening, Gideon?"

"Yes, my dear," said Gideon.

"Then why are you whistling and making circles with your hand?"

"I beg your pardon," said Gideon hastily. "I wasn't doing it intentionally."

"Then listen to this," said Mrs. Higsbee. "Lemuel did invest. He had a very hard time; he had to sell his house to find any money; but Lemuel gave them his money right away, because he felt that they were honest; and just as soon as Lemuel gave them the money the stock went up and up. Lemuel made thousands of dollars. I don't know how many thousand. Now what do you say to that?"

Gideon gently stroked his whiskers. He had never looked so youthful, so wholly devoid of guile.

"Do you hear me, Gideon?"

1489 said Mrs. Higsbee. "What do
1490 you think of that? You won't
1491 be able to laugh at Lemuel now."
1492 "My dear," said Mr. Higsbee
1493 —his words had never seemed to
1494 ring more sweetly; his voice had
1495 never been more dulcet—"I can
1496 only think what I thought
1497 before. Once a sucker, my
1498 dear, always a sucker." And
1499 Gideon Higsbee smiled and rub-
1500 bed his hands.
1501 Mrs. Higsbee looked startled
1502 and peered at Gideon around
1503 the coffee urn. "What do you
1504 mean, Gideon?" she demanded.
1505 "Lemuel didn't lose his money.

He made thousands and thou- 1506
sands of dollars." 1507
"What I said, my dear," said 1508
Gideon patiently. "Once a 1509
sucker, always a sucker. But 1510
I've said before, you don't 1511
understand business." Gideon 1512
smiled softly and stared at the 1513
ceiling. "I wonder," he began 1514
—"I wonder——" 1515
"What?" said Mrs. Higsbee. 1516
"Please talk louder, Gideon." 1517
"I wonder," said Gideon, still 1518
staring at the ceiling, "if Lemuel 1519
wouldn't also like to buy some 1520
mining stock." 1521

THE ANALYSIS

There are only two ways in which any story may be presented.
In one the order is chronological; in the other the order is flash-
back. The first one shows the situation or main narrative problem
emerging as a result of an interchange or interchanges; and the
explanatory matter necessary to an understanding of that main
narrative problem is presented to the reader before the main
problem itself, or simultaneously.

In the flash-back method the main narrative problem is
presented first, and the explanatory matter comes afterwards.
I am almost prepared to say that the capacity of a writer can be
judged by his ability to use the flash-back method adequately.
In discussing the story *Paradise Island* and the story *The Escape of
Mr. Trimm* I pointed out that there are two kinds of flash-back;
the one which flashes back from the main narrative question to the
explanatory matter, and the one which flashes back from an
important moment which is not the moment when the main narrative question emerges. This second type was the method used
in *The Escape of Mr. Trimm.*

Once and Always is a particularly interesting example of the
use of the flash-back by a competent and experienced writer. The
opening paragraphs from line 1 to line 70 present the chief actor
to the reader at a great moment of his life, the greatest moment,

perhaps, that can occur in the life of anybody, the moment when that person learns that he is in the shadow of death. Just as in *Paradise Island* Langley became important because he was in the shadow of death, so Gideon Higsbee instantly is made important to the reader because he is shown as about to die.

The first four steps of the interchange between Gideon Higsbee and Doctor Follenshope occupy lines 1 to 62. The fifth step, or the reflection of the actor upon what has passed, projects the main narrative purpose of the story, which is Gideon's attempts to restore to Lemuel Gower the $10,000. This step occupies lines 63 to 70. We have here the same type story as in *Paradise Island* in which the main narrative question is presented as an outgrowth of the first presentation unit, which here is an interchange, whereas in *Paradise Island* the main narrative question appears as the outgrowth of a meeting with a stimulus.

The interesting distinction between this story and the story *Paradise Island* is in the arrangement of the flash-back scenes in the remainder of the Beginning, concluding on line 852. Out of a total of 1521 lines for the story, the Beginning, containing the main narrative question and its explanatory matter, occupies 852. The especial difference between this story and *Paradise Island* in its flash-backs is this: in *Paradise Island* when the author flashes back he does it objectively. In this case, the flashing back is done not by the author but by the actor. It is a flash-back in the mind or consciousness of Gideon Higsbee.

This word "objective" would seem to take as its opposite and contrasting meaning the word "subjective." In ordinary criticism those are the two terms which are used. In discussing a poet, for example, we say that he presents his material "objectively" or "subjectively." If the poet describes a brook and makes us aware of that brook without in any way injecting into the description his own personal feeling, allowing the audience to receive whatever sensation it may from the stimuli which he presents, his presentation is "objective." Opposed to this, when he injects his own personality, and makes clear what *he* feels about the brook, then we say that his poetry is subjective.

But in dealing with the craftsmanship of short-story writing this is not an extremely important distinction. The distinction to be made is between the "objective" presentation, when the author presents the material to us, "objectively" in the same way that the "objective" poet does, and the "analytical" presentation by the author, when he indicates what is passing in the mind of an actor. Thus the terms we use in the criticism of short-story craftsmanship are "objective," and opposing the "objective" the "analytical." There are cases, of course, where the short-story writer is "subjective," but what I wish to draw to your attention is the special use of a new term, which is "analytical," as being the opposite of "objective."

Mr. Marquand is especially noteworthy for the ease with which he is able to change from the "objective" to the "analytical," or from the "analytical" to the "objective." On line 63 we learn that Gideon is thinking—that he has something on his mind—and so thinking there flashes into his mind a scene in the Agamemnon House. Beginning on line 172 the author becomes purely "objective" because this is a scene which could have been presented objectively. From lines 658 to 732 the author again becomes "analytical," because this is the fifth step of the interchange and deals with the reflections of the actor, those reflections being analyzed by the author, and rightly so. An example in this story of the flash-back scene which is presented objectively is the scene which begins on line 423 between Mrs. Higsbee and Gideon. It opens with the words, "Earlier that very morning, when he had entered the breakfast room of his brownstone house, etc." The actual interchange of that scene closes on line 648, where he says, "I hope to die if ever in my life I did a wrong to Lemuel Gower." The fifth step of that scene, on lines 649 to 657 projects him forward in time to the close of the scene with Dr. Follenshope, and as a result of that, there come his reflections on lines 658 to 750, as a result of which he presses a button on his desk for the man named George.

What every writer who is interested in analysis will find especially instructive about this story is that all of the Beginning is presented in a series of interchanges, and that those interchanges are almost invariably complete scenes, having purpose and clash to make them both narrative and dramatic, and that their fifth steps swiftly swing the reader either forward or backward into another interchange. Thus, at the close of the first interchange with Dr. Follenshope, Gideon swings the reader back to Agamemnon, Maine, some thirty years before, and out of that there grows the reflection that once a man is a sucker he will always be a sucker. The main character trait of Gideon Higsbee is immediately apparent, because he is shown as summing up the three strangers at once, and realizing that they are confidence men, whereas opposed to him is Lemuel Gower who is impressed tremendously by their distinguished bearing. This capacity of Gideon, which is his distinguishing trait, is the one which is used by the author to solve the narrative problem. It is interesting to see that the next step is a flash forward to the beginning of the interchange with Dr. Follenshope. At the close of this interchange the reader is aware of a dramatic hindrance through the reflection of Gideon that his own weakness may defeat his purpose of restoring the money.

The transition to earlier that morning is a very easy one and swings the reader into the interchange between Mrs. Higsbee and Gideon, when she tries to discover whether or not he has acted justly by Lemuel Gower, and Gideon's reflections upon that defiant, "I hope to die," again plunge the reader swiftly back to the close of the interview with Dr. Follenshope, and through that very swiftly into the interchange with George, and from that into the interchange with Mr. Altyne. At its close this interchange places emphasis upon a dramatic hindrance to the actor's main purpose when the reflections of the actor indicate that there is an opposing force to be reckoned with which may defeat the purpose which has now become paramount in importance. Thus the reader's attention is held by three different kinds of interest,—the main narrative interest of the main problem, with its hindrances at the close of each scene or interchange; the dramatic quality of the interchanges themselves as they disclose character; and the thematic interest of the story which comes from the author's feeling, expressed through the main actor in his story that once a man is a sucker he will always be a sucker, and that a basic trait will determine a character's action at almost any moment in life.

The Body of the story is composed of the interchange between Gideon and Lemuel in which the traits shown earlier in the story are again emphasized so that the reader is absolutely clear as to the kind of people engaged in the controversy. At the close of the interchange he is also aware that there has come the big moment of the story when, through the defeat of his attempt, the main actor is facing a moment of disaster which seems unavoidable and imminent. The quality of urgency is present because the reader knows that at any moment Gideon's heart may fail him completely, and that to achieve his purpose he must consummate this act of restitution in order to die happy.

The craftsmanship of portraying character consists in making clear to the reader the traits of character as shown by the reactions of an actor at any moment in life. The basic trait of Gideon—his ability to judge character,—is shown in his interchange with Mr.

Altyne after he has received his rebuff from Lemuel. He sums up Lemuel's character on line 1301 by saying "He's so damned honest and damned simple," then when Mr. Altyne says, "It's too bad you didn't sell him some of that mining stock we've got outside," Gideon instantly responds in terms of his main trait and there is born in his mind the scheme which is dependent upon his knowledge of Lemuel, who having once been a sucker will always be a sucker, and it is through his basic trait that he is able to bring about the solution to his problem.

Just as in *Jake Bolton, 551*, at the close of the final scene of the Body the main actor appears to have been defeated in his chief purpose, here Gideon appears to have been defeated in his purpose. But there was in *Jake Bolton, 551* an appended episodic meeting or interchange through which the reader learned the actual truth of the matter. Here through the interchange between Gideon and Mrs. Higsbee the reader is made aware of what actually transpired when Gideon sent Mr. Altyne and two other men up to Agamemnon, Maine, to impersonate the three strangers.

Realizing that Lemuel would not accept a straightforward offer because of this queer kink in his mind, and desiring to bring about the end he wished Gideon faked a "sucker scheme" for Lemuel for which Lemuel instantly "fell."

And just as in *Jake Bolton* the two speakers were caused to sum up the philosophy, or theme of the story, that is, what we call its significance, so here on lines 1509 to 1510 the significance is again summed up. It is that, "Once a sucker, always a sucker."

Almost any writer can learn to write the scenes for the Body of his story. The process is simply to get two opposing forces together and to make them clash, making sure that at the end of the clash the fifth step will form a crisis, preferably of hindrance, to the main narrative question. But the difficulty comes when writers try to write the long Beginning. The way out is through the flash-back method, and the flash-back method, as I have said before, consists of presenting the explanatory matter in interesting interchanges. One of the most instructive stories which any writer could read is this story, *Once and Always*. Because it is such a good model, and because it is such an example of character portrayal, I have great pleasure in including it in this volume.

There is a special device of craftsmanship which this story exemplifies, which has not been discussed before in this book. It is the Appended, as opposed to the Contained, Ending. When the Ending is Contained, the reader is shown the Conclusive Act *as it happens.* For example, in *Sunk,* the reader is aware of Jason Terwilliger's refusal to drink. In this story the reader is not aware of Gideon's device to make Lemuel accept the money *until after it has happened,* when he hears of it from Mrs. Higsbee. In the Contained Ending there is no delay between the final attempt of the Body of the Story and the Conclusive Act. In the Appended Ending another meeting intervenes.

ARCHITECTURAL CHART

OF

THE FACE IN THE WINDOW

SEQUEL	(Part 2)	Meeting. Sheriff Crumpett receives letter from Wiley.	1– 85	Effect of Conclusive Act is shown.
		Interchange. Sheriff and Joseph.	86– 108	Significance shown.
BEGINNING	Initial condition shown.	Interchange. Editor and his staff. (5th step.) Effect upon actors and observers.	109– 299 300– 320	Dangerous force appears.
	Main Actor's purpose is clear.	Interchange. Cora McBride and Duncan McBride.	312– 514	Difficulty shown. Desperate straits shown.
		Interchange (Mental). Different forces within.	515– 659	Promise of Disaster. Main Narrative Question: "Can Cora McBride capture Hap Ruggam?"
BODY	Series of attempts by Main Actor to achieve purpose, with attempts of opponent to prevent achievement.	Attempt to overcome Condition. (A natural obstacle of snow, etc.)	660– 957	Narrative Furtherance. Dramatic Hindrance. Tired.
		Attempt to overcome Hap Ruggam.	958–1370	Furtherance. Gun secured.
		Renewed attempt to overcome Hap Ruggam.	1371–1583	Cannot kill. Dramatic Hindrance.
		Scene. Hap Ruggam attempts to kill Cora. New condition formed.	1497–1583	Face appears. Furtherance.
ENDING	Conclusive Act.	Ruggam reacts to new condition. Collapses.	1584–1650	Main Narrative Question Answered: "Yes."
		Cora captures Ruggam.	1651–1665	
	Sequel (Part 1.)	Sheriff's party and Cora McBride.	1666–1702	Apparition explained. Significance shown.

THE FACE IN THE WINDOW

BY WILLIAM DUDLEY PELLEY

THE ordinary sequence of the divisions of a short-story is Explanatory Matter and Main Narrative Problem in the Beginning; Interchanges growing out of that problem, making up the Body; the Conclusive Act and its Sequel, making up the Ending. Usually when the "Flash-back" is used, it appears in the Beginning, changing the order of its subdivisions to Main Narrative Problem and Explanatory Matter. In this story the "Flash-back" is used in the Sequel, a sub-division of the Ending.

That, alone, would make *The Face in the Window* an instructive story for analysis; but in addition it contains a development of the different types of struggle that renders it especially illuminating to the student of craftsmanship.

CASE No. 9

THE FACE IN THE WINDOW

BY WILLIAM DUDLEY PELLEY

At nine o'clock this morning Sheriff Crumpett entered our New England town post-office for his mail. From his box he extracted his monthly Grand Army paper and a letter in a long yellow envelope. This envelope bore the return-stamp of a prominent Boston lumber-company. The old man crossed the lobby to the writing-shelf under the Western Union clock, hooked black-rimmed glasses on a big nose and tore a generous inch from the end of the envelope.

The first inclosure which met his eyes was a check. It was heavy and pink and crisp, and was attached to the single sheet of letter-paper with a clip. Impressed into the fabric of the safety-paper were the indelible figures of a protector: *Not over Five Thousand ($5000) Dollars.*

The sheriff read the name of the person to whom it was payable and gulped. His gnarled old hand trembled with excitement as he glanced over the clipped letter and then went through it again.

November 10, 1919.

MY DEAR SHERIFF:

Enclosed please find my personal check for five thousand dollars. It is made out to Mrs. McBride. Never having known the lady personally, and because you have evidently represented her with the authorities, I am sending it to you for proper delivery. I feel, from your enthusiastic account of her recent experience, that it will give you pleasure to present it to her.

Under the circumstances I do not begrudge the money. When first advised of Ruggam's escape, it was hot-headed impulse which prompted me to offer a reward so large. The old clan-blood of the Wileys must have made me murder-mad that Ruggam should regain his freedom permanently after the hellish thing he did to my brother. The newspapers heard of it, and then I could not retract.

213

60 That, however, is a thing of
61 the past. I always did detest a
62 welcher, and if this money is go-
63 ing to a woman to whom it will
64 be manna from heaven—to use
65 your words—I am satisfied.
66 Convey to her my personal con-
67 gratulations, gratitude and best
68 wishes.

69 Cordially yours,
70 C. V. D. WILEY.

71 "Good old Chris!" muttered
72 the sheriff. "He's rich because
73 he's white." He thrust both
74 check and letter back into the
75 long envelope and headed for the
76 office of our local daily paper at
77 a smart pace.

78 The earning of five thousand
79 dollars reward-money by Cora
80 McBride made an epochal news-
81 item, and in that night's paper
82 we headlined it accordingly—
83 not omitting proper mention of
84 the sheriff and giving him appro-
85 priate credit.

86 Having so started the an-
87 nouncement permeating through
88 the community, the old man em-
89 ployed the office phone and
90 called the local livery-stable. He
91 ordered a rig in which he might
92 drive at once to the McBride
93 house in the northern part of
94 town.

95 "But half that money ought
96 to be yourn!" protested the pro-
97 prietor of the stable as the sher-
98 iff helped him "gear up the
99 horse" a few minutes later.

100 "Under the circumstances, Jo-

101 seph, can you see me takin' it?
102 No; it ain't in me to horn in for
103 no rake-off on one o' the Lord's
104 miracles."

105 The old man climbed into the
106 sleigh, took the reins from the
107 liveryman and started the horse
108 from the livery yard.

109 Two weeks ago—on Monday,
110 the twenty-seventh of the past
111 October—the telephone-bell rang
112 sharply in our newspaper-office
113 a few moments before the paper
114 went to press. Now, the tele-
115 phone-bell often rings in our
116 newspaper-office a few moments
117 before going to press. The con-
118 fusion on this particular Monday
119 afternoon, however, resulted
120 from Albany calling on the long-
121 distance. Albany—meaning the
122 nearest office of the international
123 press-association of which our
124 paper is a member—called just
125 so, out of a clear sky, on the day
126 McKinley was assassinated, on
127 the day the *Titania* foundered,
128 and on the day Austria declared
129 war on Serbia.

130 The connection was made, and
131 over the wire came the voice of
132 young Stewart, crisp as lettuce.

133 "Special dispatch . . . Wynd-
134 gate, Vermont, October 27th . . .
135 Ready?"

136 The editor of our paper an-
137 swered in the affirmative. The
138 rest of us grouped anxiously
139 around his chair. Stewart pro-
140 ceeded:

141 "'Hapwell Ruggam, serving a
142 life-sentence for the murder of

143 Deputy Sheriff Martin Wiley at
144 a Lost Nation kitchen-dance two
145 years ago, killed Jacob Lamb-
146 well, his guard, and escaped from
147 prison at noon to-day.

148 " 'Ruggam had been given
149 some repair work to do near the
150 outer prison-gate. It was opened
151 to admit a tradesman's automo-
152 bile. As Guard Lambwell turned
153 to close the gate, Ruggam felled
154 him with his shovel. He escaped
155 to the adjacent railroad-yards,
156 stole a corduroy coat and pair of
157 blue overalls hanging in a switch-
158 man's shanty and caught the
159 twelve-forty freight up Green
160 River.' "

161 Stewart had paused. The edi-
162 tor scribbled frantically. In a
163 few words aside he explained to
164 us what Stewart was sending.
165 Then he ordered the latter to
166 proceed.

167 " 'Freight Number Eight was
168 stopped by telegraph near Nor-
169 wall. The fugitive, assuming
170 correctly that it was slowing
171 down for search, was seen by a
172 brakeman fleeing across a pas-
173 ture between the tracks and the
174 eastern edge of Haystack Moun-
175 tain. Several posses have al-
176 ready started after him, and
177 sheriffs all through northern
178 New England are being notified.

179 " 'Christopher Wiley, lumber
180 magnate and brother of Rug-
181 gam's former victim, on being
182 told of the escape, has offered
183 a reward of five thousand dollars
184 for Ruggam's capture, dead or

185 alive. Guard Lambwell was re-
186 moved to a hospital, where he
187 died at one-thirty.' . . . *All*
188 *right?*"

189 The connection was broken,
190 and the editor removed the head-
191 piece. He began giving orders.
192 We were twenty minutes behind
193 usual time with the papers, but
194 we made all the trains.

195 When the big Duplex was
196 grinding out newsprint with a
197 roar that shook the building, the
198 boys and girls gathered around
199 to discuss the thing which had
200 happened.

201 The Higgins boy, saucer-eyed
202 over the experience of being "on
203 the inside" during the handling
204 of the first sizable news-story
205 since he had become our local
206 reporter, voiced the interroga-
207 tion on the faces of other office
208 newcomers.

209 "Ruggam," the editor ex-
210 plained, "is a poor unfortunate
211 who should have been sent to an
212 asylum instead of the peniten-
213 tiary. He killed Mart Wiley, a
214 deputy sheriff, at a Lost Nation
215 kitchen-dance two years ago."

216 "Where's the Lost Nation?"

217 "It's a term applied to most
218 of the town of Partridgeville in
219 the northern part of the county
220 —an inaccessible district back
221 in the mountains peopled with
222 gone-to-seed stock and half-civ-
223 ilized illiterates who only get into
224 the news when they load up with
225 squirrel whisky and start a pro-
226 gramme of progressive hell.

227 Ruggam was the local black-
227 smith."

228 "What's a kitchen-dance?"

229 "Ordinarily a kitchen-dance is
230 harmless enough. But the Lost
231 Nation folks use it as an excuse
232 for a debauch. They gather in
233 some sizable shack, set the stove
234 out into the yard, soak them-
235 selves in aromatic spirits of dev-
236 iltry and dance from Saturday
237 night until Monday noon——"

238 "And this Ruggam killed a
239 sheriff at one of them?"

240 "He got into a brawl with an-
241 other chap about his wife.
242 Someone passing saw the fight
243 and sent for an officer. Mart
244 Wiley was deputy, afraid of
245 neither man, God nor devil.
246 Martin had grown disgusted
247 over the petty crime at these
248 kitchen-dances and started out
249 to clean up this one right. Hap
250 Ruggam killed him. He must
251 have had help, because he first
252 got Mart tied to a tree in the
253 yard. Most of the crowd was
254 pie-eyed by this time, anyhow,
255 and would fight at the drop of a
256 hat. After tying him securely,
257 Ruggam caught up a billet of
258 wood and—and killed him with
259 that."

260 "Why didn't they electrocute
261 him?" demanded young Higgins.

262 "Well, the murder wasn't ex-
263 actly premeditated. Hap wasn't
264 himself; he was drunk—not even
265 able to run away when Sheriff
266 Crumpett arrived in the neigh-
267 borhood to take him into cus-

268 tody. Then there was Hap's
269 bringing up. All these made ex-
270 tenuating circumstances."

271 "There was something about
272 Sheriff Wiley's pompadour," sug-
273 gested our little lady proof-
274 reader.

275 "Yes," returned the editor.
276 "Mart had a queer head of hair.
277 It was dark and stiff, and he
278 brushed it straight back in a
279 pompadour. When he was angry
280 or excited, it actually rose on his
281 scalp like wire. Hap's counsel
282 made a great fuss over Mart's
283 pompadour and the part it sort
284 of played in egging Hap on. The
285 sight of it, stiffening and rising
286 the way it did maddened Rug-
287 gam so that he beat it down
288 hysterically in retaliation for the
289 many grudges he fancied he owed
290 the officer. No, it was all right
291 to make the sentence life-impris-
292 onment, only it should have been
293 an asylum. Hap's not right.
294 You'd know it without being
295 told. I guess it's his eyes. They
296 aren't mates. They light up
297 weirdly when he's drunk or ex-
298 cited, and if you know what's
299 healthy, you get out of the way."

300 By eight o'clock that evening
301 most of the valley's deer-hunters,
302 all of the local adventurers who
303 could buy, borrow or beg a rifle,
304 and the usual quota of high-
305 school-sons of thoughtless parents
306 were off on the man-hunt in the
307 eastern mountains.

308 Among them was Sheriff
309 Crumpett's party. On reaching

the timber-line they separated. It was agreed that if any of them found signs of Ruggam, the signal for assistance was five shots in quick succession "and keep shooting at intervals until the rest come up."

We newspaper folk awaited the capture with professional interest and pardonable excitement. . . .

In the northern part of our town, a mile out on the Wickford road, is the McBride place. It is a small white house with a red barn in the rear and a neat rail fence inclosing the whole. Six years ago Cora McBride was bookkeeper in the local garage. Her maiden name was Allen. The town called her "Tomboy Allen." She was the only daughter of old Zeb Allen, for many years our county game-warden. Cora, as we had always known— and called—her, was a full-blown, red-blooded, athletic girl who often drove cars for her employer in the days when steering-wheels manipulated by women were offered as clinching proof that society was headed for the dogs.

Duncan McBride was chief mechanic in the garage repair-shop. He was an affable, sober, steady chap, popularly known as "Dunk the Dauntless" because of an uncanny ability to cope successfully with the ailments of 90 per cent. of the internal-combustion hay-balers and refractory tin-Lizzies in the county when other mechanics had given them up in disgust.

When he married his employer's bookkeeper, Cora's folks gave her a wedding that carried old Zeb within half an hour of insolvency and ran to four columns in the local daily. Duncan and the Allen girl motored to Washington in a demonstration-car, and while Dunk was absent the yard of the garage resembled the premises about a junkshop. On their return they bought the Johnson place, and Cora quickly demonstrated the same furious enthusiasm for home-making and motherhood that she had for athletics and carburetors.

Three years passed, and two small boys crept about the yard behind the white rail fence. Then—when Duncan and his wife were "making a great go of matrimony" in typical Yankee fashion—came the tragedy that took all the vim out of Cora, stole the ruddy glow from her girlish features and made her middle-aged in a twelvemonth. In the infantile-paralysis epidemic which passed over New England three years ago the McBrides suffered the supreme sorrow—twice. Those small boys died within two weeks of each other.

Duncan of course kept on with his work at the garage. He was quieter and steadier than ever.

394 But when we drove into the
395 place to have a carburetor ad-
396 justed or a rattle tightened, we
397 saw only too plainly that on his
398 heart was a wound the scars of
399 which would never heal. As for
400 Cora, she was rarely seen in the
401 village.

402 Troubles rarely come singly.
403 One afternoon this past August,
404 Duncan completed repairs on
405 Doc Potter's runabout. Cranking
406 the machine to run it from the
407 workshop, the "dog" on the
408 safety-clutch failed to hold. The
409 acceleration of the engine threw
410 the machine into high. Dunk
411 was pinned in front while the
412 roadster leaped ahead and
413 rammed the delivery truck of
414 the Red Front Grocery.

415 Duncan was taken to our me-
416 morial hospital with internal in-
417 juries and dislocation of his
418 spine. He remained there many
419 weeks. In fact, he had been
420 home only a couple of days when
421 the evening stage left in the
422 McBride's letter-box the daily
423 paper containing the story of
424 Ruggam's "break" and of the
425 reward offered for his cap-
426 ture.

427 Cora returned to the kitchen
428 after obtaining the paper and
429 sank wearily into a wooden
430 chair beside the table with the
431 red cloth. Spreading out the
432 paper, she sought the usual men-
433 tal distraction in the three-and
434 four-line bits which make up our
435 local columns.

436 As the headlines caught her
437 eye, she picked up the paper and
438 entered the bedroom where Dun-
439 can lay. There were telltale
440 traces of tears on his unshaven
441 face, and an ache in his discour-
442 aged heart that would not be
443 assuaged; for it was becoming
444 rumoured about the village that
445 Dunk the Dauntless might never
446 operate on the vitals of an ail-
447 ing tin-Lizzie again.

448 "Dunnie," cried his wife, "Hap
449 Ruggam's escaped!" Sinking
450 down beside the bedroom lamp
451 she read him the article aloud.

452 Her husband's name was men-
453 tioned therein; for when the
454 sheriff had commandeered an
455 automobile from the local garage
456 to convey him and his posse to
457 Lost Nation and secure Ruggam,
458 Duncan had been called forth to
459 preside at the steering-wheel.
460 He had thus assisted in the cap-
461 ture and later had been a witness
462 at the trial.

463 The reading ended, the man
464 rolled his head.

465 "If I wasn't held here, I might
466 go!" he said. "I might try for
467 that five thousand myself!"

468 Cora was sympathetic enough,
469 of course, but she was fast ap-
470 proaching the stage where she
471 needed sympathy herself.

472 "We caught him over on the
473 Purcell farm," mused Duncan.
474 "Something ailed Ruggam. He
475 was drunk and couldn't run.
476 But that wasn't all. He had had
477 some kind of crazy-spell during

or after the killing and wasn't quite over it. We tied him and lifted him into the auto. His face was a sight. His eyes aren't mates, anyhow, and they were wild and unnatural. He kept shrieking, something about a head of hair—black hair—sticks up like wire. He must have had an awful impression of Mart's face and that hair of his."

"I remember about Aunt Mary Crumpett's telling me of the trouble her husband had with his prisoner in the days before the trial," his wife replied. "He had those crazy-spells often, nights. He kept yelling that he saw Martin Wiley's head with its peculiar hair, and his face peering in at him through the cell window. Sometimes he became so bad that Sheriff Crumpett thought he'd have apoplexy. Finally he had to call Dr. Johnson to attend him."

"Five thousand dollars!" muttered Duncan. "Gawd! I'd hunt the devil *for nothing* if I only had a chance of getting out of this bed."

Cora smoothed her husband's rumpled bed, comforted him and laid her own tired head down beside his hand. When he had dozed off, she arose and left the room.

In the kitchen she resumed her former place beside the table with the cheap red cloth; and there, with her face in her hands, she stared into endless distance.

"Five thousand dollars! Five thousand dollars!" Over and over she whispered the words, with no one to hear.

The green-birch fire snapped merrily in the range. The draft sang in the flue. Outside, a soft, feathery snow was falling, for winter came early in the uplands of Vermont this past year. To Cora McBride, however, the winter meant only hardship. Within another week she must go into town and secure work. Not that she minded the labour nor the trips through the vicious weather! The anguish was leaving Duncan through those monotonous days before he should be up and around. Those dreary winter days! What might they not do to him—alone.

Five thousand dollars! Like many others in the valley that night she pictured with fluttering heart what it would mean to possess such a sum of money; but not once in her pitiful flight of fancy did she disregard the task which must be performed to gain that wealth.

It meant traveling upward in the great snowbound reaches of Vermont mountain-country and tracking down a murderer who had killed a second time to gain his freedom and would stop at nothing again.

And yet—*five thousand dollars!*

How much will a person do, how far will a normal human being travel, to earn five thou-

562 sand dollars—if the need is
563 sufficiently provocative?

564 As Cora McBride sat there in
565 the homely little farmhouse
566 kitchen and thought of the debts
567 still existent, contracted to save
568 the already stricken lives of two
569 little lads forgotten now by all
570 but herself and Duncan and God,
571 of the chances of losing their
572 home if Duncan could work no
573 more and pay up the balance of
574 their mortgage, of the days when
575 Duncan must lie in the south
576 bedroom alone and count the
577 figures on the wall paper—as she
578 sat there and contemplated these
579 things, into Cora McBride's
580 heart crept determination.

581 At first it was only a faint
582 challenge to her courage. As the
583 minutes passed, however, her
584 imagination ran riot, with five
585 thousand dollars to help them in
586 their predicament. The chal-
587 lenge grew. Multitudes of wom-
588 en down all the years had at-
589 tempted wilder ventures for
590 those who were dear to them.
591 Legion in number had been
592 those who set their hands and
593 hearts to greater tasks, made
594 more improbable sacrifices, taken
595 greater chances. Multitudes of
596 them, too, had won—on little
597 else than the courage of ignor-
598 ance and the strength of des-
599 peration.

600 She had no fear of the great
601 outdoors, for she had lived close
602 to the mountains from childhood
603 and much of her old physical

604 resiliency and youthful daredev-
605 iltry remained. And the need
606 was terrible; no one anywhere
607 in the valley, not even her own
608 people, knew how terrible.

609 Cora McBride, alone by her
610 table in the kitchen, that night
611 made her decision.

612 She took the kitchen lamp and
613 went upstairs. Lifting the top of
614 a leather trunk, she found her
615 husband's revolver. With it was
616 a belt and holster, the former
617 filled with cartridges. In the
618 storeroom over the back kitchen
619 she unhooked Duncan's macki-
620 naw and found her own tobog-
621 gan-cap. From a corner behind
622 some fishing-rods she salvaged a
623 pair of summer-dried snowshoes;
624 they had facilitated many a pre-
625 vious hike in the winter woods
626 with her man of a thousand ad-
627 ventures. She searched until she
628 found the old army-haversack
629 Duncan used as a game-bag. Its
630 shoulder-straps were broken but
631 a length of rope sufficed to bind
632 it about her shoulders, after she
633 had filled it with provisions.

634 With this equipment she re-
635 turned below-stairs. She drew
636 on heavy woolen stockings and
637 buckled on arctics. She entered
638 the cold pantry and packed the
639 knapsack with what supplies she
640 could find at the hour. She did
641 not forget a drinking-cup, a
642 hunting-knife or matches. In
643 her blouse she slipped a house-
644 hold flash-lamp.

645 Dressed finally for the adven-

646 ture, from the kitchen she called
647 softly to her husband. He did
648 not answer. She was over-
649 whelmed by a desire to go into
650 the south bedroom and kiss him,
651 so much might happen before
652 she saw him again. But she re-
653 strained herself. She must not
654 waken him.

655 She blew out the kerosene
656 lamp, gave a last glance about
657 her familiar kitchen and went
658 out through the shed door,
659 closing it softly behind her.

660 It was one of those close, quiet
661 nights when the bark of a distant
662 dog or whinny of a horse sounds
663 very near at hand. The snow
664 was falling feathery.

665 An hour later found her far to
666 the eastward, following an old
667 side road that led up to the Har-
668 rison lumber-job. She had mean-
669 time paid Dave Sheldon, a
670 neighbour's boy, encountered by
671 his gate, to stay with Duncan
672 during her absence which she
673 explained with a white lie. But
674 her conscience did not bother.
675 Her conscience might be called
676 upon to smother much more be-
677 fore the adventure was ended.

678 Off in the depths of the snow-
679 ing night she strode along, a
680 weird figure against the eerie
681 whiteness that illumined the win-
682 ter world. She felt a strange
683 wild thrill in the infinite out-of-
684 doors. The woodsman's blood
685 of her father was having its
686 little hour.

687 And she knew the woods. In-
688 tuitively she felt that if Ruggam
689 was on Haystack Mountain
690 making his way toward Lost
691 Nation, he would strike for the
692 shacks of the Green Mountain
693 Club or the deserted logging-
694 camps along the trail, secreting
695 himself in them during his pauses
696 for rest, for he had no food, and
697 provisions were often left in
698 these structures by hunters and
699 mountain hikers. Her plan was
700 simple. She would investigate
701 each group of buildings. She
702 had the advantage of starting on
703 the northwest side of Haystack.
704 She would be working toward
705 Ruggam, while the rest of the
706 posses were trailing him.

707 Mile after mile she covered.
708 She decided it must be midnight
709 when she reached the ghostly
710 buildings of the Harrison tract,
711 lying white and silent under the
712 thickening snow. It was useless
713 to search these cabins; they were
714 too near civilization. Besides, if
715 Ruggam had left the freight at
716 Norwall on the eastern side of
717 Haystack at noon, he had thirty
718 miles to travel before reaching
719 the territory from which she was
720 starting. So she skirted the
721 abandoned quiet of the clearing,
722 laid the snowshoes properly down
723 before her and bound the thongs
724 securely about her ankles.

725 She had plenty of time to
726 think of Ruggam as she padded
727 along. He had no snowshoes to
728 aid him, unless he had managed
729 to secure a pair by burglary,

730 which was improbable. So it
731 was not difficult to calculate
732 about where she should begin
733 watching for him. She believed
734 he would keep just off the main
735 trail to avoid detection, yet take
736 its general direction in order to
737 secure shelter and possible food
738 from the mountain buildings.
739 When she reached the country
740 in which she might hope to en-
741 counter him, she would zigzag
742 across that main trail in order to
743 pick up his foot-tracks if he had
744 passed her undetected. In that
745 event she would turn and follow.
746 She knew that the snow was fall-
747 ing too heavily to continue in
748 such volume indefinitely; it
749 would stop as suddenly as it had
750 started.

751 The hours of the night piled
752 up. The silent, muffling snow-
753 fall continued. And Cora Mc-
754 Bride began to sense an alarm-
755 ing weariness. It finally dawned
756 upon her that her old-time vig-
757 our was missing. The strength
758 of youth was hers no longer.
759 Two experiences of motherhood
760 and no more exercise than was
761 afforded by the tasks of her
762 household, had softened her mus-
763 cles. Their limitations were
764 now disclosed.

765 The realization of those limi-
766 tations was accompanied by
767 panic. She was still many miles
768 even from Blind Brook Cabin,
769 and her limbs were afire from
770 the unaccustomed effort. This
771 would never do. After pauses

772 for breath that were coming
773 closer and closer together, she
774 set her lips each time grimly.
775 "Tomboy Allen" had not count-
776 ed on succumbing to physical
777 fatigue before she had climbed
778 as far as Blind Brook. If she
779 were weakening already, what of
780 those many miles on the other
781 side?

782 Tuesday the twenty-eighth of
783 October passed with no tidings
784 of Ruggam's capture. The
785 Holmes boy was fatally shot by
786 a rattle-headed searcher near
787 Five-Mile Pond, and distraught
788 parents began to take thought
789 of their own lads missing from
790 school. Adam MacQuarry broke
791 his leg near the Hell Hollow
792 schoolhouse and was sent back
793 by friends on a borrowed bob-
794 sled. Several ne'er-do-wells, long
795 on impulse and short on stick-
796 ability, drifted back to more
797 comfortable quarters during the
798 day, contending that if Hap were
799 captured, the officers would claim
800 the reward anyhow—so what
801 was the use bucking the System?

802 The snowfall stopped in the
803 early morning. Sunrise disclosed
804 the world trimmed from horizon
805 to horizon in fairy fluff. House-
806 holders jocosely shoveled their
807 walks; small children resurrected
808 attic sleds; here and there a far-
809 mer appeared on Main Street
810 during the forenoon in a pung-
811 sleigh or cutter with jingling
812 bells. The sun soared higher,
813 and the day grew warmer. Eaves

814 began dripping during the noon
815 hour, to stop when the sun sank
816 about four o'clock behind Ban-
817 croft's hill.

818 After the sunset came a per-
819 fect evening. The starlight was
820 magic. Many people called in
821 at the newspaper-office, after the
822 movies, to learn if the man hunt
823 had brought results.

824 Between ten and eleven
825 o'clock the lights on the valley
826 floor blinked out; the town had
827 gone to bed—that is, the lights
828 blinked out in all homes except-
829 ing those on the eastern out-
830 skirts, where nervous people wor-
831 ried over the possibilities of a
832 hungry, hunted convict burglar-
833 izing their premises, or drawn-
834 faced mothers lived mentally
835 through a score of calamities be-
836 falling red-blooded sons who had
837 now been absent twenty-four
838 hours.

839 Sometime between nine o'clock
840 and midnight—she had no way
841 of telling accurately—Cora Mc-
842 Bride stumbled into the Lyons
843 clearing. No one would have
844 recognized in the staggering, be-
845 draggled apparition that emerged
846 from the silhouette of the timber
847 the figure that had started so
848 confidently from the Harrison
849 tract the previous evening.

850 For over an hour she had hob-
851 bled blindly. It was wholly by
852 accident that she had stumbled
853 into the clearing. And the cap-
854 ture of Ruggam had diminished
855 in importance. Warm food,

856 water that would not tear her
857 raw throat, a place to lie and re-
858 coup her strength after the chill-
859 ing winter night—these were the
860 only things that counted now.
861 Though she knew it not, in her
862 eyes burned the faint light of
863 fever. When a snag caught her
864 snowshoe and tripped her, there
865 was hysteria in her cry of resent-
866 ment.

867 As she moved across from the
868 timber-line her hair was revealed
869 fallen down; she had lost a glove,
870 and one hand and wrist were
871 cruelly red where she had
872 plunged them several times into
873 the snow to save herself from
874 falling upon her face. She made
875 but a few yards before the icy
876 thong of her right snowshoe
877 snapped. She did not bother to
878 repair it. Carrying it beneath
879 her arm, she hobbled brokenly
880 toward the shelter of the
881 buildings.

882 Her failure at the other cabins,
883 the lack, thus far, of all signs of
884 the fugitive, the vastness of the
885 hunting-ground magnified by the
886 loneliness of winter, had con-
887 vinced her finally that her quest
888 was futile. It was all a venture
889 of madness. The idea that a
890 woman, alone and single-handed,
891 with no weapon but a revolver,
892 could track down and subdue a
893 desperate murderer in winter
894 mountains where hardly a wild
895 thing stirred, and make him re-
896 turn with her to the certain pen-
897 alty—this proved how much

mental mischief had again been caused by the lure of money. The glittering seduction of gold had deranged her. She realized it now, her mind normal in an exhausted body. So she gained the walls of the building and stumbled around them, thoughtless of any possible signs of the fugitive.

The stars were out in myriads. The Milky Way was a spectacle to recall vividly the sentiment of the Nineteenth Psalm. The log buildings of the clearing, every tree-trunk and bough in the woods beyond, the distant sky-line of stump and hollow, all stood out sharply against the peculiar radiance of the snow. The night was as still as the spaces between the planets.

Like some wild creature of those winter woods the woman clumped and stumbled around the main shack, seeking the door.

Finding it, she stopped, the snowshoe slipped from beneath her arm; one numb hand groped for the log door-casing in support; the other fumbled for the revolver.

Tracks led into that cabin!

A paralysis of fright gripped Cora McBride. Something told her intuitively that she stood face to face at last with what she had traveled all this mountain wilderness to find. Yet with sinking heart it also came to her that if Hap Ruggam had made these tracks and were still within, she must face him in her exhausted condition and at once make that tortuous return trip to civilization. There would be no one to help her.

She realized in that moment that she was facing the primal. And she was not primal. She was a normal woman, weakened to near-prostration by the trek of the past twenty-four hours. Was it not better to turn away while there was time?

She stood debating thus, the eternal silence blanketing forest-world and clearing. But she was allowed to make no decision.

A living body sprang suddenly upon her. Before she could cry out, she was borne down precipitously from behind.

She tried to turn the revolver against the Thing upon her, but the gun was twisted from her raw, red fingers. The snow into which she had been precipitated blinded her. She smeared an arm across her eyes, but before clear sight was regained, talon fingers had ripped her shoulders. She was half lifted, half-dragged through the doorway, and there she was dropped on the plank flooring. Her assailant, turning, made to close and bar the door.

When she could see clearly, she perceived a weak illumination in the cabin. On the rough bench-table, shaded by two slabs of bark, burned the stub of a

982 tallow candle probably left by
983 some hunting-party.

984   The windows were curtained
985 with rotting blankets. Some
986 rough furniture lay about; rusted
987 cooking-utensils littered the ta-
988 bles, and at one end was a sheet-
989 iron stove. The place had been
990 equipped after a fashion by deer-
991 hunters or mountain hikers, who
992 brought additional furnishings to
993 the place each year and left
995 mouldy provisions and uncon-
996 sumed firewood behind.

997   The man succeeded finally in
998 closing the door. He turned
999 upon her.

1000   He was short and stocky. The
1001 stolen corduroy coat covered
1002 blacksmith's muscles now made
1003 doubly powerful by dementia.
1004 His hair was lifeless black and
1005 clipped close, prison-fashion.
1006 His low forehead hung over burn-
1007 ing, mismated eyes. From her
1008 helplessness on the floor Cora
1009 McBride stared up at him.

1010   He came closer.

1011   "Get up!" he ordered. "Take
1012 that chair. And don't start no
1013 rough-house; whether you're a
1014 woman or not, I'll drill you!"

1015   She groped to the indicated
1016 chair and raised herself, the sin-
1017 gle snowshoe still dragging from
1018 one foot. Again the man sur-
1019 veyed her. She saw his eyes and
1020 gave another inarticulate cry.

1021   "Shut your mouth and keep it
1022 shut! You hear me?"

1023   She obeyed.

1024   The greenish light burned
1025 brighter in his mismated eyes,
1026 which gazed intently at the top
1027 of her head as though it held
1028 something unearthly.

1029   "Take off your hat!" was his
1030 next command.

1031   She pulled off the toque. Her
1032 hair fell in a mass on her snow-
1033 blotched shoulders. Her captor
1034 advanced upon her. He reached
1035 out and satisfied himself by
1036 touch that something was not
1037 there which he dreaded. In hyp-
1038 notic fear she suffered that touch.
1039 It reassured him.

1040   "Your hair now," he demand-
1041 ed; "it don't stand up, does it?
1042 No, o' course it don't. You ain't
1043 *him;* you're a woman. But if
1044 your hair comes up, I'll kill you
1045 —understand? If your hair
1046 comes up, *I'll kill you!*"

1047   She understood. She under-
1048 stood only too well. She was not
1049 only housed with a murderer;
1050 she was housed with a maniac.
1051 She sensed, also, why he had
1052 come to this mountain shack so
1053 boldly. In his dementia he knew
1054 no better. And she was alone
1055 with him, unarmed now.

1056   "I'll keep it down," she whis-
1057 pered, watching his face out of
1058 fear-distended eyes.

1059   The wind blew one of the rot-
1060 ten blankets inward. Thereby
1061 she knew that the window-aper-
1062 ture on the south wall contained
1063 no sash. He must have removed
1064 it to provide means of escape in
1065 case he were attacked from the
1066 east door. He must have climbed

1067 out that window when she came
1068 around the shack; that is how
1069 he had felled her from behind.

1070 He stepped backward now un-
1071 til he felt the edge of the bench
1072 touch his calves. Then he sank
1073 down, one arm stretched along
1074 the table's rim, the hand clutch-
1075 ing the revolver.

1076 "Who are you?" he demanded.

1077 "I'm Cora McB——" She
1078 stopped—she recalled in a flash
1079 the part her husband had played
1080 in his former capture and trial.
1081 "I'm Cora Allen," she corrected.
1082 Then she waited, her wits in
1083 chaos. She was fighting desper-
1084 ately to bring order out of that
1085 chaos.

1086 "What you doin' up here?"

1087 "I started for Millington, over
1088 the mountain. I lost my way."

1089 "Why didn't you go by the
1090 road?"

1091 "It's further."

1092 "That's a lie! It ain't. And
1093 don't lie to me, or I'll kill you!"

1094 "Who are you?" she heard her-
1095 self asking. "And why are you
1096 acting this way with me?"

1097 The man leaned suddenly
1098 forward.

1099 "You mean to tell me you
1100 don't know?"

1101 "A lumberjack, maybe, who's
1102 lost his way like myself?"

1103 His expression changed
1104 abruptly.

1105 "What you luggin' *this* for?"
1106 He indicated the revolver.

1107 "For protection."

1108 "From what?"

1109 "Wild things."

1110 "There ain't no wild things in
1111 these mountains this time o'
1112 year; they're snowed up, and
1113 you know it."

1114 "I just felt safer to have it
1115 along."

1116 "To protect you from men-
1117 folks, maybe?"

1118 "There are no men in these
1119 mountains I'm afraid of!" She
1120 made the declaration with path-
1121 etic bravado.

1122 His eyes narrowed.

1123 "I think I better kill you," he
1124 decided. "You've seen me; you'll
1125 tell you seen me. Why shouldn't
1126 I kill you? You'd only tell."

1127 "Why? What have I done to
1128 you?" she managed to stammer.
1129 "Why should you object to being
1130 seen?"

1131 It was an unfortunate demand.
1132 He sprang up with a snarl.
1133 Pointing the revolver from his
1134 hip, he drew back the hammer.

1135 *"Don't!"* she shrieked. "Are
1136 you crazy? Don't you know
1137 how to treat a woman—in dis-
1138 tress?"

1139 "Distress, *hell!* You know
1140 who I be. And I don't care
1141 whether you're a woman or not,
1142 I ain't goin' to be took—you
1143 understand."

1144 "Certainly I understand."

1145 She said it in such a way that
1146 he eased the hammer back into
1147 place and lowered the gun. For
1148 the moment again she was safe.
1149 In response to her terrible need,
1150 some of her latent Yankee cour-

age came now to aid her. "I don't see what you're making all this rumpus about" she told him in as indifferent a voice as she could command. "I don't see why you should want to kill a friend who might help you—if you're really in need of help."

"I want to get to Partridge-ville," he muttered after a moment.

"You're not far from there. How long have you been on the road?"

"None of your business."

"Have you had any food?"

"No."

"If you'll put up that gun and let me get off this snowshoe and pack, I'll share with you some of the food I have."

"Never you mind what I do with this gun. Go ahead and fix your foot, and let's see what you got for grub." The man resumed his seat.

She twisted up her tangled hair, replaced her toque and untied the dangling snowshoe.

Outside a tree cracked in the frost. He started in hairtrigger fright. Creeping to the window, he peeped cautiously between casing and blanket. Convinced that it was nothing, he returned to his seat by the table.

"It's too bad we couldn't have a fire," suggested the woman then. "I'd make us something hot." The stove was there, rusted but still serviceable; available wood was scattered around.

But the man shook his bullet head.

After a trying time unfastening the frosted knots of the ropes that had bound the knapsack upon her back, she emptied it onto the table. She kept her eye, however, on the gun. He had disposed of it by thrusting it into his belt. Plainly she would never recover it without a struggle. And she was in no condition for physical conflict.

"You're welcome to anything I have," she told him.

"Little you got to say about it! If you hadn't given it up I'd took it away from you. So what's the difference?"

She shrugged her shoulders. She started around behind him but he sprang toward her.

"Don't try no monkey-shines with me!" he snarled. "You stay here in front where I can see you."

She obeyed, watching him make what poor meal he could from the contents of her bag.

She tried to reason out what the dénouement of the situation was to be. He would not send her away peacefully, for she knew he dared not risk the story she would tell regardless of any promises of secrecy she might give him. If he left her bound in the cabin, she would freeze before help came—if it ever arrived.

No, either they were going to leave the place and journey forth together—the Lord only knew where or with what outcome—or the life of one of them was to end in this tragic place within the coming few minutes. For she realized she must use that gun with deadly effect if it were to come again into her possession.

The silence was broken only by the noises of his lips as he ate ravenously. Outside, not a thing stirred in that snow-bound world. Not a sound of civilization reached them. They were a man and woman in the primal, in civilization and yet a million miles from it.

"The candle's going out," she announced. "Is there another?"

"There'll be light enough for what I got to do," he growled.

Despite her effort to appear indifferent, her great fear showed plainly in her eyes.

"Are we going to stay here all night?" she asked with a pathetic attempt at lightness.

"That's my business."

"Don't you want me to help you?"

"You've helped me all you can with the gun and food."

"If you're going to Partridge-ville, I'd go along and show you the way."

He leaped up.

"*Now I know you been lyin'!*" he bellowed. "You said you was headed for Millington. And you ain't at all. You're watch-in' your chance to get the drop on me and have me took—that's what you're doin'!"

"Wait!" she pleaded desperately. "I *was* going to Millington. But I'd turn back and show you the way to Partridge-ville to help you."

"What's it to you?" He had drawn the gun from his belt and now was fingering it nervously.

"You're lost up here in the mountains, aren't you?" she said. "I couldn't let you stay lost if it was possible for me to direct you on your way."

"You said you was lost your-self."

"I was lost—until I stumbled into this clearing. That gave me my location."

"Smart, ain't you? Damn' smart, but not too smart for me, you woman!" The flare flamed up again in his crooked eyes. "You know who I be, all right. You know what I'm aimin' to do. And you're stallin' for time till you can put one over. But you can't—see? I'll have this busi-ness done with. I'll end this business!"

She felt herself sinking to her knees. He advanced and gripped her left wrist. The crunch of his iron fingers sent an arrow of pain through her arm. It bore her down.

"For God's sake—*don't!*" she whispered hoarsely, over-whelmed with horror. For the cold sharp nose of the revolver suddenly punched her neck.

1318 "I ain't leavin' no traces be-
1319 hind. Might as well be hung for
1320 a sheep as a lamb. Never mind
1321 if I do——"

1322 "Look!" she cried wildly.
1323 "Look, look, *look!*" And with
1324 her free hand she pointed behind
1325 him.

1326 It was an old trick. There
1327 was nothing behind him. But
1328 in that instant of desperation in-
1329 stinct had guided her.

1330 Involuntarily he turned.

1331 With a scream of pain she
1332 twisted from his grasp and blot-
1333 ted out the candle.

1334 A long, livid pencil of orange
1335 flame spurted from the gunpoint.
1336 She sensed the powder-flare in
1337 her face. He had missed.

1338 She scrambled for shelter be-
1339 neath the table. The cabin was
1340 now in inky blackness. Across
1341 that black four more threads of
1342 scarlet light were laced. The
1343 man stumbled about seeking her,
1344 cursing with blood-curdling blas-
1345 phemy.

1346 Suddenly he tripped and went
1347 sprawling. The gun clattered
1348 from his bruised fingers; it
1349 struck the woman's knee.

1350 Swiftly her hand closed upon
1351 it. The hot barrel burned her
1352 palm.

1353 She was on her feet in an in-
1354 stant. Her left hand fumbled in
1355 her blouse, and she found what
1356 had been there all along—the
1357 flash-lamp.

1358 With her back against the
1359 door, she pulled it forth. With

the gun thrust forward for action 1360
she pressed the button. 1361

"I've got the gun—*get up!*" 1362
she ordered. "Don't come too 1363
near me or I'll shoot. Back up 1364
against that wall." 1365

The bull's-eye of radiance 1366
blinded him. When his eyes 1367
became accustomed to the 1368
light, he saw its reflection on 1369
the barrel of the revolver. He 1370
obeyed. 1371

"Put up your hands. Put 'em 1372
up *high!*" 1373

"Suppose I won't?" 1374

"I'll kill you." 1375

"What'll you gain by that?" 1376

"Five thousand dollars." 1377

"Then you know who I be?" 1378

"Yes." 1379

"And was aimin' to take me 1380
in?" 1381

"Yes." 1382

"How you goin' to do that if 1383
I won't go?" 1384

"You're going to find out." 1385

"You won't get no money 1386
shootin' me." 1387

"Yes, I will—just as much— 1388
dead as alive." 1389

With his hands raised a little 1390
way above the level of his shoul- 1391
ders, he stood rigidly at bay in 1392
the circle of light. 1393

"Well," he croaked at last, 1394
"go ahead and shoot. I ain't 1395
aimin' to be took—not by no 1396
woman. Shoot, damn you, and 1397
have it done with. I'm waitin'!" 1398

"Keep up those hands!" 1399

"I won't!" He lowered them 1400
defiantly. "I w-wanted to m- 1401

1402 make Partridgeville and see the
1403 old lady. She'd 'a' helped me.
1404 But anything's better'n goin'
1405 back to that hell where I been
1406 the last two years. Go on! Why
1407 don't you shoot?"

1408 "You wanted to make Par-
1409 tridgeville and see—*who?*"

1410 "My mother—and my wife."

1411 "Have you got a mother?
1412 Have you got a—wife?"

1413 "Yes, and three kids. Why
1414 don't you shoot?"

1415 It seemed an eon that they
1416 stood so. The McBride woman
1417 was trying to find the nerve to
1418 fire. She could not. In that in-
1419 stant she made a discovery that
1420 many luckless souls make too
1421 late: *to kill a man* is easy to talk
1422 about, easy to write about. But
1423 to stand deliberately face to face
1424 with a fellow-human—alive, pul-
1425 sing, breathing, fearing, hoping,
1426 loving, living,—point a weapon
1427 at him that would take his life,
1428 blot him from the earth, negate
1429 twenty or thirty years of child-
1430 hood, youth, maturity, and make
1431 of him in an instant—nothing!—
1432 that is quite another matter.

1433 He was helpless before her
1434 now. Perhaps the expression on
1435 his face had something to do
1436 with the sudden revulsion that
1437 halted her finger. Facing cer-
1438 tain death, some of the evil in
1439 those crooked eyes seemed to die
1440 out, and the terrible personality
1441 of the man to fade. Regardless
1442 of her danger, regardless of what
1443 he would have done to her if luck

1444 had not turned the tables, Cora
1445 McBride saw before her only
1446 a lone man with all society's
1447 hand against him, realizing he
1448 had played a bad game to the
1449 limit and lost, two big tears
1450 creeping down his unshaved face,
1451 waiting for the end.

1452 "Three children!" she whis-
1453 pered faintly.

1454 "Yes."

1455 "You're going back to see
1456 them?"

1457 "Yes, and my mother. Moth-
1458 er'd help me get to Canada—
1459 somehow."

1460 Cora McBride had forgotten
1461 all about the five thousand dol-
1462 lars. She was stunned by the
1463 announcement that this man had
1464 relatives—a mother, a wife, *three*
1465 babies. The human factor had
1466 not before occurred to her. Mur-
1467 derers! They have no license to
1468 let their eyes well with tears, to
1469 have wives and babies, to possess
1470 mothers who will help them get
1471 to Canada regardless of what
1472 their earthly indiscretions may
1473 have been.

1474 At this revelation the gun-
1475 point wavered. The sight of
1476 those tears on his face sapped
1477 her will-power even as a wound
1478 in her breast might have drained
1479 her life-blood.

1480 Her great moment had been
1481 given her. She was letting it slip
1482 away. She had her reward in
1483 her hand for the mere pulling of
1484 a trigger and no incrimination
1485 for the result. For a bit of

1486 human sentiment she was bung-
1487 ling the situation unpardonably,
1488 fatally.

1489 Why did she not shoot? Be-
1490 cause she was a woman. Be-
1491 cause it is the God-given purpose
1492 of womanhood to give life, not
1493 take it.

1494 The gun sank, sank—down
1495 out of the light, down out of
1496 sight.

1497 And the next instant he was
1498 upon her.

1499 The flash-lamp was knocked
1500 from her hand and blinked out.
1501 It struck the stove and she heard
1502 the tinkle of the broken lens.
1503 The woman's hand caught at the
1504 sacking before the window at her
1505 left shoulder. Gripping it wild-
1506 ly to save herself from that on-
1507 slaught, she tore it away. For
1508 the second time the revolver was
1509 twisted from her raw fingers.

1510 The man reared upward, over
1511 her.

1512 "Where are you?" he roared
1513 again and again. "I'll show
1514 you! Lemme at you!"

1515 Outside the great yellow moon
1516 of early winter, arising late, was
1517 coming up over the silhouetted
1518 line of purple mountains to the
1519 eastward. It illumined the cab-
1520 in with a faint radiance, disclos-
1521 ing the woman crouching be-
1522 neath the table.

1523 The man saw her, pointed his
1524 weapon point-blank at her face
1525 and fired.

1526 To Cora McBride, prostrate
1527 there in her terror, the impact of

the bullet felt like the blow of a 1528
stick upon her cheek-bone rock- 1529
ing her head. Her cheek felt 1530
warmly numb. She pressed a 1531
quick hand involuntarily against 1532
it, and drew it away sticky with 1533
blood. 1534

Click! Click! Click! 1535

Three times the revolver 1536
mechanism was worked to ac- 1537
complish her destruction. But 1538
there was no further report. 1539
The cylinder was empty. 1540

"Oh, God!" the woman 1541
moaned. "I fed you and offered 1542
to help you. I refused to shoot 1543
you because of your mother— 1544
your wife—your babies. And 1545
yet you——" 1546

"Where's your cartridges?" he 1547
cried wildly. "You got more; 1548
gimme that belt!" 1549

She felt his touch upon her. 1550
His crazy fingers tried to un- 1551
button the clasp of the belt and 1552
holster. But he could secure 1553
neither while she fought him. 1554
He pinioned her at length with 1555
his knee. His fingers secured a 1556
fistful of the cylinders from her 1557
girdle, and he opened the cham- 1558
ber of the revolver. 1559

She realized the end was but a 1560
matter of moments. Nothing 1561
but a miracle could save her now. 1562

Convulsively she groped about 1563
for something with which to 1564
strike. Nothing lay within reach 1565
of her bleeding fingers, however, 1566
but a little piece of dried sapling. 1567
She tried to struggle loose, but 1568
the lunatic held her mercilessly. 1569

1570 He continued the mechanical
1571 loading of the revolver.

1572 The semi-darkness of the hut,
1573 the outline of the moon afar
1574 through the uncurtained window
1575 —these swam before her. . . .
1576 Suddenly her eyes riveted on
1577 that curtainless window and she
1578 uttered a terrifying cry.

1579 Ruggam turned.

1580 Outlined in the window aper-
1581 ture against the low-hung moon
1582 *Martin Wiley, the murdered*
1583 *deputy, was staring into the*
1583 *cabin!*

1584 From the fugitive's throat
1585 came a gurgle. Some of the
1586 cartridges he held spilled to the
1587 flooring. Above her his figure
1588 became rigid. There was no
1589 mistaking the identity of the ap-
1590 parition. They saw the man's
1591 hatless head and some of his
1592 neck. They saw his dark pom-
1593 padour and the outline of his
1594 skull. As that horrible silhou-
1595 ette remained there, Wiley's
1596 pompadour lifted slightly as it
1597 had done in life.

1598 The cry in the convict's throat
1599 broke forth into words.

1600 "Mart Wiley!" he cried, "Mart
1601 Wiley! *Mart—Wiley!*"

1602 Clear, sharp, distinct was the
1603 shape of that never-to-be-for-
1604 gotten pompadour against the
1605 disk of the winter moon. His
1606 features could not be discerned,
1607 for the source of light was be-
1608 hind him, but the silhouette was
1609 sufficient. It was Martin Wiley;
1610 he was alive. His head and his

1611 wirelike hair were moving—ris-
1612 ing, falling.

1613 Ruggam, his eyes riveted upon
1614 the phantom, recoiled mechani-
1615 cally to the western wall. He
1616 finished loading the revolver by
1617 the sense of touch. Then:

1618 Spurt after spurt of fire lanced
1619 the darkness, directed at the
1620 Thing in the window. While the
1621 air of the hut reeked with the
1622 acrid smoke, the echo of the
1623 volley sounded through the
1624 silent forest-world miles away.

1625 But the silhouette in the win-
1626 dow remained.

1627 Once or twice it moved slightly
1628 as though in surprise; that was
1629 all. The pompadour rose in
1630 bellicose retaliation—the gesture
1631 that had always ensued when
1632 Wiley was angered or excited.
1633 But to bullets fired from an
1634 earthly gun the silhouette of
1635 the murdered deputy's ghost,
1636 arisen in these winter woods
1637 to prevent another slaughter,
1638 was impervious.

1639 Ruggam saw; he shrieked. He
1640 broke the gun and spilled out the
1641 empty shells. He fumbled in
1642 more cartridges, locked the bar-
1643 rel and fired again and again,
1644 until once more it was empty.

1645 Still the apparition remained.

1646 The man in his dementia
1647 hurled the weapon; it struck the
1648 sash and caromed off, hitting the
1649 stove. Then Hap Ruggam col-
1650 lapsed upon the floor.

1651 The woman sprang up. She
1652 found the rope thongs which had

1653 bound her pack to her shoulders.
1654 With steel-taut nerves, she rolled
1655 the insensible Ruggam over.

1656 She tied his hands; she tied
1657 his ankles. With her last bit of
1658 rope she connected the two bind-
1659 ings tightly behind him so that
1660 if he recovered, he would be at
1661 her mercy. Her task accom-
1662 plished, on her knees beside his
1663 prone figure, she thought to
1664 glance up at the window.

1665 Wiley's ghost had disappeared.

1666 Sheriff Crumpett and his party
1667 broke into the Lyons clearing
1668 within an hour. They had ar-
1669 rived in answer to five successive
1670 shots given a few moments apart,
1671 the signal agreed upon. The
1672 mystery to them, however, was
1673 that those five shots had been
1674 fired by some one not of their
1675 party.

1676 The sheriff and his men found
1677 the McBride woman, her cloth-
1678 ing half torn from her body, her
1679 features powder-marked and
1680 blood-stained; but she was game
1681 to the last, woman-fashion weep-
1682 ing only now that all was over.
1683 They found, too, the man they
1684 had combed the country to find—
1685 struggling fruitlessly in his
1686 bonds, her prisoner.

1687 And they likewise found the
1688 miracle.

1689 On the snow outside under the
1690 window they came upon a black
1691 porcupine about the size of a
1692 man's head which, scenting food
1693 within the cabin, had climbed to
1694 the sill, and after the habit of
1695 these little animals whose num-
1696 ber is legion all over the Green
1697 Mountains, had required fifteen
1698 bullets pumped into its carcass
1699 before it would release its hold.

1700 Even in death its quills were
1701 raised in uncanny duplication
1702 of Mart Wiley's pompadour.

THE ANALYSIS

This story contains all told 1702 lines. Of this number 659 lines are presented to the reader before he comes to the attempts or struggles which make up the Body of the Story. Of particular interest to readers is the arrangement of the first 108 lines. The main narrative problem of this story is, "Can Cora McBride capture Hap Ruggam?" The difficulties lying in her way are that she is herself weak and out of condition, and that there is between her and the place where she may hope to find the murderer, a snow covered wilderness. The dangerous opposition is clearly foreshadowed in the fact that Hap Ruggam is a murderer, who having killed twice will not hesitate to kill again, and this in itself constitutes the threat of disaster.

All this would have been made clear to the reader in that portion of the story which begins on line 109 and ends on line 659, but it is obvious that the first 108 lines are a Flash-back from line 1072, and that the happenings shown from lines 1 to 108 took place after the happenings which open on line 109. Yet it clearly is not a typical Flash-back Beginning because it does not open, as such a Beginning should, with the main narrative question, and flash-back to the explanatory matter necessary to a reader's understanding of that main narrative question's importance.

In point of time it comes not only after these, but after the actual Conclusive Act which ends the story by answering the main narrative question. That Act is clear on lines 1651 to 1665 where Cora McBride is shown tying up her victim.

There is only one division of the story which can follow the Conclusive Act; that division is the Sequel. From lines 1666 to 1702 where the sheriff's party find Cora McBride in the cabin, and find also the explanation of the face in the window, the category is Sequel. Lines 1 to 108 are, in point of time, a continuation from line 1702. The flash-back in this case, therefore, consists in splitting up the Sequel, so that a portion of it is presented in the responses of the sheriff to the receipt of the letter from C. V. D. Wylie, in lines 1 to 85, and between the sheriff and Joseph on lines 86 to 108.

The question instantly arising in the mind of a reader is, "What purpose is gained by such a method of flash-back?" The ordinary gain through the typical flash-back method is a gain in interest through presenting the main problem before the explanatory matter. In this case, however, no such gain can occur because the typical method is not used. There is, besides interest, however, another consideration in the presentation of a story. It is the consideration of plausibility. The more extraordinary the conclusion at which a reader arrives, the greater is the author's necessity for preparing his mind for its acceptance. The explanation of the porcupine was a strain upon the credulity of any reader, therefore Mr. Pelley anticipated this lack of credulity by explaining that it was one of the Lord's miracles. And, being wise in the ways of craftsmanship, he caused this explanation to come from the mouth of a character, rather than to make the statement as author. He did what lawyers do in cases where their clients are in danger of being disbelieved. He called in character witnesses. First, he has the letter from the men in which he says he thinks the woman deserves the reward, and has earned it; and then he brings in the testimony of the sheriff, who is a high-minded person, to add further plausibility.

The main condition is set forth on lines 109 to 299 in an interchange between the editor and his assistants. The fifth step is on lines 300 to 320 which shows the effect upon the actors or observers.

Following this comes the interchange between Cora McBride and Duncan. Thus he follows out the regular formula of presenting the condition or state of affairs and following it with the reaction of the main actor toward that condition.

There are, in the final analysis, only three kinds of struggles in which a character may engage. The first is a mental struggle; that is, a struggle between two different traits in the same character, one of which is urging on the purpose and the other of which is opposing that purpose. The second kind of struggle is an attempt to overcome a force of nature. The third kind of attempt is a struggle between man and man. It may be, of course, between man and woman, as it is in this particular story.

All three kinds of obstacles, mental, natural, and human, occur in this story, and lend to the main narrative question its importance and interest. On lines 515 to 659 there occurs a mental interchange, in which the desire of Cora McBride to achieve the capture of Hap Ruggam is opposed by other traits in her character. As a result of this interchange the main narrative purpose is apparent.

The Body of the story is contained in lines 660 to 1650. The attempt to overcome a difficulty which occupies line 660 to 957 is not presented as a struggle between the girl and the elements, but the effect of it was shown quite as effectively by the appearance of the girl after the struggle is over. It is interesting to note that although this attempt is successful insofar as it enables her to reach the spot where the murderer is, the sense of furtherance is almost imperceptible, and is instantly followed by the sense of a dramatic hindrance, when the reader realizes that the girl is exhausted and that tracks lead into the cabin.

In the struggle between Cora McBride and the man, Hap Ruggam, I have made three divisions; one from line 958 to 1370; the second from line 1371 to 1496; the third from 1497 to 1583. I have done this because the first division is an actual complete attempt resulting in a definite crisis of furtherance, on line 1370 when Cora secures the gun. It then ceases to be a scene of physical struggle and it becomes a scene of oral struggle between the man and the woman. From lines 1371 to 1496 this oral struggle continues, and results in a crisis of dramatic hindrance which is very effective because the woman finds that she cannot take away a life. Then line 1497 to 1583 constitute still another scene, because it is the attempt, a quite separate and distinct one, of Hap Ruggam to kill Cora McBride, the result of which is to form a brand new condition or state of affairs on lines 1582 to 1583, when Hap Ruggam has to abandon his attempt because he becomes aware of what appears to him to be the face of Martin Wylie, the murdered deputy, staring into the cabin through the window.

On lines 1584 to 1650 the reader is made aware of the fifth step of that interchange between Ruggam and Cora. It produces a furtherance and changes the condition to one which enables Cora to take advantage of the insensibility of Hap Ruggam to capture him.

The weakness in this story is that the solution is brought about by a coincidence. Strictly speaking, the short-story should show a character in a position where he has to act in order to solve a problem, and the solution should be brought about through some trait in the character, or by some capacity which the character possesses. The grave objection to having a coincidence used for a solution is that it places upon the author the necessity for making this coincidence plausible. Mr. Pelley has used a very clever device in achieving this plausibility, and for that reason I have included the story and have recommended it to those authors who find difficulty with such a problem.

While I am upon this subject of coincidence I might take the opportunity to say that there is a belief on the part of many students of the short-story form that a coincidence should never be used in a short-story. This is not at all the case. You may use coincidence as freely as you like to get your character into trouble, to bring about a main condition, or to create hindrances at the conclusion of the scenes in the Body of your story. The coincidence is not desirable as a solution of the problem, for the reason that most readers who read a story, and who find themselves in a predicament similar to that of the main actor of the story will feel cheated if they find, at the conclusion of the story, that the only way out of such a predicament is by the use of coincidence. That does not open for them a way to solve a similar problem.

But apart from this use of coincidence, the story *The Face in the Window* will be a very interesting model for those authors who wish to develop the promises of conflict which are contained in the Beginning of their story. Particularly so they will find it if they are interested in that particular portion of the story which presents the actor at a point where disaster is imminent, for there is no doubt that it would be very difficult to formulate a condition more dramatically filled with the threat of ultimate disaster than the position in which Cora McBride finds herself, when, at the mercy of this maniac murderer, she is unable to shoot him, because she cannot bring herself to take life.

ARCHITECTURAL CHART

OF

WESTERN STUFF

BEGINNING	Initial condition is set forth.	Meeting. Verena Dayson and Condition.	1– 37	Tragedy implied.
		Flash-back Interchange. City Editor and Mr. Dark. (An author flash-back.)	38– 109	Dramatic Crises o Plot are apparent t reader.
		(5th step of 38–109.) Verena's reaction to condition projected by announcement of Mr. Dark's arrival	110– 400	
	Main Actor's main purpose is presented.	This contains, within it, two flash-backs. (A. Buck and Verena, lines 243–297.) (B. Verena and hypothetical interviewer, lines 298–378.)		Main Narrativ Question: "Ca Verena recaptur her husband?
		Scene. Mr. Dark and Verena Dayson.	401–1119	
BODY	Main Actor engages in series of attempts to achieve purpose.	Scene. Verena and Buck. She attempts to make him jealous. He is unimpressed. Included here (lines 1183–1221) is a flash-back to previous evening. Buck and Mrs. Sennay.	1120–1269	Hindrance.
		(5th step. Effect upon Verena. Goes about her business.)	1270–1400	
		Scene. Verena and Buck. She tries to impress by her new wardrobe. He is indifferent.	1401–1557	Hindrance.
		Scene. Verena and Buck. She tries to impress him by her conversation. He is bored. (5th step. Effect.) Verena and Mr. Dark.	1558–1637 1638–1746	Hindrance. Dramatic Hindrance.
BODY	Attempts (Continued)	Interchanges. Verena and Mrs. Sennay. Verena and Buck. Verena, noticing that Buck looks liked a roped steer gets idea for solution. New condition projected.	1747–1925	Curiosity arouse
		Interchange. Verena enlists aid of Mr. Dark.	1926–1961	Curiosity unsatisfied.
		Scene. Final attempt. Verena and Buck.	1962–2200	
ENDING	Conclusive Act. Sequel.	He put out a dazed hand to his wife.	2200–2201	Answer to Narra tive Question "Yes."
		Buck and Verena.	2202–2259	Effect upon actor

WESTERN STUFF

BY MARY BRECHT PULVER

LEST I seem to be harping too much upon the necessity for writers to possess the ability to employ the "flash-back" method, I shall say that the peculiar variant of this method used by Mary Brecht Pulver is not my only reason for including this story, although I shall discuss this feature of it.

My chief reason for reprinting this story is that it shows the ingenuity of a competent craftsman in dealing with material which at first glance would seem to possess little scope for original adaptation. I refer to the initial Condition or State of Affairs which confronts the main actor in this story—that state of affairs which is commonly called a "situation," but which we refer to throughout this volume as a "condition."

It presents Verena Dayson, the rodeo queen, at the moment when she realizes that her husband has become enamoured of another woman. Because such a condition might be treated as a starting point for a narrative problem of either accomplishment or decision, I am including this story, in which the problem projected is one of accomplishment, in order to use it as a foil against another story, appearing later in this volume, in which the same initial condition is used to project a story in which the main narrative problem is one of decision.

CASE No. 10

WESTERN STUFF

BY MARY BRECHT PULVER

1 Although it was five minutes
2 to two and the man from the
3 Sunday *Tribune* due on the hour,
4 Verena Dayson, the rodeo queen,
5 still lay face down upon her bed,
6 just as she had flung herself in a
7 straight head-to-toe line, the
8 way a stick is thrown, when she
9 had come into the room ten
10 minutes before, slamming the
11 door so violently the water bot-
12 tle and glass on the dresser
13 clicked their heels in salute, the
14 pens on the enameled desk
15 leaped in their glass sockets, the
16 wastebasket fell over and the
17 Princesse de Lamballe, in pastel
18 colors on the wall, assumed an
19 angle of forty degrees.

20 Into her pillow had dived the
21 rodeo queen with the muscular
22 plunge and address of one of the
23 Bar-K boys bull-dogging a Texas
24 yearling. The pillow hadn't a
25 chance. But directly it was
26 thrown and subjected, it ceased
27 to be a steer and became a com-
28 forting mother in whose relaxing
29 embrace the queen had now for
30 some time been uttering what

31 she would have described as
32 some wild coyote howls.

33 "Wrong! Wrong! Wrong!"
34 she lay weeping. "All wrong
35 from A to Zed! What am I
36 going to do now—and how am I
37 going to do it?"

38 Whatever emotion she ex-
39 pressed would probably not have
40 been lightened had she over-
41 heard Mr. Blivens, the city edi-
42 tor, handing out an assignment
43 some twenty minutes earlier.

44 "I want you," said Mr. Bliv-
45 ens, addressing one of those
46 young minions of his who
47 snapped like rubber bands, in
48 any given direction, "to go down
49 to the McAlpin and interview
50 this rope-and-riding woman,
51 Mrs. Buck Dayson, who's been
52 here all week with the Dayson
53 outfit on their way back to the
54 West from Wembley. They're
55 off the front page now, but what
56 I want is a feature article for the
57 woman's section, from the wom-
58 an's viewpoint. I understand
59 Buck Dayson and his wife never
60 peel off any inside dope like this

241

—that it's all cooked up, what the public gets. 'Bout as easy to catch 'em off guard as squeezing blood from a turnip.

"But I've got a line that Mrs. Dayson'll talk. There's some kind of new policy on, I guess. Buck Dayson makes all his own contracts, and has always handled publicity; but I hear this Sennay woman who did the publicity for the movie actress Blanche Markhouse—that spectacular kidnaping of hers—has persuaded him that her services are valuable and is going to work for his show. Any stuff that Violet Sennay might offer is distinctly what we do not want. Slide to it, and catch the lady off first, before Sennay gets in her divine touch. The hour is two. Remember, she's the real rope-and-riding goods, the genuine cowgirl queen born in the saddle—her lifelong game. Never kisses a cow under a thousand dollars. Still, she must have a human side. Anyhow, go tackle her. She's about as big as a minute, I hear, and is probably a leathery, stringy little piece of dried beef. But you can dress her up. Call the stuff Jelly Bags and Saddle Bags if you like, or a Cowgirl Madonna—there are some kids in the offing. Anyway, slide."

"I'll slide," said the minion.

His name was Stanley Dark.

He was sliding now, coming slowly up in the hydraulic elevator to the cream-enamel-and-pink-brocade apartment occupied by Mr. and Mrs. Buck Dayson on their short vacation in New York, en route from France and England to the great uncharted spaces.

Mr. Dark's announcement of himself by phone had driven Verena from her recumbent position. One glance at her wrist watch, one final yip of misery and she began preparing to receive him. You don't live a life dependent on schedule, on the call boy's summons, without learning to conceal a carking secret sorrow, however terrible.

She saw that she would require some camouflage. Her hat, bought earlier in the morning in New York's Rue de la Paix on Fifty-seventh Street, was mangled; her face a mass of sodden blobs. She straightened her small frankly sun-tanned visage, dusted it with powder, adding a little hasty writing on her lips from a newly procured gold pencil—and at once erased this.

"What's the use?" she sighed. "It only makes me look like a sugared cruller trimmed with currant jelly. I always feel, anyhow, like a fresh-branded steer when I clap the red-hot iron on me."

And realizing that she had an extra minute before Mr. Dark would report, she went and stood by the open window and let the May air blow in on her hot cheeks.

Below, she could see New York if she craned and bent a little. Above, a narrow panel of pale insipid blue; lower down, vast plunging levels of architectural structure, colored with odd geometrical shafts of shifting gray-and-lavender light, with here and there a transverse plane of unobstructed yellow sun; and far, far below, a million teeming pygmy dark forms rushing on remote, ludicrous errands, foaming like disturbed ants, from Sixth Avenue and Broadway into Thirty-fourth Street. Into her ear poured the voice that is New York—a blend of horns, whistles, sirens, pounding feet, rumbling trucks, street calls, ambulances, fire signals, trolley bells, crashing Elevated, tube and Subway vibration of shaken earth, the architectonic response of vast buildings, keyed to various chords; a volume of sound in which a feminine crying spell amounted to nothing whatever; a heartless crowd in which one woman's heartache, purposes, acts, dwindled to nil. Yet it was funny, reflected Mrs. Buck Dayson, with a little sniffle, how important they remained—to your own self.

Recalled, she tore her eyes away from New York and picked up an oblong black hand bag from her dresser, opened it and drew out a worn and creased paper from one side. It was a draft of a fictitious newspaper interview. Buck had prepared it for her a year ago, in case she should be beset.

Buck never allowed her to give out interviews. He attended to this himself, just as he looked after the business end of the whole game so competently—or had before his mind had softened in this strange new way. He had given her this paper right after Wembley—prepared very carefully, based on his own experiences and idea of expediency. Buck was good at this, and thorough, as he was in everything. He had worked it out carefully —helped by a man they had met in London and played round with a lot; a Major Niles, with a handsome black mustache— dyed, Buck declared—who had been in oil, he claimed, and certainly a lot of it had stuck to his manner; and who, being a fellow American, given to sprightly red ties and a marvelous vocabulary, had dogged Buck's heels considerably—or until he had got fifty dollars off Buck. It was the vocabulary that made Buck patient.

Years ago, before they were married, Buck was known as the educated cowboy, and it was a fact that even now he was reading—though slowly —the Five-Foot Shelf.

Buck loved big words. He liked to get them off himself, surprising people. It impressed them, combined with his tall dark

229 good looks and careless out-of-
230 doors virility. Take this word
231 "hypothetical" that he had
232 caught off Major Niles last year.
233 Buck had gone crazy over it for
234 a while, and used it everywhere.
235   Verena unfolded the yellow
236 creased paper in her hand.
237 Buck had had it ticked off by
238 a typist at the Savoy.
239   "Hypothetical interview," she
240 read, "between Mrs. Buck Day-
241 son and hypothetical reporter
242 from news daily."
243   "Carry it with you in case the
244 write-up boys catch you when
245 your papa ain't around, honey,"
246 Buck had said; "keep as near as
247 you can to it. It may be a life
248 preserver."
249   What Buck meant exactly
250 was—for she had a good brain
251 and a native shrewdness of her
252 own—that it might preserve
253 what he called the beans of
254 privacy from being spilled. Buck
255 had a fierce love of privacy, a
256 staunch, almost savage desire
257 for the preservation of their
258 family sanctity.
259   "No use letting the public
260 fondle the camp cots and the
261 chuck wagon, honey. We've
262 got a right to an unmolested
263 family life. I'm a family man,
264 and that's the way I want it.
265 It's our work alone—our public
266 stuff they got a right to know
267 about. It's good enough too.
268 Our work stands on its own."
269   It truly did. All through the
270 West, all through those vast

271 reaches where those—to Eastern
272 ears—bewildering terms,
273 "butte," "mesa," "alfalfa,"
274 "arroyos," "canyon," "cactus,"
275 "gulch," and the like, forgather,
276 a region the most conservative
277 Cape Cod citizen will admit
278 holds connoisseurs in these
279 matters, the Daysons, known
280 friendly-wise as Buck and
281 Verena, were famed in rodeos,
282 stampedes, frontier days, as two
283 of the ridingest kids that ever
284 came out of Lochinvar's country.
285   Spectacular of achievement!
286 What need had they of undue
287 intimacy with an inquisitive
288 public? Hence Buck's cautious
289 hypothetical interview.
290   "Remember, honey, the boys
291 mostly begin on the same ques-
292 tion. If you hand it all back pat
293 and copious, fill 'em up pretty
294 good with what I'm told they
295 call a stickful of talk, mebbe
296 they won't have any room left
297 for the other stuff."
298   Verena read:

299 HYPOTHETICAL REPORTER:
300 Mrs. Dayson, what are your
301 impressions of London? Paris?
302 New York?—as the case may be.
303 MRS. DAYSON: My impres-
304 sion of London, Paris, New
305 York—as the case may be—is
306 that it is one of the largest, most
307 remarkable cities I have ever
308 visited. In fact, I think one of
309 the largest, most remarkable
310 cities in the world. We of the
311 West are apt to build a high

ideal of the great cities of the world, and my experience has been no different. But I was agreeably surprised in what I have found. Your city impresses me as attractive, unusual and filled with interesting sights. It is one of the most interesting places I have ever seen. I am delighted to be in your midst.

HYPOTHETICAL REPORTER: Mrs. Dayson, what is your impression of our people here in London? Paris? New York?—as the case may be.

MRS. DAYSON: It is almost too soon to digest and coördinate my impressions of the many types I have seen here in London, Paris, New York—as the case may be—but I can truly say that I find your street crowds remarkable and very interesting. Your men impress me with their manner, your women have a way that is all their own. I find them all interesting. I am delighted to be in their midst. (*To be added if just leaving country, for Buck had not forgotten the princes who shook his hand at Wembley:*) Individually, I cannot express too highly my pleasure in meeting your leading people here. I found their Royal Highnesses, Poincaré, Mayor Hylan—as the case may be—most simple and unaffected in their interest in the work we are doing. I have been received most graciously.

I was delighted to be in their midst.

HYPOTHETICAL REPORTER: Mrs. Dayson, what are your own impressions of the Far West which you have left behind you?

MRS. DAYSON: The Far West is not what it once was. Modern progress, with its hydraulic engineering, our wonderful mechanical improvements, the mighty strides we have made in elimination of time and space, have obliterated those earlier, ruder practices that tradition knows as the Wild West. The amelioration of those primitive conditions which fostered the practices and acts of the pioneer settlers and early cattlemen naturally affected it. Yet that this tradition still exists, if only in a hypothetical state, is attested by our own work here in your midst——

"The hell!" Verena choked suddenly.

The word would have cost her just one dollar's fine off her weekly increment if Buck Dayson had heard it, with his strict ideals of womanly purity of language and ladylike behavior. Only, of course, now Buck was not here to hear it. He usually wasn't—not since his mind had begun to soften.

There was a tap on the sitting-room door. Verena tore the hypothetical interview in two.

394 "Buck Dayson," she cried,
395 "I won't pay any attention!
396 You've gone your way—and I'm
397 going mine. I don't know where
398 the trail leads, but I guess it
399 points, first off, to this reporter
400 boy."

401 Even without a hypothetical
402 interview to guide us, most of
403 us would agree with Mrs. Day-
404 son that the West is not what it
405 once was. The coming of barbed
406 wire, irrigation, good roads and
407 automobiles has altered it for-
408 ever. Most of us, of the East,
409 have been out—in the last-
410 named—to have a look at what
411 is left, and we think we know.
412 Where the two-gun he-men of
413 an earlier, hairier era, mixed in
414 over their bald-face whisky,
415 where the pallid glassy-cheeked
416 dealer in faro took his guilty
417 profits in the red-blooded dives
418 of sin in the primitive settle-
419 ments, there stands now rank
420 upon rank of stucco apartment
421 houses like magnificent layer
422 cakes, with at least one five-
423 tube heterodyne and one pair of
424 golf pants per layer.

425 But there still are three strong-
426 holds of the old tradition. Holly-
427 wood—where men still are men
428 —where it's better to smile when
429 you say it, where virility still
430 snatches virtue from the arms
431 of villainy and bad men get their
432 just deserts from diamond-back
433 rattler or a poisoned pool as they
434 make a last crawl on their mis-
435 guided bellies across an equally

436 bad land; dude ranches, where
437 the West is organized as a
438 pattern for Eastern education;
439 and the famous rope-and-riding
440 outfits that follow the line of the
441 big rodeos and stampedes from
442 Calgary to the Mexican border
443 as the season alters, and who
444 conserve the brilliant art of the
445 older days at its best.

446 All this was well known to Mr.
447 Stanley Dark as he rode up
448 pensively on the hydraulic-pres-
449 sure elevator to see Mrs. Dayson,
450 and it bored him a great deal.
451 He had a poor opinion of this
452 Wild West stuff, anyhow. His
453 interests lay much deeper. Al-
454 though he was a hard-working
455 commonplace young reporter
456 outwardly, he led his own
457 magnificent interior life like a
458 great many of us, and with him
459 it was an affair of strong and
460 primal values only. The super-
461 ficial aspects of life did not
462 intrigue him, although he now
463 secured a living by interviews for
464 the Sunday supplement.

465 An aldermanic meeting, the
466 opening of a garbage-disposal
467 plant or the inspecting of a
468 drowned babe in the morgue—
469 he made his bread by this; but
470 what interested him really was,
471 briefly, human passion; primitive
472 feeling as it works itself out in an
473 inexorable track.

474 He had in fact just sent into
475 a competition a little one-act
476 drama of human passions called
477 Lust Below the Willows, and he

246

had it in mind to do shortly a subjective poetic tragedy bearing on the early love-life and frustrations of Shakespere's three *Weird Sisters*, and the emotional states that had reduced them to the condition in which the Bard was able to use them for his purpose. He was a very wise young man, the son of a minister in a little town called Coshecton, with a widowed mother and two young sisters he adored; but he was very modern, which is why the West bored him. He knew that muscular activity, sunlight and ozone are inimical to the subjective emotional states he so admired.

As he tapped on Verena Dayson's door, he took off his hat and sighed, under the pressure of his expectation and boredom. He knew what to expect from Mr. Blivens' little leathery piece of dried beef. She would be all that; and she would wear a badly made divided skirt, vaquero's boots, a white lingerie shirt waist, a green or magenta-colored neckerchief, a bead necklace, and perhaps a sugar-loaf hat.

But as the door opened, he was startled to see none of this. He was looking at one of the prettiest little girls imaginable; twenty-two or three at most, with a tiny, sturdy, but graceful figure. Above this looked back at him a small, sweet, wholesome sun-cured face whose shapely nose was decorated in a light spatterwork of ingenuous freckles, whose round cheeks were the color of two June wild roses, whose round blue eyes, trimmed with long, dark, curling lashes, frankly moist, were as blue as the Arizona heavens, and the whole framed with a swinging aureole of short, curly, sun-kissed hair whose undulation had no need of the permanent-wave octopus and appeared to have been dipped in liquid gilt. Moreover, the ensemble was dressed in strictly Eastern garments, in the most expensive-looking and most horribly arranged combination he had ever seen on a woman. One concedes a certain art, as in an automobile, in assembling the components of costume.

"How do you do?" said Mrs. Buck Dayson. "I guess you must be from the *Tribune*. Mr. Dark? Will you step in and find yourself a chair?"

Mr. Dark stepped in with alacrity.

"You know," he said, "you are amazingly different from what I expected."

"Oh, I'm amazing all right— I can see that myself! Just what were you looking for? Maybe——"

"Well," said Mr. Dark, with a little grin, "I expected to see the Wild West, I guess."

"Well, you're seeing the West, all right—and I s'pose you might

562 call it wild." A faint quiver
563 moved Mrs. Dayson's voice.
564 "At least I must be, to see you
565 at all. It has been the policy of
566 my husb—of Buck Dayson—of
567 Mr. Henry B. Dayson—who
568 I am married to, always to take
569 interviews with the reporters
570 and never to let me say any-
571 thing. We decided that before
572 —quite a while ago—when he was
573 around more. But I am going
574 to talk to you now," added Mrs.
575 Dayson firmly, "and you may
576 ask me anything. There are
577 just three things I won't answer:
578 How do I like New York? What
579 do I think of your people here?
580 And what is my impression of
581 the Far West?"

582 That, Mr. Dark explained,
583 was farthest from his intention,
584 and he set forth Mr. Blivens'
585 request for human-interest stuff
586 for women readers as persua-
587 sively as possible.

588 "I was going to call my article
589 A Madonna of the Saddle, but I
590 —I should like to change it to
591 Beauty and Her Beasts. Really I
592 should, Mrs. Dayson." Mr.
593 Dark showed his very good
594 teeth affably. "You see," he
595 swept on, "all that I know of
596 you is the figure which, as you
597 say, your husband has allowed
598 to appear in the public mind.
599 The professional woman rider
600 and rope artist, standing at the
601 top of the profession in skill and
602 salary, with a great tradition of
603 horse-womanship and long train-

604 ing; born, you might say—er—
605 in the saddle, living her life there.
606 Yet there must be—there is the
607 other side of it, the more
608 feminine, the—the usual
609 woman's reactions, the ideals,
610 hopes, tastes of a woman—er—
611 her passions——"

612 In spite of himself, Mr. Dark's
613 pet word escaped and Verena
614 caught at it.

615 "Passions!" she cried. "A
616 woman's passions and tastes and
617 ideals—the usual ones. Yes,
618 Mr. Dark, I've got 'em all, like
619 any other woman." She clenched
620 one hand tightly, with a deep
621 breath, then plunged: "That's
622 why I'm willing to talk now.
623 You want the—the other side
624 of my life and I'm going to
625 give it.

626 "Well, I am a rope artist and
627 Wild West rider, as you say; but
628 I am like other women too.
629 Although I was born in the
630 saddle, you might say, papa put-
631 ting my brother Al and me there
632 when we were only three years
633 old—where I have lived, as they
634 claim, ever since, I also live in a
635 house—when I am there! Buck
636 and I saved every cent we made
637 for five years, to build it, and
638 I'll say it's a good one. It's out
639 at Tulsa, Oklahoma. We had an
640 architect from San Francisco
641 for it. It has four bathrooms.
642 We buy the best of everything
643 too. Blue velvet overstuffed in
644 the parlor—I wish you could see it
645 —where I sit as often as possible

646 whenever out of the saddle. We
647 have an artesian well and some
648 of the best stock and horses you
649 can find anywheres in the West.
650 No trick stuff, you know. We
651 have a good manager, and Aunt
652 Ida looks after the housekeep-
653 ing—and our two children. Oh,
654 yes, you may tell that—Buster
655 and Henrietta, three years and
656 eighteen months. Two children
657 —and four bathrooms!" choked
658 Mrs. Dayson bitterly. Her
659 bridges were well ablaze now.
660 "I know horses and I know
661 riding, but I know other things
662 too. I've got the cutest babies
663 you ever saw, and—and I've
664 played with dolls in my time
665 too. Plenty. When I was
666 growing up I always wanted a
667 house with—with a linen closet
668 and a lot of jam, and little pink
669 aprons to work round in, like
670 anybody. I counted on it and I
671 got it, along with Buck. I
672 mean with my husb—with
673 Henry B. Dayson, who I am
674 married to. We wanted just the
675 same things. We knew that
676 right off when we met at Chey-
677 enne six years ago. We liked
678 each other right off. Buck
679 changed a lot of his dates right
680 away and followed my schedule
681 down the map for three months
682 before we got married. That
683 was the time we rode together
684 early every morning—out over
685 the prairie, while the sun came
686 up, or up into the hills." Here
687 Mrs. Dayson paused abruptly,

having apparently a slight con- 688
striction of the throat. She 689
swallowed twice and repeated 690
in a rather high, thin, strained 691
tone, "Riding out together in the 692
mornings that way—over the 693
prairie or up in the hills." 694
Mr. Dark, whose pencil had a 695
minute earlier been fleetly chas- 696
ing her revelation in his note- 697
book, looked at her, aware of a 698
sudden tension. 699
It is a fact, as Mr. Dark well 700
knew, or any of us who ply the 701
craft, that words are the poorest 702
possible conveyancers of intent, 703
the weakest imaginable vehicle 704
of emotion or actual psychology 705
—a barrier usually raised be- 706
tween people and a smoke screen 707
rather than a revelation for the 708
soul. That is why Mr. Dark's 709
pencil poised at Mrs. Dayson's 710
commonplace phrase "riding out 711
together in the mornings." 712
Some very deep emotion 713
seemed to burn in the little rodeo 714
queen. Her blue eyes were dark 715
and soft, and perhaps a little 716
tragic. They shone with the 717
memory of some older loveliness, 718
now denied to her; perhaps the 719
picture of two young figures—a 720
tall, swarthy, supple shape, god- 721
like, superior, bending to a little 722
slim eager companion with a frec- 723
kled, wild-rose, pink-and-tan face 724
under rough gilt curls. Figures 725
that turned to each other like 726
Clytie to the sun, in an age-old 727
idyl, their horses touching 728
shoulder to shoulder, light feet 729

repudiating the yielding turf, where dew still clung to grass and wild flower in silver meshes; where the air blew sweet with early morning perfume and was filled with whistle and song of lark and quail.

Mrs. Dayson resumed after a moment: "It was then that Buck and I planned our lives; to build a house and to do our stuff together; to sell it on itself without any publicity or fussing; Buck to manage our business and fix all contracts. And we have never changed from this until now. Everything," said Mrs. Dayson, "is changed now. Everything we planned as far as up to when we got on the boat at Liverpool is ruined and spoiled. We were on our way out to our house—to Buster and Henrietta. We are not going now. We were on our way to a stampede in the Central West circuit. We are not going now. I may possibly never see the West again. I may never see Buster and Henrietta. I don't know about this. I don't know anything."

"Mrs. Dayson—why not?"

"Because," said Verena, "Buck, my husb—— Mr. Henry B. Dayson has gone East--or, you might say, loco. Because we are going to stay East, right here in New York for a year at least, and maybe longer, on contract with this new Castle Garden Theater, to perform our stuff on a platform—on tanbark, mind you—with canvas scenery round us. And that's not all. We have never done such a thing before, but we will begin our contract by a special advertising feature—a kidnaping—of myself. I'm to go in a taxicab down to Pell Street and be stolen by two Chinamen. Can you beat it? To call public attention to me!"

"Mrs. Dayson! How singular! What an idea—for Mr. Dayson!"

"Don't lay it to Mr. Dayson. It isn't his." Verena bent closer and two great tears like flat silver disks slipped from beneath her eyelashes. "It belongs to a woman we met on the boat coming over; a regular publicity woman, now attached to our outfit. Her name is Sennay—Violet Sennay—and she always—for everybody begins with a kidnaping, to get attention. But not for herself. I wish to God she would. She—she's cruel, good-looking, b-beautiful, and her clothes——" Mrs. Dayson swallowed hard. "Clothes!" she choked. "What is the matter with me—with mine, I mean, Mr. Dark?"

But she didn't wait for an answer. She crumpled down and wept wildly again.

"She calls him Buck dear and mong chair, and it's only been three weeks she's known him. Oh, Mr. Dark, what'll I do? What'll I do?"

815 This, you will admit, is no
816 way to receive the press.
817 Mr. Dark laid down his note-
818 book. His official capacity
819 ceased here. He found himself
820 patting Mrs. Dayson's hand as
821 he would have patted any pretty
822 distressed girl's, as he would
823 have wished his sister's patted.
824 "What you need," said Mr.
825 Dark, "is a friend."
826 The rodeo queen agreed. It
827 was true. She had no friend, no
828 soul in New York to confide in.
829 "It's this repression stuff,"
830 sobbed Verena, "that you're
831 always reading about. You hold
832 in and you hold in till you nearly
833 burst, until a time comes when
834 you cut loose in the wrong place.
835 Think of telling your secrets to a
836 reporter! Oh, I beg of you,
837 don't print this! I should have
838 held my tongue, but I'm so
839 miserable. Forget what I said.
840 I—I shall not say another
841 word!"
842 Whereupon she entered upon
843 a rather lengthy and impassioned
844 monologue provoked by Mr.
845 Dark's kindness and sympathy.
846 Into her monologue she wove
847 many and divers references—
848 Buster and Henrietta, Buck's
849 good looks, his prowess, his
850 previous, loyalty, their happy
851 life, his passion for elegant
852 long words, incidents that had
853 occurred at the Pendleton
854 and Salinas roundups, tricky
855 horses they had ridden, how
856 they bought up all the bad ones

857 so they could really test their
858 stuff; tales of a certain star-faced
859 buckskin used at Wembley, a
860 roan that had tried to kill Buck
861 last year; a white cayuse, a
862 California sorrel. Terms like
863 crow-hopping, fanning, hazing,
864 sunfishing, got all mixed to-
865 gether with the blue velvet
866 overstuffed, some fine French
867 mirrors, Aunt Ida, the artesian
868 well and the bathrooms, with
869 certain concluding mention of
870 clothes and her great handicap
871 here. In feminine fashion, her
872 clothes were the first matter she
873 had thought of.
874 It was, she explained, part of
875 Buck's policy for them both
876 while on tour to wear their show
877 clothes. It was lots of fun, and
878 going around together made it
879 plenty easy. Also, speaking as
880 a cowgirl, she was, if she said so
881 herself, the niftiest dressed rid-
882 ing artist on any circuit. She
883 could afford it, and made a point
884 of it. Still, it got her nothing
885 here in New York. Beside the
886 beauty and sophistication of
887 Mrs. Sennay—who had in addi-
888 tion a line of talk of the kind
889 Buck loved—beside anybody,
890 the way they looked here, she
891 was nothing at all.
892 She related what had hap-
893 pened yesterday afternoon when
894 —alone, as she always was now
895 —she had stepped out to a Sixth
896 Avenue news stand for a paper,
897 wearing a costume that would
898 make any female riding artist

899 ache with envy. A divided skirt
900 and blouse lately cut by an
901 English tailor, over a Laramie
902 pattern, of pale supple pearl
903 doeskin stuff; her very best
904 neckerchief and white sugar-
905 loaf hat, lovely handmade high-
906 heeled teetering Mexican boots
907 of soft pale-gray leather, set
908 with little bronze and turquoise
909 patterns, a rattlesnake belt with
910 a massive hand-tooled silver
911 buckle, pale soft gauntlet gloves.
912 Some little flappers passing
913 made open fun of her. They
914 wore, Verena declared, little
915 short tight shimmies of color-
916 splashed silk and apparently no
917 stockings above high-heeled tot-
918 tering black-satin slippers.
919 There were pieces of fur or
920 colored strips of silk fastened
921 around their necks, and their
922 arms were bare to the shoulders.
923 Colors were mottled on their
924 faces, too, and little gay bowls
925 of cheap felt pulled over their
926 eyes.
927 "I could have laughed," sighed
928 Verena; "honestly, they looked
929 so funny to me, and if they
930 hadn't laughed at me and
931 pointed at me so people stop-
932 ped——"
933 She had defended herself, as
934 she could.
935 "I stopped and said to the
936 worst one right out loud, 'I
937 paid three hundred dollars for
938 my felt hat—how much was
939 yours?'"
940 Not that it made a bit of
941 difference, in the long run.
942 Whether she dressed herself
943 West or East, she was, ap-
944 parently, out of it; out of every-
945 thing that her old life knew.
946 The situation, so banal, so
947 bourgeois and—outside the
948 range of the darker, more exotic
949 forms of emotion—so normal,
950 one might say, almost bored
951 Mr. Dark in its simplicity but
952 for the fact that Mrs. Verena
953 Dayson's pretty blue eyes, moist,
954 appealing, unfortunate, chal-
955 lenged and pleaded with him to
956 consider her case. He patted
957 her hand again.
958 "Well," said Mr. Dark, "it's
959 simply that there's a lot you
960 get out of practice—er—from
961 being in the know. There's a
962 knack about it which—er—I
963 should say you hadn't learned,
964 not that your instinct wasn't
965 sound. I'll tell you what, Mrs.
966 Dayson, there's nothing at all
967 to worry over, really. I know Vi
968 Sennay. Everybody on the
969 newspapers knows Vi. She's a
970 one-story man, though a nifty
971 looker. She hasn't any tricks,
972 no real imagination. Every
973 time she joins up on a case, she
974 pulls a kidnaping, as you've
975 said; after that it's a general
976 diminuendo. Only she's got a
977 lot of appeal, and she's a good
978 dresser and talker. I went to a
979 studio crush she gave once, with
980 a friend. She—she dressed the
981 part. Edgar Saltus stuff—a
982 little. She had her bed on a little

platform, with a bearskin thrown over, and three little wooden steps painted orange going up, and one of those wrought-iron torcheres. But you've nothing to worry over, because people all get sick of her. Vi's a home wrecker on Monday, but by Friday she's the landlord collecting three months' back rent, with any fellow."

"Well, but," gulped Verena —"but it's only Tuesday now. I've got to live through the rest of the week. She's got Buck going strong yet. He's going to sign this contract in ten more days; she's got him a practice ground down on a tanbark pen at Mullahey's. She's got Buck caring whether it's black or white ties at dinner. I'm losing my husband, Mr. Dark, and I want to go home—to Buster and Henrietta."

"You'll go," said Mr. Dark confidently, "and I'll tell you why—because I'll help you. We'll put it over together. It amounts to a formula, almost; purely mechanical. You can follow it anywhere you like in the fiction of the day," he explained a little meanly. "You must put on a sketch and meet the lady on her own terms— outdo her, y'understand; put it over—go one better! Roughly speaking, the rescue of a husband divides itself into three parts— raiment, culture, jealousy." Mr. Dark waved his straw hat negli-

gently. "You must outdress Mrs. Vi Sennay, you must outcharm her, you must outflirt her."

"Outdress her! But look at me!"

"I know the very lady to help you—Mrs. Pat Field, a buyer, with Blaine & Holding. She'd be tickled to look you over— put you together. She'd know your type. I'll just make a note to phone and asked her to call today."

"But you said—outcharm her!"

"I mean you must cultivate the sort of stuff Vi talks, her line of vocabulary. I will coach you. I am interested in creative writing and will give you samples to work from."

"But outflirt her? With who? I only know the boys with our outfit. Buck wouldn't get jealous enough to buy a bag of peanuts. And this Mr. Wirtheimer who wants the contract—he's a perfect sixty-six."

"You know me," said Mr. Dark significantly.

"You don't mean—not seriously!"

"Not seriously, of course," Mr. Dark waved his hat again. "But I'm perfectly willing to help you here, to work out this formula, beginning tomorrow. You can't work it alone. I can arrange to give you a good bit of free time in the coming week, as it happens, and—the thing would be rather fun. Another proof of the mechanistic laws governing psychology—the inevitable interweaving of given cause and effect. Your husband, Mrs. Dayson, at present a little fascinated by the novelty Mrs. Sennay offers, thinks of you only in the aspects he's always known. When he sees beside him a comparative stranger, beautifully groomed, cultivated and charming, a little cool and indifferent to him, and especially, admired, courted by another man—well, just wait and watch."

"Yes, but," objected Verena, "what I mean is, Mr. Dark"— and she looked as Penelope might if summoned on Ulysses' peril to pack her suitcase and go and rival Circe—"do you think Buck'll be sure to notice that I'm doing it? Being that he knows me so well, being—I mean that we've been married over five years, and he's got kind of used to me."

Mr. Dark laughed and again referred to watchful waiting. It was, he told her, a practically infallible formula, used a thousand times by creative artists because of its soundness.

"Don't worry; human nature never alters. We'll give it a chance. I'll call you up tomorrow and begin our campaign. In the meantime trust me—with your confidence." As a matter of fact, Verena had forgotten he was a reporter. "I shall arrange a dignified interview for you, coached in language your husband will only be proud and envious of. As a matter of fact, it is because of a certain intellectual sympathy that we shall be drawn together, hereafter, in our little affair. Oh, trust me to manage it, Mrs. Dayson, and don't worry."

She was worried, however, all over, waking early the next morning. Or at least she thought it was morning. That was the awful part of New York. You couldn't tell whether it was night or day, with artificial lights all the time, and the ceaseless outer roar. You couldn't even tell if it was rainy or fair.

What had waked her, thinking it was pouring, was only Buck's nostrils collaborating with the radiator. Buck lay asleep in the companion bed. The dark virile head of the educated cowboy lay revealed above a cylindrical roll of pink brocade coverlet, a pastel court scene of Louis XIV above him. An effete setting for Buck of the crow-hopping, sunfishing, squealing broncos.

Lying under her own pink brocade, with her hands, so muscular and capable on the bridle and now impotent in this situation as two wax lilies, tightly clenched in her palm, Verena cried, and swore a little, and reviewed last evening. Never, never would she forget how Mrs. Sennay looked standing downstairs by the elevator with Mr. Wirtheimer! A picture to linger in anyone's—a man's especially—observing eye.

Buck himself had made unwontedly careful toilet. Ordinarily it was hard to make Buck go even a black tie. Plain business clothes were good enough, he claimed, capped by a tall gray soft hat. But ever since he had known Mrs. Sennay he had been on soup-and-fish after six—things he had bought in Piccadilly, that Wales himself would not have blushed for.

They had planned to go to the Persian Nightingale, on Wirtheimer's suggestion. It was a night club, really, and Verena at first refused on pretense of feeling ill.

But when Buck merely said, "All right, Rena, if your head aches, better stay," she had hastily donned a pink-and-blue-shot taffeta with a lot of lace and a rather bunchy skirt in which she resembled a boudoir lamp, and had tagged along. She had tasted only gall.

Against the foil of Mr. Wirtheimer, the perfect sixty-six, Violet Sennay looked like a Cyprian deity. A tall, supple, voluptuously made woman, with black glossy hair poured tightly on her head, curving in two forward horns upon her fruitlike cheeks. Her dress was perfectly plain—easy, yet also poured, of lustrous black satin, that ended in a little pointed fin. Her perfect arms swung negligently indifferent. On one white wrist was looped a bracelet thread of brilliants; one hand held a long careless sweep of cerise-dyed vulture feathers. Mrs. Sennay's feet and ankles, incased in cobweb black silk hose and pointed black slippers with brilliant-studded heels, invited all eyes to perfection. Her large, rather theatrically shadowed brown eyes, suggested at once mood and mystery. She had floated forward.

"Buck, my dear boy, how you've kept us!" Without a word for Buck's companion lamp shade.

"And yet," reflected Verena, "I'm the one to be kidnaped, taken to Pell Street and rustled by Chinks, stowed away by chuck-wagon boys. How do I know she'll even return the body? No, I won't, I won't, I won't!"

Buck stirred a moment under his cover. "'S that, Rena?"

A dozen truthful lies fought in Verena for utterance, after the fashion of all women in like plight: "Buck, I'm sick of your carrying on with this woman! Buck, tell me the truth, are you in love with Mrs. Sennay? What's going on here? Buck, are you tired of me? What's in your mind about me? What about our kids, our home?" and the like."

1235 And like other women in like 1236 plight, she feinted and circled 1237 for the answer.

1238 "I d'know," cried Verena with 1239 a gay little laugh. "I just woke 1240 up and got to thinking. I got 1241 to thinking about such a nice 1242 fella I met yest'day. He was 1243 a newspaper reporter, Buck, one 1244 o' these New York boys. I 1245 guess they're all pretty fast too. 1246 Anyway, he wanted to talk to 1247 me for the Sunday paper, and 1248 after a while he asked me out to 1249 lunch today and—I hope you 1250 don't mind—well, I said I 1251 would."

1252 She cocked an eye at the pink 1253 brocade cocoon, to see what 1254 manner of emotional butterfly 1255 it would hatch. Buck only 1256 yawned and burrowed the 1257 deeper.

1258 " 'S right, do," he murmured, 1259 "though I don't know why you 1260 wake me up to talk 'bout it. 1261 You know, wantcha have good 1262 time, Rena, help 'self." And he 1263 was off on his duet with the 1264 radiator. Wouldn't you know? 1265 thought Verena, and yet three 1266 weeks ago—mention of an un- 1267 protected luncheon with a gay 1268 fast New York man and a 1269 reporter!

1270 Nevertheless, she had an al- 1271 most happy morning, shopping 1272 with Mr. Dark's friend, lunching 1273 and preparing a campaign with 1274 Mr. Dark himself.

1275 Two o'clock found her in the 1276 tanbark pen at Mullahey's, with 1277 Dick and Dan bringing out a 1278 cow pony for her. In her rough 1279 riding clothes, working breeches 1280 and shirt, Verena was always 1281 happy. Now she proceeded to 1282 do a few practice turns, just a 1283 little exercise stuff to keep her 1284 in training. Anyone who had 1285 been present would have been 1286 quick to agree that it was a 1287 class of stuff far above the 1288 deserts of the average theater 1289 patron. It was riding for riders 1290 that the rodeo queen proceeded 1291 now to do; an exquisite con- 1292 noisseurship in her art that hung 1293 her name in big electrics of 1294 opinion at Denver, Calgary, 1295 Salinas.

1296 Ordinarily, in any prolonged 1297 stop, Buck and she went through 1298 their training drill together, but 1299 today he was not here. He had 1300 mumbled something about a 1301 conference on the kidnaping with 1302 Wirtheimer and Mrs. Sennay, so 1303 his wife had plenty of room to 1304 kick up dust, ample opportunity 1305 to pull all the tricks she knew. 1306 She went through them all, 1307 evolving every possible trick 1308 from her pony. She raced and 1309 loped and let it buck and crow- 1310 hop. She climbed round and 1311 over it, now in and out of saddle. 1312 She ducked and bent and 1313 doubled. She rode now on its 1314 back, now in one stirrup. She 1315 crawled under its belly as she 1316 raced, dropping from one side, 1317 reaching a hand under for a stir- 1318 rup, coming up on the other, flying hoofs thrashing, flashing near her head. Round and round she flashed and whirled, courting death carelessly as a part of the day's routine, and when she was tired she uncoiled the rope on her saddle and sent a spinning curvilinear dark serpent into the air.

If Verena Dayson's riding was a legend in the West, her rope work was no less. Buck had taught it all to her. Now, re-membering all those long, happy, careful instructions, Verena, as another woman might look over romantic ballroom souvenirs— a wan pressed tuberose, an old glove, a scented note—repeated each supple, graceful, intricate figure in the air, calling up the sweet association of older, more untroubled hours with the big brown-skinned boy she loved. When she had gone through all this—all the parabolas, figure eights, dancing jennys; when she had finished writing hiero-glyphics in the air, she put on that final sketch that set specta-tors roaring, their hats fanning; that had been her particular show stunt at Wembley, that even Buck always watched anx-iously, a little nervously, as performed by her tiny childish figure.

From a chute arranged at one side of the pen Dick and Dan released a steer; a wide-horned, sinister, browned figure that rushed forward, paused, head low, staring, then jerked madly away in a blind race.

Verena halted a moment, then bending low on her pony, her rope swaying out before her in a small perfectly arranged loop, was after it, horse and rider like one creature, centaur fashion; one moment the small loop float-ed in readiness, the dashing steer plunging away; the next, and the lasso curled out in the air, the loop settling over the running creature.

There came a tightening swerve and turn of the pony, and the steer, leaping up, the rope checking it in midrise, was knocked from its feet, fell heavily on its side in as perfect a bust as you could wish. Light as a thistle the rodeo queen lit on the ground in a flying leap, loosen-ing a smaller rope from her belt. With a half dozen motions she had it bound neatly around the steer as a housewife trusses a Sunday fowl for roasting. There were only two women in the country besides herself who could do it.

"Who," inquired Verena, a little breathlessly, as the boys ran up now—"who says I can't rope, throw, tie and deliver— yes, and stamp and take to the parcel post?"

But it was only a rhetorical question, there being no one of any importance to answer it.

It was five o'clock, anyhow, and time for the rodeo queen

257

1403 to begin formally her new pro-
1404 gram. Verena hurried back to
1405 her hotel to dress for dinner.
1406 No walking lamp shade tonight.
1407 She put on with trembling fingers
1408 and a final sense of ecstasy the
1409 lovely things Mr. Dark's kind
1410 friend had helped her choose.
1411 What looked out of the mirror
1412 finally was Titania herself, a
1413 figure of almost unearthly
1414 delicacy, fragility and brillance.
1415 Sparkling silver lace, fine as Jack
1416 Frost spins on the windowpane,
1417 formed the tiny bodice, the
1418 filmy soft-falling long skirt.
1419 From this emerged Verena's
1420 pretty little-girl arms and throat,
1421 covered now with a languorous
1422 siren coat of powder. Her curly
1423 gilt-tipped hair clung decorously
1424 to her shapely head, bound by
1425 a single thread of brilliants. On
1426 one wrist fell a bracelet loop
1427 of brilliants. The other hand
1428 held a great fan of brilliant-
1429 studded silver gauze painted in
1430 faint pink flowers. Little silver
1431 slippers peeped beneath her lace
1432 skirt, the heels set with rhine-
1433 stones. Over a near-by chair
1434 hung a cloak of soft pink velvet,
1435 lined with silver lamé, a great
1436 collar of pink fox. A pink fox!
1437 Verena had whistled aloud when
1438 she saw it. At this moment
1439 Henry B. Dayson entered, and
1440 as Verena looked at him, all her
1441 heart stirred to realize how fit
1442 an accompaniment Buck Day-
1443 son was for any woman at her
1444 very gladdest.

1445 "Buck," screamed her heart
1446 as he spoke to her and turned
1447 away, "notice my dress!" Then
1448 she remembered Mr. Dark's
1449 counsel.
1450 "Oh, Buck," she drawled, "I
1451 was waiting for you, to—to show
1452 you my new costume. Rather a
1453 pretty affair, don't you think?
1544 I think the lines are lovely. It's
1455 after a Boucher print." She
1456 pronounced it Booshay very
1457 carefully.
1458 Buck turned and gave the
1459 dress a careful consideration.
1460 "It's nice," he pronounced;
1461 "It's down-right pretty—if you
1462 like it. You don't sort of look
1463 natural to me. What I mean is,
1464 I like you in your workin' pants
1465 best—or one of your ginghams,
1466 back home, I guess. Some
1467 women take to being hossed up
1468 more than others, I reckon.
1469 But you look good all right,
1470 Verena."
1471 "Well," said Verena airily,
1472 "you ought to know—from your
1473 study of the different kinds of
1474 women. But I can assure you,
1475 Buck, this is a perfect costume.
1476 It's the dern-ee-ay cree, and
1477 that's, after all, what I want in
1478 a New York onsomble. If I'm to
1479 be metropolitan, as you seem to
1480 desire"—Verena curved a pretty
1481 little arm toward the glass—"I
1482 naturally want to do it in the
1483 best possible metropolitan form.
1484 I shouldn't care to have New
1485 Yorkers cherish the hypothesis
1486 that a—that a Western woman

is not adaptable and cannot conform to sophisticated Eastern standards. Anyhow, I was stung enough jack—what I· mean, I think it's very appropriate for a dinner dance or theater, and if we go to the Persian Nightingale again tonight——"

"Look here, Rena"—Buck stirred uneasily—"would you— would you mind—the fact is we didn't get our plans finished off this afternoon—I mean about the kidnaping, and Vio—Mrs. Sennay suggested we conclude 'em at dinner tonight. Wirtheimer would like it too. He's got an appointment and has to leave early, but we three could finish off. It's a fact it would be dumb slow for you. What I mean is"—Buck grew more uneasy and refused her his eyes—"what we—I thought was —being you complained yest'day of being so tired, I thought you might like to rest tonight and have dinner sent up."

"I see," said Verena slowly. "Well, I admit I've been in a kind of peaked sickly state lately, falling off a little, and not able to lift a feather, as you might say, and you may be right. Anyhow, I guess I can try it—our eating separate tonight if you want it. Only, I don't believe I'll be eating alone. You remember, I spoke this morning of a charming boy I met who asked me to lunch.

Well, we've got awfully on rap- poor together—oh, a lot really. I mean, he's tremendously interesting as a type, rather stunning to look at too. But since I'm to be alone, if you don't mind——"

She caught up the pink cloak and crushed the pink fox from No Man's Land beneath her pretty bitter little face. Buck looked at her in honest relief. "Why, not at all, Rena. That's the very ticket. Business'd be awful dull for you— you don't wanta know all the details about this Pell Street stuff. Go ahead an get this dude and play with him."

It was not Buck Dayson speaking—that she knew by the look of his eyes.

There's a weed that grows upon the plains, and Western tradition has it that a horse grazing thereon goes loco. Buck Dayson had certainly eaten of the loco weed. Was there any cure?

In the next ten days the rodeo queen followed with the most careful consistency the program young Mr. Dark indicated. If there was any subtle phase of the corrective ritual young Mr. Dark had proposed in his friendly interest in young Mrs. Dayson, as a tonic and alterative for Mr. Henry B. Dayson, it has never been recorded.

As an artist, a student and

veteran analyst of all subjective human passions, Mr. Dark, out of his great fund of experience, his familiarity with literature and wide social observation, in the next few days left no stone unturned, Verena following faithfully, in his proposed effort, mechanistically speaking, to turn Mr. Dayson, as a matrimonial delinquent, back to the fold.

With no effect whatever! The three great levers of human conduct which he had indicated here —beauty, charm and male jealousy—were pumped on to the fullest extent, and made as much impression as a fly alighting on the proverbial wheel.

Some husbands are built like this. Queen Penelope's startled cry, summoned to out-rival Circe, might not have been unfounded. Mr. Henry B. Dayson was a husband who knew all about the girl he had married—a fatal position, we are often told, yet unescapable in many instances.

He knew that his Verena was pretty; he would have knocked anyone down who claimed otherwise. Costuming might create some small advantage, but he had been well enough suited with Verena's costumes. Her beauty was sweet and native, and beyond any longer surprising him. The complete new line of dazzling correctly classy raiment which she proceeded to air passed completely over him.

Her mind he already knew as well. They had lived in the closest intimacy—equally, we are told, fatal to attraction. Her boyish candor, her slang, native spice and pep were as natural and comfortable to him as old shoes, as accepted a part of his life and thinking as his own mentality.

Verena, in new cultured aspects, trained by Mr. Dark to conversational expressions she had never used before, to little touches of sophistication, including polysyllables and foreign expressions, was noticed at first by her husband in a sort of daze, then very shortly, figuratively, slapped and put in place.

"What makes you talk so dumb, Rena?" he asked one evening. "You've been goin' round lately spoutin' like a gusher. Come to earth, girl, I don't like it."

As for jealousy, Verena had long since made the most fatal error of all. She had revealed to her husband how much she loved him. His faith in his invincibility here would have required mountains to move— a great deal larger mountain than Mr. Stanley Dark. Death alone, or its threat, could have aroused him suddenly, as with many husbands, to a realization of her special qualities—and the rodeo queen did not propose to die to secure her end.

Sitting with young Mr. Dark disconsolately at dinner one

evening a week later, they reviewed together their lack of progress and Buck's impregnability.

"It must be," said Mr. Dark, running a desperate hand through his dark hair, "that your husband is extra—er—bull-headed, Mrs. Dayson. Er— possibly as a Western man, that type is stronger. Anyhow, no man ought to be so blind as not to perceive—what has been going on here," he added indignantly. It was an outrage, a personal insult actually.

"I don't know. Maybe it's just that Buck ain't ready to see things. Mebbe a man's got to be ready. You forget he's— he's still kind of interested in Mrs. Sennay. He's busy, too, with somebody calling him up all the time arranging things. Anyhow, it ain't working, is it? Suits this Sennay all the better, I guess, what I've been doing; and it'll soon be too late——"

"No," said Mr. Dark. "About that, I've explained—in Vi Sennay's history. The men she plays round with get tired and break off with her."

"But they can't break off with a contract she gets 'em to sign meantime. Day after tomorrow is the time Wirtheimer's set to clinch everything. That's the evening picked I'm to mix in with the Chink boys. Buck told me something else this morning—we're to look for an apartment in Park Avenue. He said I could have Buster and Henrietta all next winter, with a trained nurse. I guess Sennay thinks that would keep me busy. She'll have Buck doin' his rope act in a frock coat with a gardenia soon."

"Well," said Mr. Dark, "something may happen to help us yet. Who knows?"

"At least, I don't," sighed Verena. "What could happen? Our time's up. I s'pose I'll just have to stand round and take my medicine in this like other girls do—let it wear away itself. Only, it's goin' to be a darn hard year. But don't think I'm not grateful. You've been my friend."

"I hope I'll always be your friend," cried Mr. Dark quickly, moved by the pretty distressed little face. "Anything that I can do at all—always! Anything!" he added warmly.

Verena sighed and shook her head. She was due now at what Mrs. Sennay called her studio— her private and anomalous apartment at the top of a house in West Thirteenth Street. Because, at last, they couldn't get along without herself in their plans.

After all, reflected Verena sarcastically, as Mr. Dark put her in a taxi and she rattled away down to Thirteenth Street, whither Buck and Wirtheimer had preceded her, you can't pull a kidnaping unless something is kidnaped; and it might be, maybe, that—just at the last moment—the victm might be allowed a word or two—listen in—on proceedings. It might be so! Possibly—perhaps!

Mrs. Sennay lived in a house with the door painted pea green, and when you opened it there were four flights before you reached her studio. Climbing these four flights slowly and more and more sarcastically, Verena felt with every step an accumulating fund of rage against Mrs. Sennay—this blandishing, poised woman who had come up on the boat, had flattered and followed Buck, ignoring her, preëmpting him for her own, dragging him to a new life.

It was her first visit to Mrs. Sennay's studio, and Verena batted her eyes carefully. It would probably not be the last. Mrs. Sennay gave little studio parties here—and very likely all next winter! Buck, she knew, had had a conference here at least once before—at least one time that he had mentioned.

A large room with a fanlight, a baby grand, a piece of armor and—yes, an alcoved platform, or dais, with a couch under a bearskin, three steps painted yellow and a wrought-iron torchère. The air was thick with smoke, for Wirtheimer, a man named Stendahl, a Miss Lester, Mrs. Sennay and Henry B. Dayson were already convened and engaged on tobacco. But a place was made for her, and Mrs. Sennay was very gracious, very sweet.

"Little Rena must hear what we have decided," she cried at once. "We've been so full of our plans and with insuring success, before our opening here for the summer, that we haven't been able to talk competently; but now we know what to do with you, *chérie*, you must, you really must hear."

What little Rena then heard was really a simple proceeding. A very kind Eurasian friend had agreed to turn over to them his perfectly appointed, really comfortable apartment in the Chinese region for a few hours for the completion of the plan. At nine o'clock, in a taxicab, on the given night Mrs. Dayson and a friend—no other than Mr. Stendahl—desirous of a visit to Chinatown, should have the conveyance stopped before the Eurasian's home in order to permit Mr. Stendahl a purchase of cigarettes. Gone not more than five minutes, in that brief interval a tragedy should ensue! Two men would rush from the Eurasian's home, overpower, bind the taxi driver and drag young Mrs. Dayson into the building.

"To perfect safety, my dear!

The apartment will be entirely empty except for Lydia Lester here, who will be there to receive you. Mr. Wirtheimer's car will be at the next corner, and at once you and Lydia, leaving by a side passage, heavily veiled, will be placed in it and driven up to Yonkers, where you will lie perdu for three days with friends of mine—perfectly lovely people named Mitchell. But the police, notified of course within a few minutes of this by Mr. Stendahl, will have their hands full for an interval—the newspapers furnish plenty of space—before your discovery and return on a plausible basis we have worked out."

"How nice!" trembled Verena.

"My dear friends, let us drink to success!" cried Mrs. Sennay, whose faultless wrist and arm looked so well lifted in public attention.

They drank, because Mrs. Sennay had supplied not only tobacco but wherewithal for a toast, together with dishes of hors d'œuvres to eat—suitable to æsthetic studios. Such, for instance, as sweet ripe olives filled with garlic and anchovy paste; dabs of bread spread with caviar, and the like. We mention these because it is quite likely that without them the rodeo queen would never have had the idea that suddenly came to her.

She was watching Buck, as she always did in Mrs. Sennay's presence, and as Buck put down his toast—set down his glass, that is—he reached over and helped himself to some of Mrs. Sennay's hors d'œuvres. That is, in easy plain-man fashion, he treated it as food. He practically filled his mouth with the ripe olives stuffed with garlic and anchovy. And something very curious and terrible happened in his face. To Verena, acquainted connubially with its least shading, it took on a blending of agony, solicitation, surprise, frustration, utter horror and panic that made him look desperately though elusively familiar.

Buck had large handsome brown eyes. They rolled up slightly for a second above the blank dismay and consternation in his face. Of what did he remind her? What did Buck look like? Where had she seen a look like that before?

She got it in a flash of illumination. Buck looked like a steer, jerked to a fall, pinned on the rope, with herself running up to tie. She had seen a face—eyes like that, in their wildness and anguish, a hundred times before. Her knowledge shook her because of an accompanying flash of inspiration.

"Buck," she asked suddenly, in a level tone across the smoke, "do you approve of this? Do you believe that a couple of artists like us ought to pull a stunt

263

of this kind—that our work will go better for it?"

"I do," said Buck, refusing his eyes again. "I've never held that policy before, Rena, but I have changed my views. I am strongly in favor of a kidnaping feature. I've told you so before a dozen times. As an advertising headliner for Dayson & Dayson's summer work——"

"Then," said Verena quietly, "if that's the case, and I'm to be the goat, mebby Mrs. Sennay here'll call a cab and let me slip up to the hotel again. I want to rest up all I can and get in good fix, and I'm not needed here any more."

It was not to rest, however, that Verena retired. She summoned Mr. Dark. If Mrs. Dayson, the troubled wife, had earlier thrown herself upon his mercy, it was the rodeo queen who demanded his coöperation now.

"You said you'd help," she cried, "always—that's what you said, and I've got to have help. It'll take a lot of fixing with money—the door man, this proprietor and all the damage. I've got the money, but I want a man. Besides, I've got to have some atmosphere. You told me you acted in a dramatic society. It's little enough to do. And last of all, I'm a lady and I'll want to be chaperoned."

"Chaperoned!" cried young Mr. Dark dazedly. "I'll help you—why, yes, I said I would, but I don't think you need it—a chaperon—doing cave-woman stuff."

"Cave-woman stuff!" cried Verena. "Why, a cave woman was a gumdrop! She let a man beat her up and knock her down all he pleased—just as he pleased. No, sir, I wouldn't say cave-woman stuff. Let's call it all I know—Western stuff."

If you are a patron of those forms of light relaxation beloved of the æsthetic artistic set in New York, you are already acquainted with the Persian Nightingale, that Oriental garden and rendezvous of delightful dalliance with the subtler forms of evening pleasure, which is set like a jewel in the smart aloofness of the Sixties and approached like a guarded citadel by pass-word and listed membership only. If you are not, it may be necessary to mention the famous mural decorations, by the Arabian Quenjidian, depicting love scenes—drawn so smartly, with no perspective—between a Persian troubadour and a princess of ancient Ecbatana, and capped by old legends from Hafiz; that a great many Hamadans, and Ferahans are draped around appropriately; that there are bulbuls painted on the china; that the air is musty, sweet, heavy with spice, the lights passionate, a reddish violet in color, the stringed orchestra really excellent; that Fisoshian has designed the fountain—a dancing bronze goatherd. And that the cover charge is as stiff as any night club's in New York.

Here, after the show, the lights of the theater burn to a very early hour, assisted by such kindred spirits as affect the midnight oil. Here come also more prosaic hangers-on, those of the half-world of the arts, the agents, publicity campaigners, go-betweens, and the like—the Mrs. Violet Sennay type. Here, on the evening preceding the closing of the contract, she came with, as had often happened of late, her latest affinity—her dashing cowboy.

Of the outer appearance of Mr. Buck Dayson at this point in Mrs. Sennay's interest, of his tall, easy, good-looking figure correctly valeted in smart evening wear, accompanied by a natural and attractive grace and topped by a picturesque well-shaped head, which included a rather stubborn jaw and handsome brown eyes that could certainly, under stimulus, resemble a profoundly scared steer's—it may be said that he was easily the handsomest man in the room.

Of his intellectual state, his subjective condition, as he followed Mrs. Sennay to the allotted table, it would have been more difficult to surmise. Not even the arts of divination of a Mr. Dark would have been quickly certain.

The educated cowboy looked in all respects like a man of the world, perfectly content with it and at ease. He would have been quick to claim that this was correct, yet actually a secret, hardly defined gloom weighed upon him; the sort of gloom a bridegroom knows on the eve of the fatal day and which he seeks to dispel by the factitious jollity of the stag dinner.

Mr. Henry B. Dayson, a humble understudy of Alexander the Great—who had pined for new worlds to conquer—who had responded so quickly to Mrs. Sennay as pathfinder, was aware of a slight undertone or reaction based on that impending contract. Light dalliance with a lady like Mrs. Sennay is one thing—light as air and of the emotions purely—but the lady on the dollar is a solider female, and flirtation with her as embodied in Eastern contracts and removal from more familiar paths of practice—— In fact, brought up short, Mr. Henry B. Dayson, facing his actual crisis, as an erstwhile man of sound practical sense, was undergoing a slight case of cold feet, the while he drummed upon the table, affected interest in a cigarette, the potation placed before him, the seductive lan-

2075 guors of the Lilli Lehmann music
2076 floating near.

2077 It is well that this was so. It
2078 is possible that it had its con-
2079 tributing influence on the success
2080 of Mrs. Dayson's plan. It may
2081 well be that, as Mrs. Dayson
2082 once propounded, a man must
2083 be ready. What that was, and
2084 what its dénouement, there will
2085 never, I fear, be two similar
2086 testimonies at the Persian Night-
2087 ingale.

2088 There is, in the middle of the
2089 room, an open space de-
2090 voted to acts of entertainment,
2091 which, witnessed by leisured,
2092 drinking, smoking guests, has
2093 been the scene of many an
2094 odd divertissement; yet I think
2095 nothing like that supplied by
2096 two figures, who appeared sud-
2097 denly, quite silently, between
2098 the double doors at 12:30 that
2099 evening and who moved on the
2100 actual space.

2101 They were figures not in
2102 keeping with either Persian
2103 Nightingales or gardens. Say,
2104 rather with the atmosphere of
2105 the Shooting of Dan McGrew.
2106 At least it was suggested by the
2107 more masculine of the two
2108 mounted riders who, masked
2109 over the mouth by spotted
2110 handkerchiefs, faced the gay
2111 idlers, on respectively a speckled
2112 cow pony and a cayuse. Of this
2113 shape, there were some who
2114 averred later that for bushiness
2115 of clothing, quantity of re-
2116 volvers, redness of bandanna

2117 and height of sombrero it tran-
2118 scended anything seen this side
2119 of the Rio Grande after '49.

2120 But the other, the feminine
2121 figure was not less grim. Small
2122 as a child, beautifully strong,
2123 correctly accoutered in gray
2124 cow-girl's clothes, she appeared
2125 to be doing something with a
2126 thin dark rope on her wrist. It
2127 formed suddenly in a small oscil-
2128 lating flat ring beyond her hand,
2129 trembled, swayed in the air,
2130 moved forward with a settling,
2131 beautiful precision, like a slender
2132 licking tongue.

2133 It is here that testimony varies
2134 so greatly. There are some who
2135 state that the circle of rope
2136 swooped down unswervingly and
2137 selectively, snatching its victim
2138 as he sat; others who claim he
2139 rose, pale, startled, and ad-
2140 vanced a little toward it from
2141 the end of the room. But all are
2142 agreed on the confusion of the
2143 next instant.

2144 The rope settled, clutched its
2145 victim tightly above the elbows;
2146 the cow pony sidled and feinted
2147 and circled, as the rider began
2148 to wind. Tables, chairs were
2149 pushed aside, diners receded with
2150 mingled shrieks, china crashed,
2151 bulbuls flew into the air, glass
2152 shivered, silver jingled, music
2153 stopped; there was crying out,
2154 scuffle, as the West gave battle
2155 with the East. In less time than
2156 it takes to tell, a man's figure,
2157 neatly triced yet compellingly
2158 drawn at the horn of a saddle

by a small gray amazon, was clearly realized—a figure bewildered, outraged, yet drawn irresistibly to the door by a small hand that, firm, yet subtly practiced, adjusted the leverage to poundage with just enough skilled compulsion to keep it on its feet.

"Featuring," cried a gay voice at the door, "ladies and gentlemen, Dayson & Dayson; rope-and-riding artists in their big spectacular advertising act — kidnaping in the Western style, or extracting a husband from quarters that do him no good."

Everybody is agreed on this. Only a few near the door heard the passionate exhortation the small gray figure made from her saddle to the roped-and-tied man before her.

"Buck Dayson," she flamed, "you wanted a kidnap—and you got it. I am going home. There's a train at midnight, and our trunks are at the Pennsylvania. Do I go alone? Out to Buster and Henrietta and our house. Out to our two babies— and four bathrooms. Out West, where we rode together in the mornings——"

Language is a poor conveyancer of feeling; but Buck, looking at his little rodeo queen with that memory of cold feet, that now stirring gale of laughter in the Persian room behind— needed none. He was coming out of it. He put out a dazed hand to his wife.

As I say, there is a conflict of testimony.

Two figures—a cowgirl and a handsome man in evening clothes, it is claimed—got into a waiting car. But the more desperate of the Western desperadoes, it is said, remained standing on the curb. One man claimed overhearing the farewell message:

"—— when we see you next summer, Mr. Dark, out at Tulsa —don't you forget. Never can thank you enough for helping me! It was bang-up help, too, and reg'lar stuff, even if you did put your chaps on hind end to."

With the omniscience of our kind, there is no reason, however, why we should not follow Buck and Verena, two of the ridingest kids the West ever knew, on their flight away from the lures and the voice of New York.

Not that Buck at once forgave Verena. He raged and sulked at the hurt to his dignity as far as Pittsburgh; he gloomed beyond Indianapolis; he was injured and reserved through Illinois; but when they had crossed the Mississippi and the freer airs from stretches of wheat blew on his forehead, he began to relent. He admitted error, he became a little sheepish, he finally laughed, as they neared Kansas.

And Verena, who had hoped

2242 and prayed and battled and lost
2243 —and finally used her last arrow
2244 —like any wife, relaxed with a
2245 fearful joy.
2246 "I guess—I guess," grinned
2247 Buck, "you were right. I don't
2248 wanta see the East again.
2249 Goddy, some of the eats are
2250 awful! I like to try new things.

2251 But Goddy! I guess—I could
2252 say it—you were right, Verena.
2253 I don't know what else I can do."
2254 For answer Verena flung her-
2255 self on him like a Bar-K boy
2256 bulldogging a Texas yearling.
2257 "You could kiss me, I guess,
2258 Buck," sobbed the little rodeo
2259 queen in her relief.

THE ANALYSIS

From a technical point of view this story makes an interesting exhibit. Within the Scene which occupies lines 110 to 400 there are interpolated two Flash-back Scenes. One is a flash-back by the actor. It occupies lines 243 to 297 and is an actual flash-back interchange between Buck and Verena. In this there is nothing of any especial importance to the student, which has not already been discussed; but a rather unusual device is the hypothetical interview which is a somewhat original substitute for a Flash-back Scene. It occupies lines 298 to 378; and the fifth step is also the fifth step of the preceding presentation unit. This fifth step occupies lines 379 to 400.

Another example of a flash-back occurs on lines 1183 to 1221, and is interesting because it is not a flash-back used to give explanatory matter for the Beginning of the story, but is a flash-back which occurs in the Body of the story, where it is used to give information that will make clear to the reader the importance, not of the main situation, but of the scene situation. That scene situation projects Verena's attempt to bring about her main purpose by making her husband jealous through telling him about Mr. Dark.

The writer of this story must have had a great deal of fun in writing it, and every writer must get a great deal of amusement from reading it. The writer takes an old narrative problem, used again and again, and takes the answers which have been used again and again, and pokes fun at them as solutions for such a narrative problem. In the Beginning of the story, which occupies lines 1 to 1119, the condition is made clear to the reader. Verena Dayson, rodeo queen, realizing that her husband is under the spell of a metropolitan publicity woman tells a reporter, who persuades her that to win him back she must outflirt, outdress, and outcharm her rival, Mrs. Sennay. Those three methods of winning back an erring husband have been the solution offered time and again by writers of fiction. The fact that numerous stories have been written and accepted about this central condition is sufficient evidence that plot is not nearly so important in presenting stories as are the scenes which go to make up the story.

But Mrs. Pulver, being a competent and experienced writer, realized that the solution to a narrative problem should be one growing out of the capacity of the main actor that distinguishes her from other actors. The chief capacity possessed by this Verena Dayson, is her ability to ride and rope. So Mrs. Pulver takes each of the tried and true methods and proves that in this special case each one is a failure. In so doing, she is enabled to make each attempt serve as a scene in the Body of the story, and to cause the result of it (its fifth step) to form a hindrance to the main narrative purpose. The first attempt, which is to arouse jealousy is met by indifference on the part of Buck. The next attempt, in which Verena tries to impress him with her specially chosen clothes, finds him also indifferent; and in its fifth step it shows that she seems to have reached the point where disaster is imminent. Then she uses the other method, which is to beat the opponent at her own game, that is to outcharm her. Her newly acquired sophisticated conversation simply arouses the amused tolerance of her husband, who says, "What makes you talk so dumb, Rena?" The fifth step of this interchange is shown in an episode between Verena and Mr. Dark in which, summing up the state of affairs she sees no hope. She then, being in a position where she has virtually abandoned hope, goes to the conference at Mrs. Sennay's and notices that Buck looks like the steer whom she has roped. Then, just as Gideon Higsbee, in *Once and Always*, responded to the stimulus of the suggestion that he should sell some fake mining stock to Lemuel Gower in order to solve his problem, so Verena Dayson responds to the image conveyed by this idea and responds to it in terms of a solution of her problem. And just as Gideon Higsbee enlisted the aid of his friends in his enterprise, so she enlists the aid of Mr. Dark in her enterprise. Nowhere more than in the craftsmanship of short-story writing is it true that "necessity is the mother of invention." When the character has reached the big moment in the story where disaster seems imminent and inescapable the necessity for invention is greatest. All the old methods of escaping from a predicament must be abandoned and a new one, which is inherent in the capacity of the character must be invented either by the character or by the author, which, of course, is the same thing because the author invents the character. For sound craftsmanship this invention must involve a capacity already planted by the author in the early part of the story. This is true in the case of *Western Stuff*. Mrs. Pulver having through the action of her character laughed at all the tried and true methods for solving this old narrative problem, presents a new and entertaining version of a method for winning back an erring husband; and it is essentially one which is based upon the character and capacity of the particular actor in this story, Verena Dayson.

For one other reason this story is also interesting. I spoke before of the difference between objective and analytical writing, and I mentioned that the older formula for criticism was "objective" and "subjective." In this case the treatment is in many cases "subjective" because the personality of the author is apparent. This is true particularly on line 2220, where the author says, "With the omniscience of our kind" thus injecting her own personality into the story.

I have taken pleasure in including this story because it raises and answers many questions which authors will find of interest.

SECTION II

STORIES OF DECISION

WHEN we begin to consider the story of Decision as a distinct classification from the story of Accomplishment we will see the importance of the special nomenclature that we have agreed to use. I have in mind our special use of the word "condition" or "state of affairs" to replace the older and more generally used term "situation." The distinction between the two types of stories lies in the response of the chief actor to the main condition or main state of affairs, and that response projects what we agree to call a "narrative Situation." It is for this reason that I have closed the first section of this book with the story *Western Stuff*, because the condition to which the main actor responds in terms of a narrative problem or narrative situation is the same condition to which the main actor responds in the story *Women are Wiser*, by Frank R. Adams, which opens the second section.

The condition is, in both stories, that the wife realizes that she is in danger of losing her husband. In *Western Stuff* the reaction is instantaneous, and is in terms of purpose. That purpose is to win him back from the other woman. The narrative situation is one of accomplishment. In *Women are Wiser* the narrative problem or narrative situation is one of decision or choice. In *Western Stuff* there is no question in the mind of the main actor as to what course to pursue. In *Women are Wiser* there is a very definite uncertainty as to which course to take, or what decision to make.

People often ask "How may I tell whether a story is a story of accomplishment or a story of decision?" There are several ways in which to tell. Every story has its general large division of Situaation, Explanatory Matter, Struggle, Conclusive Act, and sometimes Sequel to the Conclusive Act. The Sequel is not a distinguishing feature, because it may occur in either story, and it may be the same in either story. But in the Beginning of the story of Accomplishment the main narrative problem is one of accomplishment. In the Beginning of the story of Decision, the main narrative problem is one requiring decision, or might be said to be one of indecision or uncertainty as to what action is to be taken. But confusion may arise in the mind of a reader who finds that in certain stories there is set forth a narrative problem and there is in the mind of the reader an uncertainty, but this uncertainty is followed by certainty, and then a number of struggles arise as a result of the course of conduct decided upon. There is an example of this in the story by William Dudley Pelley, *The Face in the Window*, reprinted in the accomplishment section of this book. In this story the main condition is set forth, and the main actor, Cora McBride, is uncertain as to what course of conduct she will pursue. Had the story ended at the close of line 659, where Cora McBride leaves the house it would be a story of Decision. In the story of Decision no struggles grow out of the Conclusive Act. In the story of Accomplishment it is this Conclusive Act of Decision which projects the struggles of the story. The story of accomplishment only begins when the character decides to do something, in the story of Decision the story then ends (except, of course, for the Sequel). In the Ending of the story of Accomplishment the Conclusive Act is one that tells the reader that the actor has either accomplished his purpose, (that purpose is already known,) or has abandoned that already known purpose. In the Ending of the story of Decision there is a decision arrived at. The character is no longer uncertain, and then the story is over.

In the Body of the story of Decision we find its greatest difference from the story of Accomplishment. The Beginning of either story may have a number of presentation units leading up to the main problem, and each one of these presentation units may, at its crisis, show that there is the promise of conflict, or of a difficulty to be overcome, or of disaster. The difference in the Body of the two types of story is that, in the first, each one of these promises may be developed into a struggle between two people, but in the story of Decision the only possible conflict which can occur is a mental conflict between traits in the same person, one urging him toward one choice, another urging him toward another choice, even though that choice may be inertia. This mental struggle is, of all types of struggle, the least interesting, because it appeals to the intellect and not at all, or to a very slight extent, to the emotions or sensations. Such appeal to the intellect is usually fatal to interest. Theoretically, writers presenting stories of Decision should present a mental struggle leading to that decision. Practically they do not, because the theory defeats their purpose, to write an interesting story, and does not square with the facts.

Many writers who are inexperienced, and who realize instinctively that a story of Decision is almost certain to be an interesting story, are defeated because they try to apply a theory to the presentation of such a story. They clog the interest of the story by presenting as the Body of the story a prolonged mental struggle between different traits in the character of the chief actor. They here are led astray by an instinct which is sound; but are defeated because their knowledge of craftsmanship is insufficient.

The first clarifying step toward mastery of the craftsmanship of the story of Decision, which they would assume to have a Body showing indecision, is a realization that ordinarily the Body Scene is omitted. This is rather a startling discovery to the novices. They do not seem to see the justification for such a method. "If," they say, "the story is concerned with the uncertainty, then that uncertainty ought to be shown in the Body of the story." Here again Necessity is the mother of Invention. There was once a newly enlisted soldier in the colonial army, who did not realize that the rigid discipline of the army made it necessary for him to keep from voicing his opinion of an officer for whose abilities he had very little respect. He voiced his opinions by saying, "That officer is a damned fool." Reprimanded for this, he inquired why he should not say what he believed. "Can't I say he's a fool if I think he's a fool?" he asked. "Not at all," he was told. "You can think what you like so long as you don't say it." "All right," he said, "I think he's a damned fool."

He had devised a way of showing his thoughts. In the story of Decision if you wish to indicate the thoughts of the main actor it is better to *show* those thoughts in a scene in which he expresses them *through his speech*, and that will be an interchange with somebody else. In that way you will avoid the mental scene.

It is, of course, much easier to point out to you through the special cases which make up the remainder of the book just how this is brought about; so I shall abandon a theoretical discussion of it to illustrate by the case method. But before doing so I want to make one or two observations. If the scene in the Body of the story of Decision is eliminated, and if the scenes in the Body of the story of Accomplishment usually occupy a large portion of the space, "Where," you may ask, "is the length so taken away, made up?" It is made up either in the Beginning, or in the Ending, or in the Sequel. But your greatest advance in craftsmanship will come with the realization that in the story of Decision the interest must come chiefly from the *Scenes* of the story rather than from the

Plot. This is particularly true in the story of Decision which is presented chronologically; because when the decision is made the story is over. Therefore the bulk of such a story must be presented in interchanges or scenes which are unsupported in their interest by any knowledge on the part of the reader of the main narrative question, which comes only after there have been presented to him those Scenes which make up the Beginning of the story of Decision. Now let us abandon theory for actual illustration.

ARCHITECTURAL CHART
OF
WOMEN ARE WISER

BEGINNING	Initial condition presented.	Meeting. Faith and condition.	1– 87	Need for Decision apparent.
		Flash-back Interchange. Faith and Roger.	88–136	Difficulties in way of easy decision shown.
	Necessity for Choice is shown.	Scene. Faith and Mr. Brennon.	137–377	Choice No. 1 apparent.
		Scene. Faith and Mrs. Brennon.	378–612	Choice No. 2 apparent. Narrative Question: "What choice will Faith make?"
ENDING	Decisive Act.	Faith telephones Mrs. Brennon.	613–617	Narrative Question Answered. "She refuses to humiliate her husband."
	Sequel.	Interchange. Faith and Roger.	618–679	
		Interchange. Mrs. and Mr. Brennon.	680–733	

WOMEN ARE WISER

BY FRANK R. ADAMS

ONE reason for choosing this story was that it shows how the same author may turn with ease, provided he is a competent craftsman, from one type of story to the other: from the story of accomplishment as exemplified in *Spare Parts* to the story of decision as exemplified in *Women are Wiser*.

A further reason for including this story is that it contains the same initial Condition as the story *Western Stuff* by Mary Brecht Pulver. In this story the Condition projects a main narrative problem of Decision by the chief actor. In *Western Stuff* it projected a main narrative problem of Accomplishment.

From the point of view of analysis it is especially worthy of study because it illustrates so clearly how such a story is dependent for its interest upon scenic structure and scenic presentation. The plot can be summed up in a very few words. The Condition confronting Faith is that she realizes that her husband is slipping away from her, and that there is placed in her hands a weapon which she may use to cow him forever after. This realization makes it necessary for her to choose immediately. She finally chooses.

Now let us turn to the story in order that we may see in detail just how Mr. Adams, as a craftsman, met the problems which here confronted him in developing and presenting this story from its bald plot outline.

CASE No. 11

WOMEN ARE WISER

BY FRANK R. ADAMS

1 The Roger Brennon marriage
2 had stood a five-year breaking
3 strain pretty well. That is, it
4 had not broken.

5 This had taken considerable
6 effort on the part of Faith Bren-
7 non, but presumably all matri-
8 monial pack-loads are carried on
9 the shoulders of women. Men
10 have other things to think about
11 and usually do.

12 That, for instance, was the
13 case of Roger Brennon. He
14 thought about golf, poker, busi-
15 ness, chorus-girls, bootleggers
16 and himself. Naturally he
17 couldn't pay any more attention
18 to the institution of matrimony
19 than an occasional glance in the
20 direction of the engineer to see if
21 she was at her post with one
22 hand on the throttle and the
23 other putting ribbons on her
24 bonny brown hair.

25 Of the things mentioned which
26 occupied Roger's attention the
27 word chorus-girls is generic.

28 It covered a multitude of
29 women with perhaps no real
30 chorus-girl among them. We

31 think of gay ladies as chorus-
32 girls. Heaven knows why. It
33 is a survival, perhaps, of the days
34 when it was considered wicked
35 to be on the stage.

36 There were a couple of reasons
37 why Roger attracted the roving
38 attention of everyone, including
39 women. One of them was that
40 he was an only son and had been
41 accustomed to demand and get
42 a lot of admiration ever since he
43 had worn his first safety-pin.
44 The other reason was that God
45 had made him lovable enough so
46 that you had to care for him in
47 spite of the fact that you knew
48 darn well that he ought to spend
49 all of his leisure moments in the
50 electric chair.

51 It is only in old-fashioned
52 plays and stories that heroes are
53 all virtuous. Recent explora-
54 tions in the labyrinths of the
55 human mind have unearthed the
56 not very astonishing fact that
57 there is about an equal amount
58 of virtue and villainy in every-
59 body. And that everybody pre-
60 fers to wear the mask of virtue

until it is torn off. A real criminal is an ordinary man whose mask has been destroyed so that he can't fool anyone any more—not even himself.

Roger had no illusions about himself. But on the other hand, and Faith knew this, he never asked for mercy. As well as his limitations of character permitted, he lived gallantly. Indications were that he would die the same way—and at a comparatively early age unless someone continued to protect him.

Faith had taken over the job from Roger's father five years before.

Now it looked as if the elder Brennon was about to reassume some of the responsibility.

At any rate Faith had a curt note from him in the mail that morning asking her to call "with reference to the current misbehavior of your husband and my son."

She got the summons shortly after Roger had left for the office. She tried to think back over their breakfast together to see if there had been any symptoms of guilt in Roger's behavior. There seemed to be nothing out of the ordinary. But probably there wouldn't be under any circumstances. Roger had a duck's-back sort of conscience and an infinite capacity for playing without retrospection whatever game was on at the time.

That very morning he had awakened her by acting an elaborately jumbled fairy-story in which he was the Middle-sized Bear who had found Little Red Riding Breeches sleeping off an enchanted bun in the other half of his twin bed.

"What's this?" he had exclaimed. "As I live, it's the Princess of Peruna under a spell—a rose-colored crêpe de Chine spell. I wonder what will arouse her."

Faith had kept her eyes shut and answered faintly, "She is bewitched and can be awakened only by the kiss of the right bozo. Any other who tries will die with a horrible tummy ache."

" 'Tis too great a risk," he had decided, after deliberation. "But cold water is a sovereign remedy for witchcraft and methinks I'll drop her in a tub of it."

He had picked her up and would have done it, too, if she had not decided then and there to come out of the spell without any further magic rites.

Decidedly Roger, as a playfellow, would be an exceedingly difficult person to be without. Especially after you had once become accustomed to him.

He was not much like his father. Faith felt as if she were appearing before the Supreme Court whenever she entered Mr. John Brennon's presence. Mr. Brennon, senior, always reminded Faith of a Pilgrim landing on a Plymouth

Rock—and pulverizing it. He was the embodiment of stern and dignified virtue. In the community in which he lived he was the head and personification of militant reform. All of the worthier campaigns for civic decency were sponsored and even frequently captained by him. All in all, as Faith had occasionally reflected, he was a wonderful influence in the city but undoubtedly a hard man for his family to live up to. He would pray with you, but even in his prayers there was concealed a punitive lash. The word "compromise" had never been written into his vocabulary.

She called at the house that morning and Roger's mother took her into her husband's private study. Mrs. Brennon used a crutch handily in getting around the house. Out-of-doors she ordinarily was wheeled in a chair.

Mr. Brennon had retired from the active presidency of his bank and now conducted most of his business from his home.

But he was sitting back of a big desk much as if he were in an office. Bankers and business men in general feel more secure behind an oak or mahogany barricade. Take away all the flat-top desks in the world and the casualties among capitalists would be appalling.

To lay down the law, you've got to get behind something. Even ministers, you may remember, are more authoritative in a railed pulpit.

John Brennon dominated his study just as he dominated his family and his world. He was the only upright thing in a landscape that he had personally flailed flat. This was illustrated by the fact that although his wife was in the room she said nothing, but sat, a little twinkling figure on a straight chair near the wall, much as if she were an office boy awaiting orders.

There was a lot of formality about this meeting between Faith and her father-in-law. She felt a little as if the proceedings ought to be opened with prayer. Mr. Brennon was dressed as meticulously as a hanging judge and his pouchy jowls were shaved a faint pink. Under his eyes were undisguisable circles.

"Faith," he began, "you have, for five years, been burdened by cares which, before you assumed them, made an old man of me."

"If you mean Roger," interrupted Faith, "you needn't apologize. He's a very amusing husband."

"I rather imagined that marriage would sober him down," Mr. Brennon continued imperturbably, "but I regret to say that I find it has not. His conduct with this Winterbottom woman is disgraceful, disgusting and inexcusable."

"The Winterbottom woman?"

229 Faith repeated questioningly. "I
230 don't remember—yes, I do, too.
231 Peggy Winterbottom was her
232 name and someone brought her
233 to a country club dance last
234 fall. But we haven't seen her
235 since."

236 "*You* haven't," corrected her
237 father-in-law, "but Roger has."

238 Faith mulled that over in her
239 mind. "Perhaps he has had
240 some business dealings with her.
241 I seem to remember that they
242 said she did something for a
243 living."

244 "Not something — somebody.
245 No. Roger has not been seeing
246 her on any business but her own.
247 Unfortunately she has a hus-
248 band, a traveling salesman, who
249 returned unexpectedly and dis-
250 covered them in—in conference,
251 so to speak."

252 Mr. Brennon paused as if to
253 give her a chance to recover
254 from this shock before feeding
255 her any more indigestible infor-
256 mation.

257 Faith wished that she might
258 be alone for a few moments so
259 that she could be privately
260 hysterical. It was more of a
261 shock to her than she could
262 publicly confess—it probably is
263 to every woman when she first
264 finds that her husband is almost
265 exactly like other men whom she
266 has heard about.

267 But she steadied her voice and
268 assumed a certain composure.
269 "I don't think there is anything
270 I can do about it."

271 "No," Mr. Brennon conceded.
272 "This particular case has been
273 taken care of by me. There is
274 no danger. I have bought off all
275 the parties concerned, even the
276 husband, who seemed to think
277 ten thousand dollars was ample
278 recompense for the loss of a
279 wife.

280 "But your part is the future.
281 You've got to prevent this from
282 happening again. If I did not
283 think that you could do it I
284 never should have mentioned
285 the matter to you at all. You
286 would probably be happier not
287 to know."

288 Faith happened to look up at
289 the elder Mrs. Brennon just at
290 that moment and caught a curi-
291 ous, unfathomable look in her
292 eye, the expression of a woman
293 who has been startled momen-
294 tarily out of a lifetime pose. It
295 interested Faith so much that
296 she almost forgot to pay atten-
297 tion to Mr. Brennon's next
298 words.

299 Mechanically she had said,
300 "How could I do anything that
301 would prevent Roger from doing
302 unwise things?"

303 "Put the fear of God into
304 him," her father-in-law thun-
305 dered. "Make him realize what
306 sort of fool he has been and con-
307 stantly remind him of the wrong
308 he has done to you. It is only
309 because men forget the punish-
310 ment that they transgress."

311 "I'm afraid," Faith began,
312 "that I don't know how to——"

313 "Fortunately I do," the stern
314 old man interrupted. "And I
315 have all the weapons you need.
316 They cost me enough so that
317 they ought to be put to some
318 good use." He produced a pack-
319 et of perhaps half a dozen letters
320 held together with a wide rubber
321 band. "These are in the hand-
322 writing of your husband and are
323 worth about two thousand dol-
324 lars apiece."

325 Faith seemed to have no re-
326 action to express, not even grati-
327 tude for the supervision of her
328 affairs under most trying cir-
329 cumstances.

330 "Are you suggesting that I use
331 them as evidence in a divorce
332 suit?" she finally managed to
333 ask.

334 "N-n-no," Mr. Brennon re-
335 plied with final decisiveness,
336 "there will be no divorce scandal
337 in my family. I would never
338 have brought up this subject
339 unless I had thought you were
340 too proud and sensible to con-
341 sider such a thing. All you have
342 to do is to keep him in order.
343 I suggest that you memorize a
344 few phrases from this mess of
345 expensive rubbish so that you
346 can quote an occasional passage
347 to him whenever you suspect
348 that he has strayed even men-
349 tally from the narrow highway
350 of integrity which, heaven
351 knows, I have always tried to
352 train his footsteps to tread."

353 That was quite rhetorical and
354 Faith had a grotesquely incon-
355 gruous thought that he had for-
356 gotten that there was only one
357 of her and was visualizing an
358 audience.

359 The interview seemed to be
360 ended.

361 He gave her the letters and
362 escorted her and his wife to the
363 door. "A delegation from the
364 Women's Civic Improvement
365 Society is waiting to see me. If
366 you want any further advice or
367 instructions in this or any cor-
368 relative matter, I'll be ready to
369 help you."

370 As the two women stood in the
371 doorway Mr. Brennon leaned
372 down unexpectedly and kissed
373 his wife with sudden and genuine
374 tenderness.

375 "I'll be through here in plenty
376 of time for a gallop in the park
377 before luncheon."

378 Mrs. Brennon led the way
379 from the study, which was on the
380 main floor, toward the stairway.
381 Faith was headed for the door,
382 but the older woman indicated
383 silently that she was to come up.

384 Imitating her silence but won-
385 dering nevertheless, Faith fol-
386 lowed her up the staircase. Mrs.
387 Brennon's private sitting-room
388 was so different from the study
389 of the *paterfamilias* that it
390 scarcely seemed possible that
391 they could be under the same
392 roof. There was nothing austere
393 about the wife's apartment,
394 nothing even very modern or in
395 any particular scheme of deco-
396 ration. The only quality in

283

397 common that every article in
398 room had was that of comfort
399 and womanly gentleness.

400 The lady of the house disposed
401 of her crutch and seated herself
402 in what was apparently her ac-
403 customed chair. She indicated
404 another near by for Faith. "Did
405 you notice," she queried mus-
406 ingly, "what John said just as
407 we left?"

408 "About a gallop in the park
409 before luncheon?"

410 "Yes. That's his way of tell-
411 ing me that he loves me just as
412 much as he did when I was
413 young and, I'm afraid, lovely in
414 his eyes and when I really could
415 ride a horse instead of a rubber
416 tired perambulator. I just want-
417 ed you to remember what he
418 said because it has quite a lot to
419 do with what I may say to you."

420 "May?" Faith repeated.
421 "Meaning that there is some
422 condition attached?"

423 "Not exactly. But sometimes
424 it is difficult for a wife and the
425 mother of the man she marries
426 to understand each other very
427 perfectly. In the first place, do
428 you feel that you want a divorce
429 from Roger?"

430 "On account of these letters?"

431 "On any account."

432 "I might use them the way
433 Mr. Brennon suggested."

434 "Could you?"

435 "I don't know. Why not?"

436 The older woman, who was
437 also the smaller, spread her
438 hands out in a curious gesture

across her skirt. Mothers have 439
done it from time immemorial 440
as an invitation to a child to sit 441
on their laps. 442

Faith had a flash vision of her 443
husband, as a little boy, hugged 444
tight to that forgiving bosom. 445

"You might much better get a 446
divorce," she said gently. 447
"Much better than to hold those 448
letters over Roger's head as a 449
threat." 450

"But I really love him, I 451
think, or anyway I did up to a 452
few minutes ago, and if I give 453
him another trial I might win 454
him back," Faith told her. 455

"Not the way Mr. Brennon 456
suggested. You might keep 457
Roger, but you would lose him. 458
What every woman knows is 459
that her husband is really just a 460
little boy. But what she has to 461
learn is to let him think he is a 462
great big noble man. The min- 463
ute a woman lets a man know 464
she is holding him under her 465
thumb—and he stays there—she 466
hasn't a man at all. 467

"In the hope that you really 468
will understand, I'm going to tell 469
you something that I have never, 470
heretofore, breathed to a soul, 471
especially not to my husband. 472
Will you take my keys"—she 473
extended them—"and unlock the 474
right-hand drawer of my desk?" 475

Faith did as she was told and 476
awaited further instructions. 477

"There are several packages 478
of letters there, most of them 479
tied with bits of old ribbon— 480

those are from my husband both before and after marriage. But there is another with a rubber around it, much like the packet you hold in your hand. That is the one I want. Do you find it?"

"Yes." Faith handed it to her.

"Mr. Brennon, as you know, is a great influence for good in this city. His example is an inspiring one, even to himself.

"That last phrase may sound incomprehensible so I will try to explain. Long ago I discovered that he was a human being and not a sort of deputy of God. By that I don't mean that he is a hypocrite. Most of his instincts are right and he really lives up to the standard he sets—most of the time. Any deviations from that standard are more surprising to himself than to anyone else and he has been his own severest judge and jailer.

"But there have been many temptations. He is a strong man, a very masculine one, and his self-imposed tasks of civic reform have brought him into contact with women. Sometimes some of them confused the cause for which they were working with the man who was at the head of it, and have brought their tribute to the priest instead of laying it on the altar which he serves.

"Devotion from a woman is something which a man finds it difficult to trip over without noticing the way she does her hair and takes care of her complexion. After a man notices a woman, nature has a high-handed way of ignoring the laws with which men have fenced off the jungle.

"The letters in this package are probably quite similar to the ones which you have in yours. The only difference is that these are twenty-five years old. Mr. Brennon has never seen them, at least not since they have been in my possession.

"We can take those letters in to him and by merely laying them on his desk we can humiliate him so that he will crawl to me and to you. What shall we do? We women talk much of emancipation from the control of men. Here are we, two of us, who have the power and the opportunity to wield a lash that will make our husbands forever subject to our slightest wish.

"If we use our power we will have no more need ever to ask for anything or to exchange our love for livelihood. All we have to give up is the curious whimsical devotion which men, as part of their pose, like to bestow on those who they think are standing on the stair just one step lower than themselves.

"I have faced the problem alone for a good many years, as you can see, and I have been fearfully weak about making a decision. As it is, we are living in a little play with make-up covering our defects even from each other, speaking lines, even, that have been prepared in advance, and with scenery that is beautiful only on the painted side.

"What shall I do, what shall we do, you and I—tear off the masks, turn the scenery around to show that it is only canvas and never listen again to lying poetry, or shall we go on with the conscious dream with this little ache in our hearts to tell us that it isn't all quite true? I don't know. What do you say?"

Mrs. Brennon had not been at all emotional in stating her case. On the contrary, she had been very matter-of-fact, with her wrinkled old hands lying lightly clasped in her lap.

In view of those wrinkled, nearly useless hands Faith's question seemed almost absurd. "You do love him?"

"Yes. Quite as much as I love Roger and in much the same way. Women always are older. Nature puts age into our hearts at birth just as she keeps spring always burning in the breasts of men. I don't know why. Marrying a man is much the same as giving birth to him and quite as painful. And they forget. My dear, that is the worst, they forget. And women must never notice—not if they want them to come back."

Faith left the house still carrying the package of Roger's letters. They were in her hands, unread, when she got home. There, at last, she laid them on her tiny desk.

Before dinner she telephoned to her mother-in-law. "I have burned them," she said briefly. "And I'm going to try to be one-half as lovely as you are."

Roger was a little late for dinner. During the interval of waiting Faith had a few bad moments of indecision. Part of it was wondering if perhaps, after all, it might not be better to bind him to her more closely by fear; the other was the pure stage-fright of an actor about to play a part for the first time.

Fortunately Roger had something else to occupy his mind so he did not notice her nervousness.

"Dad has been down to the office all the afternoon," he explained. "He even drove me home. Acted kind of sorry for me and apologetic as if he had been putting a little cyanide in my tonsil alcohol. The last thing he did was to give me a fifty percent increase in pay and drive me around to a florist's and pick out these orchids for you. Something has made him darn sentimental. Got any idea what it is?"

Faith shook her head.

"And you still love your old man," he questioned, kneeling at

649 her feet, "even if he has got
650 whiskers?"
651 "Yes," Faith declared, holding
652 his head tight against her body.
653 In her eyes, which he did not
654 see, was misty light, the light
655 that babes wake up to find in
656 those of the mother who bends
657 over them. "I do, I do," she
658 declared, repeating it as if to
659 reenforce her own faith.

660 He picked her up bodily—it
661 was convenient to grab her by
662 the knees the way she stood—
663 and swung her over his shoulder.
664 "All right, then, I'll ride you
665 up-stairs and you can sit on the
666 dresser and catch the bristles as
667 they fall to stuff a sofa-pillow
668 with. I bought a new can-
669 opener today that's just the
670 thing to shave with."

671 Faith finally began to laugh.
672 Maybe it was the way she had
673 been jounced up and down on
674 his shoulder. Maybe it was
675 sheer relief at realizing that she
676 was going to go on listening
677 to his nonsense until her hands,
678 too, were wrinkled and useless
679 but not very sad. Perhaps——

680 Half across the city his father
681 came into his wife's room and
682 bent over for a kiss. His eyes
683 were haggard, too, and the circles
684 under them were darker. He
685 clung for a moment to the
686 wrinkled hand that lay in her lap.
688 "I'm worried, Dear, and
689 afraid," he said. All the high
690 authority, the dominance was
691 gone from his voice. "I'm won-

dering if we did the right thing 692
for our boy." 693

She considered a moment. 694
Then she gently disengaged her 695
fingers from his clasp and 696
touched his head soothingly. 697
"Yes, Dear, I'm quite sure that 698
we have done the right thing for 699
our boy." 700

Before they went down to din- 701
ner he noticed the packet of an- 702
cient envelopes fastened with a 703
spiritless rubber band. 704

"What's this," he asked, with 705
a return to his more familiar, con- 706
fident mood, "a collection of love 707
letters to the queen by the court 708
jester while the king was in the 709
counting-house?" 710

"No," she answered. "Per- 711
haps you had better look at 712
them." 713

He started to remove the 714
elastic. It came apart in his 715
hands and the envelopes fell, 716
disordered, on the table. He 717
picked up one and opened it. 718
He looked at the folded sheets 719
within, then picked up another 720
and another and scanned them 721
rapidly. 722

"But these are only blank 723
sheets of your new stationery 724
folded up and put in a lot of old 725
envelopes. What on earth did 726
you do that for?" 727

His wife smiled; finally she 728
laughed as she smoothed her 729
skirt as mothers do. 730

"That, John dear," she said, 731
"is something I am never going 732
to tell you." 733

THE ANALYSIS

The production of a story of Decision calls for all the knowledge of craftsmanship which a writer possesses. It calls especially for the ability to write Scenes. It is essentially a problem of enlarging simple outlines into the five to seven thousand word short-story. Writers who have difficulty with the Beginnings of their stories had better stick to some type other than the Decision, that is to an Accomplishment story, because the writing of a decision type story calls for expert knowledge in presenting Beginnings interestingly. You will remember that I mentioned earlier in this book that there were two kinds of curiosity to which the writer might appeal. The one is general curiosity, the other narrative curiosity. Since the use of narrative curiosity is ordinarily denied to the writer who presents the story of Decision chronologically, he must therefore, be able to make the appeal to the other kind of curiosity. In addition to this he must be able to appeal to the dramatic instinct in people which is aroused by the appearance of probable disaster, or conflict.

Mr. Adams's story *Women Are Wiser* falls very readily into its major divisions of Beginning, and Ending. It is one of the Decision type stories which does not bore the reader with a Body scene made up of psychological analysis of the actor's uncertainty. The Beginning occupies lines 1 to 612, the Ending occupies lines 613 to 733, the Decisive Act occupying lines 613 to 617, the Sequel occupying lines 618 to 733. A glance at the chart which precedes the analysis of the story will show that the story is divided into the very same sort of blocks as is the story of accomplishment, these blocks being presentation units. The first block, lines 1 to 87 is concerned with setting forth the condition which confronts the main actor. It contains the probability of disaster, and expecially in that paragraph which tells of the attractions of Roger, and the difficulty of blaming him, it sets before the reader the difficulty lying before Faith in making a choice. It is evident that the choice is not easy because she is very much in love with her husband; at the same time he appears to be a man who ought "to spend all his leisure moments in the electric chair." In the first paragraph of the story the reader's curiosity is aroused. He does not know what the whole thing is about, yet he is not bored, because the introduction is not too long. It sets forth the main condition and it presents the main actor. It shows also the urgency and the immediacy of the need for action. Then there is a flash-back interchange between

Faith and Roger, occupying lines 88 to 136. This is not a typical flash-back Beginning because it does not present the main problem of the story and then flash-back in order to give the information necessary to the reader's understanding of the problem, picking up the chronological order again at the moment when the choice or decision must be made. Instead it goes back and gives a certain amount of information, which is that Faith and Roger are on excellent terms and that he is very necessary to her. This is a flash-back interchange in which the promise of disaster is a turning point at the close of the interchange, but it does not then resume the story at the point where the decision must be made. Before that point is reached, there are two other interchanges. It would have been a typical flash-back had the meetings been arranged in this order: meeting lines 1 to 87, meeting lines 137 to 377, meeting lines 378 to 612, then a flash-back to interchange lines 88 to 136 which would bring the reader back to the main narrative problem. This interchange lines 88 to 136, is now an interchange to avoid the use of summary, a device of craftsmanship of which Mr. Adams is a master.

For the purposes of this book, therefore I shall regard this story as a story of decision presented *chronologically*. At the close of the first meeting which shows that Faith is aware of a certain condition, we do not know that she has to make a choice between courses of conduct. We do not realize that she is uncertain in her mind as to what to do. No uncertainty is shown. When we have read the flash-back interchange we realize the disaster that will occur should she decide to do anything that will smash up the marriage. At the close of the interchange lines 137 to 377, between Faith and Mr. Brennon, we see, however, a very definite choice apparent. The course of conduct is clearly outlined for her by Mr. Brennon. It is that she shall humiliate her husband sufficiently to assure his faithfulness thereafter. At the close of the interchange between Faith and Mrs. Brennon, from 378 to 612, we see that a second choice is possible, and now we are aware that the heroine is torn between two courses of conduct, that she has to make a definite choice.

Because Mr. Adams is a competent and experienced writer he does not bore us with an interchange showing this uncertainty or indecision. Instead he swiftly carries us through to the Decisive Act, which is now lines 613 to 617, when Faith is shown telephoning Mrs. Brennon.

The lesson to be learned from the analysis of this story is that the story of Decision is dependent almost entirely upon the ability of the writer to write interchanges, which are preferably complete scenes. There is a certain amount of leeway available in the opening of a story which may be used by the author and presented in a meeting to indicate to the reader all the information in regard to the character and much of the problem. But this cannot be prolonged. It must be swiftly made a transition to an interchange. It is essential also for a writer who contemplates writing a story of decision to realize that the problem must be one which is of interest to a large number of people. It is essentially a problem of conduct. It must be a clearly defined clash between the affection and a standard of conduct or convention. In this case it is exactly that. Faith is extremely fond of her husband, yet the conventions demand that she shall not permit him to be lax in his duties to her. The decision she makes, and the reason for making that decision are made clear by the author.

This is an extremely interesting example of the Decision story in which the Beginning takes the place of both the Beginning and Body of the ordinary story of accomplishment. Had this been a story of Accomplishment, the first meeting would have set forth the main condition. That meeting and its flash-back would have made up the Beginning, which would be composed of the main problem with explanatory matter necessary to its understanding.

Then the Body of the story would have been made up of the two interchanges between Faith and Mr. Brennon and Faith and Mrs. Brennon. At the conclusion of one there would have been a crisis of hindrance. In this case it is a crisis of choice. At the conclusion of the interchange between Faith and Mrs. Brennan there would have been another crisis of hindrance, at which point disaster would have threatened. In this case there is a crisis of choice, because another choice is apparent; and as in the story of Accomplishment, the close of the Body scenes show a moment when disaster threatens, here again there is such a moment.

The story having no Body achieves its length in the Beginning. It is made up of 733 lines. Of this number the greater proportion, lines 1 to 612, occupy the Beginning. Now I shall ask you to turn to the next story, *Jetsam*, by John Russell.

ARCHITECTURAL CHART

OF

JETSAM

	Meeting. Junius Peabody and condition. Finds himself broke at Fufuti.	1– 123	General curiosity aroused. Unusual and striking moment catches reader's attention.
	Flash-back Interchange. Junius and Bendemeer.	123– 139	Hopelessness of condition is shown.
Explanatory matter presented to the reader in order that he may understand the line-up of forces which will determine the final choice.	Interchange. Junius and the Sydney Duck. (His response is to wish to begin again.)	140– 428	Emphasis upon depth of degradation.
	Interchange. Junius and the Sydney Duck Fight over lump Junius has found.	429– 543	New beginning possible. Disaster threatens.
	Interchange with Bendemeer. Is repudiated.	544– 792	Disaster seems sure.
	Interchange. Sydney Duck and Willems, followed by Junius's attack.	793–1037	Now new beginning seems possible.
	Interchange. Junius and Bendemeer. Bendemeer sets forth two definitely exclusive choices.	1038–1256	Narrative Question: "How will Junius choose?"

BEGINNING

ENDING

Conclusive Act.

Junius decides upon Nukava.	1257–1263	Answer to Narrative Question is: "He chooses Nukava."

Sequel.

Meeting. Bendemeer and condition.	1264–1296	Ironic significance clear.

JETSAM

BY JOHN RUSSELL

I HAVE chosen this story because I felt that to leave Mr. Russell out of any collection of stories would be to ignore one of the most competent craftsmen in America today.   But I had another reason for including this story—a purely technical interest—which caused me to seize upon the splendid opportunity this story presented of showing how two writers may take the same materials, and using the same Ending, may write different types of stories, and different types of Beginning.

Now turn to the story and I will point out to you just what I have in mind.

JETSAM

BY JOHN RUSSELL

I HAVE chosen this story because I felt that to leave Mr. Russell out of any collection of stories would be to ignore one of the most consistent craftsmen in America today. But I had another reason for installing this story—a purely technical interest—which caused me to seize upon the splendid opportunity this story presented of showing how two writers may take the same materials, and using the same plots, may write different types of stories, and different types of literature.

Now turn to the story and I will point out to you just what I have in mind.

CASE No. 12

JETSAM

BY JOHN RUSSELL

1 It is likely that at some time
2 in his extreme youth Junius
3 Peabody was introduced to those
4 single-minded creatures, the ant
5 and the bee. Doubtless he was
6 instructed in the highly moral les-
7 sons they are supposed to illus-
8 trate to the inquiring mind of
9 childhood. But it is certain he
10 never profited by the acquain-
11 tance—indeed, the contempla-
12 tion of such tenacious industry
13 must have afflicted his infant
14 consciousness with utter repug-
15 nance. By the time he was
16 twenty-seven the only living
17 thing that could be said to have
18 served him as a model was the
19 jellyfish.

20 Now, the jellyfish pursues a
21 most amiable theory of life,
22 being harmless, humorous, and
23 decorative. It derives much en-
24 joyment from drifting along
25 through the glitter and froth, as
26 chance may direct. It does no
27 work to speak of. It never needs
28 to get anywhere. And it never,
29 never has to go thirsty. But
30 some day it may get itself

31 stranded, and then the poor
32 jellyfish becomes an object quite
33 worthless and fit only to be
34 shoveled out of sight as soon as
35 possible—because it lacks the
36 use of its legs.

37 Thus it was with Junius Pea-
38 body, who awoke one morning of
39 his twenty-eighth year on the
40 roaring coral beach at Fufuti, be-
41 low Bendemeer's place, to find
42 that all the chances had run out
43 and that the glitter had faded
44 finally from a prospect as drab
45 as the dawn spread over a but-
46 ternut sea before him. . . .

47 Mr. Peabody sat up and
48 looked about from under a cor-
49 rugated brow, and yawned and
50 shivered. His nerves had been
51 reduced to shreds, and even the
52 fiercest heat of tropic suns
53 seemed never to warm him, a
54 symptom familiar enough to
55 brandy drunkards. But he had
56 had such awakenings before,
57 many of them, and the chill that
58 struck through him on this par-
59 ticular morning was worse than
60 any hang-over. It was the soul

61 of Junius Peabody that felt cold
62 and sick, and when he fumbled
63 through his pockets—the subtle
64 relation between the pockets
65 and the soul is a point sadly
66 neglected by our best little
67 psychologists—he uncovered a
68 very definite reason. His last
69 penny was gone.

70 Under the shock of conviction
71 Mr. Peabody sought to cast up
72 the mental log, in the hope of
73 determining where he was and
74 how he came to be there.

75 The entries were badly blurred,
76 but he could trace himself down
77 through Port Said, Colombo,
78 Singapore—his recollections here
79 were limited to a woman's face
80 in a balcony and the cloying
81 aroma of anisette. He remem-
82 bered a stop at Sydney, where
83 he made the remarkable discov-
84 ery that the Circular Quay was
85 completely circular and could be
86 circumnavigated in a night.
87 After that he had a sketchy im-
88 pression of the Shanghai race
89 meeting and a mad sort of trip
90 in a private yacht full of Aus-
91 tralian sheep-something—kings,
92 perhaps; tremendous fellows,
93 anyway, of amazing capacity.
94 And then Manila, of course, the
95 place where he hired an ocean-
96 going tug to urge a broken date
97 on the coy ingénue of a traveling
98 Spanish opera company. And
99 then Macao, where he found and
100 lost her again, as coy as ever,
101 together with his wallet. And
102 after that the hectic session when

103 he and a Norwegian schooner
104 captain hit the bank at fan-tan
105 and swore eternal friendship
106 amid the champagne baskets on
107 the schooner's decks under a
108 complicated moon. It was this
109 same captain who had landed
110 him finally—the baskets having
111 been emptied—at the point of a
112 boot on the strand where now he
113 sat. So much was still quite
114 clear and recent, within range of
115 days.

116 Always through the maze of
117 these memoirs ran one consistent
118 and tragic motive—a dwindling
119 letter of credit, the fag end of his
120 considerable patrimony. It had
121 expired painlessly at last, the
122 night before if he could trust his
123 head, for there had been a noble
124 wake. He recalled the inscrut-
125 able face of the tall white man
126 behind the bar who had cashed
127 it for him after a rate of exchange
128 of his own grim devising. And
129 he recalled, too, a waif bit of
130 their conversation as he signed
131 the ultimate coupon.

132 "You can date it Fufuti,"
133 suggested Bendemeer, and
134 spelled the name for him.

135 "And where—where the devil
136 is Fufuti?" he asked.

137 "Three thousand miles from
138 the next pub," said Bendemeer,
139 with excessively dry significance.

140 The phrase came back to him
141 now. . . .

142 "In that case," decided Junius
143 Peabody, aloud, "—in that case
144 there's no use trying to borrow

145 car-fare, and it's too far to walk.
146 I'm stuck."

147 Some one sniffed beside him
148 and he turned to stare into a face
149 that might have been a distor-
150 tion of his own yellow, haggard
151 image.

152 "Hello," he said—and then,
153 by natural sequence: "Say, you
154 don't happen to have a flask
155 anywhere handy about you—
156 what?"

157 His neighbour scowled ag-
158 grievedly.

159 "Do I *look* like I 'ad a flask?"
160 The belligerent whine was
161 enough to renew the identity of
162 the mangy little larrikin whose
163 couch on the sand he had shared.
164 The Sydney Duck, they called
165 him: a descriptive title which
166 served as well as any. Junius
167 did not like him very well, but
168 he had lived in his company
169 nearly a week and he had long
170 forgotten to make effective dis-
171 tinctions. Brandy is a great
172 democrat.

173 "It's my notion I'm going to
174 have the fantods," explained
175 Junius. "I need a bracer."

176 "My word, I could do with a
177 nip meself just now," agreed
178 Sydney. " 'In't y' got no more
179 credit with Bendemeer?"

180 Peabody made an effort.

181 "Seems to me I was thrown
182 out of Bendemeer's last night.
183 Is that right?"

184 "You was, and so was me and
185 that big Dutchman, Willems—
186 all thrown out. But it was your

187 fault. You started playin' chuck
188 farthin' among his bottles with a
189 bunch of copper spikes. . . . I
190 never see a man 'old his liquor
191 worse."

192 "Well, I paid for it, didn't I?"
193 inquired Junius, without heat.
194 "And I believe you had your
195 share. But what I'm getting at
196 is—if he threw me out, the credit
197 must be gone."

198 This was simple logic and un-
199 answerable. "Maybe y' got
200 something else he'll tyke for th'
201 price," suggested Sydney.
202 "Damn 'im—'e's keen enough to
203 drive a tryde!"

204 Junius went through the form
205 of searching, but without any
206 great enthusiasm, nor was Syd-
207 ney himself notably expectant—
208 a fact that might have seemed to
209 argue a rather sinister familiarity
210 with the probable result.

211 "I did have some cuff links and
212 things," said Peabody vaguely.
213 "I wonder what's become of
214 them."

215 "I wonder," echoed Sydney.
216 As if some last possible claim
217 upon his regard had been dissi-
218 pated, he let his lips writhe in
219 mockery. "Ah, and that's a
220 pity too. You got to learn now
221 what it means bein' on the beach
222 and doin' *without* drinks—'cept
223 as you kin cadge them off'n 'alf-
224 caste Chinymen and such. You
225 won't like it, you won't."

226 "Do you?" asked Junius.

227 "Me? I'm used to it. But,
228 Lord, look at them 'ands! I'll

229 lay you never did a day's work
230 in your life."

231 "Did you?" inquired Junius
232 Peabody equably.

233 "Garn!" retorted Sydney with
234 a peculiarly unlovely sneer.
235 "W'y, you don't know yet what
236 you've come to, you don't.
237 'Jaimes, fetch me me mornin'
238 drawft!'—that's your style.
239 Only there 'in't no Jaimes no
240 more, and no drawfts to be 'ad.
241 Ho! . . . You're only a beach-
242 comber now, mytey. A lousy
243 beachcomber! And you needn't
244 expect me to do none of your
245 beggin' for you, for I won't—
246 no fear!"

247 Junius observed him with at-
248 tention, with rather more atten-
249 tion than he could remember
250 having bestowed upon any spe-
251 cific object for a long time. He
252 examined the features of the
253 Sydney Duck, the undue prom-
254 inence of nose and upper lip, the
255 singularly sharp ridge of the
256 whole front face—whittled, as it
257 might have been; the thin, pink
258 ears and the jutting teeth that
259 gave him something of the feeble
260 ferocity of a rat. And with new
261 perception he saw Sydney Duck,
262 not only as an unpleasant
263 individual but as a type, the
264 fitting comrade and associate for
265 such as he.

266 "It's a fact," said Junius Pea-
267 body; "I've fallen pretty
268 low. . . ."

269 He looked out again upon that
270 unprofitable dawning. To right
271 and left stretched the flat, dim
272 monotony of the beach, lined in
273 misty surf and hedged with slim
274 palms like a tufted palisade.
275 From behind drifted the smokes
276 from scores of homely hearths.
277 Down by Tenbow Head the first
278 pearling luggers were putting out
279 under silver clouds of sail. Sea
280 and land stirred once more with
281 the accustomed affairs of busy
282 men, but here between land and
283 sea was the fringe of things, the
284 deserted domain of wreckage and
285 cast-off remnants. Here lay a
286 broken spar half buried in the
287 sand, part of the complex fabric
288 that once enabled some fair ship
289 to skim the waves. And here
290 among the kelp and the bodies of
291 marine animals he saw the loos-
292 ened staves of a barrel limply
293 spread and upthrust like the fin-
294 gers of some dead giant, with an
295 empty bottle near by as if fallen
296 from that slack grip. And here,
297 lastly, he was aware of Junius
298 Peabody, also on the beach,
299 washed up at the far edge of the
300 world like any other useless bit
301 of jetsam: to stay and to rot.

302 "Pretty low," said Junius Pea-
303 body.

304 But Sydney took no offence,
305 and seemed, on the contrary, to
306 extract a certain degree of pleas-
307 ure from the other's recognition
308 of his lot.

309 "Oh, it 'in't so bad," he de-
310 clared, with a quite human im-
311 pulse to reverse the picture.
312 "There's easy pickin' if you

313 know 'ow. Nobody starves 'ere
314 anyw'y, that's one thing. No
315 nigger will let a man starve—
316 a soft lot of flats that w'y, the
317 niggers. Often you fall in with
318 a weddin' or a birthday or some-
319 thin'; they're always 'avin' a
320 feast, and *they* don't care who
321 comes—they 'in't proud. Then
322 you got nobody aharryin' of you
323 up and down and askin' you wot
324 for, that's a comfort—my word!
325 And once in a while there's sure
326 to be a new chum come along
327 with a bit of brass—some flat
328 who's willin' to stand the
329 drinks."

330 "Like me," suggested Junius.

331 "Oh, there's plenty like you,"
332 nodded the Sydney Duck. "It's
333 the pearlin' brings 'em, though
334 it 'in't so soft as maybe they
335 think, you see. When they're
336 stony they mostly tyke a job
337 till they find a chance to get
338 aw'y again—that's if they're able
339 to do anything at all."

340 For the first time in his life,
341 probably, Junius Peabody con-
342 sidered his accomplishments with
343 a view to estimating their value
344 in the open market.

345 "I once won the fancy diving
346 event at Travers Island," he
347 said. "And I used to swim the
348 four-forty in a trifle over six
349 minutes."

350 "That must 'a' been several
351 seasons back," grinned Syd-
352 ney.

353 "Not so many," said Junius
354 slowly. "I forgot to add that
355 I was also an excellent judge
356 of French brandy."

357 He got to his feet and began
358 to divest himself of the spotted
359 remains of an expensive white
360 silk suit.

361 "What's the gyme now?"

362 "Morning bath. Have you
363 had yours yet?"

364 The Sydney Duck laughed,
365 laughter that was strangely un-
366 mirthful and so convulsive that
367 Junius blinked at him, fearing a
368 fit of some kind.

369 "You're a rare 'un," gasped
370 the Sydney Duck. "I seen a
371 good few, I 'ave, but none as rare
372 as you. Mornin' bawth—and
373 'ave I 'ad mine yet! . . . On
374 the beach at Fufuti!" He wag-
375 gled his hands.

376 "Well, if it seems so queer as
377 all that why not blow yourself?"
378 offered Junius with perfect good
379 nature. "You can't tell, you
380 might like it. Come along."

381 "Garn!" snarled the other.

382 So Junius turned away and
383 walked down the strand alone.
384 Outward the ground swell broke
385 and came rushing in with long-
386 spaced undulations, and as he
387 stood at the verge, shrinking in
388 his nakedness, the east flamed
389 suddenly through its great red
390 archway and turned all the world
391 to tinted glory. Fair across to
392 him was flung a shining path.
393 It seemed as if he had only to
394 step out along that straight way
395 of escape, and for an instant he
396 had a yearning to try. Never

397 in his life had he followed a single
398 course to a definite end, and
399 what could be better now than
400 to choose one at last, to follow,
401 to go on following—and not to
402 return?

403 He looked down at his body
404 and saw as a revelation the piti-
405 ful wasting of his strength—how
406 scrawny he was of limb, how
407 bloated about the middle, and
408 his skin how soft and leprous
409 white. He made an ugly figure
410 under the clear light of the morn-
411 ing, like the decaying things
412 around him, where the carrion
413 flies were beginning to swarm in
414 the sun. And there came upon
415 him then a sudden physical
416 loathing of himself, a final sense
417 of disaster and defeat.

418 "If I could only begin
419 again—" thought Junius Pea-
420 body, and stopped and laughed
421 aloud at the wish, which is old
422 as folly and futile as sin. But
423 he had no relief from laughter
424 either, for it was the same he had
425 heard from the Sydney Duck, a
426 sort of hiccup. So he stopped
427 that too, and strode forthright
428 into the wash. . . .

429 Something flung against his
430 shin and tripped him. He
431 sprawled awkwardly from a sin-
432 gular impact, soft though quite
433 solid. He could see the object
434 floating on the next wave
435 and was curious enough to catch
436 it up. It was a rough lump of
437 some substance, a dirty grayish-
438 brown in colour, the size of a

439 boy's football. The touch of it
440 was rather greasy.

441 Junius stayed with the trove
442 in his hands and the tingling of
443 an odd excitement in his mind.
444 His first instinct rejected the
445 evidence. He had a natural sus-
446 picion that events do not hap-
447 pen so. But while he brought to
448 bear such knowledge as he
449 owned, facts read or heard, he
450 found himself still thrilled.

451 There was a sound from the
452 shore and the Sydney Duck hur-
453 ried up behind him to the edge
454 of the water, both hands clawed,
455 his little eyes distended.

456 "You've got it!" He took
457 two steps after a retreating
458 wave, but the next drove him
459 hopping. It was strange to see
460 the fellow drawn by a frantic
461 eagerness and chased again by
462 the merest flicker of foam, lifting
463 his feet as gingerly as a cat.

464 "What have I got?" asked
465 Junius, standing at mid-thigh
466 where the surf creamed in be-
467 tween them.

468 "It's the stuff! Chuck it over
469 —wha-i-i!" Sydney's voice rose
470 to a squeal as a frothing ripple
471 caught his toes.

472 Junius came wading shore-
473 ward, but he did not relinquish
474 the lump when the other felt
475 and paddled it feverishly, bab-
476 bling.

477 "Look at that—look at that!
478 All smooth an' soft—an' kind
479 of slimy, like. Oh, no, we 'in't
480 struck it fair rich this time,

481 for nothin'—oh, *now!* . . . My-
482 tey, I tell you—by Gaw', I tell
483 you it's the real stuff!"

484 "But oughtn't there be an
485 odour—a perfume?"

486 "Not yet—not while it's fresh.
487 That comes after. And any'ow,
488 what else could it be—'ey?"

489 Junius shook his head.

490 " 'Ere, I'll show you, you poor
491 flat!" The larrikin raged about
492 like a man in a strong temper.
493 "Where's a nail? Gimme a nail
494 or a piece of wire—'ell, I'll show
495 you!"

496 He snatched up a strip of
497 planking from the sand and
498 wrenched a rusty spike from it.
499 With swift jerky gestures he
500 gathered a few dry chips and
501 splinters, whipped a match, and
502 set them alight. In this brief
503 blaze he heated the spike and
504 then applied it to the lump. It
505 sank smoothly, leaving a little
506 melted ring around the hole.

507 "Ambergris!" he yelped.
508 "Worth near two pound an ounce,
509 right 'ere in Fufuti. . . . And
510 the 'arf of it's mine," he added,
511 with a startling shift to the most
512 brazen impudence.

513 Junius regarded him, incred-
514 ulous.

515 "What? That's wot! Wasn't
516 I here? 'In't I been pallin' along
517 of you? It's a fair divvy. W'y,
518 damn your soul," he screamed
519 in a sudden febrile blast of fury,
520 "you don't think you're goin' to
521 'og my 'arf an' all!"

522 "*Your* half!" repeated Junius.

523 "Huh—nothing small about you,
524 is there? Why, you weren't any-
525 where near when I found it.
526 Didn't you pass up the swim?"

527 Just here the Sydney Duck
528 made his mistake. Had he pro-
529 ceeded with any finesse, with any
530 understanding of his man, he
531 might have done about as he
532 pleased, and it is likely that
533 little of moment would have
534 transpired on Fufuti beach that
535 morning. But he acted by his
536 lights, which were narrow and
537 direct, and he hit Junius Pea-
538 body suddenly in the smiling
539 face of him and knocked him
540 reeling backward. The next in-
541 stant he was running for the
542 nearest palms with the prize
543 tucked under one arm.

544 Junius sat on the sand and
545 blinked, and at first he felt rather
546 hurt, for he was not used to
547 being treated so, at least not
548 while he was sober. And there-
549 after he grinned, for such was his
550 way of turning aside a casual un-
551 pleasantness, and the thing un-
552 deniably had its humorous
553 aspect. But finally came the
554 throb of a strange new emotion,
555 as if someone had planted a small,
556 hot coal in his breast.

557 It is a fact worthy of note that
558 never before had Junius Peabody
559 known the sting of a living anger.
560 But never before had Junius Pea-
561 body been reduced to a naked
562 Junius Peabody, dot and carry
563 nothing—penniless, desperate,
564 and now cheated of a last

565 hope. That made the dif-
566 ference.

567 "Hey!" he protested. "See
568 here, you know—Dammit!"

569 He struggled up and climbed
570 anyhow into trousers, coat, and
571 shoes, and set off at a shambling
572 trot, with no clear notion of
573 what he meant to do, but keep-
574 ing the larrikin in sight.

575 Sydney dodged in among the
576 trees, found them too scant for
577 cover, paused to fling a yellow
578 snarl over his shoulder, and
579 swung up the shore. He turned,
580 questing here and there, shout-
581 ing as he ran, and presently
582 raised an answering shout from a
583 hollow whence another figure
584 started up to join him, a bearded,
585 heavy-set rogue, whose abnor-
586 mally long arms dangled like an
587 ape's out of his sleeveless shirt.
588 Junius recognized Willems, the
589 third of their party the night
590 before, and he knew where the
591 interest of that sullen big Hol-
592 lander would lie. He had a
593 coalition of thievery against him
594 now. The two beachcombers
595 ran on together, footing briskly
596 past the long boat sheds and the
597 high white veranda of Bende-
598 meer's place. . . .

599 Under this iron thatch stood
600 the man Bendemeer himself, cool
601 and lathy in spotless ducks,
602 planted there, as was his morn-
603 ing custom, to oversee and com-
604 mand all his little capital. And
605 in truth it was a kingdom's
606 capital, the center of a trading

607 monopoly of the old type, and
608 chief seat of as strange and ab-
609 solute a tyrant as the world still
610 offers room for; rich, powerful,
611 independent, fearing nothing be-
612 tween heaven and hell, and at
613 once the best-loved and the best-
614 hated individual in his sphere
615 of influence.

616 Bendemeer, trader, philan-
617 thropist, and purveyor of rotgut,
618 was one of those unclassed
619 growths of the South Seas that
620 almost constitute a new racial
621 type. Nobody could have placed
622 his nationality or his caste or his
623 accent. His name was of a piece
624 with the grim self-sufficiency
625 that gave nothing and asked
626 nothing: an obvious jest, bor-
627 rowed from the Persian song of
628 an Irish poet, but the one touch
629 of fancy about him. Somewhere,
630 somehow, he had taken a cynic
631 twist or a rankling wound that
632 had turned his white man's blood
633 once for all. They tell stories of
634 such cases up and down the is-
635 lands, and mostly the stories
636 are very ugly and discreditable
637 indeed. But not so concerning
638 Bendemeer; against whom was
639 no scandal; only curses and bit-
640 terness. For his peculiarity took
641 the especially irritating form of
642 fair dealings with some thou-
643 sands of brown-skinned natives
644 and no dealings at all with any
645 man of his own color—except
646 to beat him at strict business and
647 then to sell him as much villain-
648 ous liquor as he could at the

highest possible price. As he leaned there indolently in his doorway, with arms folded and cheroot between his thin lips, he could measure his own land as far as he could see on either side, a small part of his holdings in plantations and trading stations throughout the archipelago. Offshore, behind the only good strip of barrier reef and near the only navigable channel on the south coast, lay anchored his *Likely Jane*, flagship of a smart little navy. His gang of boys was hustling cargo out of her in surfboats, and both boys and boats were the handiest and ablest that could be found anywhere for that ticklish work. He had only to turn his head to view the satisfactory bulk of his sheds and dependencies, solid, new-painted. The house at his back was trim, broad, and comfortable, and in the storeroom underneath lay thousands of dollars' worth of assorted trade goods, all of which would eventually become copra and great wealth.

This was the man, decidedly in possession of his own legs and able to stand and to navigate on the same, to whom Junius Peabody appealed in his wretched need. . . .

Junius stumbled up to the steps. The burst had marrow-drawn him, his lungs laboured pitifully as if he were breathing cotton wool. It was hot, for the sun had sprung wide like an opened furnace gate, but he had not started a pore.

"I've been robbed," he wheezed, and pointed a wavering hand. "Those chaps there—robbed——!"

Bendemeer glanced aside up the strand after the disappearing ruffians and then down at the complainant, but otherwise he did not move, only stayed considering from his lean, leathery mask, with still eyes, outward-looking.

"What do you care?" he said idly. "You'll be dead in a month anyhow."

Junius gaped toward him dizzily. The fellow was the local authority, and besides had taken his money. He could not believe that he had heard aright. "But say—they've stolen my property!"

Bendemeer shot a blue ring of smoke into the sunshine. "In that case you've lost it. They're heading for the Rocks, and once they've gone to earth there you never could find them—you'd be torn to pieces if you did."

He flicked the ash of his cheroot in a pause. "I suppose you mean I might help you," he continued. "I might, but I won't. I've seen a good many of your kind before, drift stuff that gets washed up on the beach. You're not worth it. And now, since you have no further business with me, I'd be obliged if you'd kindly get the hell out of my

733 front yard. You're interfering
734 with the view. . . ."

735 Junius Peabody found himself
736 groping away through the sun-
737 light on Fufuti beach once more.
738 A dead calm held the air. Under
739 the steady, low organ note of the
740 reef he could hear only the drag
741 of his own steps, the curious,
742 unforgetable "shr-ring" of boot
743 leather on coral.

744 It was borne upon him then
745 that he had just acquired a lib-
746 eral education, that he had
747 learned more essential facts with-
748 in the last hour than he had ever
749 gained before in his twenty-odd
750 years—a tabloid of life—and too
751 late to be of any use. Such ab-
752 stractions are sometimes valu-
753 able to a man, but they are not
754 the sort that brings a lump in his
755 throat and a winking in his eyes.
756 The thing, the sheerly heartfelt
757 thing that Junius Peabody said
758 to himself, sniffling, was this:
759 "And he didn't—didn't even
760 offer me a drink!"

761 There was nothing to draw
762 him any farther—no help, no
763 promise of success, not even a
764 single witness to shame with a
765 grin or to urge with an expectant
766 stare—nothing outside himself.
767 Fufuti beach lay stark and
768 aching white before him. The
769 two thieves had long since lost
770 themselves among the palms.
771 Down by the water's edge a
772 couple of Bendemeer's boat boys
773 were salvaging odds and ends
774 lost overboard in an upset in

775 yesterday's heavy surf. They
776 did not waste a thought or a look
777 on him. He was many degrees
778 less important than a lot of other
779 rubbish around there. He might
780 just as well, he might much bet-
781 ter, slump down in a sodden
782 heap amid the rest of the jetsam.
783 And yet he did not. . . . And
784 he did go on. For some obscure,
785 irrational human reason, he did
786 go on. Perhaps because of the
787 tiny coal in his breast, blown red
788 by Bendemeer's blasting con-
789 tempt. Perhaps because, after
790 all, no man ever quite achieves
791 a complete resemblance to a
792 jellyfish.

793 On the southern tip of Fufuti
794 stands Tenbow Head, the end of
795 a rough little jut of land known
796 locally as the Rocks. To speak
797 by the book, there is neither rock
798 nor head, but the abyss turned in
799 its sleep once, and shouldered
800 half a mile of Fufuti's shore line
801 to a height of thirty feet—
802 enough for a mountain in this
803 sea of humble atolls. Inciden-
804 tally it smashed the elevated
805 reefs like chalk in a mortar.
806 Tenbow is a wreck of shattered
807 coral terraces clad in the eager
808 growths which profit by its tri-
809 fling rise and which alone do
810 profit. For the rest it remains
811 the island jungle, a section apart
812 and untouched, almost impene-
813 trable.

814 Junius Peabody began his ex-
815 ploration of this cheerful region
816 by falling on his face in a gully

817 and bruising his nose very griev-
818 ously. He found no trail to guide
819 him up the slope. It was pitted
820 like slag, deceitful as old honey-
821 comb. The footing crumbled;
822 tempting beds of moss and fern
823 slipped away at his clutch;
824 twisting lianas caught his ankles
825 and sent him asprawl. The very
826 ground seemed armed against
827 him with a malignant life of its
828 own. He had to creep among
829 jagged teeth that sliced his
830 flimsy garments and his putty-
831 soft flesh. And when a loosened
832 mass slid gently over at a touch
833 and crushed an arm he scarcely
834 wondered whether any personal
835 power had directed. It was all
836 the same.

837 For a long time he lay looking
838 at his pulped fingers and the
839 driven drops of blood from the
840 quick of his nails, sensing the
841 exquisite pain almost as a lux-
842 ury, hugging it to him. But at
843 length he stirred and began to
844 wriggle forward again.

845 "If I'm going to die anyway,"
846 said Junius Peabody, "I'm going
847 to die doing this." Which was
848 an extraordinary remark on all
849 accounts. . . .

850 And so by dint of following
851 something, and still following
852 with unlimited purpose over a
853 limited terrain, he ran it down
854 in the end and came to the
855 hiding place he sought.

856 A rooted instinct of the poten-
857 tially criminal, which prompts
858 them to be ready to flee though

859 no man pursueth, had moved the
860 beachcombers of Fufuti long
861 since to prepare their snug re-
862 treat in the heart of the Rocks.
863 On the inward shore of the
864 promontory they had found a
865 level bit of shelf screened by lush
866 vegetation, with the green-
867 stained cliff for wall and the
868 sapphire waters of the lagoon be-
869 low for forecourt. Hither they
870 repaired in the intervals of lesser
871 lawbreaking and free entertain-
872 ment, always secure of hearth
873 and shelter where the broad pan-
874 danus spreads its shingles. And
875 hither, straight as merry men to
876 their shaw, they had brought the
877 great treasure of the morning.

878 A truly homelike scene was
879 that on which Junius Peabody
880 peered from ambush above. . . .

881 From the convenient branch
882 of a tree the Sydney Duck had
883 suspended by its middle a single
884 stout stick. At one end of the
885 stick he had slung the stolen
886 lump in a fiber net. At the other
887 he had attached a battered tin
888 can of the kind that the benefi-
889 cent enterprise of an American
890 oil company had spread to most
891 of the dark parts of the earth.
892 On this balance of an ancient and
893 primitive design he was engaged
894 in weighing his ill-gotten gains,
895 squatting to the task.

896 "A gallon of water weighs a
897 good eight pound," he declared.
898 "I figger five quarts an' a 'arf.
899 And five is ten and the 'arf is
900 one——"

Willems stood beside him in an attitude of stolid skepticism. There was no mistaking the breed of this big derelict. He had managed to assert it on a Pacific isle by fashioning himself somehow a pipe with a clay bowl and a long stem of the true drooping line. He looked quite domestic and almost paternal as he shuffled his broad feet and towered over the little larrikin. But the fists he carried in the pockets of his dungarees bulged like coconuts, and his hairy arms were looped brown cables. A tough man for an argument was Mynheer Willems.

"Yaw," he was saying. "But how you know you got five quarts and a half?"

"W'y, any fool could guess near enough!" cried Sydney, with the superfluous violence that was his caste mark. "And you—y' big Dutchman—'in't you swilled enough beer in your time to judge? Besides, the bally can 'olds three gallon—bound to. There's one sure measure. . . . I say we got, anyw'y, eleven pounds of this stuff, and I 'appen to know that Bendemeer's fair crazy after it. He'll pay big. We ought to 'ave two thousands dollars Chile to split. . . . Two thousands silver dibs!"

It was a cue to friendly feeling, that luscious phrase. The two men beamed upon it as Sydney dumped the balance and swung the fiber net. But it was also a cue of another kind, for it brought Junius Peabody on stage. He arrived by the simple process of sliding on a bundle over the brow of the cliff.

"That's mine," he announced.

The beachcombers stayed stricken, which was pardonable. Surely there never showed a less heroic figure or a stranger defiance than that of Mr. Peabody, torn, bedraggled, and besmeared. There was nothing muscular or threatening about him. He took no pose. He offered no weapon. He came on at them limping, with quivering lip and empty hands, even with open hands. And yet the incredible fact remained that he did come on at them and continued to come.

"It's mine," repeated Junius. "All mine, and I'm going to have it—all!"

Amazement held them motionless for as long as it took him to cross the ledge—pleased amazement, as they knew him better. There are few things more congenial to certain gentlemen than a chance to maul an easy victim. And here was the easiest victim that either of these gentlemen had seen in many a day. He was no match for them, could be no possible match. Since he would have it so, they accepted joyously, closed in upon him from either side and started to drag him down as a preliminary to trampling the

lights out of him. . . .
But they counted without the
absolute simplicity of a man who
has found an objective for the
first time in his life and has set
himself to reach it, regardless.
Mr. Peabody did not pause to
fight or to wrestle. He let them
get a good grip on him and then
took the unexpected way by
keeping right on—and, pinion-
ing their arms, merely walking
them over the edge into space.
For an instant the three
seemed to hang suspended, in-
terlocked amid smashing vines
and taut creepers, and then top-
pled toward the lagoon.
Even before they struck, Sydney's despairing yell rang out.
Their plunge drowned it and
gave way to the cries of startled
sea birds, knifing the air in flung
white crescents and circling
about the troubled spot that
boiled like blue champagne. But
when he came up again the unfortunate larrikin loosed shriek after
bubbling shriek and floundered
madly for shore, all else forgotten
in his dominant terror.
Willems was made of sterner
metal. He grappled Peabody as
they rose and sought to use his
long arms, reaching for the
throat. He learned better presently, however, and he learned
too, how much chance he had
against a man who had once
won a fancy diving title at Travers Island. Junius took him
down by the feet and held him

down until there was no spring
and no temper left to him, only
a large and limp and very badly
frightened Hollander who wanted to get out of the wet. He was
quite willing to paddle after the
Sydney Duck. Meanwhile Junius gathered up an object in a
fiber net that was floating near
by and swam on to follow his
purpose. . . .

The man Bendemeer was
standing behind his little
zinc bar when a shadow
sifted in through the doorway,
and, looking up, he took a backward step that nearly cost him
his stock of glassware. The man
Bendemeer was not used to stepping back from anything, but the
red and dripping ruin that confronted him was beyond usage
of any kind. Junius Peabody
looked as if he had been run
through a mangle. His dress
was fragmentary. Most of the
skin had been flayed from the
more prominent curves of his
anatomy. His left arm hung
useless. He crawled in and
propped himself to keep from
falling, and called for brandy in
a voice scarcely recognizable.
"Peabody—is it?" demanded
Bendemeer, incredulous.
"Will you keep a customer
waiting?" rasped Junius. "You
needn't stare." He laughed
weakly. "You can't order me
off now, Bendemeer. I'm a pay-
ing customer again."
"As how?"

1070 Junius lifted a fist and dropped
1071 the sopping net on the bar.
1072 "Ambergris—eleven pounds of
1073 of it. My property."

1074 Bendemeer inspected the
1075 brownish lump, and as he under-
1076 stood, his thin lips pleated and
1077 his glance quickened. "Oh, ho!"
1078 he said. "Was it *this* they
1079 robbed you of?"

1080 Peabody nodded.

1081 "You got it back from them—
1082 yourself?"

1083 "There's the stuff."

1084 "So I see. But I'm asking—
1085 did you take it away from those
1086 two cutthroats alone, without
1087 any help?"

1088 "I did. And now I've come to
1089 talk business. It's a good prop-
1090 osition, Bendemeer."

1091 The tall, grim white man stud-
1092 ied him with a narrow regard
1093 glinting like a probe and equally
1094 cool, detached, and impersonal.
1095 He had the air of a surgeon who
1096 approaches a clinical experiment.
1097 "I'm inclined to think it may
1098 be," he decided. "Yes—a sport-
1099 ing risk; though I'm certain
1100 enough of the result, Peabody,
1101 mind that. I believe I might
1102 make a bit of a gamble with my-
1103 self, just to see that I'm right.
1104 Come now—what do you want?"

1105 "A thousand silver," said
1106 Junius.

1107 "I haven't so much about me.
1108 Suppose we say a standing credit
1109 for a thousand drinks instead."

1110 Junius stiffened against the
1111 bar.

"It amounts to the same thing, 111
doesn't it?" continued Bende- 111
meer: "Why should you trouble 111
about dollars—mere tokens? 111
You can't get away from Fufuti. 111
The *Jane* out there, she's due to 111
sail this morning on a round of 111
my plantations. She's the only 111
ship clearing for a month at 112
least. . . . By the time you'd 112
drunk yourself to death I'd sim- 112
ply have the money back again." 112

Peabody stared, and a streak 112
of crimson leaped into his cheek 112
as if a whiplash had been laid 112
across it. 112

"Damn you—!" he cried shak- 112
ily. "Give me that brandy— 112
I'll pay for it. Here's the stuff. 113
It's mine. I went after it and I 113
got it. I earned it myself, and 113
fairly!" 113

"To what end?" Bendemeer 113
cut in. "So you can pickle your- 113
self before burial?" · 113

Junius Peabody writhed. 113
"What's it to you how I spend it 113
afterward? I'm a free agent. I 113
can do as I like." 114

"That," said Bendemeer with 114
quiet emphasis, "is a lie." 114

Holding his quivering sub- 114
ject, impaled on his glance as it 114
seemed, he reached a black, 114
square bottle. He shoved a glass 114
in front of Junius Peabody and 114
poured a generous measure. 114
With one hand he kept the glass 114
covered and with the other 115
pointed out through the doorway. 115

"I'll say you lie, and I'll 115
demonstrate: 115

"You see my schooner out there? That's her boat on the beach. She leaves in half an hour; her captain's come now for final orders. She goes first from here to an island of mine a hundred miles away. I planted it with coconuts five years ago, and left a population of maybe a dozen Kanakas to tend them— it's going to be worth money some day. Nukava, they call it, and it's the edge of the earth, the farthest corner, and the loneliest and the driest. There's not a drop of anything on the place except water, scant and brackish at that. But a white man could live there, if he were fit to live at all, and wanted to badly enough.

"Now I'll make you an offer. I'll buy this lump of stuff from you, and I'll buy it either of two ways. A half interest in Nukava and you go there at once to take charge as agent. . . . Or else— here's your brandy and I'll keep you perpetually drunk as long as you last."

Junius swayed on his feet. "Agent?" he stammered. "To go away——?"

"Now. And once there you can't escape. You're stuck for a year on a coral gridiron, Peabody, to sit and fry."

"What for? You—! What for?"

Bendemeer shrugged.

"Because it amuses me. Because I please. Because—I know what you'll do. I've been watching men of your sort all my life, and I know what they're worth—drift on the beaches, scraps, trash, jetsam. Regeneration, eh? Rot and drivel! You can't save yourself any more than you could lift yourself by your own boot straps. It suits me to prove it to you this way."

He lifted his hand away from the glass. Peabody's stare dropped from that cryptic regard to the waiting brandy before him, the red liquor, odorous and maddening. Peabody's lips moved, and he wet them with the tip of his tongue and gripped the bar with straining white fingers.

"You're wrong," he breathed. "You lose, Bendemeer. I can do it—I've just learned I can do it. And, by God," he added, prayerfully, "I will."

Bendemeer took up the netted lump.

"Very well," he said, offhand. "Just a moment, while I chuck this stuff in the storeroom."

He turned and tramped out through the rear without a glance behind him—and left Junius Peabody there alone before the bar.

He was gone perhaps five minutes, quite as much as that, an ample space of time. When he came back there was no glass in sight. It had vanished, and the room reeked with the fumes of a very flagrant distillation of

1238 French brandy. He looked his
1239 customer up and down and his
1240 lids lowered a trifle.

1241 "Well, how did you like the
1242 flavour?"

1243 The face of Junius Peabody
1244 was like a death's-head, but the
1245 eyes in his sockets blazed with a
1246 light all their own, and, standing
1247 there erect, standing square on
1248 his two legs with his feet braced
1249 apart, he swore—somewhat in-
1250 expertly, it was true, but still
1251 quite heartily; good, crisp pro-
1252 fanity such as one able man may
1253 use with another—until Bende-
1254 meer's puzzled gaze caught the
1255 sparkle of broken glass lying in
1256 a great splash of liquid in a cor-
1257 ner of the floor. "I'm going to
1258 Nukava!" cried Junius Peabody.
1259 "And you see—you see there are
1260 some scraps thrown up on the
1261 beach that are worth something
1262 after all, and be damned to you,
1263 Bendemeer!"

1264 Bendemeer's grip shot out as
1265 if against his volition, and after
1266 an instant's hesitation Peabody
1267 took it. He did not yet know all

the trader had done for him,
perhaps would never know, but
on the inscrutable front of that
remarkable man was a faint
glow curiously unlike a loser's
chagrin.

"So it seems," acknowledged
Bendemeer. "So it seems"—
and smiled a little, rather
oddly. . . .

Bendemeer was still smiling
that way, all by himself, an hour
or so later when he had watched
the *Likely Jane* lay her course
for Nukava with the new agent
on board and had gone down into
his storeroom to put the place
to rights. There was a clutter of
odds and ends of cargo that had
been spilled from an upset surf-
boat the day before. Most of it
had been salvaged by his Kanaka
boys along shore, but a certain
broken tub containing tallow had
lost part of its contents. However, he was able now to restore
a large lump weighing perhaps
eleven pounds or so, which made
the tally nearly good.

The Analysis

The Beginning of *Western Stuff* and the Beginning of *Women are Wiser* you will remember had the same initial condition; but one was treated as a story of Accomplishment and the other as a story of Decision. The story *Jetsam* and the story *Sunk* have the same Ending, that is, they have the same Conclusive Act. In each one a man conquers the temptation to take a drink, and in each case the Conclusive Act is a dramatic one. Mr. Worts, however, wrote a Beginning of accomplishment and Mr. Russell wrote a Beginning of decision or choice.

It is almost impossible to write a story of Decision without falling into the necessity for some sort of flashing back. In all cases the competent craftsman will cause this flash-back to be an interchange. If you will look at the chart preceding this story, you will see that of the 1296 lines, making up the total story, 1256 are Beginning. Lines 1257 to 1263 are the Conclusive Act, and lines 1264 to 1296 are the ironic Sequel. This story will repay reading because it is an excellent illustration of the story which opens with setting forth the condition which is unusual and apparently holding the threat of inevitable disaster. Lines 1 to 123 show that Junius Peabody, at 28, finds himself broke at Fufuti. There is a flash-back interchange with Bendemeer and Junius on lines 123 to 139, and immediately following this there is the interchange with the Sydney Duck. As a result of that interchange the response of Junius is to wish for a chance to begin again. On lines 429 to 543 there is an interchange with the Sydney Duck growing out of the finding of the lump which seems to present to Junius the chance to begin again for which he has wished. The fifth step of the interchange with the Sydney Duck is again an interchange with Bendemeer who this time repudiates Junius, who continues on in the hope that he may bring about his wish. Lines 793 to 1037 show an interchange, which is quite exciting, between Junius and the Sydney Duck and Willems as a group. As a result of this interchange Junius recovers the lump. Then the interchange between Junius and Bendemeer on lines 1038 to 1256 results in Bendemeer making clear unmistakably the choice that lies before Junius Peabody of giving up the opportunity to drink or of drinking himself to death. On lines 1154 to 1205 this is made clear. He decides upon reform; and then in the Sequel there is presented, on lines 1257 to 1296, the ironic Significance that after all this the stimulus which caused the initial impulse was only a lump of tallow. Nobody better than Mr. Russell knows the effectiveness of this type of Sequel. As a case in craftsmanship the reader will find this story particularly interesting as a companion story to Mr. Worts' story *Sunk*. He will also find that in its general structure it follows the lines of the story of Decision which Mr. Adams employed in his story *Women are Wiser*, and that in both *Women are Wiser* and in *Jetsam* the Flash-back is not a typical Flash-back in the sense in which we use the word, but it is a Flash-back by the character and not a Flash-back by the author. In this case it is a Flash-back of the character's thoughts presented by the author in an interchange to avoid summary.

311

These two stories are of the decision type story which show a conflict between the affections on the one hand and a standard of conduct or of conscience on the other. In the case of *Women are Wiser* this is quite clear, in the case of *Jetsam* the decision is really between affection for oneself, or self-indulgence and a desire for a standard of conduct which involves denying this desire. In both cases it is a standard of conduct built up by the world rather than by the individual. It is for this reason that these two stories show a variation from the stories which follow them, in which the decision is between a standard of conduct and an opportunity to profit, a much more common type of story, perhaps because it is a much more easily understood problem than the two preceding, and certainly much more clear-cut from the point of view of treatment. In the story, *Women are Wiser* in particular, there might be some question in the mind of a reader as to whether that course of conduct adopted by the actor was a wise one. In the course of conduct which has been made a possible choice in the stories which are to follow, there is a quite definite standard as to what ought to be done, even though it is not always done by the actor.

OTHER TYPES OF CHOICE ABOUT WHICH
STORIES OF DECISION ARE BUILT

The next five stories fall into the type of Decision Story which is concerned with the decision between a standard of conduct and an opportunity to profit.   They are a logical outcome of the story of Accomplishment. The story of Accomplishment, in its most usual form, deals with the desire of somebody to accomplish something, to achieve his wish.   That is to say it is a story of wish-fulfilment. These stories which I am about to analyze go beyond this, to the moment when there is an opportunity to achieve wish-fulfilment or an opportunity to profit, but which show that the main actor is prevented from seizing this opportunity by some trait of character which has established for him a standard of conduct.   A clear-cut example of this is *Gentility*, by Thomas Beer.

313

ARCHITECTURAL CHART

OF

GENTILITY

	Scene. Between all the Kent family and the condition arising from man in attic. Reported chiefly through the responses of Stukely.	1– 578
Series of Inter- changes giving the back- ground for the reader's under- standing of the im- portance of the choice to be made by Stukely.	Interchange. Joe and Rudy Kling.	579– 620
	Interchange. Rudy and Kent family.	621– 844
	(5th step. Comment of Kents upon Ru- dy. Interchange Norah and father.)	845– 951
	Interchange. Hester and Rev. Gavin Kent.	952–1010
	(5th step. Stukely's reflections.)	1011–1088
	Interchange. Stukely and Alphenius.	1088–1117
	Stukely and Joe.	1118–1148
	(5th step. Effect upon Kent family).	1149–1226
	Interchange. Stukely and Central Office.	1226–1271
	Continued by Norah.	1272–1315
	(5th step. Comments of Kent family.)	1316–1443
	Interchange. Stukely and Alphenius.	1444–1470
Choice presented.	Interchange. Stukely and Rudy Kling.	1471–1629
Decisive Act.	Stukely seizes Rudy.	1630–1651
Sequel.	Rudy fights. Mrs. Kent saves situa- tion.	1652–1812

BEGINNING

ENDING

Stukely's pride in the gentility of the Kent family is es- tablished through the series of reflec- tions in which he in- dulges at the close of the different in- terchanges.

Stukely has two choices offered. Narrative Question: "Which choice will he make?"

Answer is: "He rejects bribe."

Ironic significance.

314

GENTILITY

BY THOMAS BEER

I HAVE chosen this story because it indicates so definitely the type of story about which I have just spoken, and because it is so clearly dependent upon the quality of its interchanges for its effectiveness. I am often asked, "Who is the writer that I ought to study," to which I always reply, "There is no one writer that you ought to study. The thing to do is to study all the writers, and from each learn what he does most effectively." There is nobody writing in America today who can present scenes so effectively as Thomas Beer. Those scenes give the illusion of reality perhaps more clearly than do the scenes of any other writer. In general, writers may be divided into two classes: those whose stories are good because of their plot, and those whose stories are good because of their scenes. Mr. Beer is essentially of this second class, his scenes being connected only by a very slight thread of plot. Now read the story.

CASE No. 13

GENTILITY

BY THOMAS BEER

1 Stukely merely yawned at his
2 mother's first scream. A mos-
3 quito resumed its threatening
4 song somewhere in the darkness
5 not far from his wet face and he
6 waved an arm slowly, until Mrs.
7 Kent screamed again with an
8 abandoned violence that might
9 mean something positive, for she
10 usually woke herself. He swung
11 a leg from bed as feet bumped
12 the floor of his sister's bedroom
13 and Joe Fancher said, "Uh-huh,
14 woman, I heard it." On the
15 third wail Stukely jumped for his
16 bath robe and the baby raised a
17 distinguished yell of anger at the
18 hall's eastern end. Light shone
19 under the door while Stukely
20 pulled his hot body into thin
21 silk and wound the robe's cord
22 around his waist. Another week
23 of this indecent heat and he
24 would be down to a hundred and
25 sixty pounds or less. Silk stuck
26 to his chest as he blundered to
27 the doorway and entered bright-
28 ness, jarring Norah, in some
29 drapery of green stuff that spar-
30 kled dramatically.

"Do look where you're going, 31
Stuke!" 32

"How did I know you'd be 33
right outside my door, idiot?" 34
he snorted, and shoved past her 35
slimness toward his mother's 36
room. 37

"My dear Grace," said the 38
Rev. Gavin Kent in a composed 39
but annoyed cadence of his bary- 40
tone, "you very seldom scream 41
as loudly as that, even over a rat 42
in the cellar. There must have 43
been something!" 44

Mrs. Kent apologized in rapid 45
little gasps, inside the dark bed- 46
room. 47

She said, "No, no, Gavin! I 48
thought I heard something, but 49
it wasn't anything. I was just 50
dreaming, of course. I'm so 51
sorry! I'm so sorry, Joe! Do 52
turn the light out and go back to 53
bed, dear. I'm ever so sorry!" 54

"Goodness gracious mamma," 55
Joe Fancher yawned, filling the 56
hall with the folds and loops of a 57
whole sheet, "I wasn't sleepin' 58
any. Yeh, this Norah was doin' 59
all the sleep in our room. I was 60

317

61 kinda recumbent on the couch,
62 wonderin' if it's any hotter'n this
63 down in Gawgia. Stuke, your
64 mamma says she meant nothin'
65 whatsoever by yellin'. You can
66 go back to bed if it's any good to
67 you, son."

68 Doctor Kent observed from
69 the unseen bedroom, "It's fright-
70 ful for June. . . . Is that the
71 new bath robe Norah's been
72 making for you, Joe?"

73 "No, rev'rend. This is just a
74 sheet, sir. Winter'll come an'
75 I'll be twenty-five or so when
76 your no-account daughter has
77 that bath robe finished on me.
78 Yeh, the kid'll be talkin' an'
79 reachin' for a cigarette when it's
80 all done. . . . Want some ice
81 water, mamma?"

82 "Oh, no thank—I really would
83 like some, Joe," said Mrs. Kent
84 pathetically and suddenly, "if
85 it's not too much——"

86 "Not any, ma'am," the long
87 man drawled, and wandered
88 majestically in his sheet down
89 the green stairs, fading into the
90 blackness of the living room be-
91 low as a rooster gave an inspired
92 cry on the next farm and the
93 rooster Androcles answered from
94 Doctor Kent's henhouse.

95 "Daybreak," said the old man
96 with a sigh, "and it's the longest
97 day in the year. Grace, you'd
98 best go down to Southampton,
99 My dear, if this heat keeps up."

100 Norah Fancher grinned at her
101 brother in the hallway, lighted
102 by three little bulbs, and leaned

103 on the wall in a fluctuation of
104 the green robe strewn with spots
105 of silver embroidery. Their
106 mother heroically remarked that
107 she wouldn't think of going to
108 Uncle George's house at South-
109 ampton. The tomatoes would
110 be ripe soon and Joe and Stukely
111 would need help, and the new
112 nursemaid wasn't broken to the
113 eccentricities of Joseph Fancher,
114 Jr.; and if she went to South-
115 ampton the Rev. Gavin Kent
116 must come with her. If the high
117 farm was impossible for her, it
118 was just as hot for him; and any-
119 how, this was Sunday and it
120 might be better to wait until
121 Monday to travel. She said all
122 this with diminishing vigor and
123 concluded, "I do hope it will be
124 cool at Southampton when we
125 get there."

126 Then she went to sleep with a
127 short moaning noise and at once
128 began her delicate repressed
129 snore, a gently modulated, sooth-
130 ing little noise that always made
131 Stukely proud of her; she was a
132 lady even when asleep. He
133 gathered his blue silk robe be-
134 tween his knees and sat down on
135 the planks of the ancient floor to
136 wait for Joe Fancher and the
137 iced water, wondering whether a
138 snore could be controlled by sur-
139 gery or mental suggestion, and
140 whether roosters were glad to
141 wake with the first threat of
142 dawn or if it was something of a
143 burden on their sense of duty.
144 And did the roosters yell down

ninety miles to New York pro-
gressively or were there rooster-
less intervals where some cock
woke in silence and started the
traveling noise on his own account? Then he looked at a
drop of sweat that trickled on
his right thumb's brown curve
from the soaked blue sleeve.
The drop fell on the planks beside his foot and was immediately covered by a slipper of
worn gray leather. The boy put
back his black head and stared
up at Doctor Kent, a tremendous
figure in white pajamas, which
his gaunt body left unrumpled,
immaculately neat.

"Stuke?"

"Don't step on me, dad,"
Stukely whispered.

"My dear boy," said the retired
rector of St. Philip's Church, "I
had no intention of doing so.
I can't find my glasses, and I'm
so blind without them——
What I was going to say—Is
that you, Norah? Don't be
alarmed, my dear girl!—was
that I'm afraid there's somebody
in the spare bedroom." He
paused and finished with civility,
"I can hear him, you know,
through the wall where the old
door's papered over."

Norah Fancher clasped her
hands on her green breast and
said delightedly, "Father, you're
really wonderful! I think if the
house caught fire you'd apologize
for waking us. Stuke, go see
what it is. If it's a burglar

tell him he ought to wait for
cool nights."

"Quit bein' frolicsome,"
Stukely grunted, getting up from
the floor with its illusion of coolness. Norah had painted it a
somber gray and imitated the
broken squares of a paved walk
on its length. His father caught
his arm and the boy said, "Oh,
come off it, daddy! How can
anybody get in there with the
door locked? It's the new rat;
the one Joe saw in the cellar yesterday—I mean day before yesterday. I don't see how you
have the gu-courage to wear pajamas on a night like this."

"It's his conventionality,"
Norah sighed.

"My dear boy," said the old
man, nervously holding his son's
right biceps, "wait until Joe
comes up with——"

"I can face this rat all by myself, sir," Stukely assured him,
and strolled twelve steps down
the gray floor to the painted
door of the spare bedroom. He
yawned and turned the key under the glass knob which looked
so pleasantly like ice against the
green wood, and was even a little
cool in his palm when he shut his
hand on it. But the door did not
stir. Directly a rasping fall of
sand slid down his back and he
said loudly, "Oh, yeh—other
way," in what sounded the fals-
est voice of known time. The
door had been unlocked and he
had locked it. Now he must

229 unlock it and carelessly go into
230 the black room full of masked
231 men, armed unpleasantly. His
232 blue bath robe seemed perilously
233 thin. And why had Joe gone
234 downstairs just when a former
235 sergeant of marines was demand-
236 ed by this situation. After three
237 years of friendship Joe might
238 have stuck to him in an emer-
239 gency instead of sneaking down-
240 stairs after iced water. The key
241 turned. The door swung briskly
242 inward and Stukely set a hand
243 on the wall's dry paper, hunting
244 for the button of the lights.
245 Two bulbs flared through the
246 yellow silk of a tall lamp beside
247 the bed, and the room was empty
248 from the vermilion floor to the
249 wooden ceiling on which Norah
250 Fancher's hand had drawn a
251 number of fat golden fishes.
252 Smells of hot cloth and lavender
253 welled from the bed and from a
254 shallow cupboard set in the deep
255 wall between two windows.

256 "G-golly," said Stukely, "but
257 the place smells to heaven!
258 Nothin' here, daddy." He spoke
259 in the tone of comfortable benev-
260 olence, while five drops of sweat
261 went wandering the middle of
262 his chest and relief swelled his
263 lungs. "If any rat wants to stay
264 in here, he's trying to lose
265 weight. I'll open the windows.
266 It might start a draft through."
267 The vermilion floor seemed
268 sticky underfoot. Stukely wres-
269 tled with the weight of fine
270 chintz curtains in each window

and undid the locks. Outside a 271
sedate grayness glowed behind 272
the heavy timbers of the water 273
tower beside an oak whose foli- 274
age rustled vaguely in the pas- 275
sage of an exhausted wind. The 276
river below the orchard made a 277
little sound as though the water 278
tired of pebbles and flat rocks. 279
Earth yawned, he thought, at 280
the promise of another weary 281
day, more heat, more breathless 282
air. He stretched over the sill of 283
the second window and reached 284
an idle hand to the iron spikes 285
which made a ladder up one cor- 286
ner of the water tower's skeleton. 287
His fingers could not quite touch 288
the iron, and the boy drew him- 289
self back across the ledge of win- 290
dow sill without interest in the 291
failure. 292

"You know the tower's too 293
close to these windows," he said 294
listlessly; "if anybody did want 295
to get in, dad, this would be the 296
way." 297

"I suppose so," said Doctor 298
Kent, blinking up at the gilded 299
fishes; "and I suppose this room's 300
hotter because the ceiling's noth- 301
ing but the floor of the attic. 302
Yes, a house built in 1803 offers 303
inducements to rats. But what 304
a fine piece of building it is, 305
Stuke! I have to praise my own 306
investment, you know. We've 307
been here three years, and liter- 308
ally nothing in the way of re- 309
pairs. . . . Is that you, Joe? 310
I decided that I heard a burglar 311
in here. It was just a rat, but he 312

conveyed an impression of weighing hundreds of pounds. I think
he must be a very big rat, really
to make such a noise."

"Some rats," Joe assured him
in the sleepiest drawl, "are tal-
ented 'bout noises. Oncet in
that war they had in France I an'
forty to a hundred other guys
were kep' awake all night in a
very damn uncomfortable trench
by just one rat. He was tryin'
to saw off an old post outa sight
in the dark with his teef."

"Teeth, lamb," said Norah;
"don't be so Southern just because it's——"

Joe rounded his turquoise eyes
in his brown face and gave the
beautiful woman a long, offended
glare. He trailed his sheet over
the vermilion floor and said as
he walked, "Girl, grandmamma
raised me to be polite to women,
but you've no call to be rude at
me. For one cent, Mex'can, I'd
tear your hair offa your dumb
head. I married you for pity,
anyhow. . . . Here's a lotta
flood, rev'rend. . . . Ace, give
your poppa a drink."

Stukely took a glass from the
tray and got it firmly in his
father's grasp. The Rev. Gavin
Kent was helpless without spectacles that marred his fine long
face by daylight. He bent his
curly head to drink iced water
and a tiny feather floated down
to rest on his white curls.

"Regards from the angels,"
Joe drawled, hitching up the
green trousers of limp silk that
covered his long legs. He drew
a fold of the sheet higher up his
white chest, hiding the crooked
purple scar that roamed his ribs,
and blinked up toward the ceiling. Then he yawned and
rubbed tanned fists in his eyes.
"Yuh! Gimme credit, poppa.
I behaved all decorous, like the
father of a fam'ly oughta. Many
an egg would have loped out in
the corridor bare-nekkid on a yell
like that, but I fetched this sheet
wiv me."

"It's extremely becoming,"
Norah said, with her wild black
hair close to Joe's shoulder;
"you look like Demosthenes or
one of those classic people making an oration about something,
except that your nose isn't as
Greek as theirs."

"My nose," Joe asserted, wrinkling it, "is better'n most noses,
female! Many dames have told
me it's an int'resting kinda nose.
As for a sheet as clothes, no.
The Greeks didn't have many
fires to run to or they'd ha' never
wore anything so sorta clingy.
Go back to bed. You've been
makin' noises like a sawmill in
trouble all night. Your mamma
snores like a lady, but you're no
gentleman when you're asleep.
G'on back to bed. I'm gonna sit
in the creek until it's time to
milk. . . . Rev'rend, it's my
sad dooty to say that old Her-
mione's days as an asset on this
farm are over. She's a good,

³⁹⁷ kind, well-meanin' cow, but too
³⁹⁸ sorta ven'rable. I expect she's
³⁹⁹ twenty or so. Bought her with
⁴⁰⁰ the place, didn't you, sir?"

⁴⁰¹ "Hermione," said Doctor
⁴⁰² Kent, "is that obstreperous
⁴⁰³ black cow that used to give
⁴⁰⁴ Stuke so much trouble when he
⁴⁰⁵ was learning to milk. Yes, I
⁴⁰⁶ bought her from Mr. Kling with
⁴⁰⁷ the farm. Well, we've had her
⁴⁰⁸ three years. I don't know, Joe,
⁴⁰⁹ what one does with a venerable
⁴¹⁰ cow. As a useless relic, I have
⁴¹¹ a sentiment for Hermione, of
⁴¹² course, a natural fellow feeling—
⁴¹³ tempered, perhaps, with our hu-
⁴¹⁴ man superiority. At least I
⁴¹⁵ can't be eaten or sold to the tan-
⁴¹⁶ nery at Poughkeepsie, if there is
⁴¹⁷ one there. Can we pension
⁴¹⁸ Hermione?"

⁴¹⁹ "Good gracious, rev'rend," Joe
⁴²⁰ murmured, kicking the sheet
⁴²¹ around his feet, "it's no question
⁴²² of slayin' this dame. No, she's
⁴²³ a very orn'mental cow. All your
⁴²⁴ fool friends from New York al-
⁴²⁵ ways admire her a lot. She
⁴²⁶ reminds me of grandmamma
⁴²⁷ comin' outa church whenever
⁴²⁸ daddy had wrung tears from his
⁴²⁹ sinners down in Gawgia or out
⁴³⁰ in Eutropius. Yeh, Hermione
⁴³¹ an' grandmamma are similar.
⁴³² Very dignified an' kinda
⁴³³ haughty. All I meant was that
⁴³⁴ we gotta getta new cow, sir.
⁴³⁵ 'At means you don't have
⁴³⁶ mamma write any checks for
⁴³⁷ homes to shelter blind Episcopal
⁴³⁸ choir boys this monf. Hear me,

⁴³⁹ rev'rend? This place has got to
⁴⁴⁰ pay in more cash if you're gonna
⁴⁴¹ have mamma write any moh
⁴⁴² three-hundred-dollar checks for
⁴⁴³ blind choir boys, sir. We're a
⁴⁴⁴ dairy an' veg'table farm, poppa,
⁴⁴⁵ an' not a distillery."

⁴⁴⁶ The Rev. Gavin Kent shuffled
⁴⁴⁷ his slippers on the vermilion
⁴⁴⁸ paint and said, humbly, "Yes,
⁴⁴⁹ Joe, I—er—am afraid that was
⁴⁵⁰ rather reckless of me. You and
⁴⁵¹ Stukely make the farm pay so
⁴⁵² nicely that——"

⁴⁵³ "Good gracious, poppa," Joe
⁴⁵⁴ crooned, "you can't help bein' a
⁴⁵⁵ gentleman. Babe, take that
⁴⁵⁶ feather offa your poppa's ear.
⁴⁵⁷ Makes him look friv'lous. No,
⁴⁵⁸ rev'rend, you give away nuffin'
⁴⁵⁹ moh until middle of July. After
⁴⁶⁰ mamma's dividends come in, you
⁴⁶¹ can have a spree an' send checks
⁴⁶² to char'ties. Right now we have
⁴⁶³ to get us a new cow. I knew a
⁴⁶⁴ cow in France named"—a cloud
⁴⁶⁵ of feathers drifted prettily past
⁴⁶⁶ Doctor Kent's white curls and
⁴⁶⁷ the melodious flow of Joe's voice
⁴⁶⁸ slowed for a second. His eyes
⁴⁶⁹ changed suddenly to emeralds un-
⁴⁷⁰ der the bleached arcs of his eye-
⁴⁷¹ brows, and he stared upward, go-
⁴⁷² ing on—"Peritonitis. She——"

⁴⁷³ "It doesn't sound a very
⁴⁷⁴ French name, Joe," the old gen-
⁴⁷⁵ tleman objected. "Peritonitis?"

⁴⁷⁶ "Near as I can come to it,
⁴⁷⁷ poppa. My b'talion kinda
⁴⁷⁸ adopted her. She was all sad by
⁴⁷⁹ the roadside, with an elderly
⁴⁸⁰ dame along who sold her for a

481 hatful of francs. We were new
482 to Frawg money then an' the old
483 dame looked so sorta des'late
484 that it touched us a lot. Cal-
485 c'latin' afterward, we made out
486 that Perry cost us about three
487 thousand dollars American mon-
488 ey. I chipped in a pretty grand-
489 lookin' sorta purple bill that
490 looked fine in Porky Olsen's hel-
491 met. Yeh, I was seventeen in
492 those days, an' extravagant.
493 Only 'at old French dame was
494 downright immoral, 'cause this
495 cow had given down her last shot
496 of milk when Robert E. Lee and
497 the late Ulysses Grant were ar-
498 guin' around Richmond. Other-
499 wise she was an awful nice cow
500 an' useda lick my face real
501 friendly. It was the French lady
502 whose conduct was vulgar."
503 Stukely heard all this easy
504 chatter while cold sand seemed
505 to slide down his broad shoulders
506 under the moist silk of his bath
507 robe. He looked up at the open
508 square trap in the ornamented
509 ceiling. It shouldn't be open,
510 and feathers would not float
511 down from the ancient pillows
512 stored in the low attic unless
513 something had disturbed them.
514 A feather roved and made a
515 white point on the crust of Joe's
516 cropped pale hair. . . . Yes,
517 this burglar had heard the
518 shrieks and had jumped into hid-
519 ing through the ceiling. He
520 might be squatting above them,
521 scowling down, with a revolver
522 rested comfortably on his knee.

523 "The morality of the French
524 lady's dealings with the marine
525 corps," said the Rev. Gavin
526 Kent in his best manner, "is
527 open to question. Perhaps you
528 should say her *mores* are——"
529 "Her—huh, sir?"
530 "*Mores*," the old gentleman
531 intoned. "The word implies the
532 social customs of a race, such as
533 chewing gum, eating mission-
534 aries, attending or not attending
536 religious services, polygamy,
537 polyandry, human sacrifice and
538 cheating innocent strangers in
539 bargains. Probably she thought
540 herself justified by local custom
541 in taking anything she could get.
542 Morality is the individual's sense
543 of honorable conduct; the *mores*
544 are merely habits."
545 Joe balanced from white foot
546 to foot, watching the trap above
547 Doctor Kent's white head, and
548 evenly crooned, "Poppa, my
549 daddy's very eloquent when he
550 gets goin', but I gotta say you
551 have him plastered flat wiv a
552 ton of bricks on his belly when
553 it comes to sudden information.
554 . . . Yeh, it horrified the
555 Frawgs to see us chewin' gum,
556 but they d'vour snails in jelly.
557 Out in Eutropius, when I was
558 young—Norah, honey, run along
559 back to bed, dear."
560 "I shall do nothing of the
561 kind," said Norah, brushing her
562 hair's black masses back from
563 her face with its enormous eyes.
564 "D-daddy, you'd better go to
565 bed, though. You'll be too tired

566 for church in the morning.
567 W-won't he, Stuke? Please go
568 to——"

569 Her voice became the thinnest
570 whisper as fresh feathers floated
571 in a whirling shower.

572 "Oh!" said the old man after
573 a hot second. He sat upright
574 on the mattress and blinked at
575 Joe's restless movement three
576 yards from him. "I see! What's
577 happened, Stukely? No, I
578 shan't go to bed, Norah!
578 Stuke?"

579 Joe Fancher dropped the sheet
580 and hitched his green trousers
581 higher up his flat waist.

582 He said lightly, "Poppa
583 there's a guy up in the attic, sir.
584 Babe, take your daddy out in the
585 passage an' gimme my gun from
586 my room. You up there," he
587 drawled, his voice rising to a
588 falsetto rasp, "I was five years
589 in the m'rines an' I gotta mean
590 disposition an' a medal for
591 revolver shootin'. I'm a preach-
592 er's kid an' when I get nasty, oh,
593 you ain't any idea, son, how
594 nasty I get! Yeh, come down
595 an' be fast or——"

596 "I'll come down," a man said
597 weakly; "but don't rough me up,
598 pal. I ain't doin' any harm."
599 He coughed close to the trap and
600 went on drearily, "If the old
601 gentleman'll get out from under-
602 neath, why——"

603 Stukely drew his father from
604 the mattress and Joe dropped
605 his hands on the painted green
606 of the bed's foot, grinning up-

607 ward, with his small ears wrig-
608 gling on the round of his head.
609 All the muscles of his white chest
610 bobbed in a single motion as a
611 black suitcase tumbled from the
612 ceiling. Then he watched black
613 shoes and radiant socks descend.
614 A little person dropped through
615 the square trap and knelt on the
616 bed, plucking feathers from his
617 blue coat. Norah produced a
618 long giggle that lifted into a
619 squawk before she pressed her
620 hands on her mouth.

621 "Why," said Doctor Kent,
622 straining his dull eyes, "it's a
623 mere child!"

624 "Yeh, poppa," Joe mused,
625 "the mountain snorted an' a
626 mouse come out. . . . Stranger,
627 tell us your *mores* after scarin'
628 nine pounds offa me like that.
629 I'd get me a hairbrush an' wallop
630 you for two cents, fella!"

631 The small person said in a ter-
632 rible whimper.

633 "You leave me be! This is
634 my folks' house, and I s'pose
635 they've rented it to you guys
636 or sumpin. Only I wasn't
637 doin' nothin'. Only you scared
638 me, yellin'. My name's Rudy
639 Kling, an' this is my room. . . .
640 Where's mamma?"

641 Stukely became extremely shy
642 and embarrassed. Joe towered
643 six feet at the bottom of the bed-
644 stead. The Rev. Gavin Kent
645 was quite as long and his son had
646 only an eighth of an inch to gain.
647 They must seem terrific to this
648 minute creature crouched on the

649 mattress. Norah suppressed an-
650 other giggle.

651 "Oh," said the Rev. Gavin
652 Kent, "are you a member of Mr.
653 Otto Kling's family who for-
654 merly lived here?"

655 The little thing gave out a
656 horrid sound and asked, "They
657 ain't all dead, mister? Aw no!"
658 with his soiled hands flattened
659 on the mattress.

660 "No, no," the old man said
661 hastily; "no! In fact, Mrs.
662 Puddy had a postal from your
663 mother only the other day. Mrs.
664 Puddy, you know, across the
665 road. No, they're all very well.
666 But I don't understand——"

667 Joe Fancher put a brown
668 thumb on the little man's shoul-
669 der and affably commanded,
670 "Tell your yarn, Aloysius, an'
671 don't improve it any moh'n you
672 can help. You're kin to this
673 Mr. Kling that Rev'rend Kent
674 bought him this farm offa? Go
675 on, fella an' be plain wiv me.
676 I'm a hard hound 'at bites
677 babies."

678 "I'm Rudy Kling. I ain't
679 been home in five years since pop
680 kicked me out last time. I—I
681 came home," the soiled person
682 babbled, moving back from Joe's
683 finger; "this used to be my room.
684 Th-the front door was open. I
685 just walked in an' came on up.
686 I was huntin' for the gas when
687 the lady screamed. I see you
688 guys have put in electric light.
689 And then I heard you all talkin'
690 and knew sumpin was wrong.

691 When you've been in jail twice
692 you ain't so anxious to be in
693 again and"—he gulped—"I
694 jumped up through the trap.
695 . . . Wher've my folks gone
696 to?"

697 "California," Doctor Kent
698 said, slowly blinking. "We've
699 been here three years and three
700 months. How old are you?"

701 "Twenty-four, sir," the little
702 man said, and was silent on the
703 mattress, with his nose twitch-
704 ing and his fingers working gent-
705 ly. A rosy color had come back
706 into his round face; he was sud-
707 denly a rather pretty fellow,
708 Stukely saw. His thick hair was
709 black and waved around his
710 forehead in a becoming untidi-
711 ness that made him childish.
712 But he had been twice in jail
713 and his romantic socks an-
714 nounced in determined red and
715 green stripes that he was hope-
716 lessly vulgar. The socks were
717 inexcusable and inexpensive.

718 "You've not been home in
719 five years?"

720 "No, sir," said Rudy Kling in
721 the same dreary voice; "I came
722 home five years back. Only I
723 got in a muss over a poker party
724 an' pop kicked me out. Oh, I
725 ain't sayin' he was hard on me!
726 Naw! I ain't any good. The
727 Puddys or anybody will tell you
728 that. My brothers got all the
729 good there was in the fam'ly.
730 I'm a kind of a left-over. I'm
731 the youngest."

732 "Ran off pretty young, fella?"

733 Joe asked, gathering up his sheet.
734 "Yeh, I was fourteen. And
735 then my wife used to beat me up
736 pretty bad," the young man said
737 dolorously, rubbing his pert nose
738 with a green silk handkerchief,
739 "so pop let me come home.
740 Only I got in this fight over a
741 poker game an' knocked Ralph
742 McCarthy's eye out with a chair.
743 I expect you'd know him if
744 you've been here three years.
745 His folks have a farm over
746 by——"
747 Joe said soothingly, "Yeh,
748 fella. His glass eye's a pretty
749 fair match for his real one.
750 You're real frank."
751 Rudy Kling looked up at the
752 tall man with a sort of scorn and
753 wailed, "It wouldn't be any good
754 lyin' to you guys. You're all
755 gentlemen. I can string it out
756 pretty fair with tough eggs, but
757 it's no good lyin' to classy peo-
758 ple." He looked briefly at
759 Norah's green gauzes and said,
760 "I'm sorry I made you yell,
761 lady."
762 "Oh, that was my mother,"
763 Norah brightly mentioned. She
764 considered the trivial person fav-
765 orably and inquired, "So you've
766 been in jail a good deal?"
767 "Twice," Mr. Kling answered
768 sulkily; "but not lately. I had
769 a good job at a track. I'm a
770 pretty fair jockey, only I ain't
771 enough nerve for big races."
772 Stukely shivered. Dawn rose
773 in color behind the water tower's
774 plain gauntness and new light

775 mingled with the glow of lamps
776 in this stifling room. He had a
777 sleepy feeling of something quite
778 unreal under the gilded fishes of
779 the blue ceiling. This shameless
780 person was Joe's age—four years
781 older than himself; but his trivial
782 body had been in jail and beaten
783 by some awful wife and jounced
784 on race horses. And he had no
785 nerve and said so! He was en-
786 tirely strange. Of course any-
787 body got scared now and then.
788 But you didn't sit and say so to
789 people in night clothes or sheets.
790 "Any chance I could get a
791 drink of water, pal?" Mr. Kling
792 asked Joe Fancher. "Them
793 feathers in the attic nearly——"
794 "Take him downstairs, Joe,"
795 said Doctor Kent, in the oddest
796 tone, "and give him some water.
797 ... What time are the Puddys
798 likely to get up?"
799 "Any minute, poppa. Puddy
800 thinks unfriendly of the sun if
801 it's later'n three o'clock in sum-
802 mertime."
803 "Then," said the old gentle-
804 man, "Puddy will be able to
805 identify Mr. Kling. If Mr.
806 Puddy identifies you," he said
807 directly to the intruder, "we
808 have no reason to detain you,
809 sir. Good morning."
810 Mr. Kling picked up his little
811 suitcase. It could hold nothing
812 much, and Stukely wondered
813 whether it had been chosen to
814 match its owner's lack of bulk.
815 Rudy slipped from the mattress
816 and gave Norah a look of sharp

interest, as he asked, "I don't suppose you know where my folks moved to in California?"

"It happens that I do. Your father is so kind as to send me Christmas cards each year. They live at Los Altos. It's below San Francisco somewhere. Los Altos—can you remember?"

"Yeh," said Mr. Kling; "I was through there oncet with a circus. . . . Honest, mister, the front door was open."

"I fear that it was," Doctor Kent nodded. "I'm afraid that I left it open. Good morning. . . . Joe, please take Mr. Kling over to see if Mr. Puddy is able to identify him."

"Puddy can identify me all right. Always hated the sight of me," the trivial person sighed.

Norah swished her green skirt and gave the intruder a nod of farewell as he followed Joe's sheet through the doorway.

He ducked his head and vanished.

With a tremendous sigh the Reverend Gavin Kent sat down on the mattress and said softly, "Ugh! I hope, really, that he wasn't as offensive as his voice, Norah."

"Dad, he was perfectly charming! He had purple socks with jade embroideries on them, and he looked exactly like a doll baby. His hair's the same as Stukely's, only he oils it, and his eyelashes are an inch long. I don't think he's more than five feet high. He'd break if Stuke or Joe slapped him."

"Oh, no, he wouldn't, Norah," Stukely protested sleepily; "he's hard as wire. One of those rather pretty kids, daddy. Weak face."

"I adore you, lamb," said Norah, "when you get frightfully mature! You're twenty and he's twenty-four. Pretty kid!"

The Reverend Gavin Kent fumbled his old silver case from the pocket of his white jacket and tapped a cigarette on its shimmer. He musically remarked, "My dear daughter, Stuke is unusually mature for twenty. Joe thinks so, and Joe is the least immature boy of twenty-four now alive in the United States. It interests me to hear that our visitor is muscular. He sounded so feeble. I expect he was acting a little."

"Of course he was, daddy," Norah agreed; "he laid it on thick. So should I in his shoes! If I were only an inch high and saw two big brutes like Joe and Stuke standing over me—and Joe looks simply terrific when his eyes get green—I'd simply have groveled on the floor and kicked my heels. He's a coward anyhow. And he—— Oh, precious angel bunny!"

"I beg your pardon, daughter?"

"She's talkin' to Junior, dad," Stukely explained; "he's just rolled in, sir."

901 Joseph Fancher, Jr., rolled on 902 the door sill and waved a deter-903 mined fist at his relatives, say-904 ing ferociously, "Yattakow!" A 905 muddled white garment incased 906 his fat legs. He was otherwise 907 bare and visibly cross, after a 908 crawl down the corridor from 909 his low crib beside the eastern 910 windows and his nurse's door. 911 He said "Yattakow!" again, and 912 inflated himself for a howl of 913 rage, shutting his black eyes.

914 "Yes, darling," Norah gur-915 gled; "Uncle Stuke'll give you a 916 glass of water. Thank heaven 917 there is some! Hurry, Stuke! 918 Yes, lamb! There," she said, 919 settling the dark infant on her 920 green lap, "drink that and tell 921 us what you think. There was 922 a nice burglar here and your 923 fond grandpapa let him go be-924 cause our manners are perfect in 925 the Kent family. He just told 926 us a lot of awful lies and Papa 927 Joe has taken him outdoors so 928 that his hair oil won't smell any 929 more. . . . Yes, spill it on 930 mother, darlin' ducky."

931 "So you think he was lying, 932 daughter?"

933 "Certain of it, daddy. . . . 934 Oh, Hester," she said to an 935 apparition in a blue gown out-936 side the door, "baby got out of 937 his crib. Just put him back and 938 go on giving him this water. He 939 doesn't want it, of course, but it 940 soothes his egoism. Here, angel, 941 nursie wants you."

942 The nursemaid picked up her charge with indeterminate, 943 pretty noises of reproach and 944 said "Yes'm. Some noise woke 945 me up. . . . Did he bump him-946 self gettin' out of bed? My!" 947 while Junior clung to his glass of 948 water and chirped triumphantly 949 when he contrived to kick Norah 950 in the face. 951

"Ah, Hester," said the Rever-952 end Gavin Kent, "you were ac-953 quainted with the Klings of 954 course. Yes? Was there a 955 Rudy Kling in the family?" 956

"Rudy? I should certainly 957 say there was," the girl said, 958 bundling Junior in her arms; 959 "my, yes! Yesterday when I 960 was down home to see mamma's 961 sore foot we were talkin' about 962 him. 'Cause the doctor stuck 963 some co-cocaine into her toe 964 when he lanced it—yes." 965

"He's a pretty little thing 966 with big black eyes, Hester?" 967

The nursemaid giggled, 968 "Yes'm. He looked awful sissy, 969 but all the big fellas were scared 970 of him 'cause he fought so hard. 971 Yes'm. He was just a dreadful 972 boy. . . . No, baby. . . . The 973 other Kling boys were nice fellas, 974 but Rudy was a tough. He—— 975 Now, Junior, be good!" 976

Junior plunged his whole arm 977 into the glass, found that it 978 wouldn't come out with his fist 979 doubled and raised a horrid lam-980 entation in which traces of the 981 word "Mamma!" mingled with 982 mere breath. Mrs. Kent ap-983 peared as a wraith in lavender, 984 and the howling baby retired with all his social apparatus down the hallway.

"The day," said the Reverend Gavin Kent, "has begun, Stuke. And what the thoughts of Mr. Kling were while he listened to our conversation from the attic we shall probably never know. Probably we're nothing but an episode in his career. Is it egotism to wonder whether he relied on our gentility in surrendering? His story was silly. Few people would have gone through the form of believing it. I think it was Ludovic Halévy who remarked that well-bred people are utterly helpless in their dealings with rogues. . . . Meantime, my dear boy, you might run down and look at the silver for safety's sake."

"Yes, sir," his son said, through a yawn; "time to milk anyhow."

He crossed the hallway drenched in fresh heat and echoing with notes of admiration from Junior's nursery. The black-haired baby was being adored for his latest cleverness. Historically, Stukely thought, several million babies had stuck their doubled fists in glasses of water and hadn't been able to pull them out again. A stream of babies passed in his misty speculation, each with a doubled fist in a glass. He pulled off his soaked bath robe and stood with a lazy wind playing on his brown body through slats of his closed shutters. In Babylon, in otiose Corinth, in Roman villas beside white Naples, in the grim Middle Ages and throughout the rational eighteenth century, babies had gone on sticking their fists in glasses, and innumerable women had adored them for doing what seemed, on any calm consideration, one of the most obvious things you could do.

He hauled limp cotton trousers up his legs and hunted out a shirt of no intrinsic value from his closet. . . . Perhaps people were often admired for doing rather obvious things. It was really nothing extraordinary that Joe and he managed fifty acres of farm and made the land pay. Lots of people had done that before. His mother's unexampled talent for screaming at sudden noises was really rarer than the common sense needed to manage cows, eggs, tomatoes and apple trees. It might have to be classified as an entirely useless accomplishment. The boy laced on his canvas shoes in a drowsy speculation. What accomplishments were always useful? He had taken three prizes at school in French composition, and now he sprayed apple trees contentedly. Numbers of thoughts flowed together without relation in his mind as he descended the green stairs into the living room, lined with books. Nobody had touched the silver ranged in the

329

old sideboard of the dining room. He yawned ten times, picked a pipe from the table below Bishop Stukely's portrait beside the open front door and idled into the pillared porch. The dewy roofs of Gossetville twinkled down the shallow valley's hot reaches, and the red hair of young Alphenius Puddy, the hired boy, twinkled near at hand. Alphenius diligently left his father's farm when the multitude of Puddys rose in summer, but he usually craftily waited for Joe or Stukely to appear before he began to milk the twelve cows. However, Norah liked the boy's hair and he sometimes worked. This morning he had an appearance of prim virtue, sitting on the low step of the porch, and he said with discretion, "I'll help you carry him in, Stuke. Only he's certainly awful drunk."

"Who's drunk, Alphenius?"

"Well," said Alphenius in soprano, defensively, "he's lyin' down in the yard with nothin' on him but some p'jama pants, an' his head in a bucket. I says 'Are you drunk, Joe?' only he just kicked at me an' kind of cussed."

"But where's Rudy Kling, Alphenius?"

Alphenius remarked in a surprised barytone, "How d'I know, Stuke? Somebody saw him in Coney Island last summer. Maybe he's in jail."

"Then Joe didn't bring him over to your father's?"

"Naw," said Alphenius, with indignation; "pop'd kick him off the place if anybody fetched him in. He was sellin' that cocaine stuff to the kids in——"

His stomach became an icy balloon in Stukely's middle. He went loping down the flagged walk to the white fence of the barnyard and vaulted its solid height. Immediately Joe said hollowly, "Gettahell 'way from me, y'——" And the voice trailed into wasted vowels. He lay stretched on ruts of the yard with his naked shoulders twitching, and his head was hidden in a tin pail.

"Joe," said Stukely dizzily, "wh-what on earth are you—— Joe!" The body heaved in its vivid trousers.

Joe said, "'At you, babe? Find me my gun, boy. Gonna——" A lovely line of scarlet picked its way down his brown neck and seemed to hesitate among the dimpling muscles of his shoulders. Stukely dropped back his head and howled three times so that his throat burned. Joe said "Gracious! Quit 'at yawp, ace!" and then said nothing more for a whirling time. The clocks of Gossetville struck four.

At ten it occurred to Stukely that he would die if he didn't get to sleep. Farmers flooded up and down the pillared porch,

1153 ducking their heads when light-
1154 ning showered violet flares
1155 through the rain that fell with a
1156 vexatious steadiness. The blood-
1157 hound from Poughkeepsie sat in
1158 dignity on the hearth of the liv-
1159 ing room under Bishop Stukely's
1160 portrait and moved its ears
1161 whenever rolls of thunder banged
1162 in the valley.

1163 Norah observed the beast
1164 with sympathy and told it,
1165 "Poor dear! Did the nasty rain
1166 wash all the scent away? Stuke,
1167 maybe it's thirsty."

1168 "The hell I care," said Stuke-
1169 ly, lighting a cigarette.

1170 "My dear boy," his father in-
1171 toned, "as this is primarily—
1172 and secondarily—all my fault,
1173 don't be so miserable. . . . Grace,
1174 darling, please don't scream so
1175 loudly!"

1176 "Gavin," said Mrs. Kent, "I
1177 simply abominate lightning!
1178 And Joe's door is shut. Stuke,
1179 is he really fond of chicken
1180 broth? You're so much more
1181 observant than the rest of us.
1182 I must ask the doctor about soup
1183 when he comes back this eve-
1184 ning."

1185 "Mother," Norah assured her,
1186 "his digestion is not affected at
1187 all. He's had three cups of
1188 coffee and four pieces of toast.
1189 Being hit on the head with a
1190 horseshoe doesn't affect the
1191 stomach. I think Rudy was too
1192 frightfully clever to jam a pail
1193 over his head afterward. But I
1194 don't understand what he want-

1195 ed with that sheet. It's not a
1196 good one. Joe uses it on his cot
1197 on hot nights. . . . Precious angel
1198 bunny," she told the baby, "go
1199 bite the niceums bloodhound.
1200 Rudy improves the more you
1201 hear of him. He sells cocaine
1202 to kids in schools. He knocks
1203 people's eyes out and if Joe
1204 wasn't indestructible, of course
1205 he'd have fractured his skull."

1206 Mrs. Kent screamed with re-
1207 straint, picking up Junior from
1208 beside the bloodhound's tail, and
1209 gaspingly said, "No, baby! I
1210 must say that I think you were
1211 all a little idiotic last night. You
1212 find a terrible creature in the
1213 house and——"

1214 "My dear Grace," said the
1215 Reverend Gavin Kent, dusting
1216 ash from his black coat, "I was
1217 the idiot. The children looked
1218 to me for an attitude. I chose to
1219 turn this person loose. If I had
1220 known that he sold cocaine to
1221 people, of course—— There's
1222 the telephone."

1223 Several neighbors leaked in
1224 through the open door and gazed
1225 at Stukely picking up the tele-
1226 phone. A brisk person remarked
1227 that he was the central office in
1228 New York City, and then de-
1229 manded Mr. J. Fanchetti.

1230 "If you mean Joseph Fan-
1231 cher," Stukely growled, "he was
1232 knocked on the head with a
1233 horseshoe this morning and he's
1234 ill in bed."

1235 "Yeh," said the telephone,
1236 "him. We got a call from your

331

1237 chief of police up there about
1238 this thing. This man Klung
1239 he speaks of——"
1240 "Kling," said Stukely, in bit-
1241 terness.
1242 "Yeh, this man Klieg is de-
1243 scribed as very small, kind of,
1244 with dark hair an' eyes. Kind
1245 of a round face. Age about
1246 twenty-three or four."
1247 Stukely yawned, "That's cor-
1248 rect. Yes?"
1249 "Well," the telephone said,
1250 "he's wanted for assault. It's in
1251 yest'day's papers. This lady he
1252 'saulted is able to describe him
1253 this mornin'. She's come to.
1254 He married her under the name
1255 of Thomas Edwards in Boston
1256 last week. Only she says he's
1257 got R. J. K. tattooed on his right
1258 arm. He'll have two em'rald
1259 rings set in platinum, and——"
1260 "Set in what?"
1261 "Platinum," the telephone re-
1262 peated with an air of authority;
1263 "one gold lip stick with a rooby
1264 in the bottom of it. One dia-
1265 mond lavaleer——"
1266 "A what?"
1267 The telephone groaned; then
1268 asked: "Is there a lady there?"
1269 "Norah," Stukely urged,
1270 "come and listen to this—this
1271 stuff."
1272 Norah assumed the telephone
1273 and told it briskly, "Tell me all
1274 about it. Poor Stuke's so sleepy
1275 he can't stand up straight. . . .
1276 This is Mrs. Fancher. . . . No,
1277 not Franceshi. . . . Yes, with
1278 a horseshoe. . . . Kling, not

Klieg. . . . How characteristic 1279
of him!. . . Oh, no, we only met 1280
him last night. . . . He was hid- 1281
ing in the attic. Attic, the 1282
top of a house, you know. . . . 1283
Garret is the same thing. Yes, 1284
you're quite right. . . . Married 1285
her? Was she old and rather 1286
idiotic? . . . I thought so. 1287
Set in platinum? . . . Stuke, 1288
give me a pencil. . . . Diamond 1289
lavallière. . . . Real pearls or syn- 1290
thetic? . . . Yes, she'd naturally 1291
say they were real. . . . Yes, 1292
he's very well known around 1293
here. He sold cocaine. . . . Oh, 1294
five years ago!. . . No, his fam- 1295
ily moved to California. We're 1296
living in their house. We found 1297
him hiding in the attic at three 1298
this morning. . . . That's what 1299
the neighbors tell us. They 1300
found that he'd been selling co- 1301
caine to children in the schools 1302
here. His father ordered him 1303
out. . . . Oh, yes, the police tele- 1304
phoned everywhere. We have a 1305
bloodhound from Poughkeepsie, 1306
only it doesn't work. The rain, 1307
you know." She beamed over a 1308
shoulder at the bloodhound. 1309
"Yes, I can. He was wearing a 1310
dark blue suit, purple socks and 1311
a green tie. . . . Yes, green. . . . 1312
And is his wife going to recover? 1313
That's nice. . . . Yes. . . . Thanks, 1314
awf'ly. . . . Good-by." 1315
"What's all that?" Joe 1316
drawled from the green stair- 1317
case. He scowled as Mrs. Kent 1318
screamed, and said, "Mamma, 1319
don't! My head's like a tea- 1320

kettle awready. Yeh, babe gets his talent for yellin' offa you. I'm all melancholy and you leave me 'lone. What's that on the telephone, girl?" He sat down on the stairs abruptly and touched the cap of white bandage that hid his fair eyebrows with tremulous fingers. "Is Rudy gummed up down in New York?"

Norah fluttered her fresh gown up the green treads, saying gayly, "Yes, lamb. He married some imbecile hag in Boston and then robbed her and beat her a good deal on Friday. So the poor dear was trying to hide. . . . Come back to bed, you unutterable idiot!"

"Yeh, some dizzy dame marries this fella an' he bungs her frame. He's a nice man. Where's all our p'licemen we had here?"

"They're out looking for Rudy, Joe," said Stukely, yawned twice and finished: "In cars an' things. . . . Go back to bed, for heaven's sake!"

"Won't either!" Joe growled, getting his head on Norah's shoulder. He closed his eyes and drawled, "This fella sold dope, somebody was sayin'. . . . Aw right. And he was up in the attic makin' noises like a rat. I bet he's got him some dope hid out in the attic right now. Babe, you shinny up in the attic and look for dope. It'll do you good, bud. I'm so mis'rable I

want everybody to be unhappy too. Rev'rend, next time you wanta be all kinda magnanimious and let Rudy outa this house, you're gonna be surprised how nasty I'll act. I'll be mean and ungentlemanly."

"My dear boy," said the clergyman, "you won't—wouldn't be half as mean as I should."

"G'on, fella," Joe snorted; "it ain't in you! You ain't had any experience. Girl, unless you quit usin' sandalwood on your hair, I'll quit you cold an' marry a fat blonde. Babe, go look for dope in the attic. Nice an' hot up there an' you'll like it. Honey, get me back in bed. I'm a rooined woman."

Stukely trotted up the stairs, dragging Alphenius Puddy with him. Joe's weight seemed terrific as the long man sagged back on Stukely's shoulder and stumbled into the bland splendors of Norah's gilded Spanish bed. He recited absently:

"There, little pimple, don't y'cry!
Gonna be a sore boil by and by."

Norah urged, "Don't be so coarse, darling. You've no idea what words you used when the doctor was stitching your poor head."

"Yes, I have, female! I s'lected them careful 'cause poppa was in the room. Stuke knows I can do lots better'n that. . . . Alphenius, you worfless an'mal, go and help Stuke

1404 hunt dope in the attic. If you
1405 work hard, boy, an' keep at it
1406 steady, you'll be as bad as this
1407 Rudy when you're his age, even
1408 if your folks are Baptists."
1409   "Yes-sir," said Alphenius, in-
1410 vestigating Norah's dressing ta-
1411 ble. "What's cocaine look like?"
1412   "Toof powder," Joe moaned;
1413 "Toothbrush Fallon in my com-
1414 p'ny kep' his in a toof—tooth—
1415 teef-powder box, over in that
1416 war they had in France. He
1417 was extremely good for nothin'
1418 an' died grand, all full of cocaine,
1419 shootin' at trees. He was a
1420 tough kid outa Kentucky. They
1421 got a mon'ment to him in his
1422 home town where he was run
1423 out by the sheriff back in 1912.
1424 It's kinda sarcastic. The cap-
1425 tain was just gonna put him in
1426 arrest when the Dutch started
1427 firin'. She's an ill wind 'at
1428 don't blow somebody's dirty
1429 laundry down the creek. . . .
1430 Babe, go look in the attic. If
1431 Rudy Kling wasn't just hidin'
1432 out here, he came for somethin'.
1433 In his class of s'ciety dope's as
1434 good as cash. Me, walkin'
1435 ahead of this pinyap like I was
1436 ten years of age an' not too
1437 bright at that! I could expire
1438 of shame if my dome wasn't
1439 fallin' in on me. I told you
1440 those green p'jamas were bad
1441 luck, girl! Only you'll dec'rate
1442 or die. Get outa here, ace, an'
1443 snoop for snow in the attic."
1444   Stukely went dutifully into
1445 the spare bedroom, blinking at a

final flare of lightning through 144
the wet windows. His dazed 144
legs mounted the bed and he 144
raised his dirty hands to the 144
trapdoor. Then he stopped to 145
scratch an ear and wonder 145
whether cocaine was a durable 145
drug. He had never seen any. 145
Would it degenerate, stored in 145
an attic for five years? 145
  "I wonder if cocaine keeps?" 145
  "I dunno," said Alphenius, 145
industriously gathering a feather 145
from the vermilion floor. "Will 145
I go ask Doctor Kent, Stuke?" 146
  "You might just as well, Al- 146
phenius. Your assistance is 146
mostly spiritual anyhow," Stuke- 146
ly yawned; "you're an awf'ly 146
good witness for a dollar a day." 146
  "I know I am," the hired boy 146
assured him; "Joe says I encour- 146
age him a lot clippin' trees. I'll 146
go ask your father about the 146
cocaine." 147
  He politely closed the door. 147
Stukely pondered the value of 147
sarcasm as applied to the adol- 147
escent mind and then paused to 147
yawn some more. He would 147
gratify Joe by a cursory look 147
around the attic and then he 147
would sleep. He would sleep im- 147
mensely, probably for the rest 147
of the day. If Alphenius came 148
to tell him that the cows needed 148
milking or that chickens had 148
died of lightning, why, Alphenius 148
might be slapped on a prominent 148
ear. He lifted his arms to the 148
sides of the trapdoor and mutely 148
stared into the white face with 148

its black eyelashes fluttering. Rudy Kling looked down at him silently and licked his lips twice. A wave of thunder passed above the house and one feather from the stored pillows came fluttering out of the black attic past the tiny man's head.

"Oh, I see," said Stukely; "yeh—yes! You banged Joe an' then you ran around behind the house an' climbed up the tank onto the roof. Yes, nobody ever thought of that, of course!"

"Aw, keep your shirt on, kiddy! Let's talk business, pal," Mr. Kling murmured; "don't get excited, either. . . . Who's downstairs?"

"About half the men in the county," Stukely whispered.

"All right. Now," the pretty man said rapidly, "when it gets dark get a car—you got one, ain't you?—get a car up the north fence by the bunch of poplars. I'll be on the roof. Toot the horn oncet. I'll get down an' you drive me inta C'necticut. Two hundred to you when we get there, pal, and I'll tell you where's there's easy a couple of hundred dollars of snow in the house here. Be a gentleman and——"

"Are you crazy?" the boy asked after a gulp.

The white face stooped down a little farther. Mr. Kling said in his whining whisper, "No, I've been in an' out of this house five times since you guys have been livin' here! You never lock up right. I could have swiped your silver an' your sister's kid any time without wakin' up a soul. I had near a hundred ounces of coke hid here when my old man kicked me out. I still got nine or ten. You can sell it to a feller over in Brooklyn. Sands Street. I forget the number. Now have the car up the north fence, pal, about eight o'clock."

"What did you want with Joe's sheet?" Stukely inquired.

"To lie on, pal! Gee," said Mr. Kling morosely, "you guys don't ever clean this garret! I'm all over feathers! And the trap in the roof leaks too! If you was real farmers, you'd look after things better. . . . Now, kiddy, don't get excited and tell anybody I'm up here, 'cause it'll be hell in the papers if I'm caught in this dump, see?"

He licked his lips again. Stukely yawned. He was not asleep. This was real and interesting, but he drowsed with his hard fingers on the edges of the trap and wearily wondered what the tiny rogue meant.

"You're a lot of swells out of New York, pal."

"I don't know," said Stukely; "Uncle George is awf'ly rich— mother's brother. Father had Saint Philip's Church until he retired, and, of course, we know a lot of smart people. But——"

"Stuff a gun with it," Mr.

1572 Kling commanded; "you're
1573 swells. Your sister's named
1574 Norah and she's married to that
1575 yella-headed devil that talks like
1576 a nigger. Get me in front of a
1577 judge an' I'm an old friend of the
1578 lady. Picked her up at a dance
1579 parlor in the city years back. I
1580 phoned the lady I'm in trouble.
1581 She leaves the door open for me,
1582 see? . . . See? . . . See?"

1583 Stukely said, "Yes, I see.
1584 That's awf'ly interesting."

1585 "All right. And I'm good-
1586 lookin'. Tell me nobody'd be-
1587 lieve it and I'll tell you they
1588 will, pal! It'll be all over the
1589 papers. . . . What d'you say?
1590 It's a gentleman's offer. Two
1591 hundred——well, I'll make it
1592 two hundred and fifty to run me
1593 into C'necticut. And I'll tell
1594 you where the dust is. All you
1595 need is a chisel and ——"

1596 "And suppose you just bang
1597 me on the head when we're up
1598 the road a couple of miles an'
1599 then drive into Canada, h'm?"
1600 Stukely asked.

1601 "Aw, pal, I ain't even got a
1602 gun with me!"

1603 "Careless of you. . . . Excuse
1604 me," Stukely said after a yawn,
1605 "but why should I trust you?
1606 They want you in New York
1607 for——"

1608 "What the hell d'you think
1609 I'm doing here? Playin' pin-
1610 ochle? I ran for this place.
1611 You got me. What's the good
1612 in turnin' me over, pal? You
1613 won't make a cent, see? This

1614 way you'll be in three or four
1615 hundred at the very least," Mr.
1616 Kling insisted, "and——"

1617 "And if I go down and tell
1618 them you're here," Stukely
1619 broke in, "you'll be cad enough
1620 to lie about my sister?"

1621 "Pal," said Mr. Kling, brush-
1622 ing a feather from his ear, "don't
1623 talk any of that morality on me!
1624 I'm a cad and all that hooey.
1625 All right; only I'm not goin' to
1626 jail another stretch. You guys
1627 are gentlemen. If you want your
1628 sister in the papers for bein' in
1629 love with a——"

1630 Stukely slapped him over the
1631 mouth and got his hands in the
1632 man's drooping coat miraculous-
1633 ly at the same time. The light
1634 body came down from the ceiling
1635 on him in a remarkable limp-
1636 ness, then changed to a tangle of
1637 fighting muscles as the bedstead
1638 cracked and collapsed. A suffo-
1639 cating shower of dust and feath-
1640 ers followed Rudy Kling's tum-
1641 ble and his infantile suitcase
1642 smacked on Stukely's head, then
1643 rattled on the red floor, spilling
1644 two fat pears and a pair of horn-
1645 rimmed spectacles as the fall
1646 jarred it open. Stukely saw this
1647 revelation over the man's shoul-
1648 der. He seemed to be waltzing
1649 with Mr. Kling on the gray mat-
1650 tress, over bedposts and incon-
1651 venient pillows.

1652 Alphenius Puddy opened the
1653 door and stood civilly gaping
1654 with a slab of chocolate cake in
1655 his hand.

"Call yourself a gentleman!"

"Oh, don't be so damn silly!" said Stukely. "Alphenius, go and call——"

Alphenius turned into the hallway and said timidly, "Oh, Mis' Fancher! Oh, Jo-oe! Hey, Stuke's fightin' a fella up here!"

Mr. Kling stumbled, or Stukely stumbled. There was an indeterminate clatter and a whirling movement that left Stukely sprawling on the tiny man in a corner by the windows. He was embarrassed by Mr. Kling's size. Eventually it seemed best to sit on him, although a constant writhing made the matter uncomfortable, and it was supremely irritating that a number of men who came in sat on their heels and watched Stukely sit on the noisy body. Alphenius Puddy got up on the dresser of blue enamel and ate some cake.

His large father said, "Well, we got him," in an utterly fatuous tone of complacency, as though he had attended to all this.

"Well, do something about it, please!"

A hairy long youth from the orchard second on the left up on the north road practically suggested, "Otto, you take his legs. Sam, you catch his arm. Keep away, Doctor Kent! Hey, Rudy, quit, will ye? Be a gentleman! Hold his head on the floor, Stuke! Aw, Rudy, behave!"

Stukely tried to drag his hand from the teeth set in its side and woke fully in the pain. The tiny man was biting his hand, biting it violently too!

The boy said, "Stop that! Stop it or I'll hurt you! Say, stop it!" while he wondered whether he should hammer the mad black eyes with his free fist. No, he was too big. Wouldn't be fair. Ouch! He said "Oh, stop it!" and then something bright descended with a thump on the flushed face inclosing his hand. The teeth parted. Stukely got up in a cloud of blue shirts and stared incredulously at his mother holding a silver-backed hairbrush in both hands.

"Good heavens, Grace!" said the Reverend Gavin Kent, lifting his yellow spectacles.

"Gavin," Mrs. Kent panted, "I do not care! Will some of you please take this person out of our house? H-he has absolutely no manners!"

"Grace," the old gentleman intoned, "the poor creature is crazy with fear. Get up, young man. Nobody will hurt you."

Alphenius Puddy, on the dresser, said to someone in the hallway, "Mrs. Kent, she soaked him on the nose. He was bitin' Stuke."

"If he doesn't behave himself," Mrs. Kent cried, gripping her weapon, "I shall certainly hit him again!" She screamed a little and added, "And I hope that his nose is broken! Norah,

1740 you must see after this that your
1741 father does not leave the front
1742 door open again. It's entirely
1743 your fault, Gavin! I'm sorry to
1744 seem disagreeable, but you must
1745 be careful about locking up. You
1746 see what happens!" She lifted
1747 her lavender apron with its
1748 futile pockets and jammed its
1749 hem into her mouth, repressing
1750 a shriek, then took it out and
1751 said, "I shall be hysterical unless
1752 someone takes this man away."
1753 Rudy Kling rose from the
1754 vermilion floor with a hand on
1755 his nose and gazed at Mrs. Kent
1756 in silence.
1757 After a moment he gabbled,
1758 "Yeh! It's that lady—it's your
1759 daughter left the door open for
1760 me. I and——"
1761 "How can you have the im-
1762 pudence to say that? Gavin,
1763 he's trying to make a scandal!
1764 It's like that horrible man who
1765 was caught at the Milliman's
1766 house in Lenox and said that
1767 their governess had let him in.
1768 How dare you?" said Mrs. Kent,
1769 tightening her slim fingers on the
1770 hairbrush. "If you say that
1771 again I shall hit you! Norah,
1772 please be serious!"
1773 "Mother," Norah gurgled
1774 through her fingers, "I—I can't
1775 be! . . . Please, take him away.
1776 . . . I—he—it——"

1777 Stukely sat down on the
1778 wrecked bed in a murmur of
1779 voices and studied a crescent of
1780 blue marks on his hand. He had
1781 a sense of something incredibly
1782 wonderful, a performance in a
1783 dream. Yes, he had seen his
1784 mother, the daughter of a bishop,
1785 hit a man in purple socks on the
1786 nose with a hairbrush. The
1787 room cleared on some order from
1788 Joe Fancher in the hallway.
1789 Everything was gone, and in the
1790 vacancy Joe drawled feebly,
1791 "Mamma, I've never said any-
1792 thing of you but that you're a
1793 gentleman. Yeh, and it takes a
1794 lady to be that. No common
1795 sorta female can! It's more'n
1796 most men can manage, at that!"
1797 "Good heavens," said Mrs.
1798 Kent, "this terrible creature was
1799 simply gnawing Stuke! And the
1800 poor boy wouldn't hit him be-
1801 cause he was so little, or one of
1802 those idiotic reasons that men
1803 have for things, and somebody
1804 had to do something, and if
1805 you dare to tell me, Gavin, that
1806 it wasn't ladylike, I shall
1807 scream!"
1808 "My dear," the Reverend
1809 Gavin Kent said violently, "I
1810 never admired you so much in
1811 all my life!"
1812 Mrs. Kent screamed.

THE ANALYSIS

Gentility has a total length of 1812 lines. Of these 1629 are
occupied by the Beginning, only 23 by the Decisive Act, and 161

by the Sequel. The Ending, you will remember, includes both the Decisive Act and the Sequel. The story of Decision resembles the story of Accomplishment in this respect.

A glance at the chart will show that this story is presented entirely in interchanges with the single exception of lines 1011 to 1088 which show the reflections of Stukely upon the interchanges that have just passed. Attention is instantly concentrated upon the central character, Stukely, and it then shows how he reacts to the Scene which is contributed to by the whole Kent family, from lines 1 to 578. Lines 579 to 620, which are an interchange between Joe Fancher and the burglar, Rudy Kling, follow immediately after Stukely has become aware that there is a burglar in the attic. This interchange between Joe and the burglar occupies lines 579 to 620. Lines 621 to 844 are again an interchange between Rudy and the Kent family. The fifth step of the lines 845 to 951, is the comment of the Kents upon Rudy's statement, and includes the interchange between Nora and the Reverend Gavin Kent. Following this is the interchange between Hester and the Reverend Gavin as a result of which Stukely's reflections are presented. All these interchanges are made to contain the probability of conflict or clash, and to show the dangerousness inherent in the apparently innocuous burglar. The interchanges between Stukely and Alphenius, lines 1088 to 1117, between Stukely and Joe Fancher, lines 1118 to 1148, are also intended to make this same feeling of danger and disaster apparent. The fifth step is the effect upon the Kent family in lines 1149 to 1226. The interchange between Stukely and the central office, the interchange between Nora and the central office, again lead to the comments of the Kent family on lines 1316 to 1443. Then the interchange between Stukely and Alphemius presents to Stukely a moment of danger into which he enters bravely. After this the interchange on lines 1471 to 1629, between Stukely and Rudy Kling, set forth very definitely the main narrative problem of the story which shows that Stukely has to choose between accepting a bribe in order to keep his sister from scandal, or to preserve the gentility of the Kent family, which is the same thing, and the other course of turning Rudy over to the police. Accepting a bribe would preserve the gentility which he appears to value so highly, and turning Rudy over to the police will involve conflict with a man who has shown that he is a dangerous opponent.

The Decisive Act is contained in lines 1630 to 1651. The Sequel is contained in lines 1652 to 1812, which show that Mrs. Kent whom he considered the acme of gentility, is the one person who, in this rough and tumble scrap, does exactly the right thing, a thing which he would have hesitated to do and which he would not in the slightest degree have connected with his mother.

I have reprinted this story because it is such a clear example of the story of Decision told chronologically without any attempt whatsoever at flash-back, dependent entirely for its interest upon the interchanges. The main narrative problem is not apparent until lines 1471 to 1629. All the material preceding that has to stand upon its own feet, and a reader of this story will do well to realize that there is no hope for a person trying to write a story of Decision until he is able to write interchanges which are in themselves interesting. As in the previous stories the narrative question is one of choice. The narrative question can always be phrased, in the Decision story, "What course will the main character adopt confronted by various choices, or by two choices at least?"

It is obvious that the Beginning, therefore, must be concerned with making clear to the reader these choices that lie before the main actor. Because this story does this so well I am sure that it will repay analysis by writers interested in writing the story of Decision.

THE HAUNTED LADY

BEGINNING	Main condition is shown as placing Main Actor in a dilemma.	Gretchen Innes and Burke. Flash-back. Interchange Maurice Greer and police. 284–521 (5th step 522–584) Gretchen tells of being with Greer at time of murder.	Reader learns of the difficulty, struggle, and probable Disaster which any choice is likely to cause.

1– 907

BODY	Mental struggle.	Fifth step of preceding interchange shows mental struggle between two desires in Gretchen.	Choices each have something to commend them.

908– 980

ENDING

Decisive Act.

Interchange. Gretchen and District Attorney. Choice made. 981–1048

Answer to Narrative Question is: "She will make public avowal."

Sequel.

Interchange. Barney and others. 1049–1148

Interchange. Barney and Burke Innes. 1149–1167

Interchange. Gretchen and Abbie. 1168–1237

Interchange. Gretchen and Burke. 1238–1344

5th step. Comment of Observers. 1345–1366

Interchange. Gretchen and Burke. 1367–1442 Significance.

THE HAUNTED LADY

BY ADELA ROGERS ST. JOHN

In compiling this volume I have tried, wherever possible, to include companion stories; because such stories are extremely illuminating.

Sunk and *Paradise Island* are companion stories in that the main narrative purpose of each is the same.

Sunk and *Jetsam* are companion stories in that their Conclusive Acts are the same.

The most interesting parallelism in the volume, however, is that between *The Haunted Lady* by Adela Rogers St. John, and *The Trouble with Men* by Lucian Carey.

That parallelism, alone, would have been sufficient justification to include in this volume *The Haunted Lady;* but I have another reason for including it, which is that it is an excellent example of a story of Decision which achieves its length not so much from the Beginning as from the Ending; and particularly from that portion of its Ending which in our nomenclature we refer to as the Sequel—that portion which follows the Decisive or Conclusive Act.

CASE No. 14

THE HAUNTED LADY

BY ADELA ROGERS ST. JOHN

1 The man looked up, startled
2 by the muffled crash of glass
3 shattering upon the exquisite
4 blendings of a Bokhara prayer-
5 rug. It was a very small crash,
6 yet it echoed in the warm
7 intimacy of that charming, book-
8 lined room. It spoke so in-
9 evitably of some shameful, vi-
10 olent, secret thing—some un-
11 heard-of, shameful thing that
12 had no right to be there.

13 The man's eyes—fine, clear,
14 gray eyes that were just a little
15 stern—rested upon his wife for
16 a moment, and then went back
17 to the pages of his book. He
18 simply could not sit and stare
19 at her, because she had obviously
20 forgotten him and it couldn't
21 be fair to violate her privacy
22 like that.

23 But, though he was no longer
24 looking at her as she sat there,
25 taut as a wire that has been
26 stretched and stretched little by
27 little to the breaking-point, he
28 could still see her. His eyes
29 could not strike through the
30 memory of her face to the

31 printed words that he tried to
32 find—her face that was so small
33 and sweet and secret. And he
34 could still see that gallant
35 struggle of hers to keep her firm
36 tight mouth from twitching,
37 and the way her bright color
38 lost ground and wavered to a
39 moon pallor along her high
40 cheek-bones.

41 The glass had fallen from her
42 hand upon the Bokhara rug—
43 a rug they had once chosen to-
44 gether in their happy rambles
45 about the world. And it was
46 plain that it had fallen because
47 the hand trembled so it could
48 no longer hold it.

49 She was not reading. Lately,
50 she had ceased to read on these
51 evenings when they stayed home
52 together. Instead, she sat quite
53 still in a big velvet chair that
54 was her favorite, her dark blue
55 eyes fixed half angrily upon
56 some phantom in the fire. When
57 his eyes glimpsed her in the brief
58 space of turning a page, it
59 seemed to him that her jaw,
60 always too sharp and powerful

345

for beauty, was etched raw against the darkness. For when her own reading-lamp was off, her corner of the room lay in shadow.

And yet, she used always to read. In those days, if she put down her book, it was to caress and maul the great Dane, who always lay as close to her small feet as he could get, in the hope that she would remember his existence and vouchsafe him a word or two. Or to come and sit upon the arm of Burke's leather chair and indulge in one of her whirlwinds of talk—colorful, pungent, witty talk, full of a bright malice and a gay sophistication. But usually he had to take her book away from her, when the fire had quite died down and he himself was the victim of one prodigious yawn after another.

But now—these silences in the dusk of the lampless corner. This broken glass.

And on the nights when they did not stay at home together—Gretchen, who had always been so aloof, so easily bored, so impersonal; Gretchen, who had disdained so much and so many; Gretchen, of whom lesser people were wont to say: "Personally, I do think that young Mrs. Burke Innes is an awful snob. She does think herself grand, doesn't she?"

But young Mrs. Burke Innes didn't think herself grand, nor was she a snob, though she had some slight justification for being socially a little exclusive; after all, she had been Gretchen Hunt-Douglass, and Burke Innes's money, which allowed him to spend his life in the pursuit of sport upon the tennis-court and the polo field, was at least three generations old. It was only that Gretchen looked upon the multitude with a clear, cool gaze and too often found them wanting in everything worth while. A self-sufficient woman, Gretchen Innes.

But now—this sparkling, incessant talk, almost gushing, with people she had been wont to forget existed. Almost as though she were bidding for favor, for popularity. This surrender of her cool, aloof disdain. This broken glass.

But he went on reading or trying to read, pretending to read. It was part of his code—and men who had met him in the heat and danger of a polo game or in the strain and high tension of a championship tennis match declared that Burke Innes was the finest sportsman in America—it was part of his code that a man must never interfere with another man's game. Even more particularly a woman's, and that woman his wife, whom he loved.

Suddenly she said: "Burke!"

The great Dane got up, rigid, his eyes fastened upon her. But

346

she put him down with a firm little hand on his swelling neck.

The man laid down his book with a smile. He was almost good-looking when he smiled. The sweetness of it softened the stern lines of his tanned, lean, sharp face. The gray eyes lifted under the line of black brows that met above his nose and that, without a smile, made him look a little fierce.

"Yes, my darling?" he said.

"I can't stand it any longer," said Gretchen, and she pushed back the lion-cub mop of hair from her forehead.

At the tone of her voice, the man opposite, who loved her better than all the world, felt his heart turn over within him. For as a rule Gretchen had the most charming of voices, low and crisp, with a thousand dainty lights and shades.

He had first fallen in love with her voice, that day almost ten years ago when she had come out on the tennis-courts just as he had finished a hard set. He had heard her voice before he saw her, and it had struck deep into his heart, telling him that the woman with such a voice might possess all those things he had been seeking in a woman. Now, tonight, her voice was raw and panic-stricken and it broke because the breath back of it failed. But that was not what made Burke's heart quail and almost stop beating. It was the shame and guilt with which the voice was laden.

He didn't say anything. He could not look at her. To see Gretchen's eyes—those dark blue eyes that were so full of pride, so secret of inner thoughts. To see shame upon that brave, imperious mouth.

"I can't stand another night of it," she said swiftly, as though she wanted to be rid of them, those shameful words. "I can't. I shall go mad. I sit here—I sit here—night after night, thinking about it, strangling with it. I go to bed and lie there, suffocating, haunted with it. I am haunted. I tell you, I shall go mad."

Burke Innes got up and stood half turned from her. There was something inflexible about him—something inflexible besides his lean, hard strength. A man of honor, a man of principle, a sportsman playing life's game according to a rigid code. In no way did he betray his thoughts, his feelings.

The voice went on passionately. "I should have told you then. But I couldn't. I thought it would kill me to tell you. I think I was living in a mist. And, Burke, though I know you love me and I love you, I do not always know what you will think. Besides, I didn't want the decision to rest upon your shoulders. I couldn't—couldn't

228 bear to hurt you. I thought
229 you need never know."
230 Burke Innes made a swift
231 gesture of appeal. His iron
232 control wavered just that much.
233 The menace of this unknown
234 shame and guilt that weighted
235 his wife's voice, the menace
236 which he now realized had been
237 hovering above him for weeks,
238 months, had approached near
239 and become a monstrous night-
240 mare. If she would only give a
241 name to this horror. But he
242 would not ask her. It was fair
243 that she should be allowed to tell
244 him whatever she had to tell in
245 her own way.
246 "Do you know where Maurice
247 Greer was between twelve and
248 four the night his wife was
249 murdered? Do you know? Do
250 you want to know?"
251 He turned then and looked
252 full at her. Amazement had sent
253 him white beneath the heavy
254 tan. Amazement. Nothing more
255 yet. Just sheer, incredulous
256 amazement.
257 Gretchen Innes had risen and
258 stood facing him. Her face was
259 working, but her voice sounded
260 angry.
261 "He was here—with me."
262 The great Dane growled, deep
263 in his throat, whimpered, began
264 to whine dismally. Gretchen
265 touched him with the toe of her
266 silver slipper and he was quiet.
267 The man and woman stood
268 looking at each other. Maurice
269 Greer. For an instant the man

270 flashed before Burke Innes.
271 That smooth, fair Greek head,
272 with a touch of the faun about
273 it, and the dark, smiling eyes,
274 the wistful mouth. And the face
275 of the wife who had been murder-
276 ed, with its unwholesome ugly
277 beauty, its heavy eyelids, its half
278 open, painted lips.
279 In the still room, the man
280 whose wife had said to him:
281 "He was here—with me," tried
282 slowly, painfully, to understand
283 just what those words meant.
284 At four o'clock on a certain
285 night in June now almost a year
286 ago, Maurice Greer had tele-
287 phoned to the police station.
288 They had gone to the Greer
289 bungalow in Montecito which
290 the police knew well because, in
291 spite of the tangled grounds that
292 surrounded it, neighbors had
293 sometimes phoned to protest
294 against the hilarity and jazz
295 which disturbed their slumbers.
296 It was a glorified bungalow,
297 set well back from the highway
298 rambling about among the live
299 oaks and the yuccas and the
300 stiff little palms, and on the long,
301 uncovered veranda they found
302 Maurice Greer, walking up and
303 down, up and down.
304 Even as the car swung into
305 the drive, they saw him make
306 a swift turn and walk back,
307 and turn again swiftly and
308 walk, as though something
309 drove him close.
310 He was hatless, and his blond
311 hair was as smoothly groomed as

348

though he were just starting for some exclusive little dinner party. His dinner clothes were immaculate and worn as only Maurice Greer could wear them. He was smoking a cigaret, with all the ease and nonchalance for which he was famous.

But for all that, he looked, in the half light from the porch lamps, haggard and desperate.

Inside, they found Veronica Greer.

"I—haven't touched anything," said Maurice Greer, in a desperate, nonchalant voice.

They had seen her often enough——handsome, black-haired Veronica Greer. Some of them had even known her before she was Veronica Greer, when she was little Veronica Talamantes, last of a distinguished old Spanish family, beautiful with that ripe, luscious beauty of the Spanish-Californian, noted already in her teens for her escapades and indiscretions. Already a little cold-shouldered, there where her fathers had once ruled as kings over hundreds of thousands of acres.

But on that June night she lay quite still, her black hair, that was her greatest beauty and that she still wore long flung about her like some lace mantilla such as her grandmothers might have worn.

She had been shot through the heart and probably had never known that her swift, passionate, reckless young life was ending.

There was a gun—a gun that Maurice Greer explained he always kept in the house. The bungalow was distant from its nearest neighbors. He was away a great deal in the evening. His wife was nervous.

Followed, inexorably, those awful days after the tragedy, which for sheer horror and ugliness and humiliation always so far surpass the tragedy itself.

The coroner had fixed the hour of Mrs. Greer's death as sometime between two and three in the morning. The servants, whose quarters were some distance from the house, had heard voices sometime after midnight. They did not know exactly what time. Hilarious voices. Then angry voices. They didn't recognize the voices. They didn't pay any attention, because there were often voices in the bungalow. Also they had heard vaguely a sound which might have been a shot, but which they took for an automobile exhaust on the highway. Mrs. Greer had had a guest for dinner, but he had left duly by the front door and his hat and coat had been presented to him by the Japanese houseman. The guest was fortunately able to account for his movements from that time on. The servants knew nothing of any-

396 one who had come after his
397 departure.

398 Mr. Greer had not been at
399 home for dinner. They did not
400 know what time he had returned.
401 He was driving his own car.

402 Maurice Greer said that he
403 had telephoned the moment he
404 came home, and the telephone
405 at the police station had rung at
406 exactly ten minutes after four.
407 He had left the Samarkand,
408 where he had been playing
409 bridge with some Easterners
410 who lived there, at a little after
411 eleven. He had disappeared,
412 swiftly, in the big black car.
413 At four o'clock he had tele-
414 phoned the police station.

415 Five hours.

416 The thing had torn Santa
417 Barbara wide open.

418 No one believed—at least no
419 one who knew them—that
420 Maurice Greer had shot Ve-
421 ronica. If he had been going
422 to shoot her, he would have
423 done it years before. There had
424 been cause enough.

425 In fact why Maurice Greer,
426 who might have married almost
427 anyone, had ever married Veron-
428 ica Talamantes, no one in Santa
429 Barbara had ever quite under-
430 stood. It was even rumored
431 that he might have married the
432 famous heiress, Janet Grant.
433 Janet herself knew that no-
434 thing but the fact that he had
435 never asked her had kept him
436 from it. He was that kind of a
437 man—a throw-back to all that

438 was romantic, all that was
439 poetical, able somehow to melt
440 the hearts of women with that
441 tender, wistful, unscrupulous
442 smile of his.

443 And with all that, he had
444 suddenly married Veronica Tala-
445 mantes, whom lesser men had
446 never taken the trouble to
447 marry.

448 The truth was that he had
449 loved her. And he had married
450 her, as she knew, because being
451 what he was himself, Maurice
452 Greer could not find it in some
453 secret, chivalrous corner of his
454 heart to judge or condemn any
455 woman. One night Veronica
456 Talamantes had spoken broken-
457 ly, bitterly, of the odds that life
458 had stacked against her. And
459 that strange chivalry in Mau-
460 rice that made him every wo-
461 man's champion, except against
462 himself, sent him to his knees be-
463 fore this girl whom all the world
464 condemned, this bedraggled, bit-
465 ter damsel in distress.

466 But it was not long before
467 he knew himself tricked and
468 cheated.

469 There were people in Santa
470 Barbara who said that Veronica
471 could not help herself, that her
472 heritage of bad blood was too
473 much for her. And they, of
474 course, were not surprised when
475 they heard how she had been
476 found that June dawn, in the
477 cluttered, perfumed room.

478 But that Maurice, after six
479 years of playing the game as

Veronica played it, after six years of taking his fun where he found it while she did the same, should suddenly have shot his tawdry, unfaithful, unloved wife —that was too silly. Everyone said so. Everyone except the police.

They merely said, very politely: "Of course, Mr. Greer there won't be any trouble about your telling us exactly where you were between eleven and four that night."

Maurice Greer laughed. "Our old friend the alibi, eh?" he said, his eyebrows making a very sophisticated but rather pathetic question mark in his forehead.

"If you don't mind," said the district attorney—it had been taken over by the district attorney by that time— "I should like to know especially about the hours between two and four. It was after two that Mrs. Greer was shot."

"An alibi," said Maurice Greer, musingly. "I should have thought of that. I dare say there are a number of people who would have lied for me. Good society melodrama, this. I understand society melodrama's very popular in the movies just now." He lighted a cigaret and made the other man a little bow. He was always a bit of an actor. "I'm sorry, my dear sir; I have no alibi."

And that was that.

"Of course," said Mrs. William Wosley Grant when she heard of it: "it's all perfectly ridiculous. I've read of such things, but I certainly never thought one would happen to us. He was with some woman. Anyone can see that. Evidently with some woman he had no business to be with. Maurice always found that kind the most interesting. But it's silly of him not to tell now. As if a woman who would receive Maurice Greer, with his reputation, between two and four in the morning, deserved any protection. At least I hope she'll have the decency to own up."

But she did not own up.

Of course at first there seemed no real necessity. Maurice Greer wouldn't be convicted. Everyone was sure of that. Possibly that was why he was convicted.

Maurice Greer was convicted and sentenced to spend the rest of his life behind the walls of San Quentin, instead of in the pursuits of pleasure which had hitherto occupied him. Even then, the woman did not own up.

"The thing I hate most," said Mrs. Grant vindictively on the afternoon when she had allowed her well-known weakness for Maurice to influence her to the extent of permitting Janet to go and say good-by to him, "is thinking that Veronica may

563 know of all this and be laughing
564 at us. The little beast."

565 Janet Grant, heiress to all the
566 Grant millions and the social
567 prestige that went with them,
568 only continued to look out the
569 window, her homely, freckled
570 little face pinched. At last she
571 said: "I wonder who the woman
572 is."

573 The world—the whole news-
574 paper-reading world—also
575 wondered. For seven days.
576 Then it forgot.

577 Only Janet Grant wondered
578 about the women who wait at
579 prison gates. Would a man be
580 glad to see even the wrong
581 woman then, if she had proved
582 herself? Janet did not forget.
583 And one other woman could
584 not.

585 And so Burke and Gretchen
586 Innes stood face to face in the
587 warm intimacy of their firelit
588 library—Burke and Gretchen
589 Innes, whom everyone knew to
590 be the happiest of married
591 couples: Burke, with his rigid,
592 old-fashioned code of honor and
593 conduct, his standard of clean
594 sportsmanship; and Gretchen his
595 wife, whose name was like a star
596 among the Japanese lanterns of
597 the women of her set.

598 Between them lay those five
599 words, "He was here—with me."

600 So, having remembered all
601 those things which it was neces-
602 sary for him to remember, Burke
603 Innes thrust his hands deep into
604 the pockets of his gray house-

605 coat and said very quietly to his
606 wife: "Then he was here when
607 his wife was shot. Where"—he
608 was fighting hard to keep his
609 voice level and steady, that it
610 might remind him that he was a
611 gentleman and not a savage—
612 "where was I?"

613 "Don't you remember? You'd
614 gone to Los Angeles to play in
615 the tournament for the state
616 championship."

617 "Oh, yes. And while I was
618 away—Maurice Greer came
619 here——"

620 Gretchen set her jaw, look-
621 ing at him angrily, miserably.
622 Words were so hard for
623 Gretchen. She hated words.
624 They were so inadequate. Why,
625 they had been married for years
626 before she ever found the aban-
627 don to say to Burke the million
628 love thoughts—wild, gorgeous
629 love thoughts—that all the time
630 had seethed in her heart and
631 head for him.

632 And besides, it had been their
633 way, a secretly mutual, secretly
634 understood way, to avoid talk
635 of serious things. Now she must
636 attempt to throw a bridge of
637 words across the hell that
638 yawned between them, and she
639 felt it to be a flimsy, treacherous
640 thing that would cast her head-
641 long into the depths.

642 Finally she said, "Burke, per-
643 haps I could make you under-
644 stand——" Her voice died, of
645 hopelessness and agony and
646 shame.

647 Those dark brows of Burke
648 Innes's drew down heavily
649 over his eyes. "I didn't know
650 you and Maurice Greer were
651 friends."

652 "We weren't. Of course we
653 weren't. How silly——"

654 "Then——"

655 He waited for her. Gave her
656 every chance. Would not con-
657 demn her unheard. Would not
658 hurry her. But something of
659 what that waiting cost him
660 wrote itself in the sharp lines
661 that carved themselves from
662 his nostrils to his lips.

663 Gretchen flung across the
664 room because she could not
665 stand there before him, even
666 though his eyes were upon the
667 Bokhara rug at his feet.

668 How like Gretchen to pretend,
669 now, to be angry. She had
670 pretended, so, to be angry when
671 the birth pangs tore her, and
672 angrier still when death hovered
673 so very close above her small,
674 disordered head. It was self-
675 d e f e n s e , t h a t a n g e r of
676 Gretchen's.

677 He wondered, in deepest
678 misery, what had betrayed them
679 into this horrible place.

680 Maurice Greer—of all men.
681 The sort of man they called a
682 sheik. All Burke's young, clean
683 manhood revolted from the
684 thing. Why, he was probably
685 soft all over from lack of exer-
686 cise. It would be easy to take
687 him in one hand and break him
688 in two.

689 He dragged his mind back
690 from that flaming desire. For
691 Maurice Greer was in prison.
692 He had gone to prison because
693 some woman did not speak when
694 he might not.

695 "I can never make you under-
696 stand," said Gretchen's voice,
697 harshly despairing. She sat on
698 the arm of the chair, one silver
699 toe moving back and forth across
700 the body of the great Dane.
701 "I'm such a fool at talking. And
702 nobody can explain the unex-
703 plainable. But I'll try. For
704 God's sake, listen—listen.

705 "They plead temporary in-
706 sanity as a defense for murder,
707 don't they? Well, there are
708 other things that ought to have
709 temporary insanity as a de-
710 fense, too. They ought, they
711 ought.

712 "Years ago, before I knew you,
713 Maurice and I were—oh, no-
714 thing. Only, one night at a
715 dance he kissed me. That's
716 all. And I liked it and so did
717 he. He was the only man before
718 you that ever made me *feel*—
719 I think, Burke, he was the only
720 man who ever kissed me. I
721 wasn't a girl who let men kiss
722 me——"

723 The little appeal choked her,
724 but she stiffened herself again.

725 "Well, when Maurice kissed
726 me it thrilled me so that I was
727 afraid—because it was new, and
728 I did not like him. I did not.
729 I went home and lay awake all
730 night, remembering it and not

731 liking him. But whenever I
732 saw him, my breath always
733 stopped and I felt that dizzy
734 little thrill, and I knew he
735 could move me, terribly. I
736 think he must have known it,
737 too.

738 "But then—you came. And
739 you were my love and my man,
740 and I had been created for you
741 and I had been waiting for you
742 always, and you loved me, and
743 my real life began then.

744 "But when you have kissed
745 a man like that, it's an un-
746 finished thing. It's like a snake
747 lying in a shell waiting to hatch.
748 You forget it, but it lies there.
749 When we met there was always
750 just a little something between
751 us—a little secret understanding.
752 I know it now.

753 "And on that night I had been
754 sitting for hours under the
755 pomegranate trees. You know,
756 Burke, how heavenly it can be
757 down there? I could see the
758 moon on the water, a silver
759 mantle of romance. And the
760 garden was so sweet.

761 "The rest—is harder to tell,
762 Burke. Harder. But I had
763 been reading some silly poetry,
764 and some sillier sophisticated
765 stories. And there came to me
766 a foolish, foolish thought such
767 as women have sometimes. I
768 wondered if I had missed part of
769 the glory of life and love because
770 I hadn't had—many loves. I
771 wondered if I had been listen-
772 ing all the time to one melody,

773 when there were many melodies
774 if only a woman cared to open
775 her ears to them. I felt—this
776 was my greatest sin, darling—I
777 felt as if our love were dull
778 and domestic and drab because
779 it was safe and sane and right-
780 eous. And it seemed to me
781 that all the romance in the
782 world was dead and I would
783 never know it again. And that
784 made my heart ache with the
785 queerest, saddest ache I had
786 ever known. It was all be-
787 cause of that silly poem I had
788 been reading about a woman
789 of—many loves.

790 "I don't think I had been
791 dozing—just dreaming. Any-
792 way, when I saw it all again, the
793 world didn't seem real at all.
794 It was a world crying for
795 romance—crying.

796 "He saw me sitting there and
797 he stopped his car by the wall
798 below the pomegranate trees.
799 He jumped the wall and came
800 in. I remember he didn't wear
801 any hat and his hair was smooth
802 and glistening in the moonlight.
803 He looked so young and hand-
804 some and fair—not as though
805 he could possibly be evil. He
806 kissed my hand, there in the
807 garden."

808 Again Burke had to listen to
809 the death of that hot, breaking,
810 shameful voice.

811 "Cheap. Cheap and common
812 and shameful it was. But,
813 Burke, I forgot I was a married
814 woman. I even forgot you. I

354

even forgot"—but that name she could not name in this one story—"I just remembered that old, unfinished kiss and I was a silly girl again.

"I cannot explain to you about Maurice. No woman could explain Maurice to a man. Only there is something that stirs your pulses, and swamps you in a fire of tenderness. And——"

The poor, worn voice whispered now, the shameful secret of it all.

"And, Burke, maybe women have a beast within, just as men have. Only he is more tightly chained and there is less chance for him to break forth and wreak havoc—havoc. But because women do not know he is there, when he does clamor, they have less defense, because they do not know.

"When he kissed me again——

"I must have been mad. I tell you I must have been mad. Don't you see? I am not cheap. I am not common. I am not untrustworthy. My whole life says I am not. Am I then to be judged by one moment of madness?

"And then I hated him. I hated him. I hate him now. I could kill him. When a man has been drunk and finds some low woman beside him, doesn't he hate her and hate himself, and want to kill her and himself?

"Because that is the way I felt about Maurice, when he left me.

"I had my name to think of, my son, you—and I hated him. I hope he rots in a prison cell. But I wish he would not haunt me so—in prison. In prison. I thought at least you would never have to know. But he has made me tell you—by haunting me."

The broken glass cried out beneath her restless feet.

"Then you and he didn't agree about this—silence?" said Burke.

His voice was cold. His face was severe enough now, his lean, dark face that could be so forbidding in spite of its youth.

And she saw accusation in his eyes.

Gretchen went scarlet, painfully, horribly. Shame was upon her, enveloping her. Shame was in the aching breath he saw her draw, in the hands that twisted and untwisted.

"I never saw him again," she cried at him. "I hope I will never see him again. I can see in your face that you—can't forgive me, but I tell you——" She stopped.

Quietly he said: "I'll have to think this thing out, Gretchen. I want you to think it out. We must see what we can do about it. I must go away, until we can think this thing out."

She started toward him. The pain in his dark face. The suffering in his gray eyes. And she could not comfort him.

900 The door closed behind him,
901 not loudly, but with a horrible
902 finality.

903 Gretchen staggered.

904 "He's—gone" she said to the
905 great Dane, who rose and came
906 close to her, pressing himself
907 against her knees to console her.

908 Above the wind that shook
909 the tree tops she heard the car
910 purr away—away.

911 But all the time, strangely,
912 the mist seemed to be clearing
913 from her brain. Well, this was
914 the end—the end of everything.
915 She had told him. That was
916 necessary. And now he had
917 gone away, and there had been
918 accusation in his eyes.

919 But she was no longer
920 haunted. Not as she had been.
921 Only for the first time, now,
922 she began to think of Maurice
923 Greer without that murderous
924 film of scarlet hatred.

925 He had not told. He had
926 taken a life sentence in prison
927 rather than tell. It must be
928 terrible to be shut up in prison,
929 to face the long years of life
930 from behind those steel bars.

931 And she had shut him there.

932 The old arguments filed past
933 her. But she knew them now
934 for what they had always been
935 —part of her hatred, part of her
936 revenge.

937 "Oh God, what a rotter I've
938 been!" she cried to the silent
939 night.

940 Then a new fear walked in, to
941 keep her ghastly company.

942 If she told now! Perhaps,
943 after a while, Burke might for-
944 give her. Perhaps time might
945 soften that judgment that had
946 looked out of his eyes. He had
947 loved her greatly. Perhaps some
948 day he might forgive her, as
949 other men had forgiven their
950 wives, and they might wipe
951 out the past and be happy as
952 they had been.

953 But if she cried her shame to
954 the world, she made that impos-
955 sible. If she dragged that proud
956 name of his into the gutter, if
957 she took upon herself this
958 scandal that had rocked the
959 whole nation, she would shut
960 herself from him forever.

961 He could never forgive the
962 woman whom the world would
963 know as Maurice Greer's alibi.

964 And still that inner conviction
965 grew and grew.

966 She shuddered away from the
967 coldnesses, the insults, most of
968 all from the fellowship, the
969 equality of cheap women whom
970 she had loathed and who would
971 welcome her now as one of
972 themselves, whether she would
973 or no.

974 But none of these things
975 mattered, now that the mist
976 was gone. Clear-cut as a gallows
977 against the sun, the things that
978 she must do stood forth. Only
979 when it was done could her soul
980 know peace with itself.

981 The district attorney of Santa
982 Barbara County was a little
983 surprised the next morning when

a slightly flustered stenographer came in to tell him that Mrs. Burke Innes wanted to see him at once. He told the stenographer to show her in and was almost instantly aware of a lady standing in the doorway.

A very arrogant, imperial lady, in a short white skirt with an indefinable distinction about it, and a woolly orange sweater, buttoned up high about her throat, and an impudent orange hat, pulled far down over her right eye.

But for all her perfection of grooming, all her smart arrogance, the district attorney somehow got the impression that this lady had not slept, had certainly not closed those dark blue, angry eyes all night long. And he felt that the scarlet bow of her mouth had been painted on over gray lips.

"I want to tell you something," she said in a cold, crisp voice.

Now the district attorney had heard many astounding confessions in that unpretentious office. As a rule, he spurred men and women on to those confessions. That was his business.

But looking at this haughty orange and white lady, with the impudent orange hat pulled down over her right eye, he felt a desire, an imperative desire, to keep her from speaking. He did not want to hear what she had to say. He had never felt like that before.

"Maurice Greer," said the lady—and now the scarlet bow of her lips was plainly painted like a scarlet letter upon her white face—"Maurice Greer was with me on the night his wife was murdered. He was with me from midnight until four o'clock. He was with me between two and three, when she was killed. He did not kill her. Will you be kind enough to make out the necessary papers or—or whatever is correct legally, and I will do whatever it is essential for me to do."

She looked, this orange and white lady, with that impudent orange hat pulled so rakishly over her right eye, like a woman who knows that she has just signed her own death warrant.

The group of men lounging in the club dressing-rooms turned at the sound of the shrill whistle and the horrified "My God!" that followed it. There were five or six men in the dressing-rooms. It was noon of the day of the finals in the men's singles.

Big Jim Turner was there, looking at the comic section of the morning paper and giving forth riotous guffaws like a fourteen-year-old schoolboy. With him were the Renny brothers, slim and a little shy, their mild blue eyes and straw hair indicating nothing of their demon swiftness and accuracy upon

1067 the tennis-courts; and wizened,
1068 dried-up little Phil Dellivan, be-
1069 ginning to go bald, but still a
1070 wizard in the art of the un-
1071 expected.

1072 With Burke Innes, they were
1073 the ranking tennis stars of the
1074 State—a state, moreover, that
1075 had produced some tennis
1076 champions.

1077 Burke Innes had been there
1078 himself only a moment before,
1079 long and lean and dark and
1080 dangerous—the personification
1081 of the best in American athletes.
1082 He always looked younger, too,
1083 in his tennis clothes, and almost
1084 handsome, because of his fine
1085 shoulders and slender waist.

1086 The large fat man who had
1087 whistled came forward. In his
1088 hands he held a futuristic after-
1089 noon extra, bright pink paper
1090 from which black and green
1091 headlines screamed.

1092 "I say," he gasped, "this is
1093 terrible!"

1094 The youngest Renny brother
1095 was looking over his shoulder
1096 and his face had gone pale.
1097 Even Jim Turner, upon whom
1098 things dawned slowly off the
1099 tennis-court, had finally been
1100 jarred into nervousness.

1101 "What is it?" he said.

1102 "Burke Innes's wife," said
1103 Barney. "I wouldn't have be-
1104 lieved it. This is terrible!"

1105 "You said that once already,"
1106 said Little Phil. "Is she dead?"

1107 "No. Worse. Much worse."

1108 He read it, wheezing with
excitement between paragraphs. 1109
There was a little comprehend- 1110
ing, shamefaced pause when he 1111
finished. 1112

"Where's Burke?" said Little 1113
Phil. 1114

"He was here just a minute 1115
ago," said Jim Turner. "I guess 1116
we better put off the matches." 1117

"He had a paper," said the 1118
older Renny brother. "I saw 1119
him take it from the boy. I 1120
didn't know——" 1121

"It wouldn't be fair for him to 1122
play today," said Jim Turner 1123
slowly. "Especially the finals. 1124
Gosh, it must have taken a lot 1125
of nerve for a woman to do that. 1126
To walk right up and tell on 1127
herself." 1128

"What else could she do, for 1129
God's sake?" said Little Phil. 1130
"Let a guy spend the rest of his 1131
life in jail for something he 1132
didn't do?" 1133

"I wonder what we'd better 1134
do about the matches," said 1135
Barney, perspiring freely; "this 1136
is terrible. The biggest crowd 1137
we've ever had, too. Mrs. 1138
Grant's here already—giving a 1139
luncheon. And I tell you, this 1140
will be just like throwing a 1141
bombshell. The Burke Inneses 1142
of all people. She was always so 1143
strict, too. Now Maurice will 1144
be out, and I wonder if he'll 1145
marry Janet Grant. I suppose 1146
everybody'll make a hero out of 1147
him." 1148

At exactly that moment Burke 1149
Innes strolled in. He had the 1150

afternoon paper in his hand. His face was set like a mask, but his eyes were alight, unreadable but brilliant.

"Great crowd we've got, Barney," he said in his level, steady voice; and then to Jim Turner, "And I'm going to beat you this afternoon if it takes a leg." And he smiled.

"Then," said Barney, wiping his forehead, "we aren't going to call the matches off?"

Burke Innes looked at him coldly.

"Why," he asked, "should you call the matches off?"

Gretchen Innes folded a black and gold kimono and laid it carefully in the shining black leather suitcase. Then she folded one of the chiffon nightgowns that Abbie had laid out so carefully on the bed. She was just smoothing it absently when Abbie came in.

As she came in, Abbie said, "That was Mr. Innes on the phone, Miss Gretchen."

Gretchen's hand turned to stone.

"Yes?" she said, and she felt that the beating of her heart must shake her voice.

"He said it wasn't necessary for him to speak to you," said Abbie in a matter-of-fact way. "He just wants you to come right on over to the Country Club as soon as you can. He said to be sure to come, because he's playing Jim Turner in the finals this afternoon and he wants you there."

"Is that all he said?"

Abbie laid a little pile of silk and lace on the floor. "You need some more of those brassieres, Miss Gretchen," she said, "but I guess these'll do till you get home. Oh, he said tell you be sure to come. Not to let anything interfere." Then, as her mistress did not stir, "Here's your hat," said Abbie. "You haven't got time to change. Anyway, that looks all right for a tennis match."

Mrs. Burke Innes pulled the orange sport hat far down over her right eye and tucked the unruly lion-cub mop under it, so that only the edges of it showed.

"My gloves, Abbie," said Mrs. Burke Innes, and her voice had the desperate determination of a woman who has pulled herself up to it by her boot straps— "my gloves."

She drew them on, angrily controlling the hands that would have trembled.

"My bag," said Mrs. Burke Innes, and Abbie thought she had never seen anything so defiant and yet so frightened as the way Mrs. Innes swung the bizarre trifle over her wrist.

"Will you be in for dinner, Miss Gretchen?" asked Abbie.

"I don't know, Abbie," said Mrs. Burke Innes. "Oh—I don't know."

But to herself she was saying,

1235 over and over, "Has he seen the
1236 papers? Oh God, has he seen
1237 the papers?"

1238 The Country Club stands
1239 were packed so that not an inch
1240 of boards showed between the
1241 smart sport skirts and the
1242 smarter white flannels and tweed
1243 golf trousers. Everybody who
1244 was anybody, whether they
1245 knew anything about tennis or
1246 not, had come to the tourna-
1247 ment.

1248 As Barney had predicted the
1249 afternoon paper had exploded in
1250 Santa Barbara and Montecito
1251 like a bombshell. Every now
1252 and then between games, that
1253 rushing, sibilant roar, like the
1254 hissing of many serpents, swept
1255 the fashionable throng.

1256 That Burke Innes should play
1257 had seemed the crowning sur-
1258 prise of the day that had
1259 witnessed the biggest shock they
1260 had ever known.

1261 "That's Burke Innes's idea of
1262 good sportsmanship," said Mrs.
1263 Grant with a sniff. "I might
1264 have known that. I hope he
1265 realizes that Maurice Greer was
1266 something of a sport himself."

1267 But when, just in the pause
1268 between sets—Jim Turner had
1269 won the first set and Burke
1270 Innes by magnificent service
1271 and sheer, blinding speed had
1272 captured the second one—when
1273 a lady came across the strip of
1274 lawn from the clubhouse and
1275 entered her box alone, the whole
1276 stands were literally flabber-

1277 gasted, literally struck dumb for
1278 the space of an entire minute.

1279 They watched her in be-
1280 wildered silence, this arrogant
1281 orange and white lady, who
1282 flung her white coat so non-
1283 chalantly over a chair and
1284 settled herself so unconcernedly
1285 in another. Her sharp little
1286 chin was held very high, and she
1287 did not seem to see the hundreds
1288 of faces that stared at her—
1289 stared and stared.

1290 They could not see, of course,
1291 how her heart-beats were ac-
1292 tually shaking her whole body,
1293 or how each breath cost her such
1294 a struggle that she believed she
1295 could never, never take another.

1296 They could only watch her
1297 haughtiness and her indifference,
1298 and then the silence broke in a
1299 gasp, and the gasp was followed
1300 by that hissing, rushing sound
1301 as of many waters.

1302 Gretchen did not see them.
1303 She knew they were there, like
1304 horrible creatures in a night-
1305 mare. But she was really con-
1306 scious of only one thing—the
1307 lean, dark, hard figure on the
1308 tennis-courts in the sun.

1309 Had he seen the paper?

1310 "Well," said Mrs. Grant, rub-
1311 bing her nose in a way that was
1312 characteristic but hardly aristo-
1313 cratic, "I didn't think she'd
1314 dare."

1315 "Why not?" said Janet Grant
1316 bitterly. "I'd be glad to be able
1317 to do what she's done."

1318 The match ended.

And then Burke Innes did one of those things that a Burke Innes never does. One of those theatrical, dashing things that might have been done—oh, by a Maurice Greer, for instance. But, being Burke Innes, he did it well, so boldly and impressively that everyone in the grand stands held their breath.

For he came off the court where he had played so brilliantly, and went straight to his wife and bowed gallantly above her little white and orange glove. Being the victor, it had almost the air of a knight coming to receive the reward of conquest.

And he said, loud enough so that many people about could hear and thus repeat later: "If I won, my dear, it's only because I wanted to pay tribute to the standard of gameness and good sportsmanship that you have set me today?"

"Ah," said Mrs. Grant, when some excited bystander had carried the speech to her box, where she still lingered, "that is very clever. He is trying to becloud the issue. He means to stand by her and make us like it. That's all very fine, but I shan't do it. I think Maurice is quite the most heroic of them all, and I shan't do it."

"Well," said her daughter, with the first defiance of twenty-five years, "I shall."

And so it happened that Janet Grant slipped her arm through Gretchen's, and they walked, laughing and talking very brightly indeed, the length of that inquisitorial grand stand, with Burke Innes strolling beside them.

In the car Gretchen said explosively, "You did that so wonderfully, Burke! But—what about just you and me?"

Her husband smiled at her. "You're funny, Gretchen," he said.

"Maybe," said Gretchen, "but—does that mean, Burke, that you've forgiven me?"

"It looks rather like it, doesn't it?" said Burke Innes, very busy piloting the big roadster out of the grounds through the crowds of expensive automobiles.

"Then you've—seen the papers?"

"Of course."

"And you forgive me in spite of my telling the district attorney——"

"In spite of your telling the district attorney!" said Burke Innes, turning utterly astonished gray eyes upon her. "Good God, Gretchen, did you think I could ever have forgiven you if you hadn't done that?"

"You mean—you wouldn't have forgiven me if I hadn't proved Maurice's alibi?" she gasped at him.

"There was never anything else to forgive," said Burke Innes. "I can't talk a lot of rot, you know. But no man is

1403 capable of judging the tempta-
1404 tions and defeats and victories
1405 of a woman's soul, Gretchen.
1406 And—women are so much better
1407 than we are. I wasn't so dumb
1408 I didn't understand your tempo-
1409 rary insanity defense, Gretchen.
1410 Every man could understand
1411 that if he didn't hang on to his
1412 man-pride too tight. I felt sorry.
1413 But—men and women aren't
1414 different, they're just human
1415 beings. I tried to do as I know
1416 you would have done if I'd—
1417 made that mistake. I shall
1418 always be sorry, but I knew
1419 every word you said was true,
1420 and that you had loved me—
1421 and only me—always.
1422   "But of course I could never

1423 have forgiven you for that—
1424 missing alibi. That was why I
1425 left last night. Because of
1426 course that was just a matter of
1427 clean sportsmanship."
1428   "Burke," said Gretchen and
1429 he knew that she was weeping
1430 at last, "I do think you're a
1431 funny man."
1432   The car swung around the
1433 curve and into a shadow cast by
1434 the low-hanging oak trees. The
1435 man leaned down and crushed
1436 her very close to him, so that her
1437 small, weeping face was hidden
1438 on his shoulder.
1439   "And I do think," he said,
1440 "that you're a very game wo-
1441 man, Gretchen, and the best
1442 sport I know."

THE ANALYSIS

The Haunted Lady occupies altogether 1442 lines. Of these lines 1 to 907 are the Beginning of the story. Lines 908 to 980 show a mental struggle which is the Body of the story. This mental struggle is in the mind of the character between two possible choices set forth in the Beginning. One choice is to refrain from telling the District Attorney in the hope that she may profit by retaining the love of her husband, who will forgive her after a while. The other is that she must adhere to a standard of conduct by telling the District Attorney and, as she thinks, thus sacrifice the possibility of her husband's forgiveness.

The Ending, containing the interchange which shows the Conclusive Act, together with the other interchanges which show the Sequel, occupies lines 981 to 1442. Lines 981 to 1048 contain the Conclusive or Decisive Act which shows the decision that she has arrived at—to tell the District Attorney.

Particularly interesting to the student of craftsmanship is the fact that the Ending occupies 462 lines of which 394 are Sequel; the Beginning occupies 907 lines, and the Body occupies 73 lines only. This is an interesting example showing that in the story of Decision the length can never come from the Body. It must come from either the Beginning or the Ending.

It is extremely interesting to notice that this story in its Beginning contains, on lines 284 to 521, a Flash-back interchange between Maurice Greer and the police, which is interpolated within the interchange between Gretchen Innes and Burke Innes, occupying lines 1 to 907. The fifth step of this Flash-back interchange is on lines 522 to 584, after which the interchange between Gretchen and Burke Innes is again taken up. In fact, it is almost impossible to write a story of Decision in which the Beginning occupies any length, without resorting to the flash-back method in some way. This is not a Flash-back in the typical sense because it does not come after the main problem has been made apparent to the audience. It is a Flash-back to avoid summary.

The interchange on lines 908 to 980 is a mental one between the two traits in the same character. This is a rather unusual thing to be included in the story of Decision. Ordinarily this is omitted.

The interchange between Gretchen and the District Attorney on lines 981 to 1048 is the interchange used by the author to show that the actor has come to a decision and has acted upon it. As in the other stories of Decision quite outstanding is the evidence that such a story depends entirely upon the capacity of the writer to present interchanges and to make people who are taking part in those interchanges seem like actual human beings. The story of Decision depends for its success upon characterization; and characterization is merely the portrayal of definite traits of character in action as the actors respond to various stimuli. Particularly interesting are the first 22 lines of the story because they show just how a competent author is enabled by a knowledge of craftsmanship to set at once before the reader a character trait. She causes Burke Innes to respond to the stimulus, which is the crash of the glass, by looking up, but she causes him to withdraw his eyes because his basic character trait is that he is sportsmanlike, and it would not be fair to violate the privacy of his wife. This character trait, planted at the Beginning of the story, gives an authenticity to the significance of the story which is presented in the Sequel.

In discussing the composition of the Concord Hymn, President Emeritus Charles W. Eliot of Harvard spoke of the action therein described and its "infinite reverberations." In this story the Decisive or Conclusive Act, by which the main actor answers the main narrative question of the story has "infinite reverberations," and the story is not finished until these "infinite reverberations" have been made clear to the reader. There are more people involved than the main actor; and furthermore, no story is really ended until all the questions, either of narrative or other curiosity, raised in the Beginning or Body of the story have been answered. In this way the story varies from the scenes within the story. In the Scene ordinarily only one conflict is foreshadowed, and only one problem is presented to the reader. Only one possibility of disaster is apparent, only one minor narrative question is raised. At the end of that scene this minor narrative question is answered. In the main story, however, many questions are raised in the reader's mind. They may be answered one by one through the scenes in the Body of the story. That is the ordinary way. In this case, however, they must be answered in the Ending of the story, because the Body of the story does not present such an opportunity to the writer. There is virtually no Body to this story.

The question that arises at once in the mind of the aspiring author at this point is, "How can I keep such meetings or interchanges interesting enough to hold the reader when I am denied the use of suspense which usually comes with clash with an opposing force, which makes up the Body of the story of Accomplishment?"

The author of *The Haunted Lady* answers this query of the aspiring author by showing that while suspense *ordinarily* comes from clash, it is fundamentally concerned with the outcome of a meeting between two hostile forces, or forces regarded as hostile. The uncertainty as to this outcome keeps up the interest of the reader. This interest will be intensified in proportion as this hostility has been emphasized or this threat of disaster made apparent; but it will always be as it affects the main actor in the story.

Taking each group of forces in this story you will see that such hostility has been foreshadowed by the author in the consciousness of the main actor. The effect upon the main actor is the chief interest of the reader. This is kept in suspense. While the effect upon Burke Innes is that he goes on playing the game as always, Gretchen Innes does not know whether or not he has heard the news of the confession. Upon this depends the outcome of the story from the point of view of Gretchen. On lines 861 to 963 the author makes clear to the reader that Gretchen believes that Burke "could never forgive the woman whom the world would know as Maurice Greer's alibi." On lines 522 to 538 the hostility of Mrs. William Woolsey Grant is evident when she says, "As if a woman who would receive Maurice Greer, with his reputation, between two and four in the morning deserves any protection." Thus there is added the promise of disaster to disaster already foreshadowed.

The episode with the maid is merely stage business, purely preparatory for the interchange with the group representing the "whole world," who would thereafter know Gretchen as "Maurice Greer's alibi." But throughout all these interchanges the uncertainty as to the outcome as it affects the main character's happiness is still in doubt. It is not until the final interchange between Gretchen and Burke Innes that the reader is made aware beyond question, as Gretchen is made aware also beyond question, that to a person of Burke Innes's standards of sportsmanship the very action by which Gretchen thinks she has ruined her whole life and her whole future happiness is in reality an action which guarantees that future happiness.

This story is an extremely valuable one for the person who is interested in writing stories of "character," who wants to show the reactions of actors under the stress of great emotional crises. It is unnecessary, of course, to reiterate that a story of decision must deal with a great emotional crisis in the life of an actor. This story illustrates that the Ending may be prolonged provided that there is suspense in the interchanges, or growing out of questions raised in the story; but this suspense must be a legitimate suspense and must have a definite bearing upon the main narrative problem of the story. For such readers this story will have an additional interest, however, because it is a companion story to the one which I am about to present to you, *The Trouble with Men*, by Lucian Carey.

ARCHITECTURAL CHART

OF

THE TROUBLE WITH MEN

		Condition stated by author, projecting interchange.	1–128	Unusual and interesting series of happenings project the necessity for a decision, which once made only proves to be the inception of a new and greater dilemma.
		Interchange. Philip Maple and Gertrude Woolcott.	129–288	
BEGINNING	Initial condition presented, together with the responses of Main Actor, which show that she realizes that condition forces her to make choice.	(5th step. Effect upon actors.)	289–306	
		Interchange. Gertrude and Frieda. Possible choice.	307–464	
		Interchange. Archie and Gertrude. Frieda observes.	465–515	
		(5th step.)	516–541	
		Interchange. Gertrude and John Powell.	542–656	
		Interchange. Gertrude and Archie.	657–721	
		Effect upon actors.	722–765	
		Interchange. Gertrude and Frieda. (Begun by phone, and continued in house.)	766–948	Choice presented.
ENDING	Conclusive Act.	Gertrude proceeds to admit guilt.	949–952	Choice made. Answer to Narrative Question is "She will admit guilt even though innocent, to preserve love."
	Sequel.	Archie and Gertrude. He has overheard.	953–981	Ironically, sacrifice is unnecessary.

THE TROUBLE WITH MEN

BY LUCIAN CAREY

I SHOULD not wish any reader of this volume to get the impression that the only reason for studying this story is that it is a companion story to *The Haunted Lady*.

The problem of craftsmanship confronting Mr. Carey was a very difficult one indeed. In order to reach his initial condition or basic problem of Decision he had to present to his readers all the series of events which were contained in the story by Mrs. St. John.

That he was able to do so without loss of interest is a high tribute to his craftsmanship. The story presents material for study which will be amply repaid.

CASE No. 15

THE TROUBLE WITH MEN

BY LUCIAN CARY

The Woolcotts lived in East Harwich, which is one of those Long Island places favored of actors, bankers, scenario writers and people who go in for tournament golf.

You couldn't call East Harwich a Bohemian community because Bohemians are people who live in attics and drink red ink in basements, whereas actors, bankers, scenario writers and people who go in for tournament golf live in country houses and drink a combination of grain alcohol, water and creosote labeled Scotch. You couldn't call it suburban because a suburb is a place from which all the able-bodied men depart on the 8:10 train, and almost nobody commuted from East Harwich. You couldn't call it a fashionable summer colony because people would think you didn't know about Southampton. East Harwich is just Long Island-after-the-War. Which means that it is the home of melodrama.

Archie Woolcott was one of those chaps who used to be described as a he-man, meaning a big, honest, sentimental fellow who is scared to death of women and has the same romantic notions about life at thirty-five that he had at fifteen. He had no doubts about what is right and what is wrong, or what is probable and what is improbable. If he had been born in the time of Richard the Lionhearted, he would have spent his life happily mounted on a draft horse and wearing a couple of hundred pounds of steel plate and chain mail. He was built to handle a mace, or the favorite medieval form of meat cleaver called a gisarme. As it was, Archie Woolcott went in for the only bone-breaking sport there is left. He rode to hounds and averaged a collar bone a season.

Gertrude Woolcott was the kind of clever woman who has sense enough to marry a man like that. She loved his size and strength. He wore so well that

369

air of masterful protectiveness that means so much to a woman so long as she runs the whole show. She loved his boyish helplessness. When some other woman teased him into kissing her he always imagined he was in a serious predicament and hurried home to tell Gertrude all about it and beg her to extricate him. But above all she loved his being so completely in love with her. He had had in the beginning a childlike trust in her, and this trust had grown with the years. It was deeply gratifying to be so needed.

For the rest, she had her children, her garden and her abiding interest in other people's troubles.

This summer the troubles had been those of the Maples. Philip Maple was an actor who always played the lover in polite comedies. He was handsome, agreeable, and he had a voice with a throb in it. When he made his entrance the round of applause was followed by a sound like that of a summer breeze blowing through a poplar tree. It was the sound of the people in the audience whispering to their neighbors that Philip Maple made love as effectively off the stage as he did on it and naming the lady for whom he was then exercising his gift. The mere list of conquests which were attributed to him by his audiences would have required a newspaper page to print. Only his most intimate friends knew the disillusioning truth, which was that there had never been other than one woman in his life and that woman his wife.

Jane Maple had been born to the theatre; for several seasons she had ruled there as the first of comediennes. But she had lost her place. She was a dipsomaniac who had ruined a first night once too often. And she refused to do anything about it. She would not take a cure; she would not consult a psychoanalyst; she would not brook interference with her desire for oblivion. Gertrude Woolcott had reluctantly decided that there was nothing to do about Jane. She would inevitably drink herself to death. The only question was whether Philip would survive the process.

Gertrude had been enjoying the luxury of a silent house of a night in late August. Archie had been spending the week in Virginia searching for a hunter up to his weight. He had wired that he was coming home the next day. The children and the servants were asleep. Gertrude was deep in a new and engrossing novel when the telephone beside her bed buzzed. She reached for the receiver without taking her eyes from the page.

"I'm sorry if I've waked you up," Philip Maple said, "but

145 I want awfully to see you."

146 Gertrude glanced at the little
147 clock on her table. It was a
148 minute before midnight.

149 "Where are you?" she asked.

150 "I'm at home—I could drive
151 over in fifteen minutes."

152 "Very well," Gertrude agreed.
153 "I'll meet you in the garden."

154 She allowed herself ten
155 minutes to finish the chapter
156 in her novel; dressed in five
157 minutes, and slipped out of a
158 French window into the garden
159 a moment before the lights of
160 Philip Maple's car swung into
161 the drive.

162 He got wearily out of the car.
163 Gertrude knew at once that
164 something quite devastating had
165 happened. They walked side
166 by side to the summerhouse at
167 the back of the garden. Philip
168 lit a cigarette. Gertrude re-
169 flected that it was a night for
170 something to happen—a hot
171 August night with no stars
172 visible, and the moon riding
173 high and pale in a misty halo,
174 and in the distance flashes of
175 heat lightning against the clouds.

176 "You know I've been in
177 Washington all week trying out
178 the new play," he said. "I got
179 home half an hour ago. The
180 house was in the most terrible
181 mess. I should guess that six
182 or seven people have been hold-
183 ing a drinking bout for days.
184 Empty whisky bottles on the
185 drawing-room mantel. Dirty
186 glasses beside every chair in the

library. The butler's pantry 187
full of dirty dishes. One room 188
after another turned upside 189
down. Every door, every 190
drawer open. Every rug and 191
coverlet and table top burned 192
where a cigarette stub had 193
dropped. I don't know whether 194
the servants left or if she fired 195
them." 196

Philip paused, his head in his 197
hands. "You see," he con- 198
tinued, "I haven't told you the 199
worst. I couldn't bear to. She's 200
been running around with the 201
lowest crew she could find on 202
Broadway—race-track touts and 203
bootleggers and dope fiends. 204
She's been trying morphine. 205
I've been afraid she'd be ar- 206
rested any night in—in some 207
raid." 208

Gertrude put her hand on his 209
bowed head. She wanted to 210
comfort him. And yet she felt 211
that he must at last face the 212
fact that his wife was a hopeless 213
dipsomaniac who ought to be 214
shut up in a sanitarium. 215

Philip threw up his head, and 216
in the pale light of a far-off 217
flicker of lightning Gertrude saw 218
that the tears were running down 219
his cheeks and his mouth was dis- 220
torted with pain. 221

"Why," he cried, "why does 222
she want to humiliate me so?" 223

"She doesn't want to humil- 224
iate you, Philip. She can't help 225
herself." 226

"Why can't she help herself? 227
What does it mean when a wo- 228

man as fine as Jane, a woman with nice instincts and delicate sensibilities, a trained artist, falls so low?"

Gertrude stroked his sleek head. She had no answer except the answer that Jane had gone insane.

"Why," Philip went on, "two years ago she was playing in 'Captain Brassbound's Conversion'—playing the part that Shaw wrote for Ellen Terry. And how she did play it! There isn't an actress living who could play the lady as she could. She just was that sort—a lovely creature, with grace and wit and manner. And now——"

"I know," Gertrude said. "I remember." What Philip said of her was true. The change in Jane was incredible.

"She's ruined herself," he cried bitterly, "and I don't care. I don't care what she does or what she is. Let her go to the devil. I don't care."

"But you do care, Philip," Gertrude said gently.

"I hate her," he said through shut teeth. "Oh, God, how I hate her!"

"You hate her because you still love her," pronounced Gertrude emphatically.

"What else can I do?"

"You can think of her and treat her as a person who is desperately ill—mentally ill. You can face the truth, and when you do face it you will no longer feel humiliated, and you will no longer hate, but you will quite simply and courageously do the thing that you have to do."

They talked about that endlessly. Gertrude went over and over the same ground with him, trying to make him see that he could no longer salve his pride by concealing the facts about Jane. She had to lead him back again and again to the idea of permitting Jane's condition to become public. It was four o'clock in the morning when he looked at his watch and apologized for keeping her so late.

Gertrude felt that she had won her case—that if Jane Maple had come home Philip would lock her in her room and look at once for a lawyer and a physician and begin the process of having her committed to a sanitarium. Meanwhile she was tired. Back in her own room she picked up her novel. But she could not read. She remembered that she had the next day a luncheon engagement in town with Frieda Remington. Frieda was her best friend. And Archie would be coming in on his way home from Virginia. Gertrude fell asleep. . . .

Gertrude entered the lobby of the St. Francis promptly at one o'clock, but for once Frieda's bright head was there before her.

"My dear," Frieda cried, and her face took on the deepest

concern, "you haven't heard."

"I haven't heard anything awful," Gertrude said.

Frieda put her hand on Gertrude's arm as if to steady her against a shock. Gertrude saw that Frieda had a hastily folded newspaper in the other hand.

"Jane Maple is dead."

"Wha-a-at!" Gertrude cried.

"Come," Frieda said, "let's get a table in a corner where we can talk."

"Suicide?" Gertrude asked.

"Apparently not," Frieda said. "Come—let's get a table."

"Let me see that paper."

"Wait till we've found a corner," Frieda insisted.

"Let me see that paper!"

Frieda reluctantly unfolded the newspaper. It was an early edition of one of the more lurid afternoon papers. Clear across the top in big black letters ran the headline:

Jane Maple Shot. Husband Held!

Gertrude skipped to the first paragraph of the story as they walked into the café of the St. Francis.

Philip Maple had telephoned the police of the East Harwich station at half past four in the morning to notify them that he had found his wife with a bullet through her heart. The police surgeon declared that Jane Maple had been dead for from three to four hours when he examined her body at five o'clock in the morning. Philip Maple said that he had been out of town; had returned shortly before midnight to find the house empty; had gone out again. When he got back after four o'clock in the morning he had found his wife dead. But when he was asked to tell where he had been between midnight and four o'clock he refused. The police had promptly arrested him.

Gertrude looked at Frieda.

"You don't think he shot Jane?"

"I can't believe it," Frieda said, and hesitated. "But," she concluded, "why won't he tell where he was?"

"Because he's a man and therefore a fool," Gertrude said sharply.

"You think he was with some other woman?"

Gertrude felt suddenly calm. Philip's refusal to tell where he was had made everything as difficult as possible. His impulse had been to shield her from scandal. He had made it certain that when the truth came out some people would think she had been having a love affair with him. But she was innocent. If she told the truth quite boldly and simply, no one who mattered would doubt her.

"I know he was with another woman, Frieda," she said. "He was with me."

Frieda's eyes got big and round.

397 "Heavens!" she said.

398 "He called me up about mid-
399 night and asked if he could come
400 over. I met him in the garden.
401 He was terribly upset because
402 Jane had been having a wild
403 booze party while he was in
404 Washington. I was trying to
405 make him see that he'd have to
406 get Jane committed to a sani-
407 tarium."

408 Frieda's eyes narrowed
409 thoughtfully.

410 "You know, Gertrude, I can't
411 help thinking that if you told
412 the whole story people would
413 believe you."

414 "I think they would," Ger-
415 trude said. "And what if they
416 did think I was guilty? As long
417 as Archie knew it was all right,
418 and the people I care about, I
419 could stand anything the news-
420 papers said."

421 Frieda impulsively reached
422 across the table and took Ger-
423 trude's hand in hers.

424 "Of course," she said, "no-
425 body who knows you would
426 doubt you. And"—she laughed
427 —"nobody who knows Philip
428 Maple doubts that he was com-
429 pletely wrapped up in his wife.
430 I don't suppose he ever talked
431 to another woman about any-
432 thing else."

433 Gertrude smiled back at
434 Frieda. It was a relief to put
435 the tragedy of the Maples out of
436 her mind for a moment and smile
437 at Philip Maple's reputation.

438 "No," she said, "I don't sup-
439 pose he ever did talk about any-
440 thing else. His only interest in
441 other women was in being patted
442 on the head a little while he
443 talked himself out about Jane.
444 Isn't it absurd that people
445 always pick out that sort of man
446 to make into a Don Juan?"

447 "It's partly because he's an
448 actor and plays the lover so
449 gracefully in the theatre," Frieda
450 said.

451 "I know. And men more
452 than women make that mistake
453 about him. Most men feel so
454 awkward about making love
455 that they take it for granted a
456 man who can do it gracefully
457 would make love to every wo-
458 man he saw. I shouldn't be
459 surprised if Archie thinks Philip
460 couldn't be trusted along
461 with——"

462 Frieda stopped Gertrude with
463 a gesture.

464 "Here comes Archie now."

465 Gertrude turned and saw her
466 tall, broad-shouldered, bronzed
467 husband threading his way be-
468 tween tables toward them. He
469 had a newspaper in his hand,
470 and he looked grim.

471 "Have you heard?" he asked
472 as he reached the table. "I
473 must say Maple is more of a man
474 than I ever thought he was.
475 He's a gentleman."

476 "What do you mean, Archie?"
477 Frieda asked.

478 Archie sat down and looked
479 pityingly at Frieda. "I mean
480 that he's in an awfully tight

481 place, and if he's willing to
482 stand the gaff rather than tell
483 on the lady I respect him—
484 which is more than I ever ex-
485 pected to do."

486 Gertrude and Frieda ex-
487 changed a significant glance.

488 "You take it for granted he
489 was with a lady?" Frieda asked.

490 "I take it for granted he was
491 with a lady," Archie said, with
492 irony.

493 "He might have been with a
494 lady quite innocently," Gertrude
495 said.

496 "From midnight until four in
497 the morning?" Archie asked.
498 "Not Philip Maple."

499 Again Gertrude and Frieda ex-
500 changed a glance.

501 "Of course," Archie went on,
502 "it is sort of up to the lady to
503 come forward." He interrupted
504 himself to order lunch for the
505 three of them. "Not," he con-
506 tinued when the waiter had
507 gone, "that I can blame her for
508 hesitating to ruin her reputa-
509 tion."

510 "I don't think her reputation
511 would necessarily be ruined,"
512 Gertrude said.

513 "Neither do I," Frieda added.

514 "A lot you women know about
515 life," said Archie.

516 For the first time in the ten
517 years of their marriage Gertrude
518 doubted her ability to manage
519 Archie. She felt herself up
520 against a conviction in him so
521 naïve, so spontaneously arrived
522 at, so unthinking that she could

523 not imagine herself arguing
524 against it successfully. And
525 when Frieda spoke again she
526 knew that the same thought
527 had been running in Frieda's
527 mind.

528 "It's possible," Frieda said,
529 "that Philip won't need the alibi.
530 After all, it will be possible to
531 show that he was fond of his wife,
532 and there is no evidence against
533 him."

534 When, late that afternoon,
535 Gertrude got a chance to talk to
536 Frieda she was forced to agree
537 that the only wise thing to do
538 was to wait. The legal process
539 would take weeks, perhaps
540 months. A good lawyer might
541 put off the trial until spring.

542 It was a sunny afternoon in
543 April when Gertrude Woolcott
544 went down to Broad Street to
545 see the great John Powell.

546 Gertrude looked at the man
547 who had devoted his life to
548 defending men accused of
549 murder. He had a magnificent
550 head, with large features, thick
551 white hair and the voice of a
552 man who has talked much in
553 public. He smiled and when he
554 smiled Gertrude trusted him.

555 "I've come to tell you that I
556 am the woman Philip Maple was
557 with the night his wife was
558 shot."

559 He gave her a slow, appraising
560 glance in which there was not the
561 slightest surprise.

563 "I suppose you knew," she
564 said.

565 "No," he said. "Philip has
566 never told me."

567 "I wish he had told in the first
568 place," Gertrude said. "It
569 would have made everything so
570 much easier."

571 "You mean you are willing to
572 testify in court?"

573 "Yes," said Gertrude, "I am."

574 "Have you thought what it
575 will mean to your reputation?"

576 "I am quite innocent," Ger-
577 trude said.

578 "Being thought innocent isn't
579 the same thing," John Powell
580 said. "The prosecuting attorney
581 is trying to make capital out of
582 this case, as prosecuting at-
583 torneys usually do. He will see
584 that your testimony has ruined
585 his case and he will turn on you
586 and do everything he can to
587 make you appear in a bad light.

588 Gertrude threw up her head.

589 "I'm willing to stand it—if
590 it's necessary," she said.

591 John Powell leaned back in
592 his chair and put the tips of his
593 fingers together and frowned
594 thoughtfully with half-shut eyes.

595 "It isn't—*necessary*," he said
596 suddenly.

597 "You mean he will be acquit-
598 ted, any way?"

599 "I think so. And if he should
600 be convicted I could get an
601 appeal on the strength of new
602 evidence and win the appeal."

603 "But suppose you do get him
604 off—what will people think?"

605 "People will think what they
606 always think when a man is tried

607 for murder—they will think a
608 clever lawyer got him off."

609 "Then I want to testify,"
610 Gertrude said.

611 "What sort of man is your
612 husband?" John Powell asked.

613 "He's a big, athletic man who
614 rides to hounds and trusts me
615 completely."

616 "Does he know?"

617 "Not yet."

618 "Will he still trust you when
619 you have testified in court?"

620 "I—I think so," Gertrude
621 said.

622 John Powell gave her a shrewd
623 look.

624 "It's important to you that he
625 should continue to trust you," he
626 said.

627 "Yes," Gertrude admitted
628 with a little involuntary catch
629 in her voice.

630 "I see it is," John Powell said.

631 "I love him," Gertrude said,
632 and tears came to her eyes in
633 spite of herself. "And—and—
634 he loves me."

635 "Is he a man of the world?"

636 "Not a bit," Gertrude said
637 and smiled. "He's a romantic
638 boy—a boy who has never
639 grown up—a he-man."

640 John Powell shook his head
641 slowly.

642 "I'm sorry," he said. "I'm
643 afraid he will doubt you. And
644 I feel it's only fair to warn you
645 of what you are getting in for.
646 Because, of course, I am going
647 to accept your offer. In the
648 interest of my client I've got to."

649 "Very well," Gertrude said,
650 and her voice trembled.

651 "I shall call you as a witness
652 to-morrow morning."

653 "To-morrow morning," echoed
654 Gertrude, and her heart sank.

655 John Powell nodded, and Ger-
656 trude went home to tell Archie.

657 There happened to be no
658 guests at dinner. But Gertrude
659 put off telling him. There hap-
660 pened to be no one in that even-
661 ing. But still Gertrude put off
662 telling him. They sat in the
663 library. She read a novel.
664 Archie was studying the pedi-
665 grees of several hunters. Every
666 five minutes she looked up at
667 him over her book and opened
668 her mouth to speak. And each
669 time her heart failed her.

670 At midnight she went and sat
671 on the arm of his chair and
672 stroked his hair.

673 "Archie," she said, "I've been
674 trying to tell you something for
675 months."

676 Archie leaned back and took
677 her free hand in his.

678 "What, old thing?" he asked.

679 "That I was the woman Philip
680 Maple was with the night Jane
681 was shot."

682 His face hardly changed its
683 expression, but she felt the
684 muscles in the hand that held
685 hers contract, felt his whole
686 body stiffen.

687 "He came to talk to me about
688 Jane and what he should do. It
689 was the most innocent thing in
690 the world. I was advising him,
691 trying to make him see that he
692 would have to put Jane in a
693 sanitarium. He was so upset.
694 We talked from midnight till
695 four in the morning."

696 Archie rose and paced up and
697 down the room, avoiding her
698 eyes.

699 "You will have to testify in
700 court," he said.

701 "I've already told John Powell
702 that I would testify. I saw him
703 this afternoon. I am going on
704 the stand to-morrow."

705 Archie walked back and forth.
706 Jane watched him breathlessly.
707 He paused. He came over to
708 her. He held out his hand. She
709 took his hand in hers. He wrung
710 her hand as if she were a man.

711 "I—I always knew you were
712 a gentleman, Gertrude," he said
713 huskily.

714 Gertrude burst into tears. He
715 didn't believe she was innocent.
716 He would never believe. He
717 would never say so, but he would
718 never believe. His trust in her
719 was gone. He could only praise
720 her for the masculine virtue of
721 taking the consequences.

722 The moments on the witness
723 stand did not prove as withering
724 as John Powell had predicted.
725 The district attorney did not
726 turn on her and try to make it
727 appear that she was a guilty
728 woman. Her testimony so thor-
729 oughly smashed his case that his
730 shoulders drooped in defeat. He
731 dismissed her after a superficial
732 cross-examination.

733 Gertrude drove home from the
734 court-room with Archie.

735 "I must say," he said, "I was
736 proud of you."

737 He did not smile. He did not
738 smile in the week that followed.
739 He made an attempt to treat
740 her as he always had and
741 succeeded in being courteous.
742 Gertrude could not name a single
743 difference in his manner or his
744 attitude. But the old, simple,
745 loving harmony was broken.

746 Gertrude could only weep.
747 She who had been so wise about
748 other people's troubles had no
749 answer to her own. There
750 seemed no way to penetrate
751 Archie's reserve. Frieda prom-
752 ised to talk to Archie if she got
753 half a chance. But Gertrude
754 could not imagine Archie's dis-
755 cussing the subject of their
756 relations with a third person.
757 His code forbade it. His idea
758 of what a gentleman should be
759 required him never to mention
760 his strong or intimate emotions.
761 Now, when he needed most to
762 talk, he withdrew even from
763 Gertrude. She came on him in
764 odd corners of the house sitting
765 staring into space.

766 Gertrude stood it for ten days.
767 And then one night Archie did
768 not come home. She lay in bed
769 beside her telephone listening.
770 He had never in ten years stayed
771 away without telling her in
772 advance where he was going.
773 The children and the servants
774 were long since asleep. The

775 house was very still, so still that
776 Gertrude felt she could hear a
777 mouse run across the floor if
778 there had been any mice. Twice
779 she got up and walked all
780 through the house to see if
781 Archie could have got back
782 without her hearing him.

783 She was trembling with
784 anxiety, with fear of she knew
785 not what, when she heard a car
786 drive in. She turned off the
787 light beside her bed and went to
788 the window and looked out. It
789 was Archie. Gertrude slipped
790 back into bed and waited. She
791 heard him come in; after ten
792 minutes he came upstairs; he was
793 moving about in his own room,
794 the room next hers. When the
795 sounds ceased and she guessed
796 that he had gone to bed Gertrude
797 turned on the lamp to look at
798 the little clock on her table. It
799 was four o'clock in the morn-
799 ing.

800 Where had he been? Gertrude
801 could not guess. She was still
802 making wild surmises when she
803 went to sleep.

804 Gertrude was awakened at
805 ten the next morning by the
806 buzzer of the telephone. It was
807 Frieda.

808 "Oh," Gertrude cried, "I must
809 see you."

810 "I'm coming right over,"
811 Frieda said, and something in
812 her voice heartened Gertrude.
813 It was a hint of laughter.

814 "What's happened, Frieda?"
815 she asked.

816 "I'll tell you when I see you,"
817 Frieda promised.

818 "Tell me now," Gertrude beg-
819 ged.

820 Frieda's answer was to hang
821 up the receiver.

822 Gertrude lay in bed listening
823 for Frieda's car, listening for any
824 sound that would indicate Archie
825 was awake in the next room,
826 listening for anything that would
827 break the tension of anxiety.

828 Frieda came running up the
829 stairs and burst into Gertrude's
830 room.

831 "Oh, my dear," she cried, "do
832 you know where your husband
833 was last night?"

834 "No," Gertrude said. "I only
835 know he didn't come in till four
836 o'clock this morning."

837 Frieda burst into laughter.

838 "Sh-h-h!" said Gertrude,
839 "you'll wake him up."

840 "He was with me, my dear.
841 And he talked! Oh, how he
842 talked."

843 "What did he say?" Gertrude
844 cried. "Tell me what he said."

845 Frieda's answer was to laugh.
846 Gertrude could have slapped her.

847 "I don't see what's funny,"
848 she said testily.

849 "I'm sorry, Gertrude. But it
850 it is funny. And it makes every-
851 thing simple. I know what you
852 must do, now. You see, he can
853 forgive you for having an affair
854 with Philip Maple. There's no
855 convincing him you didn't. But
856 he can somehow accept it. The
857 thing he can't forgive you for is

858 lying to him about it. He wants
859 to forgive you, but he can't."

860 "Do you suppose he still loves
861 me?" Gertrude asked.

862 "Of course he does, you little
863 idiot. He's crazy about you—
864 as he always was and always
865 will be. I told him he was a fool.
866 I told him I knew you were in-
867 nocent. And all he would say
868 was, 'It doesn't stand to rea-
869 son.' "

870 Gertrude burst into tears;
871 Gertrude wept until Frieda be-
872 came impatient and shook her.

873 "Come out of it, Gertrude,"
874 she said sharply. "Come out of
875 it and use your head."

876 "I have used my head,"
877 Gertrude cried. "I've thought
878 and thought and thought. And
879 there just isn't anything to do
880 with a fixed idea like that. He
881 just can't believe that a man
882 and a woman could be together
883 alone from midnight till four
884 o'clock in the morning in-
885 nocently."

886 "Oh, I don't know," Frieda
887 said. "I twitted him about it
888 last night. He talked to me
889 until a quarter to four."

890 Gertrude shook her head.

891 "I know," she said. "But
892 having the experience himself
893 won't convince him. He thinks
894 Philip Maple is different. He
895 thinks Philip Maple is simply
896 irresistible to women."

897 "Then let him think it,"
898 Frieda said.

899 "What?" Gertrude gasped.

"What on earth do you mean?"

"I mean take him at his word. He says the thing he can't forgive you is telling him you are innocent. Tell him you are guilty."

"Tell him I'm guilty!" Gertrude cried.

"Why not? He believes it, anyhow. Let him feel that you trust him enough to confess to him."

Gertrude tried to consider the idea seriously.

"Don't you see, Gertrude? It's one of the oldest situations in the world. I have read a dozen stories about it. The woman is always guilty. The chivalrous man practically admits her guilt by refusing to tell her name. He would rather be hanged for murder than give her away. And then when she is given away everybody is sure she is guilty. It's the tradition. It's the thing men believe— about other men. You can't fight it. Well, my answer is, don't fight it. Let them keep their romantic notions. Let them go on believing that a woman can't be with a man at an unconventional hour unless there's a guilty passion in it."

Gertrude thought, and the more she thought the more inclined she was to accept Frieda's view of it. The only difficulty was she couldn't quite imagine bringing herself to the point of going through with it.

"It's what you'd tell me if I were in your predicament, Gertrude."

"I know it is," Gertrude said suddenly.

"Go and tell him—go and tell him quickly."

"I will," Gertrude said. "I will tell him now."

She rose and washed her face and powdered her nose.

She was interrupted in this last process by a knock on her door. It was Archie.

"Come in," she said.

Archie stood in the doorway.

"I—I——" he began.

"Have you been listening?" Gertrude cried.

Archie swallowed twice. In his code it was the last crime to listen in on a private conversation.

"I have," he said. "And I——"

With a little rush, Gertrude was in his arms. He took her in his arms gladly.

"Oh, Archie," she cried, "I was going to tell you I was guilty."

"I know," he said gently. He kissed her. "I was a fool."

Tears rolled down Archie's cheeks for the first time since he was a little boy. Gertrude sobbed in his arms. But she sobbed happily. She had got the old, harmonious, loving relationship back.

380

The Analysis

Of the total number of lines in this story(981), lines 1 to 948 comprise the Beginning, lines 949 to 952 comprise the Decisive Act, and with the Sequel, lines 953 to 981, make up the Ending. There is no Body scene in this story. In comparison with the story by Mrs. St. John this story will show that whereas her story ended with the confession to the district attorney, this story does not begin until after that confession has been made and the effect of that confession upon the actor is shown. What Mr. Carey set out to prove was that this problem as presented by Mrs. St. John was presented from a man's angle,—a purely abstract standard of conduct—whereas in this story the story is presented from a woman's angle, specific and personal considerations triumphing over abstract, which is rather a curious anomaly, considering that the man's angle story was written by a woman and the woman's angle story was written by a man.

Lines 1 to 128 set forth a condition which is stated by the author in a way to project the interchange which comes between Philip Maple and Gertrude Woolcott. This, it seems to me, might have been presented as an interchange between Gertrude Woolcott and either her husband or Frieda, purely on the ground that an interchange is usually more interesting than a statement. In this case, the author is enabled, because he is a competent writer, to keep the statement from dullness, but an author using statement rather than interchange always runs the risk of dullness.

Once, however, this initial condition is stated, the story is, as every story of decision must be, a series of interchanges, first between Philip Maple and Gertrude on lines 129 to 288 then with Gertrude and Frieda, then with Archie, Gertrude, and Frieda as an observer, then with Gertrude and John Powell. Following this is the one between Gertrude and Archie; and this, with its effect upon the actor shown in lines 722 to 765, would be the corresponding structural units in this story that occur in Mrs. St. John's story from lines 981 to 1442. But Mr. Carey, taking this as his point of departure, in the interchange between Gertrude and Frieda, caused Frieda to set forth to Gertrude the choice which is now presented to her by this unexpected condition. Lines 949 to 952 show the conclusive Act, while lines 953 to 981 show the Sequel, which fortunately makes everything come out right for everybody.

There is always a challenge to the inventiveness of a writer when somebody says, didactically, that such and such things cannot happen. I think it was Frank Norris who said that there were only three cities in the world in which romance was possible, and scoffed at the idea of romance being the theme for a story written about Nashville, Tennessee. To this O. Henry took exception, and wrote a story about Nashville. Writers are always saying that this situation has been worked out, that nothing more can be extracted from it. Then along comes Mary Brecht Pulver and takes the oldest situation in fiction, which is of the woman trying to regain the erring husband, and upsets the apple-cart by showing that something else can be got out of this apparently worked-out vein. Then, following her, comes Mr. Carey, and, taking another old situation, of the woman who has to choose between telling or not, works out of it an entirely new solution in the light of modern psychology.

It is interesting to see that these two writers consciously recognized that they were working over old situations and put in the mouths of their characters this statement in self-defense. On lines 1011 to 1015, Mrs. Pulver causes Mr. Dark to say that, "It amounts to a formula, almost purely mechanical. You can follow it anywhere you like in the fiction of the day." On lines 915 to 917 Mr. Carey causes Frieda to say to Gertrude, "Don't you see, Gertrude, it's one of the oldest situations in the world? I have read a dozen stories about it."

Because it is in this way a companion story to Mrs. Pulver's in showing that there is no condition or situation which a competent craftsman cannot work out to some new solution, this story will be most interesting to that group of writers who feel discouraged when they are told that there is nothing new to write about. Here is evidence that it doesn't matter a bit whether or not there is anything new, a writer with originality can always give a new twist to something which has always been regarded as old, and apparently abandoned as worthless.

		Interchange. Stroude and Mountaineer.	1– 181	Possible choice shown.
		(5th step. Stroude reflects upon what has passed.)	181– 285	Wavers toward return.
BEGINNING	In a series of interchanges, all the factors of the problem are presented. Necessity and urgency are indicated.	Meeting. Stroude considers wife's ambitions.	285– 354	Wavers toward remaining.
		Interchange. Stroude and wife.	355– 755	Two possible choices clear.
		Interchange. Stroude with Laflin and Wilk.	756– 973	Opportunity to profit. Agrees to remain.
		Interchange. Stroude and wife, over Laflin's remark, leading to reading of letter, which introduces a new stimulus. Sacredness of promise recalled.	973–1097	Standard of conduct. New forces enter.
BODY	Struggle.	Interchange. Mental struggle. Standard of conduct versus opportunity to profit.	1098–1183	
ENDING	Conclusive Act.	Interchange with wife. Says he will go.	1184–1218	Answer to Narrative Question is: "He will keep his promise."
	Sequel.	Interchange. Boyce and Stroude.	1219–1258	Significance shown.

SHADOWED

BY MARY SYNON

I AM including *Shadowed* because it is a type of Decision story, presented chronologically, which comes nearer to having a Body equivalent to the Body of the Accomplishment story than any other type. Where the story of Accomplishment has furtherances and hindrances at the conclusion of the interchanges, in the Body, this story has a Beginning which is architecturally the same as the Body of the story of Decision. The difference is that at the close of the interchanges the fifth step shows a wavering between choices upon the part of the main actor. Crises of character decision take the place of narrative crises of furtherance and hindrance.

The character, at the close of each scene, appears to be about to come to a certain decision, and is plunged into a meeting with another person before that decision can be crystallized into action. At the close of this new interchange he appears to be about to come to another decision.

Thus, at the close of the different meetings the advantages or disadvantages of each choice is made apparent; and eventually there is a Conclusive Act.

The illuminating discovery which a writer will make from a study of this story in that *mental wavering should never be shown through dull analysis of thoughts.*

CASE No. 16

SHADOWED

BY MARY SYNON

All the way down from the Capitol, Stroude knew that he was being followed. From the moment he had come out of the Senate office-building upon the plaza, fragrant with forsythia in the March moonlight, he had been conscious of the man who trailed his sauntering footsteps. He had led him down a winding way past the Marshall statue and into the deserted wideness of Pennsylvania Avenue. He had thought to lose him when he stepped into the lobby of a big hotel, pausing for a word there with men he knew, men who made their greetings casual or portentous, according to their knowledge of the turning of the inner wheels of Washington; but he found the other man some twenty paces behind him as he crossed Lafayette Square, and his amused acceptance of the situation curdled to annoyance at the possibility of having to deal with an irresponsible crank determined on an interview.

The day had been more than ordinarily difficult, one of the hardest Stroude had known since the turmoiled times of war. He had suffered under the sense of impending crisis, knowing that his future hung on to-morrow's balance; and his temper, always drawn like a taut bow, had been ready to snap a hundred times through the afternoon's battle in the Senate chamber. Now, in the doorway of his house, that limestone palace of Georgian severity which loomed in stately classicism among the older residences of the neighbourhood, he poised the arrow of his wrath as he turned to confront the man behind him. "What do you want?" he snapped at him.

The man came nearer. By the dim light of the hall lantern Stroude saw his shambling listlessness, and his hand went to his pocket with a thought of relief that the other sought only alms. The man, seeing the gesture, put up his hand arrestingly. "Remember me?" he inquired, almost too nonchalantly. His voice, for all its soft slurring of the consonants, was threaded with a fibre of steel which edged the menace of his quiet poise.

"Why not?" Stroude asked sharply, his shoulders lifting as if for defense.

"Then I reckon you're none too glad to see me?"

"You haven't come here to ask me that. You might as well tell me first as last what you want from me."

"Nothing you'll call the sheriff about," the man told him. He faced the Senator squarely, revealing even in the half-darkness a certain racial resemblance to him which made them equals on the instant. For all Stroude's grooming and the stranger's shabbiness, they were strangely akin in their antagonism, bound not by family ties but by broader, more basic associations. Each of them, tall, thin, lithe, gazed on the other with unflinching blue eyes. Each of them kept watch with wildcat tenacity. From each of them emanated the recklessness of personal courage that takes no count of law beyond its own code. In their sudden springing to guard, the predominant characteristics of the two men, the Senator and the shambling shadower, flared up stronger than their setting, and although the lights of the White House gleamed golden across the Square, they were mountaineers facing each other in the hate of vendetta. The years and the place fell away from Stroude, leaving him stripped to the bone of his clan's creed.

"We've settled our own affairs before," Stroude said. "We can do it now."

As if the words gave him advantage, the other man seized them swiftly. "Let's do it, then," he replied. "I've come here to get you to do something you won't want to do. Will you fight me for it?"

"Not till I know the stake."

"Didn't you get her letter?"

"Whose?"

"There's only one woman I'd be coming to you about, I reckon."

"I've never heard from her since the day she went back to you. That was twenty-six years ago last May."

"The fourteenth."

"Why should she have written me now?"

"She's dying." The man's voice sounded in a softer timbre. "A month ago the doctor from the moonlight school told her that she had only a little while to live. She's been pining ever since, not about dying, for she's as brave as any man, but for something I couldn't guess until she told me. She wants to see *you.* She wrote you a letter, but she was afraid you might not get it, and so she sent me. 'Tell him,' she said, 'that I won't rest easy in my grave over there on the side of Big Stony, if he don't come to me before I die. He told me once,' she said, 'that he'd come when I'd call. I'm calling now.' That's her message."

His tone lifted from its softer depth. "Are you coming to her?"

"I can't."

"Why not?"

"I've a thousand duties. I've— It's ridiculous."

"Then you're not coming?"

"How can I, Martin? I'm not my own man. I'm here for my State, for my country. I have work to do. I can't let any personal obligation interfere with it. Besides——"

"It couldn't hurt your wife, not even if she knew it. And Dell's dying."

"I'm sorry, Martin. I am, honestly. Will you tell Dell that I——"

"I'll tell her nothing but that you wouldn't come. Nothing else matters. And I think you owe her that, at least."

"But——"

The other man turned away, crossed the street and walked back across the Square. Stroude could see him swinging on between the bushes, and the remembrance of another trail which Boyce Martin would climb rushed over him. More plainly than the crocus-bordered path to the White House shone the moonlit path up to the cabin on Pisgah where Dell Martin had been used to wait for his own coming, the cabin where she waited for death. The memory of that way, twisting among laurel and rhododendrons, stabbed him more sharply than had Boyce Martin's words; but with the old habit of setting aside disturbing thoughts, he tried to thrust the memory from his brain as he unlocked the door of his house.

A servant, coming forward at the sound of his key in the lock, gave him a message with a careful precision which bespoke respect for the executive management that directed his tasks. "Mrs. Stroude wishes you to be told, sir, that she is at the theatre, and will see you when she comes in. And she made an appointment, sir, for Senator Manning and two other gentlemen to see you to-night on their way from the Pan-American dinner. She said it was very important."

He thanked the man, and went upstairs to the library, switching on light after light to dispel its shrouding gloom. He tried to read, but the pages of the periodicals he took up ran into dullness. He chewed his cigar savagely, finding it flavourless. He strove to concentrate on his impending interview with Manning and his companions, realizing its portent, but he could not focus his attitude. Impatiently he thrust away the work which always waited his attention on his homecoming—findings of

229 committees, digests of newspaper
230 editorials, confidential reports
231 on public interest in various
232 measures, letters from men who
233 had constituted themselves his
234 captains. He frowned at the
235 framed photograph of his wife,
236 the only decoration she had
237 placed upon his table; and he
238 grimaced at the portrait of him-
239 self which Rhoda had set above
240 the immaculate mantel. He was
241 weary with work, he told him-
242 self, crossing the room and
243 flinging wide open the windows
244 which looked down on the Square.
245 The thrill of the night wind,
246 prematurely warm as it crossed
247 the Potomac, and burdened with
248 elusive odours of a southern
249 March, caught him unawares.
250 For a moment he stood drinking
251 deeply of the immortal beauty
252 of the recurrent springtime.
253 Memories he had thought long
254 dead and buried went over him.
255 Pictures more vivid than those
256 on the walls framed themselves
257 in the darkened greenery of the
258 little park: a girl in a faded
259 gingham dress waving him wel-
260 come on a hill road, a girl with
261 eyes brighter than mountain
262 stars telling him her love, fling-
263 ing away all thought or care of
264 herself, giving him everything
265 and glorying in the gift, even to
266 the last sacrifice of her departure
267 from him. Not as she was now,
268 Boyce Martin's wife dying in
269 that far-away little community
270 of his native hills, but as she had

been when she had defied their 271
little world to come to him, 272
Stroude saw her. In the thought 273
of what she had been to him, he 274
flung out his arms. "After all 275
these years," he muttered, "after 276
all these years!" And as if 277
drawn by a power stronger than 278
his will, he crossed to the table, 279
and picking up the telephone, 280
called the information desk of 281
the Union Station. "What time 282
does the Mountain Mail on the 283
C. & O. go out now?" he asked. 284
"One o'clock? One-fifteen." He 285
hung up the receiver, and saw 286
again the photograph of his wife. 287
He studied it with suddenly 288
arrested attention. What would 289
she think of his desire to leave 290
Washington at a time when, 291
according to her fundamental 292
ideas, his presence was impera- 293
tive for the fulfilment of his 294
ambition? Or was it her ambi- 295
tion? He gazed at the pictured 296
countenance, seeing the deter- 297
mination of the uplifted chin, 298
meeting the challenge in the 299
steady eyes. Rhoda was 300
certainly her father's daughter. 301
Old Peter Armond's indomitable 302
will and shrewdly calculating 303
brain lived on in her. For the 304
fourteen—or was it fifteen?— 305
years of their marriage she had 306
managed Stroude's career as 307
cleverly as ever her father had 308
directed one of his lieutenants, 309
and he had acknowledged his 310
debt to her with a certain at- 311
titude of amusement. Now, 312

facing the last triumphal stage of its development, he felt an angry distaste of Rhoda's maneuvering. It might bring him, he conceded, to the goal, but he wished he might have traveled a simpler path.

He had been an obscure Congressman of fiery political rectitude when he had met Rhoda Armond. She, and her group, and the circumstances the Armond connection had conjured for him, had made him into a statesman. Or was it only that they had made it possible for him to plant his own standards on the heights? At any rate, he owed her something, he thought. She was his wife, even though her attitude toward him was that of a director of destinies. She had given him, after all, what he had desired from her. She had made the upward road smooth, and she had dowered him with loyal faith in his ability. It wasn't fair to compare her attitude toward him with Dell's. He had never given to Rhoda what he had given Dell. Poor little Dell! But what good could he do her now by going to her? Twenty-five years would have changed her as they had changed him. They had had their day, and the sun of it had set long since. "I won't go; I can't," he said, and turned back to the work on his desk, not looking up until his wife entered the room.

She came, a tall, consciously beautiful woman, bringing with her an aroma of power as subtle and as pervasive as the perfume of her toilet. She gave to Stroude the greeting of a perfunctory kiss on his brow, and stood off for his admiration. It was, however, not the product of her personality as much as her satisfaction in the work which struck him as he watched her. Rhoda's thought of herself as well as of him, was that of a sculptor of his masterpieces. Stroude accepted it with the affectionate tolerance of a long marital relationship, feeling somehow sorrier for Rhoda than she would ever feel for herself, since she would never know what she had missed from life. "I was playing your game to-night," she told him.

"Isn't it yours too?" he smiled.

"In a way, yes," she acknowledged, "but this involved real sacrifice, and I want reward. I went to the theatre with the Covingers."

"Was the play deadly?"

"No, but the Covingers are."

"He isn't a bad sort, and——"

"Oh, I know that he'll have the delegation from his State and that it's one of the big States; but oh, my dear, have you ever had to listen to his wife?"

"She isn't so terrible, Rhoda."

"Oh, of course, if you will look

396 at people as characters rather
397 than as social factors, you won't
398 see the awfulness of the Mrs.
399 Covingers of Washington. But
400 really——"
401 "Did Manning hint at why he
402 had to see me to-night?"
403 "At nothing but the import-
404 ance of seeing you. He is bring-
405 ing, he said, Mr. Laflin and
406 Senator Wilk."
407 "He probably said Senator
408 Wilk and Mr. Laflin, but you
409 know the field well enough to
410 put them in the order of their
411 importance. Laflin's the new
412 factor, a shrewd wolf raised in a
413 wild forest."
414 "Does it mean"—she leaned
415 forward, tapping the table with
416 her fan in eagerness—"that they
417 are going to ask you to take the
418 nomination?"
419 "They haven't the entire giv-
420 ing of it, my dear."
421 "Don't be silly, Burton. You
422 know that they are the architects
423 of presidential nominations."
424 "But even architects——"
425 "Oh, Burt, don't quibble.
426 You know that you're the logical
427 man for the place. You're
428 squarely based in party
429 politics——"
430 "Safe, and steady." His tone
431 was whimsical.
432 "But picturesque enough to
433 be a good campaigner."
434 "Barefoot boy from the
435 mountains. Good American
436 stock with fine traditions. Reads
437 rhetorically, doesn't it?"

438 "And a border State gives
439 you strategic advantage."
440 "Someone has coached you
441 well."
442 "I was coached before I ever
443 knew you, Burt dear. My father
444 taught us politics as religiously
445 as my mother taught us sewing.
446 It wasn't as practical, perhaps,
447 as yours, but——"
448 "There haven't been many
449 men more practical in their
450 politics than Peter Armond,"
451 Stroude said dryly.
452 "Even if he did grow
453 wealthy," his daughter defended,
454 "you know how high he kept his
455 standards."
456 "I can guess," Stroude said,
457 but his tone gave her no handle
458 to catch for controversy, and she
459 swung into off-side statement.
460 "Mrs. Covinger let slip some-
461 thing that may be vital to us,"
462 she told him.
463 "If it's vital, she let it slip
464 with due deliberation," he de-
465 clared. "Don't under-estimate
466 her brains, Rhoda, even if she
467 wasn't raised by the Armond
468 code. What did she say?"
469 "I don't believe I'll tell you."
470 "Yes, you will."
471 "We do run in double harness,
472 don't we? Well, she said that
473 Covinger wasn't going back to
474 New York until to-morrow
475 night, as there was a tremend-
476 ously important conference at
477 noon to-morrow. Seven men
478 will be there, and they will
479 decide the fate of the nation.

392

480 That's exactly what she said.
481 She's bombastic, you know."

482 "Seven? Then they're letting
483 Covinger in?"

484 "You knew about it?"

485 "Not that it would be to-
486 morrow."

487 "Is that why Senator Manning
488 is coming to-night?"

489 "Probably."

490 "Then that means—" Her
491 voice broke in excitement.

492 "That our fate hangs in the
493 balance."

494 "Does it?"

495 "It looks like it." He smiled
496 at her through the smoke of his
497 cigar. Her eyes shone with
498 myriad points of light. "Not
499 planning what you'll wear at
500 the inauguration, are you?" he
501 teased her.

502 "No," she said, "but wonder-
503 ing what you'll say. It's wonder-
504 ful, isn't it?"

505 "Don't count your chickens
506 yet, Rhoda," he warned her.
507 "We, both of us, know the
508 thousand slips between the cup
509 of consideration and the lip of
510 nomination. We've gone through
511 it all for other offices."

512 "But we've won every time,"
513 she said solemnly. "You've
514 never been beaten, Burt. Don't
515 you see what an advantage that
516 is, now? You've been going up
517 and up, and up."

518 "The Senate's a rather high
519 plateau, at that."

520 "But not the high mountain.
521 Oh, Burt, think of it! It seems

522 almost unbelievable, and yet
523 I've always known you were
524 destined for it. I knew you'd
525 be great. Why, even in those
526 first days here, you promised it.
527 You knew it, too. You had
528 the look of a man who was
529 dedicated to something beyond
530 the immediate, the look of one
531 who is going to travel far and
532 high. I believe that was one of
533 the reasons why I loved you.
534 And you—" She leaned over the
535 table, and spread out the brilliant
536 feathers of her fan, gazing at their
537 splendour and not at her husband
538 as she went on: "Did you love
539 me when you married me?"

540 "Why else do men marry wo-
541 men?" he countered, letting the
542 smoke veil his eyes.

543 "To put other women out of
544 their lives, sometimes," she said.

545 "Well?" He drew hard on
546 the cigar.

547 "I never knew until to-day
548 who she was," she said. "I
549 opened a letter by mistake.
550 You may see from the envelope
551 how easy it was for me to think
552 it was addressed to me when I
553 found it in my mail. It was
554 directed merely to Washington,
555 and the post office sent it to the
556 house here."

557 "I quite understand," he said,
558 and held out his hand for Dell
559 Martin's letter.

560 His wife drew it from the gay
561 bag she had borne, and gave it
562 to him. For a moment he looked
563 at the pitiful missive, contrast-

564 ing it with the appointments of
565 the table before him. "She's
566 dying," Rhoda said, "and she
567 asks you to go to her."
568 "Yes," he said, "I know it."
569 "But——"
570 "How did I know? Her
571 husband followed me down from
572 the Hill to-night. He demanded
573 that I return with him."
574 "Then she married, after——"
575 "She was married," he said,
576 "when I met her."
577 "Oh!" She snapped shut the
578 great fan, twisting its tortoise-
579 shell handle between her lithe
580 fingers. "When was that?"
581 "Before I knew you." He
582 sank down into his chair, staring
583 forward as if he were a judge
584 considering a decision. "I was
585 twenty-two years old, teaching
586 school in the mountains, and
587 studying law with old Judge
588 McLaurin, when I met Dell
589 Martin. She had been married
590 to Boyce against her will, as
591 plenty of the girls in the hills are
592 married. She was lonely, and
593 wretched, and lovelier than a
594 wild rose. I was young, and
595 reckless. I fell in love with her,
596 and I made her love me. Boyce
597 found it out. He drew me into
598 a fight, and I won it. He shot
599 me then. Dell came to nurse me,
600 and I wouldn't let her go. Boyce
601 wouldn't get a divorce, and she
602 couldn't, but she stayed with
603 me. We had two years of utter
604 happiness. I'd have gone
605 through hell to win them."

606 A stick of the tortoise-shell
607 handle of the fan broke in
608 Rhoda's hands. "But you left
609 her?"
610 "No," he said. "She left me.
611 She saw before I did that it
612 couldn't go on. She saw in me
613 the ambition that I thought I
614 had buried in my love for her.
615 She knew that if I stayed with
616 her, I'd never be anything but a
617 miserable shyster, living from
618 hand to mouth, despising myself
619 and all I did, coming perhaps
620 in time to hate her because she
621 had been the cause of my degra-
622 dation. She went to Judge
623 McLaurin, and asked him to tell
624 her the truth. He told her, old
625 Covenanter that he was. Then
626 she went up the mountain to
627 Boyce, and asked him if he wanted
628 her to come back to him. She
629 knew that it was the only action
630 I'd consider final. He told her to
631 come. She told me that she was
632 leaving me. I pleaded with her
633 all that night, but she went with
634 the dawn. I couldn't hold her.
635 I went up Pisgah with her till
636 we came to the trail to Boyce's
637 cabin. We could see the wood-
638 smoke curling up above the
639 masses of shining green leaves
640 and pink clusters of the laurel.
641 'You're going away from me,'
642 she said, 'far away, and you'll
643 climb a higher mountain than
644 Pisgah.' I begged her to come
645 with me, but she shook her head.
646 'I'm giving you up for your sake,'
647 she told me. 'But you need me,'

I pleaded. 'Not now,' she said. 'But some day I shall, and then I'll call you. And no matter where you are, you'll come, won't you, Burt?' I promised her that I would. The last I saw of her was as she climbed the trail to Boyce's cabin. From that day to this,"—he touched the crumpled little white letter, —"she has sent me no word."

"It's strange, isn't it," Rhoda said, her voice not quite steady, "that a woman may live with a man through long years, and never really know him at all?"

"Should I have told you?"

"I don't know," she said. "I suppose I'd have married you, even if you had. It's not deception, perhaps, when you've never seen her nor written to her since you married me; and yet— Are you going to her, Burt?"

"To-morrow's the conference. I must be there if I am to be the man chosen."

"Do you want to go?"

"I wonder," he mused, "if you'll understand me when I tell you that, other things being equal, I should go to-night. It's with no sense of failing you, and with no idea of helping her, but I promised her—that I'd come if she called."

"Even if there weren't the conference," Rhoda said, "you're a marked man now. You couldn't go back to a little village in the mountains without it being known, and the reason for it blazoned. It wouldn't do, would it?" She could not quite succeed in making her tone judical. Her own eagerness palpitated back of the assumed impartiality. "You've wanted the presidency too long to throw away the chance of it."

"I've never wanted it," he said.

"You don't mean," she demanded, her vexation rising into view, "that I've urged you to seek something you haven't desired?"

"It's more complex than that," he shrugged. "I suppose it's simply that I married the Armond hope as well as you. Old Peter set a standard for your family which has kept you all up on your toes. If the dead see, he must chuckle sometimes over its way of working."

"Why?" she flared, letting her annoyance catch at a point of difference less vital than the main issue. "He gave his whole service to his country. He was one of the really great men of his generation, wasn't he? You've never known my father as I knew him. You've always let yourself be influenced by the demagogic attacks on him. You've thought that because he made a great fortune he couldn't be an idealist. Haven't you seen that, if he had been a materialist, he wouldn't have trained his family as he did?

732 Why, it's been his torch that
733 I've tried to keep alight, and if I
734 have done anything for you,
735 Burton, it has been by that
736 torch's flame."
737 "You've done a very great
738 deal, Rhoda," he said. "I'm
739 not questioning the number or
740 the brightness of the candles
741 you've burned in my game.
742 I'm only questioning the value
743 of the game itself. Power's like
744 money. If you give up all else
745 to possess it, then it possesses
746 you."
747 "But——"
748 "I know. I should have
749 chosen long ago. I'm not turn-
750 ing back now. I owe you that,
751 I think. If I'm anything at all
752 beyond a struggling lawyer in a
753 little city—" He broke off
754 suddenly as the young servant
755 came to the library curtains.
756 "Senator Manning and two
757 other gentlemen," he announced.
758 They came almost on his
759 heels, three men with the aspect
760 of dignitaries: Manning tall,
761 thin, almost cadaverous, with
762 the eye and the hand of a
763 Richelieu; Wilk heavy, ponder-
764 ous, inscrutable as a great
765 Buddha; Laflin, a blend of
766 college professor and Wall Street
767 lawyer, hiding a predatory keen-
768 ness behind horn-rimmed spec-
769 tacles. Characteristically,
770 Stroude felt, they fell into place,
771 Wilk into the nearest easy-chair,
772 Manning into an Italian seat
773 which put him in the centre of a

774 softly lighted stage, and Laflin
775 back in the shadows. After a
776 moment of casual conversation
777 Rhoda rose to leave them.
778 Stroude halted her. "I have
779 an idea," he said, "that these
780 gentlemen have come to me on
781 an errand which concerns you as
782 well as myself.—Do you mind if
783 she stays?"
784 "Not at all," said Manning
785 suavely. Laflin nodded, and
786 old man Wilk grunted assent.
787 Rhoda went over beyond Laflin
788 as far outside the group as she
789 could, and just out of her
790 husband's line of vision; but he
791 turned his chair a little, that he
792 might encompass her in his sight
793 as Manning began to speak.
794 "It makes it a little easier for
795 us," he said, "that you have
796 guessed something of our mis-
797 sion."
798 "I couldn't help knowing,"
799 Stroude swung back, "when
800 every other man in the Senate
801 has known it for days."
802 "Not definitely," boomed
803 Wilk. "There's always talk, of
804 course, and often more smoke
805 than fire."
806 "Sometimes it's only a screen
807 for the protection of a real issue,"
808 Manning went on, "but in this
809 case the fire is burning. You
810 know, I am sure, that the con-
811 ference to determine the best
812 candidate for the next term of
813 the presidency is to be held here
814 in Washington to-morrow."
815 "At noon," smiled Stroude.

"Your information," Manning said, "is speedy as well as accurate. The time was not determined until seven o'clock this evening. Seven men know it."

"And their wives," cut in Laflin, peering at Rhoda.

"We have canvassed the field thoroughly before coming to you," Manning continued with his air of authoritative spokesmanship. "We have eliminated, for one reason or another, all the men who have been under consideration. Bannister is too old. Maxwell is too radical. Vandringham is too theatrical. Stearns is too variable. Durham is too light. Landreau lacks the necessary tradition. Penn comes from the wrong location. Jarvis jumped the party. The process brings us to you."

"How about Corliss?"

"I don't mind telling you," Manning said, "that Carmichael is fighting desperately for Corliss, and that, without Covinger's help, he *might* be able to swing the conference. Mr. Laflin, Senator Wilk and I have never swerved from our determination to have you. Carmichael has Bennett and Franklin with him. Covinger is the determining vote. You have him."

"Are you sure?"

"Certain. He's attending on Parker's proxy. We won that point this afternoon. He's solidly with you."

"Even against Corliss? Corliss is from his State."

"Even against him."

"Why?"

"Well, it seems that Corliss has an old scandal against him which frightens Covinger. He's afraid that it might make an election issue. By the way— You're not interested in these affairs, Mrs. Stroude?"

"Very vitally," she said, "and there's nothing you need fear to discuss before me."

Manning cleared his throat, and old man Wilk stirred uneasily in his chair. Laflin's mobile mouth twisted.

"Go on," said Stroude. "What's the charge?"

"Carmichael says," Manning stated, "that there's an old story back in your own State, Stroude, that might explode. We've all known you a good many years, all of us but Laflin, and we've never heard a whisper of it. I have told him that I do not believe it. So has Senator Wilk."

"What's the story?" Stroude's fingers, lighting a match, did not tremble.

"Well, if you insist——"

"I do."

"Carmichael says that you stole another man's wife."

"There was no theft about it. She came with me. Later she went back to her husband. I left the place, started to practise law, and married. My wife never heard the story until to-

397

night." He looked down at Dell Martin's letter, not yet read by him, topping the documents on the table in front of him. "It's an old story," he said, "and one not likely to explode unless——"

"Unless what?" Laflin demanded from the gloom.

"Unless I choose to revive it by an overt act," Stroude retorted. "It all happened more than twenty-five years ago in a tiny community in the mountains. I know the people there. They're my kind, my stock. They won't talk to strangers coming in. There's only one way the newspapers could get the story. I'd have to lead them to it."

"That's true," old man Wilk grunted. "I know the mountains."

"Then it's settled," Manning said with evident relief. "I fancy a story as old as that, cut off altogether by the time between, could not be a very appalling Banquo's ghost." He arose a little wearily. "You'll be at the conference to-morrow?" He named the time and place. "It's necessary that you should be. Without you, Covinger may switch. You may have to combat Carmichael directly. You'll be ready?"

"If I'm—if it's necessary," Stroude said.

The other two men stood up, Wilk unwieldily, Laflin with quick ease, smiling at Stroude as he held out his hand. "This was a real star-chamber session," he said, "according to the best rules of old Peter Armond. Wouldn't the old pirate have loved to sit in a ten-minute game of four men who decided the next President?"

"What do you mean?" Rhoda's voice rang out in challenge, and Manning and Wilk rushed to speech to head off Laflin, but he went on in almost boyish unconcern: "Old Peter trained me, you know, and I've always had a soft spot for him in my heart, although I've known what a wolf in sheep's clothing he was. We have to hand it to him, though, that with all his grafting and his materialism, he was a great party builder. He was the first of the Warwicks in American national life. We're just rattling around in his shoes, but we'll do our best to put you over."

He moved off, almost pushed by Manning's eagerness to depart, but his voice seemed to linger in the room after the three of them had gone. Stroude sat toying with a paper-knife. Rhoda, deep in the shadows, did not stir. A clock in the hall boomed twelve. Stroude, sighing, put his hand over Dell Martin's letter. Then Rhoda spoke. "Is Mr. Laflin telling the truth about my father," she asked Stroude, "or what he thinks is the truth?"

"The truth."

985 "That he wasn't an idealist—
986 a patriot?"

987 "Well, if he was——"

988 "I understand. And you've
989 known it always?"

990 "Since before I knew you."

991 "Then do you mean"—she
992 came back to the chair beside
993 the table—"that through all
994 these years my standards have
995 meant nothing to you? That
996 you have known them to be
997 false?"

998 "They aren't false," he said.
999 "The standards are true
1000 enough."

1001 "But the man who gave them
1002 to me wasn't?"

1003 "Well, he didn't live up to
1004 the code."

1005 "Your own code?"

1006 "I've tried to hold to it."

1007 "The one Judge McLaurin
1008 taught you?"

1009 "The very one. The one
1010 Judge Foxwell taught *him*. *He*
1011 got it, I believe, from John
1012 Marshall. Don't think about it,
1013 Rhoda. Those old boys lived in
1014 different days. Sometimes I
1015 think that I'm an anachron-
1016 ism." He sought to smile at
1017 her, but the smile faded before
1018 her intensity. "Don't let a
1019 chance word of Laflin's bother
1020 you," he counseled. "He didn't
1021 know you, of course, as your
1022 father's daughter, or he'd have
1023 cut out his tongue before saying
1024 what he did."

1025 "It doesn't matter who said
1026 it," she declared. "It's not that

1027 alone that hurts; it's the know-
1028 ledge that I've meant so little to
1029 you that cuts deep—now. I
1030 used to think, Burt, even when
1031 I knew that you didn't love me,
1032 that I was giving you something
1033 fine and splendid. I let myself
1034 believe that the Armond tradi-
1035 tion was the beacon which was
1036 lighting your way. I thought
1037 that if I couldn't give you any-
1038 thing else, I was at least giving
1039 you that torch. And now, I find
1040 out that the light I was holding
1041 for you was only marsh fire.
1042 You've never needed me!" Her
1043 voice rose to accusation.

1044 "Oh, yes," he countered, but
1045 he could not put verity into his
1046 tone.

1047 "No," she said. "You don't
1048 owe me anything for the playing
1049 of the game. I've loved that for
1050 itself."

1051 "But you thought you were
1052 giving me the other——"

1053 "And I wasn't. It's really a
1054 joke, isn't it? A buccaneer
1055 teaching his family the Golden
1056 Rule, and the family passing it
1057 on!"

1058 "It isn't a joke, Rhoda. I've
1059 always taken it in the measure of
1060 your intention."

1061 "And been sorry for me?"

1062 "Yes."

1063 "I've never sought pity."

1064 "None of us do."

1065 "It's funny, isn't it," she
1066 mused, "that one woman who
1067 loved you set you free, so that
1068 another woman whom you didn't

love might take away that freedom?"

"I've had as much freedom as most men," he said, but his eyes went back to the crumpled missive. Rhoda's glance, following his, saw its significance. "Read it," she challenged him. He hesitated an instant, as if doubting his desire to read it before her watchfulness, then drew the letter from its envelope.

Pale tracing on common paper met his gaze. *"Burt,"* he read, *"you're a great man now, and maybe you've forgotten me. I've never forgotten you. Every morning and every night I've prayed for you. Boyce has been good to me, better than I deserved; but oh, Burt, all that my life has been since I left you is just a hope that eternity will bring us together again. I used to believe it would, but I'm getting afraid, now that it's coming near. Won't you come to me for just one hour before I go? You told me once that hell wouldn't keep you if I——"*

Before the pathos of the call something in Stroude's soul trembled. He didn't love Dell now, he told himself as he came to the end of the page. He hadn't loved her in twenty years. There was no thrill of remembered passion rising from the white page to stir his heart, but there was something deeper, more poignant than romance in the plea which this woman in the mountains had sent him across time and distance. Through those long years she had never wavered in her belief in him and in the promise he had made to her. Out of the depths of his spirit he had told her that he would come to her if she should ever need him. It was a promise given not only to the woman who had heard and heeded it, but to the God of his faith and his fathers. If he failed to keep it, no matter what the cost, he would be violating more than an old love. He would be tearing down his own code. Through whatever glory might come to him he would know himself as a man who failed in the one virtue on which he had always prided himself, the keeping of his word. It was an oath he had taken to Dell Martin, just as he would take an oath to uphold the Constitution of the United States if—if he climbed the mountain of Rhoda's vision!

Realization of the immediacy of his problem came to him with the sight of his wife's fan, broken, lying beyond the letter in his hand. He looked up to find Rhoda's eyes studying him. But he must not fail her, he told himself, snatching at the straw of conventionality in the current of emotion. The very fact that he had not given her love put him under obligation to her. Because of her, because of the expectations she had harboured for him, because of the time and thought and labour she had spent for the advancement she had thought he sought, because of her very disillusionment now, he could not fail her. He must go to the conference, even if it meant the breaking of a vow he had made before the altar of his one great love. It was part of the price, he reasoned, that all men pay for power; but he felt that something within him was dying as he turned the page of Dell Martin's letter.

"—if I called for you," he picked up the thread. "That was why I didn't call when I needed you before, when our boy was born. I couldn't let you know about him. You'd never have let me go if you'd known. But it doesn't matter now, does it? And oh, Burt, I need you so! If you'll only hold my hand again, I won't fear the crossing. And perhaps when you come to die, you'll find the going easier if you have the memory of this hour you'll give me. Won't you come?" It was signed waveringly, "Dell."

He folded it back into the envelope, and put it in his pocket. "You aren't going?" Rhoda asked him, her voice strangely strained.

"Yes," he said, "I'm going."

"But to-morrow——"

"It's the long years afterward I'm thinking of," he told her.

"And the nomination——"

"Sometimes the things we put out of our lives," he said, "are the only things we really keep."

"That's ridiculous," she said. "I can't understand you at all to-night, Burton. Why should a man give up the highest honour a nation can give him——"

"There are other kinds of honour, Rhoda."

"To go to a woman he hasn't seen for twenty-five years?"

"She is the—" he began, then halted quickly in the fear of the hurt his word might give her.

"I understand," she said.

She picked up her broken fan, and moved toward the door, but before she reached it, turned back. Her face was stonily calm. "Shall I telephone Senator Manning in the morning that you will not be there?" she asked him.

"If you will," he said.

As his car bore him past the shadowy white pile on the other side of the Square, Stroude sighed. A man does not live with a dream—even the dream of another—through season after season without catching some gleam of its radiance; but in Boyce Martin's straight look as he met him at the train gate, Stroude began to drink of his justification.

"You Stroudes always kept your word," the other man said.

"We aim to," said Stroude, unconsciously slipping back into the vernacular of his youth. "It was her letter," he explained. "I

1237 never knew about the boy."
1238 "I know," said Martin. "I
1239 —I've loved him as if he'd been
1240 the child I've never had. That's
1241 why I came for you." He held
1242 out his hand, and Stroude
1243 grasped it. "You're one of us,
1244 after all."
1245 As the train slid past the
1246 Potomac and threaded the low
1247 pines of the Virginia river-lands,
1248 Stroude pondered the moun-
1249 taineer's tribute. In the light of
1250 it he saw the path to Dell
1251 Martin's cabin leading higher
1452 than the way across the Square.
1253 For the first time in many years
1254 he felt the surge of freedom ris-
1255 ing in his soul. A thousand
1256 shackles fell away as the last
1257 lights of Washington slid down
1258 on the horizon.

THE ANALYSIS

A glance at the chart will show you that this story contains 1258 lines. Of these the Beginning is made up of 1097 lines, the Body 86 lines, the Ending 75 lines, 35 for the Decisive Act and 40 for the Sequel.

The first interchange is between Stroude and the mountaineer and occupies lines 1 to 181. At the close of this interchange a possible choice is shown, and Stroude appears about to make a decision; but as he reflects, which is the fifth step occupying lines 181 to 285, he wavers toward the return. Then there is the consideration of a condition, which is shown as a meeting, when Stroude becomes aware of the stimulus, which is to consider a state of affairs involving his wife. Then he wavers toward remaining in Washington. Following this is an interchange between Stroude and his wife, and at the close of it, after lines 355 to 755, two possible choices are clear. The interchange between Stroude and Laflin and Wilk, occupying lines 756 to 973, shows at its close an agreement to remain. The decision is practically consummated, but, after the interchange between Stroude and his wife brought about by Laflin's remark which leads to the reading of the letter in which he recalls the sacredness of his promise, there comes, in lines 1098 to 1183, a mental struggle between his standard of conduct as opposed to his opportunity for wish fulfilment or profit, which makes up the Body of the story.

At the conclusion of the struggle he says, on line 1189, "Yes, I am going." That is the Decisive Act, and in the Sequel there is an interchange between the Senator and Boyce Martin in which Martin voices the reason that caused Stroude to make this decision. It is that, "You Stroudes always kept your word," (line 1231).

This story would have been improved had this trait been indicated in the interchange between Stroude and the mountaineer early in the story.

This story is particularly interesting because it is told in straight chronological form. There is no flash-back whatsoever; but the analytical reader will observe that it is made up of an extremely important situation, that it is a clear-cut case of an opportunity to profit as opposed to a standard of conduct, and that the interchanges are prolonged and dramatic because they are important. One other special reason for its inclusion is that it shows a variation from the other stories of this type in that the decision is made after the actor has become aware of a stimulus of which he was not aware at the opening of the story. At the opening of the story he knew that the woman had sent for him, but it was not until on lines 1168 to 1183, when he read the letter, that he became aware that the woman was depending upon him to keep his sacred promise. Then that trait in his character which made that standard of conduct more important to him than his opportunity to profit came to the front and defeated the other trait.

ARCHITECTURAL CHART

OF

SHODDY

BEGINNING	Main Actor is shown in characteristic responses. Condition which calls upon him to decide is presented.	Interchange. Claypool and waiter.	1– 38	
		(5th step. Claypool's reflections. Interchange with waiter.)	39– 95	
		Interchange. Krohn and Claypool. Krohn offers opportunity to profit.	96–493	Main Narrative Question: "What choice will he make?"
		Martin Claypool accepts.	484–487	Choice apparently made. Loophole left by writer.
		Interchange. Claypool and Krohn, regarding tailor.	494–574	
		Meeting. Claypool sees and buys loud goods.	575–637	
		Interchange. Claypool and tailor.	638–907	
		(5th step. Reflections. Claypool aware of photograph.)	908–963	
	Upon reflecting Claypool reverses decision. Decisive Acts.	Interchange. Telephones Tailor.	963–972	
		Interchange. Telephones Krohn.	973–988	Decision made.

404

SHODDY

BY RICHARD CONNELL

THE story *Shoddy* is an especially interesting variant of the type story illustrated by *Shadowed*. It is the story of a man who has apparently made up his mind and has come to a definite decision, but who becomes aware of a new stimulus as a result of which he reverses his original decision.

It is extremely interesting in the way in which it carries along two separate stories, linking them cleverly together. One is the story of Martin Claypool and the poor tailor; the other is the story of Martin Claypool and Mr. Krohn.

CASE No. 17

SHODDY

BY RICHARD CONNELL

Martin Claypool went directly from his suite on the world's largest—and most costly—liner to the suite engaged for him in London's largest—and most costly—hotel. He always took a suite wherever he went.

He sent for a waiter, and with a gold-mounted pencil ticked off the dishes for his dinner on the right-hand, or price, side of the menu: Beluga caviar, fillet of sole Marguery, a squab Lucullus, asparagus, an alligator-pear salad, a bit of old Stilton, hothouse grapes. He said to the waiter, "And a bottle of your best wine."

"Yes, sir. What sort, sir?"

"The best," said Martin Claypool.

"Does the gentleman prefer a sauterne? Or perhaps a claret?"

"Bring me the best you have."

The old waiter regarded Martin Claypool appraisingly. "A half bottle of Château Yquem '06," he murmured reverently, "and a half bottle of Romanée '11?"

"Yes, yes," said Martin Claypool impatiently. "That's it."

"And a liqueur, sir?"

"Yes, yes."

"What sort, sir?"

"Let me see now——"

"We have some prime '76 brandy, sir."

"That will do."

When the waiter had bowed himself away Martin Claypool stretched the long legs which supported his powerful frame, and paced his suite. He took from a thin platinum case a very long and strong cigar, lighted it. It had no band on it, because he had had it made specially for him.

In front of the long glass in one of his bedrooms he paused to survey himself. He patted the spot where vest and trousers met, reflectively. Not so bad for a fellow past forty. The golf had helped. If he could keep the circumference of his waist two inches smaller than his chest he'd be doing better than most men of his years and habits, he mused. He rubbed his head.

61 Hair going fast, despite the
62 violet-ray treatments of that
63 high-priced specialist. Still, he
64 had a good fresh color. Plenty
65 of vigorous years ahead of him—
66 years of progress and success.

67 He adjusted the black pearl
68 pin in his necktie—a rather florid
69 necktie. He was reminded of
70 something. He took off his suit
71 —it was gray, pronouncedly
72 striped with white—and changed
73 to his dinner clothes. The shirt
74 he put on had been made to order
75 for him in St. Louis. It was
76 heavily pleated. He had had
77 two dozen made, at thirty-six
78 dollars each.

79 His dressing finished, he was
80 poking the ends of his black tie
81 under the wings of his collar
82 when his dinner arrived. He
83 gazed approvingly at his image
84 in the mirror. Before he sat
85 down to dinner he telephoned to
86 Mr. Krohn. Yes, Mr. Krohn
87 could come to his suite at nine.
88 Good! Good-by.

89 "Telephone service here is al-
90 most as bad as in St. Louis," he
91 remarked to the waiter.

92 "Yes, sir. Sorry, sir," said
93 the waiter, who up to that
94 moment had always thought of
95 St. Louis as a man.

96 Krohn was prompt. Pre-
97 cisely at nine he came in, bowed
98 to Martin Claypool, held out a
99 long-fingered hand. Krohn was
100 a lean, sallow man, meticulously
101 dressed, and of no particular age
102 or nationality.

103 "Delighted to see you, Mr.
104 Claypool," he said.

105 "Pleased to meet you, Mr.
106 Krohn. Sit down and have a
107 cigar."

108 "Thanks."

109 "How about a little drink?"

110 Krohn shook his head. "I
111 leave spirits to the Americans.
112 They suit their temperament,"
113 he said. "Glass of port after
114 dinner is my limit. But please
115 don't let me deter you."

116 Martin Claypool mixed him-
117 self a highball. Then he turned
118 to Krohn.

119 "Now then," he said, "let's
120 talk turkey."

121 "I beg your pardon?"

122 "That means, in American,
123 let's get down to business,"
124 laughed Martin Claypool.

125 Krohn inclined his dark head.
126 "By all means," he said. "There
127 is really no great hurry though.
128 You see, Mr. Claypool, I've just
129 come from China, where time is
130 nothing."

131 "And I," said Martin Clay-
132 pool, "have just come from
133 America, where time is money—
134 and money is everything."

135 "But now that you are here,
136 you plan to look round a while,
137 I hope. It's your first visit to
138 England, isn't it?"

139 "Yes."

140 "You'll be taking a bit of vaca-
141 tion then, I expect; see London
142 —Paris." Mr. Krohn pro-
143 nounced "Paris" with a sug-
144 gestion of a leer.

145 "No," said Martin Claypool
146 "You deserve a rest, Mr. Clay-
147 pool. I've heard how tremen-
148 dously you work."
149 "That's no lie," said Martin
150 Claypool. "I've always worked
151 hard all my life. I wouldn't be
152 on top today if I hadn't. But I
153 don't intend to slacken my pace
154 now, Mr. Krohn. No, sir! I'll
155 save my sightseeing till I'm
156 sixty-five or so and am thinking
157 of retiring. My present trip is
158 strictly business. I'm booked to
159 sail for home a week from
160 tomorrow."

161 "You Americans are wonder-
162 ful," remarked Mr. Krohn. "It's
163 a pleasure to do business with
164 you. You see straight and you
165 go directly to the point."

166 "Have to," said Martin Clay-
167 pool, drinking his highball.
168 "Competition. It's devil take
169 the hindmost where I come
170 from, Mr. Krohn. We don't
171 bunk ourselves about what we
172 are in business for. I don't,
173 anyhow. I admit I'm not in
174 business for my health. I'm in
175 the game to make money. The
176 more money I make, the better
177 I like it."

178 "That's common sense," said
179 Mr. Krohn.

180 "Common-sense College is
181 where I got my schooling," said
182 Martin Claypool, pouring him-
183 self another drink. "It's a tough
184 school. I wasn't born with any
185 silver spoon in my mouth, Mr.
186 Krohn. Nothing was ever hand-
187 ed to me on a platter. I had
188 to grab it. Yes, sir!" He raised
189 his glass, smiled expansively.
190 "I was born a poor boy," he
191 said. "I'm not ashamed of it.
192 I didn't stay poor. My dad was
193 a puddler in a steel mill. I went
194 to work in the mill myself when
195 I was a kid. See this chest and
196 these shoulders? Well, I didn't
197 get them from lying round a
198 country club and eating cream
199 puffs. I earned them, like every-
200 thing else I have. I've had no
201 bed of roses, I'll tell you. I've
202 known what it is to be hungry.
203 Yes, and I've seen the day when
204 I had but one shirt to my back
205 and not a dime in my pockets.
206 I know what poverty means."

207 "Really?"

208 "Yes, sir. I guess that's why I
209 know the value of money. Don't
210 let anybody kid you, Mr. Krohn.
211 Money is the only thing that
212 counts. People don't ask you
213 where or how you got it. All
214 that interests them is that you
215 have it. The more you have, the
216 better they like you. Why, do
217 you know that there are plenty
218 of families in St. Louis today who
219 wouldn't have let me in their
220 back doors when I was a lad
221 juggling steel rails for a living,
222 who today invite me in their
223 front doors and are damn glad
224 to see me too?"

225 "Indeed?"

226 "Yes, there's a lot of differ-
227 ence between Martin Claypool,
228 puddler, and Mr. Claypool, head

229 of Martin Claypool, Inc., Loco-
230 motive Builders. Yet I'm the
231 same man. The answer is—I've
232 done something. I've built a
233 big corporation out of nothing.
234 I've developed and perfected the
235 best engine in the world. I'm
236 mighty proud of that."
237 "You have every right to be,
238 Mr. Claypool."
239 "I wanted money—and I got
240 it," finished Martin Claypool.
241 "And I'm going to get more too."
242 Mr. Krohn's thin lips formed
243 a knowing smile. "I shouldn't
244 wonder," he said. He studied
245 Martin Claypool, whose great
246 torso was sprawled in an easy-
247 chair. "Mr. Claypool," he said,
248 "shall we—what is it now?—
249 talk turkey?"
250 "Shoot!" said Martin Clay-
251 pool.
252 "The Kiang-su-Kiang-si Rail-
253 road Syndicate has left every-
254 thing in my hands," said Mr.
255 Krohn.
256 "Good!"
257 "The money to buy rolling
258 stock for the new road has been
259 provided."
260 "Good!"
261 Mr. Krohn inserted a long
262 cigarette in a still longer holder,
263 lighted it and said, "The ques-
264 tion which I now must decide is:
265 Where shall I buy the locomo-
266 tives?"
267 "That's easy," said Martin
268 Claypool. "The Claypool loco-
269 motive is the best in the world."
270 Mr. Krohn nodded. "I

271 think," he said, "that you'll find
272 few who will dispute that. Even
273 our Chinese directors know its
274 reputation and are in favor of
275 buying Claypools. It's the best,
276 beyond doubt. That's just the
277 trouble."
278 "What do you mean?"
279 Mr. Krohn smiled blandly.
280 "It's too good," he said.
281 "You want the best, don't
282 you?" demanded Martin Clay-
283 pool. "Any fly-by-night outfit
284 can sell you a bunch of junk that
285 won't last five years."
286 "True," said Mr. Krohn.
287 "But, Mr. Claypool, isn't there
288 a difference in your mind be-
289 tween 'too good' and 'good
290 enough'?"
291 Martin Claypool regarded Mr.
292 Krohn with his shrewd blue
293 eyes. "You've got some sort of
294 proposition," he said. "What
295 is it?"
296 Mr. Krohn smiled admiringly.
297 "It would have taken weeks of
298 negotiation, hinting, circumlocu-
299 tion, to get this far in an inter-
300 view with a Chinese," he said.
301 "Well, I'm no Chinaman," re-
302 marked Mr. Claypool. "Put it
303 in plain words."
304 Mr. Krohn hitched his chair
305 nearer Martin Claypool. "What
306 I mean is this," he said in a con-
307 fidential tone: "If you supply
308 standard Claypool locomotives,
309 made according to the rigid spe-
310 cifications you sent us, at the
311 price we can pay, you can't make
312 much profit on the transaction."

313 "Don't expect to," said Mr.
314 Claypool promptly. "I'll tell
315 you just how it is, Mr. Krohn.
316 Business is slack in my works
317 now. I want to keep them run-
318 ning full time. That's why I
319 sent a bid to you. I want to get
320 into the Far East market. I
321 want the people out there to
322 learn by experience how good
323 the Claypool locomotive is.
324 There'll be more railroads built
325 in China—a lot more. I'm out
326 to win that business, even if at
327 first I only break even."

328 "But," said Mr. Krohn,
329 "you'd like to make money—a
330 lot of money—out of this pres-
331 ent deal—now wouldn't you?"

332 "Does a cat like cream?"

333 "There's cream in this, Mr.
334 Claypool."

335 "Show me!"

336 "Your bid was four million
337 dollars, wasn't it?"

338 "Yes."

339 "Suppose you could deliver
340 those engines to us at a cost to
341 you of, say, three million?"

342 "No chance," said Martin
343 Claypool. "I can't cut the price
344 of labor and material."

345 "No," said Mr. Krohn, closely
346 watching his face, "but you can
347 change the kind of labor and the
348 kind of material." Martin Clay-
349 pool frowned. "Of course," said
350 Mr. Krohn hurriedly, "I don't
351 wish to suggest——"

352 "I get you," said Martin
353 Claypool. "You mean I could
354 cheapen the quality of the Clay-
355 pool locomotive. That's it,
356 isn't it?"

357 "Well, since you believe in
358 plain speaking—yes." Martin
359 Claypool's frown deepened. "You
360 see," said Mr. Krohn, "I've a
361 plan by which you could make
362 around a million dollars."

363 Martin Claypool ceased to
364 frown. "Let's hear it," he said.

365 "Remember," said Mr. Krohn,
366 "we are dealing with a lot of
367 rich Chinese who know nothing
368 about the practical side of rail-
369 roading. They accept me as an
370 expert. Now listen. If I say the
371 engines you ship me are O. K.,
372 well, they are O. K. and no ques-
373 tions asked."

374 Martin Claypool gestured with
375 his cigar that he got that much
376 and wanted to hear more.

377 "My technical staff is under
378 my thumb," went on Mr. Krohn.
379 "No trouble there. They didn't
380 go to China because they love
381 the country or the work. They
382 went there for the same reason
383 I would or you would—to make
384 money. The Chinese officials
385 won't interfere. There's a pleas-
386 ant custom in China called the
387 squeeze, and the highest man-
388 darins are not above taking a
389 squeeze when they can. They
390 expect us to do the same. It's
391 business ethics out there. When
392 in Rome, you know—eh, Mr.
393 Claypool?"

394 "About that million," said
395 Martin Claypool.

396 "That's up to you," said Mr.

411

397 Krohn. "You make the loco-
398 motives—make them as cheaply
399 as you can—make them so they
400 look right and will run a while.
401 You'll get the contract on the
402 specifications you have sub-
403 mitted. Well, somehow, the set
404 of specifications in my office will
405 get mysteriously lost. The Chi-
406 nese will never know the differ-
407 ence. If the engines don't stand
408 up well, we'll blame it on the
409 climate and on the fact that the
410 native engineers don't know how
411 to treat them. We'll give them
412 the merry devil for abusing the
413 Claypools. Sound scheme,
414 what?"
415 Martin Claypool chewed his
416 cigar. A hard smile came to his
417 face. "A million, eh?" he said.
418 "That's worth thinking about.
419 You and I have something in
420 common, Mr. Krohn. We both
421 play the game for all we can get
422 out of it."
423 "Quite so."
424 "I'm thinking about your
425 proposition. I'm looking at it
426 from a practical point of view.
427 I'm not one of these moon-struck
428 idealists. I'm out for the dough,
429 first, last and all the time; and
430 what's more, I'm honest enough
431 to admit it. These big million-
432 aires can yap about service, but
433 you'll notice they didn't start to
434 yap till they'd served themselves
435 pretty well first. I know these
436 philanthropists. You have to be
437 a hard-headed trader first, and
438 get yours. You can't give away

439 what you haven't got. That's
440 sense, isn't it?"
441 "Right!"
442 "As you point out," went on
443 Martin Claypool, "the Chinese
444 market is different. They half-
445 way expect to be stung. Now
446 the only reason I make the Clay-
447 pool locomotive so well is because
448 I have to if I want to get busi-
449 ness in America. If I can do
450 business in China with an in-
451 ferior article, and clean up—
452 well, why not?"
453 "An eminently sensible point
454 of view," agreed Mr. Krohn
455 warmly.
456 "Now," asked Martin Clay-
457 pool abruptly, "where do you
458 come in?"
459 Mr. Krohn waved his long
460 cigarette delicately. "Thirty per
461 cent of your saving would sat-
462 isfy me," he said.
463 Mr. Claypool's teeth tightened
464 on his cigar. "Twenty per cent
465 seems right to me," he stated.
466 "I run risks," said Mr. Krohn,
467 the temperature of his voice fall-
468 ing many degrees.
469 "So do I."
470 "There are many people I will
471 have to—satisfy," said Mr.
472 Krohn, more coldly.
473 "Twenty per cent," repeated
474 Martin Claypool.
475 "Twenty-five," said Mr.
476 Krohn, his voice touching zero.
477 "Other firms would give more."
478 "Well, then," said Martin
479 Claypool, "call it twenty-five.
480 That means about three-quarters

of a million to me. Not so bad."

Mr. Krohn thawed. "Not at all bad," he said.

"We won't sign anything now," said Martin Claypool. "I'll have to do some figuring and cabling."

"I'll be at your service whenever you are ready," said Mr. Krohn. "The formal contract is waiting for your signature." He bowed low and started for the door.

"Mr. Krohn?"

"Yes, Mr. Claypool."

Martin Claypool's manner held a hint of embarrassment in it. "I'd like to ask you a personal question," he said.

"Certainly."

"I've been noticing the fit of that coat of yours," said Martin Claypool. "Now I thought I'd stock up on clothes while I'm in London. Could I ask who your tailor is?"

"Well"—Mr. Krohn hesitated —"that's a rather delicate question to ask a Londoner. We guard the secret of our tailor's name as zealously as you, in the States, might the name of a bootlegger who had genuine Scotch. But since it's you, Mr. Claypool, I'll let you in on my secret; and mind you, it's a secret worth knowing."

"Thanks."

"I get my clothes from an artist," said Mr. Krohn, smoothing a flawless coat. "He's a queer old bird with a tiny shop in Albemarle Street. Been a tailor fifty years, and his father and grandfather were tailors before him. He does all the cutting and fitting himself; and what beautiful work! He could have built up a huge business, but he keeps to a small clientele so, as he says, he can give every garment his personal attention. Old guild spirit, I suppose you'd call it. His prices——"

"They don't matter if he's good," put in Martin Claypool.

"He's the best I know about," said Mr. Krohn. "And, incidentally, his prices are not high. He has excellent materials, or you can take your own cloth to him to make up. Now I don't ordinarily send people to him, but I happen to know that he needs work badly now. He's getting old, you see, and can't produce very fast. He'll be glad to get your order."

"I expect to give him a big one," said Martin Claypool—"a complete outfit."

"I'll give you a letter of introduction to him," said Mr. Krohn.

"Lord save us, do I have to have a letter of introduction to a tailor?"

"You do to this one," said Mr. Krohn, sitting down at a desk and picking up a pen.

"Back home they hound you for business," observed Mr. Claypool.

"This old fellow will be a new experience for you then,"

565 said Mr. Krohn, writing. "You
566 can safely leave everything to
567 him. His taste is excellent.
568 Here you are."
569 "Thank you," said Martin
570 Claypool. "J. Tavistock,——
571 Albemarle Street. I'll drop in
572 and see this paragon tomorrow."
573 "You won't regret it," said
574 Mr. Krohn. "Good night."
575 London was having one of its
576 fair days when Mr. Claypool
577 woke next morning. After a
578 regal breakfast of bloaters and
579 other cheering things, he wrote
580 some business letters and then
581 sauntered out. He strolled down
582 the Strand, gazing idly into shop
583 windows.
584 "Bum lot of stuff," he decided.
585 "Not up to Fifth Avenue."
586 He had passed St. Paul's,
587 bound east, when he stopped
588 sharply in front of a shop win-
589 dow—rather, he was stopped.
590 It was a large shop, with a garish
591 new sign which announced that
592 it supplied you with cloth Direct
593 From the Mill at Prices that
594 Will Astound You!
595 Martin Claypool's eyes had
596 been arrested by a piece of tweed
597 on display in the window. Its
598 pattern was the sort calculated
599 to start a runaway, or stop one.
600 The prevailing tone was saffron
601 —a gaudy, bellicose saffron. It
602 had been surveyed and marked
603 off into square lots by lines of a
604 rich, poisonous green. It was as
605 rough and shaggy as the coat of
606 a collie; and, indeed, at a quick

607 glance, it looked somewhat like a
608 collie that had fallen into a kettle
609 of alphabet soup. Small vermi-
610 celli-like excrescences of divers
611 bilious hues leaped out from it to
612 smite and burn the eyes of pas-
613 sers-by. At a distance anyone
614 daring enough to wear a suit of
615 it must inevitably look like a
616 hairy man suffering from acute
617 jaundice complicated by some
618 strange and violent form of
619 measles.
620 It somehow fascinated Martin
621 Claypool. "It certainly would
622 make the boys at the country
623 club sit up and take notice," he
624 said. "A bit loud, maybe; but
625 a man in my position can get
626 away with anything."
627 He went into the shop. The
628 price of the fearsome stuff was,
629 indeed, astoundingly low. Mar-
630 tin Claypool bought enough for
631 a suit. The clerks followed him
632 with their eyes as he went down
633 the Strand with his purchase
634 under his arm, as if they expected
635 to see him arrested for carrying
636 incendiary material in the public
637 streets.
638 He found Albemarle Street
639 after questioning six bobbies.
640 Before his number he stopped
641 uncertainly. It was a plain, neat
642 brick house of two stories, with
643 a small bare shop window. On
644 the door he located a tiny name
645 plate, a venerable brass sign
646 worn by years of polishing, and
647 there in old-fashioned script was
648 the name, J. Tavistock.

649 Mr. Claypool knocked and
650 waited. Presently a small faded
651 man with white hair came to the
652 door. He did not look at Mar-
653 tin Claypool's face. He looked
654 at the lapels of his coat. They
655 seemed to sadden him.

656 "I've a letter to Mr. Tavis-
657 tock," Martin Claypool an-
658 nounced.

659 "Yes, sir. I'll take it. Step
660 in, please." His voice was small
661 and faded too.

662 He conducted Martin Clay-
663 pool into a dim parlorlike room,
664 furnished with two chairs and a
665 desk. It was all very solemn,
666 Mr. Claypool thought.

667 "Now, sir?" said the small
668 faded man.

669 "Are you Tavistock?"

670 "Yes, sir." He read the letter.
671 It brightened him. He bowed
672 to Martin Claypool. "Now,
673 sir?" he said again.

674 Martin Claypool was enter-
675 tained. He was accustomed to a
676 more aggressive type of sales-
677 manship. "The general idea,"
678 he said, "as you may gather
679 from the letter, is that I came
680 here to have you make me some
681 clothes."

682 "Very good, sir."

683 "I'll want a lot of them," said
684 Martin Claypool. "First, some
685 business suits—a dozen, any-
686 way. Then three or four evening
687 suits. Then golf clothes, sport
688 clothes, riding habits—you know
689 —a complete gentleman's out-
690 fit."

691 "I'll do my best for you, sir,"
692 said the tailor. "Will you step
693 this way, please?"

694 He conducted Martin Clay-
695 pool to a back room, larger than
696 the front one and a bit brighter.
697 It was furnished with a long mir-
698 ror; that was all. The tailor
699 stood for some minutes, his
700 white head cocked on one side,
701 studying Martin Claypool's im-
702 pressive proportions with a pen-
703 sive pale-blue eye. Then from
704 drawers he took little books of
705 cloth.

706 "For lounge suits for you, sir,
707 I'd advise this and this and
708 this," he said, indicating sam-
709 ples. "Now this blue would be
710 good, and I rather fancy this
711 brown herringbone and this gray
712 flannel for your type."

713 "A bit quiet, aren't they?"
714 remarked Martin Claypool.

715 "They are on the quiet side,
716 sir," said Tavistock. "But a
717 big man like you, sir, should
718 favor the conservative patterns.
719 Now here's a splendid suiting—
720 this nut brown—to go with your
721 complexion."

722 "You're the doctor," laughed
723 Martin Claypool. "Guess I'd
724 better leave it to you, eh?"

725 Tavistock nodded. "Yes, sir."
726 He did a lot of minute measur-
727 ing. "I'll start to work at once,
728 sir," he promised. "I'm not
729 very—well, rushed at the mo-
730 ment, you see."

731 "Now about the prices,"
732 began Mr. Claypool.

733 "I send out my bills once a
734 year," said Tavistock. "The
735 garments will be sent to you
736 directly they are finished."

737 "Good!" said Martin Clay-
738 pool. He was starting to leave.

739 "Is this your package, sir?"

740 "Well, I almost did forget
741 that. You'll make me up a sport
742 suit from some material I
743 bought?"

744 "If you wish, sir." Martin
745 Claypool unwrapped his new-
746 bought tweed. As it emerged
747 from the paper like some great,
748 hirsute, leprous caterpillar, Mr.
749 Tavistock audibly gasped. "Is
750 this the material, sir?" he asked.
751 His voice shook a trifle.

752 "That's it," said Martin Clay-
753 pool.

754 The tailor backed away from
755 it. He retreated to a corner and
756 looked on the defensive, as if he
757 expected the tweed to spring at
758 him and do him bodily harm.

759 "I—I really think, sir, if you
760 don't mind my saying so, that
761 you wouldn't like this," he
762 faltered.

763 "But I do like it," said Martin
764 Claypool.

765 "I mean, it wouldn't make up
766 very well."

767 "It might be a bit noticeable,"
768 granted Martin Claypool.

769 "Noticeable, sir? Of, yes—
770 yes, indeed. It would positively
771 call attention to you, sir. I
772 really wouldn't like to see you
773 in it."

774 "Well," laughed Martin Clay-
775 pool, "I'm the one who will have
776 to wear it. You need never see
777 me in it. I won't wear it outside
778 the state of Missouri."

779 "I'm sure, sir," said Tavistock
780 gravely, "it would be a serious
781 mistake to wear it anywhere."

782 "I'll take the blame for the
783 error then," said Martin Clay-
784 pool. "Let's see now; I'll want
785 a belted coat and patch pock-
786 ets——"

787 He saw the slight form of the
788 old tailor stiffen. "I'm very
789 sorry, sir," Tavistock said, "but
790 I could not make it for you."

791 "Why not?"

792 The old tailor approached the
793 goods, stretched out a wary and
794 reluctant finger and touched the
795 tweed.

796 "You see, sir," he explained,
797 "it isn't only the pattern that
798 makes it unsuitable; it's the
799 quality of the goods. Why, sir,
800 it's—shoddy!"

801 He said the last word as if it
802 were something almost too
803 terrible to mention.

804 "Oh, it didn't cost much and
805 I don't expect it to last for-
806 ever, you know," said Martin
807 Claypool, feeling somehow net-
808 tled. "Besides, I won't hold
809 you responsible for its wear;
810 only for its cut."

811 Tavistock shook his head.
812 "I'm sorry, sir," he said
813 firmly, "but I just couldn't
814 put my shears into a piece
815 of goods like that. And I
816 certainly could not put my

817 name on a suit made from it."
818 Martin Claypool had attained
819 his position in life by generally
820 getting his own way. He grew
821 more impatient.

822 "Look here," he said, "do
823 you want my order, or don't
824 you?"

825 "Of course I do, sir. To be
826 frank with you, sir, I need the
827 work badly. Times are hard in
828 England now, you know. My
829 business has fallen away to al-
830 most nothing. Now couldn't I
831 show you some real homespuns
832 or tweeds with a good bit of life
833 in them for that sport suit?"

834 Martin Claypool compressed
835 his lips. His jaws set stubborn-
836 ly. His associates knew this was
837 a sign to stop arguing.

838 "No," he said. "I want a
839 suit made of that material."

840 Tavistock sighed and shook
841 his head. "I'm very sorry, sir,"
842 he said. "You'll find tailors in
843 London who will make it up for
844 you. I can't."

845 "Can't, eh?" Martin Claypool
846 snapped. "What do you mean
847 —you can't?"

848 "Mr. Claypool," said Tavis-
849 tock in his faded voice, "I've
850 been a tailor all my life. I
851 haven't grown rich, but I've
852 been proud of my work always.
853 I inherited a tradition from my
854 father, who had it from his. In
855 a hundred years the name Tavis-
856 tock has never been put on a
857 suit of poor fit or poor material.
858 I hope it never will be."

859 "Oh, never mind putting your
860 label in this suit if that's what
861 is worrying you," said Martin
862 Claypool, half amused, half
863 angry. He always tried to win
864 a contest of wills.

865 "That isn't the point, sir,"
866 said the tailor. "You see, sir, if
867 I may say so, I look upon my
868 work as—well, as a sort of art.
869 You wouldn't ask a painter to do
870 a cheap and nasty picture, would
871 you, sir?"

872 "He'd do it if he needed the
873 money," said Martin Claypool.
874 "That's the thing that counts in
875 this world—the old brass. I
876 know the world. I've found
877 that out."

878 "If you'll pardon my saying
879 so, sir," said the old tailor, "I'm
880 a great deal older than you; and
881 I have a notion which may be
882 old-fashioned, but which I have
883 found to be true, and that is that
884 a good name is better than great
885 riches. Good day, sir."

886 The little tailor bowed stiffly.
887 Martin Claypool felt an unrea-
888 soning surge of rage. He
889 surged angrily toward the door.
890 The tailor's voice stopped him:
891 "One minute please, sir."

892 Martin Claypool stopped,
893 turned. "Changed your mind,
894 eh?" he grunted.

895 "No, sir. I merely wanted to
896 ask you to take this away." The
897 tailor pointed at the scrofulous
898 tweed. "I really shouldn't want
899 to have it about my shop, sir."

900 Martin Claypool gathered up

the cloth and stalked out. He was not a man of even temper. He was mad now, mad all through; and yet he was critical enough of his own emotions to realize that his anger was out of all proportion to its cause.

"There are thousands of tailors in London," he growled, as he strode toward his hotel. "I don't need to bother with that old fool. Why should I let him upset me? He's nothing but a stick-in-the-mud, a failure. Him and his art! Cutting out pants an art? Bunk!"

Once in his suite, he flung the tweed on a chair, where it clung like a flat serpent.

"Why should that old fossil of a vest cutter get my goat so?" Martin Claypool demanded of himself. "Better get to work and forget him."

From an elaborate pigskin portfolio he took papers, blue prints, photographs and studied them. "Let's see now——" He wrote down figures. "Suppose now, I substituted. . . . Let's see now—six times nine is fifty-four—— Big saving there. Not so good, of course. Apt to break any time. Good enough for a lot of Chinks though."

He picked up a photograph from the pile in front of him. It was a picture of the newest Claypool locomotive. He ran his eyes over its powerful lines. His eyes stopped at the name plate, set in the side. He could read it, clearly:

CLAYPOOL. Built and Guaranteed by Martin Claypool, Inc.

He got up and walked across the floor and poured himself a glass of water. The piece of tweed tripped him and he kicked it aside. Then he stooped, picked it up, ran his fingers over its surface, held it to the light. He dropped into a chair, still holding the cloth in his hand, and sat there, staring at it. He was thinking now of the first locomotive he had built and of how he felt when he saw it steam past him, and read the name—his name—engraved on the plate in its giant side. He must have sat there, staring, motionless, for an hour. He sprang up suddenly, reached for the telephone.

"Hello, Tavistock! This is Mr. Claypool. . . . Yes, that's right, Claypool. Go ahead with that order of mine. Forget about that sport suit. I've been examining the tweed and I find it isn't up to standard. . . . You're welcome. Good-by."

He called up another number:

"Mr. Krohn? This is Martin Claypool. Listen, that deal we discussed last night is off. . . . Yes, all off. I'll take your contract, but I'll fill it with A-1 locomotives, real Claypools, or nothing. . . . Yes, I'll pass up that money. All right, Krohn,

982 you can give the order to a
983 Swede, or a Czech or the devil
984 if you want to. But get this,
985 Krohn—if you ever buy a Claypool locomotive you are going to 986
get the real thing. No shoddy. 987
No, sir!" 988

THE ANALYSIS

A glance at the chart will show that his story contains 988 lines. There is in this story no Body scene, because there is no clash of traits shown within the character. The Beginning occupies lines 1 to 963 and the Ending occupies lines 963 to 972 and 973 to 988. The Ending is particularly interesting because it shows *two* Decisive Acts; one in regard to the problem set before Martin Claypool by the tailor, the other the problem set before Martin Claypool by Krohn.

In the Beginning the bulk of the presentation units are interchanges. Lines 1 to 38 is an interchange between Martin Claypool and the waiter, lines 39 to 95 are the fifth step of that interchange and show Claypool's reflections. This is the one weak spot in the Beginning of the story. Here the basic trait which determines the main outcome ought to have been planted and it ought to consist of a pride in the name of Claypool. It could have been brought about by some such device as having him known to the waiter or having him sign his name and having the waiter look awed or extremely respectful because of what is conveyed to him by the name Martin Claypool on the check. Then, this pride in name being emphasized, we would have been prepared later for the Decisive Act of the story.

The interchange between Krohn and Claypool is quite definitely one intended to set forth the possibility of profit for Martin Claypool. The interesting thing about it as a variant from the other stories we have discussed is that Martin Claypool definitely comes to a decision then and there. The fifth step of that scene is the interchange between the two in regard to the name of the tailor, and here again the effect upon Martin Claypool of the mention of his own name could have been emphasized a little more strongly than it is, his pride in his name being an extremely important factor in his character to account for the solution of the story. The interchange which follows, between Claypool and the clerks, in which Claypool buys the loud goods is one in which he is made to be rather proud of his own ability, as Martin Claypool, to carry off any situation, and in this respect it is good, as it prepares the way for the final decisive act. In the interchange between Claypool and the tailor, the fifth step brings about his reflections which come nearer to being a Body scene than anything else, and they project his awareness of the stimulus, which is the photograph of the Claypool locomotive with the name-plate, which brings to his mind, as a perfectly new stimulus, the thought that he is proud of that name.

Then there follow swiftly the two conclusive Acts; one the calling of the tailor on the telephone, the other the calling on the telephone of Krohn.

This story is the last of the series of this type story of Decision. It is illuminating because it shows that it is of the second type of characterization story. In the first type the story interprets character, and it shows that that character is, throughout, the same. In this case, the story shows a development of character. In the first case the characteristics of the actor remain unchanged. The story deals with the manipulation of events by the character, through the exercise of a trait already in his character. In the second case, there is an actual growth of characteristics. Certain traits, not hitherto a part of the actor's character, emerge and determine the outcome. We may see, therefore, already four distinct types of story. One, the Accomplishment story, which requires only that the happenings shall be interesting and highly exciting, but not greatly significant.

Two, the second type Accomplishment story, in which the moment in life shall be both interesting and exciting, but shall in addition, have a certain significance of characterization. This is the type of the Mary Brecht Pulver and of the John Marquand stories, in which the outcome is brought about through the accomplishment of an actor who evidences in that accomplishment a certain definite and individual trait of character, or a capacity not inherent in anybody who might be confronted with that problem.

The third type is the Decision story in which the great moment of the story is one in which there is a conflict of emotions, and the basic character trait emerges.

Then there comes this fourth type, which Mr. Connell has presented, in which the character becomes aware of a new stimulus, and there is presented to the readers an evidence of certain traits in his character not hitherto known to the reader, and it is through the exercise of those new characteristics that he solves the problem of conduct facing him. We often hear statements to the effect that the American short-story is not as important or poignant as the Continental short-story. The chief evidence upon which such critics base their comparison is that the American short-story so often has a happy ending and the Continental short-story so frequently has an unhappy ending. The critics say that the American short-story goes deep into the life. They make the distinction between "realism" and "romance" which in a final analysis is no distinction at all. As a matter of fact the Continental short-stories do not go very deep, for the simple reason that they take a single great moment and show how a character reacted at that moment. When they so render the responses of a character they say that their rendering is true to life. They fail to realize that readers cannot actually know the character of any person from a single reaction at a single great moment. Writers and critics tell you that a certain reaction of a character at a single great moment is true to life because "it actually happened." In adducing such evidence they fall into the error of confusing accuracy with truth to life. Accuracy is simply the exact rendering of a fact. Truth goes beyond accuracy and presents as sincerely as possible the relationship of one fact to all other facts within the limitations laid down by the artistic purpose of the teller of the story.

The isolated fact that a certain character, at a great moment of his or her life, found his purpose achieved, or on the other hand found his purpose frustrated, may be accurate; but it is not essentially true to life. Therefore, to say that accomplishment, which is a happy ending, and frustration, which is an unhappy ending, are opposed as representing truth and untruth is not at all a fair conclusion. One single instance of either accomplishment or frustration is not a real test of character. To show the conduct of a person at a given moment is not so important as to show the characteristic of the person that dictated his conduct. Conduct is merely a surface indication of character, and like all surface indications, is likely to be misleading.

The critics who make this distinction between American and Continental stories have failed to realize that usually American stories which they say do not go deep, are stories which deal with accomplishment, whereas the stories which really go beyond accomplishment or "wish fulfilment" into the depths of character, are stories which deal with a real test of character when a choice has to be made between an opportunity to profit and a standard of conduct. The important short-story in America is that which is important anywhere. It is the short-story which deals not with Accomplishment as material, but with Decision. As the most important moment in a short-story is one of decision, so it is in any form of fiction, whether that be play or novel or short-story or moving picture. The moment when a character has to choose is what is known in the movies as the "big moment" of the story. The decision is between a possibility of achievement and has opposed to it frustration; but the frustration is brought about through a generous act of abnegation on the part of the character, and not through the stepping in of fate as in the Continental short-story. Therein lies the essential difference between the American and the Continental attitude toward life. There may be in this country frustration; but it is frustration which is brought about by a character's actions or by some basic trait under his control. The characters are not regarded as supine puppets moved about by fate. There is, however, in our newer knowledge of psychology, a justification for feeling that a character can act only in a certain way, and that at great moments only basic traits determine conduct. It is for that reason that I am including in this volume the next two stories, as companion stories, *The Roads We Take*, by O. Henry, and *The Mummy*, by John Galsworthy.

THE ROADS WE TAKE

BEGINNING	Main Actor's necessity for choice is presented.	Series of Incidents, setting forth condition.	1–110	Readers' interest captured by unusualness of happenings.
		Interchange. Effect upon Bob Tidball and Shark Dodson.	111–252	Choices apparent.
ENDING	Decisive Act.	Shark Dodson shoots Bob Tidball.	253–265	Choice made. Answer to Narrative Question is clear.
	Sequel.	Dodson rides away on Bolivar.	266–270	Cupidity triumphs.
BEGINNING	Necessity for choice presented.	Interchange. Dodson and Peabody, showing choices apparent.	271–318	Choice is required.
ENDING	Decisive Act.	Shark Dodson insists upon settlement.	319–328	Answer is clear. Cupidity triumphs

THE ROADS WE TAKE

BY O. HENRY

THERE is great scope for conjecture in wondering how successful O. Henry might have been in this modern age with our newer knowledge of the pyschological laws of character superimposed upon his capacity for observation and his talent in presentation.

O. Henry was especially interested in a philosophy of character which John Galsworthy has since summed up very succinctly by saying that "Behind conduct lies the main trend of character." By this he meant that the basic trait of a person's character determines that person's responses to the great moments of life.

Very early in his career O. Henry wrote a story called *Roads of Destiny*, in which he showed that when a boy came to three forks in a road the outcome was the same. Showing his progress along each successive road, O. Henry caused him in all three cases to be shot by a bullet from the same pistol. This story was a groping toward this theory of predetermination, with the exception that, here, Fate determined the outcome.

In the stories which I am including under what I call the "basic trait" category, *The Roads We Take* and *The Mummy*, it is not an outside Fate, but a basic trait of character in the main actor which determines the outcome. As an example of this type of story, *The Roads We Take* will be very informative, especially in comparison with *The Mummy*.

CASE No. 18

THE ROADS WE TAKE

BY O. HENRY

1 Twenty miles west of Tucson
2 the "Sunset Express" stopped at
3 a tank to take on water. Be-
4 sides the aqueous addition the
5 engine of that famous flyer
6 acquired some other things that
7 were not good for it.

8 While the fireman was lower-
9 ing the feeding hose, Bob Tid-
10 ball, "Shark" Dodson, and a
11 quarter-bred Creek Indian called
12 John Big Dog climbed on the
13 engine and showed the engineer
14 three round orifices in pieces of
15 ordnance that they carried.
16 These orifices so impressed the
17 engineer with their possibilities
18 that he raised both hands in a
19 gesture such as accompanies the
20 ejaculation "Do tell!"

21 At the crisp command of
22 Shark Dodson, who was leader
23 of the attacking force, the
24 engineer descended to the
25 ground and uncoupled the engine
26 and tender. Then John Big
27 Dog, perched upon the coal,
28 sportively held two guns upon
29 the engine driver and the fire-
30 man, and suggested that they
31 run the engine fifty yards
32 away and there await further
32 orders.

33 Shark Dodson and Bob Tid-
34 ball, scorning to put such low-
35 grade ore as the passengers
36 through the mill, struck out
37 for the rich pocket of the express
38 car. They found the messenger
39 serene in the belief that the
40 "Sunset Express" was taking on
41 nothing more stimulating and
42 dangerous than aqua pura.
43 While Bob was knocking this
44 idea out of his head with the
45 butt-end of his six-shooter Shark
46 Dodson was already dosing the
47 express-car with dynamite.

48 The safe exploded to the tune
49 of $30,000, all gold and currency.
50 The passengers thrust their heads
51 casually out of the windows to
52 look for the thundercloud. The
53 conductor jerked at the bell
54 rope, which sagged down loose
55 and unresisting, at his tug.
56 Shark Dodson and Bob Tidball,
57 with their booty in a stout
58 canvas bag, tumbled out of the
59 express car and ran awkwardly

60 in their high-heeled boots to
61 the engine.

62 The engineer, sullenly angry
63 but wise, ran the engine, accord-
64 ing to orders, rapidly away from
65 the inert train. But before this
66 was accomplished the express
67 messenger, recovered from Bob
68 Tidball's persuader to neutrality,
69 jumped out of his car with a
70 Winchester rifle and took a
71 trick in the game. Mr. John
72 Big Dog, sitting on the coal
73 tender, unwittingly made a
74 wrong lead by giving an imita-
75 tion of a target, and the mes-
76 senger trumped him. With a
77 ball exactly between his shoulder
78 blades the Creek chevalier of
79 industry rolled off to the ground,
80 thus increasing the share of his
81 comrades in the loot by one-
82 sixth each.

83 Two miles from the tank
84 the engineer was ordered to
85 stop.

86 The robbers waved a defiant
87 adieu and plunged down the
88 steep slope into the thick woods
89 that lines the track. Five
90 minutes of crashing through a
91 thicket of chaparral brought
92 them to open woods, where the
93 three horses were tied to low-
94 hanging branches. One was
95 waiting for John Big Dog, who
96 would never ride by night or
97 day again. This animal the
98 robbers divested of saddle and
99 bridle and set free. They
100 mounted the other two with the
101 bag across one pommel and

102 rode fast and with discretion
103 through the forest and up a
104 primeval, lonely gorge. Here
105 the animal that bore Bob Tidball
106 slipped on a mossy boulder and
107 broke a foreleg. They shot him
108 through the head at once and
109 sat down to hold a council of
110 flight.

111 Made secure for the present
112 by the tortuous trail they had
113 traveled, the question of time
114 was no longer so big. Many
115 miles and hours lay between
116 them and the spryest posse that
117 could follow. Shark Dodson's
118 horse, with trailing rope and
119 dropped bridle, panted and
120 cropped thankfully of the grass
121 along the stream in the gorge.
122 Bob Tidball opened the sack,
123 and drew out double handfuls
124 of the neat packages of currency
125 and the one sack of gold and
126 chuckled with the glee of a child.

127 "Say, you old double-decked
128 pirate," he called joyfully to
129 Dodson, "you said we could do
130 it—you got a head for financing
131 that knocks the horns off of any-
132 thing in Arizona."

133 "What are we going to do
134 about a hoss for you, Bob?
135 We ain't got long to wait here.
136 They'll be on our trail before
137 daylight in the mornin'."

138 "Oh, I guess that cayuse of
139 yourn'll carry double for a
140 while," answered the sanguine
141 Bob. "We'll annex the first
142 animal we come across. By
143 jingoes, we made a haul, didn't

we? Accordin' to the marks on this money there's $30,000— $15,000 apiece!"

"It's short of what I expected, said Shark Dodson, kicking softly at the packages with the toe of his boot. And then he looked pensively at the wet sides of his tired horse.

"Old Bolivar's mighty nigh played out," he said slowly. "I wish that sorrel of yours hadn't got hurt.

"So do I," said Bob, heartily, "but it can't be helped. Bolivar's got plenty of bottom—he'll get us both far enough to get fresh mounts. Dang it, Shark, I can't help thinkin' how funny it is that an Easterner like you can come out here and give us Western fellows cards and spades in the desperado business. What part of the East was you from anyway?"

"New York State," said Shark Dodson, sitting down on a boulder and chewing a twig. "I was born on a farm in Ulster County. I ran away from home when I was seventeen. It was an accident my comin' West. I was walkin' along the road with my clothes in a bundle, makin' for New York City. I had an idea of goin' there and makin' lots of money. I always felt like I could do it. I came to a place one even' where the road forked and I didn't know which fork to take. I studied about it for half an hour and then I took the left-hand. That night I run into the camp of a Wild West show that was travelin' among the little towns, and I went West with it. I've often wondered if I wouldn't have turned out different if I'd took the other road."

"Oh, I reckon you'd have ended up about the same," said Bob Tidball, cheerfully philosophical. "It ain't the roads we take; it's what's inside of us that makes us turn out the way we do."

Shark Dodson got up and leaned against a tree.

"I'd a good deal rather that sorrel of yourn hadn't hurt himself, Bob," he said again, almost pathetically.

"Same here," agreed Bob; "he sure was a first-rate kind of a crowbait. But Bolivar, he'll pull us through all right. Reckon we'd better be movin' on, hadn't we, Shark? I'll bag the boodle ag'in and we'll hit the trail for higher timber."

Bob Tidball replaced the spoil in the bag and tied the mouth of it tightly with a cord. When he looked up the most prominent object that he saw was the muzzle of Shark Dodson's .45 held upon him without a waver.

"Stop your funnin'," said Bob, with a grin. "We got to be hittin' the breeze."

"Set still," said Shark. "You ain't goin' to hit no breeze, Bob.

227 I hate to tell you, but there
228 ain't any chance for but one of
229 us. Bolivar, he's plenty tired,
230 and he can't carry double."
231 "We been pards, me and you,
232 Shark Dodson, for three years,"
233 Bob said quietly, "We've risked
234 our lives together time and
235 again. I've always give you a
236 square deal, and I thought you
237 was a man. I've heard some
238 queer stories about you shootin'
239 one or two men in a peculiar
240 way, but I never believed 'em.
241 Now if you're havin' a little
242 fun with me, Shark, put your
243 gun up, and we'll get on Bolivar
244 and vamoose. If you mean to
245 shoot—shoot, you black-hearted
246 son of a tarantula!"
247 Shark Dodson's face bore a
248 deeply sorrowful look.
249 "You don't know how bad I
250 feel," he sighed, "about that
251 sorrel of yourn breakin' his leg,
252 Bob."
253 The expression on Dodson's
254 face changed in an instant to
255 one of cold ferocity mingled with
256 inexorable cupidity. The soul
257 of the man showed itself for a
258 moment like an evil face in the
259 window of a reputable house.
260 Truly Bob Tidball was never
261 to "hit the breeze" again. The
262 deadly .45 of the false friend
263 cracked and filled the gorge with
264 a roar that the walls hurled back
265 with indignant echoes.
266 And Bolivar, unconscious ac-
267 complice, swiftly bore away the
268 last of the holders-up of the

269 "Sunset Express," not put to the
270 stress of carrying "double."
271 But as Shark Dodson galloped
272 away the woods seemed to fade
273 from his view; the revolver in
274 his right hand turned to the
275 curved arm of a mahogany
276 chair; his saddle was strangely
277 upholstered, and he opened his
278 eyes and saw his feet, not in
279 stirrups, but resting quietly on
280 the edge of a quartered-oak desk.
281 I am telling you that Dodson,
282 of the firm of Dodson & Decker,
283 Wall Street brokers, opened his
284 eyes. Peabody, the confidential
285 clerk, was standing by his chair,
286 hesitating to speak. There was
287 a confused hum of wheels below,
288 and the sedative buzz of an
289 electric fan.
290 "Ahem! Peabody," said Dod-
291 son, blinking. "I must have
292 fallen asleep. I had a most
293 remarkable dream. What is it,
294 Peabody?"
295 "Mr. Williams, sir, of Tracy &
296 Williams, is outside. He has
297 come to settle his deal in X. Y. Z.
298 The market caught him short,
299 sir, if you remember."
300 "Yes, I remember. What is
301 X. Y. Z. quoted at to-day,
302 Peabody?"
303 "One eighty-five sir."
304 "Then that's his price."
305 "Excuse me," said Peabody,
306 rather nervously, "for speaking
307 of it, but I've been talking to
308 Williams. He's an old friend of
309 yours, Mr. Dodson, and you
310 practically have a corner in X.

311 Y. Z. I thought you might—
312 that is, I thought you might
313 not remember that he sold you
314 the stock at 98. If he settles at
315 the market price it will take
316 every cent he has in the world
317 and his home too to deliver the
318 shares."

319   The expression on Dodson's
320 face changed in an instant to
321 one of cold ferocity mingled
322 with inexorable cupidity. The
323 soul of the man showed itself
324 like an evil face in the window
325 of a reputable house.
326   "He will settle at one eighty-
327 five," said Dodson. "Bolivar
328 cannot carry double."

The Analysis

One of the characteristics of the story of Decision is that it almost always forces the writer to open with a series of incidents presenting the main condition confronting the actor. The chart of this story will show that it is made up of practically parallel stories; one the story of Shark, Dodson and Bob Tidball, the other the story of Dodson and Peabody. The complete story occupies 328 lines, of which the first 111 lines are occupied with setting forth the incidents which portray the main condition. Then the fifth step of this awareness of the actor is an interchange between Tidball and Shark Dodson at the close of which the two choices are apparent; one, of abandoning his partner, the other, of assisting him. The Ending occupies lines 253 to 270 and shows a Decisive Act, lines 253 to 265, in which he shoots his partner, and the Sequel (266–270) which is that he rides away on Bolivar. And here we have cupidity as the character trait which is triumphant.

Now, we notice when we come to the parallel story that there are no series of incidents setting forth the conditions, but that they are set forth in an interchange. This is because they have already been set forth in the opening part of the story. This interchange is between Dodson and Peabody, and it shows the choices which he may make. Again the Decisive Act follows swiftly, and shows that he insists upon settlement, and that cupidity is again triumphant. This is what I should call a transitional story in the development of the character or choice story which is based upon the assumption that "behind conduct lies the main trend of character." It is a companion story to the one which follows:—*The Mummy*, by John Galsworthy.

Main Problem Presented.	Meeting. Eugene Daunt at 66 finds himself facing death.	**Main Narrative Question is: "What course will he take?"**
		1– 50
	(Flash-back Beginning shows previous choices in similar circumstances—a development of the type of parallel character decisions, of which *The Roads We Take* is an example.)	
BEGINNING A series of parallel meetings or interchanges at the close of which the Main Actor is faced by a problem of conduct similar to the Main Problem of conduct confronting him.	Interchange. Eugene and Mollie. At 28 he finds that he must make effort or marry Mollie.	His effort takes form of going on yachting cruise. (a game)
		51–232
	Interchange. Eugene and Mollie. At 38 he finds that he must make effort or elope with Mollie.	His effort takes form of going to Boer War. (a long day's hunting)
		233–391
	Meeting. Eugene, at 49 becomes aware of curtailed income.	His effort consists of playing billiards systematically. (a game)
		392–417
	Interchange. Eugene, at 54, and recruiting officers.	Effort takes form of stalking innocuous persons.
		418–484
	Meeting. Eugene, at 57, and condition of poverty.	Effort takes form of making bets.
		485–519
	Interchange with Mollie. He must make effort or accept her proposal.	Turns again to playing billiards.
		520–590
	Meeting. Eugene and condition of shakiness.	Turns to raising dogs.
		591–705
	(End of flash-back.)	
ENDING Conclusive Act.	Eugene, at 66, is finally down and out Throwing contest.	Answer to Narrative Question: He meets great crises as he has hitherto met minor crises. He avoids effort by turning to some form of sport.
		706–836

THE MUMMY

BY JOHN GALSWORTHY

THIS story is included because it shows the "basic trait" type of story at its highest point of development. The quality of the "basic trait" type of story that distinguishes it from other types is that it is a series of parallel scenes tied together by character traits. At the end of each scene there is a struggle of character traits; and always the same type trait is triumphant. It is what the older school of teachers used to call the "dominant trait."

The immediately distinguishing feature of this story as opposed to the O. Henry story is that this story is a real "flash-back" decision story. It opens with the moment when the character has to act. There is no evasion or delay possible. This urgency is an essential quality of interest in the good story of Decision.

The obvious disadvantage of opening at such a moment of urgency is that in the ordinary story of Decision the Conclusive Act comes immediately after the moment when the character becomes aware of the urgency. Such a story would be extremely short. The only way in which length can be added to such a story is to make a "flash-back" between the moment of urgency and the moment of Decision.

Because this story shows the method of presenting such a "flash-back," I am extremely anxious that every reader shall examine it with the greatest care.

CASE No. 19

THE MUMMY

BY JOHN GALSWORTHY

In the end shelter of that Devon watering-place Eugene Daunt had been sitting for two days and nights. At sixty-three, and with his lack of adipose, any but the southwest wind in late October must have "sewn him up" long before. He sat, huddled in his worn blue overcoat with belt tight-drawn, peaked golfing cap over his eyes, and his skinny brown hands deep-thrust into his pockets, dozing or staring before him.

This end shelter was out of range of lamplight, and few passed it even in the daytime. For these reasons he had chosen it. He had ceased to wonder how much longer he could "stick it." His nodding thoughts were free from the tortures of effort. The cards were hopelessly against him, and he just wanted to be let alone. Nothing so definite as suicide was in his drowsing mind. Suicide meant effort, and he had always avoided effort, except in the playing of games. He played this last game—conserving the ebbing vitality of his body, ribby as a greyhound's. Neither was he bitter, sitting there. Natural that the "Johnnies" of whom he had borrowed scantily these last five years should be "fed up." He would have been "fed up" himself. Natural that his old landlady should have come to him crying—"poor old soul"; a wonder she hadn't, long ago! He had shifted two watering-places down to the coast, to sit it out where he was not known. On his lean brown face lurked a sort of grin. He looked a little like a Red Indian; had there ever been one who needed their stoicism more — or needed it less?

Only child of an Indian civilian, Eugene Daunt had been born in India, and taken home at the age of five. While at a private school he lost both parents, killed in an accident, and fell under the protection of his father's sister, an unmarried lady who lived at Baymouth, and

435

60 doted on him. He remained at
61 this private school till he was
62 fourteen. He was given to dys-
63 pepsia, and apt at games, good-
64 looking, assured, stoical; he won
65 races, made scores, had indiges-
66 tion whenever there was an
67 examination. It was thought
68 that he would go into the army
69 or the diplomatic service. On
70 leaving school, however, he was
71 such a comfort to his aunt, and
72 it was so difficult to find a tutor
73 who did not give him instant
74 dyspepsia, that he was found
75 suddenly too old to go in for
76 either. His aunt rejoiced; she
77 would have missed him too
78 much, and he was now perma-
79 nently free for the sports, handi-
80 caps, drives, and matches of the
81 neighborhood, whence he could
82 bring home those cups, cigarette
83 cases, and other rewards of
84 which she was so proud. She
85 had a verandaed house called
86 Eglamont, in a pleasant garden.
87 Eugene had his own rooms and
88 key, his spirits and tobacco, his
89 fox terrier and spaniel, a day's
90 hunting when he wished; he shot
91 well, and was welcome with his
92 gun, to the landed neighbors; or
93 on the local yachts where he
94 looked to the life in a yachting
95 cap. He had no patrimony, but
96 his aunt had enough for two. A
97 singularly placid woman she
98 concerned herself entirely with
99 seeing that time made no changes
100 in the life of him on whom she
101 doted. No girls, however much

102 he impressed them, lean in his
103 very good clothes, detached him
104 from her roof. It was less dan-
105 gerous to prefer, platonically at
106 least, the society of barmaids and
107 married women. So the years
108 passed by him, embalmed in her
109 affection, in sport, and cigar-
110 ettes; till at the age of twenty-
111 eight, he fell in love with the
112 wife of a naval commander with
113 whom he yachted and played
114 billiards. She was a gray-eyed
115 young woman, with great good
116 humor, and an admirable figure.
117 They had leased a house within
118 a stone's throw of "Eglamont"
119 before the naval commander re-
120 tired to the China station for
121 two years. Not, indeed, till
122 after his departure was Eugene
123 aware of his feelings. Loyal to
124 one with whom he had played
125 games, he took himself in hand
126 at once, and would sit gloomily
127 pulling his fox terrier's ears and
128 smoking cigarette after cigarette,
129 sooner than go and see her. In
130 1890 the phrase "playing the
131 game" had not as yet come in,
132 and he was confined to fortifica-
133 tion by the term "not sporting."
134 The young woman, however,
135 whose name was Mollie, had
136 Venetian red hair; and he was
137 startled one morning by her ap-
138 pearance with a letter in her
139 hand. She had come to read
140 him a message from her husband.
141 After that it seemed natural that
142 she should often come. The
143 effort of saying: "Look here, you

144 know, you mustn't; I'm gone on
145 you," exhausted his defenses;
146 nor was it easy to remember a
147 man who, after all, was too old
148 for her, and would not be back
149 for two years. They remained,
150 however, on platonic terms, part-
151 ly because of their loyalty to the
152 absent commander, and partly
153 because he was not accustomed
154 to any form of energy outside
155 sport. So he would sit in his
156 long chair, a cigarette between
157 the yellow-stained fingers of one
158 hand, and his fox terrier's ear
159 between his yellow-stained fin-
160 gers of the other hand, staring
161 at her and casting out between
162 his filed-looking teeth, his short
163 laughs and answers to her rally-
164 ing talk. So it might have gone
165 on for the two years, if her hair,
166 one evening, had not been too
167 much for Plato.

168 Eugene woke up next morning
169 genuinely shocked—he had not
170 been "sporting." And yet, it
171 was impossible to resist her. For
172 a fortnight the affair proceeded,
173 till one morning she arrived with
174 a telegram in her hand, and on
175 her face an expression remorse-
176 ful, elated, tearful, glad. The
177 commander had died on a boat
178 expedition up a Chinese river.
179 The news was three weeks old.
180 "Gene," she said, "isn't it
181 awful, and isn't it—isn't it won-
182 derful, in a way! After all, we—
183 we haven't committed—and we
184 can—we can be—" She
185 stopped; his face was copper-

186 colored. He stammered out:
187 "Poor Bink! Poor old chap!"
188 She went away dreadfully up-
189 set. Next day he had violent
190 dyspepsia.

191 During the following weeks of
192 seclusion under his aunt's care,
193 he had time to see the matter in
194 all its bearings; it had become
195 evident to him that he was on
196 the edge of being married. It
197 would need inertia almost
198 amounting to effort to avoid that
199 fate. Had he enough? Think-
200 ing of her hair, he felt a sinking
201 in that part of him nourished
202 just then solely on Benger's
203 food. In the third week it came
204 to him by inspiration that he
205 knew a "Johnny" about to start
206 on a six weeks' yachting cruise.
207 That evening, eluding his aunt,
208 he made his way to the "Lion's
209 Tail" and over a game of bil-
210 liards proposed to the "Johnny"
211 and was accepted. That night
212 he was free from pain for the first
213 time.

214 Leaning over the side in the
215 sun, on his friend's yacht, a week
216 later, he felt a kind of regretful
217 deliverance. He wrote from
218 Fowey:—

219 "Dear Mollie,
220 "I have been very seedy, but
221 am feeling as right as rain again.
222 This is a nice little hooker. We
223 shall be hanging about in her
224 most of the summer. The
225 weather is jolly, at present. I
226 hope you are fit. It was a

227 shock to me to hear about poor
228 old Bink. Poor old chap! What
229 awful luck!

230   "With the best,
231   "Yours ever,
232   "Gene."

233   He did not return to Bay-
234 mouth till October. He hardly
235 knew whether to be glad or sorry
236 that she had left. A letter in-
237 formed him that she could not
238 live on her "moldy pension" and
239 had started a milliner's shop.
240 He admired her pluck, her ener-
241 gy. She sent her love and hoped
242 that his "poor tummy" was
243 stronger. She mentioned thea-
244 tres—she was evidently having
245 quite a good time. Just one
246 sentence began: "Gene, don't
247 you ever——" It had been
248 crossed through. He felt that
249 she had "sand."
250   He settled down to the
251 sports of the season; and time
252 passed like a game that is
253 played.
254   He was thirty-eight, a little
255 more dried, with a gray hair or
256 two, when she came down to
257 Baymouth again with her second
258 husband, an old sportsman of
259 fifty with any amount of brass,
260 and a dicky chest. He was no
261 end glad to see her, looking "so
262 jolly fit" with her hair as red as
263 ever. "The old sportsman"
264 played quite a good game of
265 bridge—just then coming in.
266 They resumed their relations
267 quietly under his nose. She had

268 never stopped loving him all this
269 time, she said. He was touched
270 and flattered, and would sit in
271 his long chair with a cigarette
272 between the yellow-stained fin-
273 gers of one hand, and the ear of
274 his spaniel between the yellow-
275 stained fingers of the other hand,
276 staring up at her, and emitting
277 his rather high cackles, while she
278 laughed lovingly at his taci-
279 turnity.
280   The Boer War began—he had
281 thought "those Johnnies" could-
282 n't ride or shoot "for nuts"; he
283 became surprised. It got on his
284 mind a good deal. In December
285 he noticed a great change in
286 Mollie; she grew excitable. And
287 then one day, clinging to him,
288 she said it couldn't go on, they
289 would have to "kick over"; she
290 couldn't bear that old man any
291 more. Gene must take her away
292 —he must! Divorce and all, it
293 wouldn't take a year until they
294 could be married. Extremely
295 copper-colored, he smoothed her.
296 "Easy on!" he muttered.
297 "You're off color, old girl.
298 What's the matter with the old
299 sportsman? He seems a harm-
300 less sort of old Johnny."
301   She flung off his hand. Oh!
302 yes; what did he know—what
303 did he care? He had no blood in
304 him! She was altogether unjust.
305 He told her not to be a little
306 juggins. She clung to him—she
307 called him a "mummy." He
308 said: "If you don't shut up,
309 I'll spank you!" She raved at

him. Couldn't he see—couldn't he feel—she was only thirty-three—to be taken away from Gene—to be tied to that old man—with his—and his—and his——!

He smoothed her again; told her to go "steady over the stones!" They were very well off as they were.

"Yes," she said suddenly, "but he suspects."

"Oh!" he said, and sat down in his long chair. He had seen, suddenly, an effort before him. He had a pain in his diaphragm. He lighted a cigarette. His teeth at that moment looked very filed.

The effort before him took shape in the watches of the second night. Enlist! After all, what would it be? Only, as it were, a long day's hunting, the exertion of it nothing compared with that of running away with Mollie to an ultimate marriage. He had four days' severe dyspepsia—then took an early train to Exeter, and joined the Imperial Yeomanry. They wanted fellows of his stamp who could ride and shoot. His aunt was horrified; it seemed to her the end of the world. He rallied her. It would be a "picnic." She admired his patriotism. They wanted him at once, he said. He left without having again seen his young and ardent woman. He wrote to her from Plymouth, on his way out:—

"Dear Mollie,

"I was awfully sorry not to see you to say good-by. The Johnnies in my troop ride pretty well, but they can't shoot for nuts. We're all as keen as mustard to give these Boer jokers a knock. I hope you'll have a good winter, and get some hunting. I shall think of you riding the chestnut. Well—so-long, Mollie.

"Yours with the best,
"Gene."

He rather enjoyed the campaign, and developed a talent for stalking. He had drilled three of those "jokers" when he himself received a bullet through the calf. While in hospital he developed enteric, and when convalescent was discharged and invalided home. Leaner and browner than ever, he lay in a long chair with a cigarette in his yellow fingers, staring at some conversationalist of the female sex with his steel-colored eyes, and occasionally emitting a little high laugh. He felt "full of steam," and enjoyed the voyage "like smoke."

"Well, Aunt Susan," he said on reaching Baymouth. His aunt shed tears of rapture. He renewed his life as if it had never been broken. The young woman and her husband were no longer there. And ten more years passed like a game that is played.

He was forty-nine when his

393 Aunt Susan died. It upset him; 394 she was a "good old soul." 395 "That old josser," her lawyer, 396 worried him awfully about busi- 397 ness. She seemed to have been 398 living on her capital. All he 399 would have would be the pro- 400 ceeds of the house. It was sold 401 under his feet. He and his fox 402 terrier were compelled to move 403 out. They moved to lodgings 404 close to the "Lion's Tail." He 405 experienced almost at once the 406 lack of Aunt Susan; he had to 407 think of money. It was "an 408 awful bore." His billiards and 409 bridge became systematic. He 410 could no longer afford to hunt 411 unless a friend mounted him. 412 Still, he got along—there were 413 few evenings when he did not 414 make his five to ten shillings 415 over the green baize—large and 416 small. And five years passed 417 as a game that is played.

418 He was fifty-four when the 419 Great War broke out. It roused 420 him as nothing had ever roused 421 him yet. Those German "jos- 422 sers" wanted a good hiding. 423 Sitting in his long chair with a 424 cigarette between the yellow fin- 425 gers of one hand and his cocker 426 spaniel's ear between the yellow 427 fingers of the other, he nerved 428 himself for an effort. Two or 429 three months passed in the pro- 430 cess, then he journeyed up to 431 London, and presented himself 432 at the headquarters of an Offi- 433 cers' Training Corps. He asked 434 for a commission on the strength

of his service in the Boer War. 435 They were sorry—they wanted 436 men of his stamp, but he was 437 too old for a commission. He 438 persisted that he could ride and 439 shoot. They looked at him, and 440 somebody remarked: "Yes, but 441 can you think?" 442

He went very copper-colored, 443 looked at them deeply, and left 444 the room. If those "poopsticks" 445 thought they were going to win 446 the war by thinking—! He 447 traveled back to Baymouth, and 448 enrolled himself as special con- 449 stable. It was his duty to 450 guard a culvert. He did it sit- 451 ting on a shooting-stick, with a 452 cigarette between the yellow fin- 453 gers of one hand, and the yellow 454 fingers of the other hand playing 455 with the ears of his cocker 456 spaniel. 457

Think! He had plenty of 458 time to think, out there week in, 459 week out, in various weather. 460 He would listen to the dripping 461 stillness, or the soughing of the 462 wind in the neighboring spinney, 463 and wish that one of those "Hun 464 Johnnybirds" would appear and 465 give him sport. Now and again 466 he stalked some innocuous per- 467 son who came near his culvert; 468 but there was never anything 469 "really doing." In sheer bore- 470 dom he took to thinking about 471 how to improve his income. 472 What little he had could easily be 473 doubled, he was sure, by any 474 "juggins who knew the ropes." 475 He set himself to know them, by 476

477 reading newspapers. And three
478 years passed as a game that is
479 played. During those years he
480 doubled his income—on paper—
481 but owing to circumstances that
482 no juggins could have foreseen,
483 he was receiving less of it than
484 before he began to increase it.
485 He was literally compelled to
486 seek for a paid job. They gave
487 him something in connection
488 with a hospital. In 1919 the
489 hospital was closed; the war
490 being over, there was nothing
491 for anybody to do, and his in-
492 come was now just half the
493 insufficient amount it had been
494 before he increased it. In fact,
495 it was about a pound a week;
496 and prices double what they had
497 been. He shot his dog Quiz—
498 —"poor old chap;" sold his gun,
499 and changed to a back bedroom
500 in a by-street, where he could
501 sit in what sun there was, and
502 settle down to live on "fags" and
503 billiards. "Bet you a lunch"
504 was his formula, varied by "Bet
505 you fifty cigarettes"—he seldom
506 lost. His clothes were still those
507 he had worn in the days of
508 Aunt Susan, pressed under his
509 heavy leather trunk, and only
510 put on when he went out to the
511 "Lion's Tail" at noon. The
512 mornings he spent in an old blue
513 dressing-gown, smoking cigar-
514 ette after cigarette, and conning
515 some derelict paper picked up
516 in the bar. He never pitied him-
517 self, but he would now and again
518 go copper-colored, thinking of

his income and the newspapers. 519
On the parade, in the spring 520
of 1921, a lady sat down beside 521
him. He recognized her at once 522
—his old flame Mollie, and 523
"pretty long in the tooth," too! 524
He made no sign of recognition— 525
he hadn't forgotten her calling 526
him a "mummy" last time he 527
had seen her, and that his clothes 528
were not what they had been. 529
But suddenly she turned and 530
said: "Why, it's Gene! So 531
you're still here!" It seemed to 532
him odd. Where else should he 533
be? And how was he? She her- 534
self hadn't been at Baymouth 535
since. She was a widow again. 536
"Oh, and aren't we old! Why 537
you're quite white, Gene; and so 538
should I be, if I didn't——" 539
He grinned. Old Mollie had 540
always been a "sport." 541
"And to think you nearly 542
knocked me out twice, Gene!" 543
She looked him over slowly: 544
"Poor old Gene, you look rather 545
'on your uppers'!" 546
He became copper-colored, 547
showed his filed teeth, and said: 548
"What damned cheek! You 549
always were a cheeky kid!" 550
Something came into her eyes 551
—a sort of light. 552
"You must come and dine 553
with me, Gene. I'm at the 554
Courtfield." 555
He answered stiffly: "Thanks." 556
He still had an old dress suit, 557
and one white shirt with cuffs 558
intact. In the next few days he 559
used it several times. She could 560

561 never elicit from him where he
562 lived. He just grinned, or
563 emitted his high laugh. He
564 began to perceive that she had
565 "tumbled to" his one dress shirt,
566 and pitied him. He did not like
567 it. One evening after dinner,
568 while he was sitting in a long
569 chair with a cigarette in the
570 yellow fingers of one hand and
571 the other hand dangling to the
572 floor, she proposed to him. He
573 grinned and called her "a little
574 juggins." Next day he was
575 down with a severe attack of
576 dyspepsia. There was some-
577 thing disgusting to him in her
578 wanting at her age to marry
579 him out of pity. If she thought
580 he was "such a tail-down
581 Johnny," she was jolly well mis-
582 taken. For a fortnight he stayed
583 in his room, reading old *Pink
584 'Uns*, and living on Benger's and
585 cigarettes. Only when he had
586 none left did he emerge. To
587 his relief, she was gone. He had
588 seldom played billiards better
589 than in the week that followed.
590 Then a real disaster befell him.
591 His hands suddenly began to
592 shake—he couldn't play "for
593 nuts." It meant that he must
594 live on a pound a week. He
595 began to sit stiller than ever,
596 thinking of what he could do.
597 "Bear-leading some young cub"
598 —something in a riding school;
599 he even thought of wheeling a
600 bath chair, of billiard-marking,
601 of clerking to a bookmaker. But
602 all such occupations would neces-

603 sitate his leaving Baymouth; he
604 was too well known. The exer-
605 tion of such uprooting was be-
606 yond him. Besides, he had no
607 interest anywhere else, and for
608 such careers interest was neces-
609 sary. In a sort of coma, time
610 went by. Five shillings bor-
611 rowed here and there, "tick"
612 with his old landlady—"poor old
613 soul;" the sale of little odd bits of
614 salvage from Aunt Susan's days,
615 eked out his existence for the
616 next six months. And then he
617 plunged. A "josser" of his ac-
618 quaintance who bred dogs was
619 going out of business. Selling
620 out his one remaining stock of
621 value, he bought it. With the
622 paid help of a "joker" out of a
623 job, he put up extra kennels. It
624 was the most definite work he
625 had ever done. In memory of
626 his shot spaniel, Quiz—"poor old
627 chap!"—he bred cockers. For
628 over a year nearly everything
629 went well—he spent most of his
630 capital, and had three large lit-
631 ters of pedigree pups. He passed
632 hours among the "little beg-
633 gars," a cigarette between his
634 lips, his yellow fingers crump-
635 ling their ears or feeling their
636 points, while their little avid
637 tongues licked all of him within
638 reach. They were a great pleas-
639 ure to him, not the less so for
640 their promise of ten pounds
641 apiece, and twenty pounds if
642 over distemper. He debated
643 whether to have them inoculated
644 and sell them with a guarantee.

645 Nature took the matter out of
646 his hands before he had made the
647 effort of decision. The violent
648 distemper of that season came
649 down like a wolf on his pups; all
650 but two died. "The poor little
651 black beggars!" For the first
652 time since he went to school he
653 almost shed tears. He had sat
654 up with them night after night,
655 had buried them one after the
656 other. It was "rotten luck."
657 When the holocaust was over he
658 was compelled to sell the kennel,
659 lock, stock, and barrel, to pay
660 the bills he had run up. He
661 had fifty pounds left. The ef-
662 forts of that past year and its
663 final disaster had produced in
664 him a perfect fatalism. For
665 fourteen months he lived on the
666 fifty pounds, his watch, his fam-
667 ily seal, the remains of his ward-
668 robe. He never mentioned his
669 condition, and would sit whole
670 afternoons on the high seat in
671 the billiard room of the "Lion's
672 Tail," watching the game being
673 played, and thinking: "They
674 can't play for nuts." What peo-
675 ple thought of him sitting there,
676 lean and white-haired, with his
677 drawn copper-colored face and
678 thirsting eyes, with his grin, and
679 his well-cut clothes shiny from
680 age, he neither knew nor cared.
681 He had to sit somewhere. And
682 here he got cigarettes, and once
683 in a way a drink was offered
684 him. His friends he had ex-
685 hausted; he had borrowed from
686 them and was never able to re-

687 pay; his acquaintances began to
688 shun him for fear that he would
689 borrow. He was "down and
690 out."
691 One morning his landlady,
692 "poor old soul," came to him
693 crying. She owed money. He
694 couldn't—she supposed—pay her
695 just a little? He called her an
696 "old juggins," and told her to
697 buck up. That afternoon he put
698 his toothbrush, shaving brush
699 and razor in the pocket of his old
700 blue overcoat, sold his old bowler
701 and his spare shirt for seven-and-
702 six, bought two hundred fags and
703 a ticket down the coast. The
704 "poor old soul" would be able to
705 let his room, at least.
706 In the shelter, huddled into the
707 corner out of the increasing wind,
708 he passed his shaking hand over
709 the bone and skin of his face,
710 then diving it into his pocket,
711 brought out a paper packet.
712 Still ten cigarettes, but he felt
713 too sick and empty to smoke
714 them. If the sun would come
715 out, he would get into it and
716 have a sleep. He was "fed up."
717 Some "jokers" in his place would
718 make for a workhouse, or take a
719 brick and heave it through a
720 window, get "quodded" and fed.
721 Not much! Easier, more digni-
722 fied, to sit on, here. If only the
723 sun would come out and warm
724 him! These "dam-cold" nights
725 his heart was giving him
726 "beans." He thought with a
727 grin of his Aunt Susan—the "old
728 girl" would have a fit if she could

443

729 see him; so would "old Mollie,"
730 or his landlady, "poor old soul!"
731 He shivered, so that his teeth
732 rattled. People would notice
733 him. He would get under the lee
734 side of a fishing boat till it was
735 dark. He stood up with diffi-
736 culty, and began to move slowly
737 toward the beach. With hands
738 deep thrust into his pockets, he
739 tried to look like any other
740 "Johnny" crossing that little
741 space. He sat down exhausted
742 between two boats. An "old
743 josser" was looking down at him
744 from the parade; he took up a
745 pebble, and with a shaking hand
746 threw it at a log of driftwood
747 ten yards or so away. Nobody
748 would notice a chap throwing
749 pebbles. He threw them at
750 long intervals. His hand shook
751 so that he could not aim—could
752 not hit "the darned thing." It
753 angered him. Who would bet
754 him he didn't hit it five times
755 out of fifty? He groped slowly
756 for the pebbles, amassed a little
757 heap, and counted fifty. Yes,
758 he would hit "the darned thing"
759 five times in fifty. He began.
760 He missed his first sixteen shots,
761 then hit the log twice running,
762 and, taking out a cigarette, he
763 rested. He smoked slowly—he
764 was two pebbles up. The sun
765 had come out, and shone full
766 on him over the edge of the old
767 boat. He turned his face to it;
768 then taking up a pebble, began
769 again. His hand shook worse
770 than ever; he missed eleven

771 times, then "got it plumb cen-
772 ter." Three hits in thirty shots
773 —just up to his points. Again
774 he took a cigarette and rested.
775 Two hits to make in twenty
776 shots—odd if he couldn't win
777 that bet! Time was when he
778 would have hit that "joker"
779 every time. His cigarette went
780 out. He leaned against the boat,
781 and closed his eyes. Cold sweat
782 oozed from him; things sank
783 around him. He rested, half-
784 conscious; came to again, and
785 saw the log with the sun on it.
786 He groped up a pebble, and
787 feebly flung it. A hit—by
788 George! The devil would be in
789 it now if he couldn't make the
790 other in nineteen shots. On his
791 face, bony and copper-colored in
792 the sinking sunlight, a grin was
793 fixed. He flung and flung. Miss
794 after miss after miss—thirteen
795 running! "Curse! Couldn't
796 throw for nuts! Get the damned
797 thing or bust!" Miss after miss
798 after miss. Three more pebbles!
799 He paused.

800 The setting sun still shone;
801 a sea-gull with brightened wings
802 was passing within gunshot. As
803 a boy he remembered he had
804 shot a sea-gull—before he had
805 learned to be a sportsman.
806 Three more shots. He was
807 tempted to get up and lob them.
808 But could he get up? Besides,
809 he must "play the game" with
810 the darned old log! He had once
811 claimed a ball "out" at tennis,
812 when he knew that it was in.

813 It was the sort of thing one
814 didn't like remembering. He
815 raised his arm. Look at it
816 shaking—how could a Johnny
817 throw with an arm like that?
818 The pebble flew wide. Two
819 more! He remembered a "beak"
820 at his private school who used
821 to bowl round-arm. Nobody
822 had bowled round-arm for forty
823 years and more. Give it a
824 chance! He swung his trem-
825 bling arm three times in prac-
826 tice, then took up the last pebble
827 but one. Now for it! His
828 whole body swung with his arm.
829 Whump! A faint exultant
830 whoop came from his lips. A
831 stab went through his breast-
832 bones—it "hurt like steam!" He
833 fell back, collapsed under the
834 tarry boat, still as a mummy.
835 . . . And so next day they
836 found him.

THE ANALYSIS

Had this story been told chronologically, it would merely have been a narration of happenings in the life of a character; and instead of being a short-story it would have been a narrative of character. So arranged, it would have opened on line 51, and going through to line 705, it would have picked up the story at line 1 and then gone on to line 50, resuming again at line 706 and through to the last line 836.

On the page following the reprint of the story there is the usual chart of the story showing the arrangement of the Flash-back Beginning. The following chart will show how the Flash-back was accomplished.

Chronological	Flash-back
Lines 51–705. Events from boyhood to 66.	Lines 1–50 form main situation.
Eugene Daunt at 66 is finally down and out. Lines 1–50.	Lines 51–705. Events from boyhood to 66.
He turns to throwing contest; meets great crisis. Lines 706–836.	Lines 706–836 form Ending.

The flash-back in this type story is accomplished by writing the final scene, and then splitting it in two, putting one half of it at the opening of the story to make the main narrative situation, and putting the other half of it at the end to make the Conclusive Act.

445

Thus, the answer to the first scene's question is also the answer to the main narrative question of the story. The Flash-back Beginning then occupies the intervening space, and this Flash-back Beginning is entirely a series of interchanges at the conclusion of which a basic trait emerges; and just as in the O. Henry story cupidity emerged as a basic trait, here turning from effort to the playing of a game emerges as the basic trait of Eugene Daunt. The story opens at a moment when there seems to be no possibility of evading the issue by turning to the playing of a game. Then, in the flash-back showing him at the age of twenty-eight, he meets the condition there confronting him by going on a yachting cruise which is the equivalent of playing a game. At the next crisis he goes to the Boer War, which to him is "a long day's hunting." Next, at the age of forty-nine, he turns to the playing of billiards. At the age of fifty-four he, when he is rebuffed, turns to stalking innocuous persons at the culvert. At the age of fifty-seven he meets the condition by making bets. In 1921 he again turns to billiards, and when his hands become shaky he turns to raising dogs; and finally he meets the basic condition by a throwing contest, and thus as always he meets the issue by evading it and turning to the playing of a game instead of making an effort.

Before closing our consideration of the special type of Decision or Choice story of which *The Mummy* is such an excellent example, let us examine Mr. Galsworthy's structural handling of the scenes within the portion of the story which is the Flash-back for Explanatory Matter of the Beginning. We will find that the first four steps of the different scenes almost always occur. There are exceptions, of course. Sometimes two steps are closely merged; sometimes the order varies; occasionally one is omitted; the proportion of space taken up will vary. But these exceptions are undoubtedly the result of the author's definite choice. The purpose of these different Cases in Craftsmanship is to point out to aspiring authors the use which established craftsmen have made of their knowledge of such simple steps. If, thereafter, the aspiring author chooses to ignore them, he will do so consciously, rather than through ignorance.

It is from a close study of the use which Mr. Galsworthy makes of the fifth steps in each of his presentation units that those interested in craftsmanship will gain most. This fifth step is employed always to show the effect of the happenings making up the presentation unit upon the chief actor. It has other functions, of course; but this is the one which is our special concern just now. *The*

Mummy is a story of character, as opposed to a story of action. The purpose is to show the character of the chief actor rather than to hold interest by exciting clashes in the interchanges. In the story of action the fifth step would be employed to show that the actor's chief purpose in the story had been strengthened or weakened by the happenings making up the presentation unit immediately preceding it. In the story of action, or as it is sometimes called the story of "incident," the interchange is all-important. In the story of "character" the interchange is important only as it leads into a condition where the basic trait of the chief actor clashes with some other trait, and emerges triumphant. It is not necessary to show the clash of traits in this fifth step; it is only necessary that the basic trait shall emerge.

You will see the difference between the scenes in the two types of story—the Accomplishment story, and the Decision story,—if you will turn to the scene in *Once and Always*, by John P. Marquand, where Gideon Higsbee attempts to persuade Lemuel Gower to accept his check. That scene takes 309 lines to present its four steps. (Lines 927 to 1235.)

Now if you will turn again to *The Mummy* to the scene where Eugene Daunt, at fifty-four, applies for a commission on the strength of his service in the Boer War, you will see that the four steps occupy only 28 lines. (Lines 418 to 445.) The important unit is not the first four steps, as in *Once and Always*, but the fifth step, which shows that Eugene Daunt has turned to the nearest approximation of sport which he can devise, the stalking of innocuous persons near the culvert he is guarding.

This fifth step occurs in all the types of stories. In the story of Accomplishment it dwells especially upon crises of Hindrance or Furtherance, and by so doing knits together the presentation units into a plot.

In the story of Decision or Choice it dwells especially upon the choices to be made by the actor, and here again, gives to the story its unity as a whole.

In that special type of Decision Story which is occupied with a series of decisions involving the Basic Trait of an actor it ties together the presentation units.

My reason for dwelling at such length upon this fifth step at the close of scenes, is that it must be kept clearly in mind for a comprehension of the two stories which are to conclude this collection of Cases in Craftsmanship.

These two stories are interesting variants of the story of Decision.

ARCHITECTURAL CHART

OF

RICH MAN—POOR MAN

BEGINNING	Main condition set forth.	Scene. Jay and Marianne. Jay, a wealthy man, learns that his wife, Marianne, has been having an affair with another man. He upbraids her, saying it was all brought about by her love for perfume and gold color.	1–186	Scene. Jake and Mary Smith. Jake, a common laborer, learns that his wife has been having an affair with another man. He upbraids her, saying it was all brought about by her love for perfume and the color, yellow.	1–399
ENDING	Conclusive Act.	He leaves her, declaring:— "Had I been a poor man, a common laborer, this could never have happened to us."	187–195	He turns his wife out, declaring:— "This wouldn't 'a happened, if I'd only been a rich guy."	399–405

(These parallel stories are linked together by the ironic significance of the similarity of their happenings, and the conclusions drawn by the two men from those happenings.)

RICH MAN—POOR MAN

BY MELANIE KOLL

I HAVE chosen this story, together with its companion story, *Claire and the Dangerous Man*, because it presents an interesting variant of the Decision Story. In all the other Decision stories which I have included in this volume, the Decision has been that of a single person. The presentation units in the O. Henry story, *The Roads We Take*, and in the Galsworthy story, *The Mummy*, were tied together and unified by the same trait in the main actor. They consisted of parallel scenes given a central unity by a basic trait. This story is especially interesting because it presents parallel scenes, each of which shows an actor responding to a condition by making a choice. In this case, however, there are two people who make choices. For each there is a single great moment; but the same condition confronts each one, and the parallelism extends to a similarity in the decision made. Besides this there is an additional parallelism, in that the ironic significance of their similarity is that each actor draws from the happenings an exactly opposite significance. Whereas the two stories which we have just examined were composed of parallel scenes tied together by basic character traits, here we find that the pattern is parallel scenes tied together by ironic significance.

CASE No. 20

RICH MAN—POOR MAN

BY MELANIE KOLL

In the long oval mirror of her dressing-table Marianne watched the ivory-paneled door quietly open and give place to the tall, slender man now framed in the doorway. He came into the room, the black and white of his sharply etched dinner clothes the solitary contrasting note in the dainty feminine boudoir of ivory and gold.

"I knocked twice. Perhaps you didn't hear?"

Marianne breathed more easily. His voice was cool and crisp as always. Perhaps, then, he hadn't learned. . . . That cat of a Doris—the little beast, to phone her, Marianne, under the guise of friendship, to warn her that Jay had learned of that wild, mad—

"I should like ten minutes of your time."

Her eyelids narrowed—*that* voice didn't sound quite so casual. But she twisted up the corners of her mouth in a smile. She must be charming, lovely—

"Of course, dear." Did she fancy it, or had he winced, ever so slightly, at that last word. "I've plenty of time. Really, so much time to kill, always, that it's getting to be harder and harder to find ways to do it." She laughed ruefully. "I play such rotten bridge—have such beastly luck. Only, one must do as the others do, or just simply cease to be. You know what I mean." A silence followed; then she rattled on: "I'm dining at the Delavans' tonight, but I've plenty of time. Quite all ready for dinner, except my gown." She indicated a wickedly shimmering thing, lying there like a great golden serpent. "Isn't that a dream? Such a perfectly exquisite duck of a dream! It's just come. Madame Louise says it's quite the smartest gold-lace dinner-gown she's ever created." Playing for time, praying for time, she ran on, her mind darting now this way, now that, striving to recall each tiny telltale bit. "I'll ring for Celeste and tell

451

60 her not to come back for ten
61 minutes—"
62 "I've already told her."
63 "So good of you." Her voice
64 drawling, lazy, indolent, her eyes
65 sharp, keen, alert. "Eleanor's
66 just gone. We had such a nice
67 hour over the teacups. Eleanor's
68 just returned from China, and
69 she brought me some of the most
70 perfectly marvelous tea. I do
71 adore good tea—with plenty of
72 rum drops in it. Since she left,
73 I've been idling away a half-
74 hour trying out some new per-
75 fumes. A Frenchwoman's come
76 out with an article in one of the
77 magazines, about matching up
78 one's perfumes to one's moods."
79 She half smiled, as if at some
80 mysterious, tantalizing recollec-
81 tion, as she turned to the row of
82 gold-topped crystal bottles, fin-
83 gering them lovingly. "You
84 know how I adore perfumes,
85 don't you? I'm horribly extrav-
86 agant—"
87 "I didn't come here to talk
88 perfumes."
89 She turned quickly, a tall,
90 lovely figure, in her golden drap-
91 eries. "Of course not. Why,
92 you don't even like them, do
93 you?" Stupid of her to have
94 forgotten that. She bit her lip,
95 vexedly. It was Alfred who
96 liked them—not Jay. "But
97 you've not even admired my
98 gown. Gold lace doesn't come
99 under the ban of your disap-
100 proval also, does it?"
101 That maddening, provoking

102 little pout of hers—funny how it
103 used to make his pulses beat
104 faster, faster. Now it left him
105 quite cold. "I wonder why you
106 love gold color so?" he asked
107 curiously. "This room, all gold
108 and ivory, that gown there, your
109 negligée—" He pointed to the
110 exquisite clinging thing she wore
111 so gracefully. "Is it because
112 gold color is so like—gold—and
113 gold means wealth, power, lux-
114 ury?"
115 "Why, Jay!" Her tone was
116 sweet, pained, surprised. "What
117 a horrid thing to say—even if
118 you don't really mean it!"
119 He nodded impatiently.
120 Heavens, couldn't she under-
121 stand that he was scarcely in the
122 mood to say anything he didn't
123 mean—tonight. "I stopped at
124 the club on my way home this
125 evening."
126 "Yes?" Hard to keep her
127 voice quite steady now.
128 "I went there, to meet a man
129 on business. While I was there,
130 I heard—"
131 "A lot of gossip, didn't you?
132 You men scorn women for gos-
133 siping, but when it comes to
134 scandalmongers, give me a crowd
135 of women any time, in preference
136 to you club men."
137 "Drop it. This is between
138 you and me, Marianne. No use
139 generalizing, discussing male *ver-*
140 *sus* female. This is just—us.
141 You see, I—I learned of the
142 whole rotten mess there. No
143 use arguing, Marianne. I don't

144 wish to hear any more of the
145 details. I—"

146 "But, Jay, you don't under-
147 stand—"

148 "A trifle too well, I'm afraid!"
149 —wearily.

150 "You were away—so much—"

151 Why, her voice was pleading
152 now. How—how—queer! "And
153 while I was away, slaving to
154 give you—things—jewels, furs,
155 cars, the place in the country,
156 perfumes, all this—you—you
157 were lonely."

158 "Oh, I was, I was."

159 "Till you met Alfred—and
160 then— Yet you wouldn't have
161 a child—why, you shrank from
162 the very thought of bearing one.
163 If you hadn't, then you'd have
164 had no empty idle hours to fling
165 away to—Alfred. No,"—as she
166 started to speak,—"let me fin-
167 ish. You wanted luxury, and I
168 gave it to you—on a great golden
169 platter. You never wanted me
170 for myself, just for what I could
171 give you."

172 "You said you loved me,
172 Jay."

173 That tricky little lilt in her
174 voice that had always played
175 the devil with him, made him
176 weaken, heretofore! But the
177 time for that was over—well
178 over. "We'll not discuss that
179 now, if you please."

180 "But why—"

181 "Get the divorce on any
182 grounds you please. I'm leaving
183 here—going to live at the club.
184 Simpson will pack my things."

"Jay, Jay, you're going with- 185
out a regret, aren't you?" 186

He turned and gave her a long 187
look. "My dear Marianne," he 188
said, more gently than he had 189
yet spoken, "I am leaving, with 190
one big regret—that I happen 191
to be a wealthy man. Had I 192
been a poor one,—a common 193
laborer,—this could never have 194
happened to us." 195

"Whew!" said Mary Smith, to 196
her neighbor Mrs. O'Keefe. 197
"Them onions is something 198
fierce on the eyes, ain't it the 199
truth?" 200

Mrs. O'Keefe, watching Mary 201
slice endless onions into the fry- 202
ing-pan, nodded majestically. 203
"They sure air that," she agreed. 204
"Say, Mary, if I was you, darlin', 205
I wouldn't run around so much 206
with that no-account Al—" 207

"Now, Mrs. O'Keefe, I can 208
look out fer myself, I can. I—" 209
She stopped abruptly, as a 210
man slouched into the room. 211
Tall he was, and thin—his face 212
red with the perspiration beading 213
it, his shock of black hair awry. 214

"Evenin', Mrs. O'Keefe." He 216
nodded to her indifferently. 217
Then, curtly: "Say, I wanta 218
talk to Mary alone." 219

"Sure, I was joost goin', any- 220
how. I only joost dropped in to 221
have a dish o' tea." 222

"Then come some other day 223
an' have it, Mrs. O'Keefe." 224

"We've ahlready had it, bless 225
you—and foine tea it was, too— 226

some noo Chiny tea they give away now, wid ivery dollar's worth of groceries at McNulty's store. Well, Mary darlin', I'll be on me way. Me own stew's on the stove, and I'd best be lookin' after it, or 'tis burned 'twill be, and himself swearin' mad, to be eatin' it burned, more's the pity."

As the door creakingly closed after her, Mary turned to her husband, a little frown of disapproval wrinkling her white forehead. "Jake, ain'tcha got no manners at all, that you'd ask Mrs. O'Keefe to be leavin' like that," she reproached him, face, neck, arms, glistening with beads of moisture as she stood over the blazing stove.

"See here, Mary, I ain't come home today to be perlite nor to talk to Mrs. O'Keefe. I come home to—"

"Well, whatever it is, make yerself comf'table while ye're doin' it. Set, why don'tcha?" She ran past him on her way to the door, out of the kitchen into the bedroom and back again, while he filled a thick glass with water from the faucet, gulped it down and wiped his mouth with the back of his hand. When Mary returned, he was still standing there, a puzzled, uncertain look on his none too clean countenance.

"Why don'tcha set, Jake?"

He made a wry face—sniffed the air. Then he brought a clenched hand down heavily on the table beside him. "Thet damn' smell again!"

"I know. It's them onions." She nodded sympathetically. "Somethin' fierce, ain't it?"

" 'Tain't them onions, an' well you know it. It's thet damn' perfumery you been wastin' money on again."

"Now, Jake!" The pout in her voice, like that in a little child's.

"You know how I hate that stuff."

"But, Jake, I only put it on, to take off that there onion smell. Sure I like perfume—I'm crazy about it, but I wouldn't use it, when you don't like it, except only fer them onions. Honest, Jake."

"Honest, nothin'," he snarled. "You're a fine one to use thet word 'honest', ain't you, now? You, thet ain't got a honest bone in yer whole lyin' body."

She stiffened at that, and a look of fear crept into her gray eyes. But she spoke coolly enough. "Say, look out! Who you think ye're talkin' to, anyways, Jake? I ain't standin' fer no—"

"Ye're standin' fer whatever I want you should stand fer, see? 'Cause I got the goods on you—get thet? I dropped in at Mike Casey's fer a drink, comin' home —an' I heard—"

"What do I care what you heard? Talk about women's

gossipin'. Men is twicet as bad. What do I care fer any rotten gossip they told you?"

"You'll care all right, before I'm through. You—you—" The muscles of his face worked strangely.

"What's eatin' you, Jake? Spit it out, fer heaven's sake."

"Ye're yella, you are. Sure you are. Thet's why you was always wantin' yella walls in here, wearin' yella dresses—even got a yella apern on now!" He glared furiously at the innocent yellow gingham. "You betcher sweet life, yella's yer color all right, all right."

Her chin went up defiantly. "Sure, I like yellow, sure I do. I love it. For why? 'Cause it's all happy—like the sunshine—it ain't a mean, cold color—it's happy—happy—like I wanta be. I always feel good when I'm wearin' yellow—it's a happy color."

"Yeh? Well, you ain't gonna feel so happy, when I get through with what I'm tellin' you," he sneered. "I just heard all about you an' Al—"

"What you hear?" She nobly feigned a nonchalance she was far from feeling.

"Heard o' yer carryin's-on, I did. Heard o' yer goin' round with thet dancin' skunk, while I been slavin' like a dog to give you all the stuff you keep hollerin' fer—like thet damn' perfume!" he growled.

"Jake, I get so lonely here." She strove to keep the sobs out of her shaking voice. "When I'm through with my work—an' there ain't so much work, even, to fill up my time, what with only two of us to do fer—"

"Well, why's it only two? You never wanted a kid." His tone was surly.

She flared up then. "Don't you dare shoot lies like that at me, Jake. You know it's a lie! I'm crazy to have kids, lots of 'em, only I ain't ganna have 'em till I can bring 'em up decent an' proper, an' you ain't never made enough money fer that. When you do, why—"

He threw back his head and gave an ugly laugh. "When I do, hey? Well, get this—an' get it right: When I do, you ain't gonna have no share in my pile, see? You ain't gonna have no kids o' mine to spend it on, see? For why? 'Cause I'm quittin' you flat—now—right here. Maybe I ain't got such a swell name, like yer friend Al Carter. I got a plain name, Smith, Jake Smith; but anyhow, it's always been a clean name, an' no female's gonna dirty it up, see? No one's gonna have the right to throw mud on it, neither, get me? I said I was quittin' you, didn't I? Well by God, I ain't! After them pretty little stories I heard about you an' him, you're the one what's gettin' out o' here—not me! You kin go to

395 yer mother's, any place—an' I'll
396 send yer clothes after you.
397 Only"—his face worked convul-
398 sively as he spat the words at
399 her: "Only—get the hell out o'
400 here—an' hurry!" He stood

there, tense, taut, as the door 401
slammed shut, upon Mary's exit. 402
"This wouldn't 'a' happened, 403
if I'd only been a rich guy," he 404
muttered bitterly. 405

THE ANALYSIS

A reading of this story will show very quickly that here there is a story dependent not upon its reality but upon its cleverness for the thrill of pleasure which the reader receives from it. It is a refinement of craftsmanship. It is a story which calls forth the same sort of applause that is called forth by the expert magician or juggler in the vaudeville show. Professional golfers who make pitch shots of thirty or forty yards and always land the ball in a bucket cause us the same glow of respectful admiration—and envy. The formula is simple. A condition confronts an actor, requiring decision. He makes a decision. Parallel with this is another actor confronted by a similar, almost identical condition. The "kick" comes from the ironic resemblance of the two decisions.

I remember once hearing about a very distinguished old English General who had a great reputation as a bon vivant. He professed to be able to identify any drink by taste. He made a large wager that in the course of an hour his hosts could not bring him any beverage which he could not identify blindfolded. He was blindfolded, and one after another he identified Burgundy, Moselle, Champagne, Rye Whiskey, Scotch Whiskey, Ale, Stout, Beer and many others. At last his hosts brought him water. He sipped doubtfully; again more doubtfully. Then he put down the glass, saying, "Gentlemen, I have lost my wager. I cannot identify this beverage; but I venture to say, whatever it is, it will never be popular."

I feel much the same way about this type of story. I can identify it; but I venture to say that it will never be popular. Its interest is in its unusualness. It is rather too rich fare for general and continued consumption in large quantities. But as an excursion from the tried and trodden paths of the stories of Decision involving a single person it is an interesting and instructive variant.

ARCHITECTURAL CHART

OF

CLAIRE AND THE DANGEROUS MAN

BEGINNING

Skeletonized interchanges. Bahmer and Ruth set forth the condition. — 1-134

George Bahmer is confronted with a condition calling upon him to make a decision. — BEGINNING

(5th step. Interchange. Ruth and Claire. Ruth aware of a new sort of life.) — 135-272

Bahmer and Ruth. Interchange. — 273-313

Claire is confronted with a condition calling upon her to make a decision. — BEGINNING

Reader becomes aware of the factors involved in the choice to be made.

Interchange. Claire and Bahmer. (Gibson present.) — 374-543

Interchange. Bahmer and Claire. He attempts to establish friendly footing. — 544-609 Rebuffed.

Interchange. Another try. — 610-831 Rebuffed.

Interchange. Bahmer and Claire. Re Bright Treasure. — 832-904 Claire less cautious.

Meeting. Bahmer responds to new atmosphere as did Ruth Wilson. — 905-974 Claire off guard.

Interchange. Bahmer and Claire. After party. — 975-1084 Forgiven after rebuff.

Interchange. Bahmer and Claire. He declares love. — 1085-1874 Need for choice is apparent.

Claire makes reservations. — 1875-1932 She cuts off affair.

Effect upon Actors. "George Bahmer had been merely a minor incident in a busy life." (Line 1988-1990.) — 1933-1990

ENDING

Bahmer delivers final dismissal. — 314-317 — Decisive Act. — Narrative Question Answered: "He will cut off affair."

Effect of interchanges upon actors. "Ruth had been only an incident." — 318-373 — Sequel. — 371-373 Significance.

Conclusive Act. / Sequel. — ENDING

458

CLAIRE AND THE DANGEROUS MAN

BY FANNIE KILBOURNE

BECAUSE it is such an interesting example of the type of Parallel Decision Story; and because its author's consummate craftsmanship gives it the breath of life and reality I am including *Claire and the Dangerous Man.* Unlike the story *Rich Man—Poor Man,* it does not depend for its success exclusively upon the ironic significance of the fifth step of the parallel decisions. This ironic significance, tying together the Decisive Acts of Claire and of George Bahmer, is additional value given by the author. The difference between the two stories is that in one there were parallel *scenes*, while in the other there are parallel *stories*.

CASE No. 21

CLAIRE AND THE DANGEROUS MAN

BY FANNIE KILBOURNE

1 Sooner or later Claire was sure
2 to meet George Bahmer. Every
3 young New York business wo-
4 man meets some George Bahmer
5 —the out-of-town man who
6 comes to New York once or
7 twice or half a dozen times a
8 year on business; who buys
9 tickets for the musical shows at
10 speculator prices; who goes to
11 the revues and the night clubs,
12 usually with some girl only a
13 little older than his daughter,
14 whom he tells, of course, that his
15 wife doesn't understand him.

16 Claire knew all about George
17 Bahmer before she met him.
18 Or, if not all, enough, at least,
19 so that she might have been on
20 her guard. She knew, of course,
21 that he came from Chicago, that
22 he was traveling representative
23 —and a very successful one—
24 for the huge tannery that sup-
25 plied most of the leather for
26 Gibson shoes, that he and D. E.
27 Gibson worked together, hand
28 in glove, to their mutual profit
29 and satisfaction. As the still
30 fairly new advertising manager

31 for Gibson shoes, Claire knew
32 this. As a young woman, she
33 knew also that George Bahmer
34 was, so far as young women
35 were concerned, a dangerous
36 man.

37 And it was to the obviously
38 nice girls that Bahmer was the
39 most truly dangerous. This,
40 despite the fact that he knew
41 a nice girl when he saw one, and
42 behaved toward her accordingly.
43 The others, of course—the soft-
44 cheeked, pearled and furred little
45 ladies who bought their forty-
46 five-dollar slippers at Gibson's—
47 concealed the nerve and guileful
48 acumen of a slick confidence
49 man behind a perfumed smoke
50 screen of wide eyes and sweet,
51 cooing voices. A prosperous
52 Chicago man was an opportu-
53 nity, never a menace, to these
54 luxurious Persian kittens.

55 But of what George Bahmer
56 could do to a nice girl, and how,
57 all unintentionally, he could do
58 it, Claire had already learned.
59 Little Ruth Wilson, for instance,
60 one of the youngest of the

61 Gibson stenographers, a downy
62 chick just hatched out of busi-
63 ness college, as truly naïve as a
64 three-year-old, clapping chubby
65 hands at the pretty lights. She
66 wore gun-metal chiffon stock-
67 ings and powdered heavily over
68 the honest pink of her cheeks
69 and reddened her lips and
70 stiffened her eye-lashes with
71 mascaro in an earnest effort to
72 look sophisticated. An effort as
73 hopeless as it was whole-hearted.
74 Not a chance in the world of its
75 fooling an old stager like George
76 Bahmer. He enjoyed her for the
77 very freshness that she tried so
78 hard to hide. Two-thirds of the
79 fun of taking her to dinner at
80 the Ritz had been watching her
81 try to make him think she'd
82 been there before.

83   D. E. Gibson, who was as
84 conventional as a small-city
85 banker, would have given the
86 child a fatherly warning if he had
87 known that she was going out
88 with George Bahmer; might, if
89 she had failed to heed it, even
90 have fired her eventually. So
91 she had a wonderful young time,
92 feeling secretive and surrepti-
93 tious and wicked. And all the
94 time she was really as safe as
95 she could have been with an
96 amused and indulgent grand-
97 father.

98   For the five days Bahmer was
99 in town Ruth lived the social
100 life she had read about in her
101 highly colored magazines and
102 always dreamed of knowing.

She learned the thrill of being 103
led to a restaurant table by an 104
obsequious head waiter, of tak- 105
ing a taxi for a short three 106
blocks. She saw Bahmer care- 107
lessly pay more for two theater 108
tickets than she would have 109
dared spend for a winter coat; 110
caught a furtive, awed glimpse 111
of his check at the Palms after- 112
ward—supper for two, and half a 113
dozen dances that cost a month's 114
rent on the four-room flat she 115
and her mother lived in, up in 116
One Hundred and Twenty-third 117
Street. 118

Bahmer had had fun, too, in 119
giving her things; lavish, highly 120
proper gifts—candy in a mahog- 121
any box with dull metal fast- 122
eners; such sweets as she had 123
never tasted, little candied 124
violets, chocolates that seemed 125
to be wrapped in flexible irides- 126
cent glass and were so rich that 127
even her unspoiled young sweet 128
tooth had been satisfied with 129
one or two; perfume, priced by 130
the drop and sold by the ounce, 131
and an atomizer, delicately 132
lovely enough to stand alone in 133
a jeweler's window. 134

Ecstatic over it all, the young- 135
ster had had to tell somebody 136
and had, oddly, chosen Claire. 137
Or perhaps there had been no- 138
thing odd about this. She would 139
have been afraid to tell any of 140
her fellow stenographers in the 141
office, who would, she felt sure, 142
have been jealous and might 143
have been, accordingly, indis- 144

145 creet in sharing her confidences
146 till they might eventually have
147 come to Gibson's ears. But
148 there was a warm friendliness in
149 Claire's smile and a steadiness
150 in her eyes, a combination both
151 inviting and reassuring. One
152 knew that she would listen and
153 not tell.

154 "He says he likes to give me
155 things," the child confided, "be-
156 cause I don't hint for them.
157 Why, he says you'd be surprised
158 at the way most girls do.
159 'Platinum diggers,' he calls
160 them." She giggled breathless
161 appreciation. "He says gold
162 diggers are all out of date.
163 Girls don't use anything as
164 cheap as gold any more, except
165 maybe to fill a back tooth."
166 She giggled excitedly again.
167 "But he doesn't mind, because
168 he knows how to deal with them.
169 He just lets them hint and hint,
170 and pretends he doesn't know
171 what they're getting at. Then,
172 just before he's ready to go
173 home, when they've about given
174 up hope, he gets them something
175 grand that they've never even
176 mentioned. He says it's lots of
177 fun to do it that way."

178 "It must be," Claire agreed
179 dryly.

180 "And he's been so sweet to
181 me. You just wouldn't believe
182 it! Even mother thinks he's
183 grand now, though at first she
184 didn't like the idea of my
185 going out with him, him being
186 married and all."

187 " 'And all,' meaning how
188 many children?"

189 "Two. Both boys. One is
190 twelve and the other is at
191 Andover. That's a school."

192 Claire nodded. She could see
193 exactly how piquant such fresh-
194 ness must be to a jaded palate.
195 Bahmer had respected the youth
196 and innocence, too; had gone
197 back to Chicago without any
198 more than a little hand holding,
199 perhaps; or, at the very most, a
200 good-by kiss in the downstairs
201 hallway of her flat building;
202 going back in the comfortable
203 consciousness of having behaved
204 both handsomely and decently.

205 And yet, in those five days he
206 had ruined little Ruth Wilson as
207 devastatingly as any movie
208 villain could have done. For in
209 that brief time he had made her
210 own life almost unendurable to
211 her.

212 It would have required some-
213 thing of character which little
214 Ruth did not have, to go back
215 contentedly from casually sum-
216 moned taxis to the twice-a-day
217 jam in the Subway, from
218 lobster *à la Newburg* sizzling
219 over a chafing-dish flame, and
220 avocados in subtly blended
221 dressing to watery tomato soup
222 and a minced-ham sandwich
223 on a stool at a soda-fountain
224 lunch. The two-dollar-a-week
225 raise which had seemed so well
226 worth working and hoping for
227 had become a niggling insult, the
228 merest waiter's tip. Saturday-

evening jaunts with the young man she had been thinking of marrying, an eighty-five-cent table-d'hote in some crowded Italian restaurant, and balcony seats in one of the big movie theaters—once a glorious weekly climax whose prospect had cast an anticipatory glow over even Thursday and Friday, was now something merely to be openly ashamed of.

And as for the young man himself whom she had been thinking of marrying—a mechanic who actually proposed setting up housekeeping on a weekly wage that wouldn't have paid for the embroidered shawl Bahmer had bought her as the merest souvenir; an uncouth barbarian who thought tea in the afternoon or a decent manicure was sissy; whose manners, after Bahmer's suave ease, seemed those of a frolicsome baboon! Oh, unquestionably, little Ruth's own life had been ruined for her.

Claire watched her during the three months that intervened before Bahmer's next visit, convincing herself that she was in love with him. Claire's hints, even her frank counsel, fell on deafened ears. Little Ruth would have none of it. By the time Bahmer was due again she had completely convinced herself that she was the victim of a grand passion. As the day of his arrival approached she became fairly ecstatic with anticipation.

And when Bahmer actually did arrive he didn't see Ruth at all—didn't really see her, that is. A friendly nod as he passed her typewriting desk in the big outer office on his way into Gibson's sanctum, and that was all. There had been a mistake in a shipment of pastel kids, and Bahmer, the busiest and most absorbed of business men, had no time for pretty girls. By his next trip he would have forgotten Ruth altogether.

Claire happened, by the merest chance, to see a bit of the end of the incident. She had worked late in her own office and had slipped out through the deserted salesroom. It was sleeting, and she paused in the entryway just outside the door, to find a nickel for the Subway, to put up her umbrella. And as she stood there in the early winter darkness she recognized two other figures, also pausing in the shelter under the shop's ornate entrance. The girl was Ruth, the man was obviously Bahmer.

"If I've done anything to make you angry," Ruth was saying in a tight, strained little voice, "won't you tell me?"

Hastily Claire fitted her key into the lock, slipped back into the empty dark salesroom. She had no desire to play eavesdropper, but she was not quick enough to miss Bahmer's answer, half amazed, half irritated: "But I've told you, over and over, I'm not angry at you; I've never even thought of such a thing."

Had he been honest enough to go on and assure her that he had never even thought of her at all? Claire wondered. She found herself speculating sympathetically on the probable remainder of this little scene. Would Bahmer be wise enough to realize that what little Ruth was in love with was not himself but the glimpse of a different sort of life he had shown her? Would he be kind enough to be sorry for the havoc he had wrought? Had he liked her well enough to feel guilty now, for a fleeting moment or so, because though he was so rich in all the things she wanted, he could really do little to change things for her?

Even if he were both wise and kind, even though he sincerely liked the child, Claire couldn't see just what he could do to help matters now. He might, of course, call Ruth's attention to certain precious things she had —her youth, for instance. But that sort of reasoning seldom helps much. Probably it was just as well for him to step right out of the picture, definitely and abruptly, leaving little Ruth to start at once, picking up the pieces, making such adjustment as she could to whatever she could make out of

her own life. He would have to do that sooner or later, anyway, and there never was much point in trying to taper off the inevitable.

Well, kind and wise or not, that was about what he would probably do. And he would probably forget pretty much about the whole incident, long before Ruth would. Not that he would necessarily mean to; but he was a man of many and varied interests. Granted all the sympathy that could possibly be expected, one incontrovertible fact would remain. The fact that Ruth had been only a minor incident in a busy life.

As to Bahmer's previous New York visits, Claire had had neither leisure nor interest for speculation. He had been coming on some three or four times a year for the past fifteen years. Undoubtedly there had been plenty of Ruths as well as plenty of others. Except for feeling awfully sorry for the Ruth she knew, Claire would never have given a moment's thought to George Bahmer one way or another. As it was, however, she knew well enough, when he asked her to go to the theater with him, that even at his best and most chivalrous he was a dangerous man.

A considerable spice of mischief was mingled with Claire's acceptance of the invitation— because D. E. Gibson was

397 present when it was tendered.
398 The invitation had been, in fact,
399 tendered to D. E. first. But
400 D. E. was feeling the first pre-
401 monitory twitches of neuritis
402 and was pretty sure that by
403 theater time he would have to
404 be tucked up with an electric
405 pad under his shoulder.
406   Bahmer had looked from D. E.
407 to the slim, trim young advertis-
408 ing manager who had been called
409 in to explain the exact kind of
410 white ooze leather the new French
411 designer had in mind. There
412 was nothing the matter with the
413 young French designer's mind or
414 what he might have in it, but
415 when he tried to put this into
416 English he needed help. The
417 Frenchman had gone back to his
418 studio in the rear of the office
419 floor; Claire had been just leaving
420 D. E.'s office. Bahmer looked at
421 Claire and spoke to Gibson.
422   "I don't suppose you've
423 enough pull with Miss Deming."
424 he suggested, "to dare urge her
425 to go with me in your place?
426 I'm afraid to ask her myself."
427   Claire smiled—she had a very
428 naïve, very white-toothed smile.
429 And it was, right now, a very
430 genuinely amused smile.
431   The sight of the conflicting
432 emotions which suddenly came
433 to battle all over Gibson's face
434 was downright funny. It was
435 a conflict with which Claire had
436 already become familiar, but
437 which never ceased to amuse her
438 —the battle of the old-fashioned
439 gentleman and the new-fash-
440 ioned business man.
441   Gibson was approaching sixty,
442 and for forty of his sixty years he
443 had been a shoe man. Starting
444 out as a salesman for prison-
445 made footwear in the days when
446 men still wore boots and all
447 ladies wore black kid, winding
448 up as owner of one of the
449 smartest shoe shops on Fifth
450 Avenue—a thoroughly successful
451 business man—he had kept his
452 business senses alert and his
453 business mind flexible. No
454 Canute, he, to stand on the
455 shore of fashion and command
456 the waves to fall back—not D. E.
457 of Gibson shoes. He was canny
458 enough to build him a good sea-
459 worthy craft and sail to success
460 with the wind and the tide.
461   As a gentleman, though, he
462 had done his best to play Joshua
463 and make the sun stand still.
464 In regard to women, for instance,
465 he had made his opinions at
466 about the time he had stopped
467 making boots, and he had never
468 allowed himself to see any reason
469 for changing one of them. Such
470 inconsistencies as being a suc-
471 cessful business man had forced
472 upon him had never made a dent
473 on the firmness of his beliefs.
474 He had been forced to hire young
475 women stenographers, but he
476 had not allowed this to interfere
477 with his conviction that woman's
478 place is in the home.
479   A young and even attractive
480 woman advertising manager had,

of course, been engaged by the business man who couldn't quite blink at ability when he saw it. But it caused the old-fashioned gentleman to do considerable blinking. It was difficult, for one thing, to pay her practically the same salary he would have had to pay a young man, and yet to remain convinced that the sun was standing still.

He was blinking hard right now, which was what was amusing Claire. As a gallant and fatherly employer of a young girl, he knew that it was his duty to protect her from just such men as George Bahmer. But as owner of D. E. Gibson shoes, if George Bahmer wanted to take the advertising manager to the theater, D. E. wanted her to go. Every now and then, of a May or November, even a very successful shoe retailer is likely to need a little temporary financial backing. This, Bahmer had always been able to persuade the tannery to advance. The tannery had lost nothing by it, of course. With the shoes which Gibson bought with this advance went the requirement that they should be made of leather from the tannery. It was a mutually profitable arrangement, but one which would have been quite as profitable to the tannery if made with any competing retailer. George Bahmer was Gibson's friendly and important intermediary. Oh,

just as a matter of prudence, Gibson earnestly hoped Claire would accept Bahmer's invitation. And as he looked at her, so fresh and girlish in her new tan spring suit, his conflict was writ large on his face.

Bahmer spoke to Claire direct, "Won't you take pity on a solitary out-of-towner?" he asked. "Going to the theater alone is such a dreary business."

There was a really charming humility in his voice. Dangerous men, of course, usually do have charming manners. That is what makes them so dangerous. Claire glanced at D. E.

"Thank you," she said. "I'd be very glad to."

Bahmer chose the Frivolities, of course. Claire had been sure he would. Just as she had felt sure that, during the first intermission, he would attempt to establish a more personal, more provocative relationship between them. His manner coming up in the taxi had been perfectly that of pleasant, impersonal business friendliness. But Claire, being a woman, knew that she was much more attractive after she had taken off her coat. Her black dinner dress was simple and three years old, but it had come from an excellent shop originally and it made her neck and bare arms startlingly white, just as her flame-colored scarf accentuated the blackness of her

565 hair. Besides, she knew Bahmer
566 in advance, or thought she did.
567 True to her prophecy, the
568 curtain had scarcely descended
569 for the first time when Bahmer
570 turned to her in the soft rustling
571 stir that always comes with the
572 lights.

573 "You know," he said, "the
574 moment you came into D. E.'s
575 office this morning I knew that
576 you were a person I'd simply got
577 to know."

578 "Is that so?" said Claire.
579 There was not the slightest hint
580 of rebuff in her pleasant voice.
581 It was courteous, even friendly.
582 But it would have been impos-
583 sible to convey more perfectly in
584 three short words a complete
585 and utter indifference as to what
586 Bahmer thought about her, one
587 way or the other.

588 Bahmer waited. The opening
589 of a game of this sort is as full of
590 conventional signals as a bridge
591 play. His remark had been like
592 leading the nine of spades, in-
593 dicating his strongest suit and
594 expecting the lead returned.

595 When Claire did not return it,
596 "You struck me as being entirely
597 different from any woman I had
598 ever seen."

599 Going on like a good sports-
600 man, to establish his suit despite
601 his partner's obtuse play. But
602 she went right on being obtuse.
603 After a bit Bahmer began to
604 suspect that she was playing by
605 different signals. Not till very
606 nearly the end of the show did it

607 dawn upon him that Claire was
608 simply not playing the game at
609 all.

610 During the Roaring Forties
611 number—one of those gaudy
612 affairs with a lot of radium paint
613 and flashing lights, New York's
614 sky line in the background and
615 some hundred chorus girls in the
616 fore, tiny electric stars twinkling
617 in and out in their slipper heels
618 —Bahmer stole several side
619 glances at the girl in the seat
620 beside him. He was no fool and,
621 though Claire's eyes were always
622 fixed on the stage, he began to
623 suspect that her thoughts were
624 not. There was something too
625 dutiful about the fixedness of her
626 gaze. Bahmer was suddenly sure
627 that her interest was a thousand
628 miles away.

629 "Don't you care for this sort
630 of show?" he asked.

631 "Yes, indeed," Claire an-
632 swered. "I think they're great
633 fun once in a while. This is a
634 very ingenious number, isn't it?"

635 "It strikes me that way," said
636 Bahmer; "but you're bored to
637 death with it. What's the
638 trouble?" And then suspi-
639 ciously: "You haven't seen the
640 show before, have you? I
641 thought it was a safe bet; that's
642 why I didn't ask you first.
643 It's only been running three
644 nights."

645 "I know," said Claire. "I
646 meant to play the appreciative
647 guest better. I'm so sorry you
648 found me out."

468

649 "You have seen it before,
650 then?"

651 "Why, you see," Claire ex-
652 plained, "we shoe the Frivolities
653 and I've been to such a lot of
654 rehearsals, especially this parti-
655 cular number. Our designer had
656 considerable trouble about the
657 lights in the slipper heels." She
658 laughed. "You know," she said,
659 "even as clever a number as this
660 looks better to you the first six
661 or eight times you see it."

662 Bahmer laughed too. "What
663 a rotten shame—to take a bus
664 driver out on his day off and give
665 him a nice long bus ride! I'll feel
666 rotten about this to my dying
667 day unless you let me square it
668 with you."

669 It came perversely to the tip
670 of Claire's tongue to assure
671 Bahmer that he needn't square
672 it with her, that she had only
673 gone with him in the first place
674 as a matter of business policy,
675 that she hadn't expected to
676 enjoy the evening especially
677 herself. But of course she didn't
678 say it. She couldn't so outrage
679 ordinary human friendliness,
680 even with a dangerous man.

681 "I haven't minded really,"
682 she assured him. "Part of the
683 show is colorful enough to bear
684 any amount of repeating."

685 "No." Bahmer insisted, "I
686 want to take you to something
687 you'll enjoy, not just something
688 that you won't mind. Won't
689 you let me take you to some
690 show that you really want to

691 see, some other night while I'm
692 here?" And as she hesitated,
693 "Please do," he urged. "If
694 you've got a free evening, please
695 do. Something that you'd plan
696 to go to sometime anyway."
697 And as she still didn't answer,
698 "Surely there are some other
699 shows that you want to see,
700 aren't there?"

701 "Oh, yes, of course there are,"
702 Claire admitted. "But any one
703 of them might bore you to
704 tears."

705 Bahmer did not make the
706 obvious gallant retort that no
707 evening spent with her could
708 possibly be a bore. He had had
709 too many such remarks fall dead
710 that evening. Instead:

711 "An evening alone in New
712 York is worth two cents on the
713 dollar," he said. "I'd rather
714 take a chance on being bored."
715 And again, insistently, "What
716 do you want to go to the most?"

717 "Well," Claire admitted, "I've
718 been planning all winter to see
719 Bright Treasure."

720 "Which night?" Bahmer
721 asked crisply. "I'll be here till
722 Saturday."

723 He expected Claire, of course,
724 to have great difficulty in finding
725 a free evening among her many
726 engagements. Girls always did
727 it that way, though he was
728 cynical enough to have observed
729 that they seldom missed finding
730 one eventually.

731 "I'm free any evening till
732 Saturday," Claire answered.

"Suppose we make it for whichever night you can get the best seats."

And then, where he was quite unprepared for coquetry, it seemed to Bahmer, at least, that he found it.

After the Frivolities, "Can't we go somewhere and have a bite to eat," he asked, "and a dance or two? You dance, don't you?"

"Yes," said Claire, "but I'm afraid not tonight, thank you. You see, I'm working awfully hard on my job and I'm worse than useless the next day if I stay up to all hours."

Obviously coquetry, that, Bahmer felt sure. He knew women, and women didn't pass up invitations to night clubs except in ways calculated to call forth more invitations.

As he was leaving Claire outside her apartment on West Eighth Street she said, "You won't need to go to an agency for the Bright Treasure tickets, unless it's more convenient. I'm sure you can get seats at the box office. It isn't one of the big hits."

Bahmer looked at her quizzically. "You're a funny girl," he observed. "I thought girls always wanted to see the big hits."

Claire smiled. "Girls usually choose the shows that they think will please the men who are going to buy the tickets," she told him. "You brought this on yourself, you know."

Bahmer watched her as she fitted her latchkey into the apartment-house door. No swanky, hall-boyed, all-night-service apartment house, hers. He had expected her to hand him the key, let him unlock the door for her, the usual helplessly feminine gesture of appeal.

"You don't like me very well, do you?" he guessed shrewdly.

Claire met his eyes with a distinctly uncoquettish directness. "Yes, I do," she said frankly, "though I didn't expect to. I think you'd be a very nice person, if you'd let yourself be."

Bahmer was no more surprised at this answer than Claire herself. For it was absolutely true. Spoken straight out from some instinctive reaction. Despite all her warnings, all her foreknowledge of Bahmer, for the moment she completely forgot about being on her guard against him. Though he looked exactly as she had known he would look. And behaved exactly as she had known he would behave. Good-looking without being particularly handsome, well-tailored and well-groomed. Pleasant-mannered, genial, generous, but well protected with a firm glaze of cynical, worldly-wise suspicion.

Queer that Claire should feel so suddenly sure about that

cynical glaze; so sure that it had nothing more to do with the real man underneath it than a brittle, hard coating of ice has to do with the current below. Something of this reluctant liking must, even before she recognized it herself, have crept into her manner despite her prudent intent. If she had succeeded in being quite as impersonal, as almost rudely reserved as she had planned to be, Bahmer could not possibly have been so determined to see more of her.

Bright Treasure was a charming play, witty and gay and about real people. Bahmer had lost no time, had bought tickets for the very next evening. Between acts, tonight, he did not attempt to flirt with Claire. And because he did not, Claire found herself impelled, more and more, to be herself with him—gracious, companionable, friendly.

"I knew a man once exactly like that father," Bahmer observed after the first curtain. "I used to wonder how he could expect his sons to amount to anything when he never gave them a chance to make so much as a mistake on their own."

"How did the sons turn out?" Claire asked.

"I don't know," Bahmer said, "I lost touch with them years ago, but I can guess. And I can guess just about what's going to happen to those two lads." He nodded toward the stage.

So he guessed, and Claire guessed. And they quarreled, about their respective guesses, keenly and good-humoredly. And then, through the following acts, watched the dramatist shrewdly and deftly outguess them both.

They stopped at a little Sixth Avenue rotisserie on the way home and had ginger ale and toasted cheese sandwiches.

"You know," Bahmer admitted, across the table, "I'd never have thought I'd like that play, if it had been described to me, but it was really very interesting. Let's go to another."

"I think I've already seen most of the plays that I know are especially good," said Claire, and obligingly mentioned the two or three she had enjoyed the most.

Bahmer was not interested in these, however. "I want something you'll go to with me," he said frankly. "You said you were free till Saturday. Isn't there something else that we can do together?"

Claire hesitated. Why not? She could not ask a more thoroughly delightful companion than Bahmer had been tonight.

"Come on, please do," he urged. There was something boyish, appealing, in his eagerness. It was as though he had suddenly realized that he could not buy her companionship with expensive gifts or costly enter-

902 tainment and, for some reason
903 or other, wanted it on her own
904 terms.

905 "Please," he begged, "can't
906 you think of something?"

907 "Well, they're having a block
908 party somewhere down on the
909 East Side tomorrow night," she
910 said. "A friend of mine who's
911 been doing some settlement work
912 with the children is going to
913 have a bunch of them sing
914 Neapolitan folk songs. She says,
915 though it hasn't been announced
916 that that new young Neapolitan
917 tenor at the Metropolitan is
918 going to sing. A lot of his
919 relatives live there. I thought
920 it would be great fun to go
921 down and look on. At worst,
922 it's sure to be different and
923 colorful."

924 "Great," said Bahmer. "Can't
925 we have dinner somewhere
926 first?"

927 Claire smiled. "Would you
928 like to try my pet cafeteria?"
929 she asked. "You have to
930 juggle a tray, but the food
931 is wonderful and there are
932 sure to be some nice people
933 there."

934 Oddly out of place Bahmer
935 seemed at the Round Table next
936 evening. No ready check boy
937 took his hundred-and-seventy-
938 five-dollar coat. There was no
939 obsequious head waiter to guide
940 him to the choicest table. He
941 hung his coat on a peg between
942 a sweater and a rubber raincoat,
943 obediently found a tray and a

944 knife, fork and spoon wrapped
945 in a paper napkin, and lined up
946 behind Claire at the steaming
947 counter.

948 The half dozen young people
949 already seated around a table, to
950 whom she casually introduced
951 Bahmer, accepted him quite as
952 casually. Two young men across
953 from each other continued a
954 good-humored argument about
955 the recent Pulitzer Prize award;
956 a cordial, yellow-curled girl next
957 to Bahmer directed him to the
958 ice-water cooler, showed him
959 where the empty glasses were
960 kept.

961 Little Ruth Wilson, vainly
962 trying to convince Bahmer that
963 she was used to dining at the
964 Ritz, had made no more gallant
965 effort than Bahmer himself made
966 tonight to fit in well at this
967 cafeteria dinner table. He felt
968 oddly flattered when he essayed
969 a joking comment and every-
970 body laughed. Still more flat-
971 tered when a young cover artist
972 specifically included him in an
973 invitation to dinner in her studio
974 the next evening.

975 "You'd better get something
976 to eat first," Claire cautioned
977 him privately, later in the even-
978 ing, as the two of them wedged
979 their way into a crowded trolley
980 to escape from the colorful,
981 foreign-babbling, lantern-strung
982 block party on the lower East
983 Side.

984 It had been a hilarious even-
985 ing, all colored lights and con-

986 fetti, laughter, singing. Claire
987 and Bahmer had given them-
988 selves over to the fiesta atmos-
989 phere like two children at a
990 circus, joining in on the familiar
991 choruses, drinking pop through
992 straws stuck in the bottles, buy-
993 ing chestnuts out of the braziers,
994 clinging together, arm in arm,
995 against the jolly pressure of the
996 jostling crowd.

997 "Polly means well," Claire
998 continued her warning for the
999 next evening, "but she's as likely
1000 as not to forget to order the
1001 meat."

1002 Polly proved the next night
1003 to have remembered the meat,
1004 but her whole dinner had obvi-
1005 ously been hastily assembled
1006 from the nearest delicatessen,
1007 and there wasn't enough dessert
1008 to go around. Nobody minded
1009 though. A gay young hodge-
1010 podge of an evening—dancing,
1011 laughing, wise-cracking. A
1012 smooth-faced youngster who was
1013 doing a magician act in a near-by
1014 vaudeville dropping in after his
1015 number to show them a new
1016 trick he was working on; a young
1017 professor from the big down-
1018 town university haranguing
1019 about the mysticism of the East
1020 Indian fakir; a little dancer from
1021 the Frivolities, arriving late, to
1022 dance and sing in a high, sweet,
1023 haunting voice that filled the
1024 bare studio like perfume. All
1025 fairly poor still, but all young
1026 and eager and ready for fun.

1027 At the door of Claire's apart-

1028 ment house that evening Bah-
1029 mer paused.

1030 "Tomorrow's my last evening
1031 here," he said. "Won't you have
1032 a farewell dinner with me?"

1033 "Mr. Gibson was back in the
1034 office today," said Claire. "His
1035 neuritis proved to be a much
1036 shorter affair than usual."

1037 "That's good," said Bahmer.
1038 "Well, how about tomorrow
1039 evening?"

1040 "What I was trying to suggest
1041 delicately," said Claire, "was
1042 that by tomorrow evening Mr.
1043 Gibson will be both able and
1044 eager to do the honors for the
1045 firm."

1046 For several moments Bahmer
1047 did not answer. Then: "I see,"
1048 he said stiffly. "Dining with me
1049 is the same thing as working
1050 overtime."

1051 "Oh, I didn't mean that at
1052 all!"

1053 Claire forgot all about Bah-
1054 mer's being a dangerous man, in
1055 the quick remorseful response to
1056 the unmistakable hurt under the
1057 stiffness of his voice.

1058 "Why, I'd love to have dinner
1059 with you if you want me to."

1060 "Is there anywhere you'd
1061 especially like to have it?"

1062 There had been something so
1063 unmistakably genuine in that
1064 hurt, it struck at the very root
1065 of Claire's natural kindliness.
1066 She quite forgot to be cautious
1067 and on her guard, in her eager-
1068 ness to make amends.

1069 "Wouldn't you like to come

473

here for dinner?" she asked. "I've a little kitchen in my new apartment; we could get dinner ourselves." It was her friendliest gesture. To its possible indiscretion Claire was temporarily blind.

"I'd like it better than anything in the world," the man answered. "If you'll let me be the commissary."

Claire nodded assent.

"I can get down here by 5:30," she said. "We'll do the marketing then."

At 5:30 Bahmer was waiting for her on her doorstep. "Let's have a steak," he proposed. "And I'll cook it. Lord, I haven't cooked a steak in twenty years!"

Claire cocked a dubious eye. "Smothered in onions?" she asked hopefully.

Bahmer looked at her in admiring unbelief. "Did I hear you right?" he asked incredulously. "Is there a woman in the world who would actually suggest onions?"

"I love 'em. Let's be natural and vulgar."

"Come on!"

They shopped in the great market that occupies a full block. Bahmer personally chose the steak, watched it cut off, directing its exact thickness.

"Green peas?" At the vegetable stand they bought, too, a head of lettuce as firm as a young cabbage; tomatoes, Claire pinching them with critical, housewifely fingers. They went to three different stands before they found a box of strawberries, fresh and large and red enough to suit.

"We don't want any cake with them, do we?"

"We do not," Bahmer agreed gratefully. "How about some crackers and cheese to top off with, with the coffee?"

So they stopped at a delicatessen. Here, after buying the cheese—an expensive pineapple affair—Bahmer ran quite wild. Ripe olives, wild-grape jelly, sweet butter, imported *antipasto*, spiced currants. All the expensive delicacies, and such quantities of each! He brushed aside Claire's protests as so many mosquitoes.

"You're buying a dinner, you know, not stocking a hotel."

"We want enough. Besides, you can eat up whatever's left, some other day."

She stopped him at last and, both loaded with knobby packages, they made their way back to the apartment.

It is difficult to retain any vestiges of formality between two people getting dinner together in an apartment-house kitchen. As Claire and Bahmer shelled peas and scraped potatoes and peeled tomatoes and opened up a jiggly little card table in front of the living-room fireplace, Claire forgot more and more completely to keep up any protective screen of formality. Forgot, more and more, that she was dining alone with a dangerous man.

As he tinkered with the gas broiler which exploded mildly each time instead of lighting, Claire found herself looking curiously at Bahmer, her rubber apron tied around his neck, his whole attention centered on twisting and turning the metal tube which regulated the mixture of air and gas. There was nothing about this man to suggest the George Bahmer she had heard about, the George Bahmer she had, in fact, found at first. Surely this was no cynical man about town, wise in the ways of business men and platinum diggers, complacently ignorant of everything else in life. No self-protective materialist, content to find new ways to eat, drink and be merry and forget that tomorrow we may die.

This man getting dinner in her little kitchen seemed oddly younger, oddly hungry for the very interests the other Bahmer would have passed by, unseeing or contemptuous. A very simple person, this Bahmer seemed, with all the doors of his mind standing wide open, hospitable to any vagrant wind of thought.

The steak broiled to a turn, they lighted the fire against the chill spring evening and sat down at the jiggly legged card table.

"I'm going to get a good solid table as soon as I can afford the kind I want," Claire observed. "I seldom get a meal here, except breakfast, but it's fun to, once in a while, and with this table it's like eating at sea in a hard wind."

Bahmer glanced about her living room's partial bareness— low, deep-seated wicker chairs, obviously comfortable but obviously cheap, and only two of them; the floor bare, except for one small domestic rug in front of the fireplace; a single, parchment-shaded light with an added wire length so that it could be moved about to serve wherever needed most. No room, of course, where a well-broiled steak is being served in front of an open fire is likely to seem lacking in genial hominess, but there was no blinking the fact that this room, on close inspection, was cheaply and scantily furnished.

"I used to think it would be more fun to get furniture a piece at a time," Bahmer observed. "Everything you get means something then."

Claire nodded. "I'd have to do it that way anyway. I couldn't wait any longer to have a home, but I can't put much money into it right now."

"You get a good salary at Gibson's, don't you?"

Odd, Claire realized, that such a question, coming from a Bahmer, could be asked with a frank

1239 friendliness that robbed it of
1240 any hint of impertinence.

1241 "Very good," she answered
1242 quite as frankly. "But I haven't
1243 had it so awfully long and I'm
1244 not at all sure of Mr. Gibson.
1245 He's dubious about women in
1246 responsible positions, and I'm
1247 not sure whether he'll be willing
1248 to make my job anything I'll want
1249 to stay in indefinitely. I want to
1250 have enough available money so
1251 that I'll be free to do whatever
1252 seems best when the time
1152 comes."

1253 Bahmer nodded. "That's the
1254 way to do it, all right," he said,
1255 "If you can stand out against
1256 the temptations on all sides."

1257 Claire laughed. "I spend my
1258 days breaking down other
1259 people's sales resistance and the
1260 rest of the time bolstering up
1261 my own. I like almost every-
1262 thing that money will buy, but
1263 I'm not going to have my life
1264 decided for me by the things I've
1265 bought."

1266 "There are mighty few people
1267 who have the sense to figure that
1268 out," he said, "until after they've
1269 bought them and it's too late."

1270 It was half-past eight before
1271 they finished off with crackers
1272 and cheese.

1273 "I made my dinner take as
1274 long as I could," Bahmer con-
1275 fessed, "because I wanted it to
1276 be too late to ask you if you
1277 wanted to go anywhere after-
1278 ward. I'd so much rather stay
1279 right here."

1280 "So would I," said Claire
1281 contentedly. " 'Be it ever so
1282 humble——' "

1283 "What about the dishes?"
1284 Bahmer asked.

1285 For a moment Claire stared
1286 at him as he had at her when she
1287 had suggested onions—amazed,
1288 incredulous.

1289 "Now," she said, "I know
1290 you're nice! But we don't need
1291 to bother about them, thank
1292 heaven! I've a maid who comes
1293 in Saturday mornings to clean
1294 up, and she'll do them."

1295 So they carried them out to
1296 the little kitchen, then drew the
1297 lone two comfortable chairs be-
1298 fore the fire.

1299 "Smoke?" Claire asked.
1300 "There are plenty of cigarettes
1301 over there in the box."

1302 Replete with the good dinner,
1303 almost drowsy in the warmth of
1304 the fire, they sat for some little
1305 time in an incongruous sort of
1306 companionability, Bahmer puf-
1307 fing away at a cigarette, Claire
1308 leaning forward now and then
1309 to poke the logs. In this odd
1310 sense of comradeship she forgot
1311 entirely the Bahmer Gibson
1312 knew, the Bahmer of little Ruth
1313 and the platinum diggers. Ac-
1314 cepting in his place the other
1315 Bahmer who, her common sense
1316 told her, must surely be just an
1317 illusion. But such a likable il-
1318 lusion—young, even a bit in-
1319 experienced, eager, adventurous,
1320 open-minded, frankly hungry for
1321 life. An illusion who seemed,

oddly, so much more real than the reality; with whom she could be friends unreservedly, could be herself.

It was to this friendly illusion of a man that she turned, her eyes suddenly ashine with interest when he chanced to speak of London.

"You've been to London several times!" she exclaimed. "I wonder if you've ever been to my London." She sighed. "I don't suppose you have though. I've asked so many people, and nobody ever has."

"What is your London?" Bahmer asked curiously.

"Oh, I don't suppose it really exists at all," Claire confessed. "That's why nobody's ever been there. It's just a jumble of things I've read and things I've imagined and funny ideas I got when I was a little girl. You know the kind of things."

Queer that she should feel so sure he would know. But he seemed to. He nodded. "Dick Whittington, thrice Lord Mayor of London," he suggested.

"And Vauxhall where Dobbin went with the Sedleys and Becky Sharp!"

"And Fleet Street and the Cheshire Cheese."

"And London Bridge and Kensington Gardens and Piccadilly Circus—of course they won't look the way I think they will, but——"

" 'Oranges and lemons, say the bells of Saint Clement's,' " Bahmer quoted.

" 'I'm sure I don't know, says the big bell of Bow,' " Claire finished.

They laughed, a half-amused, half-embarrassed laugh, then went on shamelessly, building up this fairy city, the London of history and phantasy, the London priceless and precious, that is owned inalienably by those who have never been to London.

"The Tower," said Bahmer— "that was the place I used to dream most about going."

"Didn't you believe you'd see the two little princes somewhere on the stone stairs in their velvet suits?"

"And Sir Walter Raleigh and Lady Jane Grey." A little pause.

"And didn't you see any of them," Claire asked half fearfully, "when you really did go to the Tower?"

"I've never been to the Tower," said Bahmer.

For a moment Claire was silent with sheer incredulity. "And you've been to London several times?"

"I had planned to go, of course, the first time," said Bahmer, "but, you see, I was there on my honeymoon and my— Mrs. Bahmer had been there two or three times before. She knew a good many people who lived in London, and it mortified her to death the provincial things I wanted to do."

1407 Bahmer laughed a little wryly.
1408 "I was a provincial who had
1409 never been anywhere before,"
1410 he said, "so, of course, I didn't
1411 want anyone to think I was. I
1412 used to think I'd slip off alone
1413 and go to the Tower, at least,
1414 by myself. But I never got a
1415 chance. We were entertained a
1416 lot, and then I had some business
1417 to see to and—well, I just never
1418 seemed to find a good chance.
1419 You see, all Mrs. Bahmer's
1420 friends were fashionable people,
1421 or trying to be fashionable, and
1422 they set great store on knowing
1423 the right people and going to the
1424 right places. I didn't know
1425 anybody at all, and all the places
1426 I wanted to go to were the
1427 wrong ones." Claire nodded
1428 understandingly. "I thought
1429 then that I'd go over to England
1430 sometime by myself and be a
1431 provincial and do all the wrong
1432 things and have a glorious time.
1433 But——"
1434 He did not finish the sentence.
1435 After a minute or two Claire
1436 asked curiously, "Why didn't
1437 you?"
1438 "Well, my next time was
1439 fifteen years later. And fifteen
1440 years is a long time. I'd for-
1441 gotten all about the little princes
1442 and Sir Walter Raleigh. I'd
1443 forgotten that I had ever wanted
1444 to see the Tower of London."
1445 Claire turned a little in her
1446 chair, looked at the man beside
1447 her as he sat staring into the fire.
1448 And suddenly her riddle was

1449 solved. The riddle of this other
1450 Bahmer, eager, friendly, open-
1451 minded, hungry for life. This
1452 illusion who had helped cook
1453 dinner in her little kitchen and
1454 seemed so oddly real. Why, of
1455 course he was real! More real
1456 than the cynical man about
1457 town whose place he had, for
1458 this one evening, taken. It was
1459 he who was sitting here right
1460 now, an ardent and romantic
1461 boy in a middle aged man's
1462 expensive clothes, wearing a
1463 worldly-wise, sophisticated face
1464 like a mask, staring into the fire
1465 through disillusioned eyes that
1466 meant no more than cloudy win-
1467 dow glass—the man that Bah-
1468 mer might have been.
1469 No wonder he seemed young
1470 and inexperienced. He had
1471 never grown up. He had just
1472 been left behind. Somewhere,
1473 along the streets of London, a
1474 quarter of a century ago, Bah-
1475 mer had walked off and left him;
1476 walked off and briskly on his
1477 way to become the ultra-success-
1478 ful salesman, the man who would
1479 learn to deal with men and
1480 handle women, the man who
1481 would forget that you can't buy
1482 friendship with a loan or love
1483 from a platinum digger.
1484 "I suppose," said Claire, "that
1485 you were awfully in love with
1486 your wife."
1487 There surely must have been
1488 some potent force to make him
1489 leave that charming boy behind.
1490 "She was very pretty," said

Bahmer, "and I was attracted to her." He paused. "She'd had a lot more advantages than I had, and that flattered me," he added honestly. "Then I had two or three rivals, and you know how competition stimulates trade. But I see now that that's quite different from being in love."

"It may be that the only way you can keep your dream of any place is by never going there. You've still got your Tower with Sir Walter Raleigh and the little princes. Maybe you'd have lost that if you'd ever seen the real one."

Claire went flying back to London on the quick wings of apprehension; in sudden realization that this quiet, firelighted apartment was no place for her and the Bahmer of today—the sporty Chicago man who tells you that his wife doesn't understand him. It had been a mistake, mentioning his wife at all. This couldn't be helped now, of course. Claire could only do her best by a hasty flight back to London and the other Bahmer, with whom she felt so unguardedly at ease.

"I came across a poem once," she went on hurriedly, "that I feel sure was written by somebody who had never been there either. There were two lines, I remember, that went something like: 'London, London, they counted me a fool—I could draw your sky line plain before I went to school.'"

Across the hearth Claire felt Bahmer's eyes on her, and she rose hastily, crossed the room, chattering determinedly.

"I think I cut it out of the magazine and saved it," she rattled on. "One verse goes something like this:

" '*As I went up to London*,' *I heard a stranger say,*
As though it were a casual thing for casual lips to say.
'*As I went up to London*'—*I'll wager many a crown*
He never took the road that I shall take to London Town.'"

She came back into the firelight with a large manila envelope, shook its clippings into her lap—bits of magazine verse from here and there, saved over a dozen years or so. She did not find the poem she was seeking among them, and as she bent her smooth dark head over the others it was with a mere pretense of attention. She was becoming with every moment more conscious of Bahmer's interest. She kept her eyes lowered over her lapful of clippings, avoided meeting the steady intensity of his gaze. But she could not avoid feeling it sweep over her, warm, vibrating, as real as the glow of the fire. She knew that in another moment he was going to rise and come across the little distance

1573 between his chair and hers.
1574 She picked up one of the bits of
1575 verse at random, passed it across
1576 to him.

1577 "Here's a good one," and as
1578 he took it tentatively: "Read
1579 it aloud, won't you?"

1580 Obediently Bahmer settled
1581 back and adjusted his glasses.
1582 Fortunately Claire's chance
1583 choice had fallen on a ballad—
1584 a long one. So she had a bit of
1585 respite as Bahmer dutifully read
1586 the lengthy rollicking account
1587 of Forty Singing Seamen in
1588 an Old Black Barque. Before
1589 he reached the "Could the grog
1590 we dreamed we swallowed make
1591 us dream of all that followed?"
1592 Claire was ready with another
1593 clipping.

1594 "Here's a spooky thing; read
1595 this!" And when he reached its
1596 concluding "I cheer a dead
1597 man's sweetheart—never ask me
1598 whose," she was ready with
1599 another. But despite the sing-
1600 ing beauty of this last choice,
1601 she could feel her reader growing
1602 restive.

1603 "My soul," she thought, in
1604 whimsical panic, "this is like
1605 that old story of grandpa's,
1606 about the time the wolves chased
1607 his cutter and he kept throwing
1608 out things to them—the lap
1609 robe, his coat, his overshoes, his
1610 shoes. I can't keep throwing out
1611 poems all night! Besides grand-
1612 pa said that after a while the
1613 wolves began to get on to him
1614 and by the time he got down to

1615 gloves they wouldn't even stop
1616 to fight over them."

1617 It had been a mistake, she
1618 realized now, these few evenings
1619 she had spent with Bahmer.
1620 Possibly she should never have
1621 accepted even that first semi-
1622 business invitation; probably she
1623 should have declined his second
1624 suggestion with a chill unfriend-
1625 liness that would have been un-
1626 mistakable, whatever bearing it
1627 had on her position as advertis-
1628 ing manager for D. E. Gibson
1629 shoes. But if these were mere
1630 possibilities and probabilities, it
1631 was a flat certainty that she
1632 should never have invited him
1633 here tonight. The informal
1634 comradeliness of the little
1635 kitchen, the unconventional
1636 friendliness of dinner on the
1637 jiggly card table and now the
1638 warm intimacy of a shared
1639 hearth fire.

1640 Someway, though, she could-
1641 n't take the situation quite
1642 seriously. Even her sense of
1643 humor continued to function
1644 quite unawed. As Bahmer ap-
1645 proached the end of the verse
1646 she pawed about for another
1647 to succeed it, and inside was
1648 laughing at herself for doing
1649 it.

1650 "I'm like the heroine in the
1651 old-fashioned novels who used
1652 to try to hold off the villain by
1653 plying him with wine. Didn't
1654 she just pretend to drink hers
1655 and keep coaxing him on till
1656 suddenly he went off into a safe

drunken sleep?" Claire bent lower over her lapful of clippings to hide her little one-sided secret smile. "I used to doubt that story, even on wine. And fancy trying it with poetry!"

Claire could smile her little one-sided smile, could make fun of herself, because she simply couldn't make herself think of Bahmer as a villain. Not even when suddenly he stopped reading, rose, scattering the clippings recklessly over the floor, crossed the bit of firelight to her chair.

"I can't go on," he said. "I'm mad about you."

So it had come. For a moment Claire considered a brisk "Nonsense, you're not really at all, you know. It's just the combination of a porterhouse steak and an open fire."

But she thought better of this before she said it. Giving a man a chance to argue about a thing of this sort is poor policy. He only convinces himself further by his own eloquence. So instead:

"I'm awfully sorry," she said simply.

He stood close beside her chair, but did not venture to touch so much as the sleeve of her trim, tan office dress.

"I didn't believe there was a girl like you in the world. I used to think there might be, years ago, when I was just a boy. Beautiful and clever and brave and good—the kind of girl who would want the same kind of life I would; that I could go anywhere with. But I decided, years ago, that it was just a dream, that women didn't come that way."

"I used to think——" Of course it was the Bahmer who used to be, who was talking now! That was why his voice was so youthfully eager, so young in its intensity. Why, too, he stood so still beside Claire, so stiff in a boyish respect. It was a very young man talking, younger even than Claire herself, the young man he had walked off and left behind somewhere in London.

"Why, we could do anything in the world together," he went on eagerly. "There's a lot in life besides just making money and spending it. As you say, you don't have to let life be decided by the things you've bought. What do you get out of a great lot of things, anyway! Here I belong to three different golf clubs, and what does it get me? I can't shoot a decent game over any one of them. Don't even know that I want to. I notice that the men I know, who can go around in ninety, have to put up five dollars a hole to keep them interested." Claire stirred uneasily in her low chair. "What is there in having a decent house and servants to run it, when it's nothing but a place that you're

1741 glad to travel to stay away
1742 from; and dinner parties that
1743 the only men you'd really like
1744 to eat dinner with aren't invited
1745 to because they don't fit with
1746 the crowd?"

1747 "It's your own crowd that
1748 they don't fit with, isn't it?"
1749 Claire asked mildly.

1750 "My own crowd!" Very
1751 young, too, was the outraged
1752 intolerance of his voice. "My
1753 own crowd! A bunch of men
1754 who all happen to live in the
1755 same suburb, in about the same-
1756 priced houses, who've all found
1757 some way of making fifteen
1758 thousand a year or over. And
1759 a bunch of women who've
1760 all been about the same kind
1761 of pickers when it came to
1762 husbands—financially, that is.
1763 That's exactly all my crowd has
1764 in common. Why, we have to
1765 have two or three stiff cocktails
1766 before we can stand each other
1767 through an evening!"

1768 Claire said nothing; there was
1769 really nothing she could say.

1770 "Traveling!" Bahmer went
1771 on with mounting bitterness.
1772 "Everybody thinks I travel a
1773 good deal. Oh, I'm abroad two
1774 or three times a year, I grant
1775 you. Paris, Cannes, Deauville
1776 —it's very broadening. I come
1777 back knowing all about whether
1778 to make up Dresden calf or
1779 Sudan lizard." He stopped
1780 short. "I've had more of what
1781 I used to think traveling would
1782 be, sitting right here in this chair

1783 tonight and talking to you about
1784 London."

1785 It was the defrauded cry of
1786 the immaterialist who has spent
1787 most of his life in the wrong
1788 camp.

1789 Claire stared into the fire un-
1790 happily. No one-sided smile
1791 tipped her lips now. The sense
1792 of humor which would have kept
1793 right on functioning through
1794 passionate love-making had flown
1795 away. Vanished, too, was the
1796 poise and common sense which
1797 could have dealt so completely
1798 with a dangerous man; could
1799 have been so safely cynical about
1800 the middle-aged philanderer who
1801 tells young women that his wife
1802 doesn't understand him. For
1803 Claire was an immaterialist, too,
1804 and she recognized plain truth
1805 when she heard it.

1806 She was suddenly afraid as
1807 she sat staring into the blaze—
1808 afraid, not of Bahmer but of
1809 herself; of the sense of aching
1810 pity that swept over her; of the
1811 wild, irrational impulse to let
1812 him take her in his arms, to
1813 comfort him, to try to make
1814 up to him for all that life had
1815 done him out of.

1816 It was a foolish, reckless
1817 impulse, she knew; it could lead
1818 to nothing but eventual sorrow
1819 for them both. But she knew,
1820 too, without having to think it
1821 out, that she was rich in all that
1822 Bahmer wanted out of life—
1823 youth, simplicity, adventure,
1824 companionship, the power to

love. She felt a poignant guilt, to sit at so rich a banquet and turn a hungry man away.

She could feel prudence, common sense, all the little wisdom she had, slipping away as Bahmer stood there beside her, not touching so much as the hem of her dress. Her knuckles whitened as she held fast to the arms of her cheap low wicker chair, trying to hold herself back, as from a perilous precipice, and knew that she was being swept closer to it every moment.

"I love you so!" Bahmer was saying tensely. "I never dreamed that being in love could be like this. I just can't go back tomorrow, go on without you, knowing that there is a woman like you in the world. I didn't mind before, when I didn't know there could be anything else—oh, I can't go on without you now! I love you so!"

Claire's hands loosed their hold on the chair arms; that terrific, tender sense of pity was too much. Wisdom could not stand against it. She lifted her eyes to the man beside her.

Suddenly the telephone shrilled, loud, insistent, at the other end of the room. For a moment their eyes clung. The telephone rang again, raucous, peremptory. Claire waited defiantly for a moment —a moment of insurrection— then habit triumphed.

"Just a moment, I'd better answer it." She rose, crossed the room.

"Yes," her voice shook a little, "yes, this is Miss Deming. . . . Good evening, Mr. Gibson." A considerable pause.

"Why, yes, I think it probably would be best for me to," Claire's voice steadying. "I'll wire the Boston papers. If the cuts are all made I'm sure we could." Another pause, a bit of commonplace arranging. "Tomorrow morning? Yes, of course I can." A brief silence. Then: "I think there's a Boston sleeper around twelve or one tonight though. It would be better if I could get that. I will, if I can. . . . All right. I'll wire you back sometime tomorrow."

Claire came back into the firelighted circle. She had been away but a brief three minutes, but she looked at Bahmer as though half surprised to find him there. Her voice was steady, her eyes cool and direct.

"I'm awfully sorry, but I've got to dash. The Boston branch store has got into a mess of some kind. Gibson wants me there in the morning. Would you mind telephoning the station for me and see if I can get a reservation while I throw some things into my bag?"

There was a long pause. Then: "I——" Bahmer began.

But Claire was already in the

next room. In the opening and shutting of bureau drawers she did not hear his tentative beginning.

"You know I suspect that Boston manager of having something up his sleeve," she observed chattily. "Because he strikes me as being too smart a man to be so incompetent. He's always doing the most stupid things, and yet he's certainly not a stupid man. It's queer."

"I——" Bahmer began again. "Mr. Gibson's giving him every chance in the world to make something good out of the branch, and yet he——"

"I——" Bahmer began once more.

"If you can't reserve a berth on that sleeper, will you find out what time the first train leaves in the morning?"

Bahmer's lips parted, but this time no sound came forth. He stood staring blankly at Claire's door, as though incredulously facing the fact that he was speaking into a dead instrument, that his connection had been cut off. For several moments he stood perfectly still, looking at the blankness of the door. From its other side came the sounds of brisk, competent packing. Claire herself had fallen silent now, but a silence that was as far from invitational as her casual words had been— the absorbed silence of a business woman, preoccupied with the business on hand.

After a few moments Bahmer crossed to the telephone, called the railway station. And after all, it was probably as wise and kind a way as could have been contrived for closing up the incident. Clare might, of course, have tried to soften the blow a little; might have pointed out to Bahmer that what he was in love with was really not herself at all, only the glimpse of another sort of life that she had shown him; might have called his attention to certain precious things he had —his boys, for instance.

But that sort of reasoning seldom helps much at the time. Sooner or later he would have to start picking up the pieces, making such adjustments as he could to his own life. And there is never much point in trying to taper off the inevitable.

And, wise and kind or not, what Claire did was exactly what she would inevitably do. And she would probably pretty much forget the incident long before Bahmer would. Not that she would mean to, but she was a young woman of many and varied interests. Granted all the sympathy that could possibly be expected, one incontrovertible fact would remain.

The fact that George Bahmer had been merely a minor incident in a busy life.

THE ANALYSIS

In the chart of *Claire and the Dangerous Man* I have placed the two distinct stories side by side to show their parallelism. There is first the story of Bahmer and the little girl Ruth Wilson. Side by side with it is the story of Claire and Bahmer, Claire occupying the same relation to Bahmer that Bahmer did to Ruth.

It is interesting to notice that the same technical treatment occurs in this story that occurred in *The Roads We Take*, by O. Henry. He presented the two stories of Shark Dodson. In the first story there was set forth a series of incidents before arriving at an interchange. The information therein contained sufficed for the second story, so that in presenting the second one the author was able instantly to present an interchange. This is true of this story. In the story of Bahmer and Ruth Wilson the information is presented in a series of skeletonized interchanges (Lines 1 to 134). The fifth step (Lines 135 to 273) are presented in an interchange between Ruth and Claire. The reader realizes that Ruth is aware of a new sort of life infinitely more desirable than her present one. This projects the interchange between Ruth and Bahmer (Lines 273 to 317). Had the author not intended to introduce the story of Claire and Bahmer she could have omitted the interchange between Ruth and Claire, and gone directly to the interchange between Ruth and Bahmer which makes it clear to Bahmer that he must take decisive action. This action he takes. The significance of this action, that Ruth had been only a minor incident in a busy life, is adroitly planted to form the ironic parallel with the other story, which follows it in structure as it does in significance.

The story of Claire and Bahmer is composed almost entirely of interchanges, as a glance at the chart will indicate. And here an interesting fact is disclosed. The author combines the technique of both the accomplishment and the decision type stories. For she keeps before the audience always the fact that Claire is setting out to play with fire, which has always before this burned other girls who played with it. The narrative question "Can she succeed?" informs all the interchanges. Although she is successful, the threat of disaster ultimately is always before the reader, to form a Dramatic Hindrance at the fifth step of each interchange. There is present, too, the Big Moment when this threatened disaster is imminent and apparently inescapable. I rather think that the author thought of this as a story of accomplishment—I deduce this from the title—and that the parallel story of Bahmer and Ruth

Wilson was merely added to give a fillip to the story of Claire. But such conjecture is idle. The lesson to be drawn from this story as from the other stories in the book is that there are only two possible Main Narrative Questions. One is "Can A Succeed?" If this is kept always before the reader, the story is one of Accomplishment. The other is "What will A do at this crisis of his life?" If this is what interests the reader, the story is one of Decision or Choice.

But whether the main Narrative Question is one of Accomplishment or one of Decision, one inescapable and inexorable conclusion is apparent. The capacity of a writer is the measure of his or her ability to write scenes. If an author can write good dramatic scenes, plotting will be an easy matter. It consists of juggling the scenes about until the most interesting and effective order of their presentation is apparent. Above all a writer, to be successful, must realize that whether the story is a Decision Story or an Accomplishment Story, there are only two ways to tell the Modern Short Story: Chronologically, or in a Flash-back.